HANDBOOK OF MIDDLE AMERICAN INDIANS, VOLUME 13
Guide to Ethnohistorical Sources, Part 2

HANDBOOK OF MIDDLE AMERICAN INDIANS

EDITED AT MIDDLE AMERICAN RESEARCH INSTITUTE, TULANE UNIVERSITY, BY

ROBERT WAUCHOPE, *General Editor*
MARGARET A. L. HARRISON, *Associate Editor*
JOSEPHITA N. BODDIE, *Administrative Assistant*
JOSEPH C. WIEDEL, *Cartographical Consultant*

ASSEMBLED WITH THE AID OF A GRANT FROM THE NATIONAL SCIENCE FOUNDATION, AND UNDER THE SPONSORSHIP OF THE NATIONAL RESEARCH COUNCIL COMMITTEE ON LATIN AMERICAN ANTHROPOLOGY

Editorial Advisory Board

IGNACIO BERNAL, HOWARD F. CLINE, GORDON F. EKHOLM,
NORMAN A. MCQUOWN, MANNING NASH, T. DALE STEWART,
EVON Z. VOGT, ROBERT C. WEST, GORDON R. WILLEY

HANDBOOK OF MIDDLE AMERICAN INDIANS

ROBERT WAUCHOPE, General Editor

VOLUME THIRTEEN

Guide to Ethnohistorical Sources

PART TWO

REF
F
1434
H3
V.13

HOWARD F. CLINE, Volume Editor

John B. Glass, Associate Volume Editor

UNIVERSITY OF TEXAS PRESS AUSTIN

Published in Great Britain by the
University of Texas Press, Ltd., London

International Standard Book Number 0-292-70153-5
Library of Congress Catalog Card No. 64-10316
Copyright © 1973 by the University of Texas Press
All rights reserved

The preparation and publication of the
Handbook of Middle American Indians
have been assisted by grants from
the National Science Foundation.

Typesetting by G&S Typesetters, Austin
Printing by Steck-Warlick Company, Austin, Texas
Binding by Universal Bookbindery, Inc., San Antonio, Texas

CONTENTS (*Continued from Vol. 12*)

ABBREVIATIONS

AAMC	—	Anales antiguos de México y sus contornos, by Ramírez.
ACAD	—	Academia de la Historia, Madrid.
AGI	—	Archivo General de Indias, Seville.
AGN	—	Archivo General de la Nación, Mexico City.
AHN	—	Archivo Histórico Nacional, Madrid.
ANP	—	Archivo de las Notarías Públicas, Puebla, Mexico.
ARSJ	—	Archivum Romanum Societatis Jesu, Rome.
BCA	—	Biblioteca Comunale dell' Archigimnasio, Bologna.
BNMA	—	Biblioteca Nacional, Madrid.
BNMex	—	Biblioteca Nacional de México, Mexico City.
BNP	—	Bibliothèque Nationale, Paris.
BNP/FM	—	BNP, Fonds Mexicains.
CDIHE	—	Colección de documentos inéditos . . . para la historia de España, Madrid.
DIA	—	Colección de documentos . . . Ibero América, Madrid.
DIE	—	Same as CDIHE.
DII	—	Colección de documentos inéditos . . . de Indias, Madrid.
DIU	—	Colección de documentos inéditos . . . de Ultramar, Madrid.
ECN	—	Estudios de Cultura Nahuatl. Universidad Nacional Autónoma de México, Seminario de Cultura Nahuatl, Mexico City.
EDIAPSA	—	Colección de estudios históricos-económicos mexicanos de la Cámara Nacional de la Industria de Transformación, Mexico City.
ENE	—	Epistolario de Nueva España.
FC	—	Florentine Codex, by Sahagún.
FM	—	Fonds Mexicains, BNP.
FPT	—	Francisco del Paso y Troncoso.
GA	—	Gesammelte Abhandlungen . . . , by Seler.
GPO	—	Government Printing Office, Washington.
HAHR	—	Hispanic American Historical Review, Durham, N.C.
HFC	—	Howard F. Cline.
HG	—	Historia general, by Sahagún.
HLAS	—	Handbook of Latin American Studies, Gainesville, Fla.
INAH	—	Instituto Nacional de Antropología e Historia, Mexico City.
JBG	—	John B. Glass.
JDE	—	Jiménez de la Espada.
JGI	—	Joaquín García Icazbalceta.
LC	—	Library of Congress, Washington.
MI	—	Monarquía indiana, by Torquemada.
MNA	—	Museo Nacional de Antropología [and predecessor institutions with varying names], Mexico City.

MNA/AH	—	MNA, Archivo Histórico.
MS	—	Manuscript.
MT	—	Manuscrito de Tlatelolco.
NYPL	—	New York Public Library, New York.
PAIGH	—	Pan American Institute of Geography and History, Mexico City.
PAL	—	National Palace Library, Madrid.
PM	—	Primeros memoriales, by Sahagún.
PNE	—	Papeles de Nueva España.
RAH	—	Real Academia de la Historia, Madrid.
RC	—	Royal cedula.
RG	—	Relaciones geográficas.
RMEA	—	Revista Mexicana de Estudios Antropológicos, Mexico City.
RMEH	—	Revista Mexicana de Estudios Históricos, Mexico City.
SMGE	—	Sociedad Mexicana de Geografía e Estadística, Mexico City.
UNAM	—	Universidad Nacional Autónoma de México, Mexico City.
UTX	—	University of Texas Library, Latin American Collection, Austin.
VR/PNE	—	Vargas Rea, Papeles de Nueva España.

HANDBOOK OF MIDDLE AMERICAN INDIANS, VOLUME 13
Guide to Ethnohistorical Sources, Part 2

GENERAL EDITOR'S NOTE

Howard F. Cline, who planned and assembled most of this volume, as well as the others in the Guide to Ethnohistorical Sources, died before all the copy was in hand to be edited and sent to the publisher. We are grateful to Mary W. Cline for her great assistance in completing the unfinished work of her late husband.

11. Published Collections of Documents Relating to Middle American Ethnohistory

CHARLES GIBSON

NLESS ONE IS CONVERSANT with the whole history of historiography, he may not be aware that historical writing based on the critical use of documents, published or unpublished, is a relatively recent phenomenon.[1] With few exceptions, documentary historiography began only with the humanistic investigations of the Renaissance. Not until the 17th century did there develop, under the stimulus of ecclesiastical scholarship, the technical methods on which our modern historical research depends.

Evolution of Documentary Collections

The first major cooperative scholarly program of modern times was initiated by the Jesuit Bollandists, under the leadership of John Bolland (1596–1665). Pressed by Protestant critics on the one hand, and on the other by humanist skeptics distrustful of the popular lives of the saints, the Bollandists undertook to collect relevant documentation, subject it to examination, and establish from it a serious and authoritative hagiography (Knowles, 1963, pp. 4–32). In addition to the diligent labors of the Bollandists in collecting and publishing sources, labors that continue to the present, they created the body of historiographical doctrine known as diplomatics, by means of which manuscript charters, official letters, and other documents are tested for authenticity.

Paralleling the Bollandist efforts at a slightly later date in the 17th century was the work of the French Benedictine monks known as Maurists, after St. Maurus, the patron of their congregation. From 1631 through 1789 they devoted themselves to the collection, criticism, and publication of historical materials relating to the Church in Europe. Again, the objective was to provide the sources on which a "true" history might rest.

The materials discovered and publicized by these 17th-century groups were primarily

[1] Ed. note: This section of the Introduction is co-authored by Gibson and Cline, in accordance with earlier plans for them to prepare the article jointly. Under a later modification, Gibson prepared the body of the text.

3

religious. The shift to secular documentation in the 18th century was closely connected with the Enlightenment, the age of revolution, and the development of modern nation-states. Until 1790 the documents written and collected by governments had been preserved not as scholarly archives but as files for the use of rulers and their advisors in the formulation and administration of policies.

With the downfall of the *ancien régime* in France came the decree of September 12, 1790, creating the Archives Nationales, through which important documents were to be collected and made available to the public. After this it was only a short step to the publication of documentary materials for wider diffusion. The revolutionists of France, and others after them, believed that the records of their struggle would provide justification for their fervor and virtue, while the documents of earlier days would reveal the iniquities that they had been seeking to redress (Schellenberg, 1958, pp. 19–24).

The prototype of modern documentary sets was the *Monumenta Germaniae Historica*, the first volume of which was published in 1826. Its originator, the Prussian statesman Karl von Stein, recognized ideological connections between German nationalism in his own time and historical knowledge of the medieval German past. In 1819 he and others created the Society for Ancient German History, which was partly funded by private subscriptions. Von Stein employed Georg Heinrich Pertz (1795–1876) and Johann Friedrich Böhmer (1795–1863) to search archives in Vienna, Rome, and other cities for chronicles, laws, charters, letters, and writings on German antiquities. The texts thus gathered were meticulously criticized and published in five subseries under the general rubric. The scholars and editors connected with the *Monumenta* put into print nearly all major sources on medieval Germany, and they simultaneously set a model of critical standards for later series

(Bresslau, 1921; Knowles, 1963, pp. 64–97). Other nations and other groups of scholars were soon to follow their lead.

Here we shall comment only on Spain and its related overseas territories. The field is not well covered bibliographically. A pioneering essay by Aznar (1938) remains nearly unique.

Although we are concerned primarily with collections of printed documents and cannot give exhaustive treatment to archival and manuscript collections, some notices of major repositories are included. With replete bibliography and useful lists of groups and individual documents, a helpful introduction to archives and archival research is provided by Lino Gómez Canedo (1961). The recently published (1966–69) two-volume *Guía de fuentes para la historia de Ibero-América conservadas en España* covers private and public collections. For Spain, Canedo's coverage is supplemented by Tudela de la Orden (1954) and Burrus (1955). For Latin America, Hill (1945, 1948), Grubbs (1936), and Carrera Stampa's translation (Schellenberg, 1958, pp. 26–36) of Schellenberg's useful manual (1957) are important. For many years the standard *Handbook of Latin American Studies* (1936–) had a separate section devoted to archival matters, edited by Hill (1938–48), and its history and other sections still carry notices of important documentary publications, especially in journals and reviews. A section on archives appears regularly in the bibliographical portion of *Revista de Historia de América* (Mexico). Especially important for Mexico is Bolton's *Guide* (1913), Carrera Stampa's *Archivalia mexicana* (1952), Millares Carlo and Mantecón's invaluable *Repertorio* (1948) and the former's later *Repertorio* (1959). Some data on United States manuscript collections of possible interest to Middle American ethnohistory appear in Robertson's *List* (1910), Hilton's *Guide* (2d ed., 1956), and other finding aids noted in Gómez Canedo (1961, 2:1–181). Supplemental for such materials are the Hamer

4

Guide (1961), Fernández de Córdoba (1956), and the revised Ricci and Wilson *Census* (1962).

In treating documents of possible value to ethnohistorical studies we can make certain general observations. First, the published ones represent only a very minor fraction of the manuscript sources available. However, the student will find that a thorough knowledge of what has already been printed on his topics will expedite his search for new and unpublished materials. Second, in general most manuscript repositories containing collections with ethnohistorical information are poorly organized, are chronically understaffed, lack finding aids, and often have capricious rules for access. Only a few have facilities for photocopying. Finally, the compilers and editors of the published sets and collections we note below did not have specifically in mind the possible needs of ethnohistorians when they selected materials for publication. Excavation of relevant data is usually a tedious, often frustrating exercise; only in the rarest cases are adequate subject or other indexes available for them.

Spain

With a characteristic passion for bureaucratic minutiae, the Spanish Crown under Philip II created as early as 1545 a general archive in the palace fortress of Simancas as a repository for official documents. Lesser administrative collections were transferred to it from time to time, but not until the advent of the Bourbon dynasty in the 18th century was an effort made to impose systematic order on the vast accumulation. Even today such attempts have not been wholly completed (Gómez Canedo, 1961, 1:139–49).

In 1780 the "enlightened" Bourbon monarch of Spain, Charles III, ordered Juan Bautista Muñoz, Royal Chronicler, to gather documentation from various holdings and to prepare a history that would contradict the anti-Spanish criticism being published by English, French, and other historians of the day. Under this authority Muñoz obtained copies of a variety of materials, filling 126 folio volumes, the bulk of which may still be consulted in the Royal Academy of History (Ballesteros y Beretta, 1954–58). Although he never completed his great work, Muñoz influenced subsequent research by persuading the Spanish Crown to establish (1785) the General Archive of the Indies in Seville. To it were to be sent from Simancas and elsewhere all important materials relating to America and the Philippines. Although the total corpus of such documentation was by no means concentrated in that one place, the archive did centralize a vast group of sources, some of which form the contents of published collections mentioned below (Gómez Canedo, 1961, 1:3–135; Burrus, 1955; Guía, 1966–69).

In his lifetime Muñoz himself published little or nothing from his collection of copies. But various copies of his copies, together with other data relating to voyages of discovery, were issued by Martín Fernández de Navarrete in a five-volume work of 1825–37. And in French translations some of the Muñoz documents came to scholars' hands in two documentary sets subsequently edited and published in Paris (Ternaux-Compans, 1837–41; 1840).[2]

New Spain and Mexico

To assist Muñoz' historiographical enterprise the Crown also ordered that documentation be provided by overseas officials. As a result an important body of colonial materials was gathered in Mexico. In 1790, under orders from Viceroy Conde de Revillagigedo II, Fathers García Figueroa and Manuel de la Vega compiled a work entitled "Colección de Memorias de Nueva España," in 32 manuscript volumes. The task was completed in 1792–93, two sets being transmitted to Spain, while one remained in Mexi-

[2] Ed. note: Several manuscripts once owned by Muñoz and Ternaux-Compans are now in the Obadiah Rich Collection, New York Public Library.

co.[3] Eleven volumes contained documents that had been specifically ordered by the viceroy in 1790; the remaining 21 were of additional antiquities, geography, and colonial history. Important maps were also included (Gómez Canedo, 1961, 1:199–201, 279). The "Memorias" have not been issued as a separate collection, but many of the particular items contained in them have since appeared in print (see especially Orozco y Berra, 1853–57).

As one of the reformist Bourbon officials, Viceroy Revillagigedo also laid the groundwork for the modern national archive of Mexico by ordering files from local depositories to be assembled in Mexico City. In 1823, shortly after Mexican independence from Spain, the public national archive of Mexico was created by decree. With various interruptions it has had a continuous history to the present, and it has issued some important sets of collected documents (Bolton, 1913, pp. 22–184; Rubio Mañé, 1940; Mariscal, 1946). Individual states of Mexico similarly organized local archives in the 19th and 20th centuries, and some also have issued documentary publications.

Central America

For Central America, the principal such depository is the Archivo General del Gobierno of Guatemala. Following an order of 1937, materials have systematically been added to it from other archives, including the Archivo Colonial and the Archivo Municipal de Guatemala. The Archivo Nacional of Honduras was created by law in 1880; that of Costa Rica dates from 1881, that of Nicaragua from 1896, and that of Panama from 1912. The national archive of El Salvador was destroyed by fire in 1889, and the

[3] Ed. note: One set is in the Royal Academy of History (Madrid); the other Spanish set is dispersed. The Mexican set is in AGN, Ramo de Historia, vols. 1–33. Tudela, 1954, pp. 17–18, and Bolton, 1913, pp. 20–59, list publication of the Memorias (Gómez Canedo, 1961, 1:1–199–201, 279).

Archivo Nacional of Nicaragua suffered a nearly complete loss of its original documents in the earthquake and fire of 1931. Further data on Central American archives and their holdings may be found in Hill (1945) and in Gómez Canedo (1961, 1:357–77).

DOCUMENTARY COLLECTIONS PUBLISHED BEFORE 1810

Legislative Compendia

Documentary collections relating to Middle America and published during the colonial period were principally compendia of laws issued for the practical use of administrators, lawyers, and judges. A helpful adjunct to their use is Altamira's *Diccionario* (1951), as is his *Manual* (1948) which contains important criticisms of collections mentioned below.

EARLY CODES. The ordinances of the first viceroy, published in Mexico City by Juan Pablos in 1548 (Mendoza, 1548) and reissued in facsimile in the 20th century (Mendoza, 1945), deal with administrative officers and their responsibilities and have only limited pertinence to Indian life. On a larger scale and of more immediate relevance for historical scholarship is Vasco de Puga, *Provisiones, cédulas, instrucciones*, published in Mexico in 1563 and now also accessible in a modern facsimile edition (Puga, 1945). This contains the major and minor legislation affecting New Spain in its first 40 years, including a large amount of legislation concerning Indians. Puga is still an excellent source for the first laws on Indian conversion, the prohibitions of Indian arms and horses, the cedula of 1549 forbidding labor in encomienda tribute, and other enactments to ca. 1560.

For Spanish America as a whole, in addition to various lesser compilations (e.g., Leyes, 1603; Ordenanzas, 1636), two major collections of law were published in the 16th and 17th centuries, preparatory to the great

Recopilación of 1681. One was Diego Encinas' *Cedulario indiano*, originally issued in 1596, but now most readily available in the facsimile published in five volumes with a study and index by Alfonso García Gallo (Encinas, 1945–53). (The term *indiano* of the title does not refer to Indians, but to the "Indies," the common Spanish term for America.) The second was the *Sumarios de la recopilación general de las leyes* of Aguiar y Acuña, issued in Madrid in 1628. The royal laws of these collections are of a diverse character, and the student must examine the volumes with some care in order to extract the quantities of ethnohistorical data they contain. The significant legislation concerns Indian tithe payments, the vulnerability of Indian agriculture to Spanish cattle, labor and tribute exaction, the carrying of loads, and other more or less expectable topics in royal legislation of the period.

RECOPILACIÓN, 1681. The foremost collection of law of the entire colonial period was the *Recopilación de leyes de los reinos de las Indias*, first issued in four volumes in Madrid in 1681, with subsequent editions, practically unchanged, appearing in 1756, 1774, 1791, and 1841. (*Recopilación de leyes*, 1943, is a facsimile of the edition of 1791.) This was the product of many years of effort and failure (Manzano y Manzano, 1950–56), and the final result stands as a major bureaucratic achievement of the 17th century in Spain.

It would be beyond the scope of this article to comment on every kind of reference made in the *Recopilación* to the native peoples of Middle America. Suffice it to say that Book VI is the one that deals directly with Indians, and that the *títulos* of this book are: Indians; Indian Liberty; Indian Reductions and Towns; *Cajas de censos* and Community Property; Indian Tribute and Taxes; Protectors of the Indians; Caciques; *Repartimientos*, Encomiendas, and Indian Pensions; *Encomenderos* of Indians; Good Treatment of the Indians; Succession to Encomiendas; Personal Service; Labor in Farms and *Obrajes*; Labor in Coca and Indigo Production; Labor in Mines; Indians of Chile; Indians of the Plata Area; the Sangeleyes of the Philippines; and Confirmations of Encomiendas. Obviously not all relate to Middle America, but the student may find in Book VI of the *Recopilación* abstracts of most of the important Indian legislation to 1680. Other portions of the work also repay examination for related subjects. Important supplementary material is provided by one of the *Recopilación*'s compilers, Juan de Solórzano, who wrote specifically on Indian matters (see Article 12, Item 17).

LATER CODES. In New Spain copies of the collection by Puga and Aguiar y Acuña had become scarce and in much demand by the last quarter of the 17th century. Accordingly, in 1677 the viceroy commissioned the *oidor* Juan Francisco Montemayor y Córdova de Cuenca to reissue the *Sumarios* of Aguiar y Acuña, and in addition to collect and publish the cedulas applying to New Spain since 1628. The Montemayor compilation appeared in 1678 as *Sumarios de las cédulas, ordenes y provisiones reales* and in the last years of the 17th century New Spain thus appeared to be well provided with printed collections of laws, for both Montemayor's *Sumarios* and the *Recopilación de leyes* were at this time up to date.

But this situation could obviously be only temporary. A century later conditions were again like those of the pre-Montemayor period. A new work, the *Recopilación sumaria* of 1787, was now published by the oidor Eusebio Bentura Beleña. This included the viceregal orders and the *autos acordados* of Montemayor, as well as the local legislation and the relevant royal orders of the period from 1677 to 1786. For the modern student the Bentura Beleña compilation is the most accessible, just as it is likely to be the most useful, of the works mentioned. Not only does it reprint material from the earlier collections, but its second volume contains the full texts of important late colonial laws: on new jurisdictions in Mexico City (1782); on rights and privileges of Indians (1784); on *obrajes* (1781); and on the establishment of the intendancies (1786).

SUMMARY. Taken as a whole the legal compilations published in the colonial period provide an enormous quantity of information on Spanish attitudes toward Indians, on administrative regulation affecting Indian life, and on Indian history itself. As one would expect, the laws have little to tell us about pre-Conquest conditions, and their substantive data on natives of the early colonial period are also relatively sparse.

These laws are not our best sources of information on Indian communities, Christianization, encomienda, or many other basic topics of Middle American ethnohistory. Only rarely does a law provide information on the activities of native peoples in particular places, and such information must ordinarily be supplemented with material from other sources if it is to be made meaningful. Moreover the abbreviated form in which most texts appear in these works does not provide for an adequate knowledge of the objectives, significance, or content of the laws. Inclusion of a given law in the *Recopilación* may frequently be most useful as an indication to the historian that such a law was issued and a notification to him that he should seek to locate the full text. But when the full text of a relevant law is given, or when a series of enactments contributes to our knowledge of how Indian peoples were treated, we have the beginnings of some useful ethnohistorical information. Thus the detailed regulations for corregidores in 1611 given by Montemayor, and the ordinances on obrajes given in Bentura Beleña, are informative both for what happened and for what the law assumed.

Other Collections

Apart from legal compilations, of which several more were issued in the late colonial period (e.g., Pérez y López, 1791–98), only

a few documentary publications appeared before 1810. Barcia's *Historiadores primitivos*, published in three volumes in Madrid in 1749, included Cortés' *cartas de relación*, Alvarado's letters to Cortés, and portions of writings by Oviedo, Cabeza de Vaca, López de Gómara, and others. The record of the ecclesiastical council of 1585 was published by royal order in Mexico as early as 1622 (Sanctum provinciale concilium, 1622), and in the 18th century Archbishop Francisco Antonio Lorenzana issued the record of the councils of 1555 and 1565 in Spanish and of the council of 1585 in Latin (Lorenzana, 1769, 1770a), with the texts of decisions reached on Indian social and religious practices (see Article 12, Item 92). These were local Mexican publications matching others issued earlier in Europe (see especially Concilium mexicanum provinciale, 1725; Sáenz de Aguirre, 1753–55). Lorenzana's own *Cartas pastorales, y edictos* (Lorenzana, 1770b) included letters of the 18th century on the treatment and conduct of native peoples, and Lorenzana also published an important edition of Cortés' letters (Lorenzana, 1770c).

Outside the Hispanic world the foremost published collection before 1810 was Richard Hakluyt, *Principal Navigations*, issued in three volumes in 1598–1600 (Hakluyt, 1598–1600) and later reprinted various times (e.g., Hakluyt, 1903–05, 1965). The collection contains the personal accounts of Englishmen who traveled to New Spain as merchants or who were captured there as Protestant intruders in the 16th century. These reports by Robert Tomson, John Chilton, Henry Hawks, and others are among the most valuable of all writing on early Mexico and their occasional comments on Indians have much ethnohistorical interest (see Article 12, Items 29–31). Finally Samuel Purchas, Hakluyt's successor, included in his series (Purchas, 1625) English translations of Herrera, Acosta, Oviedo, López de Gómara, and Codex Mendoza (see Article 12, Item 25). But none of these works should now be consulted in Purchas, for all have been more accurately published in subsequent editions.

DOCUMENTARY PUBLICATIONS OF THE 19TH CENTURY

Mexican Publications

EARLY PUBLICATIONS. Interest in Indian history was nowhere strong in the first half of the 19th century. The Romantic Age induced a certain emotional response to the exoticism of Indian life, but this tended to be superficial, distant, unconcerned with detail, and not appropriate for documentary publication. Materials published in independent Mexico from 1820 to 1850 have accordingly only a limited value. A journal, *El Museo Mexicano*, began a short-lived series (1843–44), and the editors included in its first volume the Juan Antonio Rivera diary (1676–96), with incidental data on Indian activities and most particularly on the uprising of 1692. Other texts, including viceregal *instrucciones*, travel accounts, tribute and other financial data of 1794, and another description of the 1692 uprising, were printed in subsequent issues of this journal during the next few years. The leading Mexican historian of the period was Lucas Alamán, the appendices to whose *Disertaciones* (Alamán, 1844–49) comprised one of the major collections of sources of the first half of the century. But so far as Indian materials were concerned, Alamán's selections had a distinctly conservative tone: a notice of the native artifacts sent by Cortés to Charles V; Cortés' regulation on encomienda; and genealogical and other data on the Condes de Moctezuma, who, though descendants of the Aztec emperor, were predominantly white and lived the life of aristocratic grandees in Spain.

Two *residencia* publications of the mid-century period, reflecting a continued concern with the protagonists of conquest, contained some data also on the fate of the people conquered. The first was *Procesos de residencia, instruídos contra Pedro de Alvarado y Nuño de Guzmán*, edited by J. F. Ramírez and published in Mexico in 1847 (Ramírez, 1847a). The second was the Cortés residencia papers of 1529, published in two volumes in the 1850s (Archivo mexicano, 1852–53). These works contain a large amount of contemporary fact, report, and rumor concerning official and unofficial relations between Spaniards and Indians in the early 16th century. Much of the governmental manipulation of Indian assignments in encomienda came to light in the residencias, as well as details of booty and of goods extorted from Indian towns in the early aftermath of conquest. Cortés' private relations with individual Indians, including daughters of Montezuma, were duly made part of the residencia record. It is in these documents that one may find contemporary reports of Cortés' torture of Cuauhtemoc, Alvarado's torture of Cacama, and Nuño de Guzmán's torture of Caltzontzin.

OROZCO Y BERRA (see also Article 21). In the second half of the 19th century, Manuel Orozco y Berra developed the first large-scale Mexican documentary publication. He was a serious student and collector and a writer capable of using historical texts to advantage. His *Noticia histórica de la conjuración del Marqués del Valle* (Orozco y Berra, 1853) can be thought of as a collection of documents on the 16th-century encomenderos' conspiracy, with an extended historical introduction.

But it is the *Documentos para la historia de Méjico*, published in four series of 21 (in 19) volumes (Orozco y Berra, 1853–57) that give him his chief claim as a publisher of documentary texts. The publication is still an important and useful one. Series 1 in seven volumes contains diary records of the late colonial period (by Gregorio Martín de Guijo from 1648 to 1664, by Antonio de Robles from 1665 to 1703, by José Manuel de Castro Santa Anna from 1752 to 1758, and by José Gómez from 1776 to 1798), with accounts of fiestas, epidemics, disorders, crop failures, and similar matters of importance to the Indian population, of course seen from an upper-class white point of view. All the diary materials pertain principally to central Mexico. Series 2 in five volumes includes missionary notices of the 17th and 18th centuries relating to natives and to white settlement in New Mexico and the north, and a large number of documents concerning the rebellions, which were in part Indian rebellions, in Mexico City, Puebla, and elsewhere, in 1624. The last two volumes of the series are reprints of the Mexican *Gacetas* of 1722, 1729–30, and 1730–31, with occasional scattered data for those years relating to Indian events.

Series 3 in one volume (in two parts) and Series 4 in seven volumes are rich with information on Indians of the north and frontier area. Sonora, Nueva Vizcaya, Chihuahua, New Mexico, and California in the 18th century are described in these series in a number of reports by missionaries, travelers, and administrators. For Mexicans the period was one of exceptional interest in the north, in part because of the recently completed war with the United States (1848) and the Gadsden Purchase (1853).

GARCÍA ICAZBALCETA (see also Article 21). Joaquín García Icazbalceta became the dominant figure in documentary publication in Mexico after the period of Orozco y Berra. His initial contribution was volume 1 of the *Colección de documentos para la historia de México*, published in 1858, and containing the *Historia de los indios de la Nueva España* of Motolinía, the account of the Conquest by the Anonymous Conqueror, and some letters and other texts of the Conquest period. Volume 2 of this collection, published in 1866, included significant materials of the post-Conquest 16th century: further reports and petitions of Cortés; a partial record of the Mendoza residencia, with data on the viceroy's relations with Indian society; the personal narrative of the Mixtón War by Francisco de Sandoval Acazitli, cacique of Tlalmanalco; and a large number of other valuable texts. The first document of volume 2 was the "Real ejecu-

toria de S.M." of the caciques of Axapusco, a putative cedula of 1537 granting favors to two Indian aides of Cortés. Though its authenticity was defended by José F. Ramírez, it is obviously in some degree false, and its importance for colonial ethnohistory appears to be that it illustrates the boldness of late colonial forgers and the eagerness of particular late colonial Indians to gain local privilege (García Icazbalceta, 1858–66).

García Icazbalceta's next major documentary project was the *Nueva colección de documentos para la historia de México*, published in five volumes between 1886 and 1892 (García Icazbalceta, 1886–92) and partially reprinted in 1941 (García Icazbalceta, 1941). This is an invaluable collection of source material for 16th-century ethnohistory. The abundant record of ecclesiastical writings of 1539–94 (*Cartas de religiosos de Nueva España*) in volume 1 relates at many points to Indian life, and for its time constituted by far the best collection of 16th-century material of its kind in print. Volume 2, called *Códice franciscano*, presents notices of 1569–70 on the Franciscan establishments of New Spain, the towns where they were located, and many additional data on Indian population, encomienda status, *visitas*, and the role of Christianity in Indian life. Volume 3 includes the 1582 *Relación de Texcoco* of Juan Bautista Pomar, the *Breve y sumaria relación* of Zorita, the *Historia de los mexicanos por sus pinturas*, the *Origen de los mexicanos*, and other shorter works, all of great value for Mexican ethnohistorical studies. Volumes 4 and 5 together make up the *Códice Mendieta*, a series of documents from the British Museum, with essential data from the 16th century on mission labors, tithes, visitas, Indian labor, the ecclesiastical *congregaciones*, and many other topics.

García Icazbalceta's other works demonstrate his strong predilection for documentary sources and his uncompromising scholarly purpose. He contributed to the republication of Vasco de Puga's *Provisiones*, *cédulas, instrucciones* in 1878–79 (Puga, 1878–79), an edition that initiated a long tradition of Mexican textual republication for historical and scholarly purposes. One of his major achievements in research, the biography of Zumárraga (García Icazbalceta, 1881), appeared with an extensive appendix of letters and other documents including some exceptionally important 16th-century commentary on encomienda and Indian tribute. This was reprinted in 1947 in the series *Colección de escritores mexicanos* (García Icazbalceta, 1947). His *Bibliografía mexicana del siglo XVI* (García Icazbalceta, 1886), reprinted and augmented in 1954 (García Icazbalceta, 1954) with some new materials by Agustín Millares Carlo, is essentially a listing and study of works published in Mexico to 1600, but it includes a number of passages selected from 16th-century publications and other relevant documents.

García Icazbalceta's plans for the publication of additional historical documents remained incomplete in his lifetime but were continued by his son, Luis García Pimentel, whose first major publication, the *Descripción del arzobispado de México hecha en 1570 y otros documentos* appeared in 1897 (García Pimentel, 1897). The larger portion of this work consists of a series of reports by clerics in 1569 providing exceptionally detailed information on *cabeceras* and *sujetos*, Indian populations, administration of sacraments, fiestas, other religious practices, political government, and Indian civil life in a large number of communities of the archbishopric. For its concrete ethnohistorical data, this work must be recognized as one of the most important of all those published in 19th-century Mexico.

LATER MEXICAN PUBLICATIONS. Some further documentary works made their appearance during the period of García Icazbalceta's productive activity. Among the more significant were the *Instrucciones que los vireyes de Nueva España dejaron a sus sucesores*, in two issues: a volume published in 1867 (Instrucciones, 1867), and two volumes published in 1873 as volumes 13 and 14 of the series *Biblioteca histórica de la Iberia* (Instrucciones, 1873). Although these collections were incomplete, and even though their texts have occasionally appeared in later publications, they remain today our best anthologies of the viceregal *memorias* for New Spain. Moreover they include some additional viceregal documentation that is not strictly to be included in the category of memorias. The viceroys characteristically commented on Indian affairs and Spanish-Indian relations, and they frequently did so in some detail, as in Viceroy Marqués de Montesclaros' severe indictment of clerical oppression of Indians in his letter of 1607, or Viceroy Revillagigedo's comments on tribute exaction in his *instrucción* of 1794.

Other volumes of the *Biblioteca histórica de la Iberia*, published between 1870 and 1875, include writings by Cortés, Bernal Díaz, Boturini, and Vetancurt, some of which are documentary in the present sense. Volume 20 has the interesting *Información recibida en México y Puebla* concerning the services of the Tlaxcalan Indians.

MUNICIPAL RECORDS. Not to be overlooked among 19th-century publications are the first 14 volumes of the complex series *Actas de cabildo de la ciudad de México*. The whole was issued in 54 volumes between 1889 and 1916 (Actas de cabildo, 1889–1916). This is the record of the meetings of the municipal council of Mexico City, beginning in 1524 and continuing through the 16th century and beyond. Ethnohistorical data are to be found especially for the early period, when Indians were more numerous and when the Spanish cabildo was more commonly in direct contact with native leaders. Records of urban intrusion on Indian lands, of the use of Indian labor in the city, and of a variety of other Spanish-Indian confrontations appear quite frequently in the early *Actas*. With time, such matters fell more to other administrative agencies, and the cabildo record for the 17th and 18th centuries tends to be of less interest from the ethnohistorical point of view. Moreover the published record is incomplete for these centuries. Large portions of the later *Actas*, in the Archivo del Ayuntamiento in Mexico City, remain in manuscript. Millares Carlo (1961) provides helpful information on these and other municipal records.

COLONIAL LAND LEGISLATION OF NEW SPAIN. Apart from the collections published for their historical interest there still existed a practical legal need for the printing of certain kinds of royal law, and the lawyers' and surveyors' handbooks of the 19th century therefore preserved a tradition that other kinds of publication abandoned. Examples are Colección de los decretos, 1829; Rodríguez San Miguel, 1839; Galván Rivera, 1844; Recopilación de las leyes, 1851; Manero, 1878; Labástida, 1893; Maza, 1893; and Orozco, 1895.

The laws tend to be repetitive in these compilations, but many of them, of course, do have a direct bearing on Indian history in the colonial period. Spanish land measurements, laws on relations between haciendas and Indian towns, the procedure for making a *denuncia*—these were still living issues after independence. Case after case still required interpretation of Spanish imperial law. This same law also became of interest in the United States, because legal precedents were important for business interests in Mexico itself and in the territories acquired during the Mexican War. Thus a documentary work in English translation, *The Laws of Mexico*, published by Frederic Hall in San Francisco in 1885, contains in addition to much 19th-century law the major cedulas of the colonial period on the rights of Indians, *composición*, the *fondo legal* of native towns, and related subjects. A similar work is *Spanish and Mexican Land Laws* published a decade later in St. Louis (Reynolds, 1895).

COLONIAL ECCLESIASTICAL RECORDS OF NEW SPAIN. The republication of colonial civil law was matched in the 19th century by some further documentary publication of the records of the colonial ecclesiastical councils. These were issued in Madrid in the mid-19th century by Francisco Antonio González (González, 1849–55) and Juan Tejada y Ramiro (Tejada y Ramiro, 1859–62), and in the post-Lorenzana era Mexican editions of the materials of the Third Council (1585) appeared again in 1859 (Concilio III provincial, 1859; Estatutos, 1859).

In 1879 Fortino Hipólito Vera edited a three-volume "compendium" of texts relating to the 1585 council, later adding further notes (Vera, 1893, 1897). Although some duplication in the Vera materials may be observed, these are still valuable works, for they contain many texts on conversion and on the Indian responses to missionaries beyond the material included in the formal conciliar papers. Texts on the fourth (1771) and the fifth (1896) Mexican councils appeared almost simultaneously in Queretaro (Camacho, 1898) and Rome (Acta et decreta, 1898) at the end of the century.

Of all these councils, it is the third—of 1585—that is of the most significance for ethnohistory. It was there that the ecclesiastical position on repartimiento, tribute, Indian drunkenness, and related subjects was formally and most explicitly declared, and the declarations occurred frequently in conjunction with statements containing useful ethnohistorical information. Students will ordinarily find the other conciliar materials to be less revealing, but it may be noted that the ecclesiastical councils as a whole are still incompletely documented and that further research and publication, especially of peripheral material, may yet yield data of importance.

Spanish Publications

In Spain, apart from the *Colecciones de documentos inéditos* (see below), the major publication of the period was *Cartas de In-*

dias (1877), a folio edition of documentary materials issued by the Spanish Ministerio de Fomento. The work consists mainly of official communications received in Spain from political and religious authorities in the colonies during the 16th century. In these a large share of the attention is devoted to matters relating to Indians. Southern Mexico, Yucatan, and Guatemala are included as well as the central portion of the viceroyalty. There are interesting letters on religious conversion and on the Spanish treatment of Indians, written by Martín de Valencia, Pedro de Gante, Juan de Zumárraga, and other principal figures, both political and religious, in the colony. Though published in Spain during a period of sensitivity to the Black Legend, the work evinces no tendency to suppress 16th-century criticism. Pedro de Gante's letter of 1552, for example, is a clear denunciation of abuses of Indians and disobedience of law by Spaniards.

Other Spanish items of the 19th century are of lesser interest. The *Recopilación de leyes* was again reprinted (1841), as we have seen. Other more up-to-date collections of laws were issued, such as Zamora y Coronado's *Biblioteca de legislación ultramarina* (Zamora y Coronado, 1844–46). A *nobilario de conquistadores* published in Madrid in 1892 on the fourth centenary of the discovery of America included many grants of royal arms to Mexican Indians and to Indian towns (Nobilario, 1892).

French Publications

In France the outstanding early series was the 20-volume *Voyages, relations et mémoires* of Ternaux-Compans, to which reference has already been made in connection with the collection of Muñoz (Ternaux-Compans (1837–41). Though most of this series related to other parts of the continent than Middle America, the volumes that are pertinent to our present subject reveal a concern for native history that was rare before the midcentury. They included a number of texts never before published, and even now, over a hundred years later, not all the Ternaux-Compans manuscripts have appeared in Spanish. The Ternaux-Compans versions have an historiographical interest, but they are not always reliable, and few present-day scholars refer to them. For Middle American ethnohistory the most pertinent volumes are 8 (*Crautés horribles des conquérants du Mexique*), 10 (*Recueil des pièces relatives à la conquête du Mexique*), and 46 (*Pièces sur le Mexique*). The collection also contains French translations of Zorita and Ixtlilxochitl.

In France also, Charles Etienne Brasseur de Bourbourg published various texts relating to the Maya. His edition of Diego de Landa (Landa, 1864) included parts of the *Historia de Yucatán* by Bernardo de Lizana (published in Valladolid in 1633), and his edition of the Manuscrit troano (Brasseur de Bourbourg, 1869–70) contained also some texts of Maya prayers and prophecies and a Nakuk Pech family title (see Article 18).

An important French series was the *Bibliothèque linguistique américaine*, consisting of modern and colonial dictionaries, *artes*, and works on Indian languages applying to both North and South America. Its volume 12, the *Annales* (6th and 7th Relations) of Domingo Francisco de San Antón Muñon Chimalpahin Quauhtlehuanitzin, with the Nahuatl text and a French translation by Rémi Siméon, is the most important volume of the series for Mexican ethnohistory (Chimalpahin Quauhtlehuanitzin, 1889). Eugène Boban, *Documents pour servir à l'histoire du Mexique* (Boban, 1891), is also a major French work of the period, but it is more an elaborate catalog of written documents and codices than a documentary collection.

Other European Publications

Elsewhere in Europe a small number of

13

dedicated individuals produced in the 19th century a modest body of documentary publications on Middle American Indian history. Interest centered on the Conquest and on the problems of native American linguistics.

Pascual de Gayangos, the Spanish aide of Prescott and cataloguer of Spanish manuscripts in the British Museum (Gayangos, 1875–93), published his well-known edition of Cortés' writings, including the Veracruz *regimiento* letter of 1519, the four major *cartas de relación*, and numerous other documents by and relating to Cortés (Gayangos, 1866). It is still one of our most reliable editions of Cortés materials.

A collection of ecclesiastical regulations relating to Spanish America edited by Francisco Javier Hernáez, *Colección de bulas* (Hernáez, 1879), was published in Brussels. Kingsborough's great *Antiquities of Mexico* appeared in London in the 1830s and 1840s (Kingsborough, 1831–48).

United States Publications

With respect to the United States, documentary publication was principally linguistic prior to the 20th century. After the appendix to Prescott's *Conquest of Mexico* (Prescott, 1843), the major collection was D. G. Brinton's *Library of Aboriginal American Literature* (Brinton, 1882–90), which began publication in Philadelphia in 1882. Number 1 of the *Library* is *Maya Chronicles* (Brinton, 1882), with extracts and translations of Chilam Balam books and other Maya texts. Number 3 is the *Güegüence*, a Nicaraguan ballet in Nahuatl (Brinton, 1883). Number 6 is the *Annals of the Cakchiquels* (Brinton, 1885), and Numbers 7 and 8 are publications of Nahuatl verse (Brinton, 1890a, 1890b). A number of works by Brinton include portions of Middle American texts in native languages and in English translation. A proposed set of documents on Central America edited by E. G. Squier seemingly never went beyond an initial volume (Squier, 1860).

14

Collecciones de Documentos Inéditos

Historia de España, DIE, 1842–95

The *Colección de documentos inéditos . . . para la historia de España* in 112 volumes (Colección de documentos, 1842–95, 1970a), often abbreviated in citation as CDIHE or DIE, is the foremost single published collection of documents for the history of Spain. It is not primarily a collection for Spanish America, much less for Middle American ethnohistory, but because it emphasizes the period of Charles V and Philip II it almost necessarily contains material relevant to our subject.

A table of contents may be found in Foulché-Delbosc and Barrau-Dihigo (1920–26, 2:113–79), and consultation is further facilitated through use of the Julián Paz *Catálogo* (Paz, 1930–31, reprint 1966).

Significant materials for Middle American ethnohistory in this series are: letters and other documents relating to Cortés in volume 1 (1842); further material of the same kind, perhaps particularly Martín Cortés' letter of 1538 on Indian social organization and tribute payment in volume 4 (1844); an informative *instrucción* of 1673 in volume 21 (1852); the 16th-century *instrucciones* of Viceroy Mendoza and Viceroy Enríquez in volume 26 (1855); and an account of the Indian uprising of 1692 in volume 67 (1892). Additional note may be taken of certain texts for which there are now better editions elsewhere: the *Manual de ministros* of Jacinto de la Serna in volume 104; the *Relación de Michoacán* and Motolinía's *Historia de los indios* in volume 53; and a large amount of Las Casas material, including his *Historia de las Indias* in volumes 62–66 (see Articles 12 and 13, Bibliography).

A series modeled on the 19th century one, and entitled *Documentos inéditos para la historia de España publicados por los señores duque de Alba*, first made it appearance in 1940 and concluded with 13 volumes in

1957. It contains almost nothing on the ethnohistory of Middle America.

Collections Relating to Spanish America

The equivalent large-scale collections relating to Spanish America, similarly drawn from archives in Spain, are the *Colección de documentos . . . de Indias*, in 42 volumes, now usually abbreviated as DII (Colección de documentos, 1864–84); the *Colección de documentos . . . ultramar*, in 25 volumes, normally abbreviated as DIU (Colección de documentos, 1885–1932), and the *Colección de documentos . . . Ibero-América* in 15 volumes, abbreviated as DIA (Colección de documentos, 1927–32).

Materials of the first two, from the Patronato section of the Archivo General de Indias in Seville, represent selections originally made by Muñoz. Published carelessly in some disorder, they may most conveniently be used in conjunction with the *Indice* of Ernst Schäfer (1946–47). We may note also that a chronological reorganization of the materials of the 42 volumes of the DII has been published by Benjamin Read (Read, 1914).

Documentos Inéditos . . . de Indias, DII, 1864–84

For Middle American ethnohistory the DII is the most valuable of the collections here being discussed (Colección de documentos, 1864–84, 1970b). The *Breve y sumaria relación* of Alonso de Zorita in volume 2, though also now available in other editions, is one of the basic documents for the subject. Volume 3 includes documents on the Mixtón War and on Indian baptism. Letters of Viceroy Mendoza, Francisco de Montejo, Martín Cortés, and others in volume 4, if read carefully, yield useful data on Indian life in the early colony. The descendants of Montezuma and their properties receive attention in documents of volume 6, which also has material on Indian labor. Las Casas' activities in Chiapas, Guatemala, and elsewhere are documented in volume 7. Volume 12 contains many miscellaneous materials on Cortés and his encomienda holdings, and a letter of 1532 by Ramírez de Fuenleal in volume 13 on categories of Indian sujetos and lands is most revealing. The caciques and Indians of Xochimilco are the authors of a letter of 1563 published also in volume 13.

Volume 14 includes the Pedro de Carranza report on Nuño de Guzmán's conquest of New Galicia. Various orders of Cortés on the treatment of Indians are included in volume 26, and volumes 26–29 have invaluable documentary data from Cortés' residencia. Additional ethnohistorical material from the 16th century appears in volume 41. Rich as the particular items mentioned are, they represent only a fraction of the total contained in this important collection.

Documentos Inéditos . . . de Ultramar, DIU, 1885–1932

In the DIU (Colección de documentos, 1885–1932, 1970c) the documents of Middle American ethnohistorical interest begin with volume 9, which is a collection of legislative texts, instructions to Cortés and to Luis Ponce de León, and materials on encomienda and Christian treatment of Indians in the 1520s. Volume 10 continues with documents of the same type through the 1530s, including some informative correspondence on native practices and the royal instructions to Viceroy Mendoza in 1535. Volumes 11 and 13 have the *Relaciones geográficas* of Yucatan, comprising as a group the best documentation in print for the Maya communities of the late 16th century, together with the Cristóbal de Pedraza report on Higueras and Honduras (1544).

Volumes 14–18 are the five volumes of León Pinelo's *Indice general de los papeles del Consejo de Indias*, with abundant historical information in abbreviated form (see Article 12, Item 9). The first and fifth of these volumes are most useful for Mexican studies; the fourth applies to Guatemala, Honduras, and other areas to the south.

These five volumes are indexed in volume 19. Finally volumes 20–25 comprise the *Gobernación espiritual y temporal de las Indias,* a documentary index to the files of the Consejo de Indias, with notices of a large number of Consejo orders, many relating to Indians, in the 16th century.

Documentos . . . Ibero-América, DIA, 1927–32

In the DIA the first volume is the most interesting one from the point of view of the ethnohistory of Middle America. This has much precise documentation on the early encomienda history of Mexico and a number of fascinating letters dealing with changes in Indian tributes. Other documents concern the Diego Ramírez visita in the mid-16th century, the privileges of caciques, and the structure of early colonial Indian society. The *Nobilario* of volume 2 includes a few Indian names. Manuel Josef de Ayala's *Diccionario de gobierno y legislación de Indias* in volumes 4 and 8 is a partial catalog of early cedulas, with occasional ethnohistorical data. Other volumes of the series are of limited relevance to Middle American ethnohistory.

Large General Collections of the 20th Century

Peñafiel, 1897–1904

The 20th century opened in Mexico with the publication of Antonio Peñafiel's *Colección de documentos para la historia mexicana* (Peñafiel, 1904a), the materials of which, although the final publication carried the title-page date 1904, had actually been issued in sections since 1897. The sections include the *Cantares en idioma mexicano,* the *plano* attributed to Alonso de Santa Cruz, some formal Nahuatl conversations, *Códice Aubin de 1576,* the *Anales de Tecamachalco,* and documents on Indians in Texcoco in the 16th and 17th centuries. The collection has a strong Nahuatl flavor, and it illustrates a particular tendency of the

late 19th and early 20th centuries in an ethnohistorical direction.

García Pimentel, 1903–07

García Pimentel's *Documentos históricos de Méjico* (García Pimentel, 1903–07) began to appear before Antonio Peñafiel's collection was completed. The García Pimentel series eventually amounted to five volumes, of which the first two, the *Memoriales* of Motolinía (Motolinía, 1903) and the *Relación de los obispados de Tlaxcala, Michoacan, Oaxaca y otros lugares en el siglo XVI* (García Pimentel, 1904), are the most important in the present connection. The former provided a text more or less complementary to Motolinía's *Historia,* previously published by García Icazbalceta. The latter continued the publication of local 16th-century information through reports organized by bishoprics. Other works in the series contained occasional observations on Indians of the 19th century by Eugenio de Aviraneta é Ibargoyen and José María Andrade, but without any of the systematic treatment or concentration that now characterized ethnohistorical publication on the early colonial period.

Paso y Troncoso, 1905–08

Francisco del Paso y Troncoso devoted many years to collection of documents, but unfortunately published only relatively few before his death in 1916. Details on his major series, "Papeles de Nueva España," and photoreproduced Sahagún materials are found in Article 21, especially Appendix F. His *Epistolario* is treated two sections below.

Documentos inéditos ó muy raros, 1905–11

The 36 volumes of *Documentos inéditos ó muy raros para la historia de México,* edited by Genaro García and Carlos Pereyra from 1905 to 1911 (García and Pereyra, 1905–11), though extensive, have relatively little for ethnohistory. Much of the documentation relates to political and military affairs of the independence and postindependence eras, and the documentation on the colony tends not to be concerned with Indian history. The major exceptions to these statements are to be found in volume 10 on colonial Mexican rebellions and in volume 15 on clerical activities.

Biblioteca histórica, 1936–63

The *Biblioteca histórica mexicana de obras inéditas*, first series, published in 25 volumes from 1936 to 1963, consists in part of works that are not documentary in our most strict sense. The individual volumes are sometimes entire works by distinct authors, such as *La vida económica y social de Nueva España*, written by Gonzalo Gómez de Cervantes ca. 1599 (Gómez de Cervantes, 1944). But some of the individual volumes are themselves published collections of shorter documents. Thus volumes 14 and 15, edited by France V. Scholes and Eleanor B. Adams, provide an exceptionally full documentary coverage on Diego Quijada, *alcalde mayor* of Yucatan in the 1560s (Scholes and Adams, 1938). Volume 17, edited by Nicolás León, contains data from the Archive of the Indies on relations between Indians and Vasco de Quiroga (León, 1940). Volumes 13 and 18 are archival selections on Zacatecas and Nueva Galicia. And various other volumes have ethnohistorical material in a scattered and uneven form.

Epistolario de Nueva España, 1939–42

In the second series of this same *Biblioteca histórica de obras inéditas* is the 16-volume *Epistolario de Nueva España* (Paso y Troncoso, 1939–42). We have in it one of our richest sources for ethnohistorical material. The collection reprints some of the items previously published in other collections, but in general it gives more reliable versions of them, and it adds vast quantities of new documentation to the earlier record. A detailed discussion appears in Article 21, Appendix F.

Letters by, to, and about Cortés treat many aspects of his relations with Indians. The post-Conquest activities of other conquistadores and ex-conquistadores, in encomienda, military expeditions, Indian enslavement, tribute exaction, and the like, are described in greater or lesser detail, by the individual concerned or by some external observer. The texts proceed chronologically from the 1520s and they relate to all parts of Mexico as these came to be opened and occupied. There are demographic reports, further records of the Ramírez visita, letters by caciques and other Indians in Spanish, Nahuatl, and Latin, lists of encomiendas and encomienda tributes, statements of royal and other privilege, data on the Montezuma genealogy, and occasional notices of Indian pre-Conquest conditions. The dated documents continue to the late 16th century, and the final volumes contain a number of documents *sin fecha*.

Archivo General Publications, 1910–36

The *Publicaciones* of the Archivo General de la Nación, appearing in 30 volumes between 1910 and 1936 (Publicaciones del AGN, 1910–36), form a rich series for Indian history of all parts of Mexico. Volumes 1 and 3 contain the records of early inquisitorial actions against Don Carlos of Texcoco and other Indian idolators, with some of the most detailed information in print on native attitudes, practices, and material possessions in the 1530s. Volume 27 is a collection of documents on Cortés and his family, including the absorbing record of a lawsuit between the inhabitants of Coyoacan and the second Marqués del Valle.

Volumes 29 and 30 relate wholly to the viceregal administration of Antonio María de Bucareli, in the 18th century. They include a huge number of documents relevant to late colonial official acts: *padrones*, tributes, a *bando* of 1772 designed to establish Indian schools throughout the viceroyalty, and so forth.

Other volumes of the series are also applicable to ethnohistory. There are materials

17

on missionary labors in Sonora and Arizona, a considerable quantity of documents on independence, the extremely important writings of Fray Francisco de Burgoa relating to Oaxaca (Burgoa, 1934a, 1934b), and other works of interest. The diligent student will find in this set many items of value, and he will ignore them at his peril.

In addition to the regular *Publicaciones* series, the AGN and its directors, such as López Rayón and Orozco y Berra, have issued miscellaneous volumes of documents from it. The *Libro de las tasaciones* (1952) is an example. As also noted in the last section below, its *Boletín* is a rich mine. Monographic publications of the AGN to 1940 are listed in Rubio Mañé's summary article (Rubio Mañé, 1940), with some additional data in Hill (1945).

Mexico Colonial, 1955–59

Documentos para la historia del México colonial, edited by France V. Scholes and Eleanor B. Adams, which began publication in 1955, illustrates the increasing importance assigned to ethnohistory in modern understanding of the colonial period. The volumes include *Relación de las encomiendas de indios hechas en Nueva España a los conquistadores y pobladores de ella* (1564); *Advertimientos generales que los virreyes dejaron a sus sucesores* (1590–1604); *Ordenanzas del Hospital de San Lázaro de México* (1582); *Información sobre los tributos que los indios pagaban a Moctezuma* (1554); *Sobre el modo de tributar los indios de Nueva España* (1561–64); *Moderación de doctrinas de la Real Corona administradas por las órdenes mendicantes* (1623); and *Cartas del licenciado Jerónimo Valderrama y otros documentos sobre su visita al gobierno de Nueva España* (1563–65).

Carnegie Institution of Washington Publications, 1923–39

The immense series of *Publications* of the Carnegie Institution of Washington, which includes works on many subjects, contains

several documentary items for Middle American ethnohistory. Two works edited by Ralph L. Roys, *The Book of Chilam Balam of Chumayel* (Roys, 1933) and *The Titles of Ebtun* (Roys, 1939), are important Maya texts. The latter is itself a collection of Indian documents from the archive of the town of Ebtun.

The three-volume *Historical Documents Relating to New Mexico, Nueva Vizcaya, and Approaches Thereto* (Hackett, 1923–37) is a collection of Spanish documents with English translations originally collected by Adolph F. A. Bandelier and Fanny R. Bandelier. The materials are of direct relevance to Indian history and Spanish-Indian relations of all periods, particularly for northern Mexico.

Colección Chimalistac, 1958–

Colección Chimalistac may also be cited as a series of fine modern editions of books and documents relating to colonial Mexico. Published in Madrid, beginning in 1958, the collection includes the writings of González Dávila and Vetancurt, as well as descriptions of the *Códices matritenses* of Sahagún and a large amount of material on Texas, Louisiana, California, and other parts of the north (e.g., Píccolo, 1962; Documentos, 1962; Kino, 1964).

Hakluyt Society

Finally the *Works* issued by the Hakluyt Society, continuing the publications of Hakluyt and Purchas, have given some attention to Middle America. They include the texts, in English translation, of Champlain's record of his alleged travel in Mexico (vol. 23), Cortés' fifth letter (vol. 40), Bernal Díaz (2d ser., vols. 22–25, 30, 40), and some other peripheral material.

Vargas Rea Publications,[4] 1944–

All the charges leveled by later critics at

---

[4] This section on Vargas Rea publications was prepared and inserted by the Volume Editor.

Bustamante's unsatisfactory editorial practices in the early 19th century can be applied to Luis Vargas Rea's malpractices in the 20th. Since 1944 he has published more than 400 titles on a wide variety of historical and literary topics, many of direct concern to ethnohistory, several uniquely published by him (Cline, n.d.). Hence, although the Vargas Rea publications, by flouting all recognized canons of scholarly editing, remain a public disgrace, they cannot be overlooked.

His publications are the cataloger's nightmare and the bibliographer's despair. He has issued more than 30 series and subseries, arbitrarily and whimsically initiated, erratically numbered, haphazardly paginated. Vargas Rea volumes, apparently printed in his house, appear on poor-quality paper, with slipshod binding, studded with typographical errors, and issued in small editions at high prices. Seldom is the source of a document precisely given; a particular document, under the same or variant title, may be reprinted in the same or another series or subseries without reference to its previous appearance. One student, who 20 years ago attempted to unravel the first 140 titles, noted "There is an unfortunate lack of care and thoroughness in the editorial work, and the proofreading leaves much to be desired. There would be little point in listing instances of these faults; they are legion. The work appears unduly hurried. All this is especially regrettable because of the importance and significance of the material published" (Nunemaker, 1948, p. 316).

Various portions of this "Guide to Ethnohistorical Sources" have noted or listed relevant parts of the Vargas Rea output. His several subseries containing the 1579–85 *Relaciones geográficas* are treated in Article 9 (Vargas Rea) and in Article 21 (App. F, series 2); those containing the 18th-century *Relaciones geográficas* are noted in Article 10. In progress at the Hispanic Foundation, Library of Congress, is a program to analyze and provide a bibliography of the complicated and often nearly worthless Vargas Rea production.[5]

OTHER MODERN DOCUMENTARY COLLECTIONS AND SERIES ON SPECIAL TOPICS: COLONIAL PERIOD

In this section we shall proceed chronologically and by topics, indicating the principal collections of documents relating to the various categories.

Institutional Publications

Indian history of the pre-Spanish and early colonial periods is the subject of some of the major publishing ventures of the 20th century. The series *Corpus Codicum Americanorum Medii Aevi*, published in Copenhagen, provides us with reliable facsimile editions of the manuscripts of the *Historia Tolteca Chichimeca* (1942), *Unos Annales históricos de la nación mexicana* (1945), Chimalpahin's writings (1949), and the *Memorial de Tecpan Atitlan* (1952).

Similar and related materials are contained in the *Quellenwerke zur alten Geschichte Amerikas aufgezeichnet in den Sprachen der Eingeborenen* series, published by the then Ibero-Amerikanische Bibliothek in Berlin. This consists of several volumes of the *Geschichte der Konigreiche von Colhuacan und Mexiko*, *Popol Vuh*, Sahagún, Chimalpahin, and other major texts. These are listed in Article 31.

Fuentes indígenas de cultura náhuatl, issued by the Seminario de cultura náhuatl of the Instituto de Historia, University of Mexico, presents documents by the informants of Sahagún (Sahagún, 1958a, 1958b, 1961) and other Indian records (Poesía, 1964, 1965).

The volumes in the Maya Society series are in part publications of essential Indian texts. They include the *Chronicle of Calkiní* (Gates, 1935) and the De la Cruz-Badiano herbal (Cruz, 1939).

---

[5] Ed. note: Author's text resumes.

Anthologies of Documents

Documentary sources on pre-Spanish Indian history have frequently been reprinted as separate items and occasionally gathered together in anthology form. A well-known example, with translations into English, is Paul Radin, *The Sources and Authenticity of the History of the Ancient Mexicans* (Radin, 1920).

For the area south of Mexico, Adrián Recinos, ed., *Crónicas indígenas de Guatemala* (Recinos, 1957) is perhaps the best such source.

More comprehensive is Nicolau d'Olwer's anthology of *cronista* writings relating to the native societies for all America before or at the time of white contact (Nicolau d'Olwer, 1963). With respect to Middle America the Nicolau d'Olwer work includes writings of Cortés, Bernal Díaz, Motolinía, Sahagún, Pomar, Zorita, Landa, Niza, Pérez de Ribas, Tello, Bobadilla, and Oviedo, as well as the *Relación de Michoacán*.

Native Literature

Publications of what may be called literary documents in native languages, with or without translations, comprise a special category which cannot be treated fully here. Outstanding historic examples are Brinton's *Library of Aboriginal American Literature*, previously noted; Rubén M. Campos, *La producción literaria de los aztecas* (Campos, 1936); and Luis Castillo Ledón, *Antigua literatura indígena mexicana* (Castillo Ledón, 1917). All of these are in one way or another now out of date.

To be preferred, for the quality and accuracy of the translations, are Angel María Garibay Kintana, *Poesía indígena de la altiplanicie* (Garibay Kintana, 1940), and the same editor's *Poesía*, noted above. The facsimile *Cantares en idioma mexicano*, edited by Antonio Peñafiel (Peñafiel, 1904b) should also be mentioned. The foremost guide to Nahuatl literature is Garibay Kintana, *Historia de la literatura náhuatl* (Garibay Kintana, 1953–54), which contains many quoted materials and references to texts not cited here.

A useful and convenient collection of Maya Chilam Balam texts is *El libro de los libros de Chilam Balam*, edited by Alfredo Barrera Vásquez and Silvia Rendón (Barrera Vásquez and Rendón, 1948). For a comprehensive anthology of Indian literary writings from all parts of Spanish America, José Alcina Franch, *Floresta literaria de la América indígena* (Alcina Franch, 1957) may be noted. Abraham Arías-Larreta (1964, 1967) has also provided translations of native literary and historical texts. With respect to native drama the *Teatro indio precolombino* of Cid Pérez and Martí de Cid contains the Güegüence, Rabinal, and other dramatic texts (Cid Pérez and Martí de Cid, 1964).

Conquest Literature

For the conquest period, which has always attracted preponderant attention from historians, the 20th-century documentary publications are fairly abundant.

Cortés' letters have been published in a large number of editions of all degrees of fullness and quality. In addition to the editions cited elsewhere in this article, we call attention to the facsimile of Codex Vindobonensis S.N. 1600 (Cortés, 1960) and to the Eulalia Guzmán edition (Cortés, 1958), with editorial notes that systematically question the reliability of what Cortés wrote. The *Escritos sueltos* of Cortés (Cortés, 1874) in the *Biblioteca histórica de la Iberia* series, volume 12, and the collection entitled *Hernán Cortés* edited by García de Polavieja (1889) are still valuable. Arteaga Garza and Pérez San Vicente (1949) have edited the royal cedulas relating to Cortés and *Cartas y otros documentos de Hernán Cortés*, edited by Mariano Cuevas (Cuevas, 1915), is a collection of Cortés material from the Archivo General de Indias with miscellaneous Indian data, especially on the native communities of the Marquesado del Valle in central

20

Mexico and the south. *Nuevos documentos relativos a los bienes de Hernán Cortés* (Nuevos documentos, 1946), a joint publication of the Archivo General de la Nación and the Universidad de México, also has many data on Indian peoples of central Mexico and the areas of the Marquesado.

Documents relating to the conquest of Yucatan and the Itzas have been published in English translation by Means (1917). León-Portilla is the editor of two modern documentary anthologies that express the Indian side of the conquests: *Visión de los vencidos* (1959), which has been translated into English by Lysander Kemp as *The Broken Spears* (León-Portilla, 1962); and *El reverso de la conquista* (León-Portilla, 1964), which includes Maya material as well as Aztec.

A collection of documents dealing with the Noche Triste has been edited by G. R. G. Conway (1943). A number of other collections reissue letters of conquistadores and other documentary materials relating to the subject of conquest (e.g., Crónicas, 1963).

Heraldry and Genealogy

A publication of the Museo Nacional, Mexico, *Cedulario heráldico de conquistadores de Nueva España* (Cedulario, 1933) with texts taken mainly from archives in Seville, Simancas, and Madrid, contains 145 cedulas and coats of arms, of which the first 123 relate to Spaniards and the remainder to privileged Indians of the colony. The Indian upper class is also the subject of Guillermo S. Fernández de Recas' collection, *Cacicazgos y nobilario indígena de la Nueva España* (1961), which contains documents and documentary summaries on 35 *cacicazgos* of central Mexico, Oaxaca, Guanajuato, and other areas.

Missionary Efforts

Published collections on missionary labor and the "spiritual conquest" are scarce in comparison with those of the military relations of Spaniards and Indians. We mention again the *Nueva colección de documentos para la historia de México* (García Icazbalceta, 1886–92), as well as the Zumárraga documents (García Icazbalceta, 1881), and García Pimentel's bishopric documentation (García Pimentel, 1897, 1904). The collection of primary sources on Vasco de Quiroga (Aguayo Spencer, 1939) includes the texts of the regulations governing the two "hospitals" of Santa Fe near Mexico City and in Michoacan, as well as other data on Indian slaves and on litigation involving Quiroga and the natives of Tultepec. All these are revealing for relations between ecclesiastics and Indians in central Mexico.

For the north, where the work of conversion continued for a longer time, the materials are more abundant. Lejarza's 1947 work on the spiritual conquest of Nueva Santander has a documentary section on Franciscan labors in the 18th century, and many other works on the north relate, *inter alia*, to missionary labor.

The Guadalupe literature, closely connected with spiritual conquest, is also represented in several collections that are documentary or quasi-documentary in character (e.g., Vera, 1887–89; Cuevas, 1930). An important desideratum in the field of documentary publication, however, is a serious and critically edited collection on the Virgin of Guadalupe and on other apparitions in Indian history.

Indian Tribute and Labor

The 16th-century tribute-payment history of the towns of central Mexico may be traced in the documents of *El libro de las tasaciones de pueblos de la Nueva España* (Libro de las tasaciones, 1952), a collection of detailed tribute records.

For Indian labor the largest and most valuable printed collection is the eight-volume *Fuentes para la historia del trabajo* (Zavala and Castelo, 1939–46). From the material point of view, it was as a laborer that the Indian was most important to the Spanish colonists, and the large number of texts in these volumes, drawn principally from the General de parte *ramo* of the Archivo General de la Nación in Mexico, are invaluable for an understanding of the developing labor systems of the 16th century. The volumes have good introductions and the materials are well indexed. The history is well covered from 1575 to ca. 1630, after which it runs more thinly. Other shorter collections on Indian labor include *Ordenanzas del trabajo, siglos XVI y XVII* (Zavala, 1947), and *Repartimiento de indios en Nueva Galicia* (González Navarro, 1953).

Guilds are treated in another collection, *El trabajo en México durante la época colonial* (Barrio Lorenzot, 1921), which, though not entirely accurate, is our foremost collection on *gremio* regulations and the role of Indians in the local manufacturing of the viceregal capital. It may be supplemented by other studies of gremios, especially Carrera Stampa, *Los gremios mexicanos* (1954), a work of monographic scholarship that contains selections from the texts of guild regulations in reliable form. Material of a similar nature, principally concerning Indian labor and guilds, may be consulted in *Legislación del trabajo* (Vásquez, 1938), which contains the texts of labor ordinances from 1561 to 1770.

Law and Legislation

Additional collections of royal law, or cedularios, have been published in abundance for the colonial period. For the late 17th and 18th centuries, there is Antonio Muro Orejón's *Cedulario americano del siglo XVIII* (Muro Orejón, 1956), with material from 1680 to 1800. Alberto María Carreño is the editor of *Un desconocido cedulario del siglo XVI* (1944), a collection of royal law on ecclesiastical subjects, including interesting early legislation on Indian baptism, marriage, drunkenness, and religious practices.

The three-volume *Disposiciones complementarias de las Leyes de Indias*, published by the Spanish Ministerio de Trabajo y Previsión in Madrid (1930), is an extraordi-

narily rich collection of royal orders taken from the Ayala materials of the Archivo Histórico Nacional. The editors generally excluded cedulas already contained in the *Recopilación* (it is in this sense that the laws are "complementary"). An enormous number of topics—encomienda, tribute, local government, towns, cacicazgos, *cajas de comunidad*, tithes, etc.—receive attention.

A particular collection of colonial law relating to Indians is the *Doctrinas y realidades en la legislación para los indios* (Vásquez, 1940), containing royal ordinances, laws from the *Recopilación*, and legislation from many other sources. For the legal aspects of ethnohistory this is one of the most basic and useful of all documentary publications.

Other Social and Economic Topics

Mariano Cuevas' *Documentos inéditos del siglo XVI* (1914) is a single-volume collection, principally of official letters, with some valuable commentary on native life. Letters by Mendoza, Zumárraga, and others deal with encomienda, tribute, and Indian tithes. The Meztitlan letter of Nicolás de Witte, which appears here as well as in several other collections, is a remarkable summary of information on Indian society and tribute gained over a period of 12 years by an alert and perceptive missionary. Similar letters by Motolinía and Diego de Olarte from Cholula, and by Domingo de la Asunción from Chimalhuacan are likewise included in this collection.

More theoretical aspects of Spanish understanding of the Indians are expressed in the compilation of Lewis Hanke and Agustín Millares Carlo, *Cuerpo de documentos del siglo XVI* (1943). An important documentary set relating to colonial social history, closely related to certain subjects of ethnohistory, is the four-volume *Colección de documentos para la historia de la formación social de Hispanoamérica*, edited by Richard Konetzke (1953–62).

Luis Chávez Orozco's *Documentos para*

la historia económica de México (1933–38) is a mimeographed set of 12 documentary volumes rich in material on Indian history. The subjects, in order, are textile manufacturing in the 19th century, the economy of New Spain in 1788, 18th-century salaries, intendants, cajas de comunidad, the origins of socialism, 17th-century repartimientos, mining salaries, the first steam engine, the origins of agrarianism, obrajes, and mining. Volume 11 has excellent documentation on Indian labor, especially obraje labor, from the 16th century though the colonial period.

A successor series, issued as the *Publicaciones* of the Banco Nacional de Crédito Agrícola y Ganadero (1953–58), is a documentary set relating to agriculture, credit, and prices, and it contains some basic economic data for ethnohistory. Volumes on price controls, crop crises, community funds, and hacienda economy bear particularly on Indian history.

A related collection is the *Archivo histórico de hacienda*, in five volumes, published under the direction of Jesús Silva Herzog (1943–45). It contains materials on economic history, commerce, statistics from the intendancy period, *alcabalas*, and hacienda disbursements. Though not primarily dedicated to Indian matters, the documents are revealing for such subjects as the Indian liability to particular taxes and the payments made to the descendants of Montezuma (for the subjects mentioned, see 4:269 ff. and 5:139 ff.).

Regions

NEW SPAIN (EXCEPT YUCATAN). Colonial documentation on particular regions of Mexico includes Cornejo Franco's *Testimonios de Guadalajara* (1942), an anthology of colonial writings; the *Colección de documentos para la historia de Oaxaca* (Colección de documentos, 1933), with six 16th-century documents from the materials of Paso y Troncoso; Gómez de Orozco's anthology of colonial chroniclers who dealt with the mission and Indian history of Michoacan

(1940); Joaquín Meade's *Documentos inéditos para la historia de Tampico* (1939), a small volume of 16th-century documents concerning the *alcaldías mayores* and Spanish-Indian relations in that area; José Eleuterio González' *Colección de noticias y documentos para la historia del Estado de N(uevo) León* (1867); Pérez Maldonado's edition of *Documentos históricos de Nuevo León* (1947), with materials from 1596 to 1821; Primo Feliciano Velázquez' four volumes of San Luis Potosi (1897–99); the *Biblioteca histórica jalisciense* (Alemán and Iguíniz, 1909); Roberto Ramos' 1958 *Tres documentos sobre el descubrimiento y exploración de Baja California*, an anthology of the narratives of Francisco María Píccolo, Juan de Ugarte, and Guillermo Stratford; and another brief collection of Baja California materials, *Contribución para la historia de la Baja California* (Contribución, 1928). For Puebla, the *Cartilla vieja de la nobilísima ciudad de Puebla* is an 18th-century collection of documents on the colonial history of the city (Cartilla vieja, 1961). Occasional ethnohistorical documents relating to other communities may be found in Antonio Peñafiel, *Ciudades coloniales y capitales* (1908–14) as well as in a large number of town histories. The *Actas de cabildo* of Mexico have been mentioned above.

Indian towns have occasionally published documents on their own history, usually with reference to particular land claims (e.g., Títulos principales, 1915). Somewhat akin to these are Zapotec materials published by Julio de la Fuente (1949).

The ethnohistorical content of the documentary works on local colonial history varies considerably, and much more remains to be published from local archives. But the student interested in any region of Mexico will ordinarily find it rewarding to examine whatever publications of local documents may be available to him. It should be added that these works were sometimes issued in such small editions that they are frequently now to be found only in the best and largest libraries, or in the libraries of the particular region concerned.

MAYA AREA. The Maya area also offers its particular collections for colonial history, and here because of the extensive interest in Maya Indian civilization the editions have generally been larger and the volumes are far more available. Alfredo Barrera Vásquez has edited a convenient collection for the Maya area consisting of the *Relación* of Landa and 10 *relaciones geográficas* for Yucatecan towns in the 1579–81 period (Barrera Vásquez, 1938). The *Tasaciones de los pueblos de la provincia de Yucatán* have also been published for 1549 (Tasaciones, 1941). Major collections for the area are the three-volume *Documentos para la historia de Yucatán* (Scholes and Menéndez, 1936–38), with data on conversion, congregación, visitas, and related subjects, and the *Archivo de la historia de Yucatán, Campeche y Tabasco* (Rubio Mañé, 1942), also in three volumes, with materials on 16th-century encomiendas, caciques, population, and Indian enslavement.

CENTRAL AMERICA. For the colonial areas farther to the south the student must cull relevant ethnohistorical data from standard, and very incomplete, documentary collections: *Relaciones históricas y geográficas de América Central* (Serrano y Sanz, 1908); *Colección de documentos referentes a la historia colonial de Nicaragua* (Colección de documentos, 1921); *Colección de documentos para la historia de Costa Rica* (Fernández, 1883–1907); and Vega Bolaños' edition of *Colección Somoza* (Vega Bolaños, 1954–57).

One other principal source of documentation for Central America is the justificatory publication on boundary disputes, notably the volumes edited in Europe by Manuel M. de Peralta, Minister Plenipotentiary of Costa Rica, in the late 19th century (Peralta, 1886, 1890, 1898). These contain the reports of early explorers in Central America, correspondence of colonial governors, and records of missionaries and trav-

elers, with valuable early data on the Mosquito Indians and other native peoples.

NORTHERN BORDERLANDS. Publication of Spanish colonial documents on the Indians of what is now the United States southwest properly falls outside the scope of this article, but it may be indicated in passing that such publication has been extremely abundant in the 20th century, and that many texts primarily concerned with the Indians of the southwest bear also upon the native peoples of northern Mexico.

From a long-term ethnohistorical point of view the political boundary separating the United States from Mexico is immaterial. This fact has commonly been expressed in the concept of the Borderlands, which span northern Mexico and the associated parts of the United States southwest in a single comprehensive whole. In addition to items already mentioned (e.g., Hackett, 1923–37), important documentary collections bearing in differing degrees upon the colonial native population of this region are: Bourne, 1904; Winship, 1896; Hodge and Lewis, 1907; Hammond and Rey, 1940; Bolton, 1916; Burrus, 1954; Serra, 1955–66; Portillo, 1886; Kinnaird, 1949; Haggard, 1940; and Carrasco y Guisasola, 1882.

Attention may also be called to the series *Spain in the West* and to the *Publications* of the Quivira Society, containing original chronicles, travel diaries and related materials on Texas, New Mexico, California, and adjacent regions, as well as scholarly monographs on these same areas. All have material on Indians.

MODERN PUBLICATIONS: POSTCOLONIAL PERIOD

Independence and General

The postcolonial period is far poorer in ethnohistorical documentation than is the colonial period. Independence, with some reference to Indian participation, is covered especially in the *Colección de documentos para la guerra de independencia* (Hernández y Dávalos, 1877–82), and the seven-volume *Documentos históricos mexicanos* edited by Genaro García (García, 1910–12). The bibliography on independence includes several collections dealing with Morelos (e.g., Morelos, 1927, 1965; Lemoine Villicaña, 1965), the most fully documented of the leaders of the period. Some of the collections already mentioned, such as the *Publicaciones* of the Banco Nacional de Crédito Agrícola y Ganadero, occasionally deal with 19th-century and modern topics. But it should also be said that some of the foremost collections of texts for national Mexican history, such as the *Archivo histórico diplomático mexicano*, excellent as they may be, hardly bear on ethnohistory at all.

Later 19th Century and Mexican Revolution

The later 19th century is represented by several important collections, with very uneven reference to Indian history: Puig Casauranc's edition of the *Archivos privados de D. Benito Juárez y D. Pedro Santacila* (Puig Casauranc, 1928); Tamayo's *Epistolario de Benito Juárez* (Tamayo, 1957) and *Benito Juárez, Documentos* (Tamayo, 1964); the *Colección de documentos inéditos o muy raros relativos a la Reforma en México* (Colección de documentos, 1957–58); the *Archivo del General Porfirio Díaz* (Carreño, 1947–60); the *Fuentes para la historia de la Revolución mexicana*, edited by Isidro Fabela (Fabela, 1960–67), which is the foremost documentary publication for the Revolution of 1910. The abundant materials of this last work continue to be published, and the volumes issued had reached the year 1916, in 12 volumes, by 1967.

Another kind of collection on the 20th-century Revolution is the six-volume *Historia gráfica de la Revolución*, the texts of which are photographs and other illustrations rather than written materials (Casasola, n.d.). Finally the addresses of Lázaro Cárdenas, the principal modern sponsor of Indian land reform, have been collected in the work *Cárdenas habla* (Cárdenas, 1940).

Church, Law, Legislation

Ecclesiastical texts of all periods of Mexican history to the late 19th century are published in the collection of Fortino Hipólito Vera (Vera, 1887). For civil law, the constitutions and related fundamental legislation from 1808 to the present have appeared in many publications, but are most conveniently consulted in the one-volume text by Tena Ramírez (Tena Ramírez, 1967). The *indigenismo* legislation of Mexico has been collected and edited by Manuel Gamio (Gamio, 1958). For more detailed information on legal publications, Vance and Clagett, 1945, and Clagett, 1947, should be consulted.

Local Regions and Areas

The documents of the ethnohistory of local areas are also more poorly represented for the national than for the colonial period.

Again Indian communities have occasionally published items from their town archives or engaged to collect and publish other documents that illustrate their history, as in *Al severo tribunal del público, las víctimas de Xuchitepec* (Al severo tribunal, n.d.), a rare volume of documents detailing losses of land by Xuchitepec to the mid-19th century. Another type is represented by *The Titles of Ebtun*, to which we have referred above.

At the state level should be noted the collection of legal papers relating to Indian lands, houses, lots, and *fondos legales* of Jalisco, published during the Reform period (Colección de acuerdos, 1849–68), and a series for Tabasco extending into the 19th century, published by Mestre Ghigliaza (Mestre Ghigliaza, 1916–40). Carlos Menéndez is the editor of an interesting set of documents on 19th-century Maya Indians of Yucatan who were sold as slaves in Cuba (Menéndez, 1923). And for Central American nations, the Instituto Indigenista Interamericano has issued documentary materials on indigenist legislation (Legisla-

25

ción . . . Costa Rica, 1957; Legislación . . . Guatemala, 1954; Legislación . . . Honduras, 1958).

Topics

The entire chronological history of particular topics of ethnohistorical interest has sometimes been treated in documentary publications of modern times.

Among such topics, for obvious reasons, Mexican land legislation has received principal attention. We may cite the *Cinco siglos de legislación agraria* (Fabila, 1941), and the *Historia de la tenencia y explotación del campo* of Francisco González de Cossío (González de Cossío, 1957), which include a large number of documentary selections and extracts on this subject. A somewhat similar work, designed more for the use of *campesinos* and for practical legal application, is the *Catecismo agrario* of Julio Cuadros Caldas, a compilation of laws, regulations, instructions, and other relevant documentation on land sales, *ejidos*, and other agrarian affairs. First published in 1922, the work is much better known in later editions (e.g., Cuadros Caldas, 1932). Ethnohistorical material on various subjects, including land, may also be found scattered through the large two-volume *Historia documental de México*, edited by León-Portilla and others (1964).

MODERN JOURNALS AND ADDITIONAL MISCELLANEOUS SERIES

It is impossible to comment here on all pertinent documents published in periodicals and other series. Their number and range are enormous, and the disparate character of their publication is such that they do not always fall squarely in our category of published collections of documents. We shall comment only on the principal journals that publish or have published documents more or less regularly. For further data on journals, reference may be made to Annita M. Ker, *A Survey of Mexican Scientific Periodicals to which are Appended Some Notes on*

Mexican Historical Periodicals (Ker, 1931).

MNA Anales

A major source is the massive set of the *Anales* of the Museo Nacional de México, devoted to archaeology, ethnology, linguistics, and history, almost all relating to the Indian peoples of the country. The *Anales* have been published continuously, with some minor irregularities, since 1877. The documentary publications are interspersed with articles, reports on archaeological finds, catalogs of collections, and similar materials.

The student searching for ethnohistorical sources is well advised to examine all volumes in the various series. He will be rewarded, to list only the outstanding materials of this collection, with the *Historia de los mexicanos por sus pinturas* in volume 2 (1882); *Mapa Tlatzin* and *Mapa Quinatzin* and an early published version (since superseded) of the *Anales de Cuauhtitlan* in volume 3 (1886); and the *Lista de los pueblos principales que pertenecían antiguamente a Tetzcoco* and various plates of the *Tonalamatl Aubin* in volume 4 (1897). Volume 6 (1900) contains an invaluable collection of colonial reports on Indian idolatries and superstitions: Pedro Ponce, Hernando Ruiz de Alarcón, and Jacinto de la Serna, for the central Mexican area and for Mexico in general; Pedro Sánchez de Aguilar for the Maya area; Gonzalo de Balsalobre for Oaxaca; and Pedro de Feria for Chiapas. In volume 7 (1903) are the *Historia de la Nueva España* of Francisco de Aguilar, and two native annals, the *Anales mexicanos, Mexico-Azcapotzalco, 1426–1589*, and the *Anónimo mexicano*, as well as *confesionarios* and other materials in the Tepehua, Cuitlateca, and other languages.

Volume 2 (1905) of the second epoch contains Códice Dehesa, Códice Fernández Leal, Códice Sánchez-Solís, and other Indian documents of southern Mexico. Volume 3 (1906) of this series contains Genaro García's index to Orozco y Berra's *Docu-*

mentos para la historia de Méjico (see above); and volume 4 (1907) has the same compiler's index to Hernández y Dávalos' *Colección de documentos para la historia de la guerra de independencia*. Volume 4 also includes the colonial *Relaciones geográficas* of Acatlan, Chila, and other communities of the Mixteca Baja.

The famous *Plano de maguey* is published in volume 1 (1909) of the third epoch, together with a lengthy descriptive document and *padrón* of 18th-century Churubusco. Volume 4 (1912–13) of this series includes a version of the *Cuadros de mestizos*. Volume 5 (1913) has the text of Juan Manuel de San Vicente's *Exacta descripción* of Mexico City in the 18th century, and materials from the Cuevas Collection, including Códice Cuevas.

In a long section on Francisco del Paso y Troncoso in volume 1 (1922) of época 4 may be found codical and other ethnohistorical material connected with his bibliography. Volume 2 (1923) of this series includes the important Ramón Mena catalog of Boturini manuscripts in the Biblioteca Nacional. The López catalog of Boturini items is published in volume 3 (1925). Volume 4 (1926) illustrates the Códice Mauricio de la Arena, and volume 5 (1927) contains the *Información del señor de Coyoacán*. Volume 8 (1933) has the first publication of the Códice de San Antonio Techialoyan and the pioneering study of Techialoyan materials by Federico Gómez de Orozco.

Documentary materials in época 5 include an important letter of 1556 on Indian tithe payments in volume 1 (1934). In 1939 the *Anales* initiated a new series beginning again with volume 1, and the documentary source material became less abundant, probably because opportunities for publishing such material elsewhere were by this time much more ample. But mention should be made of the Mapa de Popotla published by Alfonso Caso in volume 2 (1941–46) and the fourth *Relación* of Chimalpahin, pub-

lished in Nahuatl with Spanish translation by Silvia Rendón, as well as some Zapotec ethnohistorical data, in volume 3 (1947–48).

Obviously the student should exercise some care in the use of the documents published in the older volumes of the *Anales*. The texts and translations are not always reliable, and in some cases preferable versions are available elsewhere. But over all it is a major series, or collection of series, and it merits very serious attention from ethnohistorians. Pompa y Pompa (1962) has summarized the numerous publications of MNA, including contents of the *Anales*, *Boletín*, and bibliography of the monographic publications since 1827.

AGN Boletín

Another of the most important publications of this class is the *Boletín* of the Archivo General de la Nación in Mexico City. Published regularly since 1930, the *Boletín* is the official publication vehicle for the documents of the archive, and a perusal of the *Boletín* is like an extended tour through the archive itself. Most documents are published in full, with introductory or other commentary.

So rich and extensive is the total that any brief mention of individual items here will seem arbitrary, but the following quite incomplete enumeration may suggest the type of document to be found: Sobre los inconvenientes de vivir los indios en el centro de la ciudad (9:1–34, 1938); Mandamientos sobre indios en los obrajes, 1579–1633 (11: 9–32, 1940); Tributos de pueblos de indios (Virreinato de Nueva España), 1560 (11: 195–243, 1940); Diligencias practicadas por el obispo Zumárraga, 1536 (16:33–40, 1945); Enseñanza del castellano como factor político-colonial (17:163–71, 1946); Informe sobre pulquerías y tabernas el año de 1784 (18:187–236, 1947); Las congregaciones de indios en el siglo XVI (23:145–312, 1952); Testamento del gobernador y cacique de Santiago Tlaltelolco, Don Lucas de Santiago y Rojas, 1724 (25:59–74, 1954); Protesta de los indios de Atoyac para no ser congregados en el pueblo de Tecpan, año de 1614 (n.s.,1:535–49, 1960). Attention may also be called to the excellent introductions to the documents published in this journal in recent years, by Ernesto de la Torre Villar, Ernesto Lemoine Villicaña, and others.

Other Journals and Series

The *Journal de la Société des Américanistes de Paris* has a long record of interesting documentary publication. The *Histoyre du Mechique* and the *Leyenda de los soles* were authoritatively published in this journal in 1905 and 1906, and in the subsequent period Nahuatl documentation and codical reproduction have appeared fairly frequently.

The *Boletín del Instituto bibliográfico mexicano* is chiefly of interest for its publication of Nicolás León's *Bibliografía mexicana del siglo XVIII*, in issues of 1902 and after. León's remarkable bibliography republishes various documents: on the Hospital Real y General de los Indios, on the history of haciendas, and on a number of other aspects of Indian history. The *Gacetas* of the 18th century, with some peripheral data of ethnohistorical interest, are also republished here.

The distinguished *Memorias de la Academia mexicana de la Historia* contains in various issues a large number of ethnohistorical documents, published in whole or in part. This was the medium for the series entitled *Tlatelolco a través de los tiempos*, sponsored by Robert H. Barlow and others, with documentary publications of Indian annals, testaments, and other documents concentrating on the 16th- and 17th-century history of Tlatelolco.

The *Memorias de la Sociedad científica "Antonio Alzate,"* though not designed as a journal of history, nevertheless has occasionally printed pertinent material, such as a Cuauhtinchán annal (5:27–37, 1891–92), and some Veracruz codices (30:389 ff., 1911; 32:435 ff., 1914).

Tlalocan is also an important journal for documentary publication. In it appeared the *Titles of Tetzcotzinco* (2:110–27, 1946), the *Títulos de Cuernavaca* (2:215–22, 1946), and a number of other Indian texts.

Additional journals of various degrees of importance are *Historia mexicana, Estudios de cultura nahuatl, Revista de historia de América, Revista de Indias, Revista mexicana de estudios históricos (antropológicos), Boletín de la Sociedad mexicana de geografía y estadística, Boletín del Archivo histórico del estado de Chiapas, América indígena*, and *The Americas*.

It should be noted also that some particular journals relate to Central America: *Boletín del Archivo General del Gobierno* (Guatemala), beginning in 1935; *Anales de la Sociedad de Geografía e Historia de Guatemala*, beginning in 1924; *Revista del Archivo y Biblioteca Nacionales* of Honduras, published between 1904 and 1909, reactivated in 1927, and superseded since 1955 by the *Revista de la Sociedad de Geografía e Historia de Honduras*; *Revista de la Academia de Geografía e Historia de Nicaragua*, beginning in 1936; *Revista del Archivo General de la Nación* of Nicaragua, beginning in 1964; and *Revista de los Archivos Nacionales de Costa Rica*, beginning in 1936. Additional existing journals, and new ones as they appear, are best identified through the Anthropology, History, and Ethnohistory sections of the *Handbook of Latin American Studies*.

Marginal Collections

It remains to comment upon a large number of multi-volume collections and series that are more or less marginal to our present topic, either because they reprint material already known or because they fail in one way or another to qualify precisely as collections of documents.

A common practice is to issue works by different authors in series, as in the *Biblioteca de autores españoles*, with editions of Acosta, Las Casas, Remesal and others, and the *Nueva Biblioteca de autores mexicanos,* with or without occasional "documentary" material. Or a series that is primarily monographic may occasionally include a volume consisting of the letters or shorter writings of a given author. Materials of this nature tend to be bibliographically complex and not easily classified.

The student should be aware of the *Actas,* under various titles, of the nearly 40 meetings of the International Congress of Americanists in different cities of Europe and America. The *Proceedings* have been indexed by Comas (1954a, 1964). He has also prepared a similar guide to the proceedings of the International Congress of Anthropological Sciences, 1865–1954 (Comas, 1954b). These contain little of interest to ethnohistory.

The Academy of American Franciscan History publishes various series, including one that is bibliographical and another that is documentary. The latter has translations of important Franciscan texts, including *Motolinía's History of the Indians of New Spain,* and the writings of Junípero Serra, both of ethnohistorical interest.

Similarly the *Documents and Narratives* series of the Cortés Society contains texts of the Anonymous Conquerer and Pedro de Alvarado, as well as of the first Spanish voyages to Yucatan.

The extensive *Publicaciones* of the Centro de Estudios Americanistas in Seville, in various series which include *Estudios americanos* and the *Anuario de estudios americanos,* occasionally issues documentary materials together with its excellent studies.

The University of Mexico and its various institutes publish some complex series, and the list includes the Códice Chimalpopoca, Alvarado Tezozomoc's *Crónica mexicayotl,* the Codex Xolotl, and the Sahagún documents previously mentioned.

The *Ibero-Americana* series of the University of California has been primarily monographic, but it does include some documentary publications as appendices to monographs or as textual inserts. The principal documents for ethnohistory occur in the subseries of L. B. Simpson entitled *Studies in the Administration of the Indians in New Spain* (Simpson, 1934–40), with the text of the Laws of Burgos and documents on congregación, forced labor, and emancipation of Indian slaves.

The *Publications* series of the Middle American Research Institute of Tulane University is also monographic, but with some important documentary publications. For ethnohistory attention may be called to the "cedula" of Cuauhtemoc (Rendón, 1952) and to several native theatrical texts from Guatemala (Correa et al., 1961).

More or less similar material may be found in the series entitled *Biblioteca "Goathemala" de la Sociedad de Geografía e Historia, Biblioteca americana, Biblioteca del estudiante universitario, Colección de grandes crónicas mexicanas, Bibliotheca Novohispana, Biblioteca Tenanitla,* and *Testimonios mexicanos.* Many other published series we do not mention because they are reprint series or because they are not, or not sufficiently, documentary in nature. A number of the particular works mentioned earlier in this article and others in this Guide are titles in other series to which special reference is not made.

REFERENCES

ACTA ET DECRETA
1898 Acta et decreta concilii provincialis mexicani quinti celebrati an. dom. MDCCCXCVI metropolita illustrissimo ac reverendissimo d. d. Próspero María Alarcón y Sánchez de la Barquera. Rome.

ACTAS DE CABILDO
1889–1916 Actas de cabildo de la ciudad de México. Title varies. 54 vols. Mexico.

AGUAYO SPENCER, RAFAEL
1939 Don Vasco de Quiroga. Documentos. Mexico.

AGUIAR Y ACUÑA, RODRIGO DE
1628 Sumarios de la recopilación general de las leyes, ordenanzas, provisiones, cédulas, instrucciones y cartas acordadas, que por los reyes católicos de Castilla se han promulgado, expedido, y despachado para las Indias Occidentales, islas y tierra firme del mar océano. Mexico.

AL SEVERO TRIBUNAL
n.d. Al severo tribunal del público, las víctimas de Xuchitepec, por la inquisición de Chalco. Mexico.

ALAMÁN, LUCAS
1844–49 Disertaciones sobre la historia de la república megicana, desde la época de la conquista que los Espanoles hicieron, a fines del siglo XV y principios del XVI, de las islas y continente americano, hasta la independencia. 3 vols. Mexico. [Reprinted 1942].

ALCINA FRANCH, JOSÉ
1957 Floresta literaria de la América indígena. Antología de la literatura de los pueblos indígenas de América. Madrid.

ALEMÁN, FRANCISCO G., AND JUAN B. IGUÍNIZ
1909 Biblioteca histórica jalisciense. Guadalajara.

ALTAMIRA Y CREVEA, RAFAEL
1948 Manual de investigación de la historia del derecho indiano. PAIGH, Commission on History, Pub. 3. Mexico.

1951 Diccionario castellano de palabras jurídicas y técnicas tomadas de la legislación indiana. PAIGH, Commission on History, Pub. 25. Mexico.

ARCHIVO MEXICANO
1852–53 Documentos para la historia de México. Sumario de la residencia tomado a don Fernando Cortés, gobernador y capitán general de la Nueva España, y a otros gobernadores y oficiales de la misma. 2 vols. Mexico.

ARIAS-LARRETA, ABRAHAM
1964 Precolumbian literature: Aztec, Incan, Maya, Quiche. New World Library, Indo-American Literature, 1. Starkville, Miss.

1967 Pre-Columbian masterpieces: Popol Vuh, Apu Ollantay, Chilam Balam. New World Library. Indo-American Literature, 3. Kansas City, Mo.

ARTEAGA GARZA, BEATRIZ, AND GUADALUPE PÉREZ SAN VICENTE
1949 Cedulario cortesiano. Sociedad de Estudios Cortesianos, Pub. 1. Mexico.

AZNAR, LUIS
1938 Colecciones documentales éditas relativas a la historia de la América española. II Congreso Internacional de Historia de América (Buenos Aires), Actas, 5:40–55.

BALLESTEROS Y BERETTA, ANTONIO, ed.
1954–58 Catálogo de la colección de don Juan Bautista Muñoz. 3 vols. Madrid.

BANCO NACIONAL
1953–58 Publicaciones. 21 vols. Banco Nacional de Crédito Agrícola y Ganadero. Mexico.

BARCIA BARBALLIDO (Y ZÚÑIGA), ANDRÉS GONZÁLEZ DE
1749 Historiadores primitivos de las Indias Occidentales. 3 vols. Madrid (imprint varies).

BARRERA VÁSQUEZ, ALFREDO
1938 Relación de las cosas de Yucatán, sacada de lo que escribió el padre fray Diego de Landa.

—— AND SILVIA RENDÓN
1948 El libro de los libros de Chilam Balam. Fondo de cultura económica. Biblioteca americana, *Serie de literatura indígena*, 8. Mexico.

BARRIO LORENZOT, FRANCISCO DEL
1921 El trabajo en México durante la época colonial. Ordenanzas de gremios de la Nueva España. Genaro Estrada, ed. Secretaría de Gobernación. Mexico.

BENAVENTE, TORIBIO DE
See Motolinía.

BENTURA BELEÑA, EUSEBIO
1787 Recopilación sumaria de todos los autos acordados de la real audiencia y sala del crimen de esta Nueva España, y providencias de su superior gobierno. 2 vols. Mexico.

BIBLIOTECA HISTÓRICA DE LA IBERIA
1870–75 Biblioteca histórica de la Iberia. 20 vols. Mexico.

BIBLIOTECA HISTÓRICA MEXICANA
1936–63 Biblioteca histórica mexicana de obras inéditas. 25 vols. Antigua Librería Robredo, de J. Porrúa e hijos. Mexico.

BOBAN, EUGÈNE
1891 Documents pour servir à l'histoire du Mexique. Catalogue raisonné de la collection de M. E. Eugène Goupil (ancienne collection J. M. A. Aubin). Manuscrits figuratifs, et autres sur papier indigène d'agave mexicana. 2 vols. and atlas. Paris.

BOLTON, HERBERT EUGENE
1913 Guide to materials for the history of the United States in the principal archives of Mexico. Carnegie Institution of Washington, Pub. 163. Washington.
1916 Spanish exploration in the Southwest, 1542–1706. Original Narratives of American History. New York.

BOURNE, E. G.
1904 Narratives of the career of Hernando de Soto in the conquest of Florida. 2 vols. New York.

BRASSEUR DE BOURBOURG, CHARLES ÉTIENNE
See Article 18, Appendix A.

BRESSLAU, HARRY
1921 Geschichte der Monumenta Germaniae Historica. *Neues Archiv der Gesellschaft für ältere deutsche Geschichtskunde*, 42. Hanover.

BRINTON, DANIEL G.
1882 The Maya chronicles. *Brinton's Library of Aboriginal American Literature*, 1. Philadelphia.
1882–90 Library of aboriginal American literature. 8 vols. Philadelphia.
1883 The Güegüence: A comedy ballet in the Nahuatl-Spanish dialect of Nicaragua. *Brinton's Library of Aboriginal American Literature*, 3. Philadelphia.
1885 The annals of the Cakchiquels. The original text, with a translation, notes, and introduction. *Brinton's Library of Aboriginal American Literature*, 6. Philadelphia.
1890a Ancient Nahuatl poetry. *Brinton's Library of Aboriginal American Literature*, 7. Philadelphia.
1890b Rig Veda Americanus: Sacred songs of the ancient Mexicans, with a gloss in Nahuatl. *Brinton's Library of Aboriginal American Literature*, 8. Philadelphia.

BURGOA, FRANCISCO DE
See Article 13, Bibliography.

BURRUS, ERNEST J.
1954 Kino reports to headquarters. Correspondence from New Spain with Rome. 2 vols. Institutum Historicum Societatis Jesu. Rome.
1955 An introduction to bibliographical tools in Spanish archives and manuscript collections relating to Hispanic America. *HAHR*, 35:443–83.

CAMACHO, RAFAEL SABÁS
1898 Concilio provincial mexicano IV. Celebrado en la ciudad de México el año de 1771. Queretaro.

CAMPOS, RUBÉN M.
1936 La producción literaria de los aztecas. Mexico.

CÁRDENAS, LÁZARO
1940 ¡Cárdenas habla! Mexico.

CARRASCO Y GUISASOLA, FRANCISCO
1882 Documentos referentes al reconocimiento de las costas de las Californias desde el cabo de San Lucas al de Mendocino. Dirección de Hidrografía. Madrid.

CARREÑO, ALBERTO MARÍA
1944 Un desconocido cedulario del siglo XVI perteneciente a la catedral metropolitana de México. Mexico.
1947–60 Archivo del General Porfirio Díaz. 29 vols. *Col. de obras históricas mexicanas*, 2–3. Mexico.

31

CARRERA STAMPA, MANUEL
1952 Archivalia mexicana. UNAM. Instituto de Historia. Mexico.
1954 Los gremios mexicanos. La organización gremial en Nueva España, 1521–1861. *EDIAPSA*, 1. Mexico.

CARTAS DE INDIAS
1877 Cartas de Indias. Ministerio de Fomento. Madrid.

CARTILLA VIEJA
1961 Cartilla vieja de la nobilísima ciudad de Puebla. Pedro López de Villaseñor, ed. UNAM. Instituto de Investigaciones Estéticas, *Estudios y fuentes del arte en México*, 2. Mexico.

CASASOLA, AGUSTÍN VICTOR
n.d. Historia gráfica de la Revolución, 1900–1940. 6 vols. Archivo Casasola. Mexico.

CASTILLO LEDÓN, LUIS
1917 Antigua literatura indígena mexicana. Mexico.

CEDULARIO
1933 Cedulario heráldico de conquistadores de Nueva España. MNA. Mexico.

CHÁVEZ OROZCO, LUIS
1933–38 Documentos para la historia económica de México. 12 vols. Secretaría de la Economía Nacional. Mexico.

CHIMALPAHIN QUAUHTLEHUANITZIN, DOMINGO FRANCISCO DE SAN ANTÓN MUÑON
1889 Annales. Sixième et septième relations (1258–1612). Rémi Siméon, trans. and ed. *Bib. linguistique américaine*, 12. Paris.
1949 Diferentes historias originales de los reynos de Culhuacan, y México, y de otras provincias. Manuscrit mexicain, nr. 74. *Corpus Codicum Americanorum Medii Aevi*, 3. Copenhagen.

CID PÉREZ, JOSÉ, AND DOLORES MARTÍ DE CID
1964 Teatro indio precolombino. Madrid.

CLAGETT, HELEN L.
1947 A guide to the law and legal literature of the Mexican states. GPO. Library of Congress. Washington.

CLINE, HOWARD F.
n.d. A working list of Vargas Rea publications. Unpublished working paper, Hispanic Foundation, Library of Congress, 1961.

COLECCIÓN DE ACUERDOS
1849–68 Colección de acuerdos, órdenes y decretos sobre tierras, casas y solares de los indígenas, bienes de sus comunidades y fundos legales de los pueblos del estado de Jalisco. 2 vols. Guadalajara.

COLECCIÓN DE DOCUMENTOS
1842–95 Colección de documentos inéditos para la historia de España. Martín Fernández de Navarrete and others, eds. 112 vols. Madrid (imprint varies). [Reprinted 1970.]
1864–84 Colección de documentos inéditos, relativos al descubrimiento, conquista y organización de las antiguas posesiones españolas de América y Oceanía, sacados de los archivos del reino, y muy especialmente del de Indias. Title varies. 42 vols. Madrid (imprint varies).
1885–1932 Colección de documentos inéditos relativos al descubrimiento, conquista y organización de las antiguas posesiones españolas de ultramar. 25 vols. Madrid.
1921 Colección de documentos referentes a la historia colonial de Nicaragua. Recuerdo del centenario de la independencia nacional, 1821–1921. Managua.
1927–32 Colección de documentos inéditos para la historia de Ibero-América. 15 vols. Madrid.
1933 Colección de documentos para la historia de Oaxaca. MNA. Mexico.
1957–58 Colección de documentos inéditos o muy raros relativos a la Reforma en México. 2 vols. INAH. Mexico.
1970a Colección de documentos inéditos para la historia de España. 112 vols. [Reprint of Madrid, 1842–95, series by arrangement with Academia de la Historia, Madrid.] Kraus Reprint Co. New York.
1970b Colección de documentos inéditos relativos al descubrimiento, conquista y organización de las antiguas posesiones españolas de América y Oceanía. 42 vols. [Reprint of Madrid, 1864–84, series by arrangement with Academia de la Historia, Madrid.] Kraus Reprint Co. New York.
1970c Colección de documentos inéditos relativos al descubrimiento, conquista y organización de las antiguas posesiones españolas de ultramar. 25 vols. [Reprint of Madrid, 1885–1932, 2d series by arrangement with Academia de la Historia, Madrid.] Kraus Reprint Co. New York.

COLECCIÓN DE LOS DECRETOS
1829 Colección de los decretos y órdenes de las cortes de España, que se reputan vigentes en la república de los Estados Unidos Mexicanos. Mexico.

COMAS, JUAN
1954a Los Congresos Internacionales de Americanistas: síntesis histórica e índice bibliográfico general, 1875–1952. Instituto Indigenista Interamericano, Ediciones especiales. Mexico.
1954b Historia y bibliografía de los Congresos Internacionales de Ciencias Antropológicas: 1865–1954. UNAM. Instituto de Historia, Publicaciones, 1 ser., 37. Mexico.
1964 Una década de Congresos Internacionales de Americanistas, 1952–1962. UNAM. Instituto de Investigaciones Históricas, Cuadernos, ser. antropol., 18. Mexico.

CONCILIO III PROVINCIAL
1859 Concilio III provincial mexicano, celebrado en México el año de 1585, confirmado en Roma por el papa Sixto V, y mandado observar por el gobierno español, en diversas reales órdenes. Mariano Galván Rivera, ed. Mexico.

CONCILIUM MEXICANUM PROVINCIALE
1725 Concilium mexicanum provinciale, celebratum Mexici anno MDLXXXV, praeside d. d. Petro Moya de Contreras, archiepiscopo eiusdem urbis. Paris.

CONTRIBUCIÓN
1928 Contribución para la historia de la Baja California. Compilación de datos ordenada por Amado Aguirre, Gobernador del Distrito Sur de la Baja California. La Paz.

CONWAY, G. R. G.
1943 La noche triste documentos, segura de la frontera en Nueva España, año de MDXX. Mexico.

CORNEJO FRANCO, JOSÉ
1942 Testimonios de Guadalajara. UNAM. *Bib. estudiante universitario*, 35. Mexico.

CORPUS CODICUM AMERICANORUM MEDII AEVI
Vol. 1, *see* Historia tolteca-chichimeca, 1942. Vol. 2, *see* Unos annales históricos de la nación mexicana, 1945. Vol. 3, *see* Chimalpahin Quauhtlehuanitzin, 1949. Vol. 4, *see* Memorial de Tecpan Atitlan, 1952.

CORREA, GUSTAVO, CALVIN CANNON, WILLIAM A. HUNTER, AND BARBARA BODE
1961 The native theater in Middle America. Tulane University, Middle American Research Institute, Pub. 27. New Orleans.

CORTÉS, FERNANDO
1874 Escritos sueltos. *Bib. histórica de la Iberia*, 12. Mexico.
1958 Relaciones de Hernán Cortés a Carlos V sobre la invasión de Anáhuac. Eulalia Guzmán, ed. Mexico.
1960 Cartas de relación de la conquista de la Nueva España escritas al emperador Carlos V, y otros documentos relativos a la conquista, años de 1519–1527. Codex Vindobonensis S.N. 1600. Josef Stummvoll, Charles Gibson, and Franz Unterkircher, eds. Akademische Druck- u. Verlagsanstalt. Graz.

CRÓNICAS
1963 Crónicas de la conquista del reino de Nueva Galicia en territorio de la Nueva España. INAH, *Serie de historia*, 4. Guadalajara.

CRUZ, MARTÍN DE LA
1939 The de la Cruz–Badiano Aztec herbal of 1552. Text and figures. The Maya Society, Pub. 22. Baltimore.

CUADROS CALDAS, JULIO
1932 Catecismo agrario, recopilación completa de leyes, reglamentos, circulares, instrucciones, jurisprudencia tramitación, machotes, contabilidad, etc., en materia agraria, e índice alfabético, del léxico agrario. Puebla.

CUEVAS, MARIANO, ed.
1914 Documentos inéditos del siglo XVI para la historia de México. MNA. Mexico.
1915 Cartas y otros documentos de Hernán Cortés, novísimamente descubiertos en el Archivo General de Indias de la ciudad de Sevilla. Sevilla.
1930 Album histórico guadalupano del IV centenario. Mexico.

DISPOSICIONES COMPLEMENTARIAS
1930 Disposiciones complementarias de las Leyes de Indias. 3 vols. Madrid.

DOCUMENTOS
1940–57 Documentos inéditos para la historia de España publicadas por los señores duque de Alba.
1962 Documentos para servir a la historia del Nuevo México, 1538–1778. Madrid.

ENCINAS, DIEGO DE
1596 Provisiones, cedulas, capítulos de ordenanças, instrucciones, y cartas, libradas y despachadas en diferentes tiempos por sus magestades. 3 vols. Madrid.
1945–53 Cedulario indiano. Reproducción facsimil de la edición única de 1596. 5 vols. Madrid.

ESTATUTOS
1859 Estatutos ordenados por el santo concilio III provincial mexicano en el año del Señor MDLXXXV, según el mandato del sacrosancto concilio tridentino. Mexico.

FABELA, ISIDRO
1960–67 Documentos históricos de la Revolución mexicana. 12 vols. Fondo de Cultura Económica. Mexico.

FABILA, MANUEL
1941 Cinco siglos de legislación agraria (1493–1940). Banco Nacional de Crédito Agrícola. Mexico.

FERNÁNDEZ, LEÓN
1883–1907 Colección de documentos para la historia de Costa Rica. 10 vols. San José, Paris, Barcelona (imprint varies).

FERNÁNDEZ DE CÓRDOBA, JOAQUÍN
1956 Nuestros tesoros bibliográficos en los Estados Unidos. *Historia mexicana*, 5:123–60, 6:129–60.

FERNÁNDEZ DE NAVARRETE, MARTÍN
1825–37 Colección de los viajes y descubrimientos que hicieron por mar los españoles desde fines del siglo XV, con varios documentos inéditos. 5 vols. Madrid.

—— AND OTHERS
1842–95 *See* Colección de documentos, 1842–95.

FERNÁNDEZ DE RECAS, GUILLERMO S.
1961 Cacicazgos y nobilario indígena de la Nueva España. UNAM. Biblioteca Nacional, Instituto Bibliográfico Mexicano, Pub. 5. Mexico.

FOULCHÉ-DELBOSC, RAYMOND, AND L. BARRAU-DIHIGO
1920–26 Manuel de l'hispanisant. 2 vols. New York.

FUENTE, JULIO DE LA
1949 Documentos para la etnografía e historia zapoteca. MNA, *Anales*, 3:175–97.

GALVÁN RIVERA, MARIANO
1844 Ordenanzas de tierras y aguas, o sea formulario geométrico-judicial. Mexico.

GAMIO, MANUEL
1958 Legislación indigenista de México. Instituto Indigenista Interamericano. Mexico.

GARCÍA, GENARO
1910–12 Documentos históricos mexicanos. Obra conmemorativa del primer centenario de la independencia de México. 7 vols. MNA. Mexico.

—— AND CARLOS PEREYRA
1905–11 Documentos inéditos o muy raros para la historia de México. Librería de la Viuda de Ch. Bouret. 36 vols. Mexico.

GARCÍA DE POLAVIEJA, CAMILO
1889 Hernán Cortés. Copias de documentos existentes en el Archivo de Indias y en su palacio de Castilleja de la Cuesta, sobre la conquista de Méjico. Seville.

GARCÍA ICAZBALCETA, JOAQUÍN
See Article 21, Appendix D.

GARCÍA PIMENTEL, LUIS
1897 Descripción del arzobispado de México hecha en 1570, y otros documentos. Mexico.
1903–07 Documentos históricos de México. 5 vols. Mexico, Paris, Madrid.
1904 Relación de los obispados de Tlaxcala, Michoacán, Oaxaca y otros lugares en el siglo XVI. *Documentos históricos de Méjico*, 2. Mexico

GARIBAY KINTANA, ÁNGEL MARÍA
1940 Poesía indígena de la altiplanicie. UNAM. Bib. estudiante universitario, 11. Mexico.
1953–54 Historia de la literatura náhuatl. 2 vols. Mexico.

GATES, WILLIAM
1935 The Maya Calkiní chronicle, or documents concerning the descent of the Ah-Canul, or Men of the Serpent, their arrival and territory. In facsimile. The Maya Society, Pub. 8. Baltimore.

GAYANGOS, PASCUAL DE
1866 Cartas y relaciones de Hernán Cortés al emperador Carlos V. Paris.
1875–93 Catalogue of the manuscripts in the Spanish language in the British Museum. 4 vols. London.

GÓMEZ CANEDO, LINO
1961 Los archivos de la historia de América: período colonial español. 2 vols.

PAIGH, Commission on History, Pub. 87. Mexico.

GÓMEZ DE CERVANTES, GONZALO
1944 La vida económica y social de Nueva España al finalizar el siglo XVI. Alberto María Carreño, ed. *Bib. histórica mexicana de obras inéditas*, 19. Mexico.

GÓMEZ DE OROZCO, FEDERICO
1940 Crónicas de Michoacán. UNAM. *Bib. estudiante universitario*, 12. Mexico.

GONZÁLEZ, FRANCISCO ANTONIO
1849–55 Colección de cánones de la iglesia española, publicada en latín a expensas de nuestros reyes. Juan Tejada y Ramiro, trans. and ed. 5 vols. Madrid.

GONZÁLEZ, JOSÉ ELEUTERIO
1867 Colección de noticias y documentos para la historia del estado de N. León. Monterrey.

GONZÁLEZ DE COSSÍO, FRANCISCO
1957 Historia de la tenencia y explotación del campo desde la época precortesiana hasta las leyes del 6 de enero de 1915. 2 vols. *Bib. Instituto Nacional de estudios históricos de la revolución mexicana*, 9. Mexico.

GONZÁLEZ NAVARRO, MOISÉS
1953 Repartimiento de indios en Nueva Galicia. Museo Nacional de Historia. Mexico.

GONZÁLEZ RAMÍREZ, MANUEL
1954–57 Fuentes para la historia de la Revolución mexicana. 4 vols. Fondo de Cultura Económica. Mexico.

GRUBBS, HENRY A.
1936 A tentative guide to manuscript material in Latin American archives and libraries. *HLAS*, 1:219–30 [Mexico, pp. 228–29].

GUÍA
1966–69 Guía de fuentes para la historia de Ibero-América conservadas en España. 2 vols. Dirección General de Archivos y Bibliotecas. Madrid.

HACKETT, CHARLES WILSON
1923–37 Historical documents relating to New Mexico, Nueva Vizcaya and approaches thereto, to 1773. 3 vols. Carnegie Institution of Washington, Pub. 330. Washington.

HAGGARD, J. VILLASANA
1940 Letters and documents: Spain's policy in Texas. Translations from the Bé-

xar Archives. *Southwestern Historical Quarterly*, 44:232–44.

HAKLUYT, RICHARD
1598–1600 The principal navigations, voiages, traffiques, and discoveries of the English nation. 3 vols. [Facsimile ed. 1965.] London.

1903–05 The principal navigations voyages traffiques & discoveries of the English nation. 12 vols. Glasgow.

1965 [Facsimile reproduction of 1589.] Hakluyt Society, Extra Series, 39. [Introduction by David Seers Quinn and R. A. Skelton, and a new index by Alison Quinn.] Cambridge, Mass.

HALL, FREDERIC
1885 The laws of Mexico: A compilation and treatise relating to real property, mines, water rights, personal rights, contracts and inheritances. San Francisco.

HAMER, PHILIP
1961 A guide to archives and manuscripts in the United States. New Haven.

HAMMOND, GEORGE, AND AGAPITO REY
1940 [Narratives of the Coronado expedition, 1540–1542. *Coronado Centennial Publications*, 2. University of New Mexico Press. Albuquerque.

HANKE, LEWIS, AND AGUSTÍN MILLARES CARLO
1943 Cuerpo de documentos del siglo XVI sobre los derechos de España en las Indias y las Filipinas. Fondo de Cultura Económica. Mexico.

HERNÁEZ, FRANCISCO JAVIER
1879 Colección de bulas, breves y otros documentos relativos a la iglesia de América y Filipinas. 2 vols. Brussels.

HERNÁNDEZ Y DÁVALOS, JUAN E.
1877–82 Colección de documentos para la historia de la guerra de independencia de México de 1808 a 1821. 6 vols. Mexico.

HILL, ROSCOE R.
1938–48 Archives. HLAS, 3:45–52 (1939) and annually to 11:43–55 (1948).

1945 The national archives of Latin America. Cambridge, Mass.

1948 Los archivos nacionales de América latina. Prólogo de Emeterio S. Santovenia. Archivo Nacional de Cuba, Pub. 19 [Spanish translation of Hill, 1945]. Havana.

HILTON, RONALD, ed.
1956 Handbook of Hispanic source materi-

als and research organizations in the United States. 2d ed. Stanford.

HISTORIA TOLTECA-CHICHIMECA

1942 Liber in lingua nahuatl manuscriptus picturisque ornatus, ut est conservatus in Bibliotheca Nationis Gallicae Parisiensi sub numeris XLVI–XLVIIbis, cum praefatione in lingua Britannica, Gallica, Germanica, et Hispana atque indice paginarum editit Ernst Mengin. E. Munskgaard. [40 pp.] *Corpus Codicum Americanorum Medii Aevi*, 1. Copenhagen.

HODGE, FREDERICK W., AND THEODORE H. LEWIS

1907 Spanish explorers in the southern United States, 1528–1534. New York.

INSTRUCCIONES

1867 Instrucciones que los vireyes de Nueva España dejaron a sus sucesores. Mexico.

1873 Instrucciones que los vireyes de Nueva España dejaron a sus sucesores. 2 vols. *Bib. histórica de la Iberia*, 13, 14. Mexico.

KER, ANNITA M.

1931 A survey of Mexican scientific periodicals, to which are appended some notes on Mexican historical periodicals. Baltimore.

KINGSBOROUGH, LORD EDWARD KING

1831–48 Antiquities of Mexico, comprising facsimiles of ancient Mexican paintings and hieroglyphs. 9 vols. London.

KINNAIRD, LAWRENCE, ed.

1949 Spain in the Mississippi Valley, 1765–1794. 3 vols. GPO. American Historical Association, Annual Report for the Year 1945, 2–4. Washington.

KINO, EUSEBIO FRANCISCO

See Article 13, Bibliography.

KNOWLES, DAVID

1963 Great historical enterprises: Problems in monastic history. London.

KONETZKE, RICHARD

1953–62 Colección de documentos para la historia de la formación social de Hispanoamérica, 1493–1810. 3 vols. Consejo Superior de Investigaciones Científicas. Madrid.

LABÁSTIDA, LUIS G.

1893 Colección de leyes, decretos, reglamentos, circulares, órdenes y acuerdos relativos a la desamortización de los bienes de corporaciones civiles y reli-

giosas y a la nacionalización de los que administraron las últimas. Mexico.

LANDA, DIEGO DE

See Article 13, Bibliography.

LEGISLACIÓN . . . COSTA RICA

1957 Legislación indigenista de Costa Rica. Instituto Indigenista Interamericano. n.p. [Mexico.]

LEGISLACIÓN . . . GUATEMALA

1954 Legislación indigenista de Guatemala. Instituto Indigenista Interamericano. Mexico.

LEGISLACION . . . HONDURAS

1958 Legislación indigenista de Honduras. Instituto Indigenista Interamericano. Mexico.

LEJARZA, FIDEL DE

1947 Conquista espiritual del Nuevo Santander. Consejo Superior de Investigaciones Científicas, *Bib. missionalia hispánica*, 4. Madrid.

LEMOINE VILLICAÑA, ERNESTO

1965 Morelos, su vida revolucionaria a través de sus escritos y de otros testimonios de la época. UNAM. Mexico.

LEÓN, NICOLÁS

1940 Documentos inéditos referentes al ilustrísimo señor Don Vasco de Quiroga. *Bib. histórica mexicana de obras inéditas*, 17. Mexico.

LEÓN-PORTILLA, MIGUEL

1959 Visión de los vencidos. Relaciones indígenas de la conquista. UNAM. *Bib. estudiante universitario*, 81. Mexico.

1962 The broken spears: The Aztec account of the conquest of Mexico. Lysander Kemp, trans. Boston.

1964 El reverso de la conquista. Relaciones aztecas, mayas e incas. Instituto Indigenista Interamericano. Mexico.

——, LUIS GONZÁLEZ BARRERA VÁSQUEZ, ERNESTO DE LA TORRE VILLAR, AND MARÍA DEL CARMEN VELÁZQUEZ

1964 Historia documental de México. Universidad Autónoma de México, Instituto de Investigaciones Históricas. 2 vols. Mexico.

LEYES

1603 Leyes y ordenanzas nuevamente hechas por su magestad, para la governación de las Indias, y buen tratamiento y conservación de los indios. Valladolid.

LIBRO DE LAS TASACIONES
1952 El libro de las tasaciones de pueblos de la Nueva España, siglo XVI. AGN. Mexico.

LORENZANA, FRANCISCO ANTONIO
1769 Concilios provinciales primero, y segundo, celebrados en la muy noble, y muy leal ciudad de México, presidiendo el illmo. y rmo. señor d. fr. Alonso de Montúfar, en los años de 1555, y 1565. Mexico.
1770a Concilium mexicanum provinciale III. celebratum Mexici anno MDLXXXV, praeside D. D. Petro Moya, et Contreras archiepiscopo ejusdem urbis. Mexico.
1770b Cartas pastorales, y edictos. Mexico.
1770c Historia de Nueva-España, escrita por su esclarecido conquistador Hernán Cortés. Mexico.

MANERO, VICENTE E.
1878 Noticias y documentos sobre tierras realengas, vacantes, baldíos, ejidos, poblaciones y medidas agrarias. Tabasco.

MANZANO Y MANZANO, JUAN
1950–56 Historia de las recopilaciones de Indias. 2 vols. Madrid.

MARISCAL, MARIO
1946 Reseña histórica del AGN, 1550–1946. Mexico.

MAZA, FRANCISCO F. DE LA
1893 Código de colonización y terrenos baldíos de la república mexicana. Secretaría de Fomento. Mexico.

MEADE, JOAQUÍN
1939 Documentos inéditos para la historia de Tampico, Siglos XVI y XVII. Mexico.

MEANS, PHILIP AINSWORTH
1917 History of the Spanish conquest of Yucatan and of the Itzas. Peabody Museum of American Archaeology and Ethnology, Harvard University, *Papers*, 7. Cambridge, Mass.

MEMORIAL DE TECPAN ATITLAN [ANNALS OF THE CAKCHIQUELS]
1952 Memorial de Tecpan Atitlan (Sololá) historia del antiguo reino del Cakchiquel dicho de Guatemala. Liber in lingua Cakchiquel . . . . Bibliotheca Musei Universitatis Pennsylvaniensis . . . sub Br. 498.21/CAr 15. [96 pp.] *Corpus Codicum Americanorum Medii Aevi*, 4. Copenhagen.

MENDOZA, ANTONIO DE
1548 Ordenanzas y compilación de leyes hechas por el muy illustre señor don Antonio de Mendoza visorrey y gobernador desta Nueva España y presidente de la audiencia real que en ella reside y por los señores oidores de la dicha audiencia para la buena gobernación y estilo de los oficiales della. Juan Pablos. 45 fols. Mexico.
1945 Ordenanzas y compilación de leyes. Cultura Hispánica, *Col. incunables americanos*, 5. Madrid.

MENÉNDEZ, CARLOS
1923 Historia del infame y vergonzoso comercio de indios vendidos a los esclavistas de Cuba por los políticos yucatecos, desde 1808 hasta 1891. Justificación de la revolución indígena de 1847. Documentos irrefutables que la comprueben. Merida.

MESTRE GHIGLIAZA, MANUEL
1916–40 Documentos y datos para la historia de Tabasco, 1790–1833. 4 vols. Mexico and Tacubaya (imprint varies).

MILLARES CARLO, AGUSTÍN
1959 Repertorio bibliográfico de los archivos mexicanos y de los europeos y norteamericanas de interés para la historia de México. Mexico.
1961 Los archivos, municipales de Latinamérica, libros de actas y colecciones documentales; apuntes bibliográficos. Maracaibo, Venezuela.

—— AND JOSÉ IGNACIO MANTECÓN
1948 Repertorio bibliográfico de los archivos mexicanos y de las colecciones diplomáticas, fundamentales para la historia de México. UNAM, Instituto de Historia. Mexico.

MONTEMAYOR (Y CÓRDOBA DE CUENCA), JUAN FRANCISCO DE
1678 Sumarios de las cédulas, órdenes y provisiones reales que se han despachado por su majestad, para la Nueva España, y otras partes, especialmente desde el año de mil seiscientos y veinte y ocho, en que se imprimieron los cuatro libros del primer tomo de la Recopilación de Leyes de las Indias, hasta el año de mil seiscientos y setenta y siete. Con algunos títulos de las materias, que nuevamente se añaden, y de los autos acordados de su

real audiencia y algunas ordenanzas del gobierno. Mexico.

MORELOS, JOSÉ MARÍA
1927 Morelos, documentos inéditos y poco conocidos. 3 vols. Secretaría de Educación Popular. Mexico.
1965 Morelos, documentos. Antonio Arriaga and Manuel Arellano Z., eds. 2 vols. Gobierno del Estado de Michoacán. *Bib. michoacana*, 5–6. Morelia.

MOTOLINÍA
See Article 13, Bibliography.

MURO OREJÓN, ANTONIO
1956 Cedulario americano del siglo XVIII. Escuela de Estudios Hispano-americanos de Sevilla, Pub. 99. Seville.

EL MUSEO MEXICANO
1843–44 El museo mexicano, ó miscelanea pintoresca de amenidades curiosas é instructivas . . . . T. 1–5. I. Cumplido. Mexico.

NICOLAU D'OLWER, LUIS
1963 Cronistas de las culturas precolombinas. Fondo de Cultura Económica. Mexico.

NOBILARIO
1892 Nobilario de conquistadores de Indias. *Sociedad de bibliófilos españoles*, 30. Madrid.

NUEVOS DOCUMENTOS
1946 Nuevos documentos relativos a los bienes de Hernán Cortés, 1547–1947. UNAM. Mexico.

NUNEMAKER, J. HORACE
1948 The Biblioteca Aportación Histórica Publications, 1943–1947. *HAHR*, 28:316–44.

ORDENANZAS
1636 Ordenanzas del Consejo Real de las Indias, nuevamente recopiladas. Madrid.

OROZCO, WISTANO LUIS
1895 Legislación y jurisprudencia sobre terrenos baldíos. 2 vols. Mexico.

OROZCO Y BERRA, MANUEL
See Article 21, Appendix C.

PASO Y TRONCOSO, FRANCISCO DEL
See Article 21, Appendix F.

PAZ, JULIÁN
1930–31 Catálogo de la colección de documentos inéditos para la historia de España. 2 vols. Instituto de Valencia de Don Juan. Madrid. [Photoreproduction, 1966.]

PEÑAFIEL, ANTONIO
1904a Colección de documentos para la historia mexicana. 6 vols. Secretaría de Fomento. Mexico.
1904b Cantares en idioma mexicano. Reproducción facsimilaria del manuscrito original existente en la Biblioteca Nacional. Secretaría de Fomento. Mexico.
1908–14 Ciudades coloniales y capitales de la república mexicana. 5 vols. Secretaría de Fomento. Mexico.

PERALTA, MANUEL M. DE
1886 Costa-Rica y Colombia de 1573 á 1881. Su jurisdicción y sus límites territoriales según los documentos inéditos del Archivo de Indias de Sevilla y otras autoridades. Madrid.
1890 Límites de Costa-Rica y Colombia. Nuevos documentos para la historia de su jurisdicción territorial. Madrid.
1898 Costa Rica y Costa de Mosquitos. Documentos para la historia de la jurisdicción territorial de Costa Rica y Colombia. Paris.

PÉREZ MALDONADO, CARLOS
1947 Documentos históricos de Nuevo León anotados y comentados. Monterrey.

PÉREZ Y LÓPEZ, ANTONIO XAVIER
1791–98 Teatro de la legislación universal de España é Indias, por orden cronológico de sus cuerpos y decisiones no recopiladas. 28 vols. Madrid.

PÍCCOLO, FRANCISCO MARÍA
1962 Informe del estado de la nueva cristiandad de California, 1702, y otros documentos. Ernest J. Burrus, ed. Madrid.

POESÍA
1964 Poesía náhuatl, I. Romances de los señores de la Nueva España, manuscrito de Juan Bautista de Pomar, Tetzcoco, 1582. Angel María Garibay Kintana, ed. UNAM, Instituto de Historia, Seminario de cultura náhuatl, *Fuentes indígenas de la cultura náhuatl*, 4. Mexico.
1965 Poesía náhuatl, II. Cantares mexicanos, manuscrito de la Biblioteca Nacional de México. Angel María Garibay Kintana, ed. UNAM, Instituto de Historia, Seminario de cultura náhuatl, *Fuentes indígenas de la cultura náhuatl*, 5. Mexico.

POMPA Y POMPA, ANTONIO, comp.
1962 El Instituto Nacional de Antropología e Historia: su contribución a la

bibliografía nacional. INAH [includes MNA publications since 1827]. Mexico.

PORTILLO, ESTEBAN L.
1886 Apuntes para la historia antigua de Coahuila y Texas. Saltillo.

PRESCOTT, WILLIAM HICKLING
1843 History of the conquest of Mexico, with a preliminary view of the ancient Mexican civilization, and the life of the conqueror, Hernando Cortés. 3 vols. New York.

PUBLICACIONES DEL AGN
1910–36 Publicaciones del AGN. 30 vols. AGN. Mexico (imprint varies).

PUGA, VASCO DE
1563 Provisiones, cedulas, instrucciones de su magestad, ordenanças de difuntos y audiencia. Mexico.
1878–79 Provisiones, cedulas, instrucciones de su magestad, ordenanças de difuntos y audiencia. 2 vols. Mexico.
1945 Provisiones, cedulas, instrucciones para el gobierno de la Nueva España por el doctor Vasco de Puga. Obra impresa en México, por Pedro Ocharte, en 1563 y ahora editada en facsimil. Cultura Hispánica, *Col. incunables americanos*, 3. Madrid.

PUIG CASAURANC, J. M.
1928 Archivos privados de D. Benito Juárez y D. Pedro Santacila. Secretaría de Educación Pública. Mexico.

PURCHAS, SAMUEL
1625 Hakluytus Posthumus, or Purchas his Pilgrimes. 4 vols. London.

RADIN, PAUL
1920 The sources and authenticity of the History of the Ancient Mexicans. University of California, Publications in American Archaeology and Ethnology, 27, no. 1. University of California Press. Berkeley.

RAMÍREZ, J. F.
See Article 21, Appendix B.

RAMOS, ROBERTO
1958 Tres documentos sobre el descubrimiento y exploración de Baja California por Francisco María Píccolo, Juan de Ugarte y Guillermo Stratford. Mexico.

READ, BENJAMIN M.
1914 Chronological digest of the "Documentos inéditos del Archivo de las Indias." Albuquerque.

RECINOS, ADRIÁN
1957 Crónicas indígenas de Guatemala. Universitaria. Guatemala.

RECOPILACIÓN DE LEYES
1681 Recopilación de leyes de los reynos de las Indias. 4 vols. Madrid.
1756 Recopilación de leyes de los reynos de las Indias. 4 vols. Madrid.
1774 Recopilación de leyes de los reynos de las Indias. 4 vols. Madrid.
1791 Recopilación de leyes de los reynos de las Indias. 3 vols. Madrid.
1841 Recopilación de leyes de los reinos de las Indias. 4 vols. Madrid.
1851 Recopilación de las leyes del gobierno español, que rigen en la república, respectivas a los años de 1788 y siguientes. Mexico.
1943 Recopilación de leyes de los reynos de las Indias. Edición facsimilar de la cuarta impresión en Madrid el año 1791. 3 vols. Madrid.

RENDÓN, SILVIA
1952 Ordenanza del Señor Cuauhtemoc. Tulane University, Middle American Research Institute, Pub. 12, no. 2. New Orleans.

REYNOLDS, MATTHEW G.
1895 Spanish and Mexican land laws: New Spain and Mexico. St. Louis.

RICCI, SEYMOUR DE, AND W. J. WILSON
1935–40 Census of medieval and Renaissance manuscripts in the United States and Canada. 3 vols. (Supplement, 1962.) New York.

ROBERTSON, JAMES A.
1910 List of documents in Spanish archives relating to the history of the United States, which have been printed or of which transcripts are preserved in American libraries. Carnegie Institution of Washington, Pub. 124. Washington.

RODRÍGUEZ SAN MIGUEL, JUAN N.
1839 Pandectas hispano megicanas, o sea código general comprensivo de las leyes generales, útiles y vivas de las Siete Partidas, recopilación novísima, la de Indias, autos y providencias conocidas por de Montemayor y Beleña y cédulas posteriores hasta al año de 1820. Con exclusión de las totalmente inútiles, de las repetidas y de las totalmente derogadas. 3 vols. Mexico.

ROYS, RALPH L.
1933 The Book of Chilam Balam of Chu-

mayel. Carnegie Institution of Washington, Pub. 438. Washington.

1939 The Titles of Ebtun. Carnegie Institution of Washington, Pub. 505. Washington.

RUBIO MAÑÉ, J. I.

1940 Historia del Archivo General de la Nación. *Revista de Historia de América*, 9:63–169.

1942 Archivo de la historia de Yucatán, Campeche y Tabasco. 3 vols. Mexico.

SÁENZ DE AGUIRRE, JOSÉ

1753–55 Collectio maxima conciliorum omnium Hispaniae et Novi Orbis, epistularumque decretalium celebrarum. 6 vols. Rome.

SAHAGÚN, BERNARDINO DE

1958a Ritos, sacerdotes y atavíos de los dioses. Miguel León-Portilla, ed. UNAM, Instituto de Historia, Seminario de cultura náhuatl, *Fuentes indígenas de la cultura náhuatl, Informantes de Sahagún*, 1. Mexico.

1958b Veinte himnos sacros de los nahuas. Angel María Garibay Kintana, ed. UNAM, Instituto de Historia, Seminario de cultura náhuatl, *Fuentes indígenas de la cultura náhuatl, Informantes de Sahagún*, 2. Mexico.

1961 Vida económica de Tenochtitlan. Angel María Garibay Kintana, ed. UNAM, Instituto de Historia, Seminario de cultura náhuatl, *Fuentes indígenas de la cultura náhuatl, Informantes de Sahagún*, 3. Mexico.

SANCTUM PROVINCIALE CONCILIUM

1622 Sanctum provinciale concilium Mexici celebratum anno domini millesimo quingentesimo octuagesimo quinto. Mexico.

SCHÄFER, ERNESTO (ERNST)

1946–47 Indice de la colección de documentos inéditos de Indias, editada por Pacheco, Cárdenas, Torres de Mendoza y otros (1a serie, tomos 1–42) y la Real Academia de la Historia (2a serie, tomos 1–25). 2 vols. Consejo Superior de Investigaciones Científicas, Instituto "Gonzalo Fernández de Oviedo." Madrid.

SCHELLENBERG, T. R.

1957 Modern archives: principles and techniques. 2d ed. University of Chicago Press. Chicago.

1958 Archivos modernos: principios y técnicas. Traducción y adiciones por el

Dr. Manuel Carrera Stampa. PAIGH, Commission on History, Comité de Archivos, Pub. 4. Havana.

SCHOLES, FRANCE V., AND ELEANOR B. ADAMS

1938 Don Diego Quijada, alcalde mayor de Yucatán, 1561–1565. Documentos sacados de los archivos de España. 2 vols. *Bib. histórica mexicana de obras inéditas*, 14, 15. Mexico.

1955–61 Documentos para la historia del México colonial. 7 vols. Mexico.

SCHOLES, FRANCE V., AND CARLOS R. MENÉNDEZ

1936–38 Documentos para la historia de Yucatán. 3 vols. Merida.

SERRA, JUNÍPERO

1955–66 Writings of Junípero Serra. 4 vols. Academy of American Franciscan History. Washington.

SERRANO Y SANZ, MANUEL

1908 Relaciones históricas y geográficas de América central. Madrid.

SILVA HERZOG, JESÚS

1943–45 Archivo histórico de hacienda. Colección de documentos publicados bajo la dirección de Jesús Silva Herzog. 5 vols. Mexico.

SIMPSON, LESLEY BYRD

1934–40 Studies in the administration of the Indians in New Spain. 4 parts in 3 vols. *Ibero-Americana*, 7, 13, 16. University of California Press. Berkeley and Los Angeles.

SQUIER, E. G.

1860 Collection of rare and original documents etc. concerning the discovery and conquest of America. Albany.

TAMAYO, JORGE L.

1957 Epistolario de Benito Juárez. Fondo de Cultura Económica. Mexico.

1964 Benito Juárez, documentos, discursos, y correspondencia. 2 vols. Secretaría de Patrimonio Nacional. Mexico.

TASACIONES

1941 Tasaciones de los pueblos de la provincia de Yucatán, pertenecientes a los encomenderos de la villa de San Francisco de Campeche, hechas por la Audiencia de Santiago de Guatemala en el mes de febrero de 1549. Museo Arqueológico, Etnográfico e Histórico del Estado. Campeche.

TEJADA Y RAMIRO, JUAN

1859–62 Colección de cánones y de todos los concilios de la iglesia de España y América. 7 vols. in 6. P. Montero. Madrid.

TENA RAMÍREZ, FELIPE
1967 Leyes fundamentales de México, 1808–1967. Mexico.

TERNAUX-COMPANS, HENRI
1837–41 Voyages, relations et mémoires originaux pour servir à l'histoire de la découverte de l'Amérique publiés pour la première fois en français. 20 vols. Paris.
1840 Recueil de documents et mémoires originaux sur l'histoire des possessions espagnoles dans l'Amérique. Paris.

TÍTULOS PRINCIPALES
1915 Títulos principales del nombre y ejidos del barrio de la Magdalena Mexihuca antes barrio y hermita de Lloalatzinco Anepantla. Mexico.

TUDELA DE LA ORDEN, JOSÉ
1954 Los manuscritos de América en las bibliotecas de España. Madrid.

UNOS ANNALES HISTÓRICOS DE LA NACIÓN MEXICANA
1945 Manuscrit mexicain nr. 22; liber in lingua Nahuatl manuscriptus paucisque picturis linearibus ornatus ut est conservatus in Bibliotheca Nationis Gallicae Parisiense sub numero XXII, archetypum. Manuscrit mexicain nr. 22bis; ejusdem operis exemplum aetete posterius nonnullisque conservatum in Bibliotheca Nationis Gallicae Parisiense sub numero XXIIIbis. Cum praefatione in lingua Britannica, Gallica, Germanica, et Hispana atque indice paginarum editit Ernst Mengin. [26 pp.] *Corpus Codicum Americanorum Medii Aevi*, 2. Copenhagen.

VANCE, JOHN T., AND HELEN L. CLAGETT
1945 A guide to the law and legal literature of Mexico. GPO. Library of Congress. Washington.

VASQUÉZ, GENARO V.
1938 Legislación del trabajo en los siglos XVI, XVII y XVIII. Relación entre la economía, las artes y los oficios en la Nueva España. Departamento Autónomo del Trabajo, *Historia del movimiento obrero en México*, 1. Mexico.

1940 Doctrinas y realidades en la legislación para los indios. Departamento de Asuntos Indígenas. Mexico.

VEGA BOLAÑOS, ANDRÉS
1954–57 Colección Somoza. Documentos para la historia de Nicaragua. 17 vols. Madrid.

VELÁZQUEZ, PRIMO FELICIANO
1897–99 Colección de documentos para la historia de San Luis Potosí. 4 vols. Imprenta del Editor. San Luis Potosi.

VERA, FORTINO HIPÓLITO
1879 Compendio histórico del concilio III mexicano, o indices de los tres tomos de la colección del mismo concilio. 3 vols. Amecameca.
1887 Colección de documentos eclesiásticos de México, o sea antigua y moderna legislación de la iglesia mexicana. 3 vols. Amecameca.
1887–89 Tesoro guadalupano. Noticia de los libros, documentos, inscripciones, &c. que tratan, mencionan ó aluden á la aparición y devoción de Nuestra Señora de Guadalupe. 2 vols. Amecameca.
1893 Apuntamientos históricos de los concilios provinciales mexicanos y privilegios de América. Mexico.
1897 Notas del compendio histórico del concilio III mexicano. Amecameca.

WINSHIP, GEORGE P.
1896 The Coronado expedition, 1540–1542. Fourteenth annual report of the Bureau of American Ethnology, pp. 329–637. GPO. Washington.

ZAMORA Y CORONADO, JOSÉ MARÍA
1844–46 Biblioteca de legislación ultramarina en forma de diccionario alfabético. 7 vols. Madrid.

ZAVALA, SILVIO A.
1947 Ordenanzas del trabajo, siglos XVI y XVII. UNAM, Instituto de Investigaciones Históricas, *Serie de historia novohispana*, 2. Mexico.
—— AND MARÍA CASTELO
1939–46 Fuentes para la historia del trabajo en Nueva España. 8 vols. Fondo de Cultura Económica. Mexico.

12. An Introductory Survey of Secular Writings in the European Tradition on Colonial Middle America, 1503-1818

J. BENEDICT WARREN

URING THE 15th and 16th centuries a great surge of exploration and discovery opened new vistas to the inquiring European mind, recently awakened to new quests for practical knowledge by the humanism of the Renaissance. As the explorers pushed back the curtains on the previously unknown reaches of Africa, Asia, and America, their reports were in great demand in the literate circles of Europe. This interest quickened as the European nations entered a struggle for control of the new-found regions. The demand for more enlightenment regarding the new lands and peoples and the desire of the explorers and conquerors for recognition and favors conspired to produce a great number of narratives, chronicles, and histories of the new discoveries and of the expansion and development of European domination in them.

This article aims to present biobibliographical studies of authors whose works relate to the ethnohistory of Middle America.[1]

We have limited ourselves to those who wrote during the period of Spanish domination, from 1503 to 1818. Works dealing principally with the history of religious orders, native and Mestizo authors, and collections of printed documents are treated in other articles and hence are not included here except for a few minor chronicles not mentioned elsewhere. Only those works of an author which have a direct bearing on the ethnohistory of Middle America in the colonial period are listed here.

Because they have been given extensive treatment elsewhere in this volume, two major colonial writers do not figure below: Sahagún (Article 14) and Torquemada (Article 16).

[1] I wish to express my gratitude to Howard F. Cline and the staff of the Hispanic Foundation, Library of Congress, for their generous assistance in the preparation of this study. Appreciation is also expressed to France V. Scholes, Charles Gibson, John B. Glass, and others for review and helpful suggestions on earlier versions of this article.

Some of the works considered here went through a great number of editions, but not all these editions appear in the unannotated bibliography which accompanies these biobibliographical studies. The aim has been, rather, to list the first complete edition, a good modern edition, an English translation when available, and other editions of particular significance. References are given to more extensive studies of individual authors or works where readily known, but no effort has been made to be comprehensive.

In the preparation of this article many works have been consulted. Often the scholarly introductions to modern editions have given the greatest help. Among general works, Francisco Esteve Barba's *Historiografía indiana* (1964) has been consulted most frequently. It is an excellent study of the colonial historiography of Spanish America, although it suffers from some significant oversights. Manuel Carrera Stampa's article "Fuentes para el estudio de la historia indígena," which appeared in the second volume of *Esplendor del México antiguo* (1959), has been an important guide, even though it contains a number of factual errors; he amplified that work by a series of articles which appeared in the *Memorias* of the Mexican Academy of History during 1962–63. A cursory study of the sources of Hispanic American history is found in A. Curtis Wilgus, *Histories and Historians of Hispanic America* (1942). Wilgus studied some of the writers of the 16th century more at length in a series of articles entitled "Some Sixteenth Century Histories and Historians of America," which appeared in the *Bulletin of the Pan American Union* between 1933 and 1941.

A work such as the present one cannot be prepared adequately without reference to José Mariano Beristáin de Souza's *Biblioteca hispano americana septentrional* (1816–21, 3d ed. 1947) or to José Toribio Medina's *Biblioteca hispano-americana (1493–1810)* (1898–1907) and his *Imprenta en México*

(1539–1821) (1907–12). These authors drew heavily upon earlier works such as Antonio de León Pinelo's *Epítome de la biblioteca oriental y occidental, naútica y geográfica* (1629), Nicolás Antonio's *Biblioteca Hispana sive Hispanorum* (1672), and Juan José de Eguiara y Eguren's *Bibliotheca Mexicana* (1755).

The *Handbook of Latin American Studies* (1936–) was an important aid in locating recent publications, especially items which have appeared in periodicals. Other biobibliographical sources of a more limited nature which deserve mention include Manuel Ballesteros, *Escritores de Indias* (2 vols., 1940–49); Rómulo D. Carbia, *La crónica oficial de las Indias Occidentales: Estudio histórico y crítico acerca de la historiografía mayor de Hispano-América en los siglos XVI a XVIII*; Berta Flores Salinas, *México visto por algunos de sus viajeros (siglos XVI y XVII)* (1964); Ángel María Garibay K., "Los historiadores del México antiguo en el virreinato de la Nueva España," *Cuadernos americanos* (1964), 132:129–47; *Estudios de la historiografía de la Nueva España*, edited by Ramón Iglesia (1945); Ramón Iglesia, *Cronistas e historiadores de la conquista de México: El ciclo de Hernán Cortés* (1942); Luis Nicolau d'Olwer, *Cronistas de las culturas precolombinas: Antología* (1963); Víctor Rico González, *Historiadores mexicanos del siglo XVIII: Estudios historiográficos sobre Clavijero, Veytia, Cavo y Alegre* (1949). Henry R. Wagner has a good introductory study of the sources for the history of the conquest of Mexico in *The Rise of Fernando Cortés* (1944). Of great assistance for finding biographical data on some of the more obscure figures were the *Enciclopedia universal illustrada europeo-americana* (1907?–30) and the *Diccionario Porrúa de la historia, biografía y geografía de México* (1964).

The present survey was prepared in the fall of 1967. Since that time there has appeared Benjamin Keen's masterful study of the bibliography regarding the Aztecs, *The*

Aztec Image in Western Thought (New Brunswick, N.J., 1971). The reader is referred to it for a more extensive treatment of many of the authors discussed here, as well as for a coverage of some of the remote European writers on the Aztecs whose works are not included here.

To facilitate reference, authors treated (except anonymous) have been given an item number. The following alphabetical listing of authors serves as an index to the items.

Writers and Writings Treated in Article 12, with reference item number.

EARLIEST ACCOUNTS [see also Item 39]

1. Christopher Columbus (1451–1506)

The Discoverer of America was the first known European to come into contact with the Indians of Middle America. On his fourth voyage to the New World he explored the coast of Central America from Honduras to Panama (1502–03). On July 7, 1503, he wrote a letter from Jamaica to the King and Queen of Spain concerning this fourth voyage, in which he gave information regarding his contacts with the Indians on the east coast of Central America.

This letter appeared in Spanish at a very early date, but the first edition seems to have disappeared. An Italian translation was printed in Venice in 1505, but the letter did not become widely known until Navarrete published a Spanish text in 1825. His source was a manuscript copy which was later given to the Library of the Royal Palace in Madrid. The Spanish text was republished from the same manuscript, with extensive annotations, by the Reale Commissione Colombiana in 1894. An English translation by R. H. Major was published by the Hakluyt Society in 1847 and was reprinted in paperback form (1961).

More firsthand data on the same voyage may be found in the report of Diego de Porras, the will of Diego Méndez, and the *Histories* of Ferdinand Columbus. A convenient collection of these and other documents regarding Columbus' fourth voyage was published by the Academia de Geografía e Historia de Costa Rica in 1952.

2. *Ferdinand Columbus* (1488–1539)

Ferdinand Columbus was born in Córdoba, Spain, on August 15, 1488, the illegitimate son of Christopher Columbus and Beatriz Enríquez de Arana. After his father's first voyage of discovery he was named a page in the royal court. He accompanied his father on the fourth voyage (1502–04) and also went to the Indies with Diego Columbus in 1509. Later he traveled extensively through Europe and collected a large library, which at the time of his death totaled 15,370 volumes. In 1524 he was a member of the commission established to arbitrate the claims of Spain and Portugal to the Moluccas. He set up his household in 1526 in Seville on the banks of the Guadalquivir River, where he died July 12, 1539, and was buried in the cathedral. His books formed the basic collection of the Biblioteca Colombina, now housed within the patio of the cathedral of Seville.

Ferdinand wrote a number of works of geographical interest and some items connected with the lengthy lawsuits of the Columbus family for their rights as heirs of the Discoverer. But his most important work was a biography of his father, which he apparently wrote toward the end of his life and had not entirely completed at his death. This biography is of particular interest in regard to the Admiral's explorations along the coast of Central America, as Ferdinand was

a member of the expedition. He recorded the first contact with the Indians of the mainland, which occurred when the expedition encountered a large trading dugout, apparently from present-day Honduras (chap. 89). The Central American exploration is described in chapters 90–100.

The Spanish original of this biography was never published and has unfortunately disappeared, although fragments of it were included in the *Historia de las Indias* of Bartolomé de las Casas. The work was preserved through an Italian translation by Alonso de Ulloa, published in Venice in 1571. The first Spanish translation was published only in 1749, when Andrés González de Barcia included it in his *Historiadores primitivos*. A good modern Spanish edition, prepared by Ramón Iglesia, was published in 1947. The work was translated into English and annotated by Benjamin Keen (1959).

During the late 19th century a literary controversy arose over whether the biography was truly the work of Ferdinand Columbus. Most scholars now accept its authenticity. José Torre Revello has written an excellent biobibliography of Ferdinand Columbus, in which he discusses this controversy.

General Works
Official Chroniclers

3. *Peter Martyr d'Anghiera* (Petrus Martyr ab Angleria, Pedro Martir de Anghiera, Pietro Martire d'Anghiera) (1457–1526)

Peter Martyr was born in Arona, Milan, probably in 1457. He was educated in Milan by Giovanni Borromeo and in 1477 went to Rome where he became acquainted with the Conde de Tendilla (1486). With the Conde he went to Spain in 1487. There he joined the royal court of Queen Isabella and conducted school for the children of the court. He was present at the conquest of Granada in 1492. Apparently in 1494 he was ordained a priest. He carried out an embassy to Hungary in 1495 and to Egypt in 1501. After Queen Isabella's death he remained in the court as an important counselor of the Crown. In 1518 he was appointed to the Council of the Indies and in 1520 he was named royal chronicler. Under the Emperor Charles V he was given many honors in the court and in the Church. He died in 1526.

Because of his position in the court, Peter Martyr had immediate access to reports of the discoveries in the New World and was able to interview many of the explorers and conquerors personally. His humanistic and literary interests led him to report these happenings in Latin letters to the high churchmen and nobility with whom he was acquainted. His letters were published in two collections: *De Novo Orbe Decades*, which contains eight lengthy relations concerning the New World, written between 1493 and 1525; and *Opus Epistolarum*, a collection of 812 letters on various matters.

Both sources contain a great deal of information concerning the first contacts between the Spaniards and the Indians. In the *Decades*, book 4 of decade 3 tells of Columbus' voyage; large parts of decades 4–8 are devoted to the first explorations and conquests of Middle America. In the *Opus Epistolarum* there are many references to New Spain, beginning with Letter 634. Martyr took a great interest in information regarding the natives of the New World—their customs, religious ceremonies, temples, art, and artifacts. The descriptions that he gives of Indian artifacts have some firsthand value, since he saw the gifts which the explorers and conquerors sent back to the court. Owing to the fact that Martyr's writings are contemporary reports, the materials on any particular area are scattered, and an edition with a good index is a great help to utilizing them efficiently.

The first edition of the *Opus Epistolarum* and the first complete edition of the *Decades* were published in Alcalá de Henares in 1530. The *Decades* went through many editions and translations. A good English translation is that of Francis Augustus Mac-Nutt (1912). A modern Spanish translation by Agustín Millares Carlo, with an introductory study and appendices by Edmundo O'Gorman, was published in Mexico in 1964. It also contains a bibliography of editions of Peter Martyr's works by Joseph H. Sinclair. A Spanish translation of the *Opus Epistolarum*, prepared by José López de Toro, was published in Madrid in 1953–57 as volumes 9–12 of *Documentos inéditos para la historia de España*. A facsimile republication of the original editions of Peter Martyr's principal works (*Legatio Babylonica, De Orbe Novo Decades Octo*, and *Opus Epistolarum*) appeared in Graz, Austria, in 1966. Henry Raup Wagner has written a lengthy biobibliography of Peter Martyr.

4. Gonzalo Fernández de Oviedo y Valdés (1478–1557)

A chronicler who united a classical humanistic education with extensive experience in the New World was Gonzalo Fernández de Oviedo y Valdés. As a youth he entered the service of Alphonso of Aragón, nephew of Ferdinand the Catholic, and soon afterward he became a page of Prince John, the son of Ferdinand and Isabella. Throughout his life he retained close contacts with the royal court. He was present at the return of Christopher Columbus in 1493. He traveled and studied in Italy. He went to the New World in 1514 in the expedition of Pedrarias Dávila as supervisor of gold-smelting. During his life he held many offices in the New World—regidor of Nuestra Señora de la Antigua, governor of Cartagena, regidor and alcalde of the fortress of Santo Domingo—and he crossed the ocean a dozen times. He died in Valladolid, Spain, in 1557.

Oviedo's humanistic curiosity led him to note down the novelties of the land, nature, and peoples of the New World, as well as the history of the discovery and conquest. He began to write his *Historia general y natural de las Indias* during his second stay in

47

the Indies (1520–21). In 1526 he published a brief work which is known as the *Sumario de la natural historia de las Indias*. It gained him the attention of the Emperor, who appointed him official Chronicler of the Indies in 1532. All the authorities in the Indies were obliged to send him whatever relations and information he requested. He did a large part of his writing in Santo Domingo.

The first 19 books of his *Historia general y natural de las Indias* were printed in Seville in 1535. The twentieth book did not appear until 1557, perhaps because of the bitter opposition of the influential Bishop Las Casas (Item 12). The complete 50 books of the history were printed only in 1851–55. A new edition was published in Madrid in 1959, with a lengthy introductory study by Juan Pérez de Tudela Bueso. A modern edition of the *Sumario* appeared in 1950. No complete English translation of the *Historia* was ever published. An English translation of the *Sumario* by Sterling A. Stoudemire appeared in 1959. An annotated bibliography for Oviedo has been published by Daymond Turner (1966).

For the ethnohistorian Oviedo's *Historia* is one of the most valuable of the early chronicles. He is especially important for southern Middle America, where he had considerable personal experience. For other areas he used many firsthand sources which are now lost to us. The strongest criticism that has been directed against him is that he followed his sources uncritically and is more a mere chronicler than an historian. But because of his interest in all aspects of the New World, he recorded much that is of interest to the student of Indian life at the time of Contact. Of particular interest for Middle America are books 28–35 and 40–43, but there are also valuable ethnological data in the books that are devoted to natural history (bks. 7–15).

5. Alonso de Santa Cruz (fl. 1511–67)

A brief narrative of the discovery and conquest of Yucatan and Tenochtitlan is found in the *Islario general de todas las islas del mundo*, written by Alonso de Santa Cruz about 1540. Santa Cruz had studied cosmography in Salamanca (1511) and had sailed to the Rio de la Plata with Sebastian Cabot in 1525 as Royal Treasurer. He returned to Seville in 1530 where he continued his labors as a cosmographer and was named *Cosmógrafo mayor*. In 1539 he was attached to the royal court as a *contino*. At about this time the Emperor Charles V commissioned him to write the *Islario general*, which was not completed until the reign of Philip II. Santa Cruz also prepared many other works, among them a chronicle of the reign of Charles V. In the court at Valladolid he gave lectures on cosmography which were attended by the king and the nobles. As cosmographer he began the collection of reports and memorials from the New World which would later furnish material for the chroniclers of the Indies. He died in 1567.

The materials on the New World from the *Islario* were published by Franz R. v. Wieser in Innsbruck in 1908. The complete work was published in Madrid by the Royal Geographic Society in 1918 with text and atlas in separate volumes.

6. Juan López de Velasco (fl. 1571–91)

The position of official chronicler of the Indies as a post in the Council of the Indies was established as a result of the Visitation of the Council by Juan de Ovando. The first to hold the office, in connection with that of cosmographer of the Indies, was Juan López de Velasco, who was appointed in 1571. He remained in the post until 1591, when he was transferred to the Secretariat of the King. His principal work was the *Geografía y descripción universal de las Indias*, completed in 1574, of which a compendium was made, entitled *Demarcación y división de las Indias*. His own works were principally of geographic interest, although they contain considerable material of interest to the ethnohistorian, especially data concerning the population and customs of the natives. As noted in Article 5, he was primarily responsible for the program which brought into being the valuable *Relaciones geográficas* (1578–85).

His works remained in manuscript until the 19th century, although his successor as chronicler, Antonio de Herrera y Tordesillas (Item 7), drew on them for his *Historia*. The *Demarcación* was published in 1871 from a manuscript in the National Library, Madrid. The manuscript of the *Geografía* came into the possession of Archbishop Francisco Antonio de Lorenzana (Item 92) and with his books it later went into the Provincial Library of Toledo, Spain. It was published from this source by Justo Zaragoza in the *Boletín de la Sociedad Geográfica de Madrid*, starting in 1880. Zaragoza then published it in book form in 1894.

7. *Antonio de Herrera y Tordesillas* (1559–1625)

See Article 15.

8. *Gil González Dávila* (1570–1658)

The post of official chronicler of the Indies fell to Gil González Dávila in 1643. He had been born in Ávila in 1570. As a youth he went to Rome in the household of Cardinal Pedro Deza, but returned to Castile when he was 20 years old and occupied a position in the cathedral of Salamanca. He prepared works on the antiquities of Salamanca and the ecclesiastical history of the cities and cathedrals of Spain. In 1617 he was appointed Chronicler of Castile and continued his writings on political and ecclesiastical history. He was 73 years old when he was appointed *cronista mayor de Indias*. In this post he prepared his *Teatro eclesiástico de la primitiva iglesia de las Indias*. The first volume, which treated of the dioceses of Middle America, the West Indian Islands, and Venezuela, appeared in print in 1649. The second volume, which comprehended the rest of Spanish South

America, was published in 1655. The author died three years later in Ávila.

González Dávila utilized materials that had been sent in to the court as a response to royal cedulas of December 31, 1635, and November 8, 1648, in which Philip IV had commanded all the prelates of the Indies to submit relations of their dioceses to the official chronicler. He gives a brief history of each diocese and its bishops, but the user must be careful in regard to the information, as it is not without errors. (See Article 5.)

The part of the work which described the dioceses of New Spain was republished in Madrid in 1959.

9. *Antonio de León Pinelo* (1596–1660)

The successor of Gil González Dávila in the post of chronicler of the Indies was Antonio de León Pinelo, appointed in 1658. Unfortunately he died within a year after assuming the office, without having produced anything during his tenure, but the works that he had completed prior to his appointment make him deserving of inclusion here.

León Pinelo was probably born in Valladolid, Spain. He went with his parents to Rio de la Plata and from there he moved to Tucuman, Chuquisaca, and Lima. In Lima he entered the Jesuit college in 1612 and later studied laws at the university. He traveled extensively in the Andean region, served as corregidor and alcalde mayor of Oruro and as assessor of the corregidor of Potosi. In 1621 he went to Spain, where he was put in charge of compiling the *Recopilación de leyes de Indias*. He spent the rest of his life in Madrid, occupied with various writing projects. He produced many works, which in general show him more as a compiler of facts than as a great writer.

Three of his works are of interst here. In 1629 he published the *Epítome de la biblioteca oriental y occidental, naútica y geográfica*. This was a compendium of a larger work which is now lost. It was the first attempt to produce a comprehensive independent bibliography of works on the Indies, East and West. It listed printed and manuscript materials from public and private collections and recorded the existence of items which would otherwise be unknown. In 1737–38 Andrés González de Barcia published a much enlarged edition in three volumes. A facsimile edition of the 1629 edition was published in Washington, D.C., 1958.

A brief work by León Pinelo concerning efforts to pacify the Lacandón and Manché was published about 1639. It sums up the history of contacts between the Spaniards and the Lacandón up to that time. It was published in 1960 by France V. Scholes and Eleanor B. Adams in conjunction with a relation of the same area by Martín Alfonso Tovilla (*Item 9a*; see also Item 142).

A work by León Pinelo which remained in manuscript until the 20th century is his *El paraíso del Nuevo Mundo*, written between 1640 and 1650. In it he attempted to prove that the location of the Garden of Eden was in the New World. It is interesting not so much for its conclusions as for the data which he assembled to support them. It contains many references to the antiquities and natural history of Middle America, but it is not at all critical regarding the marvels that were reported. It was published by Porras Barrenechea in 1943.

10. Antonio de Solís y Rivadeneyra (1610–86)

In 1661 Antonio de Solís was appointed to succeed Antonio de León Pinelo as chronicler of the Indies. He was a native of Alcalá and had studied classics, philosophy, and laws there and in Salamanca. He served as secretary to the Conde de Oropesa and, after 1654, as *Oficial* of the first Secretariat of State. His writings prior to his appointment as chronicler were of a literary nature, principally dramatic and poetic. His work as chronicler showed the influence of his literary background. He at first intended to

write a continuation of Herrera's *Historia*. In preparing himself for this he found a prejudice in the works of foreigners and such a lack of conformity among writers of his own nation that he decided to rewrite the story of the conquest of Mexico, which he found most in need of revision. His work, therefore, was affected by two elements which damaged its historical value: his desire to write a well-balanced literary work and his determination to defend the Spanish national honor.

The result of his labors was his *Historia de la conquista de México, población y progreso de la América Septentrional conocida con el nombre Nueva España*, which appeared in 1684. The actual content of the work does not come up to the indications of the title. Solís was able to complete only the first part, which told the history of the conquest of Mexico, 1519–21. He was working on the continuation of the work when he died in Madrid in 1686.

Solís' *Historia* has been called a poem without verse, as it is written in epic style, with a great central hero and with the facts selected according to the needs of the story. It became the standard literary version of the Conquest until it was replaced by Prescott's history and other later works. It went through numerous Spanish editions and was translated into the major European tongues. An English translation appeared in 1724. A recent Spanish edition was published in Buenos Aires in 1944. A lengthy study of Solís and his history, by Luis A. Arocena, saw publication in Buenos Aires in 1963.

Other General Works by Spaniards

11. Martín Fernández de Enciso (1469–ca.1530)

An early geographic work which gives limited information regarding Central America is the *Suma de geografía* of Martín Fernández de Enciso. The author was born in Spain, probably in 1469. After gaining a baccalaureate in laws, he went to Santo Domingo early in the 16th century. In 1509 he took part in Alonso de Ojeda's expedition to colonize the northern coast of South America. He returned to Spain in 1512 but was back in the New World in 1514 in the expedition of Pedrarias Dávila. He soon went back to Spain again, where he published his *Suma de geografía* in 1519. He died about 1530.

The *Suma* is composed of three parts, the last of which describes the New World as far as it was then known. An antique English translation by Roger Barlow was published by the Hakluyt Society in 1932. A modern Spanish edition, with a biobibliographical study by José Ibáñez Cerdá, appeared in Madrid in 1948.

12. *Bartolomé de las Casas* (1474–1566)

Bartolomé de las Casas, whose long years as an active polemicist for the rights of the Indians merited for him a prominent place in the history of Latin America, also made significant contributions to its historiography.

He was born in Seville in 1474, the son of Francisco Casaus, who would later go to the New World in the second expedition of Christopher Columbus. Having received an education in Salamanca, Bartolomé himself sailed to the New World in 1502 with Nicolás de Ovando. Like most of his fellows, he took a strong interest in the quest for riches. In 1510 he was ordained as a secular priest and began his priestly activity in Cuba, where he was an advisor of Diego Velázquez, but he continued to use the Indians for his own enrichment. In 1514 he experienced a conversion, renounced his encomienda, and began to work for the defense of Indian rights. He went to Spain in 1515, where he was given a sympathetic hearing by Cardinal Cisneros. He returned to the Indies in 1517 with the title of Universal Protector of the Indians. He was granted permission to colonize 200 leagues of the northern coast of South America in 1520, but his effort failed miserably in 1521.

Soon afterward he entered the Dominican Order, making his religious vows in 1523. In 1534 he undertook missionary work in Guatemala and there, in 1537, he put into effect his theories of proselytism without the support of military force, converting the province of Tuzulatlan. The region which had been known to the Spaniards as *Tierra de Guerra* was changed into the province of Vera Paz. He was named bishop of Chiapas in 1543, much to the dismay of the Spanish colonists, but he renounced his bishopric in 1547 to return to Spain, where he continued his polemics in favor of the Indians from the friary of San Gregorio in Valladolid. The most outstanding results of Las Casas' years of work for the Indians were seen in the New Laws of 1542 and in the Instructions published in Valladolid, May 13, 1556. He died in the friary of Atocha, Madrid, in 1566, at the age of 92.

Las Casas' three writings of greatest importance for the ethnohistorian are *Brevísima relación de la destrucción de las Indias*, *Apologética historia . . .* , and *Historia general de las Indias*. Only the first was published during his lifetime. It appeared in 1552, one in a series of tracts which Las Casas put into print at that time. It painted a very dark, one-sided picture of the Spanish treatment of the native peoples of the New World. For this reason it was immediately exploited by Spain's enemies in northern Europe and was translated into many languages, forming a large part of the documentary basis for the Black Legend of Spanish colonial rule. The first English translation appeared in 1583. A modern translation is included in the appendix of Francis Augustus MacNutt's biography of Las Casas. A new Spanish edition of the *Tratados* by Las Casas was published in 1965, with facsimiles of the Seville imprints and modern transcriptions on facing pages.

The compete texts of the *Apologética historia* and the *Historia general* were not published until modern times, but fortunately Las Casas' own manuscripts of each had survived. The *Historia general de las Indias* was first published in Madrid in 1875–76. It tells of the discovery and conquest of the New World from 1492 to 1520. Las Casas had intended to complete the narrative down to 1550 in six parts, but he had completed only three parts at the time of his death. For the ethnohistorian of Middle America it is valuable principally in regard to the early explorations in southern Central America. His narrative does not go beyond the first exploratory phases of the Cortés expedition along the Mexican coast. A good modern edition, with a valuable analytical index, was published in 1951 in Mexico and Buenos Aires.

The *Apologética historia*, which was originally intended as a part of the *Historia general*, first came out in Madrid in 1909. It contains a great deal of information regarding the religious customs of the tribes of Middle America. The author aims to show that the Indians did not compare unfavorably with the pagans of Greece and Rome in their level of civilization.

A good edition of the collected works of Las Casas has been published in the "Biblioteca de Autores Españoles" (Madrid, 1957–58). It includes critical editions of the *Historial general* and the *Apologética historia*, based on Las Casas' manuscripts, as well as the *Tratados* and other smaller works, with indexes of persons and places. A critical edition of the *Apologética historia*, edited by Edmundo O'Gorman, with extensive biographical, textual, and bibliographical studies by the editor, was published in Mexico in 1967.

The figure of Las Casas has continued to be the center of polemics during the four centuries since his death. The struggle shows no sign of abating. An extensive bibliography of materials by and about Las Casas was published by Lewis Hanke and Manuel Giménez Fernández in 1954, but it was soon out of date, owing largely to renewed publication from the observance in 1966 of the fourth centenary of the bishop's death and controversies over the attack on the stability of Las Casas' personality by Ramón Menéndez Pidal (1963).

13. Jerónimo Román y Zamora (ca. 1536–97)

One of the first comparative studies of the religious and social practices of the Indians of the Americas was the *Repúblicas de Indias* of Jerónimo Román y Zamora, published in 1575 as part of his *Repúblicas del mundo*. Román, who was born in Logroño, joined the Augustinian Order in Haro. He was a prolific writer and he traveled extensively in Spain and other parts of Europe to gather materials for his histories. He was named chronicler of his Order in 1573. He died in Medina del Campo.

As sources for his study of the Indians he indicated Peter Martyr, Oviedo, Gómara, and Las Casas, as well as many letters of Cortés and the Pizarros. But he also had access to a great number of other reports, as he says very explicitly: "Tengo por cosa dudosa que alguno particular tenga en el mundo tantas memoriales como yo de aquella gente."

The *Repúblicas de Indias* is divided into three books. The first treats of the religious practices of the Indians; the second, of their government; and the third, of their social customs. It was republished in Madrid in 1897 as volumes 14 and 15 of the *Colección de libros raros o curiosos que tratan de América*.

14. Gregorio García (fl. 1607–27)

Almost from the time of the discovery the question of the origin of the American Indians occupied the minds of those who wrote about the New World. At the end of the 16th century Fr. Acosta considered the problem at some length in his *Historia natural y moral de las Indias* (see Item 75), but the author who gave it the most extensive study was a Dominican priest, Gregorio García. He was a native of Baeza, Spain, where he joined the Dominican Order. He worked as a missionary in the provinces of New Spain and Peru. He traveled through much of Middle America, noting data on Indian customs and antiquities. Later he returned to Spain where he published his works. He died in Baeza in 1627.

His two works which contain material on Middle America are the *Origen de los indios del Nuevo Mundo e Indias Occidentales* (Valencia, 1607) and *Historia eclesiástica seglar de la India Oriental y Occidental y predicación del Santo Evangelio en ella por los Apóstoles* (Baeza, 1625). Like his contemporaries, he based his conclusion on a large Scriptural and classical background and a rather limited knowledge of anthropology. In the first work he discussed many opinions regarding Indian origins and preferred the opinion that they were originally Hebrew, with later additions of Greek and Roman blood. In Book Five of the second work he discussed evidences of pre-Spanish Christian evangelization in Middle America. The importance is not so much in their conclusions as in the observations with which the author supported them.

In 1729 Andrés González de Barcia (*Item 14a*) brought out a second, enlarged edition of García's *Origen de los indios*. During the intervening century the question of Indian origins had been discussed by a number of northern Europeans, such as Hugo Grotius, Joannes de Laet (Item 26), and Georg Horn. Utilizing these and other works, Barcia interpolated lengthy additions into García's work in order to bring it up to date with the state of the literature on the subject at his time.

15. Alonso Fernández (1572–after 1627)

Alonso Fernández, born in Malpartida de Plasencia in 1572, joined the Dominican Order in 1589. He resided in various Dominican friaries in Spain during his whole life, writing a great number of works. He was appointed preacher-general in his Order at its Chapter in Lisbon in 1598. He died sometime after 1627.

Among Fernández' works is an *Historia eclesiástica de nuestros tiempos* (1611). It is divided into three books. The first treats of the conversion of the New World; the second, of Catholicism in Asia and the Pacific islands; and the third, of Catholicism in Europe. The most extensive treatment in the first part is given to Mexico and Guatemala, with accounts of works written by the missionary friars in the Indian languages.

16. Antonio Vázquez de Espinosa (fl. 1612–30)

A general description of Spanish America, written at a time when the Conquest had been completed in its main outlines, is found in the *Compendio y descripción de las Indias Occidentales* by Antonio Vázquez de Espinosa. The author was a Carmelite priest, a native of Jerez de la Frontera, Spain, born during the last third of the 16th century. He became an eminent theologian in his Order, but, desirous of an active missionary life, he went to the New World, laboring among the peoples of both Mexico and Peru from 1612 to 1621. About 1622 he returned to Spain, residing afterwards in Madrid and various towns of Andalucia. He died in Seville in 1630.

After his return to Spain from the New World, Vázquez de Espinosa wrote down his description of the Indies in two parts. The second part does not interest us here, since it was devoted entirely to South America. In the first part, after a general discussion of the origin of the Indians, he described the districts subject to the Secretariat of New Spain, i.e., the Audiencias of Santo Domingo, Mexico, Guadalajara, Guatemala, and the Philippines. Included are brief histories of the Spanish domination of the various areas, as well as valuable material on the economy, population, and ethnography of each region.

The manuscript of the work was found in 1929 by Charles Upson Clark in the Berberini Collection of the Vatican Library. In 1942 Clark published an English translation of the work, followed by his publication of the Spanish text in 1948.

17. Juan de Solórzano Pereira (1575–1655)

The work of Juan de Solórzano is of interest here both because of the record that it contains of the legal status and condition of the Indians during the early 17th century and because of the influence that it had on Spanish legal thought relative to the Indies.

The author was born in Madrid in 1575, the son of a bureaucrat of noble lineage. He entered the University of Salamanca about 1587, where he gained a licenciate in law in 1599. He began to teach in the same university in 1602 while still studying for his doctorate, which he received in 1608. In 1609 he was named oidor of the Audiencia of Lima, a position which was given to him principally so that he might gain a fuller comprehension of the laws of the Indies in order to organize them better. He arrived in Lima in mid-1610, where he was to remain for 18 years. He married a creole woman there, but he considered life in Peru as an exile. He became more and more dissatisfied, as he saw himself passed over for preferments in Spain. During these years, however, he prepared the first volume of his *De Indiarum Iure*, which he sent to Spain in April 1626.

That same year he was given the coveted permission to return to Spain to a position in the royal court. In February 1628, he was named fiscal of the Hacienda, and in June 1629 he was transferred to the same position in the Council of the Indies. In October 1629, he was appointed Councilor of the Indies in the place of Rodrigo de Aguiar, to continue the latter's work of organizing the laws of the Indies. Also in 1629 the first volume of *De Indiarum Iure* appeared in print. The second volume was published in 1639, after he had satisfied some critics who thought him too severe regarding the Spanish treatment of the Indians.

In 1642 he was named honorary Counci-

lor of the Council of Castile, retaining his position on the Council of the Indies. He continued to work on organizing the laws of the Indies, and in 1646 he had a large *recopilación* ready for the press, although it did not appear in print. In 1648 he published his *Política indiana*, a reworking in Spanish of his *De Indiarum Iure*. He died in Madrid on September 26, 1655. His work of collecting and organizing the laws of the Indies was continued in the Council of the Indies, although little credit was given to the importance of his contribution when the *Recopilación de leyes de Indias* appeared in 1681.

The first volume of *De Indiarum Iure* is composed of three books. Book 1 is a general introduction to the history and law of the Spanish New World. Book 2 (pp. 225–642) is a lengthy tract on Spain's right to conquer the New World. Book 3 (pp. 643–751) treats of Spain's right to retain its New World possessions. The second volume, in five books, deals with the question of the liberty of the Indians and the correlative problem of the various systems of enforced labor (bks. 1, 2), the Church (bk. 3), the civil government (bk. 4), and the royal treasury (bk. 5). The work is of great importance for the history of such institutions as the encomienda and repartimiento, although because of Solórzano's background he tends to explain these questions more in terms of Peru than of Middle America.

No true translation of the *De Indiarum Iure* has ever appeared, and it has generally been neglected because of the greater accessibility of the Spanish version. But the *Política indiana* does not contain the second and third books of the first volume of the *De Indiarum Iure*, and many other sections were made more succinct in the Spanish version. On the other hand, the book on the royal treasury was expanded considerably in the revision.

An important later edition of the *Política indiana* appeared in two volumes, 1736–39, with notes by Francisco Ramiro de Valenzuela (*Item 17a*). It was republished in 1930 in five volumes with a prologue by José M. Ots Capdequí. In 1945 Ricardo Levene published the *Libro primero de la recopilación de las cédulas, cartas, provisiones y ordenanzas reales* (2 vols., Buenos Aires) which Solórzano had prepared while oidor in Peru. A valuable biobibliographical study by Javier Malagón and José M. Ots Capdequí appeared in Mexico in 1965. It was originally intended as an introductory study for a scholarly edition of the *Política indiana*, which unfortunately has not appeared.

18. *Bernabé Cobo* (1580–1657)

Bernabé Cobo, born in Lopera, Jaen, Spain, sailed to the New World in 1596 in an expedition which set out to find El Dorado in northern South America. It seems that he spent some time in Española and Panama, traveling on to Lima in 1599. There he studied for two years in the Jesuit College of San Martín and in 1601 he entered the Society of Jesus in Lima. He was ordained a priest in 1613, apparently in Cuzco, and was sent back to Lima, where he began to show an interest in matters of natural and political history. In pursuit of this interest he traveled through various parts of Peru. In 1629 he went by way of Nicaragua and Guatemala to New Spain, where he remained until 1642. Returning to Peru in 1642, he put the finishing touches on his monumental *Historia del Nuevo Mundo*, which he completed in 1653. He died in Lima.

Cobo spent 40 years in the preparation of his *Historia*. It was composed of three parts, containing a total of 43 books. The first part described the natural history of the New World and its native peoples. The second part was devoted principally to the history and geography of Peru; the third part discussed primarily the history and geography of New Spain and other parts of North America. Unfortunately only the 14 books of the first part and three books on the foundation of Lima are now known. The books on natural history contain a considerable amount of information regarding Middle America.

These 14 books were first published in Seville in 1890–95 in an edition by Marcos Jiménez de la Espada. They were republished in the "Biblioteca de Autores Españoles" (vols. 91–92; 1956) with a biobibliographical study by Francisco Mateos. A letter from Cobo, relating his journey from Guatemala to Puebla, was published by Mariano Cuevas in 1944.

19. *Juan Díez de la Calle* (fl. 1645–48)

Juan Díez de la Calle was second official of the Secretariat of the Royal and Supreme Council of the Indies in 1646 when he published his *Memorial y noticias sacras y reales de las Indias Occidentales*. He had served in this capacity for 22 years and had taken advantage of his position to note down many facts regarding the jurisdictions subject to the Secretariat.

The *Memorial* is principally a manual of statistics regarding the civil and ecclesiastical political structures of the jurisdictions of Santo Domingo, Mexico, Guadalajara, Guatemala, and the Philippine Islands. It also includes items of interest regarding history, population, and encomiendas of Indians.

A second edition of the *Memorial* was published in Mexico in 1932.

20. *Pedro Murillo Velarde* (1696–1753)

Pedro Murillo Velarde, born in Laujar, Almeria, Spain, joined the Jesuits in 1718. A few years later he went to the Philippines, where he became professor of theology and canon law at the University of Manila. He returned to Europe as procurator of the Philippine province in Rome and Madrid. He was a man of broad interests and wrote works in such varied fields as law, history, geography, and cosmography. He died in Puerto de Santa María, Spain.

In 1752 Murillo Velarde published a 10-

volume *Geografía histórica*, the ninth volume of which was devoted to the Americas and adjacent islands. He gives a general geographic and ethnographic picture of each area, with a history of the conquest of each. For the City of Mexico he has a description of the city before the Conquest and at the time of writing.

21. Domingo Muriel (pseud. Cyriacus Morellus) (1718–95)

Domingo Muriel, born in Spain in 1718, joined the Jesuits in 1734. He went to the Jesuit missions in Paraguay and taught in the University of Cordoba, Tucuman. He returned to Madrid and Rome as procurator of the Jesuit Province of Paraguay, going back to Paraguay later to assume the direction of his province. He was deported to Italy at the time of the general expulsion of the Jesuits and died in Faenza in 1795.

Muriel's *Fasti Novi Orbis et ordinationum apostolicarum ad Indias pertinentium breviarium* (1776) contains a brief chronicle of the explorations and conquests in the New World up to the middle of the 18th century, but the greater part of it is a summary of ecclesiastical legislation pertaining to the Indies.

22. Antonio de Alcedo y Bexarano (1736–1812)

One of the first attempts to prepare a complete encyclopedic dictionary of the Spanish possessions in the Western Hemisphere was the *Diccionario geográfico histórico* of Antonio de Alcedo y Bexarano. The author was born in Quito, the son of an important Spanish official, Dionisio de Alcedo y Herrera. He was in Panama with his father from 1742 to 1750. He went to Madrid in 1752 and entered the Royal Spanish Guards as a cadet. He studied mathematics in the Colegio Imperial de Madrid, later pursuing courses in languages, history, and exact sciences. In 1760 he went to France to study medicine but returned to Spain to follow a military career. He became *mariscal del campo* (1800) and governor of La Coruña in Spain (1802). Between 1786 and 1789 he published the five volumes of his dictionary, on which he had worked for 20 years. In volume 5 he included a supplementary appendix of Americanisms and items on natural history. G. A. Thompson translated this work of Alcedo into English and published it, with extensive additions, in 1812–15. Publication of a new Spanish edition of the *Diccionario* was begun in Madrid in 1967 in the *Biblioteca de autores espanoles*.

Alcedo proposed to include a catalog of authors at the end of the last volume of his dictionary, but the catalog grew into an extensive independent work. Two manuscript versions survive, one in the Angrand Collection, Bibliothèque National, Paris, dated 1791 (photostatic copy, Library of Congress), and another in the New York Public Library, from the collection of Obadiah Rich, dated 1807. The latter version, which is the more finished of the two, was published in Quito in 1964–65. It is entitled *Bibliotheca americana: Catálogo de los autores que han escrito de la América en diferentes idiomas y noticia de su vida, patria, años en que vivieron, y obras que escribieron*. It is especially valuable for authors of the late 18th century.

José de Onís published a biobibliographical study of Alcedo and the *Bibliotheca americana* in 1951. The introductory study to the new Spanish edition of the *Diccionario* treats of both Antonio de Alcedo and of his father, who was an author in his own right.

23. Benito María de Moxó y de Francolí (1763–1816)

During the final decade of the colonial period a Catalan churchman who was in Mexico for a short time took an interest in the antiquities of the area. Benito María de Moxó y de Francolí, born in Cervera, Spain, on April 10, 1763, studied at the Benedictine college in Barcelona and then took a degree in philosophy at the University of Cervera. He joined the Benedictine Order, studied in Italy for four years, and returned to Spain to teach in the Colegio de San Pablo, Barcelona. He was appointed professor of humanities in the University of Cervera in 1792. In 1802 he gained the attention of King Charles VI when he officiated at a welcome for the monarch at the university. He was appointed auxiliary bishop of Michoacan and went to Mexico, where he was consecrated bishop. He was unable to assume his post because of the death of the bishop of Michoacan, and in 1805 he accepted an appointment as archbishop of Charcas. During his year in Mexico he interested himself in Indian antiquities, and wrote of them in his *Cartas mejicanas*, which he sent to Spain from Lima in 1806. He took possession of his archdiocese in 1807, but his tenure was seriously disturbed by the revolutionary upheavals of the time. He was exiled to Salta in 1815 and died there April 11, 1816.

In the *Cartas mejicanas* the author's attention was directed principally toward idolatry, human sacrifice, and cannibalism. He also described a Tarascan painting which he had studied. The letters were not published during the author's lifetime. In 1828 they were published in Barcelona by Moxó's nephew under the title *Entretenimientos de un prisionero* . . . , as though they were principally the nephew's work. In 1837 they appeared in Genoa with the original title and the name of the author. A good biobibliographical study of Moxó was published in Buenos Aires by Rubén Vargas Ugarte in 1931.

General Works by Northern Europeans

24. *André Thevet* (1502–90)

Spain made serious efforts to prevent detailed knowledge of her American possessions from reaching her political and commercial rivals in northern Europe. But gradually, through Latin works, translations of

Spanish narratives, and the writings of travelers, enough material became available to northern Europeans for them to write significantly concerning Spanish America.

A 16th-century cosmographer who expanded European knowledge of the New World was André Thevet. Born in France, he joined the Franciscan Order as a youth. He obtained permission of his superiors to visit Italy, and from there he went on to Constantinople, Asia Minor, Greece, and the Holy Land, returning to France in 1554. The next year he went with an expedition to Brazil. Later he was chaplain of Maria de Medici and finally historiographer and cosmographer of the French king. He died in Paris.

In 1575 Thevet published his great *Cosmographie universelle*, the fourth part of which was devoted to the New World. He included an interesting description of the geography and peoples of Central America and Mexico (fols. 984v–1000r). Among his sources he mentions Peter Martyr (Item 3), Hernando Cortés (Item 41), Diego Godoy (Item 121), Nuño de Guzmán (Item 100), Hernando Ruiz de Alarcón (Item 83), and Francisco Vázquez de Coronado. He is also known to have had other manuscript materials. The Codex Mendoza (see Article 23, no. 196) came into his possession after it had been taken from a Spanish ship by French pirates, and the *Histoyre du Mechique* (Article 27B, Item 1049) survives only in his translation.

25. *Samuel Purchas* (ca.1575–1626)

An early 17th-century English study of the pre-Spanish history and culture of Middle America is found in *Purchas His Pilgrimage* (bk. 8, chaps. 9–14) by Samuel Purchas, first published in 1613.

Purchas, who was born in Thraxted, Essex, England, studied at Cambridge, and entered the Anglican ministry. He was vicar of Eastwood, Essex, 1604–13, going from there in 1614 to St. Martin's, Ludgate, London, where he remained until his death. He inherited many manuscripts from others, especially Richard Hakluyt (Item 29). He drew on these sources and the available printed works to write his *Pilgrimage*, in which he treated of the religions of all parts of the world, but especially of those cultures which had come to the knowledge of Europeans during the previous century. In his section on Middle America he discussed the Conquest, Indian history, their idols, sacrifices and other religious rites, their calendar, and customs. As sources he used Peter Martyr (Item 3), López de Gómara (Item 54), Benzoni (Item 28), Acosta (Item 75), and Hakluyt, as well as manuscript materials. In 1625 he published a supplementary collection of narratives of travelers and conquerors which he entitled *Purchas His Pilgrims*. In this collection he included the first edition of the Mexican pictorial Codex Mendoza (see Article 23, no. 196, "Mendoza, Codex"). But neither as an author nor as an editor was Purchas really of the first rank, since in neither case was he entirely faithful to his sources.

26. Joannes de Laet (1595–1649)

One of the first general descriptions of the Western Hemisphere intended for northern European audiences was written by Joannes de Laet. The author was born in Antwerp; about 1624 he was director of the Dutch West India Company. It is supposed that he traveled a great deal, since he wrote several books about various European nations. In 1625 he first published his *Nieuvve vereldt, ofte Beschrijvinghe van West-Indien* . . . , and in 1648 he wrote a reply to Hugo Grotius' opinion on the origin of the American Indians. He died in Leiden.

In his description of the New World he devoted book 5 to New Spain, book 6 to New Galicia, and book 7 to Guatemala. In the 1625 edition he described the political divisions and geography. In the second Dutch edition of 1630 he included chapters on the natural history of New Spain and on the culture and pre-Conquest history of the Indians. He included five engravings of Aztec symbols for numbers and years, selected from Purchas' edition of the Codex Mendoza. A Latin edition of Laet's work was published in 1633, based on the 1630 Dutch edition, but with some additional engravings of items of natural history. A French translation of Laet's work, published in 1640, followed the Latin version. Among Laet's sources we find: Nicolás Monardes, Charles de L'Ecluse, and Francisco Ximénez for natural history; Acosta (Item 75), López de Gómara (Item 54), and Purchas (Item 25) for Mexican antiquities; Herrera (Article 15) for political history. The book was widely read, since it was one of the first works to give northern Europeans a general view of the whole of the Western Hemisphere, from which they had been largely shut off by the restrictive legislation of the Spanish government.

27. William Robertson (1721–93)

William Robertson was born in Borthwick, Midlothian, Scotland, and was educated at the University of Edinburgh. He entered the ministry in 1741. In 1759 he published his *History of Scotland during the Reigns of Queen Mary and King James VI*. It was very popular and led to his being named chaplain of Stirling Castle (1759), principal of the University of Edinburgh (1762), and historiographer-royal of Scotland (1762). He was an industrious researcher and produced a number of significant historical works.

Of importance to the present bibliography is his *History of America*, published in 1777. It was one of the first books in English to give a general history of Spanish and English America. The author consulted a great number of Spanish sources in preparing it, evident from the catalog of Spanish books and manuscripts which he presents at the beginning of the work. His agents in Vienna turned up the Vienna Codex of Cortés' letters which contained the then unpublished Fifth Letter of Relation and the Cabildo Letter of 1519. His work, however, was quite critical of Spanish colonial policy toward the Indians and aroused considerable resentment among Spanish writers.

Of special interest for Middle America are book 5, on the conquest of New Spain, and book 7, concerning Indian cultures, particularly those of Peru and Mexico. He published a slightly revised edition in 1778, making some additions to his notes and catalog of books. The revisions contain the first mention of Codex Borbonicus. Later editions generally followed the 1777 version. Books 9 and 10, on the English colonies, were published only in 1796 after the author's death and the termination of the American Revolution. The work was republished many times until the more advanced works of modern scholarship replaced it.

Colonial Travelers in Middle America

Travel literature has always contributed valuable insights into the life and customs of an area, because the foreign traveler often notes many aspects of the life from a fresh point of view, which the local residents lack. This type of writing is not absent for Middle America during the colonial period, in spite of Spain's strict prohibition against the presence of foreigners in the Indies. Berta Flores Salinas has written a group of worthwhile biobibliographical studies of foreign travelers in Mexico during the 16th and 17th centuries. An English work on Mexican travelers, in a more popular style, is that of William Mayer (1961).

28. Girolamo Benzoni (1518–70)

An Italian traveler who in the 16th century visited many of the islands of the West Indies as well as Central America, Venezuela, and Peru was Girolamo Benzoni. In 1541, after having traveled through Germany, France, and Spain, he embarked for the Canary Islands and soon went on from there to the New World. From that time

until he returned to Eurpoe in 1556, he wandered through parts of the Spanish colonies and experienced a great series of adventures and misadventures. After his return to Italy, he wrote down the story of his travels, including historical items that he had gleaned from his association with the conquerors. He complimented the valor of the Spaniards, but he also sharply criticized their cruelty, avarice, and other excesses. The work is garrulous and disorganized but merits attention because of the extensive experience of the author.

Benzoni's *La historia del mondo nuovo* was first published in Venice in 1565 and went through a great number of editions and translations. Theodor de Bry included it in his collection of narratives. An English translation by W. H. Smith was published by the Hakluyt Society in 1857. The original edition was republished in facsimile in Graz, Austria, in 1962, with an introduction by F. Anders. A Spanish translation by Marisa Vannini de Gerulewicz, with a preliminary study by León Croizat, appeared in Caracas in 1967.

29. Richard Hakluyt's English Travelers

Richard Hakluyt (1552?–1616), a clergyman of the Church of England, in his collection of voyages of the English nation (1589), included a number of narratives of Englishmen who had visited Mexico, principally as traders or corsairs. He also published important *relaciones* on mid-16th-century Tecuanapa, Guerrero. Two Englishmen who gave the most meaningful descriptions of the natives were Henry Hawkes and John Chilton.

30. Henry Hawkes

Henry Hawkes was a merchant who obtained permission to sell wine in the Indies about 1567. He arrived in New Spain in 1570, and later was working in the mines of Zacatecas when he was apprehended as a heretic. He was tried in the diocese of Guadalajara in 1571 and condemned to perpetual exile in the gobierno of New Spain. He escaped almost immediately and returned to England. In 1572 he gave a relation of his experiences to Hakluyt. In a short space Hawkes described the most salient aspects of the geography, natural history, and culture of New Spain.

31. John Chilton

John Chilton spent many more years than Hawkes in the New World. He sailed for New Spain in 1568 after having lived in Spain for several years. He traveled extensively through Mexico and Central America until 1586. His relation is quite succinct, considering the extent of his experience, but it gives valuable information regarding Indian population and culture at the time.

32. Juan González de Mendoza

Juan González de Mendoza, in his history of the kingdom of China, has a brief description of Mexico and its inhabitants as part of the "Itinerario" of Fray Martín Ignacio (*Item 32a*), a Franciscan who made a trip around the world in the 16th century. González de Mendoza's history was first printed in Rome in 1585 and went through many editions and translations. An English translation was published by the Hakluyt Society in 1853–54.

33. Alonso Ponce (fl. 1584–89)

Fray Alonso Ponce arrived in New Spain in 1584 with the title of Commissary General for the Franciscan Order in New Spain. From then until 1589 he traveled through the various Franciscan provinces from Guadalajara to Nicaragua, visiting friars and correcting abuses. The two friars who accompanied him successively as his secretaries noted down the incidents of his travels and observations about the various regions and peoples. It is generally accepted that the two secretaries were Alonso de San Román (*Item 33a*) and Antonio de Ciudad Real (*Item 33b*). The work is an invaluable record of life in Middle America

toward the end of the 16th century. Scattered through its pages are many items of ethnohistorical interest.

The narrative of Ponce's journey was first published in Madrid in 1873 from a manuscript in the possession of Mariano de Zabalburu. A good index was published separately in 1949 by Raúl Guerrero. Another was prepared by Grace Metcalfe and published in 1946.

34. Samuel Champlain (ca. 1567–1635)

A travel narrative that seems to be largely fiction is Samuel Champlain's story of a trip he claimed to have made to the West Indies, New Spain, and Panama. Champlain used this narrative to obtain the favor of the French king for his ventures into New France (Canada). The results of critical scholarship, however, have cast serious doubts on the authenticity of the story of his experiences in New Spain. The arguments are summed up by L. A. Vigneras (1953) and Berta Flores Salinas (1964).

There are a number of manuscripts of this work, but the one which is now in the John Carter Brown Library, Providence, Rhode Island, served as the basis for the published versions. It was translated into English by Alice Wilmere when the manuscript was still in the Public Library of Dieppe. The translation was published by the Hakluyt Society in 1859. A French edition was published in Quebec in 1870.

35. Thomas Gage (1603–56)

One of the best-known travelers of Middle America during the colonial period was the English Dominican, Thomas Gage. Born of an upper-class recusant family, he studied in Jesuit schools in France and Spain. He later entered the Dominican Order in Spain, against his father's wishes. In 1625 he joined a Dominican missionary expedition destined for the Philippines, starting the trip in an empty barrel to avoid the prohibition against foreigners in Spain's overseas possessions. When he reached Mex-

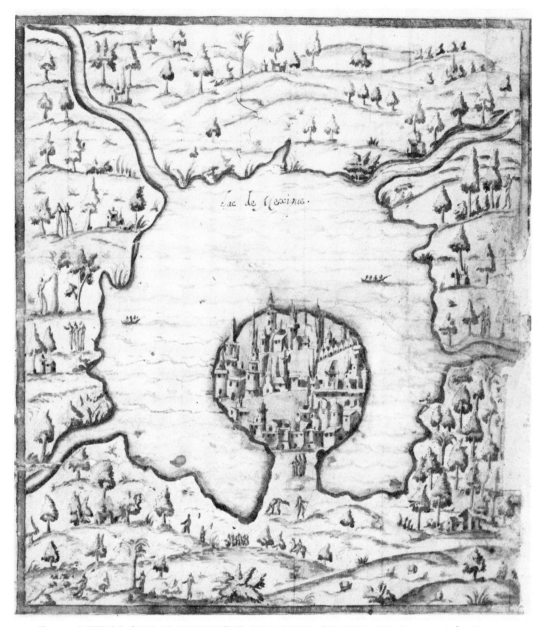

Fig. 1—MEXICO CITY AS VISUALIZED BY SAMUEL CHAMPLAIN. Courtesy, John Carter Brown Library, Brown University.

ico, he changed his mind about the Philippine missions and, deserting his companions, made his way to Chiapas and Guatemala.

This was the beginning of a 12-year period of missionary work and wanderings through Central America, during which the friar became progressively more interested in accumulating worldy goods. He returned to England via Spain in 1637. After a trip to Rome in 1639–40, he went back to England where in 1642 he recanted his Catholicism in a public sermon in St. Paul's Cathedral. He later gave testimony in court against a

61

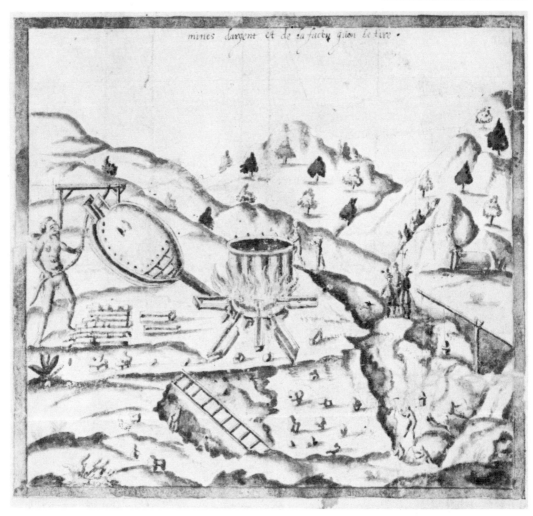

FIG. 2—A SPANISH SILVER-MINING OPERATION, ACCORDING TO SAMUEL CHAM-PLAIN. Courtesy, John Carter Brown Library, Brown University.

number of his fellow priests, sending them to their deaths. He was given the small parish of Acrise in Kent, where he wrote the story of his experiences in America. Later he became rector of the parish church of Deal, Kent. When the Puritans came to power he supported them. In 1654 he sailed to the New World in the expedition of Penn and Venables, which had been organized largely as a result of his writings. The expedition captured Jamaica, where Gage remained as chaplain of the English force. He died there in 1656.

Gage's narration of his wanderings, *The English American*, was first published in London in 1648. It was the first extensive eyewitness description of life in the Spanish colonies by a northern European, although it is not always trustworthy. It also included some grammatical notes on the Pokoman Indian language. It went through several English editions and was translated into a number of other European languages. A modern edition, somewhat abridged, prepared by J. Eric S. Thompson, appeared in 1958.

36. *Giovanni Francesco Gemelli Careri* (1651–1725)

In 1697 Giovanni Francesco Gemelli Careri, an Italian traveler, passed through Mexico from Acapulco to Veracruz as part of a trip around the world. He had been born in Naples in 1651. He was well educated, having obtained a doctorate in laws. He suffered a number of reverses in his native land and decided to travel, going first through the countries of Europe and then around the world. Starting out from Naples in 1693 he passed through North Africa, Turkey, Palestine, Persia, India, Malaysia, China, the Philippines, and New Spain before returning to Naples in 1698. He died in his native city.

Gemelli Careri wrote a lengthy narrative of his travels which was published in Naples in 1699–1700. The work shows the author as an acute observer. For New Spain (vol. 6) he assembled considerable material on the pre-Conquest and post-Contact history, for which he was able to use sources in the library of Carlos de Sigüenza y Góngora (Item 86). An English translation of Gemelli Careri's work appeared in Awnsham Churchill's collection of voyages in 1704. The section on New Spain has been published separately in Spanish translation a number of times. A good biobibliographical study of Gemelli was written in Italian by Filippo A. Nunnari (1901).

37. *Francisco de Ajofrín* (1719–89)

Francisco de Ajofrín, a native of Ajofrín, Toledo, Spain, joined the Capuchin Order in 1740 in Salamanca. In 1763 he was appointed by the Congregation for the Propagation of the Faith to go to Mexico to collect alms. He made two extensive circuits through the Mexican provinces: the first, in 1764, through Michoacan, Guanajuato, and Queretaro; the second, in late 1765 and early 1766, through Puebla, Veracruz, Oaxaca, and Guerrero. He left Mexico in August, 1766, returning to Spain, where he became chronicler of his province. He died in Madrid.

Ajofrín's diary of his travels in Mexico contains many notes of importance about the regions through which he passed, notes concerning their traditions, history, flora and fauna, economic resources, etc. The manuscript of the first pages of his diary passed into the possession of the National Library of Madrid and was published by Genaro Estrada in 1936. The complete text was published in 1958–59 by the Academy of History, Madrid, from a manuscript in their possession.

37a. *Pedro Alonso O'Crowley y O'Donnell* (1740–1817)

Pedro Alonso O'Crowley y O'Donnell was born in Cadiz, Spain, on February 21, 1740, the son of Irish immigrant parents. He received a classical education in the school of the Augustinians in Senlis, France. Afterwards he undertook the career of a merchant, in which he spent the rest of his life. He made his first recorded trip to Mexico when he was 24 years old, and repeated the journey several times during the following 10 years. At age 44 he married María Power, also of Irish ancestry, and apparently settled down to life in Cadiz. There he raised a family of nine children, gained a fortune, and achieved an important position in the society. He died there in 1817.

In 1774 O'Crowley wrote a work entitled *Idea compendiosa del Reyno de Nueva España*. It is a somewhat disorganized survey of New Spain, with sections on its Indian and Spanish history, major towns and geographical areas, and contemporary conditions of Indians and Spaniards. As illustrations he included a sketch of the Aztec temple, three pages copied from Indian pictorial manuscripts, a series of the well-known paintings of racial mixtures, pictures of flora and fauna, maps of cities, and paintings of three contemporary Indian types (caciques, common Indians, and barbarous Indians). It depends heavily on earlier published sources, but it has value because of the author's observations of conditions at his time.

The original manuscript is in the Biblioteca Nacional in Madrid and has not been published in Spanish. An English translation by Seán Galvin, who also supplied a biobibliographical introduction, was published in San Francisco in 1972.

38. *Nicolas Joseph Thiéry de Menonville* (1739–80)

A French traveler who made his way into Oaxaca toward the end of the colonial period was Nicolas Joseph Thiéry de Menonville. He was sent out by King Louis XVI of France to study the economic resources of the Antilles. In 1777 he entered Mexico by way of Veracruz and went to Oaxaca in search of cochineal. He noted down many of the interesting novelties that he observed along the way. After a great amount of trouble he succeeded in bringing back some cochineal alive. His narrative of the trip appeared in French in 1787 and in English in 1812.

DISCOVERY AND CONQUEST OF MEXICO
Exploratory Expeditions [see also Items 1–3]

39. *Juan Díaz* (fl. 1518–21)

The expedition of Juan de Grijalva in 1518 gave the Spaniards in Cuba some idea of the importance of Mexico and led to the conquering expedition of Hernando Cortés. The coast of Yucatan had previously been explored to some extent by Francisco Hernández de Córdoba in 1517. Grijalva extended the explorations to the coast of Mexico north of Veracruz toward Panuco.

Grijalva's chaplain, a secular priest named Juan Díaz, wrote a chronicle of the expedition in which he recorded many interesting facts about the Indians whom they encountered. Later this priest returned to Mexico with the Cortés expedition. Bernal Díaz mentions that Juan Díaz said Mass in the camp of Alvarado in Tacuba on the

morning when the final siege of Tenochtitlan was begun.

The Spanish original of the chronicle of Juan Díaz is lost. The text was preserved in an Italian translation which was placed at the end of Ludovico de Varthema's *Itinerario* in editions published after 1520. Joaquín García Icazbalceta published a Spanish translation in 1858, which was republished by Agustín Yáñez (1963). Patricia de Fuentes published it in English translation in 1963. In 1942 Henry Raup Wagner published studies of the expeditions of Hernández de Córdoba and Grijalva, including in each an appendix of source materials in English translation. The chronicle of Juan Díaz appears in the volume on Grijalva.

Eyewitness Accounts of the Conquest of Mexico

The conquest of the Aztec Empire of Central Mexico by a small band of Spaniards produced an extensive literature relating the history of the military campaign and telling of the wonders of the new land. The wealth of the Aztecs, their artistic, cultural, and ceremonial splendor, the novelty and, at times, repugnance of their customs to the European mind, all led to the extensive production of descriptive contemporary literature which is invaluable for one who wishes to know the civilization and culture of the Mexican Indians at the time of the Conquest.

40. *Letter of the Regimiento of Vera Cruz*

The first report that has come down to us from the Cortés expedition is the letter written to the King by the *Regimiento* of Vera Cruz on July 10, 1519. It was accompanied by a list of treasure and other artifacts which they were sending to the King. The letter was found by agents of William Robertson (Item 27) in Vienna when he was searching for materials for his *History of America*. It was first published in the *Colección de documentos inéditos para la historia de España* (1842). Since that time it

64

has generally been printed with Cortés' Letters of Relation (Item 41) as a substitute for his lost First Letter with which it was sent.

41. Hernando Cortés (ca. 1485–1547)

Hernando Cortés was born in Medellín, Spain. He was educated in Salamanca and, after possibly working as a notary's assistant there, he made his way to Santo Domingo. In 1511 he accompanied Diego Velázquez in the conquest of Cuba, where he established himself as an encomendero during the following years. In November, 1518, he took command of the expedition that he had helped Velázquez outfit to further the exploration to Mexico. He led his small army to the conquest of the Aztec empire finally in August, 1521, and was named governor and captain-general of his conquests on October 15, 1522. In 1524 he led an overland expedition to Honduras. Increasing difficulties with the royal authorities led him to return to Spain in 1528, where he partially regained royal favor and was given the titles of Captain-general and Marqués del Valle de Oaxaca. He went back to Mexico and extended his explorations into the Pacific, discovering the Peninsula of California in 1538. He returned to Spain once more in 1540 and died there in Castilleja de la Cuesta, near Seville, on December 2, 1547.

Between 1519 and 1526 Cortés wrote six lengthy narrative letters to the king, informing him and the royal court of his explorations and conquests. The first and the fifth have disappeared. We know of the existence of the fifth letter only because it is mentioned in the sixth. For this reason, it is not generally considered in the numeration of the Cortés letters and the final letter is generally called the Fifth Letter of Relation. The extant letters bear the following dates: October 30, 1520; May 15, 1522; October 15, 1524; September 3, 1526.

The second, third, and fourth letters were published individually soon after they were

FIG. 3—HERNÁN CORTÉS, 1529, AT AGE 42. From Weiditz, 1927, pl. 4, sheet 77.

received in Spain, but the last one saw publication only in 1844. The first collected edition of the letters was published in the "Biblioteca de Autores Españoles" (vol. 22) in 1852. There have been many more recent editions. A facsimile edition of the Vienna Codex (S. N. 1600) of manuscript copies of the Cortés letters was published in Graz, Austria, in 1960. A good collection of the letters of Relation, together with other writings of Cortés, was published in Mexico in 1963. There have been two good English translations of the Cortés Letters, the first by Francis Augustus MacNutt in 1908, and the second by J. Bayard Morris in 1928. The Morris translation was republished in paperback in 1962.

In using Cortés' Letters one must remember that they are the work of a man who is telling his own story to make a favorable impression on the Spanish Crown. Nevertheless, they contain invaluable ethnohistorical data as the report of an eyewitness and of the captain who brought the Aztec empire to an end. They are enlightening in regard to linguistics, ethnography, and ethnogeography.

42. Andrés de Tapia (1495–after 1528)

One of Cortés' most trusted captains in the conquest of Mexico was Andrés de Tapia. He was a young man of 24 when he sailed from Cuba to Mexico with Cortés in 1519. He took part in all the major engagements of the Conquest and afterward supported Cortés in the political struggles of the 1520s. He went to Spain with Cortés in 1528. Later he returned to Mexico, where he lived until his death.

Tapia wrote a truncated relation of the conquest of Mexico, which tells the story from the departure from Cuba to the imprisonment of Pánfilo de Narváez. It gives certain details that are not found elsewhere. López de Gómara (Item 54), Cervantes de Salazar (Item 56) and Herrera (see Article 15) used it in writing their chronicles.

Tapia's Relation was first published by García Icazbalceta in 1866. Agustín Yáñez (1963) republished it in his collection of chronicles, and Patricia de Fuentes (1963) brought out an English translation.

43. Francisco (Alonso) de Aguilar (1479–1572)

The conqueror Alonso de Aguilar spent the last 40 years of his life in the Dominican Order under the name Fray Francisco. He had come to Mexico with Cortés in 1519 and had taken part in the whole course of the Conquest. A man more than 40 years old at the time, he was one of the more mature conquerors. He was entrusted with guarding Montezuma during his imprisonment and was given a number of other responsible assignments. After the Conquest he was given an encomienda of Indians, and he opened an inn along the road between Vera Cruz and the future site of Puebla. He joined the Dominican Order in 1529 at 50 years of age and lived an exemplary life in it until his death at the age of 92.

Aguilar's Dominican brethren insisted that he share his experiences with them. At some time after 1559, when he was more than 80 years old, he composed a chronicle of the Conquest. Most probably it was dictated to one of his brethren, since Aguilar was crippled with gout for his last 35 years.

His narrative follows the story of the exploration and conquest of Mexico from the expedition of Grijalva to the final capitulation of Mexico City. A few supplementary paragraphs at the end tell of Cortés' expedition to Honduras, of the parts of Mexico that Aguilar had visited, and of the customs of the Indians. The narrative is succinct and frugal, but it contains information that is not found elsewhere.

The manuscript was preserved in the Library of the Escorial. It was first published in 1900 from a copy made by Francisco del Paso y Troncoso. The best recent edition is that of Federico Gómez de Orozco (1954), from which Patricia de Fuentes (1963) translated it into English for inclusion in her volume of chronicles of the Conquest.

44. Bernal Díaz del Castillo (1496–1584)

The narrative of the conquest of Mexico which has attracted more widespread interest than any other is that by Bernal Díaz del Castillo. The author combined the authenticity of an eyewitness with the charm of a superb storyteller.

Díaz was born in Medina del Campo, Spain, probably in 1496. He sailed to the New World in 1514 with Pedrarias Dávila. He was a member of the exploratory expeditions of Francisco Hernández de Córdoba (1517) and possibly that of Juan de Grijalva (1518). At 23 years of age (1519) he returned to Mexico in the expedition of Cortés, and in 1524 he accompanied Cortés on his march to Honduras. He returned to Spain twice, in 1540 and 1549–50. He took up residence as an encomendero in Guatemala in 1541 and made his home there until his death in 1584.

Between 1552 and 1557 Bernal Díaz began to write a narrative of the conquest of Mexico as he had experienced it, seemingly as a "Relation of merits and services" (see Item 46), but he allowed the project to lapse. Probably in the mid-1560s he read Francisco López de Gómara's *Conquista de México* (Item 54), which glorified the role of Cortés in the Conquest. Angered by this slighting of the common soldiers, Díaz took up his writing once again and completed the first draft of his *True History* in 1568.

He sent a copy of his work to Spain in 1575, but he also had a copy made for himself which he continued to revise, apparently to the end of his life. This latter copy now belongs to the Guatemalan government. In 1932 another manuscript which had once belonged to the grandson of the author came to light in Spain. Known as the Murcia, or Alegría, manuscript, it differs in some respects from the other two versions.

The manuscript which Díaz had sent to Spain was finally published in 1632 by Fray Alonso de Remón (*Item 44a*), a Mercedarian friar, who made a few interpolations to add to the luster of his confrere Fray Bartolomé de Olmedo, who had accompanied the Cortés expedition. The Remón edition remained the standard version until Genaro García published the text of the Guatemala manuscript in 1904. In 1940 the Instituto "Gonzalo Fernández de Oviedo" in Madrid published a critical edition of chapters 1–146, showing the variants between the three Spanish versions. The most popular Spanish edition is that first published in 1939 by Joaquín Ramírez Cabañas, a modernized Spanish text based on a comparison of the three Spanish versions. A deluxe illustrated Spanish edition appeared in Mexico in 1961. Besides the text it contains an introductory study, a bibliography of Spanish editions, an annotated bibliography, biographies of Indian personages mentioned by Díaz, a lexicon of obsolete words that appear in the text, and separate indexes of personal and place names.

An English translation of the Remón text was published by Maurice Keatinge in 1800. The Guatemala text, as published by Genaro García, was translated into English by Alfred Percival Maudslay and published by the Hakluyt Society (1908–16). In 1963 J. M. Cohen published an abridged version of the first 157 chapters, translated from the Ramírez Cabañas edition. A good biographical study of Bernal Díaz by Herbert Cerwin appeared in 1963. Much detailed analysis of the manuscripts and related matters, as well as important bibliography, is given in a 1967 publication by Carmelo Sáenz de Santa María.

For the ethnohistorian the narrative of Bernal Díaz gives many personal insights into Indian life at the time of the Conquest, and it is a help for establishing the ethnography and distribution of languages at the time. It is devoted principally to the story of the conquest of Mexico and the expedition of Cortés to Honduras, but it also contains information on the Spanish colonization down to the time of writing.

45. *Anonymous Conqueror* (16th century)

An interesting relation of the life and customs of the Indians of New Spain at the time of the Conquest has come down to us through an Italian translation published by Gian Battista Ramusio in 1556. The relation is anonymous, attributed only to "un gentil'huomo del Signor Fernando Cortese." Francisco Javier Clavigero, who used the work in preparing his *Historia* (Article 17), dubbed the author "el conquistador anónimo," and by this name he has come to be known.

Carlos María de Bustamante attributed the work to Francisco de Terrazas, mayordomo of Cortés, but gave no sound reason for this attribution. It is certain from internal evidence that the work was written in Spain. Federico Gómez de Orozco concluded, because of inconsistencies in the text, that the author had never actually been in New Spain. He was of the opinion that the work was a fabrication of the professional translator, Alonso de Ulloa, who compiled it from information that he had gleaned as a member of the entourage of Hernando Cortés in Spain. His argumentation against the author's having been an eyewitness is strong; his thoughts on Ulloa's authorship have considerable force, but need further study. His opinion has greater force for those who maintain that Ferdinand Columbus' biography of his father (Item 2) was also Ulloa's fabrication.

The first retranslation into Spanish, bowdlerized in places, was published by García Icazbalceta in 1858. The best Spanish edition is the one prepared by Jorge Gurría Lacroix and published in 1961. It includes a bibliography of editions by Gurría Lacroix, Gómez de Orozco's study of the authorship, Francisco de la Maza's translation of the text into Spanish, significant introductory studies from previous editions, and a facsimile reprint of the Ramusio edition of 1556. Patricia de Fuentes (1963) included an English translation of this work in her collection of Conquest chronicles.

46. Relations of Merits and Services

A type of document which is often of great value for filling out the details of the conquest of a particular area is the *Relación* or *Probanza de méritos y servicios*. These documents were judicial inquiries, made at the request of an individual, concerning his personal contributions, or those of his close relatives, in the service of the Crown. The interested party presented an itemized relation of his services before a qualified official and then brought in a group of witnesses

who were to testify about what they knew regarding each item. The itemized relation thus constituted the individual's narrative of the Conquest. Often his witnesses were his companions in the campaigns and they also contributed significant details. The danger of depending too heavily on these relations is obvious, as the object of the document was to impress the Crown with the importance of the activities of an interested party. As noted, the *Historia* by Bernal Díaz (Item 44) probably developed from such a probanza.

There are long series of these relations in the Archivo General de Indias, in the section of Patronato Real as well as in the sections of the various audiencias. A large body of such documents was found and listed by Francisco del Paso y Troncoso (Article 21). Summaries of 1,385 of these, also collected by Paso y Troncoso, were published in 1923 by Francisco A. Icaza under the title *Diccionario autobiográfico de conquistadores y pobladores de Nueva España*. A number of probanzas have seen publication in various collections of documents. Unfortunately the statements of the witnesses have sometimes been neglected in these publications. In the accompanying bibliography we have included only a sample selection of these relations: Jerónimo de Aguilar (*Item 46a*), Blas González (*Item 47*), Francisco de Montejo (*Item 48*), Juan Rodríguez Cabrillo (*Item 49*), Alonso García Bravo (*Item 50*), and Juan Vázquez de Coronado (*Item 51*; see also Item 133). We shall say a few words here about the probanza of Bernardino Vázquez de Tapia (*Item 52*).

Bernardino Vázquez de Tapia came to the New World with Pedrarias Dávila (Item 132) and served him for a while in Castilla del Oro. Later he went to Cuba, where he was given an encomienda of Indians. Preferring the prospect of adventure and possible wealth, he sailed with Grijalva as his *alférez general*. He returned to Mexico with Cortés and was sent as one of the first messengers from Cortés to Montezuma. He was a leader of the anti-Cortés faction in Mexico after the Conquest. He held various positions on the town council of Mexico as late as 1552.

Vázquez de Tapia's relation of merits and services is more extensive and detailed than most and gives a valuable view of the Conquest. It has been published twice, first by Manuel Romero de Terreros in 1939, and again by Jorge Gurría Lacroix in 1953.

Derivative Accounts of the Conquest of Mexico

The news of the discoveries and conquests that Cortés had made in New Spain was of international interest. Word of them spread through Europe by letter almost as soon as the reports reached the Spanish court. A number of these letters were immediately put into print. The most famous one was the *De nuper sub D. Carolo Repertis Insulis* (1521) of Peter Martyr (Item 3), which corresponds roughly with the Fourth Decade of his *De Orbe Novo*. Marshall H. Saville (1920) and Henry R. Wagner (1929a and 1929b) published a number of other letters in English translation. Another interesting item (*Item 53*), which tells the story through the period of Cortés' Second Letter of Relation, is *Des marches, iles et pays trouvés et conquit par les capitaines du tres ilustre . . . Charles V.* It was written in Valladolid, Spain, shortly after October, 1522, and was published in Antwerp. Often these items were based on interviews with eyewitnesses as well as on written relations, and the authors had seen the artifacts that were sent back to Spain by the conquerors.

54. Francisco López de Gómara (1511– ca. 1566)

Hernando Cortés was an outstanding leader of men, no matter how one feels about the results of his leadership. His chaplain in his later years, Francisco López de Gómara, looked upon him as a hero and wrote of him as such. While Bernal Díaz (Item 44) would later insist that Cortés

was only the first among many equally valiant men, López de Gómara wrote of him as one who stood head and shoulders above his fellows. The relative value of the treatments have been discussed at length, perhaps best by Ramón Iglesia (1942). Possibly the best conclusion would be to say that the viewpoints complement one another.

López de Gómara was born in the town of Gómara in Soria, Old Castile. He never went to the New World but spent his life principally in Spain and Italy, obtaining an excellent classical and humanistic education. In 1541 he accompanied Charles V in his campaign against Algiers, where he became acquainted with Cortés. He served as the conqueror's private secretary-chaplain until Cortés died in 1547. Afterward he retired to Gómara or Valladolid and devoted his time to writing until his death sometime after 1557 and before 1566.

López de Gómara's principal contribution to the historiography of the New World was his chronicle of the conquest of Mexico by Cortés. But, considering an introductory study necessary, he wrote a general history of the Indies to accompany his chronicle of the Conquest. This *Historia de Indias* includes rather brief summaries of the exploration and conquest of Middle America. The *Conquista de México* might better have been entitled "The Life of Hernando Cortés," since it traces the conqueror's career from birth to death and centers the whole story of the Conquest around him. As sources for his work Gómara utilized the Letters of Relation and other information given him by Cortés, the *Memoriales* of Motolinía (see Article 13), and information given him by Andrés de Tapia (Item 42). It is a fine work of history, written in the classical tradition, with a highly polished style.

The double work was published in Zaragoza in 1552 under the title *La historia de las Indias y conquista de Mexico.* An edition published in Medina del Campo in 1553 bore the added title *Hispania victrix.*

The book was almost immediately suppressed by an order of the Crown, dated November 17, 1553, possibly because of the strong opposition by Bishop Las Casas to López de Gómara's work or possibly because the Crown feared documentation of the claims of the Cortés family regarding their rights in Mexico. But the work became widely known in spite of royal opposition.

No complete English translation of the *Historia de Indias* has ever been published. A good modern translation of the *Conquista de México* is that of Lesley Byrd Simpson (1964). It is complete except for the omission of chapters 200–48, on Aztec society and religion, which López de Gómara took almost verbatim from Motolinía.

In 1858 García Icazbalceta published the Latin text and Spanish translation of a fragmentary work (*Item 55*) entitled *De rebus gestis Fernandi Cortesii*, which takes the story of the Cortés expedition only as far as his departure from Cuba. Juan Bautista Muñoz, who had found the manuscript in the Archive of Simancas, attributed it to Juan Cristóbal Calvete de Estrella (*Item 55a*), but Ramón Iglesia (1942) has shown, almost beyond doubt, that it is the beginning of a Latin version of the *Conquista de México* which López de Gómara himself was preparing at the time of his death.

56. *Francisco Cervantes de Salazar* (ca. 1515–75)

Born in Toledo during the second decade of the 16th century, Francisco Cervantes de Salazar studied humanities in Toledo and canon law in Salamanca. He traveled to Italy and Flanders and later served as Latin secretary to García de Loaysa, cardinal-archbishop of Seville, apparently until 1546. In 1550 he occupied the chair of rhetoric in the University of Osuna. About the year 1551 he went to New Spain where in 1553 he was given the chair of rhetoric in the newly created University of Mexico. In 1555 he was ordained a priest and was later given a post as canon in the Cathedral of Mexico (1563 or 1566). He also pursued studies in the University of Mexico, obtaining degrees in arts, canon law, and theology. In 1567, a year after obtaining his doctorate in theology, he was named rector of the University and he was re-elected to this post in 1573.

His principal work was the *Crónica de la conquista de la Nueva España*, but he also wrote three Latin dialogues about life in Mexico, which contain some information regarding the Indians and their customs. The dialogues were published in Mexico in 1554. An English translation, with a facsimile of the original edition, was published in 1953.

The *Crónica*, with which Cervantes was occupied apparently as early as 1554, became a project of public interest in Mexico City, where the old conquerors hoped to receive more credit than they had been given in López de Gómara's chronicle (Item 54). In 1558 the Town Council of Mexico assigned Cervantes a salary of 200 pesos annually so that he could devote more time to its composition. The work was incomplete in 1566 when the *visitador* Jerónimo de Valderrama took a copy back to Spain with him. The manuscript was in the National Library of Madrid when in 1914 the Hispanic Society of America brought out a complete edition based on a copy of Zelia Nuttall, and Francisco del Paso y Troncoso also published the first volume of a proposed three-volume edition. The polemic about the competing editions is discussed briefly in Article 21.

The *Crónica* is composed of six books. The first is an introductory description of New Spain with its peoples and their customs. The rest of the work is a history of the conquest of central Mexico and the expansion into the outer provinces. It terminates abruptly with the heading of a chapter which was to tell of the expeditions of

Juan Rodríguez de Villafuerte and Gonzalo de Sandoval into western Michoacan and Colima.

Jorge Hugo Díaz-Thomé (1945) condemned the *Crónica* roundly as a dishonest copy, with interpolations, of López de Gómara's history of the conquest (Item 54). It is true that for his story of the conquest of Tenochtitlan Cervantes copied large sections from López de Gómara, but he also went significantly beyond him and utilized a number of written and oral sources which were not available to earlier writers. For instance, Cervantes' chapters on Francisco Montaño's *entrada* into Michoacan, which Herrera incorporated almost verbatim into his *Decadas*, are apparently based on an account given him by Montaño and are not found elsewhere. He also made use of relations by Jerónimo Ruiz de la Mota, Alonso de Mata, and Alonso de Hojeda. Atanasio López (1925) was favorably impressed with Cervantes de Salazar's careful and critical use of the several sources at his disposal. Among them were two lost works by Motolinía that he used extensively, often to refute López de Gómara.[2]

As a classicist, Cervantes de Salazar wrote with a sense of the drama of the events, sometimes allowing his literary tastes to interfere with the factual relation of history. Irma Mora Plancarte (1963) has studied this dramatical aspect of his work.

57. *Juan Ginés de Sepúlveda* (ca. 1490–1573)

Another chronicler of the conquest of Mexico who never set foot in the New World was Juan Ginés de Sepúlveda, better known for his disputes with Bishop Las Casas over the justice of the conquest of the Indies (Hanke, 1959). Sepúlveda was born in Pozoblanco, northwest of Cordoba, Spain, about 1490. He studied humanities in Cordoba, philosophy in Alcala, and the-

ology in Sigüenza. In Bologna he became interested in Aristotle and proposed to translate his complete works, but he was unable to complete this project. He was a protégé of Pope Clement VII and of other patrons of Italian humanism. In 1535 he was introduced to Emperor Charles V, who appointed him his chronicler and chaplain. Later he was named as one of the teachers of young Prince Philip. He spent the rest of his life in Spain, assisting at the court or working on his literary endeavors, until his death in 1573.

The work by Sepúlveda which interests us here is his *De Rebus Hispanorum Gestis ad Novum Orbem Mexicumque*, which he finished about the year 1562. It is primarily a history of the discovery and conquest of Mexico. Of its seven books, only book 1 and book 2 (chaps. 1–9) treat of the early explorations in the Caribbean; the rest of the work is devoted to Mexico. Books 3–7 are concerned entirely with the Cortés expedition up to the fall of Tenochtitlan.

In general the author relied on Oviedo's *Historia*, but he also conferred with Cortés at least three times. He had at hand certain commentaries of Cortés which perhaps included the Conqueror's first letter. His narrative incorporates information that is not found elsewhere.

Sepúlveda's work has been neglected in the literature of the Conquest. It has been published only once—in the *Opera* of Sepúlveda, edited by the Royal Academy of History in 1780. Ángel Losada has emphasized its importance in several studies. It should be translated and reissued in scholarly form.

58. *Antonio de Saavedra Guzmán* (fl. 1599)

A 16th-century effort to record the history of the conquest of Mexico in verse was *El peregrino indiano* of Antonio de Saavedra Guzmán. The author was born in Mexico, the son of Juan Arias de Saavedra, one of

---

[2] This and the preceding sentence were added by the Volume Editor.

the earliest Spanish colonists of Mexico. Little is known of him except that he was corregidor of Zacatecas and visitador of Texcoco. Toward the end of the 16th century he made a trip to Spain. During 70 days at sea he composed his poem, for which he had been gathering materials during the previous seven years. It traces the story of the Conquest from Cortés' departure from Cuba to the imprisonment of Cuauhtémoc. Its literary value consists mainly in the fact that it is the only lengthy work in verse by a creole which survives from the 16th century. It was published in Madrid in 1599 and reprinted in Mexico in 1881.

Selections from Other Spanish Authors Regarding the Conquest

The reports of the Conquest fired the interest of other Spanish authors who included narratives of the Conquest in works on general Spanish or European history. Joaquín Ramírez Cabañas republished two such narratives in Mexico in 1940. The more extensive narrative is from the *Anales de Aragón* of Bartolomé Leonardo de Argensola (*Item 59*), first published in 1630. Also included is a chapter from the *Historia pontifical* (1565) of Gonzalo de Illescas (*Item 60*). The volume concludes with a previously unpublished short work by Hernán Pérez de Oliva (*Item 61*), "Algunas cosas de Hernán Cortés y México," from a manuscript in the Escorial. This last item was written before 1533, and the author may have known Cortés when the Conqueror returned to Spain in 1528.

62. Fernando Pizarro y Orellana (d. 1652?)

A relative of the famous Pizarros of Peru, Fernando Pizarro y Orellana was born in Trujillo, Cáceres, Spain, and studied law at the University of Salamanca, where he was later a professor. He was a knight of the Order of Calatrava, fiscal, and member of the Council of Military Orders, and later a member of the Council of Castile. He died in Madrid.

In 1639 Pizarro y Orellana published a work entitled *Varones ilustres del Nuevo Mundo* in which he drew upon the lives of certain of the conquerors as models for lessons in good government. It is not surprising to find a large part of the book devoted to four Pizarros of Peru and their relative Hernando Cortés. He terminated the volume with a legal discourse on the obligation of kings to reward the services of their vassals by favors, either to the vassals themselves or to their descendants. Cortés is the only illustrious man of Middle America included in the work.

CENTRAL MEXICO
Sixteenth Century

63. Christoph Weiditz (fl. 1529–32)

The earliest European pictorial record of the Indians of Central Mexico is found in the drawings of Christoph Weiditz, a German medalist who lived at the court of Charles V in Spain from 1529 to 1531. He left perhaps an authentic medal portrait of Cortés. In his *Trachtenbuch* he depicted the Indians whom Cortés had brought to Spain with him in 1528. The work was first published in Berlin in 1927. A selection of the items of Mexican interest was republished in 1963 by Frans Blom. In 1969 Howard F. Cline also republished the Mexican items and some additional pictures from Weiditz, accompanied by an article on the Indians who went to Spain with Cortés.

64. Andrés de Olmos (d. 1571)

Andrés de Olmos, a Franciscan missionary, came to New Spain in 1528 with bishop-elect Juan de Zumárraga. He quickly mastered Nahuatl, for which he prepared a still useful grammar in 1547. It included a collection of *Huehuetlatolli*, the didactic exhortations of Aztecs to their children, rulers, and others and the prescribed responses, partially published (1601) by Juan

Bautista, and later by Remi Simeón (1875) when he published the Olmos grammar. At the request of Bishop Sebastian Ramírez de Fuenleal, President of the Audiencia, in 1533 Olmos wrote a "copious" work on pre-Conquest rites and antiquities, based on Mexican codices and oral testimonies. All copies and the original of this great work were sent to Spain and were lost. Ecclesiastical officials persuaded Olmos to make an "epilogue" or summary of the work from memory and from his notes and native materials. This he did, and the work was utilized by Mendieta (especially bk. 2 of his *Historia eclesiástica indiana*) as well as by Toribio de Benavente (Motolinía) and Juan de Torquemada. That Olmos work is also lost. Garibay and others have attributed to Olmos wholly or partially various surviving materials, among them the *Historia de los mexicanos por sus pinturas* and *Histoyre du Mechique* (see Article 27, Items 1060, 1049); detailed study of these attributions remains to be done. Perhaps Olmos' greatest contribution was to establish the method and model for subsequent Franciscan investigators and to inspire the work of Bernardino de Sahagún, Motolinía, Gerónimo de Mendieta, and Juan de Torquemada.[3]

65. *Juan Bautista* (1555–1615)

Juan Bautista was born in Mexico and entered the Franciscan Order there in 1570. He became an expert in the Nahuatl language, in which he wrote several works related to missionary activity. He was a disciple of Fr. Bernardino de Sahagún (Article 14) and teacher of Juan de Torquemada (Article 16) and had charge of the college of Tlaltelolco. Perhaps his most important contribution to the study of Aztec social life was the publication of the native texts of the *Huehuetlatolli* (*Discursos de los viejos*) which had been collected and only partially translated in the mid-16th century

by Fr. Andrés de Olmos (Item 64). Bautista added similar materials from other sources and included the Olmos translations.

66. *Alonso de Zorita* (Zurita) (1512–ca. 1585)

Alonso de Zorita was born in 1512, probably in Cordoba, Spain. He gained a licenciate in laws from the University of Salamanca and entered the practice of law in the audiencia of Granada. In 1547 he was appointed oidor of Santo Domingo, where he arrived in June, 1548. His dedication to justice merited for him further appointments, as *juez de residencia* of the governor of New Granada (1550–52), oidor of Los Confines (1553–56), and oidor of New Spain (1556–66). In each place he was known for his protection of the Indians against the Spanish encomenderos. In Mexico he also joined the faculty of the university. In 1562 he petitioned the Crown to name him governor of New Galicia and to allow him to lead a peaceful expedition into the Chichimec country and northeast toward Florida at royal expense, but his plan was rejected. In 1566 he returned to Spain, where he spent the rest of his life in Granada, occupied with literary work. His death occurred probably about 1585.

Zorita wrote two works of ethnohistorical interest that have been at least in part published. The *Breve y sumaria relación de los señores de la Nueva España* was published very defectively in French in 1840 and in Spanish in 1864. The first adequate edition was made by García Icazbalceta in 1891. An easily accessible edition was published in Mexico in 1963. In the same year an English translation appeared in print, with an extensive biobibliographical introduction. The *Breve y sumaria relación* was written to give the Spanish Crown information regarding the government and tribute system of the Indians. It contains a great amount of valuable data on the social system of the Indians.

---

[3] Ed. note: See also Articles 13 (Religious Chroniclers and Historians), 14 (Sahagún), and 16 (Torquemada).

Zorita also wrote a more extensive work which he entitled, "Relación de las cosas notables de la Nueva España y de la conquista y pacificación de ella y de la doctrina y conversión de los naturales." It consists of four parts. Part 1 tells of the land and peoples of New Spain; part 2 is much the same as the *Breve relación*; part 3 treats mainly of the conquest of Mexico, with some material on the expansion into Guatemala and Honduras; part 4 is concerned with the Christianization of the Indians of New Spain. The work was composed mainly on the basis of other written sources, some of which have disappeared. Manuel Serrano y Sanz published part 1 in 1909 from the manuscript in the Library of the Royal Palace in Madrid. He entitled it *Historia de la Nueva España*. The remaining three parts have never been published. Serrano y Sanz wrote a lengthy biobibliographical introduction for his edition and appended an extensive group of documents relative to Zorita's work in the New World.

67. *Diego Valadés* (1533–82?)

Diego Valadés was born in Tlaxcala, the son of a conqueror of the same name and of a Tlaxcalan Indian woman. He entered the Franciscan Order in 1550. He showed great ability in Indian languages, becoming expert in Nahuatl, Otomí, and Tarascan. He worked as a missionary among the Indians, especially the Chichimecs. In 1569 he was guardian (religious superior) of Tepeji del Río, where Fr. Juan Focher was also stationed. Valadés was sent to France in 1571 as representative of his province to the General Chapter of the Franciscan Order. In 1572 he visited Fr. Jerónimo de Mendieta in Vitoria, Spain, and in 1574 he published Fr. Juan Focher's *Itinerarium Catholicum* in Seville. The next year he was chosen to be Procurator General of his Order in Rome, but because Valadés did not show adequate respect for the patronage of the Spanish Crown in obtaining

privileges from the Roman curia, in 1577 he was removed from the office under pressures from Spain. He went to Perugia where he completed his *Rhetorica Christiana*, published there in 1579. He continued to reside in Italy and apparently died there.

The *Rhetorica Christiana* was written as a textbook in rhetoric and the art of preaching, but the author included in the Fourth Part fairly extensive materials on the religious practices of the Indians and the progress of Christianity among them. He also included his own woodcuts, which illustrate various aspects of native religion and of missionary methods. These are discussed and reproduced by Francisco de la Maza (1945).

Esteban J. Palomera, S.J., has published two works on Valadés: the first on his work (1962), and the second on his life and times (1963). In the former he included a Spanish translation of the chapters of the *Rhetorica Christiana* relative to the Indians of Mexico. He also reproduced in the two volumes all the woodcuts of the original. The Valadés illustration used by Torquemada on the cover to the *Monarquía indiana* (1615) is reproduced in Article 16 (fig. 1). Palomera proposes in the future to publish a complete Spanish translation of the work.

68. *Francisco Hernández* (ca. 1517–87)

Doctor Francisco Hernández was a native of Puebla de Montalban, Toledo, Spain. He studied medicine in the University of Alcala de Henares. He practiced medicine in Seville until 1553 and later was active in Guadalupe and Toledo. In 1567 he was summoned to the Court and appointed Médico de Cámara. He was given the office of *Protomédico general* for the entire Spanish New World in 1570 and in September of that year sailed for America. He lived in New Spain from 1571 to 1577, traveling through large parts of the country, gathering medicinal plants, and studying and describing the natural history and antiquities

FIG. 4—NATIVE SACRIFICIAL RITES AS DEPICTED IN AN ENGRAVING BY THE MESTIZO FRIAR DIEGO VALADÉS. From Valadés, 1579.

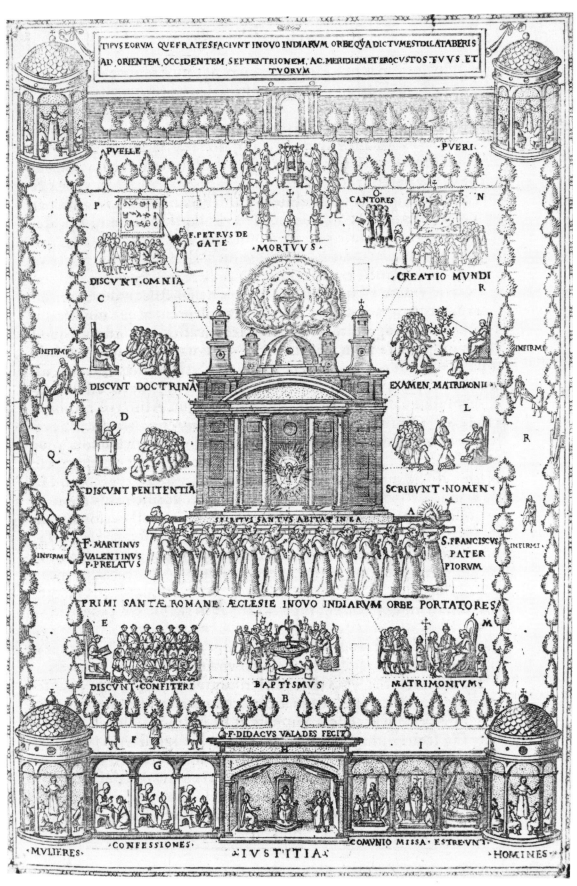

Fɪɢ. 5—RELIGIOUS ACTIVITIES OF THE EARLY FRANCISCANS IN MEXICO. From
Valadés, 1579.

of the country. He returned to Spain in 1577, but did not succeed in having any of his works published during his lifetime. He was given charge of the health of young Prince Philip, later King Philip III. Hernández died in Madrid.

The bibliography of Hernández' works is quite complicated, largely because the writings were all published posthumously. The first pieces published were included by Juan Eusebio Nieremberg in his *Historia Naturae Maximae Peregrinae* (Antwerp, 1635). One of these was a description of the structure and offices of the temple of Mexico (bk. 8, chaps. 22–27) which Hernández had excerpted from a manuscript copy of Sahagún's *General History* (bk. 1, app. 2). It gives the Nahuatl names, Latin translations, and descriptions of the 78 parts of the temple complex as well as of its various ministers. Nieremberg also drew heavily on Hernández for his natural history and utilized some of his drawings to illustrate his text.

Hernández' *Natural History*, the original of which perished in a fire at the Escorial in 1671, survived through a digest made by the Neapolitan doctor Nardo Antonio Recchi, and through a copy in the library of the Jesuit Colegio Imperial of Madrid. Recchi's digest retained little beyond the scientific skeleton of Hernández' work. A manuscript copy of this digest came into the hands of a Mexican Dominican, Fray Francisco Ximénez, who translated it from Latin into Spanish and published it, interpolating the results of his own observations. His *Quatro libros de la naturaleza* appeared first in 1615 and was republished in 1888. Recchi's Latin compendium was published in Rome in 1649 through the efforts of the Accademia dei Lincei. At the end of some copies of this edition is found the *Historia animalium et mineralium, Liber unicus in sex tractatus divisus*. This was published from a copy of Hernández' original text rather than from Recchi's compendium.

The copy of Hernández' *Natural History* which was preserved in the Colegio Imperial was partially published in Madrid in 1790.

A Spanish translation of the complete work was published by the National University of Mexico in 1962 as volumes 2 and 3 of Hernández' *Obras completas*. This edition has assembled Spanish translations of the best of the previous editions: the history of plants from the 1790 Madrid edition, the history of the animals and minerals from an edition printed in Rome in 1651 and the illustrations from the Roman edition and the *Historia naturae* of Fr. Nieremberg.

Two works by Hernández, on the antiquities of Mexico and on the Conquest, came to light in 1830. A facsimile edition of the Latin manuscripts was published in Mexico in 1926. In 1945 a Spanish translation by Joaquín García Pimentel of the two works appeared in Mexico.

Both the *Natural History* and the works on Mexican antiquities and the Conquest are of interest to the ethnohistorian. The *Natural History* contains much information about native customs and usages in relation to the plant and animal world. The studies of the antiquities and the Conquest depended on the works of Cortés (Item 41), Motolinía (Article 13), López de Gómara (Item 54), and Sahagún (Article 14), but the doctor also included the results of his own observations.

The first volume of the *Obras completas* of Hernández, which appeared in Mexico in 1959, consists of a lengthy biographical and bibliographical study of Hernández by Germán Somolinos d'Ardois, preceded by a study of Spain and New Spain at the time of Philip II by José Miranda.

69. *Pedro de Feria* (1524–88)

A native of Feria, Extremadura, Spain, Pedro de Feria became a Dominican friar and was sent to work in the Zapotec region of New Spain, where he learned the native language to perfection. He went back to

Fig. 6—A FRANCISCAN FRIAR INSTRUCTING INDIANS WITH THE HELP OF PAINT-
INGS. From Valadés, 1579.

Spain in 1570, but in 1575 he returned to Mexico as bishop of Chiapas. He was prevented from personally attending the Third Mexican Church Council (1585) because he broke his leg on the journey to Mexico.

Besides a *Doctrina* which he composed in Spanish and Zapotec, he also prepared a brief report on the problem of Indians relapsing to idolatry: *Relación que hace el obispo de Chiapa sobre la reincidencia en sus idolatrías de los indios de aquel país después de treinta años de cristianos.* The original was preserved in the Archivo General de Indias. It was published in 1899 and was republished in 1953.

70. *Juan Suárez de Peralta* (1537–after 1589)

Juan Suárez de Peralta was in an advantageous position to assemble information regarding the first contacts between the Indians and Spaniards in Mexico. Born in Mexico in 1537, he was the son of Juan Suárez, whose sister Catalina had been the first wife of Hernando Cortés. His education hardly went beyond the basics of grammar, but he developed his knowledge by reading and by personal contact with those who had participated in the Conquest. He lived in Mexico until 1579, when he traveled to Spain. He remained there at least until 1589, the year in which he completed the *Tratado del descubrimiento de las Indias.* He later returned to Mexico. The date and place of his death are unkonwn.

The complete title of Suárez de Peralta's work gives an adequate description of its contents: *Tratado del descubrimiento de las Indias y su conquista, y los ritos y sacrificios y costumbres de los Indios; y de los virreyes y gobernadores que las han gobernado, especialmente en la Nueva España, y del suceso del Marqués del Valle, segundo, Don Martín Cortés: del rebelión que se le imputó y de las justicias y muertes que hizieron en México los jueces comisarios que para ello fueron por su Majestad, y del rom-pimiento de los ingleses, y del principio que tuvo Francisco Draque para ser declarado enemigo.* It contains information on the history, religion, and customs of the Indians of central Mexico, derived largely from Oviedo (Item 4), Motolinía (Article 13), Sahagún (Article 14), and Las Casas (*Brevísima relación*) (Item 12).

When Justo Zaragoza published the work for the first time in 1878, he shortened the title to *Noticias históricas de la Nueva España.* It was republished in Mexico in 1949 with an introduction by Federico Gómez de Orozco.

71. *Diocesan Reports*

Significant information regarding native population and the distribution of linguistic groups is to be found in the descriptions of dioceses which were prepared occasionally for the information of the royal authorities. A collection of such descriptions was published in 1904 by Luis García Pinentel under the title *Relación de los obispados de Tlaxcala, Michoacán, Oaxaca y otros lugares en el siglo XVI.* They date from the period of the 1560s and 1570s and contain important material regarding the encomiendas of Indians.

A description of the archdiocese of Mexico was compiled in 1571 by Bartolomé de Ledesma (*Item 72*), administrator of the archdiocese. Ledesma, a Dominican friar who came to Mexico with Archbishop Montúfar, was later bishop of Oaxaca (1583–1604). His report, *Descripción del arzobispado de México . . .* , was partially published by Francisco del Paso y Troncoso in 1905.

73. *Diego Durán* (ca. 1537–88) [See also Tovar (Item 74) and Acosta (Item 75)]

The Dominican Diego Durán was born in Seville about the year 1537 and came to New Spain when he was seven or eight years old. He made his profession of vows in the Dominican Order in 1556, and in

1559 was serving as a deacon. Undoubtedly he was ordained a priest soon afterward. In 1561 he was assigned to the friary in Oaxaca. He served as a missionary in many towns of Mexico. Toward the end of his life he lived in the friary of Mexico where he knew Fray Francisco de Aguilar (Item 43), the former conquistador. Durán died there in 1588.

Drawing principally upon native sources, Durán wrote a *Historia de las Indias de Nueva España y islas de tierra firme*. It consists of three parts. Chapters 1–78 narrate the political and social history of the Aztecs from their legendary origins to the death of Cuauhtémoc. The second part (chaps. 79–101) tells of the religious rites of the Aztecs. The third part, which is completely distinct from the other two, is an analysis of the Aztec calendar. The second part was completed first, then the calendar (1579), and finally the first part (1581). Durán's work is an item of primary importance for studying the history and ethnology of the Aztecs. The Durán illustrations are treated in Article 23, no. 114. (For bibliographical data see Item 76.)

74. Juan de Tovar (ca. 1541–1626)

Juan de Tovar, born in Texcoco, was ordained a priest in 1570. He was prebendary of the Cathedral of Mexico City and secretary of its cabildo in 1572 when the first Jesuits arrived in Mexico. He joined the Society of Jesus in 1573, the third resident of Mexico to do so. He taught for many years in the colleges of Tepozotlan and San Gregorio de México. He was noted for his knowledge of the Nahuatl, Otomí and Mazahua languages. He died in 1626, having spent the last six years of his life in blindness.

Viceroy Martín Enríquez, wishing to know more about the people whom he ruled, commanded Tovar to write down their history with the assistance of the native historians and their books. Around 1579,

when the work was completed, Dr. Portillo, *provisor* of the archdiocese of Mexico, took it to Spain, promising to have a copy made for the author, but Tovar did not receive the copy. Later, when Father José de Acosta asked Tovar for information on the Mexicans to include in his own work, Tovar utilized the *Historia* of Durán, his relative, to refresh his memory in rewriting his previous work. His writing, then, derived a great deal from Durán but also depended on the research that he had done for his first work. He also prepared an analysis of the Aztec calendar different from that of Durán. (See Items 73, 75, 76.)

75. José de Acosta (1540–1600)

José de Acosta was born in Medina del Campo, Spain. He entered the Society of Jesus as a boy in 1552 and made his first religious vows in 1554. After a brilliant scholastic career in Spain, he went to Peru as a missionary. He gained fame as a preacher in Cuzco and La Paz. In 1576 he became provincial superior of Peru. He took a leading part in the third ecclesiastical council of Lima in 1583. Having obtained permission to return to Europe, he passed through Mexico where he spent a year (1586–87) before going on to Spain. There he knew Tovar and requested the materials mentioned above. After his return to Spain he held a number of important positions in his Society, but unfortunately he became involved in certain factionalism which led him into serious conflict with his higher superiors. During the last years of his life he devoted himself principally to literary work in Valladolid and Salamanca.

The work of Acosta which interests the ethnohistorian of Middle America is his *Historia natural y moral de las Indias*. Its importance in this context rests not so much on Acosta's own work as on the fact that he copied into it verbatim large sections of the work that Tovar had given him. (See especially Item 76.)

76. Relationship between Acosta, Tovar, Codez Ramírez, and Durán

Acosta's *Historia* saw publication long before the works from which his Mexican materials were derived. It was first printed in Seville in 1590 and went through many editions and translations. An English translation appeared in London in 1604 and was reprinted in 1880.

The *Historia* of Durán was not published until 1867, when José F. Ramírez brought it to light from a manuscript copy in the National Library of Madrid. The illustrative drawings which were scattered through the original manuscript were all placed in an "Atlas" at the end, not published until 1880 by Alfredo Chavero, who at that time also published the second volume of text. A microfilm copy of the Madrid manuscript, as well as color slides of the illustrations, is available in the Library of Congress. An English translation of the historical section of the work was published in 1964. In 1967 Angel Garibay K. edited a critical edition of the *Historia* from the Madrid manuscript, with photocolored drawings. An English translation of the nonhistorical sections (*Book of the Gods and Rites* and *The Ancient Calendar*) appeared in 1971, with a biobibliographical study of Durán by Fernando Horcasitas and Doris Heyden.

In 1856 Ramírez had also found, in the library of the friary of San Francisco, Mexico, an anonymous manuscript which treated the same materials as Durán but much more briefly. He concluded that this was the translation of an Indian chronicle from which both Durán and Acosta had drawn their material. It was published by Manuel Orozco y Berra in 1878 under the title *Codex Ramírez*. Soon, however, it became evident that this work was nearly identical with that utilized by Acosta, which he had received from Tovar.

A manuscript of Tovar's work was in the hands of the English bibliophile Sir Thomas Phillipps. He made a private printing of part of it in 1860. Later the manuscript was obtained by the John Carter Brown Library, Providence, Rhode Island. Recent studies (Kubler and Gibson, 1951) have shown that it differs in some respects from the Codex Ramírez and that the Providence version was the one used by Acosta. A careful examination of this manuscript, made by Ernest J. Burrus, S.J., indicates that the historical section is written in Tovar's own hand, whereas the calendric material which follows it is in a different hand.

The calendric material from the Providence manuscript was studied and published in facsimile, with transcription, and translation by George Kubler and Charles Gibson in 1951. At the time of this writing the complete Providence manuscript has not yet been published, although plans for publication are under way.

The suggestion has been made that Durán's *Historia*, Codex Ramírez, and the Providence version of Tovar's work are all derived from a third unknown manuscript (see Article 23, "X, Crónica," following no. 397; and Article 27B, following no. 1137). Good studies of the Durán-Tovar-Acosta literary question are found in Sandoval (1945) and in the Kubler-Gibson edition of the Tovar calendar (1951).

77. Diego Muñoz Camargo (ca. 1525–ca. 1613)

One of the best sources that we have for the pre-Conquest and early post-Conquest history of Tlaxcala was written by Diego Muñoz Camargo. He was the son of a Spanish father and of a Tlaxcalan mother of noble lineage. He was born soon after the Conquest. In 1537 he was charged with giving Christian instruction to the Indians who had come to Mexico with Cabeza de Vaca. He married María Maxixcatzin, a descendant of Texcocan and Tlaxcalan noble families. He was governor of Tlaxcala a number of times and was a friend of the leading Spanish personages of Mexico. He died about 1613.

Between the years 1576 and 1595, apparently, Muñoz Camargo wrote a "Historia de la Ciudad y República de Tlaxcala." It was composed of three books, the first on pre-Conquest history, the second on the Conquest and early post-Conquest history, and the third, quite brief, on natural history. It was circulated in manuscript and was utilized by a number of the colonial chroniclers, such as Herrera, León, Torquemada, and Clavigero, but it did not appear in print until 1870.

Alfredo Chavero published an edition in 1892 without the section on natural history. In 1947 another edition was published, based on that of Chavero but including the third book. Manuel Carrera Stampa (1945a) has written a good biobibliographical study of Muñoz Camargo and his *History*, but Gibson (1952, pp. 239–45) has a fuller bibliography.

78. *Baltasar Dorantes de Carranza* (fl. 1560–1604)

Baltasar Dorantes de Carranza, born in Mexico about the middle of the 16th century, was the son of Andrés Dorantes de Carranza, companion of Alvar Núñez Cabeza de Vaca (Item 101) on his long trek to Mexico. Baltasar was neglected after his father's death, which occurred before 1560. He made his way to Mexico City where by the time he was 16 years old he was involved in a bigamy scandal. Nevertheless, he made friends in high places and held a number of offices of importance. He was asked by the descendants of the conquerors to go to Spain as their attorney before the Crown. He died sometime between 1604 and 1613.

Dorantes compiled a work on New Spain and the families of the conquerors, apparently drawn from the material that he had collected in his position as procurator. The first part of his work is a rambling dissertation on New Spain, in which he writes in a most disorganized fashion about the peoples and history of the area. He depended heavily on Las Casas' *Apologética historia,* López de Gómara's *Historia general de las Indias y conquista de México,* and Durán's *Historia,* but he also used a number of lesser-known authors, such as the poet Francisco de Terrazas. The Dorantes work is now known as *Sumaria relación de las cosas de la Nueva España, con noticia individual de los descendientes legítimos de los conquistadores y primeros pobladores españoles,* a title given to it by José F. Ramírez, who found the manuscript, lacking the first 14 leaves. It was published in Mexico in 1902. A critical study of the work was written by Ernesto de la Torre Villar (1945).

79. *Gonzalo Gómez de Cervantes* (fl. 1599)

Little is known about Gonzalo Gómez de Cervantes beyond what he tells about himself in a report on the social and economic life of New Spain, written in 1599. He mentions being alcalde mayor in Tlaxcala, Tepeaca, and Huejotzingo (Gómez de Cervantes, 1944, p. 164). Beristáin noted he had been governor of Tlaxcala in 1598, one of three successive ones that year (Gibson, 1952, p. 70). From his report we can deduce that Gómez was well acquainted with mining and the raising of cochineal and that he had been a judge. He was apparently a man of considerable wealth and had a penetrating comprehension of economic conditions in New Spain.

The manuscript of Gómez de Cervantes' report is preserved in the British Museum, under the title "Memorial de Gonzalo Gómez de Cervantes para el Oidor Eugenio Salazar, oidor del Real Consejo de las Indias." It was published in Mexico in 1944, under the title *La vida económica y social de Nueva España al finalizar el siglo XVI,* with prologue and notes by Alberto María Carreño.

The report shows the influence of the

Spanish social and economic life on the Indians at the end of the 16th century, particularly in central Mexico.

Seventeenth Century

80. *Henrico Martínez* (Heinrich Martin) (ca. 1555–1632)

Henrico Martínez was a German printer and engineer who came to Mexico in 1589. He had been born in Hamburg between 1550 and 1560, and was known in his native land as Heinrich Martin. Later he went to Spain and traveled through a large part of Europe before coming to the New World. He formulated and initiated the project of protecting the Valley of Mexico from floods by means of a drainage system. He also served as an interpreter of the Inquisition. Many books came from his printing press between 1599 and 1611. In 1606 he printed his own work, *Repertorio de los tiempos y historia natural de la Nueva España*. He died at Cuautitlan in 1632.

His *Repertorio* is something of a mixture of astronomy, astrology, and history. It is made up of six *tratados*, the second of which follows the course of Mexican history from its pre-Conquest origins to the time of writing. For this section Martínez depended heavily on Acosta (Item 75), but he also utilized Motolinía and other religious chroniclers. The work was republished in Mexico in 1948 with an introduction by Francisco de la Maza and a bibliographical appendix by Francisco González de Cossío.

81. *Martín de León* (fl. 1574–1611)

An explanation of the Aztec calendar is found in the *Camino del cielo en lengua mexicana* (Mexico, 1611) by the Dominican friar Martín de León. Born in Mexico, León entered the Dominican Order there in 1574. He became an expert in the Nahuatl language, in which he wrote several books. The *Camino del cielo* is the best known. Vargas Rea in 1947 published

León's Aztec calendar from the manuscript of the friar's catechism.

82. *Pedro Ponce de León* (1546–?)

Pedro Ponce de León was an Indian who became a diocesan priest in Mexico during the second half of the 16th century. He gained a licenciate in theology in the University of Mexico and was pastor of Zumpahuacan (state of Mexico) from 1571 to 1626. In 1610 he was commissioned by the archbishop of Mexico to investigate cases of idolatry in the region of Teutenango (Serna, 1892, p. 288). He wrote a short work, *Breve relación de los dioses y ritos de la gentilidad*, concerning the native socio-religious practices which had survived among the Indians of his time. It was included as the second manuscript in the volume known as the *Códice Chimalpopoca*. It was first published in Mexico in 1892 and was republished in 1953 and again in 1965.

83. *Hernando Ruiz de Alarcón* (?–1646)

Many invaluable texts of Nahuatl hymns and prayers still in use in the 17th century are preserved in the original language, with Spanish translation, in the work of Hernando Ruiz de Alarcón. The author was born in Taxco, a brother of the dramatist Juan Ruiz de Alarcón. He gained a baccalaureate at the University of Mexico, became a priest, and served as pastor of various towns. About the year 1617 he was appointed an ecclesiastical judge, and in the course of his efforts to uproot surviving native socio-religious parctices in the region of the present-day state of Guerrero, he recorded many of these practices. He died while on a visitation of the mountain area near Atenango del Rio in 1646 (Serna, 1892, p. 249).

In 1629, while Ruiz was pastor of Atenango, he organized the information that he had collected into a work entitled *Tratado de las supersticiones y costumbres gentílicas que hoy viven entre los indios naturales de esta Nueva España*. It is composed of six tracts. The first tract contains general considerations of native practices, especially valuable for its treatment of the use of hallucinogenic plants. The remaining tracts deal with specific practices in detail, and are largely compilations of native texts, with accompanying explanatory paragraphs. It is of great importance for the study of the history, ethnography, and language of the Nahuatl-speaking Indians of the early 17th century. It was first published in 1892. This edition was republished in Mexico in 1953.

84. Juan de Palafox y Mendoza (1600–59)

Known more for his political struggles with the religious orders and the viceroys than for ethnohistorical writings, Bishop Juan de Palafox y Mendoza showed a deep love for his Indian charges in his *Virtudes del indio.*

Palafox was born in Fitero, Navarre, the illegitimate son of the Marqués de Ariza. He studied law in Salamanca and became *fiscal* successively of the Council of War and the Council of the Indies. He was ordained a priest in 1629 and 10 years later was appointed to the bishopric of Puebla in New Spain. He served as *juez de residencia* of three viceroys and served as viceroy himself from March to November, 1642. He was also involved in bitter jurisdictional disputes with the Jesuits. He returned to Spain in 1649, and his episcopal jurisdiction was transferred to the diocese of Osma, Spain, in 1653. He died there six years later.

His defense of the virtues of the Indians, a somewhat romantic eulogy, was prepared after his return to Spain. Even where the author admits the Indians' obvious vices, he makes every effort to excuse them. It seems to have been printed privately at first for the use of the King and Council. Palafox's collected works, which deal largely with questions of theology and the spiritual life, were published in 1762. A recent edition of his *Virtudes del indio* appeared in Mexico in 1950.

85. Diego Luis de Motezuma (1619–99)

A descendant of the rulers of Mexico, Diego Luis de Motezuma was born in Madrid on March 14, 1619. He entered the Jesuits on March 14, 1636, followed the usual ecclesiastical course of studies in humanities, philosophy, and theology, and was ordained a priest. He wrote a number of devotional works, and also *Corona mexicana, o Historia de los nueve Motezumas,* written in 1686.

This work is divided into two nearly equal parts. The first part deals with the lives of eight pre-Conquest Aztec emperors; the second treats of the life of the last Montezuma and the Spanish conquest. The author aimed to show that Mexican emperors were a legitimate dynasty in the 17th-century European sense. There is little evidence that Motezuma utilized any living traditions of his family. The authors whom he cites most frequently are Solís, Acosta, and Díaz del Castillo, although he refers to many others as well.

Motezuma's work was first published in 1941 by Lucas de Torre from a manuscript in the Biblioteca Nacional, Madrid.

86. Carlos de Sigüenza y Góngora (1645–1700)

One of the most outstanding intellectual figures of colonial Mexico was Carlos de Sigüenza y Góngora. He was born in Mexico City of Spanish parents. In 1660 he entered the Society of Jesus and two years later made his first vows in Tepozotlan. He studied philosophy as a Jesuit in the Colegio de San Pedro y San Pablo in Mexico City. In 1667 he was dismissed from the Society for some infraction of discipline. In 1672 he obtained the chair of Astrology and Mathematics in the University of Mexico. He later became a priest and in 1682 he was appointed chaplain of the Hospital de Amor de Dios. During the riot in Mexico City on June 8, 1692, he saved part of the archive of the Ayuntamiento from fire. He was named Geographer of His Majesty and in this capacity he accompanied an exploratory expedition to Pensacola Bay in 1693. A man of encyclopedic interests, he wrote on questions of astronomy, religion, geography, history, and Mexican antiquities. He collected a large library, especially rich in materials on Mexican antiquities. When he died in Mexico in 1700, he left his library to the Jesuits. Unfortunately, he took little interest in publishing his writings, and many of them were lost after his death.

In 1680 he published the *Teatro de virtudes políticas . . . ,* in which he portrayed the virtues of the ancient Aztec monarchs as examples for rulers. The work was republished in a collection of his works in 1928.

During the last decade of his life, Sigüenza wrote a work on the hospital for Indians founded by Cortés. Entitled *Piedad heróica de Don Fernando Cortés,* the work was first published at an unknown date during the 18th century. A modern edition, with a lengthy biobibliographical study by Jaime Delgado, appeared in Madrid in 1960.

A picture of the dissatisfactions of the Indians of the Valley of Mexico nearly two centuries after the Conquest is found in Sigüenza's report of the riot in Mexico City on June 8, 1692, written as a letter to Admiral Andrés de Pez. The first known edition was the English translation which Irving Leonard (1929) included as appendix B in his standard biography of Sigüenza. Leonard also published the Spanish text in 1932. This edition included a prologue by Federico Gómez de Orozco, notes by Leonard, and a documentary appendix. It was reissued among Sigüenza's *Relaciones históricas,* in Mexico (1940).

Sigüenza also wrote a brief chronology of the rulers of the City of Mexico from its founding by the Indians in 1327 down to the time of writing (about 1695). It was published in Mexico in 1948 in an extremely limited edition of only 30 copies.

A good study of Sigüenza y Góngora's library and its later history was published by Ernest J. Burrus in 1959.

87. *Jacinto de la Serna* (?-1681)

Another 17th-century priest who recorded extensive information regarding the survival of native religious customs was Jacinto de la Serna. Born in Mexico, he gained a doctorate in theology at the University of Mexico, of which he was later rector three times. As a young priest he served for 14 years in parishes of the Indians during the same time that Ruiz de Alarcón (Item 83) was making his investigations. He seems, however, to have spent most of his later career in Mexico City, where he was one of the curates of the cathedral during three periods. He held important offices in the administration of the archdiocese. He served as visitor general of the archdiocese under two archbishops.

In 1656 he composed a work entitled *Manual de ministros de indios para el conocimiento de sus idolatrías y extirpación de ellas,* published in 1892, in which he drew together the fruits of his own experience and the results of his studies. The purpose of the work was to acquaint the religious ministers with the superstitions of the Indians, so that they could better instruct their Indian charges. The work may be divided into four parts. In chapters 1–5 he traces the history of the efforts to put an end to native religious practices. In this section he gives valuable details of his own activities and of those of his predecessors, such as Pedro Ponce de León (Item 82) and Hernando Ruiz de Alarcón (Item 83). Chapters 6–11 are a study of the Aztec calendar, for which he drew heavily on Martín de León (Item 81). Boturini (Item 89) later used some of this material. Chapters 12–27 treat of religious beliefs and practices of the Indians. Large sections were taken directly or in paraphrase from Ruiz de Alarcón, including the latter's translations of Indian chants and prayers. Chapters 28–33 propose remedies against the continued practice of the native religions. The work was republished in Mexico in 1953.

Eighteenth Century

88. *José Antonio Villaseñor y Sánchez* (fl. 1733–56)

By order of Philip V, the viceroy of New Spain, Conde de Fuenclara, was commanded in 1740 to have a report prepared on the true condition of the provinces of his jurisdiction. He commissioned José Antonio Villaseñor y Sánchez to prepare the report. Villaseñor had been born in Mexico City and educated in the Jesuit College of San Ildefonso. He occupied a number of important posts: *oficial mayor* of the Contaduría de Reales Tributos, *contador general de azogues*, and cosmographer of New Spain. He wrote a number of works of mathematical and astronomical interest.

The outcome of his commission by Fuenclara was the *Theatro americano: Descripción general de los reinos y provincias de la Nueva España y sus jurisdicciones*. It appeared in two volumes in 1746 and 1748. The first volume contains introductory chapters on pre-Spanish and Spanish history of Mexico, followed by a jurisdiction-by-jurisdiction description of the archdiocese of Mexico and diocese of Puebla. The second volume continues the description for the dioceses of Michoacan, Oaxaca, Guadalajara, and Durango. The work comprehends a great mass of data regarding the ethnology and population of the Mexican provinces in the mid-18th century. A facsimile re-edition was published in Mexico in 1952. The reports on which Villaseñor y Sánchez based his work are discussed by West in Article 10.

89. *Lorenzo Boturini de Benaducci* (ca. 1702–55)

Lorenzo Boturini de Benaducci was born in Sondrio, diocese of Como, Italy. He studied in Milan and later went to Vienna, where he lived for eight years. In 1733 he went to Portugal and soon journeyed to Spain. He sailed for Mexico in 1736. There he interested himself in the history of the image of the Virgin of Guadalupe and started collecting manuscripts related to it. To carry out his project he learned the Nahuatl language. His interests expanded, as did his collection, to include the whole history of New Spain, but especially that of the pre-Conquest period. In 1743 he was imprisoned for having entered New Spain without official permission and for unauthorized efforts to have the image of Guadalupe crowned. His goods and documents were sequestered and he was sent back to Spain. There he was absolved from the charges and was appointed chronicler in the Indies. He was given permission to return to Mexico and recover his documents, but he stayed on in Spain, working on his history there.

In 1749 he presented the Council with the first volume, entitled *Historia general de la América Septentrional. Tomo primero: De la cronología de sus principales naciones*. It dealt principally with the Aztec calendar. In 1746 he had published a plan of his work under the title *Idea de una nueva historia general de la América Septentrional*, which contained a partial catalog of the materials that he had collected in Mexico. During the years immediately following his return to Spain, Boturini lived in the house of Mariano Veytia (Item 90), in whom he awakened an interest in the ancient history of New Spain. Veytia, who was later executor of Boturini's will, had access to the Italian's collection of manuscripts and based much of his own work on them. Boturini died in Madrid, and his collection in Mexico was gradually scattered. Glass identifies many of the historical and pictorial documents in the collection (see Article 29).

Boturini's *Idea* was republished in Mexico in 1871, preceded by a short biobibliographical study by García Icazbalceta. A facsimile republication of the original edition appeared in Paris in 1933. The volume of the *Historia general* which Boturini completed came into the possession of the Royal Academy of History, Madrid, where it remained unpublished until 1948, when Manuel Ballesteros Gaibrois brought it out as volume 6 of *Documentos inéditos para la historia de España*. In volume 5 of the same collection Ballesteros Gaibrois had published a biobibliographical study of Boturini and some important papers relative to his life and work, including a description of Boturini's collection, made in Mexico in 1791 by Vicente de la Rosa Zaldivar.

90. *Mariano Veytia* (Mariano José Fernández de Echeverría Orcolaga, Alonso Linaje de Veytia) (1718–79)

Mariano Veytia was born in Puebla, Mexico. His father was an oidor of the audiencia of Mexico, who saw to it that his son was well educated in Mexico City. He gained baccalaureates in arts (1733) and laws (1736) and passed the examination for lawyers in 1737, when he was only 19 years old. His father sent him to Spain on business in 1738, where he was admitted among the lawyers of the Royal Councils in the same year. It was during this period that Lorenzo Boturini (Item 89) awakened his interest in Mexican antiquities. Veytia traveled through many parts of Europe before returning to Mexico in 1750. Utilizing the manuscripts collected by Boturini, he wrote a *Historia antigua de México*. The work follows the pre-Spanish history of Mexico through the reign of Nezahualcoyotl.

In 1826 Carlos María de Bustamante published the part of it that pertains to Texcoco, with supplementary material on Texcoco added by the editor. In 1836 the entire *Historia* was published by Francisco Ortega, possibly from a different manuscript than Bustamante's. Ortega added an appendix completing the work up to the death of Cuauhtémoc. This edition was republished in Mexico in 1944. Both omit the Prologue, which has been separately published in García Icazbalceta (1927). Victor Rico González (1949) has written a biobibliographical study of Veytia, whom he criticizes for his lack of historical analysis and for carelessness in regard to historical fact. Nevertheless, in consideration of the number of documents to which Veytia had access, he cannot be neglected.

90a. *Juan José de Eguiara y Eguren* (1696–1763)

Juan José de Eguiara y Eguren was born in Mexico City, the son of a Basque merchant and of a first-generation creole mother of Basque stock. He was a brilliant youth, gaining a baccalaureate of arts in 1709 and a licenciate and doctorate in theology in 1715. He also entered the clerical state, and both in the Church and in the academic life of the University of Mexico he advanced quickly. In 1738, having made his way up through the lower positions of university teaching, he won the choice chair of morning lectures in theology; in 1749 he was elected rector of the university. In the ecclesiastical cabildo of the cathedral, he held various positions, as a canon, beginning in 1747. In 1751 he was named bishop of Yucatan, but he declined in 1752, for reasons of ill health and because of his literary occupations. He died in Mexico City.

Eguiara y Eguren's bibliography is extensive, consisting of 244 known works, of which only 15 were published. They are principally sermons or works of theology. His fame, however, rests primarily upon his *Bibliotheca mexicana . . .* , a lengthy biobibliographical dictionary, of which only the first volume was ever published. This published volume includes an extensive introduction and entries from A to C, alphabetized by the first names of the authors. The four unpublished volumes, which carried the work only through the letter J, are in the Library of the University of Texas.

It was a pioneering bibliographical work for Mexico, but because it was written in Latin, its use has been somewhat limited.

The part of the work which is of greatest interest here is the author's introduction, consisting of 20 *Anteloquia*, or prologues. In the first he explains the motivating cause of his work. Don Manuel Martí, dean of the cathedral of Alicante, had disparaged the intellectual life of Mexico in a published letter; the Mexican ecclesiastic felt constrained to defend the honor of the colony by preparing a catalog of Mexican writers. Anteloquia 2–7 deal with the intellectual attainments of the Mexican Indians in the pre-Conquest period. The remaining Anteloquia discuss the intellectual progress of the colony after the Spanish Conquest. Anteloquim 19 treats briefly of the Indians during the post-Contact era. Because of these introductory essays Eguiara y Eguren has been called "the initiator of the history of ideas in Mexico" (Hernández Luna, 1953).

The sole published volume of the *Bibliotheca mexicana* appeared in 1755 and has never been reprinted. The Anteloquia were republished in 1944, with the Latin text and a Spanish translation in parallel columns. The translations and biobibliographical studies of the author were prepared by Agustín Millares Carlo.

91. Diego García Panes y Avellán (1730–1811)

An heir to the tradition of Boturini (Item 89) and Veytia (Item 90) was Diego García Panes y Avellán. Born in Urgel, Spain, he came to Mexico in the retinue of Viceroy Agustín de Ahumada y Villalón in 1755. The next year he was sent to Veracruz as *subteniente* of artillery. He returned to Spain in 1793, where he formed a close friendship with Juan Bautista Muñoz. Later he went back to Mexico and became commander of the castle of San Juan de Ulua about 1796. He died in Veracruz.

Panes y Avellán was an avid collector of manuscripts for the history of Mexico, an interest which was undoubtedly influenced by his friendship with Mariano Veytia. Copies of some of these manuscripts are in the Muñoz Collection, Royal Academy of History, Madrid. We know of two of his works, neither of which has been published. His "Cronología de los virreyes de la Nueva España" is now in the Library of the University of Texas. In the National Library of Mexico is preserved the greater part of his "Theatro de Nueva España en su gentilismo y conquista." It is a pictorial history of Mexico from its pre-Spanish beginnings to the time of writing. Of the eight original volumes, volumes 2–7 have been preserved. Manuel Carrera Stampa (1945b) has written a documented biobibliographical study of Panes y Avellán.

92. Francisco Antonio de Lorenzana y Butrón (1722–1804)

An ecclesiastic of the first order who was also devoted to matters of Mexican history was Francisco Antonio de Lorenzana y Butrón. He was born in Leon, Spain, and studied at the University of Salamanca. In 1765 he was named bishop of Plasencia and a year later was transferred to Mexico as archbishop. There he showed a sincere zeal for the good of his clergy and people. In 1771 he presided over the Fourth Provincial Council of the Mexican Church. In 1772 he was named archbishop of Toledo, where he used the rich resources of his diocese to assist the needy, to give refuge to the clergy who had fled the French Revolution, and to promote ecclesiastical letters. He was raised to the cardinalate by Pope Pius VI, whom he assisted through the difficulties of the French Revolution. After the pope's death it was largely through Lorenzana's influence that the conclave was able to meet to elect Pius VII. Afterward he resigned his archbishopric in order to stay with the Pope in Rome. There he died in 1804.

Lorenzana served the cause of Mexican history both as a collector and as an editor. From his library, which later became the Provincial Library of Toledo, came the manuscripts for the publication of the works of Juan López de Velasco (Item 6), Juan Suárez de Peralta (Item 70), and Martín Alfonso Tovilla (Item 142). In 1769 and 1770 he published the decrees of the Mexican Church Councils of 1555, 1565, and 1585, which are of great importance for the history of the official attitude toward many problems involving the Indians. In 1770 he published an edition of the Letters of Cortés entitled *Historia de Nueva España, escrita por su esclarecido conquistador Hernán Cortés*. The volume included notes on ancient Mexican history, a list of emperors, an Aztec calendar, a list of Spanish governors of New Spain, fragments of the *Matrícula de tributos* (see Article 23, Item 368), and a relation of Cortés' voyage to Lower California, with information regarding other expeditions to California down to 1769.

93. *José Joaquín Granados y Gálvez* (1734–94)

José Joaquín Granados y Gálvez was born in Sedella, Malaga, Spain. He was related to the Gálvez family who later became prominent in the civil government of New Spain. He joined the Franciscan Order in Spain and was sent to Mexico, where he was ordained a priest. He became a member of the Franciscan Province of Michoacan, and served as religious superior of the friaries of Valladolid, Jiquilpan, and Rio Verde and its missions. He was also a member of the provincial advisory board. He was bishop of Sonora from 1788 to 1794. In the latter year he was transferred to the diocese of Durango, but he died at the hacienda of Dolores as he was approaching his see.

Before he became a bishop, Granados y Gálvez wrote a work on the history of the Mexican nation, *Tardes americanas*, presented as a dialogue between an Indian and a Spaniard. The first eight chapters were devoted to pre-Conquest history and culture, the ninth narrated the story of the Conquest, and the remainder (chaps. 10–17) traced the civil and ecclesiastical history of Mexico after the Conquest. The work favored the Indians and sympathized with their difficulties, but opposed any use of force against constituted authority. The author used all available printed sources, especially the Franciscan chroniclers. He also had access to manuscripts in Spanish and the native languages. He mentions, for instance, Ixtlilxochitl, Tezozomoc, and Chimalpahin. The work was first published in Mexico in 1778.

94. *José Díaz de la Vega* (1718–after 1783)

An unpublished 18th-century work which has aroused some scholarly interest recently is the *Memorias piadosas de la nación indiana* by José Díaz de la Vega, a Mexican Franciscan. The author was born in Huichapan in 1718 and took vows in the Franciscan Order in 1736. From 1745 to 1753 he resided in Tacuba. He composed the *Memorias* in Mexico City in 1782–83.

The work was copied as the final volume (vol. 32) of the manuscript *Colección de memorias de Nueva España*, compiled chiefly by Francisco García Figueroa, O.F.M., at the Crown's orders to Viceroy Revillagigedo. The collection was completed in 1792. There are copies in the Archivo General de la Nación, Mexico, and the Academy of History, Madrid (see Article 11).

Díaz de la Vega's *Memorias* are largely devotional, aiming to show the work of divine grace among the Indians, not only in New Spain but also in New France. Nevertheless, the author showed a sympathetic appreciation of the pre-Spanish culture of the Indians. Articles on the *Memorias* have been written by José Alcina Franch (1957) and Georges Baudot (1966), both of whom include selections from the work in their studies.

95. *Hipólito Villaroel* (18th century)

In the late 1780s Hipólito Villaroel, for whom no biographical data are available, wrote a lengthy treatise on the political infirmities of New Spain. The problem of the Indian was necessarily one of the serious questions that had to be faced repeatedly in such a discussion. The work is of importance here for its treatment of the relationship between the Indians and the Spanish political structure toward the end of the colonial period.

The work was published quite defectively by Carlos María de Bustamante in *La Voz de la Patria*, starting September 11, 1830; it was reissued in book form in 1831. It was republished by Genaro Estrada (1937) from a manuscript in the National Library of Madrid.

96. *José Antonio de Alzate y Ramírez* (1737–96)

A contemporary and schoolmate of Antonio de León y Gama (Item 97), José Antonio de Alzate y Ramírez was also principally interested in the exact sciences. Born in Ozumba near Chalco, he studied in Mexico City in the Colegio de San Nicolás and in the University, where he gained a baccalaureate in theology in 1756. In the latter year he also was ordained to the priesthood, although his interests throughout his life were more scientific than ecclesiastic. In the spirit of the Enlightenment he attacked Scholastic philosophy in the name of exact science. He was especially attracted to questions of astronomy and medicine, although his interests were encyclopedic.

As an expression of his thought Alzate did not produce any extensive individual work, but he wrote many journalistic essays, which he published either in the periodicals which he himself established or in other papers. In 1768 he began publication

of a weekly *Diario Literario de México*, which he revived in 1772 under the title *Asuntos varios sobre Ciencias y Artes*. In 1787 he published *Observaciones sobre la Física, Historia Natural y Artes Utiles*, through 14 numbers. In January, 1788, he began publication of his most important periodical, *Gazeta de Literatura*, which he continued to publish through October, 1795, numbering them as three volumes.

Through the pages of his own periodicals and of the *Gazeta de México*, Alzate carried on a public scientific conversation and controversy with the other Mexican intellectuals of his day, generally enlightening, sometimes very cutting. He included valuable data on the condition of the Indians at his time as well as some information on Indian antiquities. Alzate died in Mexico City on February 2, 1799.

The *Gazeta de Literatura* was republished in Puebla in 1831 in three volumes, with a fourth volume containing some of his writings from the earlier periodicals and from the *Gazeta de México*. A valuable index to Alzate's periodicals was published by W. F. Cody in 1953.

97. *Antonio de León y Gama* (1735–1802)

Possibly the most scientific effort to describe the Aztec calendar written during the colonial period was the work of Antonio de León y Gama, composed on the occasion of the discovery of the Aztec calendar stone under the Plaza of Mexico City in 1790. León y Gama was born in Mexico City. After some literary studies in the schools of that city, he trained himself in mathematics and astronomy, becoming one of the most capable Mexican astronomers of his day. He also interested himself in Mexican antiquities. With the discovery of the calendar stone, he was able to draw these two interests together in the book which he entitled *Descripción histórica y cronológica de las dos piedras que con ocasión del nuevo empedrado que se está formando en la plaza principal de México se hallaron en ella el año de 1790* (Mexico, 1792). A second edition, published by Carlos María de Bustamante in 1832, contained a lengthy supplementary section (145 pages) which León y Gama had left in manuscript at his death. In it he defended his previous work against the criticism of José Antonio Alzate y Ramírez (Item 96).

León y Gama's published works were principally of astronomical interest, and his works on Mexican antiquities were largely left in manuscript. Among them were a chronology of the ancient Mexicans, a study of their numerical system, and a description of Mexico City before and after the conquest by the Spaniards. This last item, together with a brief description of the diocese of Michoacan by León y Gama was published in the appendix to *Revista Mexicana de Estudios Históricos*, volume 1 (1927). In the Henry E. Huntington Library, San Marcos, California, is conserved one of his manuscripts, dated 1795 and entitled "Compendio de la historia antigua de la Nueva España, desde sus primeros pobladores hasta después de la conquista; deducido de las pinturas de los indios, de los mejores manuscritos que dejaron estos así en su idioma como en nuestro castellano y de otros documentos originales donde se refutan varias relaciones históricas," a microfilm of which is in the Library of Congress.

98. *Andrés Cavo* (1739–1803)

Andrés Cavo was born in Guadalajara, Mexico, and received his education in the Jesuit school there, acquiring a baccalaureate in arts. He entered the Society of Jesus (1758) in Tepozotlan. After teaching in Jesuit schools in Puebla, he was transferred to the missions in Nayarit in 1764. He was residing there, in the mission of Santisima Trinidad, at the time of the expulsion of the Jesuits in 1767. Cavo was taken to Spain and then allowed to proceed to Rome. In the hope of being permitted to return to his native land, he disassociated himself from the Jesuits, but the permission was not granted and he died in Rome in 1803.

Cavo wrote a *Historia de México* covering the years 1521–1766, completed while he was residing in Rome. It was the first attempt at a general history of the period of Spanish domination in Mexico. Cavo's method gives the work more the character of annals than of history. He sets down the happenings of Mexican history year by year rather than following the historical relationship between them. Further, he rarely shows the relationship between Mexican history and the history of Spain and Europe. Nevertheless, he gathered together a great deal of valuable information and led the way for later historians of Mexico.

The work was first published very defectively by Carlos María de Bustamante under the title, *Los tres siglos de México durante el gobierno español . . .* (Mexico, 1836–38). It was republished from the manuscript in the Library of the University of Texas by Ernest J. Burrus in 1949. Víctor Rico González has a biobibliographical study of Cavo in his *Historiadores mexicanos del siglo XVIII* (1949).

Nineteenth Century

99. *Alexander von Humboldt* (Friedrich Wilhelm Heinrich Alexander, Freiherr von Humboldt) (1769–1859)

The famous German scientist and traveler, Alexander von Humboldt, was born in Berlin the son of a German baron. He was educated under some of the leading intellectuals of his time, first in the paternal castle of Tegel and later in the University of Frankfurt and the school of higher studies in Göttingen. He made further professional studies in the Commercial Academy of Hamburg and the Academy of Mines of Freiburg. Afterward he was appointed Assessor of the Department of Mines in Berlin. He became famous in Europe for his writings on geology and botanic geography. In 1799 he sailed for the New World with Aimé Bonpland. They traveled through Spanish South America until early 1803 and then went to Mexico, where they spent nearly a year. From there they went on to Cuba and the United States, finally returning to Europe in 1804. After spending some time in Paris in communication with the great scientists of the day, Humboldt returned to Berlin and there continued to devote himself to his varied intellectual pursuits. His long life ended in that city in 1859.

Humboldt published two works which are of special interest in the present context. He included a number of essays on the antiquities of Middle America in his *Vues des cordillères et monuments des peuples indigènes de l'Amérique* (Paris, 1810). Here he described a number of Mexican codices conserved in Europe, as well as archaeological remains in America. The work was published in English translation in London in 1814, but only 20 of the 69 plates of the original were reproduced.

Humboldt's analysis of the Mexico of his day is contained in his *Essai politique sur le royaume de la Nouvelle-Espagne* (Paris, 1811). His observations on the condition of the native races are to be found principally in the second book of the *Essai politique*. A rather poor English translation by John Black was published in New York and London in 1811. There is a critical Spanish translation with an introductory essay and notes by Vito Alessio Robles (1941). A one-volume Spanish edition, with an introductory study by Juan A. Ortega y Medina, was published in Mexico in 1966.

99a. Guillermo Dupaix (1748 or 1750–after 1808)

A systematic study of the archaeological monuments of central and southern Mexico was attempted in the years 1805–1808 by Guillermo Dupaix, former captain of dragoons. Dupaix was born in Salm or Saln, Flanders, apparently in 1748 or 1750. He entered the military service of the Spanish Crown in 1767, rising through the ranks to that of captain, to which he was promoted in 1790. Either before or during his military career he went to New Spain and took up residence there. He seems to have retired from the service in 1800. His interest in archaeology, which he had developed during his years in the army, brought him a royal commission to study the pre-Spanish monuments. In this capacity he made three journeys through central and southern Mexico between 1805 and 1808, accompanied by Don José Luciano Castañeda, professor of design (*dibujo*) and architecture, who sketched the monuments.

The work was first published by Lord Kingsborough in his *Antiquities of Mexico*. The sketches, redrawn for the edition, were published in volume 4, the Spanish text appeared in volume 5, and an English translation was printed in volume 6. A French translation was published in 1844. In 1969 José Alcina Franch brought out a Spanish edition based on a newly discovered Spanish manuscript which is now in the Laboratorio de Arte, Faculty of Philosophy and Letters, University of Seville. Volume 1 includes a biobibliographical introduction; volume 2 consists of Castañeda's sketches.

NORTHERN AND WESTERN MEXICO

100. Nuño Beltrán de Guzmán (ca. 1485–ca. 1560)

The expansion of Spanish control into northern Mexico was initiated most determinedly by Nuño Beltrán de Guzmán. From his own day onward Guzmán has been remembered as the archetype of the cruel Spanish conquistador, although recent revisionist research has to some extent lightened his dark reputation. The son of a noble family of Guadalajara, Spain, he studied law, possibly at the University of Alcalá de Henares, and became a *contino* in the royal court. In 1525 he was appointed governor of the Province of Panuco in New Spain, where he took office in 1527. He went on to Mexico City as president of the royal audiencia in 1528, but his conflicts with the friars and the supporters of Cortés became so acute that he was soon replaced as president in 1530. But toward the end of 1529 he had left Mexico City with an expedition that passed through Michoacan and went on into the unconquered expanses to the north, which was named New Galicia. He was given the governorship of the new conquest and envisioned establishing his domain over northern Mexico in a zone extending from New Galicia on the west to Panuco on the east. In 1537, however, he was subjected to a rigorous judgment by representatives of the Crown for his activities as governor of Panuco and New Galicia. The next year he was commanded to return to Spain, where he spent the rest of his life as a prisoner in the royal court.

The published relations of Guzmán's expedition into northwestern Mexico are numerous and contradictory. He wrote a report of his own to the king from the field in 1530, which was published in *Documentos inéditos . . . de Indias* (DII) in 1870. Later he composed a Memorial which was intended as an apologia for all his activities in the New World. Francisco del Paso y Troncoso included it among the documents published in the *Epistolario de Nueva España* (1940). Relations of the expedition by Pedro de Carranza and Gonzalo López first appeared in the DII (1870). García Icazbalceta published relations by Juan de Sámano and García del Pilar and four anonymous relations (1866). The Memorial and five of the relations were republished in 1955. Ten relations of the campaign were published in a single volume in 1963. García del Pilar's relation was published in English by Patricia de Fuentes in 1963. A study of Guzmán's rule in Panuco by Donald E. Chipman (1967) has corrected a number of earlier biographical errors in regard to Guzmán.

101. Alvar Núñez Cabeza de Vaca (ca. 1510–58)

The first record of European contact with the Indians of the extreme northern frontier of Mexico is found in the work of Alvar Núñez Cabeza de Vaca.

He was born in Seville, the grandson of Pedro de Vera, conqueror of the Canary Islands. In 1527 he sailed for Florida in the ill-starred expedition of Pánfilo de Narváez. After a number of misadventures he was shipwrecked near present-day Galveston, Texas (1528). He and several companions were enslaved by the Indians, but after six years four of them escaped and made their way overland to Sonora, where they met an advance party of Nuño de Guzmán's forces. Cabeza de Vaca returned to Spain via Mexico City in 1537. He obtained an appointment as governor of Rio de la Plata but was unable to control the Spanish settlers, who sent him back to Spain as a prisoner in 1545. The Council of the Indies condemned him to exile in Oran, but the Crown intervened, even giving him a small pension. He died in Seville in 1558.

During his stay in Mexico in 1537 Cabeza de Vaca wrote a brief relation of his adventures with the Indians, which was later used by Fernández de Oviedo (Item 4). When the adventurer returned to Spain, he wrote a longer report which was published in 1547. A recent Spanish edition was published in Madrid in 1945 and reissued in 1960. There have been several English editions. A thoroughgoing study of Cabeza's journey was written by Cleve Hallenbeck (1940).

102. Marcos de Niza (fl. 1531–43)

When Cabeza de Vaca brought back rumors of rich cities to the north of the region he had traversed, Viceroy Antonio de Mendoza sent out an Italian Franciscan, Marcos de Niza, to investigate these reports. Fray Marcos had come to Santo Domingo in 1531. From there he went on to Peru at the head of the first group of Franciscans to go into that area. He was in Quito in 1534 but in April, 1537, he was in Mexico, having come by way of Guatemala. In 1539, accompanied by the Negro Estebanico who had been with Cabeza de Vaca, he set out to the north, seeking the fabled "Seven Cities of Cibola." According to his report he arrived within sight of Cibola (Zuñi Pueblo), where Estebanico, who had gone on ahead of him, had already been killed. He returned to Mexico in haste and gave a glowing report of the wealth of Cibola. His report led to the organization of the Coronado expedition into New Mexico, which he accompanied as far as Zuñi. He served as provincial of the Mexican Province of Franciscans from 1540 to 1543. He died in Mexico.

Niza's report contains valuable information regarding the Indians of Sinaloa and Sonora. It was published in Italian in 1565 but did not appear in Spanish until 1865. An English-Spanish edition was published in 1926. A vehement dispute has raged over whether or not Fray Marcos actually reached the vicinity of Zuñi, but the authenticity of the first part of his report is not contested.

103. Gonzalo de las Casas (fl. 1540s–1570s)

Gonzalo de las Casas was born in Trujillo, Spain, the son of Cortés' relative and companion in arms, Francisco de las Casas. He inherited from his father the encomienda of Yanhuitlan in the Mixteca. His activity as a writer seems to have taken place mainly in the 1570s.

Besides a work on sericulture in New Spain, published in 1581, he wrote a "Defensa de conquistas y conquistadores de las Indias Occidentales" and a *Tratado de la guerra de los Chichimecas*. The "Defensa"

is apparently lost, but two versions of a tract on the Chichimec war which seem to be his work have been published. The work probably resulted from his service in this war on the frontier.

The version of a manuscript in the National Library of Paris was published by González Obregón in 1903 from a rather extensively edited copy by José Ramírez. In 1936 Hermann Trimborn published the version contained in a manuscript of the Escorial, with some comparative passages from the Paris manuscript and the Ramírez edition. Trimborn's argumentation in favor of Las Casas' authorship of the work seems to be conclusive.

The work is divided into two parts. The first part gives a description of the various nomadic tribes of northwestern Mexico who were known by the generic name "Chichimecs," with information on their way of life and customs. The second part is a justification of the war against the Chichimecs. It includes considerable information concerning the early contact between the Indians and the Spaniards.

104. Baltasar de Obregón (1544–?)

The story of Spanish expansion into northwestern Mexico is told by a participant in Baltasar de Obregón's *Historia de los descubrimientos antiguos y modernos de la Nueva España*. Obregón was born in Mexico City in 1544 and later inherited his father's encomienda of Tezuntepec. He joined Antonio de Luna on a pearl-fishing expedition to California. In 1564 he entered the service of Francisco de Ibarra. His record of Ibarra's activities is one of the most valuable parts of his chronicle. The work is divided into two parts. The first tells of the conquest of Mexico and the northwestern expansion from 1519 to 1584. The second narrates the *entradas* of Fr. Francisco Sánchez Chamuscado and Antonio de Espejo into New Mexico.

Obregón completed his book in 1584. He hoped that it would bring him fame and royal permission to lead an expedition into New Mexico. In this it was unsuccessful. It remained unpublished until 1924, when it appeared in Spanish. An English translation by George P. Hammond and Agapito Rey was published in 1928.

105. Domingo Lázaro de Arregui (17th century)

An informative description of New Galicia was written by Domingo Lázaro de Arregui in 1621. Nothing is known about the author except what can be derived from the text itself. He was a resident of Tepic, who had extensive experience in New Galicia, although there are indications that he was Spanish in origin. He was familiar with the Indian tribes of the area and had gone among them with a number of expeditions, generally warlike.

Arregui was requested to write a description of New Galicia by Pedro de Otálora, president of the audiencia of that region. He completed it December 24, 1621, and titled it simply Descripción de la Nueva Galicia. It consists of two parts. The first describes New Galicia in general; the second describes each alcaldía mayor or province systematically. He gives a great amount of information about the Indians, their customs, languages, and geographical distribution. The manuscript of this report remained unpublished until François Chevalier brought it to light in 1946.

106. Francisco Mariano de Torres (fl. 1755–66)

A fragmentary chronicle of the Franciscan Province of Jalisco, attributed rather conclusively to Fr. Francisco Mariano de Torres, was published in Guadalajara in 1939, with a study on the authorship by Fr. Luis del Refugio de Palacio y Valois. Fr. Torres was active in the Franciscan Province of Jalisco in the mid-18th century. In 1755 he was in Cocula, having previously been superior of the friary of Amacueca. Later he was commissary of the Franciscan

Third Order in Guadalajara. In 1766 he was dispensed from attending the functions of his religious community because of his age.

In writing his chronicle he depended on Antonio Tello and Nicolás Antonio de Ornelas Mendoza y Valdivia, but he included additional material. The chronicle consisted of three books originally, but the part that has survived begins with a remnant of the seventh chapter of book 2. This book narrates the civil conquest of northern New Spain. Book 3 treats of the evangelization of Michoacan, Nayarit, and Coahuila. The work was republished in Mexico in 1960, but without Fr. Palacio's study regarding the authorship.

107. Jesuit Missions in Northwestern Mexico.

Three brief reports from the Jesuit missions in northwestern Mexico deserve mention here because of the light they throw on Indian life in the area. The anonymous Relación de la Provincia de Nuestra Señora de Sinaloa, 1601, was published by Edmundo O'Gorman in the Boletín del Archivo General de la Nación, Mexico, in 1945. It gives an informative description of the life of the Indians of Sinaloa at the time when the Jesuits first established missions among them.

The Historia de la tercera rebelión tarahumara was published in 1950 by Roberto Ramos, who attributed it to Padre Tomás de Guadalajara. It was written in 1691 about a rebellion that had occurred the previous year. Conflicts between the civil and ecclesiastical authorities seem to have been an important causative factor in the rebellion. The work originally consisted of 24 chapters, but the first five chapters and part of the sixth are missing.

Estado y descripción de la Provincia de Sonora, 1730, published by Francisco González de Cossío in Boletín del Archivo General de la Nación, Mexico, in 1945, contains detailed information regarding the population, languages, and customs of the Indians of the Jesuit missions of Sonora.

108. Juan Mateo Mange (fl. 1693–1721)

A firsthand report on the Indians of northern Sonora and southern Arizona at the time when the Jesuit missionaries first came among them is contained in the second part of Juan Mateo Mange's *Luz de tierra incognita*. Mange was a military captain who accompanied Fr. Eusebio Kino on nine exploratory expeditions into Primería Alta between 1694 and 1701. The history of seven of these expeditions is recorded in the second part of his work. The first part traces the history of the northward expansion of Spanish domination in Mexico from the Conquest onward. It contains a considerable number of historical inaccuracies. The second part contains, besides Mange's diary, three chapters on the same material by Fr. Luis Velarde, S.J. (*Item 108a*), and a final chapter describing the geography and peoples of Sonora. Mange's writings show him as a man of some erudition, although he was not always careful in regard to historical facts. Francisco Fernández del Castillo published the *Luz de tierra incognita* in 1926. An English translation of the second part, prepared by Harry J. Karns and associates, appeared in Tucson in 1954.

109. Matías Ángel de la Mota Padilla (1688–1766)

Matías Ángel de la Mota Padilla was born in Guadalajara and received his first education there, completing his studies later at the University of Mexico. In 1712 he was serving as lawyer before the audiencia of Mexico. He held many other positions: *alcalde ordinario* (1717), *asesor general* in New Galicia (1724), *alcalde mayor* of Aguascalientes (1730), *fiscal interino* of the audiencia of Guadalajara (1739), *regidor perpetuo* of Guadalajara (1746). His wife died in 1755 and he entered the priesthood in 1757. He died in Guadalajara.

In 1742 Mota Padilla completed the *Historia de la conquista del reino de la Nueva Galicia*. For the early period he depended very heavily on the chronicle of Father Tello, but he furnished some details that are not found elsewhere. After a brief description of the Indians of New Galicia, he tells at length of the conquests of Nuño de Guzmán (Item 100), the expedition of Francisco Vázquez de Coronado, and the Mixton War. He continues on through the political and religious history of the region up to the time of writing, with some information on developments in almost the whole of northern Mexico. The description of the conquest of the Nayarit seems to be derived from the now rare *Relación de la conquista de los Nayaritas* (Item 110), published in Madrid in 1722.

Mota Padilla's work remained in manuscript until 1856, when it was published quite defectively in Guadalajara. Better editions were published in Mexico in 1870 and in Guadalajara in 1924.

111–113. Alonso de León (111), Juan Bautista Chapa (112), and Fernando Sánchez de Zamora (113)

One of the most informative works regarding the Indians of northeastern Mexico is the *Historia de Nuevo León*, begun by Alonso de León, and continued by Juan Bautista Chapa, with a narrative of the discovery of Rio Blanco by General Fernando Sánchez de Zamora. Alonso de León was born in Mexico City between 1600 and 1610, and he attended the Jesuit college of San Ildefonso there. He moved to Nuevo Leon in 1635, where he became a stock raiser. He was active both in the pacification of the Indians and in exploratory expeditions. In 1654–55 he went to Spain as representative of the governor to the king. He died at his hacienda of San Mateo del Pilón in 1661.

León wrote his history of Nuevo Leon in 1649. It consists of three "discursos." The first treats of the Indians of the region; the second and third trace its history from its discovery by the Spaniards down to 1649.

The history was continued by an anonymous author down to 1690. Israel Cavazos Garza has proven rather conclusively that the author of the continuation was Juan Bautista Chapa, an Italian, born in 1630 or 1631, who came to New Spain in 1647 and settled in Nuevo Leon in 1650. He married into one of the wealthy families of the area. In 1662 he became secretary of the governor of Nuevo Leon and in 1687 he moved to Coahuila as secretary of the governor there. Chapa died in Monterrey in 1695.

Chapa included in his part of the history a relation of the discovery of the Rio Blanco by General Fernando Sánchez de Zamora. The general was a citizen of San Luis Potosi and was named *justicia mayor* of Rio Blanco in 1659. He was a miner but he also spent a great amount of time supporting the work of the missionaries and promoting the pacification and settlement of the area.

The *Historia de Nuevo León* was first published by Genaro García in 1909. It was republished in 1961 with an excellent introductory study by Israel Cavazos Garza.

114. *Vicente Santa María* (?–1813)

A valuable source of ethnohistorical data for the northern Gulf Coast of Mexico is the *Relación histórica de la colonia del Nuevo Santander y costa del Seno Mexicano*, written by Fray Vicente Santa María. The author was born in Valladolid, Michoacan, where he joined the Franciscan Order. In 1808 he took a leading part in an early conspiracy for independence, but he imprudently became too outspoken about it from the pulpit. He was arrested with his fellow conspirators December 21, 1808. He was imprisoned but managed to escape and join the forces of Morelos. He died during the storming of the Castillo de San Diego, Acapulco, in 1813.

The *Relación histórica* was apparently written between 1789 and 1794, since the dedication is addressed to the second Conde de Revillagigedo, who was viceroy of New Spain during those years. It describes the geography, native peoples, and history of the area. He gives valuable information on the many Indian tribes, with comparative inquiries into their languages and customs. He showed an advanced anthropological attitude for his day, being deeply interested in understanding the culture of the Indians and showing a sympathetic approach toward their social betterment.

The work was published in 1930 as an appendix to the documents of the visitation of the Province of Panuco and Nuevo Santander made by José Tienda de Cuervo (*Item 114a*) in 1757. The documents also contain a great amount of material on the Indians of the area toward the end of the colonial period.

115. *Alonso de la Mota y Escobar* (1546–1625)

During the 17th and 18th centuries a number of lengthy tours of inspection, or visitations, of the northern provinces were made by officials of the ecclesiastical and civil government of New Spain. Diaries of several of them have been published. They often contain notes on the population and way of life of the Indians that are not found elsewhere.

One of the first such visitations was that of Alonso de la Mota y Escobar, bishop of Guadalajara. He had been born in Mexico, the son of a conqueror, Jerónimo Ruiz de la Mota. He studied in the University of Mexico and later in that of Salamanca, Spain. On his return to Mexico he was given a series of ecclesiastical dignities: dean of the cathedral of Michoacan, dean of the cathedral of Puebla (1590), and dean of the cathedral of Mexico City (1593). He was offered the bishopric of Nicaragua but did not accept it. In 1598 he became bishop of Guadalajara. He was transferred to the diocese of Puebla in 1606, where he remained until his death in 1625.

During his tenure as bishop of Guadalajara, apparently between 1602 and 1605, Mota y Escobar made a visitation of his diocese, which then included most of northern Mexico. He wrote a record of his visitation in which he showed himself a careful observer. It is of interest because of its information on population, economic resources, and ethnography of the area. Under the title *Descripción geográfica de los reinos de Galicia, Vizcaya, y León*, it was first published privately in 1930 from a copy of the manuscript in the British Museum. In 1940 it was reissued for general consumption with modernized orthography. It was republished in 1963 on the basis of the original manuscript, with the antique orthography.

116. Pedro de Rivera y Villalón (1679–after 1742)

One of the first civil inspections of the northern frontiers of New Spain was made by Brigadier Pedro de Rivera y Villalón. Between November 21, 1724, and June 21, 1728, he visited all the more important settlements of northern New Spain, from Santa Fe in New Mexico to the missions of Sinaloa and Sonora to Nagadoches in Texas. He kept a day-to-day account of his journey, noting down the number of leagues traveled, the exact geographical location of the larger centers of population, and data concerning demography and ethnology.

Rivera had been born in Antequera, Malaga, Spain, and had elected a military career. By 1713 he had spent 34 years in the military service in Europe, in San Juan de Ulua, in the fleets, and as governor of the presidio of Veracruz (1711). He was governor of Tlaxcala in 1711, 1716, and 1723. In 1724, when he was commissioned to inspect the presidios of the northern frontier, he was serving as governor of Tlaxcala. In 1733 he became governor and captain-general of Guatemala and held the post until 1742.

Rivera's diary, entitled *Diario y derrotero de lo caminado, visto y observado en la visita que hizo a los presidios de la Nueva España septentrional el Brigadier Pedro de Rivera*, was first published in Guatemala in 1736. In 1946 a new edition was published from manuscript copies in Mexico City. Included in this latter edition were Rivera's official report to the viceroy and the regulations for the Provincias Internas which were issued as a result of Rivera's visitation.

117. Pedro Tamarón y Romeral (?–1768)

A description of northern New Spain which was the result of another episcopal visitation is the *Demostración del vastísimo obispado de la Nueva Vizcaya* by Bishop Pedro Tamarón y Romeral. The author was a native of Villa de la Guardia, Toledo, Spain. In 1719 he went to Caracas in the household of Bishop Escalona y Calatayud. There he completed his education and advanced through the stages of ecclesiastical preferment. In 1758 he was appointed bishop of Durango, where he served until his death in 1768. He died in Bamoa, Sinaloa, during the course of a visitation.

Between 1759 and 1764 Tamarón made four journeys during which he saw almost the entirety of his extensive diocese. He noted down the results of his observations and inquiries in a visitation record which is especially valuable for the information that it contains on the population of the towns and missions.

Tamarón's manuscript is in the Archivo General de Indias. It was first published in 1937 from a manuscript copy in the National Library in Mexico. Vito Alessio Robles wrote the introduction and made extensive annotations to the text, attempting to indicate the location and modern name of each of the places mentioned. A second edition was issued in Madrid in 1958.

118. Nicolás de Lafora (ca. 1730–?)

The stabilization of the northern frontier of Mexico against the incursions of the Apaches and other marauding Indians was the aim of the inspection trip of the Marqués de Rubí, 1766–68. He was accompanied by Nicolás de Lafora, a young Spanish military engineer, who wrote a diary of the expedition. Lafora was a native of Spain who had joined the Spanish army in 1746. He participated in campaigns in Italy, Oran, and Portugal. In 1764 he was sent to Mexico to assist Rubí. In this capacity he traveled through the whole area of Mexico's northern frontier in the course of two years. Afterward he gave his attention to the perennial problem of the flooding of Mexico City. He returned to Spain in 1771 or 1772 where he participated in deliberations concerning the presidios of northern Mexico. In 1774 he was appointed corregidor of Oaxaca, an office which he held for eight years. Later he seems to have retired to agricultural pursuits.

Lafora's diary of the Rubí inspection, entitled *Relación del viaje que hizo a los presidios internos, situados en la frontera de la América Septentrional, perteneciente al Rey de España*, was first published by Vito Alessio Robles in 1939 from a copy in the National Library of Madrid. An English translation was published by the Quivira Society in 1958.

Lafora's diary gives a picture of the unsettled conditions of the northern frontier of Mexico toward the end of the colonial period, when the nomadic tribes still presented a threat to settled life in the area.

119. Hugo de O'Conor (fl. 1771–76)

Another valuable record of life in the northern provinces of New Spain toward the end of the colonial period is contained in the *Informe de Hugo de O'Conor sobre el estado de las Provincias Internas del Norte, 1771–1776*. As inspector-general of the northern presidios of New Spain, Colonel O'Conor made a tour of 4000 leagues through the regions of Sonora, Nueva Vizcaya, Coahuila, and New Mexico between 1771 and 1776. In his report he recorded the existence and conditions of life of many ethnic groups, as well as important data on the climate, economy, and society of the area. The report was published in 1952, with a prologue by Enrique González Flor-

es and annotations by Francisco R. Almada.

120. Juan Agustín de Morfi (?–1783)

When the younger Teodoro de Croix formed an expedition to reorganize the frontier provinces of northern New Spain in 1776, he requested that Fray Juan Agustín de Morfi be allowed to accompany him. The Franciscan friar was a Galician by birth and at the time of Croix's request was teaching theology in the college of Santiago Tlaltelolco. He had written a number of works of historical and devotional interest. He became the chronicler of Croix's expedition, recording the events of the journey from 1777 to 1781.

Upon his return to Mexico City Morfi prepared a literary version of his diary for publication, but either he was unable to complete the work or the last part is lost, for the narrative extends only from August 4, 1777, to February 24, 1778. It stops abruptly with the expedition in the desert of northwestern Coahuila. The first adequate edition of this version of Morfi's diary was prepared by Vito Alessio Robles and published in a limited edition by Bibliófilos Mexicanos in 1935 under the title *Viaje de indios y diario del Nuevo México*. A popular version of the same edition was published in the same year. Another edition, included in *Biblioteca Indiana*, appeared in Madrid in 1958.

The manuscript of Morfi's personal day-to-day diary of the expedition was later found in the University of Texas Library. In 1967 Eugenio del Hoyo and Malcolm D. McLean published it, with the title *Diario y derrotero (1777–1781)*. It is simpler and less polished in style than the *Viaje de indios* but it contains a complete record of the journey down to the return to Mexico in 1781. The editors enhanced its usefulness with notes, indexes, and maps.

Morfi's diaries show him as an acute observer as well as a critic of social conditions. They are a valuable record, written by a man with a deep human interest in the people whom he visited. They contain important information regarding the native tribes and languages with which he came into contact.

SOUTHERN MEXICO

121. Diego Godoy (fl. 1524–25)

In 1524 Cortés sent Diego Godoy at the head of an expedition into Colonia del Espiritu Santo and Chiapas, which had revolted. Godoy succeeded in pacifying Chamollon and the surrounding territory and afterwards returned to Mexico. In 1525 Cortés named him governor of the Villa de Natividad, Honduras. Little else is known of his life.

Godoy sent Cortés at least two reports of his campaign into southern Mexico. The first is lost, but the second was published with Cortés' Fourth Letter in 1525. It was also included by Vedia in his *Historiadores primitivos de Indias* (1852), and in modern editions of Cortés' letters.

122. Gonzalo Balzalobre (fl. 1629–59)

A treatise on the surviving pagan practices in 17th-century Oaxaca was written by Bachiller Gonzalo Balzalobre, parish priest of San Miguel Sola for 20 years. In 1653 he discovered that some of his parishioners were still practicing pagan rites. With the consent of the bishop of Oaxaca he launched a full-scale investigation of the survivals of native practices. He published the results of his investigation in 1656 under the title of *Relación de las idolatrías y supersticiones y vanas observancias de los indios del obispado de esta región*. In 1659 the work was suppressed by the Inquisition because of a jurisdictional squabble. It was republished in Mexico in 1892. A recent edition appeared in Mexico in 1953. For the study of Zapotec antiquities it is invaluable and is often the only source for information on this region. Heinrich Berlin extracted it, together with related material from the Mexican Inquisition, in *Las antiguas creencias en San Miguel Solá, Oaxaca* (1957).

123. Indian Rebellions in Southern Mexico

Genaro García collected a number of rare items regarding riots and rebellions in Mexico into a single volume entitled *Tumultos y rebeliones acaecidos en México* (1907). The volume includes a relation of disturbances among the Indians of Nejapa, Ixtepeji, and Villa Alta in 1662, written by the alcalde mayor of Nejapa, Juan de Torres Castillo (*Item 124*), the narration by Antonio Robles (*Item 125*), of the efforts of Alonso de Cuevas Dávalos, bishop of Oaxaca, to pacify the Province of Tehuantepec in 1660; and a history of the same rebellion in Tehuantepec, written in 1661 by Cristóbal Manso de Contreras (*Item 126*). There is also a report of an uprising of the Indians of Tepic in 1801. All but the last item had been published previously.

YUCATAN

Fray Diego de Landa's *Relación de las cosas de Yucatán* is treated in Article 13 of this volume. Here we wish simply to mention a collection of related letters and documents (*Item 127*) published by France V. Scholes and Eleanor B. Adams under the title *Don Diego de Quijada, alcalde mayor de Yucatán, 1561–1565* (2 vols., Mexico, 1938). They throw a great deal of light on this period of severe intercultural conflict between the Mayan natives and the Spaniards, arising from the suppression of native religious practices.

A report on the diocese of Yucatan which gives considerable information on the Indians of that area was published in 1938 in *Documentos para la historia de Yucatán* (2:66–94), collected by France V. Scholes. It was written by the bishop of Yucatan, Gregorio de Montalvo (*Item 128*), in 1582.

129. Pedro Sánchez de Aguilar (1555–1648)

A treatise against the continued pagan practices of the Indians of Yucatan was prepared by Pedro Sánchez de Aguilar in 1613.

The author was born in Valladolid, Yucatan, a grandson of the conqueror Fernando de Aguilar. He received the first elements of his education in Tiximin from an educated Indian, Gaspar Antonio Xiu (discussed in Article 5). Sánchez studied in the Colegio de San Ildefonso in Mexico, was ordained a priest, and gained a doctorate from the University of Mexico. He served as a parish priest in various towns of Yucatan, was vicar-general of the diocese (1603), and later became dean of the cathedral in Merida (1613). He traveled to Spain in 1617 as representative of the Province of Yucatan. In 1619 he was named canon of the cathedral of La Plata (Sucre), Charcas. He took up the position in 1621 and remained in it until his death.

His *Informe contra idolorum cultores del Obispado de Yucatán* was published in Madrid in 1639. It is largely a juridical argument in favor of the suppression of pagan practices by forceful means, but it also contains valuable notes on the religious practices of the Mayas and on the history of the efforts to suppress them. In 1937 the work was republished in Merida, Yucatan, with an introductory note by Francisco Cantón Rosado. Another edition was published in Mexico in 1953.

A record of conditions in Yucatan and Campeche toward the end of the colonial period (*Item 130*) is found in the anonymous *Discurso sobre la constitución de las Provincias de Yucatán y Campeche, 1766.* This report was drawn up by the officials who were commissioned to visit Yucatan by the visitor-general of New Spain, José de Gálvez. It was published as Volume 3 of the *Documentos para la historia de Yucatán* (Merida, Yucatan, 1938). It presents a critical examination of the Indians and their economic resources.

CENTRAL AMERICA

Early Southern Central America

There are several rather brief letters and reports of the explorers and conquerors of the southern part of Central America. They are valuable sources regarding the Indians of that area at the time of Contact.

131. Gil González Dávila (?–1526)

Gil González Dávila arrived in Tierra Firme in 1520. In 1522–23 he led an expedition into Nicaragua, concerning which he wrote a letter to the king from Española on March 6, 1524. He returned to Honduras and Nicaragua in 1524, but he was made a prisoner by Cristóbal de Olid. Having cooperated with Francisco de las Casas in the assassination of Olid, he was made a prisoner by Las Casas, who took him to Mexico and sent him back to Spain. He died in Avila on April 21, 1526.

132. Pedro Arias de Ávila (ca. 1440–1530)

Better known as Pedrarias Dávila, a Spanish nobleman of high rank, Pedro Arias de Ávila sailed to Darien (Castilla de Oro) as governor in 1514. In 1525, probably, he wrote a letter to the king, reporting the discovery of Nicaragua. Having been removed from his previous governorship because of his severity, he occupied Nicaragua, where he was appointed governor and captain-general in 1527. He died at Leon, Nicaragua, in 1530. History has branded him as one of the most cruel of the Spanish conquerors. Pablo Álvarez Rubiano published a study of Dávila in 1944 with an extensive appendix of documents about his career.

133. Juan Vázquez de Coronado (ca. 1525–65)

Juan Vázquez de Coronado was born in Salamanca, Spain, before 1525. He was an educated and cultured man. In 1548 he went to Mexico and in 1550 to Guatemala. He occupied many offices in the government of Central America. He accompanied Ramírez de Quiñones on his expedition to the Lacandon, and in 1561 he succeeded Licenciado Juan de Cavallón as alcalde mayor of the provinces of Nuevo Cartago and Costa Rica. He was known for his kindness and generosity toward the Indians. During the years 1562–65 he wrote a number of letters, *informaciones*, and memorials regarding his expeditions into the unexplored areas of Costa Rica, Nicaragua, and Panama in the 16th century. He died in a shipwreck in October, 1565.

In 1883 Manuel M. de Peralta published a collection of valuable documents related to Costa Rica. The collection, entitled *Costa Rica, Nicaragua y Panamá en el siglo XVI*, contains many of the more important reports by or about the conquerors of southern Central America. In 1908 Ricardo Fernández Guardia published a collection of the letters of Juan Vázquez de Coronado. All but one of the letters was taken from Peralta's collection. The 1908 edition was reproduced in facsimile by the Academy of Geography and History of Costa Rica in 1964. The letter of Pedrarias Dávila describing the discovery of Nicaragua was published by the Academy of Geography and History of Nicaragua in 1946.

134. Pascual de Andagoya (ca. 1498–1548)

Pascual de Andagoya, born in the valley of Cuartango, Alava, Spain, came to the New World in the expedition of Pedrarias Dávila. He assisted in the founding of Panama in 1519. He was visitador of the Indians of Panama and explored to the south along the Pacific coast, bringing back reports of the Indians of Peru. From him Pizarro and Almagro obtained information which led them to press forward their own explorations to the south. Andagoya later went to Nicaragua with Pedrarias Dávila. He was given the governorship of Popayan in present-day Colombia, but he came into conflict with Benalcázar, who took him prisoner. In 1541 he went back to Spain, where he stayed until 1546. He returned to Peru with Pedro de la Gasca in 1546 and died in 1548.

Andagoya wrote a *Relación de los sucesos de Pedrarias Dávila en las provincias de Tierra Firme ó Castilla del Oro, y de lo ocurrido en el descubrimiento de la mar del Sur y costas del Perú y Nicaragua*. In it he told of some of the early expeditions from the south into Central America. He showed special interest in the life and customs of the natives. Navarrete (1825) published the *Relación* from the original manuscript in the Archivo General de Indias, Seville. In 1865 the Hakluyt Society published a translation, with introduction and notes, by Clements R. Markham. Hermann Trimborn (1954) has written an extensive study of Andagoya's life and work, in which he included the *Relación* in Spanish with a German translation.

Early Northern Central America

135. Pedro de Alvarado (ca. 1486–1541)

Pedro de Alvarado, one of the favorite captains of Hernando Cortés, was a native of Badajoz, Spain. He was in Santo Domingo by 1510, going on later to Cuba. He sailed in the expeditions of both Grijalva and Cortés and took a leading part in the conquest of Mexico. After Mexico had been subdued, Alvarado was placed in command of an expedition which conquered Guatemala in 1523–24. In 1527 he went back to Spain where he secured the title of governor and captain-general of Guatemala. He organized an expedition to Peru in 1534, but it failed and he sold his interests to Pizarro and Almagro. He returned to Guatemala, but in 1541 he went to the assistance of the Spaniards of Mexico in the Mixton War. There a horse fell on him and he died several days later of his injuries.

During the conquest of Guatemala Alvarado wrote two letters to Cortés, dated April 11 and July 28, 1524, telling of his campaigns. They were first published in 1525 with the Fourth Letter of Cortés. Since then they have been published many times. A good Spanish edition appeared in 1954, and an English translation was included in Fuentes' *Conquistadors* (1963). A valuable collection of letters and other documents pertaining to Pedro de Alvarado is contained in the second part (pp. 137–402) of *Libro viejo de la fundación de Guatemala, y papeles relativos a D. Pedro de Alvarado* (1934). Included are a facsimile of the 1525 printed edition of Alvarado's letters and a transcription of the same. The first part of the volume contains the acts of the cabildo of Santiago de Guatemala for the years 1524–30.

136. Diego García de Palacio (?–1595)

Acute observations regarding the Indians and archaeological remains of present-day El Salvador and the surrounding region are found in the letter of Licenciado Diego García de Palacio, written in 1576. As oidor of the audiencia of Guatemala (1572–79) he visited the section of the Pacific coast of Guatemala lying between the Michatoyat and Lempa rivers and inland as far as the city of Chiquimula and the ruins of Copan. He aspired to the office of governor of the Philippines but did not receive the appointment. He served as visitador of Yucatan. In 1579 he was appointed *alcalde de crimen* of the audiencia of Mexico. There he published two works regarding military and nautical science in 1583 and 1587. In the latter year he was appointed captain-general of an armada which was sent out from Acapulco against the English corsairs.

Antonio de Herrera (Article 15, Appendix A) copied much of García de Palacio's report into his *Historia* (dec. iv, bk. vii, chaps. 8–10) but the complete Spanish text was first published by E. G. Squier in 1860, accompanied by an English translation. Later it appeared in DII (1866) and in the *Colección de documentos para la historia de Costa Rica* (1881). The last edition was accompanied by a preface and notes by Alexander von Frantzius.

Two short but informative reports regarding the Province of Verapaz come from this same period. *Descripción de la provincia de la Verapaz*, by Fray Francisco Montero de Miranda (*Item 137*), was directed to Oidor García de Palacio. It gives a description of the geography, natural history, and natives of the area. It was published in 1955 from a manuscript in the Library of the University of Texas. Another valuable description is of the Dominican missions in Verapaz in the *Relación de la Provincia de la Verapaz hecha por los religiosos de Santo Domingo de Cobán, 7 de diciembre de 1574*, signed by Fr. Francisco de Viana (*Item 138*), Fr. Lucas Gallego (*Item 139*), and Fr. Guillermo Cadena (*Item 140*). It was also published in 1955.

A description of the towns and provinces of Guatemala was written by Juan de Pinedo (*Item 141*) in 1594. It gives valuable information on the condition of the natives and their economy. This *Descripción de la Provincia de Guatemala, año de 1594*, was first published in Costa Rica in 1939.

142. Martín Alfonso Tovilla (fl. 1623–44)

The problem of pacifying and christianizing the area of Manche, Lacandon, and Peten was very troublesome to the authorities of Guatemala during the 17th century. A summary of efforts down to 1635 is given in the *Relación histórica descriptiva de las Provincias de la Verapaz y de la del Manché* by Martín Alfonso Tovilla. The author, a native of Alcaraz de la Mancha, Spain, had served as a soldier in the Low Countries before being appointed alcalde mayor of Verapaz, Golfo Dulce, Sacapulas, and Manche in 1629. He arrived in his jurisdiction in December, 1630. In March, 1631, he was given permission to found a town in the Manche to protect the christianized Indians of the area. The town was founded in May, 1631, and given the name Toro de Acuña, but it was soon abandoned while Tovilla was away making a visitation of Verapaz. Little is known about Tovilla's later life, except that he was appointed alcalde mayor of Zapotitlan before the termination of his tenure in Verapaz and that he was alcalde ordinario in Guatemala City in 1644.

Tovilla's *Relación* is composed of two

books. The first tells of his voyage from Spain, the history of the mission efforts in Verapaz, and the author's exertions in getting permission to found a town in the Manche. The second book relates the history of his expedition into the Manche and of his visitation of his province. Many items of ethnohistorical interest are interspersed through the narrative. Parts of the work depend heavily on Antonio de Remesal (see Article 13).

The manuscript once belonged to Francisco Antonio de Fuentes y Guzmán (Item 151) and was later in the collection of Archbishop Lorenzana (Item 92), with which it went into the Public Library of Toledo, Spain. It was published in Guatemala by France V. Scholes and Eleanor B. Adams in 1960.

143. Sebastián de Caldas (Sebastián Alvarez Alfonso Rosica de Caldas) (fl. 1667)

Sebastián de Caldas arrived in Guatemala in January, 1667, as governor, captain-general, and president of the audiencia. He quickly realized that one of the most serious Indian problems of his jurisdiction was the unsettled state of the Province of Lacandon. He wrote a letter to the king on January 30, 1667, relating briefly the history of the efforts to penetrate the Lacandon and requesting permission to form an expedition to conquer the area. The letter was printed in Guatemala in 1667 and has been reproduced in the microfilm copies of the J. T. Medina Collection.

144. Andrés de Avendaño y Loyola (fl. 1695–1705)

Born in Castile, Andrés de Avendaño y Loyola joined the Franciscan Province of Burgos. Later he came to the New World and became a member of the province of Yucatan. In 1705 he was a member of the provincial council of that province.

In 1695 and 1696 Avendaño y Loyola made two entradas to the south of Yuca-

tan to contact the Cehaches and Itzas. He wrote a fairly extensive report of these journeys. An extract of the report was incorporated in Villagutierre's *Historia de la conquista de la Provincia de el Itzá* (Item 149). Large sections of it in English translation were included in Philip Ainsworth Means' *History of the Spanish Conquest of Yucatán and of the Itzas* (1917).

145. Agustín Cano, et al.

Also in 1695 Fray Agustín Cano entered the Peten region from the Province of Verapaz. An informative relation of his journey and of the incidents preceding the expedition of Don Martín de Ursúa into the Peten area are contained in the *Informe dado al Rey por el Padre Fray Agustín Cano sobre la entrada que por la parte de la Verapaz se hizo al Petén en el año de 1695*. It was published in Guatemala in 1942.

Another letter indicating the concerted effort of Spanish authorities to pacify the Lacandones was written from Nuestra Señora de los Dolores, near Lake Peten, on August 26, 1695, by the Franciscan friars Antonio Margil de Jesús (*Item 146*), Lázaro de Mazariego (*Item 147*), and Blas Guillén (*Item 148*). Seemingly it was directed to the president of the audiencia of Guatemala. It describes the methods of the Spaniards for pacification as well as Lacandon rites and customs. Under title of "A Spanish manuscript letter on the Lacandones in the Archive of the Indies at Seville," it was translated into English and published in 1913 by Alfred M. Tozzer, who presented it at the XVIIIth International Congress of Americanists (London, 1912).

149. Juan de Villagutierre Soto-Mayor (fl. 1701)

As relator of the Royal Chancery of Valladolid and later of the Council of the Indies, Juan de Villagutierre Soto-Mayor had access to many documents and relations of the region of Itza and Lacandon which are now in the Archivo General de Indias (Seville). Utilizing these and other works, he wrote his *Historia de la conquista de la Provincia de el Itzá, reducción y progresos de la del Lacandón, y otras naciones de indios bárbaros de la mediación de el Reino de Guatemala, a las Provincias de Yucatán, en la América Septentrional.* It traces the history of the region from 1525 to 1699. It was first published in Madrid in 1701 and republished in Guatemala, with an introduction by Pedro Zamora Castellanos, in 1933.

Francisco de Elorza y Rada (*Item 150*) extracted from Villagutierre's work the materials pertaining to Martín Ursúa y Arizmendi, conde de Lizárraga-Bengoa, and published them in 1714. This extract was republished in 1943. An English translation by Philip Ainsworth Means appeared in Paris in 1930.

Later Writings

151. *Francisco Antonio de Fuentes y Guzmán* (ca. 1643–1700)

The first general work on the history of Guatemala was the *Recordación florida* of Francisco Antonio de Fuentes y Guzmán, a great-great-grandson of Bernal Díaz del Castillo. He was born in Antigua, Guatemala, the son of one of the prominent families of that city. At 18 he was given the office of *regidor perpetuo* on the town council of his native city. At different times he was first alcalde and second alcalde of the city. Later he served as alcalde mayor of Totonicapan and finally he held the same office in Sonsonate, where he died.

By 1690 Fuentes y Guzmán had completed the first 16 books of the first part of his work. He had a clean copy made of this, which he sent to Madrid in the hope of obtaining the title of chronicler of the Kingdom of Guatemala. Although he apparently did not obtain the post, he continued to write. He added a 17th book to the first part and wrote a second part, consisting of 14 books. As an historian Fuentes y Guzmán has been severely criticized for his lack of

order and his inability to synthesize, but he lent an invaluable service to later historians by preserving many documents and native traditions which would otherwise have been entirely lost.

The incomplete copy of his work, which Fuentes had sent to Spain, was published in Madrid by Justo Zaragoza in 1882–83. The complete text from the original manuscript in the Archive of the Municipality of Guatemala was published in Guatemala in 1932–33. The first volume of a new edition was published in Madrid in 1969. Although the complete work of Fuentes y Guzmán did not see publication until the present century, large parts of it were copied by the diocesan priest Domingo Juarros (*Item 152*) in his *Compendio de la historia de la Ciudad de Guatemala* (2 vols., Guatemala, 1808–18). An English translation of Juarros' work appeared in London in 1823.

153. *Pedro Cortés y Larraz* (1712–86)

A picture of the condition of the Indians of Guatemala toward the end of the colonial period is found in the record of the visitation of that area by Archbishop Pedro Cortés y Larraz in 1768–70. Cortés y Larraz was born in Belchite, Zaragoza, Spain. He attended the University of Zaragoza, where in 1741 he gained a doctorate in theology. He became a priest and served in various parishes of Zaragoza, later becoming a canon of the cathedral of the diocese. In 1766 the king presented him for the post of archbishop of Guatemala. He was consecrated a bishop in Puebla, Mexico, on August 24, 1767, and took possession of his archdiocese in February, 1768. His archdiocese included the present-day republics of Guatemala and El Salvador. He made a complete visitation of the area in three trips: November 3, 1768, to July 1, 1769; November 22, 1769, to February 9, 1770; and June 6, 1770, to August 29, 1770. In his report he noted his acute observations regarding each parish and mission. At the time of the destructive earthquake of July 29, 1773, he gave great assistance to the needy and made futile efforts to prevent the transferal of the seat of civil and ecclesiastical government from Antigua to Guatemala. This dispute lasted until 1779, when the archbishop was transferred to the diocese of Tortosa in Spain. He retired to Zaragoza in 1786, where he died the following year.

The manuscript of the archbishop's description of his archdiocese is preserved in the Archivo General de Indias. The first volume of a printed edition appeared in Guatemala in 1958 under the title *Descripción geográfico-moral de la diócesis de Goathemala*, with a prologue by Adrián Recinos.

Other Writings

Two titles pertaining to the history of the Dominican friars in Guatemala are *Isagoge histórica apologética de las Indias, y especial de la provincia de San Vicente de Chiapa y Guatemala de la Orden de Predicadores* and *Antigua Guatemala: Memorias del M. R. P. Maestro Fray Antonio de Molina, continuadas y marginadas por Fray Agustín Cano y Fray Francisco Ximénez, de la Order de Santo Domingo.*

The first is an anonymous work (*Item 154*) written during the first years of the 18th century and first published in Madrid in 1892. A more complete edition appeared in Guatemala in 1935, but the final part of the original manuscript seems never to have been copied and is lost. The book is composed of two parts. In the first part the author, a Dominican friar, attempts to prove that the Indians were the descendants of the 12 lost tribes of Israel. He also discusses the medieval question of the Antipodes and traces the first steps of the exploration and missionizing of the New World. Among his speculative lucubrations one finds some interesting materials on the antiquities of Guatemala. The second part, of which chapters 1–20 and 23–29 are preserved, treats of the conquest of Guatemala and the early activities of the Dominicans there.

Antigua Guatemala is a chronicle of the activities of the Dominican Order in Guatemala during the greater part of a century (1628–1721). It was begun by Antonio de Molina (*Item 155*), who wrote the entries for the years 1628–78. Agustín Cano (*Item 156*; see also Item 145), and Francisco Jiménez (*Item 157*), continued it to 1721. It was used by Jiménez as a major source for his *Historia de la Provincia de San Vicente de Chiapa y Guatemala de la Orden de Predicadores* (see Article 13). Jorge del Valle Matheu published it in 1943 from a manuscript in his possession.

A rather simplistic solution to the social and economic problems of the native peoples of Guatemala is found in *Utilidades de que todos los indios y ladinos se visten y calcen a la española y medio de conseguirlo sin violencia, coacción ni mandato*, written by Fray Matías de Córdoba (*Item 158*; ca. 1768–1828) in 1797. The author, a member of the Dominican Order, is better known for his activities as a patriot and poet. It was first published in Guatemala in 1798 and republished there in 1937.

A valuable source of information concerning the Indians of Costa Rica at the middle of the 18th century is the *Informe sobre la Provincia de Costa Rica presentado por el Ingeniero Don Luis Diez Navarro* [*Item 159*] *al Capitan General de Guatemala Don Tomás de Rivera y Santa Cruz, año de 1744*. It first appeared in print in Guatemala in 1939.

A collection of narratives and reports regarding Central America was published by Manuel Serrano y Sanz in 1908 under the title *Relaciones históricas y geográficas de América Central* (*Item 160*) (vol. 8 of *Colección de libros y documentos referentes a la historia de América*). The first half of the volume is composed of items on Panama. The second half contains seven items on other parts of Central America, all of which include some information on the Indians. They appear in the following order: a diary of two voyages along the Mosquito Coast in 1787 by Gonzalo Vallejo; a narrative of another reconnaissance of the Mosquito Coast in 1790 by Antonio Porta Costas; a file of descriptive documents on the Rio de San Juan, the Mosquito Coast and adjacent islands, and Nicaragua (1791–1804); a relation of the conversion of the Xicaque Indians of the province of Tegucigalpa between 1612 and 1674, written by a Franciscan priest, Fr. Fernando Espino, and first published in Guatemala in 1674; a collection of letters from Franciscan missionaries among the Xicaques to Fr. Espino; a proposal by Ramón de Anguiano, governor intendant of Honduras, to subjugate Xicaque Indians living in the mountains, and related documents; and a description of the province of Guatemala by Juan de Pineda (1594).

BIBLIOGRAPHY

ACADEMIA
1952 Colección de documentos para la historia de Costa Rica relativos al cuarto y último viaje de Cristóbal Colón. [Ed. Jorge A. Lines.] Academia de Geografía e Historia de Costa Rica. San Jose, Costa Rica.

ACOSTA, JOSÉ DE
1590 Historia natural y moral de las Indias en que se tratan las cosas notables del cielo, y elementos, metales, plantas, y animales dellas: y los ritos, y ceremonias, leyes, y gobierno, y guerras de los Indios. Compuesta por el Padre Ioseph de Acosta Religioso de la Compañía de Iesús. Seville.
1880 The natural and moral History of the Indies, by Father Joseph de Acosta. Reprinted from the English translated edition of Edward Grimston, 1604. Edited, with notes and introduction, by Clements R. Markham. . . . 2 vols. Works issued by the Hakluyt Society, 60–61. London.
1940 Historia natural y moral de las Indias . . . . Estudio preliminar de Edmundo O'Gorman. Mexico. [Reissued in 1962.]
1954 Obras del P. José de Acosta de la Compañía de Jesús. Estudio preliminar y edición del P. Francisco Mateos de la misma Compañía. Biblioteca de Autores Españoles, 73. Madrid.

ADAMS, ELEANOR B.
1938 See Scholes and Adams, 1938.
1960 See Tovilla, 1960.

ÁGREDA Y SÁNCHEZ, JOSÉ MARÍA DE
1902 See Dorantes de Carranza, 1902.

1946 See Gemelli Careri, 1946.
1955 See Gemelli Careri, 1955.

AGUILAR, FRANCISCO (ALONSO) DE
1900 Historia de la Nueva España de Francisco de Aguilar. MNA, Anales, 1a época, 7/1:3–25.
1954 Relación breve de la conquista de la Nueva España, escrita por Fray Francisco de Aguilar, de la Orden de Predicadores. Estudio y notas por Federico Gómez de Orozco. Mexico.
1963 The chronicle of Fray Francisco de Aguilar. In Fuentes, 1963, pp. 136–64.

AGUILAR, JERÓNIMO DE
1948 Informaciones sobre Gerónimo de Aguilar, conquistador y primer lengua. Mexico.

AGUILERA, EMILIANO M.
1954 See López de Gómara, 1954.

AJOFRÍN, FRANCISCO DE
1936 Diario del viaje que hicimos a México Fray Francisco de Ajofrín y Fray Fermín de Olite, capuchinos, con una introducción por Genaro Estrada. Mexico.
1958–59 Diario del viaje que por orden de la Sagrada Congregación de Propaganda Fide hizo a la América Septentrional en el siglo XVIII el P. Fray Francisco de Ajofrín, Capuchino. Edición y prólogo de Vicente Castañeda y Alcover. Notas del P. Buenaventura de Carrocera. Archivo Documental Español publicado por la Real Academia de la Historia, 12, 13. Madrid.

ALCEDO Y BEXARANO, ANTONIO DE
1786–89 Diccionario geográfico-histórico de las Indias Occidentales o América: Es a saber: de los Reinos del Perú, Nueva España, Tierra Firme, Chile, y Nuevo Reino de Granada . . . escrito por el Coronel D. Antonio de Alcedo, Capitán de Reales Guardias Españoles. 5 vols. Madrid.
1812–15 The geographical and historical dictionary of America and the West Indies. Containing an entire translation of the Spanish work of Colonel Don Antonio de Alcedo, Captain of the Royal Spanish Guards and member of the Royal Academy of History: with large additions and compilations from modern voyages and travels and from original and authentic information. By G. A. Thompson, Esq. 5 vols. London.
1964–65 Bibliotheca americana. Catálogo de los autores que han escrito de la América en diferentes idiomas y noticia de su vida y patria, años en que vivieron, y obras que escribieron, compuesta por el mariscal de campo D. Antonio de Alcedo, Gobernador de la Plaza de la Coruña, año de 1807. Introducción de Jorge A. Garces G. Publicaciones del Museo Municipal de Arte e Historia, vol. 32, t. 1, 2. [Quito.]
1967 Diccionario geográfico de las Indias Occidentales o América. Edición y estudio preliminar por Don Ciriaco Pérez-Bustamante. Biblioteca de Autores Españoles, 205–208. 4 vols. Madrid.

ALCINA FRANCH, JOSÉ
1957 El indigenismo de Fray José Díaz de la Vega. América Indígena, 17:271–81.
1969 See Dupaix, 1969.

ALESSIO ROBLES, VITO
1935 See Morfi, 1935a.
1937 See Tamarón y Romeral, 1937.
1939 See Lafora, 1939.
1941 See Humboldt, 1941.
1946 See Rivera y Villalón, 1946.

ALVARADO, PEDRO DE
1525 La quarta relación que Fernando Cortés gobernador y capitán general por su majestad en la nueva España del mar océano envió al muy alto y muy potentísimo invictísimo señor don Carlos emperador semper augusto y rey de España nuestro señor; en la cual están otras cartas y relaciones que los capitanes Pedro de Alvarado y Diego Godoy enviaron al dicho capitán Fernando Cortés. Toledo.
1954 Relación hecha por Pedro de Alvarado a Hernando Cortés, en que se refieren las guerras y batallas para pacificar las provincias del Antiguo Reino de Goathemala. Estudio y notas por José Valero Silva. Mexico.
1963 Two letters of Pedro de Alvarado. In Fuentes, 1963, pp. 182–96.

ÁLVAREZ ALFONSO ROSICA DE CALDAS, SEBASTIÁN
1667 Copia de carta escrita a su Majestad, D. Carlos Segundo, Rey de las Españas y Nuevo Mundo, por Don Sebastián Álvarez Alfonso Rosica de Caldas . . . , gobernador y capitán general de las provincias de Goatemala, y presidente de su real audiencia. Sobre la conquista, reducción y conversión de las provincias del Lacandón, en treinta de enero de este año de mil y seiscientos y sesenta y siete. Guatemala.

ÁLVAREZ RUBIANO, PABLO
1944 Pedrarias Dávila: Contribución al estudio de la figura del "Gran Justador," gobernador de Castilla del Oro y Nicaragua. Madrid. [Appendices (pp. 395–720) contain 152 documents relative to the career of Dávila.]

ALZATE Y RAMÍREZ, JOSÉ ANTONIO DE
1788–95 Gazeta de literatura. 3 vols. (15 enero, 1788–22 octubre, 1795). Mexico.
1831 Gacetas de literatura de México. 4 vols. Puebla.

ANALES
1900 Anales del Museo Nacional de México, vol. 6 (1900). In this volume are collected, each with its own date of imprint: Balzalobre, 1892; Feria, 1899; Ponce de León, 1892; Ruiz de Alarcón, 1892; Sánchez de Aguilar, 1892; Serna, 1892. They are given individual entries below.

ANDAGOYA, PASCUAL DE
1829 Relación de los sucesos de Pedrarias Dávila en las provincias de Tierra Firme ó Castilla del Oro, y de lo ocurrido en el descubrimiento de la mar del Sur y costas del Perú y Nicaragua, escrita por el Adelantado Pascual de

Andagoya. *In* Navarrete, 1825–37, 3:393–456.

1865 Narrative of the proceedings of Pedrarias Dávila in the provinces of Tierra Firme or Castilla del Oro and of the discovery of the South Sea and the coasts of Peru and Nicaragua. . . . Translated and edited, with notes and introduction, by Clements R. Markham. Works issued by the Hakluyt Society, 34. London.

ANGHIERA, PETER MARTYR D'

1521 De nuper sub D. Carolo repertis insulis simulque incolarum moribus, R. Petri Martyris, enchiridion, Dominae Margaritae, Divi Max. Caes., filiae dicatum. Basel.

1530a Opus epistolarum Petri Martyris Anglerii Mediolanensis protonotarii Apostolici atque a consiliis rerum Indicarum: nunc primum et natu et mediocri cura excusum; quod quidem praeter stili venustatem nostrorum quoque temporum historiae loco esse poterit. Alcalá de Henares.

1530b De Orbe Novo Petri Martyris ab Angleria Mediolanensis protonotarii Cesaris senatoris decades cum privilegio imperiali. Alcalá de Henares.

1912 De Orbe Novo: the Eight Decades of Peter Martyr D'Anghera. Translated from the Latin, with notes and introduction, by Francis Augustus MacNutt. 2 vols. New York and London.

1953–57 Epistolario. Estudio y traducción de José López de Toro. 4 vols. Documentos inéditos para la historia de España, 9–12. Madrid.

1964 Decadas del Nuevo Mundo, por Pedro Martir de Angleria, primer cronista de Indias. Estudio y apéndices por el Dr. Edmundo O'Gorman. Traducción del latín del Dr. Agustín Millares Carlo. 2 vols. Mexico.

1966 Opera: Legatio Babylonica; De Orbe Novo Decades Octo; Opus Epistolarum. Introduction by Dr. Erich Woldan. Graz, Austria.

ANONYMOUS CONQUEROR

1556 Relatione di alcune cose della Nuovo Spagna, & della gran cittá di Temestitan Messico; fatta per uno gentil'huomo del signor Fernando Cortese. *In* Ramusio, 1556, ff. 245r–259r.

1858 Relación de algunas cosas de la Nueva España, y de la gran ciudad de Temestitán México; escrita por un compañero de Hernán Cortés. *In* García Icazbalceta, 1858–66, 1:368–98.

1961 Relación de algunas cosas de la Nueva España y de la gran ciudad de Temestitán México, hecha por un gentilhombre del Señor Fernando Cortés. Mexico.

1963 The chronicle of the Anonymous Conquistador. *In* Fuentes, 1963, pp. 167–81.

ANTONIO, NICOLÁS

1672 Biblioteca hispana sive hispanorum, qui usquam unquamque sive latina sive populari sive alia quavis lingua scripto aliquid consignaverunt noticia, his quae praecesserunt locupletior et certior brevia elogia, editorum atque ineditorum operum catalogus duabus partibus continens, quarum haec ordine quidem rei posterior, conceptu vero prior duabus tomis de his agit qui post annum saecularem MD ad praesentem diem floruere. 2 vols. Rome.

AROCENA, LUIS A.

1963 Antonio de Solís, cronista indiano: Estudio sobre las formas historiográficas del barroco. Buenos Aires.

ARREGUI, DOMINGO LÁZARO DE

1946 Descripción de la Nueva Galicia. Edición y estudio por François Chevalier. Prólogo de John Van Horne. Seville.

AVENDAÑO Y LOYOLA, ANDRÉS DE

1917 Relación de las dos entradas que hizo a la conversión de los gentiles Itzaes y Cehaches . . . del 2 de junio y 13 de diciembre de 1695, al 6 de abril 1696. [English translation of most of this item is included in Philip Ainsworth Means, *History of the Spanish conquest of Yucatán and of the Itzas*, pp. 103–74. Cambridge, Mass.]

ÁVILA, PEDRO ARIAS DE

1883 Relación de la tierra que se envía a Su Majestad, León de Nicaragua, 15 de enero de 1529. *In* Peralta, 1883, pp. xi–xiii. [See also the two letters of Licenciado Francisco de Castañeda in Peralta, 1883, pp. 36–82, regarding the governorship of Pedrarias in Nicaragua.]

1946 Carta de Pedrarias al Emperador, refiriendo el descubrimiento de Nicaragua, [1525]. *Revista de la Aca-*

demia de Geografía e Historia de Nicaragua, 8/3:1–12.

AYALA ECHAVARRI, RAFAEL
1948   See Relación histórica, 1948.

BAILY, J.
1823   See Juarros, 1823.

BALDWIN, PERCY M.
1926   See Niza, 1926.

BALLESTEROS GAIBROIS, MANUEL
1940–49   Escritores de Indias. 2 vols. Zaragoza.
1947a   Los papeles de Don Lorenzo Boturini Benaducci. In Documentos inéditos para la historia de España, 5:xli–lxvii. Madrid.
1947b   Papeles referentes al caballero Lorenzo Boturini Benaducci. In Documentos inéditos para la historia de España, 5:89–189. Madrid.

BALZALOBRE, GONZALO DE
1656   Relación auténtica de las idolatrías, supersticiones, varias observaciones de los indios del obispado de Oaxaca. Y una instrucción y práctica que el Ilustrísimo y Reverendisimo Señor M.D.F. Diego de Hevia y Valdés, Obispo . . . de la Santa Iglesia de Antequera, Valle de Oaxaca . . . piadosa y afectuosamente envía a los venerables padres ministros seculares y regulares de indios para el conocimiento, inquisición y estirpación de dichas idolatrías, y castigo de los reos. Mexico.
1892   Relación de las idolatrías y supersticiones y vanas observaciones de los indios del obispado de Oaxaca. Mexico.
1953   Relación auténtica de las idolatrías. . . . In Paso y Troncoso, 1953, 2:337–90.

BANCROFT, HUBERT HOWE
       See Article 19, Appendix A.

BARCIA [CARBALLIDO Y ZÚÑIGA], ANDRÉS GONZÁLEZ DE
1749   Historiadores primitivos de las Indias Occidentales, que juntó, tradujo en parte, y sacó a luz, ilustrados con eruditas notas y copiosos índices, el ill mo. Señor Don Andrés González de Barcia. . . . Madrid.

BARDASANO, JOSÉ
1961   See Díaz del Castillo, 1961.

BARLOW, ROGER
1932   See Enciso, 1932.

BAUDOT, GEORGES
1966   Les antiquités mexicaines du P. Díaz

de la Vega, O.F.M. Melanges de la Casa de Velázquez, 2:283–310.

BAUTISTA, JUAN, ed.
[1601]   Huehuetlahtolli. . . . Santiago Tlatelolco.

BENZONI, GIROLAMO
1565   La historia del mondo nuovo de Girolamo Benzoni. La qual trata del' isole, et mari nuovamente ritrouati et delle nuove citta di lui proprio vedute, per acqua et per terra in quattuordeci anni. Venice.
1857   History of the New World, by Girolamo Benzoni, of Milan. Shewing his travels in America, from A.D. 1541 to 1556, with some particulars of the island of Canary. Now first translated and edited by Rear-Admiral W. H. Smith. Works issued by the Hakluyt Society, 21. London.
1962   La historia del Mondo Nuovo. Photomechanischer Nachdruck der Ausgabe Venedig 1572, Einleitung von Dr. F. Anders. Graz, Austria.
1967   La historia del Mundo Nuevo. Traducción y notas de Marisa Vannini de Gerulewicz; estudio preliminar de León Croizat. Biblioteca de la Academia Nacional de la Historia, 86. Caracas.

BERISTÁIN DE SOUZA, JOSÉ MARIANO
1816–21   Biblioteca hispano americana septentrional; o, Catálogo y noticia de los literatos que o nacidos, o educados, o florecientes en la America Septentrional española, han dado a luz algún escrito, o lo han dejado preparado para la prensa. 3 vols. Mexico.
1947   Biblioteca hispano americana septentrional. . . . 5 vols. in 2. Mexico.

BERLIN, HEINRICH
1957   Las antiguas creencias en San Miguel Solá, Oaxaca. Hamburg.

BERNAL, IGNACIO
1964   See Durán, 1964.

BIBLIOTHECA INDIANA
1958   Viajes y viajeros: Viajes por Norteamérica. Bibliotheca indiana: Libros y fuentes sobre América y Filipinas, 2. Madrid.

BLACK, JOHN
1811   See Humboldt, 1811b.

BLÁQUEZ, ANTONIO
1918   See Santa Cruz, 1918.

BLOM, FRANS
1963   See Weiditz, 1963.

BOTURINI BENADUCCI, LORENZO

1746 Idea de una nueva historia general de la América Septentrional, fundada sobre material copioso de figuras, símbolos, caracteres y geroglíficos, cantares y manuscritos de autores indios ultimamente descubiertos. Madrid.

1870 *See* Muñoz Camargo, 1870.

1871 Idea de una nueva historia general de la América Septentrional. Mexico.

1933 Idea. . . . Facsimile de la edición original de 1746. Collection des textes relatifs aux anciennes civilisations du Mexique et l'Amérique Central, publié sous la direction de Mr. Jean Genet, 2. Paris.

1948 Historia general de la América Septentrional por el caballero Lorenzo Boturini Benaducci, Señor de la Torre y de Hono, Cronista Real en las Indias. Edición, prólogo y notas por Manuel Ballesteros Gaibrois. Documentos inéditos para la historia de España, 6. Madrid.

BRASSEUR DE BOURBOURG, CHARLES ÉTIENNE
See Article 18.

BURRUS, ERNEST J.

1949 *See* Cavo, 1949.

1959 Clavigero and the lost Sigüenza y Góngora manuscripts. *Estudios de Cultura Nahuatl*, 1:59–90.

BUSTAMANTE, CARLOS MARÍA DE

1826 *See* Veytia, 1826.

1831 *See* Villaroel, 1831.

1832 *See* León y Gama, 1832.

1836–38 *See* Cavo, 1836–38.

CADENA, GUILLERMO

1955 *See* Viana, Gallego, and Cadena, 1955.

CALDAS, SEBASTIÁN DE
See Álvarez Alfonso Rosica de Caldas, Sebastián.

CANO, AGUSTÍN

1942 Informe dado al Rey por el Padre Fray Agustín Cano sobre la entrada que por la parte de la Verapaz se hizo al Petén en el año de 1695, y fragmento de una carta al mismo sobre el propio asunto. *Anales de la Sociedad de Geografía e Historia de Guatemala*, 18:65–79.

CANTÓN ROSADO, FRANCISCO

1937 *See* Sánchez de Aguilar, 1937.

CARBIA, RÓMULO D.

1934 La crónica oficial de las Indias Occidentales: Estudio histórico y crítico acerca de la historiografía mayor de Hispano-América en los siglos XVI a XVIII; con una introducción sobre la crónica en Castilla. La Plata, Argentina.

CARRANZA, PEDRO DE

1870 *See* [Guzmán, Nuño Beltrán de,] Relations, 1870.

CARREÑO, ALBERTO MARÍA

1944 *See* Gómez de Cervantes, 1944.

1946 *See* Gemelli Careri, 1946.

CARRERA STAMPA, MANUEL

1945a Algunos aspectos de la Historia de Tlaxcala de Diego Muñoz Camargo. *In* Estudios de historiografía (1945), pp. 91–142.

1945b El "Teatro de la Nueva España en su gentilismo y conquista" de Diego Panes. AGN, *Boletín*, 16:399–428.

1955 *See* Guzmán, 1955.

1959 Fuentes para el estudio de la historia indígena. In *Esplendor del México antiguo*, 2:1109–96, edited by Carmen Cook de Leonard. 2 vols. Mexico.

CARROCERA, BUENAVENTURA DE

1958–59 *See* Ajofrín, 1958–59.

CASTAÑEDA, CARLOS EDUARDO

1953 *See* Cervantes de Salazar, 1953.

CASTAÑEDA, JOSÉ LUCIANO

1830 *See* Dupaix, 1830a.

1834 *See* Dupaix, 1834.

1969 *See* Dupaix, 1969.

CASTAÑEDA Y ALCOVER, VICENTE

1958–59 *See* Ajofrín, 1958–59.

CAVAZOS GARZA, ISRAEL

1961 *See* León, Chapa, and Sánchez de Zamora, 1961.

CAVO, ANDRÉS

1836–38 Los tres siglos de México durante el gobierno español, hasta la entrada del Ejército Trigarante, obra escrita en Roma por el Padre Andrés Cavo de la Compañía de Jesús. Publícala con notas y suplemento, el Lic. Carlos María Bustamante. . . . 4 vols. Mexico. [The third and fourth volumes of this edition are Bustamante's *Suplemento a la Historia de los tres siglos de México* . . . , in which Bustamante continued Cavo's chronicle down to 1821.]

1949 Historia de México. Paleografiada del texto original y anotada por el P. Ernesto J. Burrus, S.J., con un prólogo del P. Mariano Cuevas, S.J.

CERVANTES DE SALAZAR, FRANCISCO

1554 Francisci Cervantis Salazari Toletani,

ad Ludovici Vivis Valentini exercitationem, aliquot Dialogi. Mexico.

1914 Crónica de la Nueva España que escribió el Dr. D. Francisco Cervantes de Salazar, cronista de la Imperial Ciudad de México. [Prologue by M. Magallón.] Hispanic Society of America. Madrid.

1914–36 Crónica de Nueva España, escrita por el doctor y maestro Francisco Cervantes de Salazar, cronista de la Ciudad de México. 3 vols. *Papeles de la Nueva España*, compilados y publicados por Francisco del Paso y Troncoso, 3d ser., *Historia*, 1–3. Madrid and Mexico.

1953 Life in the imperial and loyal City of Mexico in New Spain and the royal and pontifical University of Mexico as described in the dialogues for the study of the Latin language prepared by Francisco Cervantes de Salazar for use in his classes and printed in 1554 by Juan Pablos. Now published in facsimile with a translation by Minnie Lee Barrett Shepard and an introduction and notes by Carlos Eduardo Castañeda. Austin, Tex.

CERWIN, HERBERT
1963 Bernal Díaz, historian of the conquest. Norman, Okla.

CHAMBERLAIN, ROBERT S.
1948 *See* González, Blas, 1948.

CHAMPLAIN, SAMUEL
1859 Narrative of a voyage to the West Indies and Mexico in the years 1599–1602 . . . by Samuel Champlain. Translated from the original and unpublished manuscript, with a biographical notice and notes by Alice Wilmere. Edited by Norton Shaw. Works issued by the Hakluyt Society, 23. London.

1870 Bref discours des choses plus remarquables que Samuel Champlain de Brovage a reconneues aux Indes Occidentales au voyage qu'il en a faict en icelles en l'année mil vc.iiijxxxix & en l'année mil vjc.j. comme ensuit. Quebec.

CHAPA, JUAN BAUTISTA
1909 *See* León, Alonso de, 1909.
1961 *See* León, Alonso de, 1961.

CHAVERO, ALFREDO
1892 *See* Muñoz Camargo, 1892.
1947 *See* Muñoz Camargo, 1947.

CHEVALIER, FRANÇOIS
1946 *See* Arregui, 1946.

CHILTON, JOHN
1589 [1965] A notable discourse of Master John Chilton, touching the people, manners, mines, cities, riches, forces, and other memorable things of the West Indies, seen and noted by himself in the time of his travels, continued in those parts the space of 17 or 18 years. *In* Hakluyt, 1589 [1965], pp. 587–94.

CHIPMAN, DONALD E.
1967 Nuño de Guzmán and the Province of Pánuco in New Spain, 1518–1533. Glendale, Calif.

CHURCHILL, AWNSHAM
1704 *See* Gemelli Careri, 1704.

CLARK, CHARLES UPSON
1942 *See* Vázquez de Espinosa, 1942.
1948 *See* Vázquez de Espinosa, 1948.

CLAVIJERO, FRANCISCO JAVIER
See Article 17.

CLINE, HOWARD F.
1963 *See* Fuentes, 1963.
1969 Hernando Cortés and the Aztec Indians in Spain. *Quarterly Journal of the Library of Congress*, 26:70–90.

COBO, BERNABÉ
1890–95 Historia del Nuevo Mundo por el P. Bernabé Cobo . . . , publicada por primera vez con notas y otras ilustraciones de Marcos Jiménez de la Espada. 4 vols. Seville.

1944 Cartas del P. Bernabé Cobo, de la Compañía de Jesús, escritas a un compañero suyo residente en el Perú. *In* Vázquez de Espinosa, 1944, pp. 195–214.

1956 Obras del P. Bernabé Cobo de la Compañía de Jesús. Estudio preliminar y edición del P. Francisco Mateos de la misma Compañia. 2 vols. Biblioteca Autores Españoles, 91, 92. Madrid.

CODEX RAMÍREZ
1878 *See* Tovar, 1878.
1944 *See* Tovar, 1944.

CODY, W. F.
1953 An index to the periodicals published by José Antonio Alzate y Ramírez. HAHR, 33:442–75.

COHEN, J. M.
1963 *See* Diáz del Castillo, 1963.

COLUMBUS, CHRISTOPHER
1505 Copia de la Lettera per Columbo mandata a Serenissimi Re et Regina

di Spagna: de le insule et luoghi per lui trouate. Venice.

1825 Carta que escribió D. Cristobal Colón, Virey y Almirante de las Indias, a los Cristianísimos y muy poderosos Rey y Reina de España, nuestros señores, en que les notifica cuanto le ha acontecido en su viage; y las tierras, provincias, ciudades, ríos y otras cosas maravillosas, y donde hay minas de oro en mucha cantidad, y otras cosas de gran riqueza y valor. *In* Navarrete, 1825–37, 1:296–312.

1894 Copia de la carta que escrivio don Cristóval Colón, virrey y almirante de las Indias, á los cristianíssimos i mui poderosos rei i reina de España. . . . *In* Reale Commissione Colombiana, 1892–96, pt. 1, vol. 2, pp. 174–205.

1961 Four Voyages to the New World. Letters and selected documents. Bilingual edition. Translated and edited by R. H. Major. Introduction by John E. Fagg. New York. [This text is a paperback reprint of the translation published by the Hakluyt Society, 1847.]

COLUMBUS, FERDINAND

1571 Historie Del S. D. Fernando Colombo; Nelle quali s' ha particolari, et vera relatione della vita, et de' fatti dell' Ammiraglio D. Christoforo Colombo, suo padre: Et dello scoprimento, ch' egli fece dell' Indie Occidentali, dette Mondo Nvovo; hora possedute dal Sereniss. Re Catolico: Nuouamente di lingua Spagnuola tradotte nell' Italiana dal S. Alfonso Vlloa. Venice.

1749 La historia de D. Fernando Colón en la qual se da particular, y verdadera relación de la vida, y hechos de el almirante D. Cristóbal Colón, su padre, y del descubrimiento de las Indias Occidentales, llamadas Nuevo Mundo, que pertenece al serenísimo rey de España, que traduxo de español en italiano Alonso de Ulloa; y ahora por no parecer el original español, sacada del traslado italiano. *In* Barcia, 1749, 1:1–128 [i.e., 134].

1947 Vida del Almirante Don Cristóbal Colón, escrita por su hijo Hernando Colón. Edición, prólogo y notas de Ramón Iglesia. Mexico and Buenos Aires.

1959 The life of the Admiral Christopher Columbus by his son Ferdinand. Translated and annotated by Benjamin Keen. New Brunswick, N. J.

CÓRDOBA, MATÍAS DE

1798 Utilidades de que todos los indios y ladinos se vistan y calcen a la española y medios de conseguirlo sin violencia, coacción, ni mandato. Memoria premiada por la Real Sociedad Económica de Guatemala, el 13 de diciembre de 1797. Guatemala.

1937 Utilidades. . . . *Anales de la Sociedad de Geografía e Historia de Guatemala*, 14:211–22.

CORTÉS, HERNANDO

1852 Cartas de relación de Fernando Cortés sobre el descubrimiento y conquista de la Nueva España. *In* Vedia, 1852, 1:1–153. Madrid.

1908 Letters of Cortés. The Five Letters of Relation from Fernando Cortés to the Emperor Charles V. Translated, and edited, with a biographical introduction and notes compiled from original sources by Francis Augustus MacNutt. New York and London.

1928 Hernando Cortés: Five Letters, 1519–1526. Translated by J. Bayard Morris, with an introduction. London. [Republished, New York, 1962.]

1960 Cartas de Relación de la conquista de la Nueva España escritas por Hernán Cortés al Emperador Carlos V, y otros documentos relativos a la conquista, años de 1519–1527. Codex Vindobonensis S. N. 1600. Geleitwort: Josef Stummvoll. Introduction and bibliography by Charles Gibson. Kodikologische Beschreibung: Franz Unterkircher. Graz, Austria.

1963 Cartas y documentos. Introducción de Mario Hernández Sánchez-Barba. Mexico.

CORTÉS Y LARRAZ, PEDRO

1958 Descripción geográfico-moral de la diócesis de Goathemala hecha por su arzobispo, el Illmo. Sor. Don Pedro Cortés y Larraza del consejo de S.M. en el tiempo que la visitó y fue desde el día 3 de noviembre de 1768 hasta el día 1o de julio de 1769, desde el día 22 de noviembre de 1769 hasta el día 9 de febrero de 1770, y desde el día 6 de junio de 1770 hasta el día 29 de agosto del dho. 1770. Prólogo del Licenciado Don Adrián Recinos. Vol. 1. Guatemala.

COVEY, CYCLONE
1961 See Núñez Cabeza de Vaca, 1961.

CROIZAT, LEÓN
1967 See Benzoni, 1967.

CUEVAS, MARIANO
1924 See Obregón, 1924.
1944 See Vázquez de Espinosa, 1944.
1949 See Cavo, 1949.

DELGADO, JAIME
1960 See Sigüenza y Góngora, 1960.

DES MARCHES
1522? [1919] Des marches, iles et pays trouvés et conquit par les capitaines du tres illustre . . . Charles Ve. Antwerp. [Americana series: photostat reproductions by the Massachusetts Historical Society, no. 5. Boston, 1919.]

DÍAZ, JUAN
1520 Itinerario de larmata del re catholico in India uerso la isole de Iuchathan del anno. M.D.XVIII. allaqual fu presidēte & capitan general Ioan de Grisalua elqual e facto per el capellano maggior de dicta armata a sua alteza. In Varthema, 1520, pp. 78–100.

1858 Itinerario de la armada del Rey Católico a la isla de Yucatán, en la India, el año 1518, en la que fue por comandante y capitán general Juan de Grijalva, escrito para Su Alteza por el capellán mayor de la dicha armada. In García Icazbalceta, 1858–66, 1:281–307.

1963a Itinerario de Juan de Grijalva. In Yáñez, 1963, pp. 3–23.

1963b The chronicle of Juan Díaz. In Fuentes, 1963, pp. 5–16.

DÍAZ DE LA VEGA, JOSÉ
See Alcina Franch, 1957; Baudot, 1966.

DÍAZ DEL CASTILLO, BERNAL
1632 Historia verdadera de la conquista de la Nueva España escrita por el Capitán Bernal Díaz del Castillo, uno de sus conquistadores. Sacada a luz por el P. M. Fr. Alonso Remón, predicador y coronista general de Orden de Nuestra Señora de la Merced Redención de Cautivos. Madrid.

1800 The true history of the conquest of Mexico, by Captain Bernal Díaz del Castillo, one of the conquerors. Written in the year 1568. . . . Translated from the original Spanish by Maurice Keatinge. London.

1904 Historia verdadera de la conquista de la Nueva España por Bernal Díaz del Castillo, uno de sus conquistadores. Única edición hecha según el códice autógrafo. La publica Genaro García. 2 vols. Mexico.

1908–16 The true history of the conquest of New Spain. By Bernal Díaz del Castillo, one of its conquerors. From the only exact copy made of the original manuscript. Edited and published in Mexico by Genaro García. Translated into English, with introduction and notes, by Alfred Percival Maudslay. 5 vols. Works issued by the Hakluyt Society, 2d series, 23–25, 30, 40. London.

1939 Historia verdadera de la conquista de la Nueva España. Introducción y notas por Joaquín Ramírez Cabañas. 3 vols. Mexico.

1940 Historia verdadera de la conquista de la Nueva España por Bernal Díaz del Castillo. Edición crítica. Vol. 1. Madrid.

1961 Historia verdadera de la conquista de la Nueva España escrita por el Capitán Bernal Díaz del Castillo, uno de sus conquistadores; ahora añadida con las estampas de José Bardasano y noticias bibliográficas. [Introducción, catálogos, noticias bibliográficas e índices elaborados por Federico Gómez de Orozco . . . , Guadalupe Pérez San Vicente . . . , y Carlos Saban Bergamín.] Mexico.

1963 The conquest of New Spain. Translated with an introduction by J. M. Cohen. The Penguin Classics. Baltimore. [Abridged version translated from the Ramírez Cabañas edition.]

DÍAZ-THOMÉ, JORGE HUGO
1945 Francisco Cervantes de Salazar y su crónica de la conquista de la Nueva España. In Estudios de Historiografía, 1945, pp. 15–47.

DICCIONARIO PORRÚA
1964 Diccionario Porrúa de historia, biografía y geografía de México. Mexico.

DIEZ DE LA CALLE, JUAN
1646 Memorial y noticias sacras y reales del imperio de las Indias Occidentales, al muy católico . . . rey de

las Españas . . . D. Felipe IV. N.S. en su real y supremo Consejo de las Indias, Cámara y Junta de Guerra . . . comprende lo eclesiástico, secular, político y militar, que por su secretaría de la Nueva España se provee: presidios, gente, y costas, valor de las encomiendas de indios, y otras cosas curiosas, necesarias y dignas de saberse. Madrid.

1932 Memorial y noticias sacras y reales de las Indias Occidentales. 2d ed. Mexico.

DIEZ NAVARRO, LUIS
1939 Informe sobre la Provincia de Costa Rica presentado por el Ingeniero Don Luis Diez Navarro al Capitán General de Guatemala Don Tomás de Rivera y Santa Cruz, año de 1744. *Revista de los Archivos Nacionales*, 3:579–600. Costa Rica.

DISCURSO, 1766
1938 Discurso sobre la constitución de las Provincias de Yucatán y Campeche, 1766. Documentos para la historia de Yucatán, vol. 3. Merida, Yucatan.

DOCUMENTOS INÉDITOS
1864–84 Colección de documentos inéditos relativos al descubrimiento, conquista y organización de las antiguas posesiones españolas de América y Oceanía, sacados de los archivos del Reino, y muy especialmente del de Indias. 42 vols. Madrid.

DORANTES DE CARRANZA, BALTASAR
1902 Sumaria relación de las cosas de la Nueva España con noticia individual de los descendientes legítimos de los conquistadores y primeros pobladores españoles por Baltasar Dorantes de Carranza. La publica por primera vez el Museo Nacional de México, paleografiada del original por el Sr. D. José María de Ágreda y Sánchez. Mexico.

DUPAIX, GUILLERMO
1830a Monuments of New Spain. From the original drawings executed by order of the king of Spain. *In* Kingsborough, 1830–48, vol. 4.
1830b Viages de Guillermo Dupaix sobre las antigüedades mejicanos. *In* Kingsborough, 1830–48, 5: 207–343.
1831 Monuments of New Spain. *In* Kingsborough, 1830–48, 6:421–86.
1834 Antiquités mexicaines. Relation des trois expéditions du capitaine Dupaix, ordonnées en 1805, 1806, et 1807, pour la recherche des antiquités du pays, notamment celles de Mitla et de Palenque, accompagnée des dessins de Castañeda . . . et de une carte du pays exploré. . . . 2 vols. Paris.

1969 Expediciones acerca de los antiguos monumentos de la Nueva España. Edición, introducción y notas por José Alcina Franch. Colección Chimalistac de libros y documentos acerca de la Nueva España, 27–28. 2 vols. Madrid.

DURÁN, DIEGO
1867–80 Historia de las Indias de Nueva-España y islas de Tierra Firme por el Padre Fray Diego Durán, religioso de la Orden de Predicadores (escritor del siglo XVI). La publica con un atlas de estampas, notas e ilustraciones José F. Ramírez. . . . 2 vols. and atlas. Mexico. [Reprinted, Mexico, 1951, 1965.]

1964 The Aztecs: The history of the Indies of New Spain by Fray Diego Durán. Translated, with notes, by Doris Heyden and Fernando Horcasitas. Introduction by Ignacio Bernal. New York.

1967 Historia de las Indias de Nueva España e islas de la Tierra Firme. Edited by Angel María Garibay K. 2 vols. Mexico.

1971 Book of the gods and rites and the ancient calendar. Translated and edited by Fernando Horcasitas and Doris Heyden. Norman, Okla.

EGUIARA Y EGUREN, JUAN JOSÉ DE
1755 Bibliotheca Mexicana, sive eruditorum historia virorum, qui in America Boreali nati, vel alibi geniti, in ipsam domicilio aut studiis asciti, quavis lingua scripto aliquid tradiderunt: Eorum praesertim qui pro Fide Catholica et pietate amplianda fovendaque egregie factis et quibusvis scriptis floruere editis aut ineditis. Tomus primus, exhibens litteras A B C. Mexico.

1944 Prólogos a la Biblioteca mexicana. Nota preliminar por Federico Gómez de Orozco. Versión española anotada, con un estudio biográfico y la bibliografía del autor por Agustín Millares Carlo. Biblioteca americana de obras latinas (ediciones bilingues). Mexico.

ELORZA Y RADA, FRANCISCO DE

1714 Nobiliario de el Valle de la Valdorba, ilustrada con los escudos de armas de sus palacios y casas nobles. Con el extracto de la conquista de el Ytza en la Nueva España por el conde de Lizarraga-Vengoa, natural del Valle. Expresión del significado de toda suerte de armas y sus empresas. Pamplona.

1930 A narrative of the conquest of the province of the Ytzas in New Spain, performed by Captain Don Martín de Ursúa y Arizmendi, count of Lizarraga Vengoa, and described by Dr. Don Francisco de Elorza y Rada, abbot of Barasoaya, in his Nobiliario de el Valle de la Valdorba, published at Pamplona in 1714, now first translated into English and accompanied by a facsimile of the original edition, the translator being Philip Ainsworth Means. Paris.

1943 Conde de Lizarraga-Bengoa: Conquista del Ytza en la Nueva España. Publicada de la edición de 1714 por Vicente Fontavella. Valencia.

ENCICLOPEDIA UNIVERSAL

1907?–30 Enciclopedia universal ilustrada europeo-americana. 70 vols. in 72. Bilboa, Madrid, Barcelona.

ENCISO, MARTÍN FERNÁNDEZ DE

1519 Suma de geografía que trata de todas las partidas y provincias del mundo, en especial de las Indias, y trata largamente del arte del marear, juntamente con la espera en romance con el regimiento del sol y del norte, nuevamente hecha. Seville.

1932 A brief summe of geographie, by Roger Barlow. Edited with an introduction and notes by E. G. R. Taylor. . . . Works issued for the Hakluyt Society, 2d ser., no. 69. London.

1948 Suma de geografía del Bachiller Martín Fernández de Enciso. Madrid.

ESCALONA RAMOS, ALBERTO

1947 See Muñoz Camargo, 1947.

ESTADO Y DESCRIPCIÓN

1945 Estado y descripción de la Provincia de Sonora, 1730. Prólogo y notas de Francisco González de Cossío. AGN, Boletín, 16:587–636, map.

ESTEVE BARBA, FRANCISCO

1964 Historiografía indiana. Madrid.

ESTRADA, GENARO

1936 See Ajofrín, 1936.

1937 See Villaroel, 1937.

ESTUDIOS DE HISTORIOGRAFÍA

1945 Estudios de historiografía de la Nueva España por Hugo Díaz-Thomé, Fernando Sandoval, Manuel Carrera Stampa, Carlos Bosch García, Ernesto de la Torre, Enriqueta López Lira, Julio Le Riverend Brusone, con una introducción de Ramón Iglesia. Mexico.

EZQUERRA, RAMÓN

1962 La crítica española sobre América en el siglo XVIII. Revista de Indias, 22:159–287.

FAGG, JOHN E.

1961 See Columbus, Christopher, 1961.

FERIA, PEDRO DE

1899 Relación que hace el obispo de Chiapa (Fray Pedro de Feria) sobre la reincidencia en sus idolatrías de los indios de aquel país después de treinta años de cristianos. Anales de Museo Nacional de México, 6 (1900): 481–87.

1953 Relación que hace el obispo de Chiapa. . . . In Paso y Troncoso, 1953, pp. 380–92.

FERNÁNDEZ, ALONSO

1611 Historia eclesiástica de nuestros tiempos, que es compendio de los excelentes frutos que en ellos el estado eclesiástico y sagradas religiones han hecho y hacen en la conversión de idolatras y reducción de herejes, y de los ilustres martirios de varones apostólicos, que en estas heróicas empresas han padecido. Toledo.

FERNÁNDEZ DEL CASTILLO, FRANCISCO

1926 See Mange, 1926.

FERNÁNDEZ DE NAVARRETE, MARTÍN

See Navarrete, Martín Fernández de.

FERNÁNDEZ GUARDIA, RICARDO

1908 See Vázquez de Coronado, 1908.

FLORES SALINAS, BERTA

1964 México visto por algunos de sus viajeros (siglos XVI y XVII). Mexico.

FONTAVELLA, VICENTE

1943 See Elorza y Rada, 1943.

FRANTZIUS, A. VON

1881 See García del Palacio, 1881.

FUENSANTA DEL VALLE, MARQUÉS DE LA

1875–76 See Las Casas, Bartolomé de, 1875–76.

FUENTES, PATRICIA DE, comp.
1963 The conquistadors: First-person accounts of the conquest of Mexico. Edited and translated by Patricia de Fuentes. Preface by Howard F. Cline.

FUENTES Y GUZMÁN, FRANCISCO ANTONIO DE
1882 Historia de Guatemala, o Recordación florida, escrita en el siglo XVII por el Capitán C. Francisco Antonio de Fuentes y Guzmán, natural, vecino y regidor perpetuo de la ciudad de Guatemala, que publica por primera vez con notas e ilustraciones D. Justo Zaragoza. 2 vols. Madrid.
1932–33 Recordación florida: Discurso historial y demostración natural, material, militar y política del Reyno de Guatemala. Escríbela el cronista del mismo reyno Capitán D. Francisco Antonio de Fuentes y Guzmán. . . . Edición conforme al códice del siglo XVII que original se conserva en el Archivo de la Municipalidad de Guatemala. Prólogo del Licenciado J. Antonio Villacorta C. 3 vols. Guatemala.
1969– Obras históricas de Francisco Antonio de Fuentes y Guzmán. Edición y estudio preliminar de Carmelo Sáenz de Santa María. Biblioteca de Autores Españoles, 230. Madrid.

GAGE, THOMAS
1648 The English-American, his travail by sea and land: Or, A new survey of the West-India's, containing a journall of three thousand and three hundred miles within the main land of America . . . with a grammar, or some few rudiments of the Indian tongue, called Poconchi, or Pocoman. By the true and painful endeavors of Thomas Gage. London.
1958 Thomas Gage's travels in the New World. Edited and with an introduction by J. Eric S. Thompson. Norman, Okla.

GALLEGO, LUCAS
1955 See Viana, Gallego, and Cadena, 1955.

GALVIN, SEÁN
1972 See O'Crowley y O'Donnell, 1972.

GARCES G., JORGE A.
1964–65 See Alcedo y Bexarano, 1964–65.

GARCÍA, GENARO
1904 See Díaz del Castillo, 1904.
1907 Tumultos y rebeliones acaecidos en México. Documentos inéditos o muy raros para la historia de México, 10. Mexico.

GARCÍA, GREGORIO
1607 Origen de los indios de el Nuevo Mundo e Indias Occidentales. Averiguado con discurso de opiniones por el padre presentado Fray Gregorio García de la Orden de Predicadores. Trátanse en este libro varias cosas y puntos curiosos, tocantes a diversas ciencias y facultades, con que se hace varia historia, de mucho gusto para el ingenio y entendimiento de hombres agudos y curiosos. Valencia.
1625 Historia eclesiástica seglar de la India Oriental y Occidental y predicación del Santo Evangelio en ella por los apóstoles. Veriguada por el P. presentado Fr. Gregorio García de la Orden de Predicadores, en que hallará el lector versado en letras, discursos que deleiten su entendimiento y el curioso romancista cosas de mucho gusto, piedad y devoción particularmente desde el segundo libro de este tratado. Baeza.
1729 Origen de los indios. . . . Segunda impresión. Enmendada y añadida de algunas opiniones o cosas notables en mayor prueba de lo que contiene, con tres tablas muy puntuales de los capítulos, de las materias, y autores que las tratan. Madrid.

GARCÍA BARRAGÁN MARTÍNEZ, ELISA
1965 La conciencia mexicana en Suárez de Peralta a través de su crónica. In Noticias históricas de la Nueva España. Mexico.

GARCÍA BRAVO, ALONSO
1956 Información de méritos y servicios de Alonso García Bravo, alarife que trazó la ciudad de México. Introducción de Manuel Toussaint. UNAM, Instituto de Investigaciones Estéticas, Estudios y fuentes del arte in México, 3. Mexico.

GARCÍA DE PALACIO, DIEGO
1860 Carta dirigida al Rey de España por el Licenciado Dr. Don Diego García del Palacio, oidor de la Real Audiencia de Guatemala, año 1576. Being a description of the ancient provinces of Guazacapan, Izalco, Cuscatlan, and Chiquimula, in the Audiencia of Guatemala: With an account of the languages, customs and religion of

their aboriginal inhabitants, and a description of the ruins of Copan. Collection of Rare and Original Documents and Relations concerning the Discovery and Conquest of America. . . . Published in the original with translations, illustrative notes, maps, and biographical sketches, by E. G. Squier, 1. New York.

1866 Relación hecha por el Licenciado Palacio al Rey D. Felipe II, en la que describe la provincia de Guatemala, las costumbres de los indios y otras cosas notables. [Guatemala, 1576.] DII, 6:5–40.

1881 San Salvador y Honduras el año 1576. Informe oficial del Licenciado Diego García del Palacio al Rey de España sobre las provincias Centro Americanas de San Salvador el año de 1576. Con prefacio y notas del Dr. A. von Frantzius de Heidelberg, traducidas del alemán por Don Manuel Carazo. In Colección de documentos para la historia de Costa-Rica, publicados por el Lic. Don León Fernandez (1881–1907), 1:i–vi, 1–52.

GARCÍA GRANADOS, RAFAEL
1934 See Libro viejo, 1934.
1949 See Rico González, 1949.

GARCÍA ICAZBALCETA, JOAQUÍN
1858–66 Colección de documentos para la historia de México. 2 vols. Mexico.
1886–92 Nueva colección de documentos para la historia de México. 5 vols. Mexico.
1927 Catálogo de la colección de manuscritos relativos a la historia de América formado por Joaquín García Icazbalceta, anotado y adicionado por Federico Gómez de Orozco. Mexico.

GARCÍA MORALES, JUSTO
1945 See Núñez Cabeza de Vaca, 1945.
1960 See Núñez Cabeza de Vaca, 1960.

GARCÍA PIMENTEL, JOAQUÍN
1946 See Hernández, 1946.

GARCÍA PIMENTEL, LUIS, ed.
1904 Relación de los obispados de Tlaxcala, Michoacán, Oaxaca y otros lugares en el siglo XVI. Manuscrito de la colección del Señor Don Joaquín García Icazbalceta. Publícalo por primera vez su hijo Luis García Pimentel. Documentos históricos de México, 2. Mexico.

GARIBAY K., ÁNGEL MARÍA
1964 Los historiadores del México antiguo en el virreinato de la Nueva España. Cuadernos americanos, 132:129–47.
1967 See Durán, 1967.

GEMELLI CARERI, GIOVANNI FRANCESCO
1699–1700 Giro del mondo. 6 vols. Naples.
1704 A voyage round the world, by Dr. John Francis Gemelli Careri. . . . Written originally in Italian, translated into English. In Awnsham Churchill, A collection of voyages and travels, 4. London.
1946 Las cosas más considerables vistas en la Nueva España por el doctor Juan Francisco Gemelli Careri. Traducción de José María de Ágreda y Sánchez, revisada por los editores a la vista de la edición original. Prólogo de Alberto María Carreño. Mexico.
1955 Viaje a la Nueva España. Traducido por José María Ágreda y Sánchez. Introducción de Fernando B. Sandoval. 2 vols. Mexico.

GIBSON, CHARLES
1951 See Tovar, 1951.
1952 Tlaxcala in the sixteenth century. Yale Historical Publications, Miscellany, 66. New Haven.
1960 See Cortés, 1960.

GIMÉNEZ FERNÁNDEZ, MANUEL
1954 See Hanke and Giménez Fernández, 1954.
1965 See Las Casas, Bartolomé de, 1965.

GODOY, DIEGO
1525 See Alvarado, 1525.
1852 Relación hecha por Diego Godoy a Hernando Cortés, en que trata del descubrimiento de diversas ciudades y provincias, y guerra que tuvo con los indios, y su modo de pelear; de la provincia de Chamula, de los caminos difíciles y peligrosos, y repartimiento que hizo de los pueblos. In Vedia, 1852–53, 1:465–70.

GÓMARA, FRANCISCO LÓPEZ DE
See López de Gómara, Francisco.

GÓMEZ DE CERVANTES, GONZALO
1944 La vida económica y social de Nueva España al finalizar el siglo XVI. Prólogo y notas de Alberto María Carreño. Mexico.

GÓMEZ DE OROZCO, FEDERICO
1949 See Suárez de Peralta, 1949.
1950 See Palafox y Mendoza, 1950.
1954 See Aguilar, 1954.
1961 See Díaz del Castillo, 1961.

González, Blas
1948 Probanza de méritos y servicios of Blas González, conquistador of Yucatán. Robert S. Chamberlain, ed. *HAHR*, 28:526–36.

González, J. Natalicio
1945–46 *See* Navarrete, 1945–46.

González Dávila, Gil (d. 1526)
1883 El Capitán Gil González Dávila a S. M. el Emperador Carlos V, sobre su expedición a Nicaragua, Santo Domingo, 6 de marzo de 1524. *In* Peralta, 1883, pp. 3–26.

González Dávila, Gil (d. 1658)
1649–55 Teatro eclesiástico de la primitiva iglesia de las Indias Occidentales, vidas de sus arzobispos, obispos y cosas memorables de sus sedes. 2 vols. Madrid.
1959 Teatro eclesiástico de la primitiva iglesia de la Nueva España en las Indias Occidentales. 2 vols. Madrid.

González de Barcia, Andrés
1729 *See* García, Gregorio, 1729.
1737–38 *See* León Pinelo, 1737–38.

González de Cossío, Francisco
1945 *See* Estado y descripción, 1945.
1948 *See* Martínez, 1948.
1952 *See* Villaseñor y Sánchez, 1952.

González de Mendoza, Juan
1585 Historia de las cosas mas notables, ritos y costumbres, del gran reino de la China, sabidas así por los libros de los mismos Chinas, como por relación de religiosos y otras personas que han estado en el dicho reino. Hecha y ordenada por el muy R. P. maestro Fr. Juan González de Mendoza. Con un itinerario del Nuevo Mundo. Rome.
1853–54 The history of the great and mighty kingdom of China and the situation thereof. Compiled by the Padre Juan González de Mendoza, and now reprinted from the early translation of R. Parke. Edited by Sir George T. Staunton, with an introduction by R. H. Major. 2 vols. Works issued by the Hakluyt Society, 14–15. London.

González Flores, Enrique
1952 *See* O'Conor, 1952.

González Obregón, Luis
1903 *See* Las Casas, Gonzalo de, 1903.

Granados y Gálvez, José Joaquín
1778 Tardes americanas: Gobierno gentil y católico: Breve y particular noticia de toda la historia indiana: Sucesos, casos notables, y cosas ignoradas, desde la entrada de la gran nación tulteca a esta tierra de Anahuac hasta los presentes tiempos. Trabajadas por un indio y un español. Mexico.

Grimston, Edward
1880 *See* Acosta, 1880.

Guadalajara, Tomás de (?)
1950 Historia de la tercera rebelión tarahumara. Roberto Ramos, ed. Chihuahua.

Guerrero, Raul
1949 Índice clasificado de la Relación breve y verdadera de algunas cosas de las muchas que sucedieron al Padre Fray Alonso Ponce en las provincias de la Nueva España. Mexico.

Guibelalde, Pilar
1954 *See* López de Gómara, 1954.

Gurría Lacroix, Jorge
1953 *See* Vázquez de Tapia, 1953.
1964 Trabajos sobre historia mexicana. Mexico.

Gutiérrez, José Ireneo
1924 *See* Mota Padilla, 1924.

Guzmán, Nuño Beltrán de
1870 Carta a Su Magestad del presidente de la audiencia de Méjico, Nuño de Guzmán, en que refiere la jornada que hizo a Mechuacan, a conquistar la provincia de los Tebles-Chichimecas, que confina con Nueva España (8 de Julio de 1530). DII, 13:356–93.
1940 Memoria de los servicios que había hecho Nuño de Guzmán desde que fue nombrado gobernador de Pánuco en 1525. *In* Paso y Troncoso, 1939–42, 14:166–94.
1955 Memoria de los servicios. . . . Estudio y notas por Manuel Carrera Stampa. Mexico.

[Guzmán, Nuño Beltrán de], Relations of his expedition into New Galicia
1866 [Relations of Juan de Sámano and García del Pilar, and four Anonymous Relations.] *In* García Icazbalceta, 1858–66, 2:248–306, 449–83.
1870 [Relations of Pedro de Carranza and Gonzalo López.] DII, 14:347–73, 411–63.
1955 Apéndices. *In* Guzmán, 1955, pp. 93–193. [Includes the four Anonymous Relations and the Relation of García del Pilar.]
1963a Crónicas de la conquista del Reino

de Nueva Galicia en territorio de la Nueva España. José Luis Razo Zaragoza, ed. Dirección y dibujos de José Parres Arias. Guadalajara.

1963b *See* Pilar, 1963.

HAKLUYT, RICHARD
1589 The principal navigations, voyages and discoveries of the English nation, made by sea or land, to the most remote and farthest distant quarters of the earth at any time within the compass of these 1500 years. London.

1965 [Facsimile reproduction of the preceding entry.] Hakluyt Society, Extra series, 39. Cambridge, Mass. [Includes an introduction by David Beers Quinn and Raleigh Ashlin Skelton and a new index by Alison Quinn.]

HALLENBECK, CLEVE
1940 Álvar Núñez Cabeza de Vaca: The journey and route of the first European to cross the continent of North America. Glendale, Calif.

1949 *See* Niza, 1949.

HAMMOND, GEORGE P.
1928 *See* Obregón, 1928.

HAMPE, THEODOR
1927 *See* Weiditz, 1927.

HANDBOOK OF LATIN AMERICAN STUDIES
1936– A selective and annotated guide to recent publications. Prepared in the Hispanic Foundation, Library of Congress. 33 vols. to date. Cambridge, Mass., and Gainesville, Fla.

HANKE, LEWIS
1951 *See* Las Casas, Bartolomé de, 1951.
·1959 Aristotle and the American Indians: A study of race prejudice in the modern world. Chicago.
1965 *See* Las Casas, Bartolomé de, 1965.

—— AND MANUEL GIMÉNEZ FERNÁNDEZ
1954 Bartolomé de las Casas, 1474–1566: Bibliografía crítica y cuerpo de materiales para el estudio de su vida, escritos, actuación y polémicas que suscitaron durante cuatro siglos. Santiago de Chile.

HAWKES, HENRY
1589 [1965] A relation of the commodities of Nova Hispania, and the manners of the inhabitants, written by Henry Hawkes, merchant which lived 5 years in the said country, and drew the same at the request of M. Richard Hakluyt Esquire of Eiton in the county of Hereford, 1562. *In* Hakluyt, 1589 [1965], 545–53.

HERNÁNDEZ, FRANCISCO
1635 De partibus septuaginta octo maximi templi Mexicani, fartis, effuso sanguine, aliis ministeriis, generibus officiorum, votis, iure iurando, hymnis, ac feminis que templo inserviebant. Liber unus. *In* Nieremberg, 1635, pp. 142–50.

1649 Rerum medicarum Novae Hispaniae thesaurus seu plantarum, animalium, mineralium mexicanorum historia ex Francisci Hernandez Novi Orbis medici primarii relationibus in ipsa Mexicana Urbe conscriptis, a Nardo Antonio Recchi . . . iussu Philippi II Hisp[aniarum] Ind[iarum] etc. Regis collecta ac in ordinem digesta, a Ioanne Terrentio Lynceo . . . notis illustrata. Rome.

1790 Francisci Hernandi, medici atque historici Philippi II, Hisp. et Indiar. Regis, et totius orbis Archiatri, opera, cum edita tum inedita, ad autographi fidem et integritatem expressa. . . . 3 vols. Madrid.

1926 De antiquitatibus Novae Hispaniae, authore Francisco Hernando, medico et historico Philippi IIi. et Indiarum omnium medico primario; Códice de la Real Academia de la Historia en Madrid. Edición facsimilar. Mexico. [Also in this volume: De expugnatione Novae Hispaniae, liber unus (fols. 138r–169r).]

1946 Antigüedades de la Nueva España. Traducción del latín y notas por don Joaquín García Pimentel. Obra póstuma. Mexico. [Also in this volume: Libro de la conquista de la Nueva España (pp. 191–226).]

1959 Obras completas. Vol. 1: Germán Somolinos d'Ardois. Vida y obra de Francisco Hernández. Precedida de: España y Nueva España en la época de Filipe II, por José Miranda. Vols. 2–3: Historia natural de Nueva España. Traducción del latín de José Rojo Navarro. Vol. 4: C. Plinius Secundus. Historia natural. Trasladada y anotada por Francisco Hernández. Mexico.

HERNÁNDEZ LUNA, JUAN
1953 El iniciador de la historia de ideas en México. *Filosofía y Letras* (nos. 51–52), pp. 65–80. Mexico.

HERNÁNDEZ SÁNCHEZ-BARBA, MARIO
1958a *See* Morfi, 1958.

120

1958b   *See* Tamarón y Romeral, 1958.
1963   *See* Cortés, 1963.
HERRERA Y TORDESILLAS, ANTONIO DE
   See Article 15.
HERRERO, ANDRÉS
1837   *See* Moxó y de Francolí, 1837.
HEYDEN, DORIS
1964   *See* Durán, 1964.
1971   *See* Durán, 1971.
HISTORIA DE LOS MEXICANOS POR SUS PINTURAS
1882   Historia de los mexicanos por sus pinturas.   MNA, *Anales,* 2:83–106.
1883–84   Notes upon the Codex Ramírez,
   with a translation of the same.   By
   Henry Phillips, Jr.   *Proceedings of
   the American Philosophical Society,*
   21:616–51.
1891   Historia de los mexicanos por sus pinturas.   *In* García Icazbalceta, 1886–
   92, 3:228–63.
HISTOYRE DU MECHIQUE
1905   Histoyre du Mechique.   Manuscrit
   français inédit du XVI siècle traduit
   par A. Thévet.   Publié par M. Edouard de Jonghe.   *Journal de la Société
   des Américanistes de Paris,* n.s. 2:1–
   41.
1961   Histoyre du Mechique. . . .   Retra-
   ducción del francés al castellano por
   Joaquín Meade.   Con notas del Profr.
   Wigberto Jiménez Moreno.   *Memorias de la Academia Mexicana de la
   Historia,* 20:183–210.
HORCASITAS, FERNANDO
1964   *See* Durán, 1964.
1971   *See* Durán, 1971.
HOYO, EUGENIO DEL
1967   *See* Morfi, 1967.
HUMBOLDT, ALEXANDER VON
1810   Vues des cordillères et monuments
   des peuples indigènes de l'Amérique.
   Paris.
1811a   Essai politique sur le royaume de la
   Nouvelle-Espagne.   2 vols.   Paris.
1811b   Political essay on the kingdom of
   New Spain.   With physical sections
   and maps founded on astronomical
   observations and trigonometrical and
   barometrical measurements.   Translated from the French by John Black.
   4 vols.   London.
1814   Researches concerning the institutions
   and monuments of the ancient inhabitants of America with descriptions
   and views of some of the most striking
   scenes in the cordilleras!   Written
   in French by Alexander de Humboldt, and translated into English by
   Helen Maria Williams.   2 vols.   London.
1941   Ensayo político sobre el reino de la
   Nueva España.   Sexta edición castellana.   Edición crítica, con una introducción biobibliográfica, notas y
   arreglo de la versión española por Vito Alessio Robles.   5 vols.   Mexico.
1966   Ensayo político sobre el reino de la
   Nueva España.   Estudio preliminar,
   revisión del texto, cotejos, notas y
   anexos de Juan A. Ortega y Medina.
   Mexico.
ICAZA, FRANCISCO A., ed.
1923   Diccionario autobiográfico de conquistadores y pobladores de Nueva
   España, sacado de los textos originales [por Francisco del Paso y Tron-
   coso].   2 vols.   Madrid.
IGLESIA, RAMÓN
1942   Cronistas e historiadores de la conquista de México: El ciclo de Hernán
   Cortés.   Mexico.
1945   *See* Estudios de historiografía, 1945.
1947   *See* Columbus, Ferdinand, 1947.
ILLESCAS, GONZALO DE
1940   *See* Ramírez Cabañas, 1940a.
ISAGOGE
1892   Isagoge histórico apologético general
   de todas las Indias y especial de la
   Provincia de Sn. Vicente Ferrer de
   Chiapa y Goathemala de el Orden de
   Predicadores.   Libro inédito hasta
   ahora, que, con motivo de la celebra-
   ción del cuarto centenario del descubrimiento de América, ha mandado
   publicar el gobierno de la República
   de Guatemala.   Madrid.
1935   Isagoge histórica apologética de las
   Indias Occidentales y especial de la
   Provincia de San Vicente Ferrer de
   Chiapa y Guatemala de la Orden de
   Predicadores.   Manuscrito encontrado
   en el Convento de Santo Domingo de
   Guatemala, debido a la pluma de un
   religioso de dicha orden, cuyo nombre se ignora.   Colección de documentos antiguos del Ayuntamiento de
   Guatemala.   Prólogo de J. Fernando
   Juárez Muñoz.   Guatemala.
JIMÉNEZ DE LA ESPADA, MARCOS
1890–95   *See* Cobo, Bernabé, 1890–95.
JIMÉNEZ MORENO, WIGBERTO
1961   *See* Histoyre du Mechique, 1961.
JONGHE, EDOUARD DE
1905   *See* Histoyre du Mechique, 1905.

JUÁREZ MUÑOZ, J. FERNANDO
1935 *See* Isagoge, 1935.

JUARROS, DOMINGO
1808–18 Compendio de la historia de la Ciudad de Guatemala. Escrito por el B. D. Domingo Juarros, presbítero secular de este arzobispado. 2 vols. Guatemala.
1823 A statistical and commerical history of the Kingdom of Guatemala in Spanish America: Containing important particulars relative to its productions, manufactures, customs, . . . with an account of its conquest by the Spaniards and a narrative of the principal events down to the present time: From original records in the archives, actual observation, and other authentic sources. . . . Translated by J. Baily. London.
1936 Compendio de la historia de la Ciudad de Guatemala. . . . 3d ed. 2 vols. Guatemala.

KARNS, HARRY J.
1954 *See* Mange, 1954.

KEATINGE, MAURICE
1800 *See* Díaz del Castillo, 1800.

KEEN, BENJAMIN
1959 *See* Columbus, Ferdinand, 1959.
1963 *See* Zorita, 1963b.

KINGSBOROUGH, EDWARD KING
1830–48 Antiquities of Mexico. . . . 9 vols. London.

KINNAIRD, LAWRENCE
1958 *See* Lafora, 1958.

KUBLER, GEORGE
1951 *See* Tovar, 1951.

LAET, JOANNES DE
1625 Nieuvve wereldt, ofte Beschrijvinghe van West-Indien wt veelderhande schriften ende aen-teeckeninghen van verscheyden natien by een versamelt door Ioannes de Laet. . . . Leiden.
1630 Beschrijvinghe van West-Indien door Ioannes de Laet. Tweede druck: in ontallijcke plaetsen verbetert, vermeerdert, met einige nieuwe caerten, belden van verscheyden dieren ende planten verciert. Leiden.
1633 Novus Orbis, seu Descriptionis Indiae Occidentalis libri XVIII. Leiden.

LAFORA, NICOLÁS DE
1939 Relación del viaje que hizo a los presidios internos situados en la frontera de la América Septentrional perteneciente al Rey de España. Con

un liminar bibliográfico y acotaciones por Vito Alessio Robles. Mexico.
1958 The frontiers of New Spain: Nicolás de Lafora's description, 1766–1768. Translated and edited by Lawrence Kinnaird. Quivira Society Publications, 13. Berkeley, Calif.

LAS CASAS, BARTOLOMÉ DE
1552 Brevísima relación de la destrucción de las Indias, colegida por el obispo don Fray Bartolomé de las Casas o Casaus, de la Orden de Santo Domingo. Seville.
1583 The Spanish colonie, or briefe chronicle of the acts and gestes of the Spaniards in the West Indies, called the new World, for the space of xl yeeres, written in the Castilian tongue by the reverend Bishop Bartholemew de las Casas or Casaus, a friar of the order of S. Dominicke, and now first translated into English, by M.M.A. [Facsimile reproduction of preceding entry, Ann Arbor, Mich., 1966.]
1875–76 Historia de las Indias escrita por fray . . . , obispo de Chiapa, ahora por primera vez dada a luz por el Marqués de la Fuensanta del Valle y D. José Sancho Rayón. 5 vols. Madrid.
1909a The Brevissima Relacion. *In* MacNutt, 1909, pp. 311–414.
1909b Apologética historia de las Indias. *In* Serrano y Sanz, 1909a, 1.
1951 Historia de las Indias. Edición de Agustín Millares Carlo y estudio preliminar de Lewis Hanke. Mexico and Buenos Aires.
1957–58 Obras escogidas. 5 vols. Biblioteca de Autores Españoles, nos. 95, 96, 105, 106, 110. Madrid. [Vols. 1–2: Historia de las Indias. Texto fijado por Juan Pérez de Tudela y Emilio López Oto. Estudio crítico preliminar y edición por Juan Pérez de Tudela Bueso. Vols. 3–4: Apologética historia. Estudio crítico preliminar y edición por Juan Pérez de Tudela Bueso. Vol. 5: Opúsculos, cartas y memoriales. Ilustración preliminar y edición por Juan Pérez de Tudela Bueso.]
1965 Tratados de Fray. . . . Prólogos de Lewis Hanke y Manuel Giménez Fernández, transcripción de Juan Pérez de Tudela Bueso y traducciones

de Agustín Millares Carlo y Rafael Moreno. 2 vols. Mexico and Buenos Aires.

1967 Apologética historia sumaria, cuanto a las cualidades, dispusición, descripción, cielo y suelo destas tierras, y condiciones naturales, policías, repúblicas, manera de vivir e costumbres de las gentes destas Indias Occidentales y Meridionales cuyo imperio soberano pertenece a los reyes de Castilla. Edición preparada por Edmundo O'Gorman, con un estudio preliminar, apéndices y un índice de materias. 2 vols. Mexico.

LAS CASAS, GONZALO DE

1903 Guerra de los chichimecas. Noticia de la obra, José F. Ramírez. Conjeturas sobre quién pudo ser el autor, Luis González Obregón. MNA, *Anales*, ep. 2, 1. Mexico.

1936 Noticia de los chichimecas y justicia de la guerra que se les ha hecho por los españoles. *In* Hermann Trimborn, *Quellen zur Kulturgeschichte des präkolumbischen Amerika*, pp. 123–215. Stuttgart.

1941 [Reissue of Trimborn's text, without his notes and commentary, by Ramón Alcorta Guerrero and José Francisco Pedraza.] *In* Bibliografía histórica y geográfica del Estado de San Luis Potosí, pp. 586–612. Tacubaya.

1944 [Reissue of the Ramírez-Obregón edition by Luis Vargas Rea.] Mexico.

LEDESMA, BARTOLOMÉ DE, comp.

1905 Descripción del arzobispado de México sacada de las memorias originales hechas por los doctrineros o capellanes y compiladas por Fr. Bartolomé de Ledesma, O.S.D., administrador del mismo arzobispado. Papeles de Nueva España, publicados . . . por Francisco del Paso y Troncoso. 2d ser., Geografía y estadistica, 3. Madrid.

LEÓN, ALONSO DE, JUAN BAUTISTA CHAPA, AND FERNANDO SÁNCHEZ DE ZAMORA

1909 Historia de Nuevo León con noticias sobre Coahuila, Tejas, Nuevo México por el Capitán Alonso de León, un autor anónimo y el General Fernando Sánchez de Zamora. Documentos inéditos o muy raros para la historia de México, publicados por Genaro García, 25. Mexico.

1961 Historia de Nuevo León con noticias sobre Coahuila, Tamaulipas, Texas y Nuevo México, escrita en el siglo XVII por el Cap. Alonso de León, Juan Bautista Chapa y el Gral. Fernando Sánchez de Zamora. Estudio preliminar y notas de Israel Cavazos Garza. Monterrey.

LEÓN, MARTÍN DE

1611 Camino del cielo en lengua mexicana, con todos los requisitos necesarios para conseguir este fin, con todo lo que un cristiano debe creer, saber, y obrar, desde el punto que tiene uso de razón hasta que muere. Mexico.

1947 Calendario de los indios mexicanos con sus fiestas para los confesores. Mexico.

LEÓN PINELO, ANTONIO DE

1629 Epítome de la biblioteca oriental y occidental, náutica y geográfica. Madrid.

1639? Relación que en el Consejo Real de las Indias hizo el Licenciado Antonio de León Pinelo, relator de su Alteza, sobre la pacificación y población de las provincias del Manché, y Lacandón, que pretende hacer Don Diego de Vera Ordóñez y Villaquirán, caballero de la Orden de Calatrava, etc. Madrid.

1737–38 Epítome . . . añadido y enmendado nuevamente en que se contienen los escritores de las Indias Orientales y Occidentales, y reynos convecinos, China, Tartaria, Japón, Persia, Armenia, Etiopia, y otras partes. [Andrés Gonzalez de Barcia, ed.] 3 vols. Madrid.

1943 El paraíso en el Nuevo Mundo: Comentario apologético, historia natural y peregrina de las Indias Occidentales Islas de Tierra Firme del Mar Océano. . . . Publícalo, con un prólogo, Raúl Porras Barrenechea. . . . Lima.

1958 El Epítome de Pinelo: Primera bibliografía del Nuevo Mundo. Estudio preliminar de Agustín Millares Carlo. Pan American Union. Washington.

1960 Relación . . . sobre la pacificación y población . . . del Manché y Lacandón. . . . *In* Tovilla, 1960, pp. 251–72.

LEÓN Y GAMA, ANTONIO DE

1792 Descripción histórica y cronológica de las dos piedras que con ocasión del nuevo empedrado que se está for-

123

mando en la plaza principal de México, se hallaron en ella el año de 1790. Explícase el sistema de los calendarios de los indios, el método que tenían de dividir el tiempo, y la corrección que hacían de él para igualar el año civil, de que usaban, con el año solar trópico. Noticia muy necesaria para la perfecta inteligencia de la segunda piedra: A que se añaden otras curiosas e instructivas sobre la mitología de los mexicanos, sobre su astronomía, y sobre los ritos y ceremonias que acostumbraban en tiempo de su gentilidad. Mexico.

1832 Descripción histórica y cronológica. . . . Dala a luz, con notas, biografía de su autor y aumentada con la segunda parte que estaba inédita, y bajo la protección del Gobierno general de la Unión, Carlos María Bustamante. . . . Mexico.

1927a Descripción de la Ciudad de México, antes y después de la llegada de los conquistadores españoles. *Revista Mexicana de Estudios Históricos*, 1, appendix, pp. 8–58.

1927b Descripción del obispado de Michoacán. *Revista Mexicana de Estudios Históricos*, 1, appendix, pp. 93–100.

LEONARD, IRVING A.
1929 Don Carlos de Sigüenza y Góngora: A Mexican savant of the seventeenth century. Berkeley, Calif.

1932 *See* Sigüenza y Góngora, 1932.

LEONARDO DE ARGENSOLA, BARTOLOMÉ
1940 *See* Ramírez Cabañas, 1940a.

LEVENE, RICARDO
1945 *See* Solórzano Pereira, 1945.

LIBRO VIEJO
1934 Libro viejo da la fundación de Guatemala, y papeles relativos a D. Pedro de Alvarado. Prólogo del Licenciado Jorge García Granados. Guatemala.

LINES, JORGE A.
1952 *See* Academia de Geografía e Historia de Costa Rica, 1952.

LÓPEZ, ATANASIO
1925 Cuestionario histórico. ¿Escribió Fr. Toribio Motolinía una obra intitulada "Guerra de los Indios de la Nueva España o Historia de la Conquista de México?" *In* Archivo Ibero-Americano, 12:221–47.

LÓPEZ, GONZALO
1870 *See* [Guzmán, Nuño Beltrán de,] Relations, 1870.

LÓPEZ DE GÓMARA, FRANCISCO
1552 La [h]istoria de las Indias y conquista de Mexico. Zaragoza.

1553 Hispania victrix. Primera y segunda parte de la historia general de las Indias con todo el descubrimiento, y cosas notables que han acaecido dende que se ganaron hasta el año de 1551. Con la conquista de México y de la Nueva España. Medina del Campo.

1858 Vida de Hernán Cortés. De Rebus Gestis Fernandi Cortesii. *In* García Icazbalceta, 1858–66, 1:309–56.

1943 Historia de la conquista de México. Introducción y notas por Joaquín Ramírez Cabañas. 2 vols. Mexico.

1954 Historia general de Indias, "Hispania Victrix," cuya segunda parte corresponde a la conquista de México. Modernización del texto antiguo por Pilar Guibelalde, con unas notas prologales de Emiliano M. Aguilera. 2 vols. Barcelona.

1964 Cortés: the life of the conqueror by his secretary Francisco López de Gómara. Translated and edited by Lesley Byrd Simpson. Berkeley and Los Angeles.

LÓPEZ DE TORO, JOSÉ
1953–57 *See* Anghiera, 1953–57.

LÓPEZ DE VELASCO, JUAN
1871 Demarcación y división de las Indias. *In* DII, 1864–84, 15:409–572.

1894 Geografía y descripción universal de las Indias, recopilada por el cosmógrafo-cronista Juan López de Velasco, desde en año de 1571 al de 1574, publicada por la primera vez en el Boletín de la Sociedad Geográfica de Madrid, con adiciones e ilustraciones por Don Justo Zaragoza. Madrid.

LÓPEZ OTO, EMILIO
1957–58 *See* Las Casas, Bartolomé de, 1957–58.

LORENZANA Y BUTRÓN, FRANCISCO ANTONIO DE
1769 Concilios provinciales primero y segundo, celebrados en la muy noble y muy leal ciudad de México, presidiendo el Illmo. y Rmo. Señor D. Fr. Alonso de Montúfar, en los años de 1555 y 1565. Dalos a luz el Illmo. Sr. D. Francisco Antonio Lorenzana. . . . Mexico.

1770a Concilium mexicanum provinciale III. celebratum Mexici anno MDLXXXV. Mexico.

1770b Historia de Nueva-España, escrita por su esclarecido conquistador Hernán Cortés, aumentada con otros documentos y notas, por el Ilustrísimo Señor Don Francisco Antonio Lorenzana, arzobispo de México. Mexico.

LOSADA, ÁNGEL
1947 Una historia olvidada de nuestro descubrimiento de América. ("De Orbe Novo" de J. G. de Sepúlveda.) *Revista de Indias,* 8:509–20.

1948 Hernán Cortés en la obra del cronista Sepúlveda. *Revista de Indias,* 9:127–69.

1949 Juan Ginés de Sepúlveda a través de su "Epistolario" y nuevos documentos. Madrid.

LOS RÍOS, JOSÉ AMADOR DE
1851–55 *See* Oviedo y Valdés, 1851–55.

McLEAN, MALCOLM D.
1967 *See* Morfi, 1967.

MacNUTT, FRANCIS AUGUSTUS
1908 *See* Cortés, 1908.

1909 Bartholomew de las Casas: His life, his apostolate, and his writings. New York and London.

1912 *See* Anghiera, 1912.

MAJOR, R. H.
1853–54 *See* González de Mendoza, 1853–54.

1961 *See* Columbus, Christopher, 1961.

MALAGÓN, JAVIER, AND JOSÉ M. OTS CAPDEQUÍ
1965 Solórzano y la política indiana. Mexico.

MANGE, JUAN MATEO
1926 Luz de tierra incognita en la América Septentrional y diario de las exploraciones en Sonora. Versión, notas e índice alfabético por Francisco Fernández del Castillo. AGN, *Publicaciones,* 10. Mexico.

1954 Unknown Arizona and Sonora, 1693–1721, from the Francisco Fernández del Castillo version of Luz de tierra incognita. An English translation of part II by Harry J. Karns and associates. Tucson.

MANSO DE CONTRERAS, CRISTÓBAL
1661 Relación cierta y verdadera de lo que sucedió y ha sucedido en esta villa de Guadalcazar, Provincia de Tehuantepec, desde los 22 de marzo de 1660 hasta los 4 de julio de 1661, cerca de que los naturales indios de estas provincias, tumultuados y amotinados, mataron a don Juan de Avellán, su alcalde mayor y teniente de capitán general, y a tres criados suyos, procediendo a otros gravísimos delitos, hasta aclamar rey de su naturaleza; y de las diligencias, averiguación, castigo y perdón que con ellos se ha seguido, ejecutado por el señor don Juan Francisco de Montemayor de Cuenca, . . . oidor de la real audiencia y chancillería de esta Nueva España. . . . Escribíala don Cristóbal Manso de Contreras, regidor de la Ciudad de Antequera, Valle de Oaxaca, alcalde mayor y teniente de capitán general de dicha villa. . . . Mexico.

1907 Relación cierta y verdadera. . . . *In* Genaro García, 1907, pp. 109–229.

MARKHAM, CLEMENTS R.
1865 *See* Andagoya, 1865.

1880 *See* Acosta, 1880.

MARTÍNEZ, HENRICO
1606 Repertorio de los tiempos, y historia natural desta Nueva España. Compuesto por Henrico Martínez, cosmógrafo de su Majestad e intérprete del Santo Oficio deste reino. Mexico.

1948 Repertorio. . . . Escrita e impresa por Henrico Martínez en México, el año de 1606. Introducción de Francisco de la Maza. Apéndice bibliográfico de Francisco González de Cossío. Mexico.

MATEOS, FRANCISCO
1954 *See* Acosta, 1954.

1956 *See* Cobo, 1956.

MAUDSLAY, ALFRED PERCIVAL
1908–16 *See* Díaz del Castillo, 1908–16.

MAYER, WILLIAM
1961 Early travelers in Mexico, 1534 to 1816. Mexico.

MAZA, FRANCISCO DE LA
1945 Fray Diego Valadés, escritor y grabador franciscano del siglo XVI. Mexico.

MEADE, JOAQUÍN
1961 *See* Histoyre du Mechique, 1961.

MEANS, PHILIP AINSWORTH
1917 *See* Avendaño y Loyola, 1917.

1930 *See* Elorza y Rada, 1930.

MEDINA, JOSÉ TORIBIO
1898–1907 Biblioteca hispano-americana (1493–1810). 7 vols. Santiago de Chile.

1907–12 La imprenta en México (1539–

1821). 8 vols. Santiago de Chile.

MÉNDEZ, DIEGO

1825 Relación hecha por Diego Méndez, de algunos acontecimientos del último viage del Almirante Don Cristóbal Colón. *In* Navarrete, 1825–37, 1:314–29. [This is the concluding section of Méndez' will. The first part was later published in Reale Commissione Colombiana, 1892–96, pt. 1, 11:217–21.]

1961 An account given by Diego Méndez in his will of some events that occurred in the last voyage of the admiral Don Christopher Columbus. *In* Christopher Columbus, 1961, pp. 204–34. [Diego Méndez was a companion of Columbus on his fourth voyage and carried the news of the admiral's shipwreck from Jamaica to Española.]

MENÉNDEZ, CARLOS R.

1938 *See* Montalvo, 1938.

MENÉNDEZ PIDAL, RAMÓN

1963 El Padre Las Casas, su doble personalidad. Madrid.

METCALFE, GRACE

1946 Indice de la crónica de Fray Alonso Ponce. *Boletín Bibliográfico de Antropología Americana*, 7:56–84. Mexico.

MILLARES CARLO, AGUSTÍN

1951 *See* Las Casas, Bartolomé de, 1951.
1958 *See* León Pinelo, 1958.
1964 *See* Anghiera, 1964.
1965 *See* Las Casas, Bartolomé de, 1965.

MIRANDA, JOSÉ

1959 *See* Hernández, Francisco, 1959.

MOLINA, ANTONIO DE

1943 Antigua Guatemala: Memorias del M. R. P. Maestro Fray Antonio de Molina, continuadas y marginadas por Fray Agustín Cano y Fray Francisco Ximénez, de la Orden de Santo Domingo. Transcripción paleográfica, prólogo, índice y notas por Jorge del Valle Matheu. . . . Guatemala.

MONTALVO, GREGORIO DE

1938 Carta del Obispo don Fray Gregorio de Montalvo a Su Majestad con un memorial sobre el estado del la Iglesia de Yucatán. Mérida, 6 de enero de 1582. *In* Documentos para la historia de Yucatán, 2:66–94. France V. Scholes, C. R. Menéndez, J. I. Rubio Mañé, and Eleanor B. Adams, eds. Merida, Yucatan.

MONTEJO, FRANCISCO DE

1938 Méritos y servicios del gobernador y capitán general D. Francisco de Montejo en la conquista de Yucatán, Chiapas, Honduras. AGN, *Boletín*, 9:85–148.

MONTERO DE MIRANDA, FRANCISCO

1955 Descripción de la provincia de la Verapaz por Fray Francisco Montero de Miranda. Relación del siglo XVI. *Anales de la Sociedad de Geografía e Historia de Guatemala*, 27:342–58.

MORA PLANCARTE, IRMA

1963 Cervantes de Salazar, el dramaturgo de la conquista. Tesis que sustenta . . . para obtener el grado de maestra en historia universal. UNAM. Mexico.

MORALES PADRÓN, FRANCISCO

1959 Los grandes cronistas de Indias. *El Faro a Colón*, 10:32–59.

MORELLUS, CYRIACUS, pseud.

1776 *See* Muriel, Domingo, 1776.

MORENO, RAFAEL

1965 *See* Las Casas, Bartolomé de, 1965.

MORFI, JUAN AGUSTÍN DE

1935a Viaje de indios y diario del Nuevo México. Noticia biobibliográfica y acotaciones por Vito Alessio Robles. Mexico.

1935b Viaje de indios. . . . Segunda edición, con adiciones, de la impresa por la Sociedad "Bibliófilos Mexicanos." Mexico.

1958 Viaje de indios y diario de Nuevo México. Prólogo de Mario Hernández. Biblioteca indiana, 2:329–431.

MORFI, JUAN AGUSTÍN

1967 Diario y derrotero, 1777–1781. Edición de Eugenio del Hoyo y Malcolm D. McLean. Noticias geográficas e históricas del noreste de México, 2. Monterrey.

MORRIS, J. BAYARD

1928 *See* Cortés, 1928.

MOTA PADILLA, MATÍAS ÁNGEL DE LA

1856 Historia de la conquista de la provincia de la Nueva-Galicia, escrita por el Lic. D. Matías de la Mota Padilla en 1742. 3 vols. Guadalajara.

1870–72 Historia de la conquista. . . . Publicada por la Sociedad Mexicana de Geografía y Estadística. Mexico.

1924 Historia de la conquista del reino de la Nueva Galicia. . . . Adicionada y comentada, en vista, ya de documentos inéditos que existen en el Archivo

Municipal, ya en lo expuesto por otros historiadores, por el Licenciado José Irineo Gutiérrez. Guadalajara.

MOTA Y ESCOBAR, ALONSO DE LA

1930 Descripción geográphica de los reynos de Galicia, Vizcaya, y León. Bibliófilos de México. [Introductory study by Joaquín Ramírez Cabañas.] Mexico.

1940 Descripción geográfica de los reinos de Nueva Galicia, Nueva Vizcaya y Nuevo León. Introducción por Joaquín Ramírez Cabañas. 2d ed. Mexico.

1963 Descripción geográfica de los reynos de Galicia, Vizcaya y León. INAH, *Anales*, 16:287–364.

MOTEZUMA, DIEGO LUIS DE

1914 Corona mexicana, o historia de los Motezumas, por el Padre Diego Luis de Motezuma de la Compañía de Jesús. Madrid.

MOXÓ Y DE FRANCOLÍ, BENITO MARÍA DE

1828 Entretenimientos de un prisionero en las provincias del Río de la Plata, por el Barón de Juras Reales, siendo fiscal de S. M. en el Reino de Chile. 2 vols. Barcelona.

1837 Cartas mejicanas escritas por D. Benito María de Moxó en 1805 dadas a luz a impulsos del Revmo. P. Fr. Andrés Herrero, Menor Observante, Prefecto Apostólico de las misiones de la América Meridional y Comisario Colector por la Sagrada Congregación de Propaganda Fide. Genoa.

MUÑOZ CAMARGO, DIEGO

1870 Fragmentos de historia mexicana pertenecientes en gran parte a la Provincia de Tlaxcala, descubierto en otro tiempo por el caballero Boturini, copiado del original que existe hoy día en el conservatorio de antigüedades mexicanas y Museo Nacional de la Ciudad de México. Tlaxcala.

1892 Historia de Tlaxcala por Diego Muñoz Camargo. Publicado y anotado por Alfredo Chavero. Mexico.

1947 Historia de Tlaxcala por Diego Muñoz Camargo. Tomada de la edición de 1892, publicada por D. Alfredo Chavero. Primera edición ilustrada y anotada completa, cotejada con el original que se conserva en el Archivo del Museo Nacional de Anthropología, por Don Lauro E. Rosell y un estudio del Ing. Don Alberto Escalo-

na Ramos, con el itinerario de los primitivos tlaxcaltecas. Mexico.

MURIEL, DOMINGO

1776 Fasti Novi Orbis et Ordinationum Apostolicarum ad Indias pertinentium breviarium cum adnotationibus. Opera D. Cyriaci Morelli presbyteri, olim in Universitate Neo-Cordubensi in Tucumania professoris. Venice.

MURILLO VELARDE, PEDRO

1752 Geografía histórica, donde se describen los reynos, provincias, ciudades, fortalezas, mares, montes, ensenadas, cabos, ríos, puertos, con la mayor individualidad, y exactitud.... La escribía el P. Pedro Murillo Velarde .... 10 vols. Madrid. [Vol. 9: De la América y de las islas adyacentes, y de las tierras árticas y antárticas, e islas de los mares del norte y sur.]

NAVARRETE, MARTÍN FERNÁNDEZ DE

1825–37 Colección de los viajes y descubrimientos que hicieron por mar los españoles desde fines del siglo XV con varios documentos inéditos concernientes a la historia de la marina castellana y de los establecimientos españoles en Indias. 5 vols. Madrid.

1945–46 Colección de los viajes.... Prólogo de J. Natalicio González. 5 vols. Buenos Aires.

1954–55 Obras. Edición y estudio preliminar de Carlos Seco Serrano. 3 vols. Biblioteca Autores Españoles, 75–77. Madrid.

NAYARITAS, RELACIÓN DE LA CONQUISTA

1772 Relación de la conquista de la provincia de los Nayaritas, en el reino de la Nueva España que consiguieron las armas de su Majestad a principios de este año de 1722. Madrid.

NICOLAU D'OLWER, LUIS

1963 Cronistas de las culturas precolombinas: Antología. Prólogo y notas de Luis Nicolau d'Olwer. Mexico.

NIEREMBERG, JUAN EUSEBIO

1635 Historia naturae Maximae Peregrinae. Antwerp.

NIZA, MARCOS DE

1865 Descubrimiento de las siete ciudades, por el P. Fr. Marcos de Niza. DII, 3:325–51.

1926 Discovery of the Seven Cities of Cibola, by the Father Fray Marcos de Niza. Translated and edited by Percy M. Baldwin. Albuquerque, N. Mex.

1949 The journey of Fray Marcos de Niza, by Cleve Hallenbeck. Illustrations and decorations by José Cisneros. Dallas.

NÚÑEZ CABEZA DE VACA, ALVAR
1542 La relación que dió Alvar Núñez Cabeza de Vaca de lo acaescido en la armada donde iba por gobernador Pánfilo de Narváez, desde el año de veinte y siete hasta el año de treinta y seis que volvió a Sevilla con tres de su compañía. Zamora.
1945 Naufragios. Texto restaurado, prologado y anotado por Justo García Morales. Madrid.
1961 Cabeza de Vaca's adventures in the unknown interior of America. A new translation, with annotation, by Cyclone Covey. New York.

NUNNARI, FILIPPO A.
1901 Un viaggiatore Calabrese della fine del secolo XVII. Messina.

NUTTALL, ZELIA
1929 The causes of physical degeneracy of Mexican Indians after the Spanish conquest as set forth by Mexican informants in 1580. *Journal of Hygiene*, 27:40–43.

OBREGÓN, BALTASAR DE
1924 Historia de los descubrimientos antiguos y modernos de la Nueva España, escrita por el conquistador Baltasar Obregón, año de 1584, descubierta por Mariano Cuevas, y publicada por la Sria. de Educación. Mexico.
1928 Obregón's history of the 16th century explorations in western America, entitled Chronicle, commentary, or relation of the ancient and modern discoveries in New Spain and New Mexico, Mexico, 1584. Translated, edited, and annotated by George P. Hammond and Agapito Rey. Los Angeles.

O'CONOR, HUGO DE
1952 Informe de Hugo de O'Conor sobre el estado de las Provincias Internas del Norte, 1771–1776. Texto original con prólogo del Lic. Enrique González Flores. Anotaciones por Francisco R. Almada. Mexico.

O'CROWLEY Y O'DONNELL, PEDRO ALONSO
1972 A description of the Kingdom of New Spain. Translated and edited by Seán Galvin. [San Francisco.]

O'GORMAN, EDMUNDO
1940 *See* Acosta, 1940.

1945 *See* Relación de Sinaloa, 1945.
1964 *See* Anghiera, 1964.

OLMOS, ANDRÉS DE
1875 Grammaire de la langue nahuatl ou mexicaine, composée en 1547, par le franciscain André de Olmos et publiée avec notes, eclairicessements, etc. par Rémi Siméon. Paris.

ONÍS, JOSÉ DE
1951 Alcedo's Bibliotheca americana. *HAHR*, 31:530–41.

OROZCO Y BERRA, MANUEL
1878 *See* Tovar, 1878.
1944 *See* Tovar, 1944.

ORTEGA, FRANCISCO
1836 *See* Veytia, 1836.

OTS CAPDEQUÍ, JOSÉ M.
1930 *See* Solórzano Pereira, 1930.

OVIEDO Y VALDÉS, GONZALO FERNÁNDEZ DE
1526 La natural hystoria de las Indias. Toledo. [*See* 1959b.]
1535 La historia general de las Indias. Seville.
1557 Libro XX de la segunda parte de la general historia de las Indias. Valladolid.
1851–55 Historia general y natural de las Indias, islas y Tierra Firme del Mar Océano, por el capitán Gonzalo Fernández de Oviedo y Valdés, primer cronista del Nuevo Mundo. Publícala la Real Academia de la Historia, cotejada con el códice original, enriquecida con las enmiendas y adiciones del autor, e ilustrada con la vida y el juicio de las obras del mismo por D. José Amador de los Ríos. 4 vols. Madrid.
1950 Sumario de la natural historia de las Indias. Edición, introducción y notas de José Miranda. Mexico and Buenos Aires.
1959a Historia general y natural de las Indias. Edición y estudio preliminar de Juan Pérez de Tudela Bueso. 5 vols. Biblioteca Autores Españoles, 117–21.
1959b Natural history of the West Indies. Translated and edited by Sterling A. Stoudemire. Chapel Hill, N. C. [This is a translation of the short work of 1526.]

PALAFOX Y MENDOZA, JUAN DE
16– Virtudes del indio. N.p.
1762 Obras del ilustrísimo, excelentísimo, y venerable siervo de Dios Don Juan

de Palafox y Mendoza. . . . 13 vols.
Madrid.

1950   Libro de las virtudes del indio. Prólogo de Federico Gómez de Orozco.
Mexico.

PALOMERA, ESTEBAN J.
1962   Fray Diego Valadés, O.F.M., evange-
lizador humanista de la Nueva España: Su obra. Mexico.

1963   Fray Diego Valadés, O.F.M., evan-
gelizador humanista de la Nueva España: El hombre y su época. Mexico.

PANES Y AVELLÁN, DIEGO
1945   See Carrera Stampa, 1945b.

PARKE, R.
1853–54   See González de Mendoza, 1853–
54.

PASO Y TRONCOSO, FRANCISCO DEL
1905   See Ledesma, 1905.

1914–36   See Cervantes de Salazar, Francisco, 1914–36.

1939–42   Epistolario de Nueva España,
1505–1818. Recopilado por Francisco del Paso y Troncoso. 16 vols.
Mexico.

1953   Tratado de las idolatrías, supersticiones, dioses, ritos, hechicerías y
otras costumbres gentílicas de las ra-
zas aborígines de México. Notas,
comentarios y un estudio de Francisco del Paso y Troncoso [2a ed. ampli-
ada con importantes suplementos e
índices]. 2 vols. Mexico.

PERALTA, MANUEL M. DE
1883   Costa-Rica, Nicaragua y Panamá en
el siglo XVI: Su historia y sus límites
según los documentos del Archivo de
Indias de Sevilla, del de Simancas,
etc., recogidos y publicados con notas
y aclaraciones históricas y geográficas.
Madrid and Paris.

PÉREZ BUSTAMANTE, CIRIACO
1967   See Alcedo y Bexarano, 1967.

PÉREZ DE OLIVA, FERNÁN
1940   See Ramírez Cabañas, Joaquín,
1940a.

PÉREZ DE TUDELA BUESO, JUAN
1957–58   See Las Casas, Bartolomé de,
1957–58.

1959   See Oviedo y Valdés, 1959a.

1965   See Las Casas, Bartolomé de, 1965.

PÉREZ SAN VICENTE, GUADALUPE
1961   See Díaz del Castillo, 1961.

PHILLIPPS, THOMAS
1860   See Tovar, 1860.

PHILLIPS, HENRY, JR.
1883–84   See Historia de los mexicanos por
sus pinturas, 1883–84.

PILAR, GARCÍA DEL
1866   See [Guzmán, Nuño Beltrán de,] Relations, 1866.

1870   See [Guzmán, Nuño Beltrán de,] Relations, 1870.

1955   See [Guzmán, Nuño Beltrán de,] Relations, 1955.

1963   The chronicle of García del Pilar. In
Fuentes, 1963, pp. 196–208.

PINEDA, JUAN DE
1939   Descripción de la Provincia de Guatemala, año de 1594. Revista de los
Archivos Nacionales, 3:557–79. Costa Rica.

PINKERTON, JOHN
1808–14   See Thiéry de Menonville, 1812.

PIZARRO Y ORELLANA, FERNANDO
1639   Varones ilustres del Nuevo Mundo.
Descubridores, conquistadores, y pa-
cificadores del opulento, dilatado, y
poderoso imperio de las Indias Occidentales: Sus vidas, virtud, valor, ha-
zañas, y claros blasones. Ilustrados
en los sucesos de estas vidas con sin-
gulares observaciones políticas, morales, jurídicas, miscelaneas, y razón
de estado, para mayor autoridad de
la historia, y demostración de ella y
su utilísima lección. Con un discurso legal de la obligación que tienen
los reyes a premiar los servicios de
sus vasallos, o en ellos, o en sus descendientes. Madrid.

PONCE, ALONSO
1873   Relación breve verdadera de algunas
cosas de las muchas que sucedieron
al Padre Fray Alonso Ponce en las
provincias de la Nueva España, siendo Comisario General de aquellas partes. Tratanse algunas particularida-
des de aquella tierra, y dícese su ida
a ella y vuelta a España, con algo de
lo que en el viaje la acontedió hasta
volver a su provincia de Castilla.
Escrita por dos religiosos, sus com-
pañeros, el uno de los cuales le acom-
pañó desde España a México, y el
otro en todos los demás caminos que
hizo y trabajos que pasó. 2 vols.
Colección de documentos inéditos para la historia de España, vols. 57–58.
Madrid.

PONCE DE LEÓN, PEDRO
1892   Breve relación de los dioses y ritos de

la gentilidad, por Pedro Ponce, bene-
ficiado que fue del partido de Tzum-
pahuacan. MNA, *Anales*, 6 (1900):
3–11.

1953 Breve relación. . . . *In* Paso y Troncoso, 1953, 1:369–80. [Republished,
1965.]

PORRAS, DIEGO DE
1825 Relación del viage é de la tierra agora
nuevamente descubierta por el Almirante D. Cristóbal Colón. *In* Navarrete, 1825–37, 1:282–87. [Diego de
Porras was a member of Columbus'
company on the fourth voyage. He
and his brother Francisco led a mu-
tiny against the admiral on Jamaica.]

PORRAS BARRENECHEA, RAÚL
1943 *See* León Pinelo, 1943.

PURCHAS, SAMUEL
1613 Purchas his pilgrimage. Or, Relations
of the world and the religions observed in all ages and places discovered, from the creation to the present.
London.

1625 Purchas his pilgrims. 4 vols. London.

QUINN, ALISON
1965 *See* Hakluyt, 1965.

QUINN, DAVID BEERS
1965 *See* Hakluyt, 1965.

RAMÍREZ, JOSÉ F.
1867–80 *See* Durán, 1867–80.
1903 *See* Las Casas, Gonzalo de, 1903.

RAMÍREZ CABAÑAS, JOAQUÍN
1930 *See* Mota y Escobar, 1930.
1939 *See* Díaz del Castillo, 1939.
1940a Bartolomé Leonardo de Argensola.
Conquista de México. Gonzalo de
Illescas. Un capítulo de su Historia
pontifical sobre la conquista de la
Nueva España. Introducción y notas por Joaquín Ramírez Cabañas.
Mexico. [Also in this volume: Algunas cosas de Hernán Cortés y México,
by Fernán Pérez de Oliva.]
1940b *See* Mota y Escobar, 1940.
1943 *See* López de Gómara, 1943.
1963 *See* Zorita, Alonso de, 1963a.

RAMOS, ROBERTO
1950 *See* Guadalajara, 1950.

RAMUSIO, GIOVANNI BATTISTA
1556 Terzo volume della navigationi et
viaggi. . . . Venice.

RAZO ZARAGOZA, JOSÉ LUIS
1963 *See* [Guzmán, Nuño Beltrán de,] Relations, 1963a.

REALE COMMISSIONE COLOMBIANA
1892–96 Raccolta di documenti e studi
pubblicati dalla R. Commissione colombiana pel quarto centenario dalla
scoperta del'America. 6 parts in 14
vols. Rome.

RECCHI, NARDO ANTONIO
1649 *See* Hernández, 1649.

RECINOS, ADRIÁN
1958 *See* Cortés y Larraz, 1958.

REFUGIO DE PALACIO, LUIS DEL
1960 *See* Torres, 1960.

REGIMIENTO OF VERA CRUZ
1842 Relación del descubrimiento y conquista de Nueva España, hecha por
la justicia y regimiento de la nueva
ciudad de Vera-Cruz, á 10 de julio
de 1519. *In* Colección de documentos inéditos para la historia de España, 1:410–72.

RELACIÓN DE SINALOA
1945 Relación de la Provincia de Nuestra Señora de Sinaloa, 1601. Edmundo O'Gorman, ed. AGN, *Boletín*,
16:173–94.

RELACIÓN HISTÓRICA
1948 Relación histórica de la conquista
de Querétaro. Ed. Rafael Ayala
Echavarri. SMGE, *Boletín*, 66:109–
52.

RELACIONES HISTÓRICAS
1908 Relaciones históricas y geográficas de
América Central. [Manuel Serrano
y Sanz, ed.] Colección de libros y
documentos referentes a la historia de
América, 8. Madrid.

REMÓN, ALONSO
1632 *See* Díaz del Castillo, 1632.

REY, AGAPITO
1928 *See* Obregón, 1928.

RICO GONZÁLEZ, VÍCTOR
1949 Historiadores mexicanos del siglo
XVIII: Estudios historiográficos sobre
Clavijero, Veytia, Cavo y Alegre.
Prólogo de Rafael García Granados.
Mexico.

RÍOS, JOSÉ AMADOR DE LOS
See Los Ríos, José Amador de

RIVERA Y VILLALÓN, PEDRO DE
1736 Diario y derrotero de lo caminado,
visto, y observado en el discurso de
la visita general de presidios, situados
en las Provincias Internas de Nueva
España, que de orden de Su Majestad
ejecutó D. Pedro de Rivera, brigadier
de los reales ejércitos, habiendo tran-
sitado por los reinos del Nuevo de

Toledo, el de la Nueva Galicia, el de la Nueva Vizcaya, el de la Nueva México, el de la Nueva Extremadura, el de las Nuevas Philipinas, el del Nuevo de León, las Provincias de Sonora, Ostimuri, Sinaloa, y Guasteca. Guatemala.

1946   Diario y derrotero de lo caminado, visto y observado en la visita que hizo a los presidios de la Nueva España Septentrional el Brigadier Pedro de Rivera. Con una introducción y notas por Vito Alessio Robles. Archivo Histórico Militar Mexicano, 2. Mexico.

ROBERTSON, WILLIAM
1777   The history of America. London.
1778   The history of America. . . . 2d ed. 2 vols. London.
1885   The history of the discovery and settlement of America by William Robertson . . . , with an account of his life and writings. . . . New York.

ROBLES, ANTONIO DE
1757   Resguardo contra el olvido, en el breve compendio de la vida admirable y virtudes heroicas del Illmo. Sr. Dr. D. Alonso de Cuevas Dávalos, obispo electo de Nicaragua, consagrado de Oaxaca, arzobispo de esta imperial ciudad de México, su patria, que dejó escrita . . . su autor, el Lic. D. Antonio Robles, notario público. Mexico.
1907   Viaje que hizo el ilustrado señor Doctor don Alonso de Cuevas Dávalos, obispo de Oaxaca, a pacificar la provincia de Tehuantepec. *In* Genaro García, 1907, pp. 96–108. [Pp. 151–65 of the *Resguardo*.]

RODRÍGUEZ CABRILLO, JUAN
1935   Méritos y servicios de Juan Rodríguez Cabrillo, de los primeros conquistadores. *Anales de la Sociedad de Geografía e Historia de Guatemala*, 11:472–96.

ROJO NAVARRO, JOSÉ
1959   *See* Hernández, 1959–.

ROMÁN Y ZAMORA, JERÓNIMO
1575   Repúblicas del mundo, dividas en XXVII libros. 2 vols. Medina del Campo.
1897   Repúblicas de Indias. Idolatrías y gobierno en México y Perú antes de la conquista, ordenadas por Fr. Jerónimo Román y Zamora, cronista de la orden de San Agustín. Fielmente

reimpresas, según la edición de 1575, con una addenda de las noticias que hay en la crónica, del mismo autor, impresa en 1569. 2 vols. Madrid.

ROMERO DE TERREROS, MANUEL
1926   Bibliografía de cronistas de la Ciudad de México. Monografías Bibliográficas Mexicanas, 4. Mexico.
1939   *See* Vázquez de Tapia, 1939.
1940   *See* Sigüenza y Góngora, 1940.

ROSELL, LAURO E.
1947   *See* Muñoz Camargo, 1947.

RUIZ DE ALARCÓN, HERNANDO
1892   Tratado de las supersticiones y costumbres gentílicas que hoy viven entre los indios naturales de esta Nueva España escrito en México por el Br. Hernando Ruiz de Alarcón, año 1629 MNA, *Anales*, 6(1900):123–223.
1953   Tratado de las supersticiones. . . . *In* Paso y Troncoso, 1953, 2:17–180.

SAAVEDRA GUZMÁN, ANTONIO DE
1599   El peregrino indiano, Por D. Antonio de Saavedra Guzmán, Viznieto del Conde del Castellar, nacido en México. . . . Madrid.
1881   El peregrino indiano. . . . Mexico.

SABAN BERGAMÍN, CARLOS
1961   *See* Díaz del Castillo, 1961.

SÁENZ DE SANTA MARÍA, CARMELO
1967   Introducción crítica a la "Historia verdadera" de Bernal Díaz del Castillo. Instituto Gonzalo Fernández de Oviedo. Madrid.
1969–   *See* Fuentes y Guzmán, 1969–.

SALAS, ALBERTO M.
1959   Tres cronistas de Indias: Pedro Mártir de Anglería; Gonzalo Fernández de Oviedo; Fray Bartolomé de las Casas. Mexico.

SÁMANO, JUAN DE
1866   *See* [Guzmán, Nuño Beltrán de,] Relations, 1866.

SÁNCHEZ ALONSO, BENITO
1952   Fuentes de la historia española e hispanoamericana. 3d ed. 3 vols. Madrid.

SÁNCHEZ DE AGUILAR, PEDRO
1639   Informe contra idolorum cultores del obispado de Yucatán. Madrid.
1892   Informe. . . . MNA, *Anales*, 6(1900):13–84.
1937   Informe. . . . Precedido de una breve biografía del autor por el Lic. D. Francisco Cantón Rosado. Merida, Yucatan.

1953   Informe. . . . *In* Paso y Troncoso, 1953, 2:181–336.

SÁNCHEZ DE ZAMORA, FERNANDO
1909   *See* León, Alonso de, 1909.
1961   *See* León, Alonso de, 1961.

SANCHO RAYÓN, JOSÉ
1875–76 *See* Las Casas, Bartolomé de, 1875-76.

SANDOVAL, FERNANDO B.
1945   La relación de la conquista de México en la historia de Fray Diego Durán. *In* Estudios de historiografía, pp. 49–90.
1955   *See* Gemelli Careri, 1955.

SANTA CRUZ, ALONSO DE
1908   Die Karten von Amerika in dem Islario general de Alonso de Santa Cruz, cosmógrafo mayor des Kaisers Karl V, mit dem spanischen Originaltexte und einer kritischen Einleitung, herausgegeben von Franz R. v. Weiser. Festgabe des K. U. K. Oberstkämmer-Amtes für den XVI Internat. Amerikanisten-Kongress. Innsbruck.
1918   Islario general de todas las islas del mundo. Con un prólogo de D. Antonio Blázquez. 2 vols. Madrid.

SANTA MARÍA, VICENTE
1930   Relación histórica de la colonia del Nuevo Santander y costa del Seno Mexicano. *In* Estado general de las fundaciones hechas por D. José de Escandón en la colonia del Nuevo Santander, costa del Seno Mexicano. Documentos originales que contienen la inspección de la provincia efectuada por el Capitán de Dragones don José Tienda de Cuervo, el informe del mismo al virrey y un apéndice con la relación histórica del Nuevo Santander, por Fr. Vicente de Santa María. AGN, *Publicaciones*, 15:351–483.

SAVILLE, MARSHALL H.
1920   The earliest notices concerning the conquest of Mexico by Cortés in 1519. Heye Foundation, Indian Notes and Monographs, vol. 9, no. 1. New York.

SCHOLES, FRANCE V.
1938   *See* Montalvo, 1938.
1960   *See* Tovilla, 1960.

—— AND ELEANOR B. ADAMS, eds.
1938   Don Diego Quijada, alcalde mayor de Yucatán, 1561–1565. Documentos sacados de los archivos de España. *Bib. histórica Mexicana de obras inéditas*, 14, 15. Mexico.

SECO SERRANO, CARLOS
1954–55 *See* Navarrete, 1954–55.

SEPÚLVEDA, JUAN GINÉS DE
1780   De rebus Hispanorum gestis ad novum orbem Mexicumque. *In* Joannis Genesii Sepulvedae Cordubensis Opera, cum edita, tum inedita, accurante Regia Historiae Academia, vol. 3. Madrid.

SERNA, JACINTO DE LA
1892   Manual de ministros de indios para el conocimiento de sus idolatrías, y extirpación de ellas. MNA, *Anales*, 6(1900):261–480.
1953   Manual de ministros de indios. . . . *In* Paso y Troncoso, 1953, 1:40–368.

SERRANO Y SANZ, MANUEL
1908   *See* Relaciones históricas, 1908.
1909a Historiadores de Indias. 2 vols. Madrid.
1909b *See* Zorita, 1909.

SHAW, NORTON
1859   *See* Champlain, 1859.

SHELBY, CHARMION
1949   The cronistas and their contemporaries: Recent editions of works of the sixteenth and seventeenth centuries. *HAHR*, 29:295–317.

SHEPARD, MINNIE LEE
1953   *See* Cervantes de Salazar, 1953.

SIGÜENZA Y GÓNGORA, CARLOS DE
1680   Theatro de virtudes políticas, que constituyen a un príncipe: Advertidas en los monarchas antiguos del Mexicano Imperio, con cuyas efigies se hermoseó el Arco Triunphal, que la muy noble, muy leal, imperial Ciudad de México erigió para el digno recibimiento en ella del Excelentísimo Señor virrey, Conde de Paredes, Marqués de la Laguna, etc. Ideólo entonces, y ahora lo describe D. Carlos de Sigüenza y Góngora. . . . Mexico.
1928   Teatro de virtudes políticas. . . . *Obras*, pp. 1–148. Mexico.
1929   Letter of Don Carlos de Sigüenza to Admiral Pez recounting the incidents of the corn riot in Mexico City, June 8, 1692. *In* Leonard, 1929, pp. 210–77.
1932   Alboroto y motín de México del 8 de junio de 1692. Relación de don Carlos de Sigüenza y Góngora en una carta dirigida al Almirante don Andrés de Pez. Edición anotada por Irving A. Leonard. Mexico.
1940   Relaciones históricas. Selección, pró-

logo y notas de Manuel Romero de Terreros. Mexico.

1948 Noticia chronológica de los reyes, emperadores, governadores, presidentes, y vi-reyes de esta nobilísima ciudad de México. Mexico.

1960 Piedad heroyca de Don Fernando Cortés. Edición y estudio por Jaime Delgado. Madrid.

SIMÉON, RÉMI
1875 See Olmos, 1875.

SIMPSON, LESLEY BYRD
1964 See López de Gómara, 1964.

SKELTON, RALEIGH ASHLIN
1965 See Hakluyt, 1965.

SMITH, W. H.
1857 See Benzoni, 1857.

SOLÍS Y RIVADENEYRA, ANTONIO DE
1684 Historia de la conquista de México, población y progresos de la América Septentrional, conocida por el nombre de Nueva España. Madrid.

1724 The history of the conquest of Mexico by the Spaniards. Done into English from the original Spanish of don Antonio de Solís, secretary and historiographer of his Catholic Majesty, by Thomas Townsend. London.

1944 Historia de la conquista de México. 2 vols. Buenos Aires.

SOLÓRZANO PEREIRA, JUAN DE
1629 . . . De Indiarum iure, sive de iusta Indiarum Occidentalium inquisitione, acquisitione, et Retentione. . . . Madrid.

1639 . . . De Indiarum iure, sive de iusta Indiarum Occidentalium gubernatione. . . . Madrid.

1648 Política indiana sacada en lengua castellana de los dos tomos del derecho y gobierno municipal de las Indias Occidentales que más copiosamente escribió en la latina el Doctor Don Juan de Solórzano Pereira . . . por el mismo autor, dividida en seis libros. En los cuales con gran distinción y estudio se trata y resuelve todo lo tocante al descubrimiento, descripción, adquisición, y retención de las mismas Indias y su gobierno particular, asi cerca de las personas de los indios y sus servicios, tributos, diezmos y encomiendas, como de lo espiritual y eclesiástico, cerca de su doctrina, patronazgo real, iglesias, prelados, prebendados, curas seculares, y regulares, inquisidores, comisarios de cruzada y

de las religiones. Y en lo temporal, cerca de todos los magistrados seculares, virreyes, presidentes, Audiencias, Consejo Supremo y Junta de Guerra de ellas, con inserción y declaración de las muchas cédulas reales que para esto se han despachado. Añadidas muchas cosas que no están en los tomos latinos, en particular todo el libro sexto, que en diez y siete capítulos trata de la Hacienda Real de las Indias, regalías, derechos, y miembros de que se compone y del modo en que se administra; y de los oficiales, tribunales de cuentas, y Casa de la Contratación de Sevilla. Obra de sumo trabajo, y de igual importancia y utilidad, no solo para los de las provincias de Indias, sino de las de Espána, y otras naciones, de cualquier profesión que sean, por la gran variedad de cosas que comprehende, adornada de todas letras, y escrita con el método, claridad, y lenguaje que por ella parecerá. Con dos índices muy distintos y copiosos, uno de los libros y capítulos en que se divide, y otro de las cosas notables que contiene. Madrid.

1736–39 Política indiana. . . . Sale en esta tercera impresión ilustrada por el Licenc. D. Francisco Ramiro de Valenzuela, relator del Supremo Consejo y Cámara de Indias, y electo oidor honorario de la Real Audiencia y Casa de la Contratación de Cádiz. 2 vols. Madrid.

1930 Política indiana, compuesta por el Señor Don Juan de Solórzano y Pereyra . . . corregida, e ilustrada con notas por el Licenciado Don Francisco Ramiro de Valenzuela. . . . [Prólogo de José M. Ots Capdequí.] 5 vols. Madrid.

1945 Libro primero de la recopilación de las cédulas, cartas, provisiones y ordenzas reales. Noticia preliminar de Ricardo Levene. 2 vols. Colección de textos y documentos para la historia del derecho argentino, 5, 6.

SOMOLINOS D'ARDOIS, GERMÁN
1959 See Hernández, 1959–.

SQUIER, E. G.
1860 See García del Palacio, 1860.

STAUNTON, GEORGE T.
1853–54 See González de Mendoza, 1853–54.

133

STOUDEMIRE, STERLING A.
1959 *See* Oviedo y Valdés, 1959b.
STUMMVOLL, JOSEF
1960 *See* Cortés, 1960.
SUÁREZ DE PERALTA, JUAN
1878 Noticias históricas de la Nueva Espa-
      ña, publicadas con la protección del
      Ministerio de Fomento por don Justo
      Zaragoza. Madrid.
1949 Tratado del descubrimiento de las In-
      dias (Noticias históricas de Nueva Es-
      paña) compuesto en 1589 por Don
      Juan Suárez de Peralta, vecino y na-
      tural de México. Nota preliminar de
      Federico Gómez de Orozco. Mexico.
TAMARÓN Y ROMERAL, PEDRO
1937 Demostración del vastísimo obispado
      de la Nueva Vizcaya – 1765: Duran-
      go, Cinaloa, Sonora, Arizona, Nuevo
      México, Chihuahua y porciones de
      Texas, Coahuila y Zacatecas. Con
      una introducción bibliográfica y aco-
      taciones por Vito Alessio Robles.
      Mexico.
1958 Viajes pastorales y descripción de la
      diócesis de Nueva Vizcaya. Estudio
      preliminar y notas aclaratorias por
      Mario Hernández Sánchez-Barba.
      In Bibliotheca indiana, 2:947–1062.
      Madrid.
TAPIA, ANDRÉS DE
1866 Relación de algunas cosas de las que
      acaecieron al Muy Ilustre Señor Don
      Hernando Cortés Marqués del Valle,
      desde que se determinó ir a descubrir
      tierra en la Tierra Firme del mar Océ-
      ano. *In* García Icazbalceta, 1858–
      66, 2:554–94.
1963a Relación de Andrés de Tapia. *In*
      Yáñez, 1963, pp. 27–78.
1963b The chronicle of Andrés de Tapia.
      In Fuentes, 1963, pp. 19–48.
TAYLOR, E. G. R.
1932 *See* Enciso, 1932.
TERRENTIUS, IOANNES
1649 *See* Hernández, 1649.
THEVET, ANDRÉ
1575 La cosmographie universelle d'André
      Thevet, cosmographe du roy. Illus-
      tre de diverses figures des choses
      plus remarquables veuës par l'auteur
      et incogneuës de noz anciens et mo-
      dernes. Paris.
1905 *See* Histoyre du Mechique, 1905.
THIÉRY DE MENONVILLE, NICOLAS JOSEPH
1787 Traité de la culture du nopal, et de
      l'éducation de la cochenille dans les
      colonies françaises de l'Amérique;
      précédé d'Un voyage à Guaxaca. 2
      vols. Cap-Français, St. Dominque.
1812 Travels to Guaxaca, capital of the
      province of the same name in the
      kingdom of Mexico. *In* John Pinker-
      ton, ed., *A general collection of the
      best and most interesting voyages and
      travels*, 13:753–876. 17 vols. [1808–
      1814]. London.
THOMPSON, G. A.
1812–15 *See* Alcedo y Bexarano, 1812–15.
THOMPSON, J. ERIC S.
1958 *See* Gage, 1958.
TORRE REVELLO, JOSÉ
1945 Don Hernando Colón: Su vida, su bi-
      blioteca, sus obras. *Revista de His-
      toria de América*, 19:1–59.
TORRE VILLAR, ERNESTO DE LA
1945 Baltasar Dorantes de Carranza y La
      sumaria relación. *In* Estudios de his-
      toriografía, pp. 203–262.
TORRES, FRANCISCO MARIANO DE
1939 Fragmento de la crónica de la Santa
      Provincia de Xalisco. Guadalajara.
1960 Crónica de la Santa Provincia de Xal-
      isco. Notas de Fray Luis del Refu-
      gio de Palacio. Mexico.
TORRES CASTILLO, JUAN DE
1662 Relación de lo sucedido en las Provin-
      cias de Nejapa, Ixtepeji y la Villa
      Alta; inquietudes de los indios sus
      naturales; castigos en ellos hechos, y
      satisfacción que se dió a la justicia, re-
      duciéndolos a la paz, quietud y obe-
      diencia debida a Su Majestad y a sus
      reales ministros, que ejecutó el señor
      don Juan Francisco de Montemayor
      de Cuenca . . . mediante del celo, cui-
      dado y desvelo que aplicó a estos ne-
      gocios el excelentísimo señor Marqués
      de Leiva y de Ladrada, conde de Ba-
      ños, Virrey . . . por cuya mano la de-
      dica y ofrece . . . el gobernador Juan
      de Torres Castillo, alcalde mayor y
      teniente de capitán general de la di-
      cha Provincia de Nejapa. Mexico.
1907 Relación de lo sucedido. . . . *In* Ge-
      naro García, 1907, pp. 27–96.
TOVAR, JUAN DE
1860 Historia de los indios mexicanos por
      Juan de Tovar. Cura, et impensis
      Dni. Thomae Phillipps. Typis Medio-
      Montanis [England].
1878 Crónica mexicana escrita por D. Her-
      nando Alvarado Tezózomoc hacia el
      año de MDXCVIII. Anotada por el

Sr. Lic. D. Manuel Orozco y Berra y precedida del Códice Ramírez, manuscrito del siglo XVI intitulado: Relación del origen de los indios que habitan esta Nueva España según sus historias, y un examen de ambas obras, al cual se anexó un estudio de cronología mexicana por el mismo Sr. Orozco y Berra. José M. Vigil, ed. Mexico.

1944 Códice Ramírez, manuscrito del siglo XVI intitulado: Relación del origen de los indios que habitan esta Nueva España, según sus historias. Examen de la obra, con un anexo de cronología mexicana por el Lic. Manuel Orozco y Berra. Mexico.

1951 The Tovar Calendar, an illustrated Mexican manuscript ca. 1585. Reproduced with a commentary and handlist of sources on the Mexican 365-day year by George Kubler and Charles Gibson. Memoirs of the Connecticut Academy of Arts and Sciences, 11. New Haven.

TOVILLA, MARTÍN ALFONSO
1960 Relación histórica descriptiva de las Provincias de la Verapaz y de la Manché, escrita por el Capitán don Martín Alfonso Tovilla, año de 1635, publicada por primera vez, con la Relación que en el Consejo Real de las Indias hizo sobre la pacificación y población de las Provincias del Manché y Lacandón, el Licenciado Antonio de León Pinelo. Paleografía [y introducción] por France V. Scholes y Eleanor B. Adams. Guatemala.

TOWNSEND, THOMAS
1724 See Solís y Rivadeneyra, 1724.

TOZZER, ALFRED M.
1913 A Spanish manuscript letter on the Lacandones in the Archives of the Indies at Seville. [Audiencia de Guatemala, 69–1–2, f. 29.] XVIII International Congress of Americanists (London), Proceedings, 2:497–509.

TRIMBORN, HERMANN
1936 See Las Casas, Gonzalo de, 1936.
1954 Pascual de Andagoya: Ein Mensch erlebt die Conquista. Abhandlungen aus dem Gebiet der Auslandskunde, Band 59. Reihe B. Völkerkunde, Kulturgeschichte und Sprachen, Band 33. Hamburg.

TURNER, DAYMOND
1966 Gonzalo Fernández de Oviedo y Val-

dés: An annotated bibliography. Studies in the Romance Languages and Literature, 66. Chapel Hill.

ULLOA, ALFONSO
1571 See Columbus, Ferdinand, 1571.

UNTERKIRCHER, FRANZ
1960 See Cortés, 1960.

VALADÉS, DIEGO
1579 Rhetorica christiana ad concionandi et orandi usum accommodata, utriusque facultatis exemplis suo loco insertis, quae quidem ex indorum maxime deprompta sunt historiis, unde praeter doctrinam summa quoque delectatio comparabitur. Perugia.
1962 See Palomera, 1962.

VALENZUELA, FRANCISCO RAMIRO DE
1736–39 See Solórzano Pereira, 1736–39.
1930 See Solórzano Pereira, 1930.

VALERO SILVA, JOSÉ
1954 See Alvarado, 1954.

VALLE-ARIZPE, ARTEMIO DE
1939 Historia de la ciudad de México según los relatos de sus cronistas. Mexico.

VALLE MATHEU, JORGE DEL
1943 See Molina, 1943.

VAN HORNE, JOHN
1946 See Arregui, 1946.

VANNINI DE GERULEWICZ, MARISA
1967 See Benzoni, 1967.

VARGAS UGARTE, RUBÉN
1931 Don Benito María de Moxó y de Francolí, arzobispo de Charcas. Instituto de Investigaciones Históricas, Pub. 56. Buenos Aires.

VARTHEMA, LUDOVICO DE
1520 Itinerario de Ludovico de Varthema bolognese ne lo Egypto ne la Suria ne la Arabia deserta et felice ne la Persia ne la India et ne la Ethiopia. La fede el uiuere et costũi de le p̃fate puĩcie. Et al p̃sente agiõtoui alcũe Isole nouamẽte ritrouate. Venice.

VÁZQUEZ DE CORONADO, JUAN
1883 [Various letters, informaciones, and memorial, 1562–1565.] In Peralta, 1883, pp. 213, 221–24, 227–93, 299–303, 327–58, 363–67, 759–88.
1908 Cartas de Juan Vázquez de Coronado, conquistador de Costa Rica, nuevamente publicadas por D. Ricardo Fernández Guardia. Barcelona.
1964 Cartas de relación sobre la conquista de Costa Rica. San Jose, Costa Rica. [Facsimile reproduction of the 1908 Barcelona edition.]

VÁZQUEZ DE ESPINOSA, ANTONIO

1942 Compendium and description of the West Indies. Translated by Charles Upson Clark. Washington.

1943 La audiencia de Guatemala. Primer Parte, Libro Quinto del Compendio y Descripción de las Indias occidentales por Antonio Vázquez de Espinosa, año de 1629. Adrian Recinos, ed. Guatemala.

1944 Descripción de la Nueva España en el siglo XVII, por el padre fray Vázquez de Espinosa, y otras documentos del siglo XVII. Mariano Cuevas, ed. Mexico. [Bks. 1, 3, 4, 5 (chaps. 2–5) of *Compendio*.]

1948 Compendio y descripción de las Indias Occidentales. Transcrito del manuscrito original por Charles Upson Clark. Washington.

VÁZQUEZ DE TAPIA, BERNARDINO

1939 Relación del conquistador Bernardino Vázquez de Tapia, que publica por primera vez Don Manuel Romero de Terreros. Mexico.

1953 Relación de méritos y servicios del conquistador Bernardino Vázquez de Tapia, vecino y regidor de esta gran ciudad de Tenustitlán, México. Estudio y notas por Jorge Gurría Lacroix. Mexico.

VEDIA, ENRIQUE DE, ed.

1852–53 Historiadores primitivos de Indias. Colección dirigida e ilustrada por Don Enrique de Vedia. 2 vols. *Bib. de autores españoles*, 22, 26. Madrid.

VEYTIA, MARIANO

1826 Tezcoco en los últimos tiempos de sus antiguos reyes, o sea, relación tomada de los manuscritos inéditos de Boturini; redactados por el Lic. D. Mariano Veytia. Publícalos con notas y adiciones para estudio de la juventud mexicana, Carlos María de Bustamante. Mexico.

1836 Historia antigua de Méjico, escrita por el Lic. D. Mariano Veytia. La publica con varias notas y un apéndice el C. F. Ortega. 3 vols. Mexico.

1944 Historia antigua de México. 2 vols. Mexico.

VIANA, FRANCISCO DE, LUCAS GALLEGO, AND GUILLERMO CADENA

1955 Relación de la Provincia de Verapaz hecha por los religiosos de Santo Domingo de Cobán, 7 de diciembre de

1574. *Anales de la Sociedad de Geografía e Historia de Guatemala*, 28:18–31.

VIGIL, JOSÉ M.

1878 *See* Tovar, 1878.

VIGNERAS, L. A.

1953 El viaje de Samuel Champlain a las Indias Occidentales. *Anuario de Estudios Americanos*, 10:457–500. Seville.

VILLACORTA C., J. ANTONIO

1932–33 *See* Fuentes y Guzmán, 1932–33.

VILLAGUTIERRE SOTO-MAYOR, JUAN DE

1701 Historia de la conquista de la Provincia de el Itza, reducción y progresos de la de el Lacandón y otras naciones de indios bárbaros de la mediación de el reino de Guatimala, a las Provincias de Yucatán, en la América Septentrional. Madrid.

1933 Historia de la conquista de la Provincia de el Itza. . . . Prólogo por el General Pedro Zamora Castellanos. Guatemala.

VILLAROEL, HIPÓLITO

1831 México por dentro y fuera bajo el gobierno de los virreyes, o sea Enfermidades políticas que padece la capital de la N. España en casi todos los cuerpos de que se compone, y remedios que se deben aplicar para su curación. Manuscrito inédito que da a luz por primer Suplemento al tomo cuarto de la Voz de la Patria Carlos María de Bustamante. . . . Mexico.

1937 Enfermedades políticas que padece la capital de esta Nueva España en casi todos los cuerpos de que se compone y remedios que se le deben aplicar para su curación si se quiere que sea útil al rey y al público; con una introducción por Genaro Estrada. Mexico.

VILLASEÑOR Y SÁNCHEZ, JOSÉ ANTONIO

1746–48 Theatro americano: Descripción general de los reynos y provincias de la Nueva-España, y sus jurisdicciones. 2 vols. Mexico.

1952 Theatro americano. . . . 2 vols. Mexico. [Facsimile edition of 1st ed., with an introduction by Francisco González de Cossío.]

WAGNER, HENRY RAUP

1929a Three accounts of the expedition of Fernando Cortés, printed in Germany between 1520 and 1522. *HAHR*, 9:176–212.

1929b Translation of a letter from the arch-bishop of Cosenza to Petrus de Acosta. *HAHR*, 9:361–63.

1942a The discovery of New Spain in 1518 by Juan de Grijalva. A translation of the original texts with an introduction and notes by Henry R. Wagner. Berkeley, Calif.

1942b The discovery of Yucatan by Francisco Hernández de Córdoba. A translation of the original texts with an introduction and notes by Henry R. Wagner. Berkeley, Calif.

1944 The rise of Fernando Cortés. Berkeley, Calif.

1946 Peter Martyr and his works. *Proceedings of the American Antiquarian Society*, 56:238–88.

WEIDITZ, CHRISTOPH
1927 Das Trachtenbuch des Christoph Weiditz, von seinen Reisen nach Spanien (1529) und den Niederlanden (1531/32) nach der in der Bibliothek des Germanischen Nationalmuseums zu Nürnberg aufbewahrten Handschrift, herausgegeben von Dr. Theodor Hampe. Historische Waffen und Kostume, 2. Berlin.

1963 Hernán Cortés y el libro de trajes de Cristoph Weiditz. Frans Blom, ed. *Instituto de Ciencias y Artes de Chiapas*, 11:7–14.

1969 *See* Cline, 1969.

WILGUS, A. CURTIS
1933–41 Some sixteenth century histories and historians of America. *Bulletin of the Pan American Union*, 67:558–66, 741–49; 70:322–26, 406–11, 572–78; 72:293–99; 73:42–47; 74:392–97; 75:174–79. Washington.

1942 Histories and historians of Hispanic America. New York.

1966 *Idem*, reprinted.

WILLIAMS, HELEN MARIA
1814 *See* Humboldt, 1814.

WILMERE, ALICE
1859 *See* Champlain, 1859.

WINSOR, JUSTIN
1884-89 Narrative and critical history of America. 8 vols. Boston and New York.

XIMÉNEZ, FRANCISCO
1615 Quatro libros, de la naturaleza, y virtudes de las plantas y animales que están recebidos en el uso de medicina en la Nueva España, y la méthodo, y corección, y preparación, que para administrarlas se requiere con lo que el Doctor Francisco Hernández escribió en lengua latina. . . . Traducido, y aumentados muchos simples, y compuestos y otros muchos secretos curativos, por Fr. Francisco Ximénez. . . . Mexico.

1888 Cuatro libros de la naturaleza y virtudes medicinales de las plantas y animales de la Nueva España. Mexico.

YÁÑEZ, AGUSTÍN
1963 Crónicas de la conquista. Introducción, selección y notas. 3d ed. Mexico.

ZAMORA CASTELLANOS, PEDRO
1933 *See* Villagutierre Soto-Mayor, 1933.

ZARAGOZA, JUSTO
1878 *See* Suárez de Peralta, 1878.

1882 *See* Fuentes y Guzmán, 1882.

1894 *See* López de Velasco, 1894.

ZORITA, ALONSO DE
1891 Breve y sumaria relación de los señores y maneras y diferencias que había de ellos en la Nueva España, y en otras provincias sus comarcanas, y de sus leyes, usos y costumbres, y de la forma que tenían en les tributar sus vasallos en tiempos de su gentilidad, y la que después de conquistados se ha tenido y tiene en los tributos que pagan a S. M., y de la orden que se podría tener para cumplir con el precepto de los diezmos, sin que lo tengan por nueva imposición y carga los naturales de aquellas partes, dirigida a la C. R. M. del Rey Don Felipe Ntro. Sr. por el doctor Alonso de Zorita. . . . *In* García Icazbalceta, 1886–92, 3:71–227.

1909 Historia de la Nueva España por el doctor Alonso de Zorita (siglo XVI). Colección de libros y documentos referentes a la historia de América, 9. Manuel Serrano y Sanz, ed. Madrid.

1963a Breve y sumaria relación de los señores de la Nueva España. Prólogo y notas de Joaquín Ramírez Cabañas. 2d ed. Mexico.

1963b Life and labor in ancient Mexico: The brief and summary relation of the lords of New Spain by Alonso de Zorita. Translated with an introduction by Benjamin Keen. New Brunswick, N. J.

13. Religious Chroniclers and Historians: A Summary with Annotated Bibliography

ERNEST J. BURRUS, S.J.

THIS ARTICLE discusses selected religious chroniclers and historians, indicates briefly the contents of their works and their scope in area and time, and attempts some evaluation of them. An Epilogue serves as summary and is followed by an annotated bibliography of works by and about the authors discussed, arranged alphabetically by author in dictionary form. Accents on foreign words have been uniformly modernized, except as qualified in note 1.[1]

Biobibliographical information is arranged by the Order to which the author belonged. The Orders appear in the sequence in which they began their work in New Spain and, within the Order, by date of establishment of provinces. For each province, writers usually appear in chronological sequence, by date of composition of their work. Table 1 lists authors alphabetically and adds summary data.

[1] Ed. note: Throughout the *Handbook* accents are omitted from Spanish and Mexican place names, except in quotations and titles of publications, but are retained on personal names.

GENERAL OBSERVATIONS AND BACKGROUND

The limited manpower and economic resources available required that the various Orders, as they took up their ministries, be assigned specific geographical areas for which they had primary, if not exclusive, responsibility. Over the course of time it was found that the initial apportionment contributed to better mastery of often difficult native languages and adoption of uniform mission methods peculiar to each religious corporation.

In general the works discussed below record work among the converted or already Christianized Indians (*fieles*) and among those still to be converted (*infieles*.) The fieles were ministered to in cities and towns; the infieles lived scattered through mountain and plain. Often they were brought together in small and numerous preplanned communities known as *congregaciones*. As the chronicles detail activity among European Spaniards, Negroes, various mixed breeds, as well as Indians, the ethnohistorian must select from such information those

TABLE 1 — RELIGIOUS CHRONICLERS AND HISTORIANS*

Name	Dates	Order	Principal Areas Treated	Time Span
Alcocer, José Antonio	1749–1802	O.F.M.	New Spain, northern Mexico	1600–1789?
Aldana, Cristóbal de	1735–?	O.Merc.	New Spain, Central America	1524–1687
Alegre, Francisco Javier	1729–88	S.J.	Florida, New Spain, northern Mexico	1566–1766
Arlegui, José	fl. 18thC	O.F.M.	Zacatecas, northern Mexico	1603–1733 (1827)
Arricivita, Juan Domingo	fl. 18thC	O.F.M.	New Spain, northern Mexico	1740?–1790?
Baegert, Johann Jakob	1717–72	S.J.	Lower California (south)	1751–68
Balthasar, Johann Anton, see under José Ortega	1697–1763	S.J.	Northern Mexico, Pimeria Alta	1710–54
Barco, Miguel del	1706–90	S.J.	Lower California	1697–1767
Basalenque, Diego	1577?–1651	O.S.A.	Michoacan	1535–1644
Beaumont, Pablo de la Purísima Concepción	1710–80	O.F.M.	Western Mexico, northern Mexico, Michoacan	1523–65
Benavente, Toribio de	1482/91–1568	O.F.M.	New Spain, Central Mexico	1523–40
Benavides, Alonso de	fl. 1630	O.F.M.	New Mexico	1540?–1630
Burgoa, Francisco de	1605–81	O.P.	Oaxaca	1526–1650
Clavigero, Francisco Javier	1731–87	S.J.	New Spain, Lower California	1697–1768
Cogolludo, Diego López de	1610–86	O.F.M.	Yucatan	1640–56
Dávila Padilla, Agustín	1562–1604	O.P.	Central Mexico, New Spain	1526–92
Escobar, Matías de	16? –1748	O.S.A.	Central Mexico, Michoacan	1644–1729
Espinosa, Isidro Félix de	1679–1755	O.F.M.	New Spain, Michoacan, Jalisco, Guatemala	1565–1630; 1523–1740
Florencia, Francisco	1620–95	S.J.	Florida, central Mexico, Michoacan	1566–82
Fluviá, Francisco, see under José Ortega	1699–1783	S.J.	. . .	. . .
Franco, Alonso y Ortega	. . .	O.P.	New Spain	1591–1645
García, Esteban	. . .	O.S.A.	New Spain, Philippines	1602–75
González de la Puente, Juan	1580–16?	O.S.A.	Central Mexico, Michoacan, Orient	1535–1623
Grijalva, Juan de	ca. 1559–1638	O.S.A.	Central Mexico, Michoacan, Philippines, Orient	1533–92
Jiménez, Francisco	1666-ca. 1722	O.P.	Guatemala, Chiapas	pre-Conquest–1719
Kino, Eusebio Francisco	1645–1711	S.J.	Northern Mexico, Lower California, southwest United States	1683–1711
Landa, Diego de	1524–79	O.F.M.	Yucatan	pre-Conquest–1560
Lizana, Bernardo de	1581–1631	O.F.M.	Yucatan	pre-Conquest–1630

López de Cogolludo, Diego, see Cogolludo, Diego López de

*Compiled by Volume Editor.

139

(*Table 1, continued*)

Name	Dates	Order	Principal Areas Treated	Time Span
Medina, Baltasar de	? –1696	O.F.M.	Central Mexico	1523–1679
Mendieta, Jerónimo de	1528–1604	O.F.M.	New Spain, Central Mexico	1510–96
Motolinía, *see* Benavente, Toribio de				
Muñoz, Diego	1550–1610	O.F.M.	Michoacan, Jalisco	1565–83
Ojea, Hernando	1560–ca. 1615	O.P.	Central Mexico, Oaxaca	1592–1607
Ornelas Mendoza y Valdivia, Nicolás de	1662–ca. 1725	O.F.M.	Jalisco	1530–1722
Ortega, José	1700–68	S.J.	Nayarit, Pimeria Alta	1721–54
Palou, Francisco	1723–89	O.F.M.	Upper California	1767–80
Pareja, Francisco de	? –1628	O.Merc.	New Spain, Central America	1524–1687
Pérez de Ribas, Andrés	1576–1655	S.J.	New Spain, Sinaloa	1572–1654
Pfefferkorn, Ignaz	1725–post 1795	S.J.	Sonora	1740?–67
Píccolo, Francisco M.	1654–1729	S.J.	Lower California	18thC
Rea, Alonso de la	1610–16?	O.F.M.	Michoacan, Jalisco	pre-Conquest–1640
Remesal, Antonio de	1570–1639	O.P.	Guatemala, Chiapas, Central America, Philippines	1526–1619
Sánchez Baquero, Juan	1548–1619	S.J.	Central Mexico	1571–80
Tello, Antonio	1564?–1633?	O.F.M.	Jalisco, western Mexico	1565–1630
Torres, Francisco Mariano	fl. 18thC	O.F.M.	Jalisco, Michoacan, northern Mexico	1630–1750?
Vásquez, Francisco	fl. 1559	O.F.M.	Guatemala	1524–1600
Venegas, Miguel	1680–1764	S.J.	Lower California	1697–1739
Vetancurt, Agustín de	1620–ca. 1700	O.F.M.	Central Mexico, New Spain	pre-Conquest–1698
Villerías, Gaspar de	ca. 1562–?	S.J.	Central Mexico, Michoacan	1572–82
Ximénez, Francisco, *see* Jiménez, Francisco				

data bearing particularly on native peoples and cultures.

Each Order had particular strengths and emphasis. The Jesuits, for instance, devoted the greater part of their number and time to education, from primitive schools for Indians in the northern missions to more sophisticated colleges in the main Europeanized urban centers.

The chronicles and histories, for the most part, deal with activities solely within one province of an Order, and usually cover only a very limited time span. No chronicler attempts to record the ministry of his province during the entire colonial period, excepting only Francisco Javier Alegre, for the Jesuits. None attempted extended chronicles or history of his Order in all New Spain, much less general works for all Orders for that area.

The chroniclers show wide divergences among themselves. They vary greatly in sources consulted and cited, in the manner and exactness of quotations, cross-references, indexes, style of composition, chronological sequences, amounts of biographical, geographical, and cultural information, and, above all, in their critical acumen and spirit. Some were naïve, credulous, and given to choosing and enlarging upon all that seemed unusual and extraordinary. Such a wide range of reliability requires especially cautious use and verification of statements from all chronicles.

It was customary for each Order to appoint an official historian for each of their provinces. He had complete access to unpublished materials in the local archives of the Order, normally replete with correspondence, reports, accounts, catalogs, and other papers of the individual houses and institutions. The original biographical and other important notices in these repositories have in general been lost, except what was utilized and conserved.

Chroniclers were often missionaries who had worked among Indians. Hence they had the advantage of firsthand knowledge of their charges' daily habits, ways of thought, and emotional responses. Forced to learn native languages, they possessed a key to the complex Indian cultural world usually closed to other historians. No outsider, moreover, knew as much as they about the official terminology and legislation governing their Order.

But chroniclers were all too prone to over-defend their own religious corporation against all comers: other Orders, secular clergy, civil authorities. Unfortunately most also overstrained to "edify" their brethren and the general reader. Thus on the debit side of the chroniclers' ledger are many things. Not least among them is prolixity, with insignificant domestic chitchat, over-glorification of real or imaginary virtues of fellow members of the Order, automatic defense of it in even trivial controversies and unimportant matters. There are other weaknesses—but there are also strengths.

In most cases the chroniclers were contemporary, or nearly so, with events and episodes they record. Occasionally they were actual participants and eyewitnesses,

or were able to draw on those who were. As a rule the chroniclers were curious about Indians, and discuss their culture, customs, religion ("superstitions"), language, crafts, dress, games, character, their country and its products, and much else, however unsystematically. Collectively the combined efforts of the religious chroniclers preserve in writing many things not found elsewhere. Thus the chronicles are still an important, and not wholly exhausted, corpus of data about natives of Middle America.

Historians, of course, have in various ways utilized these chronicles and histories for many years. A discussion of this group of writers as a whole, outlining basic facts on many of the principal figures, appears in Raquel García Méndez (1930). For many purposes, however, there has been a lack of bibliographical controls and critical evaluation of these sources. Even more serious, many works still await scholarly publication. Printed texts are often corrupt, commentary superficial, and scholarship to clarify puzzling points still to be performed. With few exceptions the standard apparatus of modern scholarship is quite lacking: adequate indexes, chronological guides, concordances of unpublished data, good maps. Critical editions of the chronicles would furnish a useful tool for fruitful research.

BIOBIBLIOGRAPHICAL SOURCES

Space confines our discussion to only a few outstanding works: first general ones, then those on individual Orders.

General

The first bibliography of the New World was the *Epítome* by León Pinelo (1629). Recent studies of this important work have been made by Millares Carlo (1958) and Quiñones (1968).

The best and most complete general reference work is that of Streit (1916–67). He lists most of the religious chronicles mentioned below (and others), giving a succinct, reliable account of contents, fairly accurate biographical notices of the author, libraries in which copies may be found, and often a critical evaluation. He includes a few of the more important unpublished manuscripts, usually in a separate section or appendix. There is considerable unevenness in the Streit volumes. This may be due to his having studied some works at first hand, but for others having relied on other bibliographical compilations. He confuses several important writings. His primary purpose was to furnish a comprehensive bibliography of the history of missions, not of chroniclers.

The present article relies on Streit in many instances, but unless expressly noted, it can be assumed that a direct study of the chronicle in question was made. Where a later or more analytic account than Streit's has been published, preference for the latter will be indicated. In some instances these more detailed studies appear from the hands of an editor or other specialist who has provided biobibliographical material to an edition or re-edition.

José Toribio Medina also provides abundant bibliography on chronicles. Those which were published in Mexico City appear in his work covering the years 1539–1891 (Medina, 1909–11). A parallel work (Medina, 1898–1907) deals with those printed in Europe. These 15 volumes maintain a high level of 19th-century scholarship.

Difficult to use, but useful, are the works of José M. Beristáin de Souza. Beristáin's *Biblioteca* is a vast biobibliographical work, first published in 1816–21. It was based on Eguiara y Eguren's pioneering *Bibliotheca mexicana* (1755), and Beristáin's own material. The more readily available second edition (1883) of Beristáin was followed by a third in 1947. The last also includes a bewildering maze of relatively unorganized additions, a less than successful attempt to summarize the bibliographies of Ramírez,

Medina, Wagner, and many others, making the 1883 version preferred.

Beristáin is annoyingly inaccurate and unreliable, yet indispensable. He provides a wealth of material on manuscripts. But his titles of books are usually inexact and vague; this is especially true of those first translated from Spanish into Latin by Eguiara y Eguren, then retranslated into Spanish from the Latin by Beristáin. Numerous printed works attributed by Beristáin to exiled Jesuits can hardly be explained otherwise than as wholesale and deliberate falsification.

Usefulness of a basic work by Ricard (1933a, 1947, 1966) is limited chiefly by the short time span he covers, from 1523 to 1572. He deals critically and extensively in an initial bibliographical chapter with chronicles of the three major Orders of that period: Franciscans, Dominicans, and Augustinians. There is a Spanish translation (Ricard, 1947) of his book, with a few references not found in the original French edition of 1933. There is also a less than satisfactory English translation (1966). Here we cite the original (1933a), unless otherwise noted.

Based in large part on materials in the *Handbook of Latin American Studies*, edited by Lewis Hanke and others, Charmion Shelby in 1949 listed numerous reissued chronicles, both secular and religious, that had appeared 1937–48. Such re-editions are usually noted in the continuing annual issues of the *Handbook*, with evaluative comment.

Franciscans

The standard general biobibliographical work on the Franciscan Order is by Luke Wadding, O.F.M. (1650). This single volume has been reprinted (1806, 1906), but other hands added to it, forming a so-called second edition (1731–1886) that reached 25 volumes. Volume 15, covering 1492–1515, initiates New World material, terminating

1612–22 (vol. 25). Civezza (1879) remains an important survey of Franciscan sources and publications.

José Ascencio's monograph (1944a, b) lists manuscripts and printed chronicles by Franciscans in New Spain and dependent areas, by provinces. He makes no serious attempt to evaluate critically the numerous works included. He supplies a few biographical items, usually the vague ones of Beristáin. He includes manuscript chronicles (as a rule) only when mentioned by that compiler. Manuscripts deposited in Rome are carefully described by Borges (1959).

Superior is the series of monographic articles by Marion A. Habig, O.F.M. They appeared in *The Americas* under the general title "The Franciscan Provinces of Spanish North America" (Habig, 1944–45). Also first appearing as articles in the same journal, then published as a single volume, is the careful biobibliographical summary of Franciscan authors in Central America by Eleanor B. Adams (1953).

Other references: López-Velarde López, 1964; Ocaranza, 1933–34; Zulaica, 1939.

Dominicans

What Wadding is to Franciscan bibliography, that Quétif and Echard (1719–21) are to the Dominicans. They provide biographical data on each author, followed by a list of his manuscript and published writings (Streit, 1916, Introduction, p. 16).

Disappointing and deceptive is Roze (1878), whose title *Les Dominicains en Amérique* . . . is misleading. The only Middle American province chronicled is Santiago de Mexico. A note (Roze, 1878, p. 76, n. 1) merely indicates that the latter was subdivided to form provinces in Chiapas, Oaxaca, and the last, Puebla. Brief coverage, by provinces, is given by Asencia (1946). José M. de Agreda y Sánchez gives an excellent study of the official chroniclers of the Dominicans in New Spain in his introduction to Ojea's *Libro tercero* (Ojea, 1897).

For Dominicans in Guatemala during the colonial period Juan Rodríguez Cabal (1961) has compiled an exhaustive catalog. It lists writers alphabetically and provides biobibliographical information.

There seems to be no formal chronicle for the Puebla province. There is, however, a major printed source that appeared at four-year intervals: Acta provincilia, published in Puebla. The earliest I have seen is 1743, the latest 1796. Each contains much on the Indian ministry: villages, languages, priests, and the like of special interest to ethnohistorians. Abundant manuscript and published material on Dominicans in the Puebla area is recorded by Arce (1910–11). He carries the narrative to 1610.

Augustinians

The most complete and scholarly bibliography on Augustinian chroniclers is the multi-volume *Ensayo* by Vela (vols. 1–3, 1913–17; vols. 5–6, 1920–22; vols. 7–8, 1925–31). He supplies a good biographical sketch, with a list of the author's unpublished and published writings. When Vela has the information, he states in which repository the unpublished items were found. Printed separately (Vela, 1918a) and then used as introduction to his edition of García (1918b), his article on the Augustinians in New Spain during the 16th and 17th centuries is useful. Diego Pérez Arrilucea (1913–14) gives a history of the Order in colonial Mexio.

Jesuits

The standard Jesuit biobibliographical work is Sommervogel (1890–1930), an 11-volume work reissued (in 12 volumes) in 1960. Considerably more detailed treatment of Spanish-American Jesuits is found in Uriarte (1904–16) and in Uriarte and Lecina (1925–30). A monumental compilation of biobibliographies of 16th- and 17th-century Jesuits in Mexico began to appear in Mexico in 1961 at the hands of Francisco Zambrano;

volumes 1 and 2 deal with those who died in the 16th century; Jesuits who died in the 17th century form a second series. In 1970 the 10th volume was published (last entry is "Páez, Melchor F."). Warren (1962) from standard sources provides a summary sketch of Jesuit historians of Sinaloa-Sonora. A more extended account of similar matters is given by Burrus (1963). Burrus (1967a) discusses some 300 maps of Jesuit missions, 46 of which are reproduced in the second volume of the work (see also Burrus, 1965b).

CHRONICLES AND HISTORIES, BY ORDERS

Franciscans (O.F.M.), 1523

Two Franciscan writers of special interest to ethnohistory receive separate and extended treatment elsewhere in this volume. Because Luis Nicolau d'Olwer, Howard F. Cline, and H. B. Nicholson treat Bernardino de Sahagún in Article 14, and José Alcina Franch similarly sketches Juan de Torquemada in Article 16, these two Franciscans are not included here.

Provincia del Santo Evangelio de Mexico, 1524

Toribio de Benavente ("Motolinía"), O.F.M. (1482/91–1569)

Toribio de Benavente, who took the name Motolinía, wrote an especially important religious chronicle, one by an eyewitness. As one of them, he records the coming and work of the famous first twelve Franciscans in New Spain (1524), and continues the account until about 1540. The original of his work is now lost, but a substantial portion survives in a work that was baptized by later hands as *Historia de los indios de la Nueva España*.

He divides the work into three "treatises" (*tratados*), prefaced by a long introductory letter (*epístola proemial*) chiefly on Indian history. Much of the book is devoted to conversion of Indians. For the ethnohistorian his accounts of their culture at European contact are invaluable. In them he discusses

native ways of life, religion and superstitions, reckoning of time, human sacrifices, gods, feasts, temples, Indian character, mental and moral attitudes, and means of transportation. Adib (1949) summarizes the image of the Indian as he appears in the *Historia*.

O'Gorman (1969, pp. xxxiv–xxxvii) lists nine editions, the first of which is 1848 (Benavente, 1848, 1858, 1869, 1914).[2] A facsimile edition of Benavente, 1869, published in 1966, is also cited by O'Gorman. There are five full or partial recent editions (Benavente, 1941, 1951, 1956a, 1956b, 1964) based on the previous more or less standard 1914 Spanish edition, each with a good biobibliographical account. A scholarly, critical edition, taking into account variations beween the two principal manuscripts, *Historia* and *Memoriales*, was edited by O'Gorman in 1969, superseding earlier texts. Steck's English translation (1951) has a brief but valuable commentary and a detailed analytical index. There is also a scholarly English translation by Foster (1950).

Motolinía wrote other works of ethnohistorical interest, though not strictly religious chronicles. Seemingly as a counterpart to his account of the spiritual conquest by the clergy, he wrote a now lost volume on the military conquest. It was used by López de Gómara, Bernal Díaz, and above all by Cervantes de Salazar, who cites it frequently (López, 1925).

Motolinía also left materials that in 1903 were carelessly published under the confected title of *Memoriales*. A facsimile of the 1903 publication appeared in Guadalajara, Mexico (1967). The *Memoriales* are generally fuller in treatment of topics also found in the *Historia*. They contain a wealth of data not included in the latter. As is true of the *Historia*, the 16th-century original manuscript of the *Memoriales* is missing,

[2] The Volume Editor has substituted the following paragraphs for those submitted by the author in 1960, to reflect the important scholarly literature that has appeared since then.

but survives in part at least in a 16th-century copy (Steck, 1951, pp. 48–53; Benavente, 1969, pp. xxxiii–xxxiv). Divided into two parts, the first contains 31 chapters (of which chaps. 3–13 are missing) on pre-Contact customs and antiquities; the second part (29 chaps.) is disordered, with chapters on a variety of topics. The *Memoriales* also contain inserted materials that may not have been part of the original manuscript. Such is a long section of the calendar and a calendar wheel (discussed in Article 23, no. 388), in part 1, chapter 16, as well as lists of towns and other materials in part 2, chapter 28. Lejeal (1907) provides a concordance between the *Memoriales* and the *Historia*.

Relationships between the so-called *Historia* and Motolinía's work known as *Memoriales* are puzzling and are the subject of diverse scholarly opinion. An earlier generation of Mexican scholars, notably Joaquín García Icazbalceta (1898), hypothesized that the latter was an earlier draft of the former. In scrutinizing the texts more closely, Atanasio López (1925, 1931) concluded that there was a larger lost Motolinía work which various colonial writers had used and cited, containing similar, more extensive materials than either the *Historia* or *Memoriales*, with references to books and chapters variant with them. Taking these findings into account and adding his own results, Robert Ricard in 1933 reversed his own earlier view of 1931 that had more or less accepted the earlier simple explanation of García Icazbalceta. Ricard (1933b) corroborated that Zorita, Las Casas, Cervantes de Salazar, Suárez de Peralta, Mendieta, Juan Bautista, and Torquemada all had copied from a work now lost. Ricard considered that the *Historia* and *Memoriales* were composed about the same time, 1536–41, that the former was a hasty and imperfect extract sent to Spain, and that the *Memoriales* were drafts of the later lost work on which Motolinía continued to work. Unpublished findings by Cline (n.d.) based on examination of Torquemada, Mendieta, Zo-

rita, and others substantiated Ricard's hypothesis that Motolinía had continued to work on the larger, lost work, called by Mendieta and Torquemada *De Moribus Indorum*, which they cited frequently. From scattered data Cline partially reconstructed its contents, noting overlapping unique parts of it reflected in either the *Historia* or the *Memoriales*, or both.

O'Gorman (1969), traversing independently some of the same ground, concluded that the *Historia* was an extract of the lost work, probably made after Motolinía's death in 1569. O'Gorman attributes its compilation to a now unknown person in Spain who had access to that production, but who was unfamiliar with many of the details of native matters in New Spain treated by Motolinía. O'Gorman has recently published his views on the *Memoriales* (Benavente, 1971), which he has re-edited.

Perhaps next to Sahagún these surviving works of Motolinía provide the most extensive and penetrating coverage of late pre-Hispanic and early post-Contact coverage of Indian history and culture in central Mexico. In their historical ethnography they go far beyond the often cursory treatment usually encountered in more strictly religious chronicles.

Other references: See Article 27B under Motolinía. Streit, 1924, pp. 112–15 (confuses Benavente's *Historia* with *Relación de Michoacán*); Ramírez, 1858; López, 1915–17, 1925, 1931; Lejeal, 1906, 1907; Ricard, 1924, 1933b; Luis González, 1949.

Jerónimo de Mendieta, O.F.M. (1528–1604)

Born in Vitoria, Spain, about 1528, Jerónimo (or Gerónimo) de Mendieta arrived in Mexico in 1554, following the pioneering period of the famous twelve original Franciscans, among whom was Motolinía.[3] Mendieta began writing his chronicle in 1571, finishing it in 1596. He died in Mexico City on May 10, 1604.

---

[3] Author's text resumes.

Mendieta wrote at a time when many eyewitnesses of the initial contact between Indians and Europeans were still alive; he utilized their information. He also drew not only on the works of Motolinía, but on those by Andrés de Olmos, Bernardino de Sahagún, and others in the archives of the Convent of San Francisco. He attempted purposefully to be an historian, and his work shows a logical organization not found in Motolinía. Mendieta's *Historia eclesiástica indiana* is considered to be a major ethnohistorical source.

It remained undiscovered until 1860. The *Historia* was unpublished until 1870, when it was first issued in Mexico City by Joaquín García Icazbalceta (Mendieta, 1870). This bulky folio tome was reissued in a much more handy four-volume edition (Mendieta, 1945a).

The entire work is divided into five books. These are: (1) De la Isla Española; (2) De los ritos y costumbres de los Indios en su infidelidad; (3) De cómo fue introducida la Fe entre los Indios de Nueva España; (4) Del aprovechamiento de los Indios de la Nueva España y progreso de su conversión; (5) part 1: Las vidas de los claros varones apostólicos obreros de esta nueva conversión que acabaron en paz con muerte natural; part 2: Las vidas de los frailes menores que han sido muertos por la predicación del Santo Evangélio en esta Nueva Espana. Each book is subdivided into chapters.

The 1870 edition has a general table of contents at the beginning and an index at the end. The table of contents in the 1945 edition is distributed at the end of each volume, with the index to the whole after the text of the final volume.

García Icazbalceta's introduction is printed in both editions. A biobibliographical study, it provides a brief and accurate account of the author and a penetrating critical evaluation of the work and its sources. He also notes use of the earlier unpublished manuscript by other historians, notably Juan de Torquemada, a controversial matter discussed in Article 16 by Alcina Franch. Phelan (1970) has studied Mendieta and his works in the context of the times.

Other references: Iglesia, 1945; Larraiñaga, 1914–15; López, 1925; Pilling, 1895; Streit, 1927, pp. 605–06 (summarizing García Icazbalceta, 1870).

Agustín de Vetancurt, O.F.M. (1620–ca. 1700)

Agustín de Vetancurt wrote his name that way. Other, and later, hands render it variously: Vetancurt, Betancourt, Betancurt. His *Teatro mexicano* is a fundamental work.

A creole, Vetancurt was born in Mexico City about 1620. He entered his Order in Puebla and for over 40 years worked among the Indians in the parish of San Jose of his natal city. He was considered one of the most eminent preachers in Nahuatl. He was appointed the official chronicler of his province. He died about 1700. Thus for the 16th century Vetancurt was not an eyewitness, but for the ill-documented 17th he is especially useful.

As official chronicler, Vetancurt recorded matters of interest to his province, and much more. The chronicle proper is the fourth part of his much more ambitious work, entitled *Teatro mexicano*, first published in Mexico City in 1698.

The *Teatro* is a massive production, divided into four parts, each subdivided into treatises. A summary of the parts reveals the scope of coverage.

Part 1, "sucesos naturales," is split into two treatises: (1) De la naturaleza, temple, sitio, nombre, longitud, fertilidad y otras grandezas del Nuevo Mundo; and (2) De la fertilidad y riqueza en común de este Nuevo Mundo. Part 2, "sucesos políticos," is made up of three treatises: (1) De los que habitaron la tierra de la Nueva España antes del deluvio [*sic*] and Del origen de sus naciones después y de sus primeros pobladores; (2) Del gobierno político y doméstico de los naturales en su gentilidad; and (3) De los nombres de los falsos dioses, templos, sirvientes y ritos gentílicos de los naturales de las Indias. Part 3, "sucesos militares," has two treatises: (1) De los sucesos militares de las armas; and (2) De las batallas y conquistas que hizo el ejército de españoles y tlaxcaltecas en México y sus contornos, referring to Mexico City.

The Vetancurt chronicle proper is (as mentioned) part 4. It has five treatises: (1) De la fundación de la Provincia del Santo Evangelio en la Nueva España; (2) De las Provincias y conventos de la Provincia del Santo Evangelio de Mexico; (3) De las custodias de la Provincia del Santo Evangelio; (4) De los conventos de las monjas que administra la Provincia del Santo Evangelio de Mexico; and (5) De las entradas y misiones que han hecho los religiosos de la Provincia del Santo Evangelio, obras útiles y santas imágenes que veneran. As a supplement or appendix to part 4 Vetancurt added a *Menologio franciscano*, fully as extensive as the *Crónica* itself. Finally, there are two additional treatises in part 4: (1) De la Ciudad de Mexico y las grandezas que la ilustran después que la fundaron las españoles; and (2) De la Ciudad de la Puebla de los Angeles y grandezas que la ilustran. These final two items do not follow the same order in the editions of Vetancurt.

The two later editions of the *Teatro* are easier to handle than the bulky 17th-century folio. The 1870–71 version is in four volumes, with a biobibliographical notice by the editors, followed by Vetancurt's indication of principal sources; printed (pp. xix–xxii), manuscript (pp. xxiii–xxvii). The most accessible and useful edition is that of 1960–61, also in four volumes. Especially helpful is its analytical index.

As Vetancurt's listing of sources suggests, he leaned heavily on works by Mendieta, via Torquemada, and others of his Order. Ricard notes (1933a, p. 7) that where Vetancurt's sources can be checked, he is reliable, the presumption being that where

he does not cite a specific reference he is equally so. It may be noted that Vetancurt does more than recopy previous materials. Vetancurt's *Teatro* preserves much information about pre-Contact and colonial Indians not found elsewhere.

Other references: Atanasio López, 1922, pp. 377–80.

Provincia de San Jose de Yucatan, 1559
Diego de Landa, O.F.M (1524–79)

Sahagún and Landa are usually taken as the two Franciscan chroniclers who provide an almost inexhaustible fount of data about the ancient Aztec and the ancient Maya. Father Angel Garibay, as a Nahuatalist, feels that Sahagún is much superior (Landa, 1959); A. M. Tozzer, a noted Mayanist who worked in both sources, remarked, "With the exception of Sahagún there is no other manuscript of New Spain which covers adequately a similar range of subjects" (Landa, 1941, p. vii).

Diego de Landa was born in Cifuentes de la Alcarria, Toledo, Spain, about 1524. After coming to Yucatan in 1549 as a Franciscan friar, he held various positions of authority in the monasteries of his Order. In 1572 he was appointed bishop of Merida (the diocese including all of Yucatan), a post he held in 1579 at his death (Landa, 1938b, pp. 10–11; Landa, 1959, pp. xi–xiv).

Landa wrote his fundamental *Relación de las Cosas de Yucatán* about 1566 while in Spain, but the first printed version did not appear until 300 years later.[4] The original manuscript of the *Relación* is lost. All versions derive from an undated but probably early 17th-century manuscript copy now in the Royal Academy of History, Madrid, seemingly incomplete (Landa, 1941, pp. vii–viii). It is not certain that the order of materials in the copy is that of the original.

As printed, the *Relación* contains 52

---

[4] The Volume Editor is responsible for remaining paragraphs on Landa.

chapters. Tozzer stated, "The source material presented by Landa includes practically every phase of social anthropology of the ancient Mayas, together with the history of the Spanish discovery, the conquest and the ecclesiastical and native history together with the first accurate knowledge of the hieroglyphic writing. It is especially complete on Maya religion and rituals. . . ." (Landa, 1941, p. vii).

Landa drew from a wide variety of sources. In addition to several European works (Oviedo, Gómara, and others), Landa utilized his own personal observations and experiences, as well as oral and written materials from natives. Genet (Landa, 1928–29, 1:12–18) discusses these matters in detail. It is also interesting that numerous others used Landa's work in manuscript, including those who compiled the 1579 *Relaciones geográficas* for Yucatan; Herrera, Cervantes de Salazar, and others among colonial chroniclers derive much about Yucatan from the *Relación*. Modern knowledge about the ancient Maya tends to date from the first publication of Landa's work in 1864.

This came at the hands of the celebrated French Americanist, Abbé Brasseur de Bourbourg (Landa, 1864; see Article 18). He provided a French translation, but arbitrarily divided the work, which is incomplete in this edition. The deficiencies of the Brasseur version were critically enumerated by Brinton (1887). The importance of the *Relación* soon brought forth better editions.

Including Brasseur's there have been at least 10 published editions of Landa, usually accompanied by additional materials of considerable scholarly merit. A second French version, edited by Genet, was left unfinished (Landa, 1928–29). Two appeared in Spain (Landa, 1881, 1900), one with previously omitted texts. The first English translation by W. E. Gates (Landa, 1937) was rapidly superseded by the standard Tozzer version (Landa, 1941)

whose massive scholarly apparatus makes it especially valuable. Three Mexican editions (Landa, 1938a, 1938b, 1959) are available, of which that edited by Héctor Pérez Martínez (7th ed.) is the Spanish language standard; the 1959 version edited by Garibay is basically a reissue of it, without notes but with other materials. Y. V. Knorosov, the Soviet scientist who has been trying to decipher the Landa alphabet, translated into Russian (from Genet, 1928, and DIU, 1900) the *Relación* which the Soviet Academy of Sciences published in 1955. His notes are largely based on Tozzer and his introduction is outdated and polemical.

Other reference: Landa, 1941 (Tozzer ed.), is exhaustive.

Diego López de Cogolludo, O.F.M. (1610–86)

Diego López de Cogolludo was born about 1610 in Alcala de Henares, Spain. On March 31, 1629, he donned the Franciscan habit, and spent many years as a missionary and a superior of his Order in Yucatan. He died about 1686.

Cogolludo's experiences apparently moved him to write his *Historia de Yucatán*, more an annalistic account than a real chronicle or true history. He was familiar with previous writings on the area and had a personal interest in historiography. It might also be said that his style is diffuse, that he overloads his narrative with pious and "edifying" accounts, especially so in biographies. He only occasionally and quite vaguely alludes to his sources. Cogolludo, however, used materials not available to Landa. He carries the narrative a century further. Landa stops at 1560, Cogolludo at 1656. This is by no means a great work, but it is a very useful one.

The continuing importance of the *Historia* for local matters had produced five editions (Cogolludo, 1688, 1842–45, 1867–68, 1955, 1957). The Mexican edition of 1957 seems to supplant completely the earlier versions.

Its first part contains an erudite editor's prologue by Jorge Ignacio Rubio Mañé, a good bibliography, and a biobibliographical study of Cogolludo, with details on the earlier editions. The introductory matter is followed by 780 facsimile pages of text from the Madrid edition of 1688, together with the unpaginated original index. The second part of the 1957 *Historia*, some 569 pages, is a commentary. It provides necessary corrections in a critical study, subdivided into three parts: Los Mayas; La Conquista Español; and El Régimen Español, terminating with an analytic index.

Bernardo de Lizana, O.F.M. (1581–1631)

Beside Landa, or even the lesser Cogolludo, Bernardo de Lizana is indeed a relatively minor chronicler of Yucatan. He was born in 1581 in Ocaña, Toledo, Spain, came to Yucatan in 1606, and worked there until his death 25 years later (April 2, 1631). He is credited with mastering Maya and teaching it to many.

His bibliographical fame rests on his *Historia de Yucatán*, a chronicle first published in Valladolid, Spain (1633). For it he apparently utilized unpublished and now lost sources like Padre Alonso de Solana's "Noticias sagradas y profanas de las antigüades y conversiones de los Indios de Yucatán." A second edition (which I have not seen) was issued by the Museo Nacional, Mexico, in 1893. A French translation of portions of part 1 was published by Brasseur de Bourbourg (1864).

Other references: Asencio, 1944b, p. 10; Habig, 1944–45, p. 227; Streit, 1924, p. 453; 1927, p. 667.

Provincia de San Pedro y San Pablo de Michoacan, 1565

Diego Muñoz, O.F.M. (1550–1610)

Born in Cholula (ca. 1550), Diego Muñoz was twice provincial superior. He died in

1610 (or shortly afterwards). His chronicle or *Memorial* gives a view of Michoacan about the year 1583.

Its translated full title practically lists its contents: Description of the Province of the Apostles St. Peter and St. Paul, and of the militia, dwelling, customs and way of life of the unconverted Chichimec Indians, whose conversion the religious of our Order have been and are attending. Muñoz provides data on the subjects of his title. He also gives considerable attention to eminent Franciscans, first of Michoacan, then of Jalisco. Both Mendieta and Vetancurt used the manuscript version of Muñoz' *Memorial*.

It might be noted that Franciscans seemingly began work in Michoacan quite early (1525/26) and that there is a *Relación de Mechuacán* attributed to Martín de Jesús (or de la Coruña) about 1538/39. Data on Michoacan and Jalisco for periods before it became a province may also be found in Motolinía. Muñoz and Alonso de la Rea were the first chroniclers of the province whose writings have been preserved. Those of Muñoz remained unpublished for nearly three and a half centuries.

The Muñoz chronicle has been twice published. Atanasio López (1922) included it as the latter portion of a long article. The second edition is in book form (Muñoz, 1951) edited by José Ramírez Flores, who has also added additional useful documents (pp. 54–76) in an appendix.

Other references: For *Relación de Mechuacán*, see Article 23, no. 213; Article 27B, no. 1004.

Alonso de la Rea, O.F.M. (1610–16 ?)

Alonso de la Rea was born in Queretaro in 1610. He wrote his *Crónica* in 1637–39, providing data on Michoacan and Jalisco. For many matters he leaned heavily on Torquemada, who in turn had copied them from Mendieta. Ricard, quoting an 18th-century opinion, mentions that Rea lacked

149

interest in chronology to an excessive degree (Ricard, 1933a, p. 9). His work was, however, an official and methodical chronicle of the province, preserving considerable detail about it. Rea's *Crónica . . . 1639* was first published in 1643, and is now a bibliographical rarity.

The volume is divided into three books, totaling 92 chapters. Book 1 describes the region, products, people, their dealings with Aztecs, their general traits, religious rites, the last native emperors, and coming of the Spaniards. This is followed by arrival of the Franciscan missionaries, with biographies of some of these pioneer friars. Book 2 begins with the division of the province between Michoacan and Jalisco (1606) and contains numerous biographies of the members of that Order. Book 3 is also a series of lives, and an account of the Custodio del Río Verde.

There is a second, handy edition (Rea, 1882) published in Mexico. Neither paper nor print is fully adequate but it does include additional relevant documents in three appendices (pp. 443–75). At the end of the text there is a table of contents, but no index.

Isidro Félix de Espinosa, O.F.M. (1679–1755)

One of the more important successors to Muñoz and Rea was Isidro Félix de Espinosa. He was born in Queretaro, November 26, 1679. He served his Order in Michoacan, Texas, and his native Queretaro. There he was guardian of the famous Colegio de la Santa Cruz, where he died February 12, 1755.

Espinosa was author of two quite distinct chronicles, with which we shall deal separately. One is related to the Franciscan Province of Michoacan, the other a more general record of Franciscan missionaries in New Spain.

The Michoacan *Crónica* was written about 1752, and nominally includes materials as late as 1751. Following 1630, how-

ever, these notices are superficial; to that date Espinosa follows the same pattern as Rea, but with more details, presumably from a more fully documented base.

León pointed out Espinosa's strong reliance on Beaumont (treated in the next section), a major portion of whose chronicle he copies. Espinosa himself, however, noted his own wide use of that source and hence deflected charges of plagiarism similar to those leveled at Torquemada for incorporating much of Mendieta, and at Vetancurt for copying Torquemada.

The first publication of the Espinosa chronicle of Michoacan came nearly 150 years after its composition, edited by Nicolás León (Espinosa, 1899). León prefaced it with "Apuntamientos bio-bibliográficos," and issued a few copies printed on extremely wretched, fragile paper. In 1945 José Ignacio Dávila Garibi reissued the chronicle, as well as León's "Apuntamientos" in an excellent second edition that boasts an erudite prologue and notes, justifying its claim to be "amply improved and illustrated."

A second work by Espinosa is noteworthy for the generous amounts of ethnohistory it contains. Published in 1746, this *Chrónica . . . de todos los colegios* was a substantial folio volume, covering all of New Spain. In it Espinosa depicts his heroes, Franciscan friars, converting the Indians of several regions. It is especially strong on Central American matters, notably Guatemala, and what Espinosa calls the "Gentilidad de Talamanca." The subtitle of the work states it is "primera parte" (all that was published) of a projected three. A scholarly re-edition, with notes and introduction by Lino G. Canedo, O.F.M., appeared in 1964.

Pablo de la Purísima Concepción Beaumont, O.F.M. (1710–80)

There are only meager biographical data about Pablo de la Purísima Concepción Beaumont, whose work is a major source on Michoacan. Few go beyond Beristáin to fix a birthdate (ca. 1710). Madrid was his home city. His father was personal physician to Philip V of Spain; the surname suggests French descent. The chronicler first studied medicine in Paris, and took up practice in the royal hospital of Mexico City, after which he entered the Franciscan Order. He worked chiefly from the Colegio de la Santa Cruz (Queretaro). He died about 1780.

Despite its title "Chronicle of the Holy Apostles St. Peter and St. Paul of Michoacan," Beaumont's work in fact spans a much greater area, including much of western Mexico, northward to New Mexico, and tending toward a general history. It provides details to 1565, the date 1575 in the first edition (Beaumont, 1873–74, 1:6) being an error. Bancroft (1883, 3:726) stated that Beaumont had a prolix style and was "confused at times," but, he added, that and other drawbacks "must be overlooked, and the importance of the material [be] chiefly considered." Beaumont stated in a preliminary note to the reader that he considered Rea's chronicle much too summary, and presumably sought to correct this deficiency by a large-scale plan that he never completed.

Beaumont divided his total work into two major parts, the first, or *Aparato*, intended to be introductory to the second or the *Crónica* proper. The first seems complete, but the second was never finished.

The *Aparato* takes up fully a third of the extant Beaumont work, although nominally introductory. It deals with the discovery of America and the conquest of Mexico to the year 1521. It was twice published before appearance of the total work. Far more valuable is the *Crónica*. It consists of two books, and one chapter of book 3.

Book 1 begins with the "Discovery," followed by the Conquest, the coming of the Franciscans, the conquest of Nueva Galicia, and the first viceroy of New Spain, Antonio de Mendoza. Book 2 opens with elevation of the Mexican custodia to province

status, establishment of the custodia of Michoacan (1536), and erection of the diocese of Michoacan. Beaumont gives much attention to Franciscan educational and missionary work, both around Mexico City and in Michoacan; he also notes the important work of the Augustinians and of Vasco de Quiroga. At some length he records the expedition of Vázquez Coronado, the founding of Valladolid (Morelia), hospitals for Indians, University of Mexico, and the coming of the second viceroy. There are also biographies of prominent missionaries, churchmen, and administrators, the founding of episcopal sees, and the expedition of Francisco de Ibarra, taking events in detail through 1565. Matters of later date are occasionally mentioned. The one extant chapter of book 3 discusses maize as a source of food and drink for the Tarascans. He had hoped to bring his narrative to 1640, but sickness and death apparently intervened.

Beaumont drew on a wide variety of sources. He tells us that he gathered a large quantity of manuscripts from various Franciscan archives as well as listing 30 standard writers in printed sources (with whom at times he disagrees). He gives full copies of some of his documents, of which several have since disappeared. He speaks of obtaining a native painting (Beaumont, 1932, 2:25, 124), possibly from which his illustrations came. Of special interest are Indian paintings Beaumont included. These show incidents of the first visits of Spaniards to Michoacan, their reception by Tarascans, labors of the Franciscans, coats of arms of principal cities of Michoacan, and other matters (Bancroft, 1883, 3:726). All episodes depicted predate 1550 (see Article 23, nos. 25–26).

It is usually thought that Beaumont composed his work around 1777. That is the last date in the later copies of the original manuscript. Unfortunately his original manuscript seems to be lost. It was copied in Mexico City around 1792 to form volumes 7–11 of a 32-volume *Collection of Me-*

morias on New Spain, ordered by Viceroy Conde de Revilla Gigedo and compiled by Manuel de la Vega, O.F.M. Three partially complete sets of these Vega *Memorias* are known; from one or another of them come other recopied manuscript copies of the Beaumont work, as well as printed versions.

Editions of the work have had a somewhat unfortunate publishing history. In 1826 Bustamante published an incomplete and useless edition of the *Aparato*, attributing it to Vega, who had owned the manuscript Bustamante used. In 1873–74 a five-volume edition of both *Aparato* and *Crónica* appeared in Mexico; it lacks the Indian drawings, and was based on a secondary manuscript copy made by J. F. Ramírez that then belonged to Alfredo Chavero. A three-volume version was published by the National Archives of Mexico in 1932, based on their copy of the 1792 *Collection of Memorias*; it contains the Indian drawings and an introduction by Rafael López. The text seems slightly corrupt, but it may be near the original, as Beaumont said his Spanish was defective, owing to his Parisian rearing.

Other references: Ricard, 1933a, pp. 9–10; Chavero, 1904, 1:217–30; Rafael López, 1932, pp. 354–64.

Provincia del Santisimo Nombre de Jesus de Guatemala, 1565

Francisco Vásquez, O.F.M. (fl. 1559)

Francisco Vásquez compiled an exceptionally good chronicle. It includes a wealth of detail, with verbatim copies of numerous original documents. Its depth and scope are suggested by the subtitles of each of the first books of volume 1: Book 1, " . . . infancy of this holy Province, which contains the first forty years since the appearance of the Apostolic sons of Seraphic Religion in the extensive and very flourishing Guatemalan realm, with the first and very brave, very noble conquerors of it and its provinces, from the years 1524 to 1565, at which time erected into a Province was this

Franciscan organization. . . ." Book 2, equally florid, covers materials from 1565 through 1600.

The first edition (Vásquez, 1714–16), divided into these two books, appeared in Guatemala City. A second (Vásquez, 1938–44) supplants it. In four volumes, it has good notes, indexes, and a biobibliographical introduction by Lázaro Lamarid, O.F.M.

Provincia de San Diego de Mexico, 1599

Baltasar de Medina, O.F.M. (? –1696)

The sole published chronicle on this province is that of Baltasar Medina (1682). Despite a diffuse style, he provides a wealth of reliable information, from the coming of the first Franciscans (1523) to the year 1679. To aid chronological developments, the year he is discussing is placed by Medina in the margin, and hence it is easier to follow his materials than those of most fellow chroniclers.

In his prologue, Medina discusses his principal manuscript and printed sources. In the course of writing he points out anew the specific place from which his information is drawn. Quite useful is a map (between fols. 229 and 230) on which are sketched the 12 monastic houses he describes, extending, as he says, "From Oaxaca to Aguascalientes. Eastward [the province] is bounded by the Bishopric of Puebla and Oaxaca; on the west by Michoacan and Guadalajara, and at the north and south by the Archbishopric of Mexico."

Medina devotes considerable attention to the ministry of each of the dozen central monasteries, but the bulk of the volume, totaling 259 folios, is devoted to biographies of the more eminent Franciscans. He gives helpful lists of the general officers (*comisarios generales*) of the Order (fols. 208–10), as well as the lesser jurisdictions within the province of San Diego: chapters, custodies, ministries (fols. 211–20), followed by a "brief and panegyric" description of cities, villas, and communities in which the houses of the Order were founded (fols. 221–58).

Other reference: Streit, 1924, pp. 613–14.

Provincia de San Francisco de Zacatecas, 1603

José Arlegui, O.F.M. (fl. 18thC)

By comparison with more reliable authors, it soon becomes evident that José Arlegui is very uneven. In the earlier and more general history he is inaccurate and untrustworthy. Closer to his own 18th-century times, he evidently drew on more exact sources. His own work closes with the year 1733. As Habig (1944–45, pp. 335–37) suggests, Arlegui's work warrants more penetrating critical analysis than it has received.

He indicates early the general sources from which he draws, but thereafter he seldom specifies them further. Here and there he does insert verbatim some important documents (e.g., pp. 17–18). Ricard (1933a, p. 10) thought Arlegui superior to some other chroniclers, as he attempts to indicate chronology; Ricard adds, however, that unfortunately the chronology is not wholly accurate and is contradictory.

Arlegui's *Crónica* is divided into five parts. Part 1 details the origin of the Custodia of Zacatecas. Part 2 gives data on the monasteries and unusual episodes connected with their founding. Part 3 provides the boundaries, and discusses the customs of the "barbarian" Indians therein and the hostilities that have occurred with them to his own day. Part 4 contains biographies of friars who met death in their ministry at the hands of hostile Indians. Part 5 gives similar accounts of various famous Franciscans of the province.

In addition to the original 1737 edition there is a second one, 1851. To it has been added "Notes for the continuation of the chronicle . . . compiled by Fr. Antonio Gálvez in the year 1827." It has a table of contents (pp. 487–88).

Other references: Meade, 1962; Sotomayor, 1889.

Provincia de Jalisco, 1606

Antonio Tello, O.F.M. (1564?–1633?)

Seemingly, Antonio Tello was earlier thought to be a Mestizo or Indian, born in Guadalajara about 1564/66 and educated in Mexico City. Recent research by Gómez Canedo (1959), however, shows him to be a Spaniard who could not have arrived in the New World before 1619. He served in various Franciscan convents—Zacoalco, Tecolotlan, Cocula. Near his death (around 1633) he finished his "Miscellaneous Chronicle," which is discussed by Iguíniz (1917). Its book 1, now lost, would be especially useful as an ethnohistorical source, as it dealt with the Indians of New Spain (Brand, 1944, pp. 89, 103).

Only slowly have the surviving parts of the *Crónica* seen print. Manuscripts of books 2, 4, 5, and 6 are in the Biblioteca Pública, Guadalajara, Mexico; book 3 is in the John Carter Brown Library, Providence, Rhode Island. Apparently no parts of books 5 and 6 have been published. Book 2 was partially printed in 1866 (Tello, 1866) by García Icazbalceta, then completely in 1891 by José López Portillo y Rojas, whose Introduction questioned Tello's authorship of following books and stated that book 3 was not worth publishing. Despite that statement, José Cornejo Franco edited book 3 in 1942, and book 4 in 1945. The latter includes a study by Luis del Refugio de Palacio, O.F.M., on Tello.

In book 3 Tello gave considerable attention to Franciscan labors among Indians. He indicates only a few sources, and those vaguely. The work is chiefly a series of biographical sketches of prominent Franciscans active in Jalisco before formal establishment of the province in 1606. Book 4, a portion of which was published by García Icazbalceta (1871), details the foundation of monasteries after that date. While occasionally erring in matters of fact and interpretation, Tello's chronicle contains data not found elsewhere, and was used exten-

153

sively by Mota Padilla, Torres, and Beaumont.

Other reference: Palacio y Valois, 1935.

Nicolás de Ornelas Mendoza y Valdivia (1662–ca. 1725)

Son of a creole couple, Nicolás de Ornelas was born in Xalostotitlan, in the present state of Jalisco.[5] After making his vows, he served in various posts, and in 1719 his petition to be chronicler of the province was granted. He wrote a work which survives only in part. The partial manuscript was purchased in bad condition, and was copied (1934) by Fr. Luis del Refugio de Palacio, who first published it in 1941. A second edition with notes by him and various other documents appeared in 1962. It has helpful indexes of persons and places.

The *Crónica* has some ethnohistorical materials, especially on areas where new convents were established after the close of Tello's narrative, bringing data to 1722. Especially useful are demographic materials, and descriptions of minor places.

Francisco Mariano de Torres, O.F.M. (fl. 18thC)

Francisco Mariano de Torres attempted to carry on the Tello and the Ornelas *Crónicas*. A fragmentary manuscript portion of the Torres work is in the Biblioteca Pública, Guadalajara, Mexico. He recounts the conquest of the province of Nueva Galicia, with some data on Indian groups in Jalisco, Michoacan, Colima, Nayarit, Coahuila, and California.

The item has been published, first in 1939. To a 1960 edition Luis del Refugio de Palacio had added notes, reprinted in 1965.

Other Franciscan Chroniclers and Historians

Juan Domingo Arricivita, O.F.M. (fl. 18thC)

It will be recalled that Isidro Félix de Es-

[5] This entry has been added by the Volume Editor, at the suggestion of Alfonso Caso.

pinosa, O.F.M., wrote two chronicles, one on Michoacan which was treated above. We noted there his treatment of the work of various colegios in Christianizing the Indians. The "segunda parte," which Espinosa himself did not publish, was issued by Juan Domingo Arricivita in 1792.

With emphasis on Franciscans from the Colegio de Propaganda Fide de la Santa Cruz in Queretaro, a central establishment, it follows the same pattern as Espinosa's part 1. Arricivita records the lives of friars, with much attention to their work in the north: Sonora and areas around the Colorado and Gila rivers.

José Antonio Alcocer, O.F.M. (1749–1802)

Also chronicling the work of Franciscan friars from a different center, Colegio de Nuestra Señora de Guadalupe in Zacatecas, is the *Bosquejo* by José Antonio Alcocer. It, too, is concerned mainly with biographies of outstanding Franciscans. It is particularly useful for activities among Indians of Nayarit, Tarahumara, and Texas. Rafael Cervantes, O.F.M., has provided detailed biobibliographical study, bibliography, and notes in his 1958 edition. The work was first published in 1788. A short summary survey of Franciscan activities in northern New Spain is found in McCarty, 1962.

Alonso de Benavides, O.F.M. (fl. 1630)

Still farther north in the Borderlands we find the brief but valuable account of missionary work among the Indians of New Mexico by Alonso de Benavides. He wrote his *Memorial* in 1630 and revised it in 1634. The 1945 and 1954 English translations supersede that of 1916. There is a handy Spanish version of the 1630 work (1962). Hodge (1919) gives the Benavides bibliography.

Other reference: Wagner, 1937, pp. 227–33, 343–56.

Francisco Palou, O.F.M. (1723–89)

Palou's work deals with the 18th-century

Californias, mainly Upper or New California. His *Noticias* are divided into four parts. The first records expulsion of the Jesuits from Lower California, supplanted by Franciscans, who in turn soon handed over the missions to the Dominicans, as the Franciscans moved northward. The second part records establishment of first Franciscan missions in Upper California during the late 18th century, followed in parts 3 and 4 by descriptions of mission conditions and the founding and early history of San Francisco. Chapman (1921, pp. 496–97) mentions that the *Noticias* were meant to be a source book for Palou's life of Serra, disconnected but abounding in indispensable information.

Local historians of California have handled it considerably. The first edition (3 vols., 1857) appeared in Mexico, the second (4 vols., 1874) in San Francisco (extensively noted by Wagner, 1937, pp. 480–82). In 1926 Herbert E. Bolton issued a four-volume English translation; a critique of the translation appears in Nichols, 1929. Geiger (1959) provides a well-nigh exhaustive bibliography of California in the Palou-Serra period. The documentary materials published by Burrus (1967c) complement Palou, with much information on the period 1774–77.

Dominicans (O.P.), 1526

Provincia de Santiago de Mexico, 1535

Agustín Dávila Padilla, O.P. (1562–1604)

First published in 1596, the long title of the chronicle by Agustín Dávila Padilla indicates its purpose: to provide the history of the first Mexican Dominican province through a series of lives of its outstanding missionaries. It is considered a major or key work. The author extends his account from the first coming of the Dominicans to the very eve of his sending his manuscript to Madrid, covering therefore the rich period from 1526 through 1592.

This work is so fundamental for the early Dominican apostolate in New Spain that the other chroniclers of the Order who record the same period draw heavily from it without adding anything really substantial to Dávila Padilla (Ricard, 1933a, p. 13).

On the composition and printing of the chronicle, its author provides important information. He says that he wrote the book in the Indies [New World], and therefore it has that viewpoint. He said that some 40 years earlier Fray Andrés de Moger had begun the chronicle, and that it was extended by Fray Vicente de las Casas and Fray Domingo de la Anunciación. These materials were translated into Latin by Fray Tomás Castellar. In 1589 the General Chapter ordered Dávila to collect all the papers and write a history in "Romance," i.e., Spanish. Because of the scarcity of documents it was all the more necessary to get eyewitness accounts from the original persons. He finished the work in 1592, he states, and it was to be printed in Mexico. But the merchant fleet did not appear with the necessary paper, so the manuscript was taken to Spain where "the Lord was served by having it printed."

The various biographies stress the record of work among Indians, with much information on native matters. Dávila Padilla, in the spirit of his times and the canons of chroniclers, overemphasizes the unusual and extraordinary, as well as the numerous standard virtues of his biographical subjects. Book 1 deals with Domingo de Betanzos, founder of the province, first Provincial; with Julián Garcés, first bishop of Tlaxcala; with Domingo de la Cruz, Domingo de Santa María, and Luis Cáncer (missionary in Mexico, later Florida, where natives killed him). Book 2 takes up Bartolomé de las Casas, Tomás del Rosario, Cristóbal de la Cruz, Alonso Garcés, Pedro de Pravía, Domingo de la Anunciación, and Jordán de Santa Catalina.

There are three editions (Dávila Padilla, 1596, 1625, 1955). The first, 1596, has 815 double-columned pages, folio, not counting preliminary pages and index. The 1625 edition has 654 pages. For most purposes the 1955 version is the best. It is a facsimile of the 1625 printed text, enhanced by an excellent biobibliographical study by Agustín Millares Carlo, with a series of plates showing earlier editions and related illustrations, with a chapter index and a complementary index of names, quite detailed.

Other reference: Fernández del Castillo, 1925.

Hernando Ojea, O.P. (1560–ca. 1615)

Hernando Ojea was a pupil of Dávila Padilla, and composed a chronicle to continue that of his master. It was ready for press May 24, 1608, but actually did not see print until José M. de Agreda y Sánchez edited it for the Museo Nacional, Mexico, a thin but splendid volume (Ojea, 1897). The editor's introductory remarks not only give a scholarly account of Ojea, but provide a general sketch of all the official Dominican chroniclers of this province. To stress the continuity, Ojea's work carries the title *Libro tercero.* . . .

It is divided into 30 chapters. Like most Dominican chronicles, it emphasizes lives of prominent friars, but also devotes much attention to the monastery of Santo Domingo in Mexico City. When discussing the division of Dominican provinces into Mexico and Oaxaca, Ojea lists the 39 centers from which missionary work among Indians was being carried on among the "Mexican"-speakers, and 9 for the Mixteca (pp. 35–36).

At the close of the chronicle proper is another, distinct work. It is entitled "Información apologética de los Dominicos de Mexico en 1578."

When compared with that of fellow chroniclers, the factual, concise, and objective writing of Ojea seems especially wholesome.

Alonso Franco y Ortega, O.P.

Alonso Franco y Ortega also continued the work of Dávila Padilla in a *Segunda parte* . . . , written in 1645 but not published until more than 250 years later (Franco y Ortega, 1900). On May 16, 1637, he was commissioned by the Chapter of his province to be official chronicler. He covered the years 1591 to 1645 in a manuscript that recorded Dominican activities and that was presented to the Chapter May 5, 1645.

His work is divided into three books, chronologically arranged. Book 1 deals with the years 1591–1607; Book 2, 1608–23; and book 3, 1624–45. He has two main topics: Chapters of the province, and lives of prominent missionaries and administrators. Other matters of more general interest, both civil and ecclesiastical, are fitted into this main framework. Chronology is indicated by marginal notes of the year; hence, unlike many works of the same general title, this tends to be a true chronicle. Especially in the lives of notable Dominican missionaries appear useful linguistic and cultural data on Indians, with specific areas well indicated. The style is diffuse, and the biographies eulogistic but helpful. Some of his manuscript and printed sources are noted in the course of his narrative.

The 1900 edition printed by the Museo Nacional was expertly edited by José M. de Agreda y Sánchez. It is one of the most superb volumes of the many chronicles mentioned in this article.

Provincia de Predicadores de Antequera, Valle de Oaxaca San Hipolito, 1592

Francisco de Burgoa, O.P. (1605–81)

Of all the chronicles mentioned in this survey, the two by Francisco de Burgoa easily hold first place for inflated style and bombastic phraseology, especially the opening remarks to various chapters. Yet for the important area of Oaxaca, and the numerous subjects he treats, Burgoa's works are indispensable and irreplaceable sources.

156

Burgoa, born in Oaxaca, was related to numerous local colonial families. He took his final vows in 1625, and by 1649 was provincial of his Order. In that post he made a special effort to visit various parts of Oaxaca, especially seeking notices of Zapotecan antiquities, with the aim of writing a history of Oaxaca. Before his death in 1681 he did not complete it but left two prolix yet valuable published treatises. The two chronicles are the usually abbreviated *Palestra historial* (Burgoa, 1670, 1934a) and *Geográfica descripción* (Burgoa, 1674, 1934b). Burgoa conceived of them as a single work, but they differ in contents.

The *Palestra historial* is a typical chronicle. It begins with the arrival in 1526 of Dominicans in Mexico City, and shortly thereafter their appearance in Oaxaca. Burgoa rehearses the lives of many missionaries already biographized by Dávila Padilla, but Burgoa emphasizes their apostolate in the Oaxaca areas, even before formal establishment of the Province of San Hipólito (1592). These lives are uniformly eulogistic, but scattered through them are important bits of information on the numerous Indian groups of Oaxaca.

The *Geográfica descripción* has 80 chapters. They detail the histories of the monasteries and the work of their friars among the Indians, with much less attention to biographical detail than in the *Palestra historial*. The data run to about mid-17th century in both.

Each has two editions, the original 17th-century one and a 1934 version issued by the Archivo General de la Nación. In the latter is a biobibliographical notice of Burgoa in the *Palestra historial*, with an incomplete onomastic index for that work. The *Geográfica descripción* has a general table of contents and a defective index of proper names. Fortunately, there is a separately published, quite detailed index for each, prepared and published by Grace Metcalfe (1946a, 1964b).

Provincia de San Vicente de Chiapa y Guatemala, 1551

Antonio de Remesal, O.P. (1570–1639)

Antonio de Remesal borrowed heavily from Dávila Padilla, but goes far beyond him in detail for Chiapas and Guatemala as well as in time. Remesal's is an extensive chronicle, enhanced by inclusion of numerous civil documents, especially *cédulas reales*, and ecclesiastical ones. With varying emphasis, Remesal records data from 1526 through 1619, with a few forays into native history.

The entire work, *Historia*, is divided into eleven books. The first recounts the conquest of Mexico and Central America, and the coming of the missionaries to pioneer missionary work among the Indians. Book 2 emphasizes the work of the Dominicans in Guatemala, especially Fr. Betanzos and Bartolomé de las Casas, a matter continued in book 3 with the work of Luis Cáncer. It also notes the coming of the Mercedarians to Chiapas and Guatemala. The year 1541 opens book 4, which deals with maltreatment and enslavement of the Indians. Defense of the natives by the Dominicans is a main theme of book 5, with much on Indians of Chiapas. The history and conversion of the latter continues in book 6. The founding of new towns, the differing attitudes of bishops, secular clergy, laymen, and the Orders toward Indians are themes of book 7. It also has important statements on native ways of life, Indian character, rights, problems of conversion, and related topics.

More detail on the coming of the Mercedarians to Chiapas (Ciudad Real) is among treatments found in book 8. It also touches on encomiendas, education (especially of Indian girls), and attitudes of native caciques toward the Spaniards. Book 9 tells of the founding of San Salvador and establishment of the Dominican Province of San Vicente de Chiapa. Reaction of the Indians to Christianity, a list of Dominicans and the native languages they had mastered, and hospitals established for Indians also figure in book 9. Somewhat more general is book 10, which describes the widening area of the apostolate among the Indians as well as a controversy between Dominicans and Franciscans over the proper Indian word correctly to designate God. Pioneering Dominican efforts in the Philippines closes the *Historia* with book 11.

Like so many Middle American chronicles, there is both the old, rare original (Remesal, 1619), for which J. F. Ramírez prepared a biographical index (Ramírez, n.d.), and a more modern version (Remesal, 1932) of Remesal's *Historia*. The new edition changes the title slightly, adds a rather emotional prologue to its first volume, and two to its second. The text is adequate for most scholarly purposes.

Other reference: Fernández del Castillo, 1920.

Francisco Jiménez, O.P. (1666–ca. 1722)

Francisco Jiménez, often spelled Ximénez, extends the chronological span of Remesal in both direction: he deals more fully with pre-Contact times and carries the historical narrative further by a century, to 1719. It is a rich and useful chronicle, written in 1721–22, but not published until the 20th century, and then only in part (Jiménez, 1929–31).

The wealth of ethnohistorical data is suggested by a brief scanning of contents of the three published volumes. Book 1 is entirely devoted to Indian history of Guatemala and Chiapas prior to the coming of the Spaniards. Book 2 records introduction of Christianity and missionary efforts to establishment of the Province of San Vicente. Book 3 is missing. The year 1601 opens book 4 and gives a chronicle of the province until 1650. In it are noted principal events of the Order, the work among Indians through its

several Chapters, with added information on methods and results in the biographical sketches of prominent friars. The eventful years 1651–98 form the stuff of book 5: efforts to "reduce" the Chols, Lacandons, and Indians in Manche and Peten-Itza. Book 6, opening in 1699, covers the "Entrada al Ahitzá," as well as expeditions to the Cobojes and work in Verapaz and Yucatan, with lives of eminent Dominicans of the period. There is much in this same book on civil government in Guatemala, as well as ministry among the natives. It closes with the Chapter meeting of 1719.

Jiménez speaks of seven books, but only six appear in the Guatemalan edition. Lic. J. Antonio Villacorta C., who wrote the prologue, states (Jiménez, 1929–31, 3:429) that volume 3 includes the last part of book 5, book 6, and part of book 7 which the original history contains, "although concerning these latter two, the paleographer suppressed various chapters, believing them unnecessary." He added that the 19th-century copyist, Gavarete, took care to make synopses of them which appear in the final table of contents. Unfortunately in the published text there is no vestige of book 7, and we are uncertain how much of book 6 was "suppressed." Obviously a full, scholarly edition of this important chronicle seems highly desirable.

Augustinians (O.S.A.), 1533

Provincia del Santisimo Nombre de Jesus, 1535

Juan de Grijalva, O.S.A. (ca. 1559–1638)

Juan de Grijalva's *Crónica*, covering the "four ages" from 1533 through 1592, is the most important of the Augustinian chronicles, as well as the first published (Grijalva, 1624). He drew on abundant sources, many now lost, giving special importance to his verbatim quotation of numerous important documents. His clear style makes for ready understanding, with a chronology easy to follow by his precise indication of the year he is treating (Vela, 1913–17, 3:301–07).

The "four ages" of the title of the *Crónica* are represented by its division into as many books. Book 1 records the coming of the first Augustinians to New Spain (1533) and the Indian areas to which they devoted themselves: Mexico City, Chilapa, and the Otomi of Atotonilco, with information on other doctrinas and expeditions to the Orient. Book 2 details the *cocoliztli* epidemic that decimated natives, and discusses mission methods for Indians. More expeditions to the Orient, with the temporal and spiritual conquest of the Philippines (which was administratively attached to New Spain) are found in book 3. It also chronicles the Augustinian ministry among the Tarascans, the founding of the Colegio de San Pablo (Mexico City), the work of Alonso de la Veracruz, and the entrance of Augustinians into China. The final book contains biographies of eminent Augustinians. Grijalva himself was born in Colima, perhaps as early as 1559.

Grijalva had access to earlier histories and chronicles. Among these were a lost biography by Agustín de la Coruña, and works by Alonso de Buica and Francisco Muñoz, all apparently lost. He also utilized some materials by Alonso de la Veracruz, most of whose work remains in manuscript. Brand (1944, p. 91) notes that Grijalva may have written a special history of the Province of San Nicolás Tolentino, published posthumously 1646.

The 1624 first edition of Grijalva's major chronicle is rare, but the second (Grijalva, 1924) is adequate. It attempts to approach a facsimile reproduction, retaining spelling and abbreviations of the earlier version. Its utility is improved by two appendices by Federico Gómez de Orozco (1924), one a biobibliographical sketch of Juan de Grijalva, the other a discussion of the Augustinian provincials of this province. He includes

a brief but helpful bibliography on Augustinians of New Spain and dependent areas (pp. xci–xciv).

Here in passing might be noted the somewhat frustrated efforts of the Carmelite Order to missionize Indians in New Spain, summarized by Moreno (1966). Entering the field tardily in 1585, they had minimal results, their only contacts with natives being through their Doctrine of San Sebastián (Atzacoalco) in Mexico City, which they maintained from 1586 until 1607. At that time the Order voluntarily transferred the doctrine to the Augustinians.

Other reference: Ricard, 1933a, pp. 16–17.

Esteban García, O.S.A.

Fr. Esteban García completed the history of his Augustinian province about 1675, but it was not printed until this century (García, 1918). Like Grijalva, García wrote in a clear, straightforward style; and, following the pattern, he inserted numerous original documents, especially cédulas reales, in the text. His *Crónica* is subtitled "Libro Quinto" to indicate it is a continuation of Grijalva.

The work contains 134 chapters. It opens with an account of separation of the Province of San Nicolás de Michoacan from the mother province March 17, 1602 (García, 1918, p. 3). He pays special attention to religious beliefs of the Indians although his prime emphasis is on biographical treatment of prominent Augustinians and their successes among natives. García also treats the Philippines, considered to be offshoots from the Mexican province.

Gregorio de Santiago Vela, O.S.A., edited and published the *Crónica* (García, 1918) in very useful fashion. His preface is an excellent study of Augustinian chroniclers of New Spain during the 16th and 17th centuries (pp. vii–xxi). He has added valuable notes and documents to the text, as well as compiling an index of proper names (pp.

398–400) and a general table of contents (pp. 401–04).

Provincia de San Nicolas de Tolentino de Michoacan, 1602

Juan González de la Puente, O.S.A. (1580–16 ?)

Juan González de la Puente, born a Spaniard in 1580, undertook to chronicle the Augustinians in Michoacan and to write the lives of nine "apostolic *varones*." Part 1 of his *Chorónica* appeared not long after its composition about 1623 (Puente, 1624). In 1630 the chapter meeting of his province in Tiripitio, Michoacan, authorized him to publish a second part, but no trace of part 2 has to date been uncovered.

In the extant manuscript, he wrote the biographies of the nine friars, scattered over three books. They are Juan Bautista de Moya, Juan de Medina Rincón, Diego de Chaves, Sebastián de Trasierra, Francisco de Acosta, Juan de Montalvo, Francisco López, Pedro de Vera, and Diego de Villarubia. As a matter of fact, none of these belonged to the Michoacan province, but were from Santísimo Nombre in Mexico City; but as they had been active in Michoacan, before the latter was an officially established province, Puente included them (García, 1918, p. ix).

Book 1 contains no lives of these men, but instead is devoted to a wide range of topics. Among them is the discovery of the New World, the conquest of Mexico, and Augustinian activities in Mexico after arrival, as well as in Persia and the Orient. Book 2 contains biographies of the first five missionaries and recounts, in entire chapters, Augustinian efforts among the Indians of Michoacan, as well as to missions in China and Japan. The remaining four missionaries appear in book 3, which completes the account (to his times) of the Augustinian ministry to the Tarascans.

At the edge of the text Puente indicates his main sources. His ideas are easy to follow, but occasionally he lapses into a diffuse style, especially when extolling the virtues of his brethren. He also has a predilection for the unusual and the extraordinary.

His *Chorónica* of Michoacan appeared in the same year (1624) as Grijalva's of Mexico, although the latter province had been founded some 67 years earlier. A relatively rare work, the 1624 edition was reissued (Puente, 1909) under the general direction of Bishop Plancarte y Navarrete, with a brief biobibliographical note in it by Nicolás León, and under a slightly altered title.

Other references: Ricard, 1933a, p. 16; Santiago Vela, 1913–17, 3:239–40; 1923, pp. 128–32.

Diego Basalenque, O.S.A. (1575/77–1651)

Born in Spain, Diego Basalenque spent much of his life in Michoacan; he died in Charo, Michoacan, in 1651. He states in his introduction that he personally knew most of the persons about whom he writes. His purpose in composing their biographies was to inspire emulation. He obviously drew heavily on Grijalva, especially for earlier periods of his own *Historia*, which gives the history of his province to 1644. He pays particular attention to Augustinian work among Indians.

Basalenque divided his work into three books, titles of which indicate their contents. Book 1 reports on the state of the Province of San Nicolás de Tolentino de Michoacan when it was still part of the Province of Mexico (1533–1601). The second book covers the period after division into two provinces (1602) until about 1628. Book 3 deals with years (1629–44) when the "alternativa" between Spanish and Mexican Augustinians was permitted, alternation in the position of superiors of the Order and the religious garb of the novices.

Basalenque's *Historia* has seen three editions (1673, 1886, 1963). The 1886 version, three small volumes, has a table of contents at the end of volumes 1 and 3. Santiago Vela (1913, p. 334 ff.) provides a good critical study of Basalenque's writings. José Bravo Ugarte gives biobibliographical data and a few notes in the 1963 edition, but the index is defective.

Other references: Santiago Vela, 1923, pp. 132–33; Monasterio, 1928.

Matías de Escobar, O.S.A. (16 ?–1748)

Matías de Escobar continued the narrative of Basalenque by drawing on him, on Grijalva, and on a lost manuscript by Jacinto de Avilés. His own work has never been completely published. He brought events down to his own time, 1729. He entitled it *Americana Thebaida*, with a subtitle indicating it was to contain lives of the Augustinians of Michoacan.

Its contents fall into 61 chapters. The early ones repeat the pioneer history of the Augustinians in Mexico and Michoacan. The author devotes much attention to mission methods for Indian conversions, the founding of monasteries, and biographies of numerous Augustinian missionaries, especially from his own province. His account has a wider scope in place and time than similar Augustinian efforts. But as a stylist, Escobar is a close runner-up to Burgoa for lowest honors. His baroque sentences are overloaded with pretentions and irrelevant erudition, sacred and profane. Hence *Americana Thebaida* is seldom read for pleasure.

Escobar's work still awaits proper publication. Nicolás León twice edited the chronicle (Escobar, 1890, 1924), neither time completely successfully. Santiago Vela reissued chapter 17 of book 1 from the original manuscript, dealing with the historians of the Chapter (Santiago Vela, 1923, pp. 266–79). He also has provided critical notices of the extant editions (Santiago Vela, 1913–31, 2:332–33; 1923, pp. 129–44), in one instance providing a complete table of contents (Santiago Vela, 1923, pp. 134–43).

Jesuits (S.J.), 1572

Province of New Spain, 1572–1767

The Jesuits, whose official name is Society of Jesus (Compañía de Jesús), came to New Spain in 1572 after it had the status of a fully constituted province, which remained undivided during the colonial period. They were exiled from Spanish overseas dominions generally in 1767, and did not return to New Spain until 1816. During exile, Jesuits who had worked in New Spain composed important works on the ethnohistory of areas in which they had labored. Among the latter is the work by Francisco Javier Clavigero, given extended and separate treatment in Article 17.

Another significant group of materials by Jesuits are the *Annuae Litterae Societatis Iesu*. Streit (1924, pp. 63–64) outlined the nature and importance of these Annual Letters, and scattered entries to them throughout his bibliographical coverage. The *Annuae Litterae* are reports, in Latin, from individual provinces throughout the world, giving annual summaries. They rest, in turn, on much more detailed annual accounts from units within the province. Originals of the *Annuae Litterae* for the Province of New Spain are found in Rome, Mexico City, and elsewhere.

The published Letters cover the years 1581–1614 and 1650–54. The Bancroft Library, University of California, has filmed a relatively complete collection of the Letters, 1583–1654; in addition to photostats, they also have transcripts. Still scattered in Jesuit archives are the detailed local reports, often in Spanish, from which the *Annuae Litterae* were composed. These, of course, contain a wealth of detail on work with and among Indians.

The *Annuae Litterae* are published as part of the *Monumenta historica S.J.* series, not separately; in the case of Mexico, in

Monumenta mexicana. Under the editorship of Félix Zubillaga, S.J. (1956–71) four volumes of the *Annuae Litterae*, covering the years 1570–92, have appeared in Rome.

Francisco Florencia, S.J. (1620–95)

Born in 1620 in St. Augustine, Florida, Francisco Florencia died in Mexico City in 1695. As his *Historia* covers the years 1566–82, he was not an eyewitness to the events he recounts. He was, however, official historian of his province, and therefore had access to abundant archival and manuscript material, including the complete *Corónica* of Pérez de Ribas. One value of Florencia's writing is that he reproduces whole or partial numerous key documents, some of which are now lost. He wrote the first published history of the Jesuits in New Spain, but only the first of his planned three volumes was printed (Florencia, 1694).

The eight books give a detailed account of the Jesuit mission to Florida (1566–72), and the first decade of the Jesuits in New Spain following their coming in 1572. At that time the principal mission area of the Jesuits was the vicinity of Mexico City and main centers in Michoacan, especially Patzcuaro and present Morelia (Valladolid). Florencia gives special attention to the epidemic of 1575. The *Historia* is often diffuse. Not infrequently Florencia overstresses the exceptional and the extraordinary.

The first edition (Florencia, 1694) is rare, but the modern facsimile (Florencia, 1955) makes it more available. The latter has a biobibliographical study by Francisco González de Cossío and a supplementary proper name index.

Juan Sánchez Baquero, S.J. (1548–1619)

One of the 15 founding Jesuits who came in 1572, Juan Sánchez Baquero wrote a history of the pioneer years, 1571–80, a work of prime importance. As the author was an eyewitness and a participant of early work among Indians, especially in urban centers, the significance of his account is obvious,

improved by a clear and concise style. The history is refreshingly objective and factual.

Félix Ayuso, S.J., edited the chronicle (Sánchez Baquero, 1945). He added a biobibliographical account, notes, and a series of brief biographies of Jesuits whom Sánchez Baquero mentions. Unfortunately this version of the *Fundación* is incomplete. There is a complete original in the Museo Nacional, Mexico.

Gaspar de Villerías, S.J. (ca. 1562– ?)

The first official historian of the Mexican Jesuits, Gaspar de Villerías compiled a detailed, unpublished history of the first decade of Jesuit work in New Spain. Many of the participants were alive when, about 1602, he prepared a summary, *Relación breve*, of the larger work.

Even the *Relación breve* did not see print until 1945 (Villerías, 1945), and was then edited by Francisco González de Cossío as an "anonymous account." The more important major work still awaits publication.

Andrés de Pérez de Ribas, S.J. (1576–1655)

Andrés de Pérez de Ribas (or de Rivas) was well equipped to write two books that are outstanding. They cover the first 80 years of Jesuit ministry among the Indians of New Spain.

Born in Cordoba, Spain, in 1576, he entered the Society of Jesus in Spain (1602), then came to New Spain. For many years he was a missionary among the Indians of Sinaloa, later superior of the Jesuit Province of New Spain and its official historian. He died in 1655. Dunne (1951) has provided a biography.

Until his death Pérez de Ribas worked on a general history of the province. It appeared only in 1896, in mutilated form, under the title *Corónica y historia. . . .* It opens in 1572 and closes in 1654. He gave particular attention to work among Indians in the Jesuit province for all areas but the northern missions, subject of a specialized work noted below. Unfortunately the 1896 edition omits most of the many chapters on Indians: of a total 134 chapters originally in volume 1, 49 are lacking; and of the 150 for volume 2, 9 are wanting. Although not printed in full, the whole original manuscript is available for use in the Manuscripts Division, Library of Congress (Transcripts, no. 6).[6] Streit (1927, pp. 677–78) and Dunne (1951) also discuss these matters.

Andrés Pérez de Ribas also wrote the first and most complete history of the Jesuit missions in Sinaloa during their first half-century and the establishment of those in Sonora, entitling his work *Historia de los triumphos . . .* (Pérez de Ribas, 1645). The work is divided into 12 books.

A description of Sinaloa, its Indian groups, and coming of the first Spaniards opens the account in book 1. Books 2 and 3 deal with the first entrance of the Jesuits in 1590 and conversion of the three principal native groups along the Zuaqui River. Book 4 is the story of the "reduction" of the River Mayo groups. The bitter wars between Yaquis and Spaniards is the material of book 5. Acceptance of Christianity by the northernmost groups of Sinaloa follows in book 6.

General consideration of the character of the Indians of Sinaloa and their reactions to a new and different way of life is the theme of book 7. Book 8 studies the new mission area of Topia and Indians in its vicinity, the same approach appearing in book 9 for the mission of San Andres. The efforts to win over the Tepehuanes and the ensuing wars then come in book 10. Book 11 summarizes data on the important centers of Parras and of Laguna Grande de San Pedro and their dependent missions. Finally, book 12 is a general summing up of the work of Mexican Jesuits among unconverted Indians over the whole period, including the abortive 1566–72 efforts in Florida.

[6] Ed. note: Ernest J. Burrus and Félix Zubillaga are preparing a complete version of the *Corónica* from the Library of Congress manuscript, to be published by Porrúa in Madrid.

Because of his position as superior general and official historian of the Mexican province, Pérez de Ribas had available and used many manuscript sources. Missionary reports he put to good advantage, quoting generously from them and reproducing their texts with fidelity. In archives of Mexico City and Rome are found numerous unpublished documents, some not directly cited by him, with his notation that he had seen their contents. Nearly all historians since his time have leaned heavily on the *Triumphos* and, in verifying his statements from other sources, have found them substantially accurate. Streit (1924, pp. 488–89) discusses the *Triumphos*, as does Dunne (1951).

The first edition appeared in Madrid (Pérez de Ribas, 1645, with a second in Mexico City (Pérez de Ribas, 1944). Preceding the *Triumphos* in the latter is a work "Los naufragios" (1:1–74) by Alvar Núñez Cabeza de Vaca, causing the title of the three volumes to be generalized, although they are primarily devoted to the *Triumphos*.

Francisco Javier Alegre, S.J. (1729–88)

Francisco Javier Alegre, official historian of the Mexican Jesuits, was the first following Pérez de Ribas to produce a general history of the province. Alegre was born in Veracruz in 1729 and died in exile, in Bologna, Italy, 1788.

He was appointed in 1764 with a mandate to write a more critical and scholarly account of the Mexican province than hitherto had been published. He finished the first draft in 1766, and, when expulsion came in 1767, was revising the last part. It was not published during his lifetime.

Carlos M. Bustamante issued it first (Alegre, 1841–42). Comparison of the Bustamante text with the original manuscript (in the University of Texas) reveals that the editor changed not only the title but also the text; he misread various passages. Even in that mangled state, the Alegre work has been a main source of many historians.

The Alegre text spans exactly two centuries and deals with Jesuit work among the Indians of Florida and New Spain, 1566–1766. Nine of his ten books deal with New Spain, from 1572, documenting the rise in number of Jesuits from the original 15 to 693. He notes the establishment of permanent missions in 1590, and their spread northward and westward, reaching northern Lower California and Arizona by 1767 when the Society was banished from New Spain. Reports from mission centers, where at least one priest was in charge, each with its Indian school, tell much about native groups and their languages.

Alegre provides much detail on the Indian missions and other establishments for natives. The latter included the colegios exclusively for Indians (San Gregorio, Mexico City; San Martín, Tepotzotlan; San Miguel, Puebla), including the short-lived one at Jalatlaco, near Oaxaca.

Alegre compiled his work chronologically, based on literally hundreds of carefully examined records that still bear his notations. He cites and quotes extensively from many of the sources, with scrupulous accuracy.

His is the last of the Jesuit general histories. Other chronicles are much more limited in time and space than his *Historia*. More detail will be found in Burrus, 1963, and below for selected areas.

There is a recent, critical edition of this important work, edited by Burrus (Alegre, 1956–60). Assisted by Félix Zubillaga, Burrus published the nearly 2000 pages under its original title, and added more than 1000 pages of widely scattered documents that relate to every mission area administered by Jesuits in New Spain. The editors have tried to utilize all modern scholarly apparatus to make this major work as useful as possible.[7]

[7] Ed. note: This meticulously edited work is an outstanding model of careful scholarship.

Selected Regional Chroniclers and Historians

Eusebio Francisco Kino, S.J. (1645–1711)

Eusebio Francisco Kino was the outstanding Jesuit explorer of northwest Mexico, Lower California, and the southwest United States. He was also a foremost missionary and historian. He has been biographized by Bolton (1936) and therefore we need only state that he was born in Segno near Trent, Italy, in 1645, started work in Mexico in 1681, and died in Magdalena, Sonora, in 1711. The Bolton life contains maps related to his journeys, and a well-nigh exhaustive list of Kino's writings.

His diary and chronicle is the single most important work on various Indian groups of the Pimeria Alta, 1683–1711 (Kino, 1913–22). The two-volume translation (Kino, 1919, 1948) into English by Bolton is superior to the earlier Spanish version. Kino's letters and reports to Rome also contain much of ethnohistorical value; they were translated and published by Burrus (Kino, 1954, 1961a, 1961b, 1961c, 1964, 1965a). Of the 800 pages of *Kino and Manje, Explorers of Sonora and Arizona* (Burrus, 1971a), about 500 are of original documents, nearly all on the Indians of Sonora and Arizona.

José Ortega, S.J. (1700–86)

Jesuit activity 1721–54 in Nayarit, a relatively undocumented area, appears in the *Apostólicos afanes . . .*, compiled from various sources by José Ortega. He was missionary to the Coras, and wrote in, as well as about, their language.

The first part of the *Afanes* records the entire history of the Jesuits in Nayarit. The second part concerns the Pimeria Alta missions, reproducing a manuscript ascribed to a fellow Jesuit, Johann Anton Balthasar. This portion drew heavily on earlier manuscripts and chronicles, especially those by Kino, Sedelmayr, Keller and Consag. The direct accounts by Kino have since been published, much reducing the value of data in Ortega, but part 1 on Nayarit has not been so superseded.

Although the first edition appeared anonymously in Barcelona (Ortega, 1754), we know it was prepared for press by Francisco Fluviá, S.J. Under a variant title a more recent version was published in Mexico (Ortega, 1944).

Other references: Streit, 1927, pp. 176–77; Wagner, 1937, pp. 406–10.

Ignaz Pfefferkorn, S.J. (1725–17 ?)

Sonora is the area given monographic treatment by Ignaz Pfefferkorn. He worked mainly at Ati and Cucurpe for 11 years, 1756–67.

Born in Mannheim, Germany, in 1725, he entered the Jesuit Order in 1742 and went to New Spain in 1754. After the expulsion, he composed his work (Pfefferkorn, 1794–95) in Europe on the basis of his own materials but also included information furnished by Jakob Sedelmayr, S.J., fellow prisoner for eight years in Puerto de Santa María, Spain. Sedelmayr was a veteran explorer and missionary in the same area.

The first of two volumes is primarily a natural history. It discusses the Seri and Apache Indians, raiders into Sonora. The second volume opens with a detailed account of various Indian groups in Sonora, which is followed by chapters on the establishment of Jesuit missions and their internal administration. Pfefferkorn speaks, in his preface, of a third volume as though already completed. It was to contain a travel account of his return trip, with texts of other missionary reports: Sedelmayr, Ugarte, Consag. To now, no trace of this third volume has been found.

Pfefferkorn's *Beschreibung* forms a reliable source for their epoch written in an exceptionally critical spirit. Edited by Theodore E. Treutlein, who translated and annotated the printed original, is an excellent

modern version (Pfefferkorn, 1949), with a map, valuable brief notes, and a good index; he also gives the best biobibliographical sketch of Pfefferkorn in the introduction.

Other references: Streit, 1927, p. 341; Wagner, 1937, pp. 493–97.

Jesuit Chroniclers of Lower California

Although belonging to the same province as Jesuit writers noted above, a group who wrote about Lower California merit special though brief mention. Until expulsion in 1767, they were given exclusive responsibility, and confined their activities to the peninsula. It was not until 1849 that Jesuits entered Upper California, following its separation from Mexico by absorption into the United States. The most complete and best modern general account of the work of the Jesuits in Lower California is by Peter Masten Dunne, S.J. (1952). An important book for the history of the mainland missions was published by John Augustine Donahue, S.J. (1969). The first volume of Bandelier's history has been edited by Burrus (1969).

Until recently nearly all the chronicles of Jesuits who wrote about Lower California have remained in manuscript. That lacuna is partially filled by Burrus (1971b). The following paragraphs are notes on the main previously published accounts.

Miguel Venegas, S.J. (1680–1764)

Miguel Venegas wrote the most complete general history of the Lower California missions, from foundation in 1697 to 1739. The original work was edited by a Spanish Jesuit, Andrés Marcos Burriel, *Noticia . . .* 1739 (Venegas, 1757), who found that the long, detailed account originally entitled *Empressas apostólicas* by Venegas was too prolix even for him, so he made a summary of it, added other reports, and brought that information to his date. The *Empressa* has value in the abundance of documents quoted verbatim by Venegas. Wagner (1937, pp. 415–26) gives biobibliographical data, especially on original editions and several translations of the *Noticia*. There is a more recent version than any mentioned by Wagner (Venegas, 1944).

Miguel del Barco, S.J. (1706–90)

Miguel del Barco, while in exile (ca. 1770–75), wrote in two volumes his "Correcciones y Adiciones" to Burriel's résumé of Venegas (MS). Having spent more than 30 years in the same area, he drew on his own knowledge and that of fellow missionaries, especially Lucas Ventura, S.J. His linguistic material, especially on the Cochimíes, is superior to that of Venegas.

Francisco Javier Clavigero, S.J. (1731–87)

Another exiled Jesuit, Francisco Javier Clavigero, is best known to Middle Americanists for his *Historia antigua*.[8] He also wrote *Storia della California* (Clavigero, 1789). For it he made much use of the Barco manuscript and information from the latter's collaborator, Lucas Ventura. Clavigero's work is markedly superior to Venegas' in accuracy and in the critical spirit. Clavigero also chronicles the Jesuit missions, 1697–1768. There is a good recent translation (Clavigero, 1937). For other editions see Wagner, 1937, pp. 485–87.

Johann Jakob Baegert, S.J. (1717-72)

Johann Jakob Baegert (born in Schlettstadt, Alsace, 1717) wrote the main work on the Guaicura Indians of the southern tip of Lower California (Baegert, 1771, 1772). He worked among them from 1751 to 1768. His *Nachrichten* describe the country (part 1) and the Indians, their language and customs (part 2). Part 3 is a history of the missions in the area to 1768.

His German language work originally appeared in Mannheim, 1771, with a cor-

rected and augmented edition the following year. Two modern versions, one in Spanish, the other in English, indicate the continuing importance of the *Nachrichten*. Translated by Pedro R. Hendrichs, and with an excellent analytical introduction by Paul Kirchhoff, the Spanish edition appeared in Mexico City (Baegert, 1942). M. M. Brandenburg and Carl L. Baumann translated the work from German into English, added a few but good notes (especially biographical) and an introduction (Baegert, 1952). Both translations have good indexes; the Spanish reproduces the original map (basically that of Ferdinand Consag, S.J.).

Other Writers

Francisco M. Píccolo (1654–1729) provides much information on Indians of Lower California. Edited by Burrus, some 500 pages of his original documents appeared in 1962. Burrus also edited (1967b) an account by Ducrue concerned with the expulsion of the Jesuits from Lower California, and added a brief history of the missions there, data on the missionaries, and selections of their letters. Indians of northern Baja California (1762–78) are also described in two other works edited by Burrus, a diary and letters of Wenceslaus Linck (Burrus, 1966, 1967a).

Mercedarians (O. Merc.), 1594

Nuestra Senora de la Merced de la Nueva Espana, 1594

Francisco de Pareja, O.Merc. (? –1628)

In 1671 Francisco de Pareja was appointed official chronicler of his Order in New Spain. He finished its history by November 4, 1687, but it lingered in manuscript for nearly 200 years before publication (Pareja, 1882–83).

Under the general title of *Crónica* there are three distinct works. The first is his detailed account of the pioneer Mercedarians, Estado Primero (Pareja, 1882–83, pp. 1–64), notably Bartolomé de Olmedo, who accom-

---

[8] See Article 17.

panied Cortés, and Juan de Varillas, who came with Alonso Zuazo. The second deals with the group of Mercedarians who in 1574 came to Mexico City with the intention of forming a permanent community, the founding of the province in 1594, and its history to 1687. A third part of the printed work is a collection (140 pages) of documents added as appendices by the editors, summarizing events of the Order through 1844.

Pareja's main purpose was to demonstrate that Mercedarians came to New Spain before the Franciscans, Dominicans, or Augustinians, and to buttress the claim generally fails to distinguish beween activity of certain individual members (Olmedo and Varillas) and the province proper. Information on Indians of New Spain and Central America is scattered through accounts of the founding of missions and monasteries and their administration. Pareja reproduces some documents verbatim and cites book and chapter of some of the better-known historians.

Cristóbal de Aldana, O.Merc. (1735– ?)

The *Compendio histórico* by Cristóbal de Aldana is important only for detail on individual Mercedarians during their early years in New Spain, with relatively little ethnohistorical material. He made a compendium of Pareja's *Crónica* (then still in manuscript), corrected it by using other sources, and then had a fellow Mercedarian, Fray José Gómez, print it, presumably in the Mercedarian monastery of Mexico City (Aldana, ca. 1770). Its diminutive format is almost overwhelmed by its long title. In general its two books summarize and comment on the Estado Primero of Pareja. The title page states this is "tomo primero," and the text concludes "as will be seen in Book III." Nothing is known of the latter, in print or in manuscript.

There is a facsimile edition (Aldana, 1929), issued by the Sociedad de Bibliófilos Mexicanos. A biobibliographical study serves as introduction. A reprint of that 1929 limited edition was reissued in 1953, with added material.

EPILOGUE

In summary it may be said that the large and often scattered corpus of writings by the religious chroniclers and historians is an important body of material in the European tradition giving data about Indians and their ways. As sources they must be used with critical caution, given the main purpose of their composition: to record and often praise the role of missionaries and their Orders in Christianizing—tantamount to civilizing, according to Hispanic canons—the diverse Indian peoples and communities of Middle America. The scope and coverage of the group is summarized in Table 1.

A SELECTED, ANNOTATED BIBLIOGRAPHY OF RELIGIOUS CHRONICLERS AND HISTORIANS OF MIDDLE AMERICA compiled by Ernest J. Burrus, S.J., and augmented by Howard F. Cline

ACTA PROVINCILIA
1743–96 Acta Provincilia Sancti Michaelis Archangeli et S. Angelorum Provinciae Ordinis Praedicatorum. Puebla. [Dominican work in Puebla, appearing at four-year intervals, with much on Indian matters. Dates are the earliest and latest issues examined by Burrus.]

ADAMS, ELEANOR B.
1952 A bio-bibliography of Franciscan authors in colonial Central America. *Americas*, 8:431–73; 9:37–86. [Extremely helpful compilation.]
1953 A bio-bibliography of Franciscan authors in colonial Central America. Academy of American Franciscan History, *Bibliographical Series*, 2.

Washington. [Reprint of 1952.]

ADIB, VICTOR
1949   Los indios en la *Historia* de Motolinía. *Abside*, 13/1:89–97 (Jan.–Mar.).

AGREDA Y SÁNCHEZ, JOSÉ M. DE
1897   *See* Ojea, 1897.
1900   *See* Franco y Ortega, 1900.

AGÜERO, VICTORIANO
1898   *See* Beristáin de Souza, 1898.

ALCOCER, JOSÉ ANTONIO, O.F.M.
1958   Bosquejo de la historia del colegio de Nuestra Señora de Guadalupe y sus misiones, año de 1788. Introducción, bibliografía, acotaciones e ilustraciones del R.F. Fr. Rafael Cervantes, O.F.M. [Mexico.] [Principal value of the *Bosquejo* is its account of ministry among Indians of Nayarit, Tarahumara, and Texas. Scholarly introduction, notes, index.]

ALDANA, CRISTÓBAL DE, O.MERC.
ca. 1770   Compendio histórico chronológico de el establecimiento y progressos de la Provincia de la Visitación de Nueva España del real y militar Orden de N.S. de la Merced, estraído de la Chrónica que dexó manuscripta el M.R.P.M.F. Francisco Pareja por el P.M.F. . . . [Privately printed]. Mexico. [Based on 1687 MS by Pareja (1882–83) with additions. Printed for Aldana by José Gómez, O.Merc.]
1929   Crónica de la Merced de México. . . . 2 ed. facsimilar de la primera. [Edited by] Federico Gómez de Orozco. Sociedad de Bibliófilos Mexicanos. Mexico. [Limited edition. Facsimile, with biobibliographical data in introduction.]
1953   Crónica de la Merced de México. Introducción y notas de Jorge Gurría Lacroix. Mexico. [Limited edition. Reprints text from Aldana, 1929.]

ALEGRE, FRANCISCO JAVIER, S.J.
1841–42   Historia de la Compañía de Jesús en Nueva España. [Published by Carlos M. Bustamante]. 3 vols. Mexico. [Written 1764–67. A comparison with the original text shows that the editor changed not only the title but even the text; he misread not a few passages. The text is incomplete, but even in this state, this version has been used as a key source by historians. Replaced by Alegre,

1956–60. *See* Dávila y Arrillaga, 1888–89.]
1956–60   Historia de la Provincia de la Compañía de Jesús de Nueva España. [New edition by] Ernest J. Burrus, S.J., and Félix Zubillaga, S.J. Institutum Historicum Societatis Iesu, *Bibliotheca Instituti Historici*, 9, 13, 16, 17. 4 vols. Rome. [With commentary, numerous documentary appendices, and complete text, this edition is approximately twice that of 1841–42, which it supersedes. Definitive scholarly edition, a model of proper editing.]
1957   *See* González de Cossío, 1957.

ALVAREZ Y ALVAREZ DE LA CADENA, L.
1944a   *See* Pérez de Ribas, 1944.
1944b   *See* Venegas, 1944.

ANNUAE LITTERAE
1581–1614   Annuae Litterae Societatis Jesu. MS. Rome (and elsewhere). [See Jesuits, Letters from Missions, for LC holdings.]
1650–54   *Idem.* [Summaries, in Latin, of general annual letters sent to Rome from individual Jesuit provinces; these in turn had been compiled from detailed local reports, especially from mission areas. Bolton Papers (Bancroft Library) has over 3,000 pages of photostats, with seemingly complete collection of transcripts.]
1956–71   Annuae Litterae Societatis Jesu. Jesuit Historical Institute. *Monumenta Mexicana*. Rome. [Four volumes, edited by Félix Zubillaga, to date: vol. 1, 1570–80 (1956); vol. 2, 1581–85 (1959); vol. 3, 1585–90 (1967); vol. 4, 1590–92 (1971.]

ARCE, FRANCISCO DE LOS RÍOS
1910–11   Puebla de los Angeles y la Orden Dominicana. Estudio histórico para ilustrar la historia civil, eclesiástica, científica, literaria de esta ciudad de los Angeles. 2 vols. Puebla. [Narrative to 1610. Notes much manuscript and published material on Dominicans in the Puebla area.]

ARLEGUI, JOSÉ, O.F.M.
1737   Crónica de la Provincia de N. S. P. S. Francisco de Zacatecas. Mexico. [The chronicle closes in 1733.]
1851   Crónica de la Provincia de N. S. P. S. Francisco de Zacatecas. Mexico. [Table of contents, pp. 487–88. To

the *Crónica* has been added "Memorias para la continuación de la Crónica . . . acopiadas por Fr. Antonio Gálvez, año de 1827."]

ARRICIVITA, JUAN DOMINGO, O.F.M.

1792 Crónica seráfica y apostólica del Colegio de Propaganda Fide de la Santa Cruz de Querétaro en la Nueva España. Part 2. Mexico. [Can be considered a continuation of Espinosa, 1746.]

ASENCIO, JOSÉ

1944a Ensayo de una bibliografía de cronistas franciscanos, agustinos y dominicos. *Estudios históricos*, 3:33–58 (Jan.), 37–52 (July). Guadalajara, Mexico. [This does not include Dominicans; see his 1946. Uncritical and incomplete, with a few biographical notices.]

1944b Ensayo de una bibliografía de cronistas franciscanos. *Col. Revista estudios históricos*, Cuaderno 1. Guadalajara. [Reprint of 1944a, paged consecutively.]

1946 Cronistas dominicos. *Estudios históricos*, 7:21–38 (Jan.). Guadalajara, Mexico. [Annotated list of chronicles, MSS or printed. Arranged by provinces: Mexico, Chiapas, Guatemala, Oaxaca, Puebla, Filipinas, Peru, Quito, Chile, Buenos Aires, and "General."]

AYER, [MRS.] E. E.

1915 *See* Benavides, 1916.

AYUSO, FÉLIX, S.J.

1945 *See* Sánchez Baquero, 1945.

BAEGERT, JOHANN JAKOB, S.J.

1771 Nachrichten von der Amerikanischen Halbinsel Californien. Mannheim [Major source on Guaicura Indians, southern tip of Lower California.]

1772 Nachrichten von der Amerikanischen Halbinsel Californien. Mannheim. [Corrected and enlarged version of 1771 edition.]

1942 Noticias de la Península americana de California. [Translated and edited by Pedro R. Hendrichs]. Mexico. [Modern Spanish version. Analytical introduction by Paul Kirchhoff.]

1952 Observations in Lower California, translated by M.M. Brandenburg and Carl L. Baumann. University of California. Berkeley and Los Angeles. [Complete English translation, with introduction and notes.]

BALTASAR, JUAN ANTONIO

See Balthasar, Johann Anton.

1944 *See* Ortega, 1944.

BALTHASAR, JOHANN ANTON

1754 *See* Ortega, 1754.

BANCROFT, HUBERT HOWE

1883–88 History of Mexico. Works, 9–14. 6 vols. San Francisco.

BANDELIER, ADOLPH F.

1969 A history of the Southwest: A study of the civilization and conversion of the Indians in the southwestern United States and northwestern Mexico from the earliest times to 1700. Vol. 1: A catalogue of the Bandelier Collection in the Vatican Library. Supplement to Vol. 1: Reproduction in color of thirty sketches and of ten maps. Edited by Ernest J. Burrus, S.J. Rome and Vatican City. [The last three volumes of text are being prepared for publication.]

BARCO, MIGUEL DEL, S.J.

1770–75 Correcciones y adiciones a la historia de la California en su primera edición de Madrid, año de 1757. MS. 2 vols. Biblioteca Nazionale. Rome. [Refers to Venegas, 1757. Original data by Barco, especially linguistic materials on the Cochimíes, are important.]

BARRERA VÁSQUEZ, ALFREDO

1938 *See* Landa, 1938a.

BASALENQUE, DIEGO, O.S.A.

1673 Historia de la Provincia de San Nicolás de Tolentino de Michoacán del Orden de N. P. S. Agustín. Mexico. [Covers years 1533–1644.]

1886 Historia de la Provincia de San Nicolás de Tolentino de Michoacán del Orden de N. P. S. Agustín. 3 vols. Mexico. [Vols. 1 and 3 have table of contents at end.]

1963 Historia de la Provincia de San Nicolás de Tolentino de Michoacán. *Col. Mexico heróico*, 18. Mexico. [Bio-bibliographical introduction by José Bravo Ugarte, occasional notes, defective index.]

BAUMANN, CARL L.

1952 *See* Baegert, 1952.

BEAUMONT, PABLO DE LA PURÍSIMA CONCEPCIÓN, O.F.M.

1826 Historia del descubrimiento de la América Septentrional por Cristóbal Colón, escrito por R. P. Manuel de la Vega. Mexico. [Carlos M. Bustamante, editor, incorrectly attributed the Beaumont *Aparato* to Vega, who owned the MS utilized for the edition. Bancroft (1883, 3:727) correctly characterizes this version as "incomplete, untrue, and useless."]

1873–74 Crónica de la Provincia de los Santos Apóstoles San Pedro y San Pablo de Michoacán. *Bib. histórica de la Iberia*, 15–19. 5 vols. Mexico. [Composed in late 18th century, a major source, with details on western Mexico to about 1565. Divided between an introductory *Aparato*, and the incomplete *Crónica*. Lacks Indian drawings. Based on Ramírez copy of a copy.]

1904 *See* Chavero, 1904.

1932 Crónica de la Provincia de los Santos Apóstoles San Pedro y San Pablo de Michoacán. AGN, *Publicaciones*, 17–19. 3 vols. Mexico. [Based on copy in Mexico. Contains Indian drawings. Introduction based on Rafael López. Text slightly variant from 1873–74 edition.]

BENAVENTE, TORIBIO DE, O.F.M.

1848 Historia de los Indios de la Nueva España. *In* Kingsborough, *Antiquities of Mexico* (9 vols., 1831–48), 9. London. [First printing of a basic chronicle, written ca. 1540. Later editions are easier to handle.]

1858 Historia de los Indios de la Nueva España. *In* Joaquín García Icazbalceta, comp., *Col. documentos para la historia de México*, 1:1–249. Mexico. [J. F. Ramírez provides biobibliographical introductory matter. The MS from which this version was published is now in the University of Texas collections.]

1869 Historia de los Indios de la Nueva España. *Col. documentos inéditos para la historia de España* [DII], 53:297–474. Madrid.

1903 Memoriales de Fray Toribio de Motolinía. Manuscrito de la Colección del Señor Don Joaquín García Icazbalceta. *In* Luis García Pimentel,

ed., *Documentos históricos de México* (6 vols., 1903–07), 1. Paris. [Duplicates some material in the *Historia*, but also contains information not in it.]

1914 Historia de los Indios de la Nueva España. [Edited by] Daniel Sánchez García, O.F.M. Barcelona. [From the Escorial MS. Basis of later versions, see 1941, 1951, 1956a, 1956b, 1964.]

1941 Historia de los Indios de la Nueva España. Salvador Chávez Hayhoe, ed. Mexico. [Reprint of 1914 edition, but with new introductory materials.]

1950 History of the Indians of New Spain. Translated and edited by Elizabeth Andros Foster. Cortés Society, *Documents and narratives concerning the discovery and conquest of Latin America*, n.s., 4. Berkeley. [Scholarly translation.]

1951 Motolinía's History of the Indians of New Spain. Translated and annotated with a biobibliographical study of the author by Francis Borgia Steck. Academy of American Franciscan History, *Documentary Series*, 1. Washington. [Translated from 1914 version, compared with Texas and Escorial MSS. Important notes.]

1956a Historia de los Indios de la Nueva España. Ed. Nacional. Mexico City. [Reprints 1914 edition.]

1956b Relaciones de Nueva España. UNAM, *Bib. estudiante universitario*, 72. Mexico City. [Introduction and selection by Luis Nicolau d'Olwer. See 1964.]

1964 Relaciones de Nueva España. UNAM, *Bib. estudiante universitario*, 72. Mexico City. [Reprint of 1956b.]

1966 Ritos antiguos, sacrificios, etc. [facsimile ed. of Benavente, 1869]. Krauss [so cited in Benavente, 1969, p. xxxvii]. Vaduz.

1967 Memoriales de Fray Toribio de Motolinía. Guadalajara, Mexico. [New offset edition of Benavente, 1903, by Edmundo Aviña Levy.]

1969 Historia de los indios de la Nneva España. Ed. Porrúa, *Sepan Cuantos*, 129. Mexico City. [The best scholarly edition, by Edmundo O'Gorman, who contributes extensive biobibliographical material, appendices, notes, and index.]

1971 Memoriales o libro de las cosas de Nuevo España y de los naturales de ella. Edición preparada por Edmundo O'Gorman. 591 pp. UNAM. Mexico. [An analytical study with full scholarly apparatus.]

BENAVIDES, ALONSO DE, O.F.M.

1916 The Memorial of Fray Alonso de Benavides. Translated and edited by Mrs. E. E. Ayer, F. W. Hodge, and C. F. Loomis. Chicago. [See 1945 and 1954 for superseding works.]

1945 Alonso de Benavides' Revised Memorial of 1634. Edited and translated by F. W. Hodge, G. P. Hammond, and A. Rey. University of New Mexico Press. Albuquerque. [Elaborately annotated, with numerous supplementary documents.]

1954 Benavides' Memorial of 1630. Translated by Peter F. Forrestal, with an historical introduction and notes by Cyprian J. Lynch. Academy of American Franciscan History, *Documentary Series*, 2. Washington. [Scholarly translation, with new materials in notes. Supersedes 1916 edition.]

1962 [Memorial de 1630.] In *Documentos para servir a la Historia del Nuevo México*, pp. 1–77. *Col. Chimalistac*, 13. Madrid.

BERISTÁIN DE SOUZA, JOSÉ MARIANO

1816–21 Biblioteca hispano-americana septentrional; o, Catálogo o noticia de los literatos, que o nacidos, o educados, o florecientes en la América Septentrional española, han dado a luz algún escrito, o lo han dexado preparado para la prensa. 3 vols. Mexico. [A basic historical bibliography.]

1883 Biblioteca hispano americana septentrional. . . . 2 ed. publícala el presbítero br. Frotino Hipólito Vera. 3 vols. Amecameca. [Most useful edition. See 1897, 1898, and 1947.]

1897 Biblioteca hispano-americana septentrional. . . . Tomo IV. Comprende los anónimos que dejó escritos el autor, las adiciones del Dr. Osores y otras añadidas posteriormente por

las personas que se expresan. José Toribio Medina publícalo, ahora con una introducción biobibliográfico. Santiago de Chile. [The biobibliographical portion was also issued separately by Medina, 1897.]

1898 Biblioteca hispano-americana septentrional. . . . Adiciones y correcciones que a su fallecimiento dejó manuscritas el Sr. Lic. José Fernando Ramírez. . . . Publícanlas por vez primera el Lic. Victoriano Agüeros y el Dr. N. León. Mexico. [Luis González Obregón provides biobibliographical notes on Ramírez (pp. v–xlvii).]

1947 Biblioteca hispano americana septentrional . . . 1521–1850. 3rd ed. 5 vols. in 2. Mexico. [Reissue of 1883 edition, with additions and corrections. Added titles from various well-known bibliographical compilations, identified by symbols and confusingly arranged. Each volume indexed separately. Difficult to use. Does not fully replace 1883 edition.]

BETANC(O)URT, AGUSTÍN DE

See Vetancurt, Agustín de.

BOLTON, HERBERT E.

1919 See Kino, 1919, 1948.

1926 See Palou, 1926.

1929 See Nichols, 1929.

1936 Rim of Christendom: a biography of Eusebio Francisco Kino, Pacific coast pioneer. New York. [Standard scholarly biography. Reprinted, New York, 1960.]

BORGES, PEDRO

1959 Documentación americana en el Archivo General O.F.M. de Roma. *Archivo Ibero-Americano*, 19:5–119 (Jan.–June). Madrid. [Titles, contents, description of manuscripts relating to America, principally 17th and 18th centuries, in Franciscan General Archive in Rome. Important compilation.]

BRAND, DONALD D.

1944 An historical sketch of geography and anthropology in the Tarascan Region. Part 1. *New Mexico Anthropologist*, 6–7/2:37–108 [also issued separately]. Albuquerque. [Only part 1 issued. Detailed notes on numerous sources, with "religious" covered (pp. 85–95) for various Orders and secular clergy.]

BRANDENBURG, M. M.
1952   See Baegert, 1952.
BRASSEUR DE BOURBOURG, CHARLES ETIENNE
1864   See Landa, 1864.
BRAVO UGARTE, JOSÉ
1963   See Basalenque, 1963.
BRINTON, DANIEL G.
1887   Critical remarks on the editions of Diego de Landa's writings. American Philosophical Society, *Proceedings*, 24:1–8. Philadelphia.
BURGOA, FRANCISCO DE, O.P.
1670   Palestra historial de virtudes y exemplares apostólicos fundada del zelo de insignes héroes de la sagrada Orden de Predicadores en este Nuevo Mundo de la América en las Indias Occidentales. . . . Mexico. [Prolix chronicle of Oaxaca, less valuable for ethnohistory than the *Geográfica descripción* (1674). See 1903 for partial edition and 1934a for modern edition.]
1674   Geográfica descripción de la parte septentrional del Polo Artico . . . y sitio de esta Provincia de Predicadores de Antequera, Valle de Oaxaca. . . . 2 vols. [continuously paged]. Mexico. [Considerable ethnohistorical material buried in verbosity. See 1934b for modern edition.]
1903   Palestra historial. . . . MNA. Mexico. [Partial edition, xvi+78 pages.]
1934a Palestra historial. . . . AGN, *Publicaciones*, 24. Mexico. [For index to this edition, see Metcalfe, 1946a.]
1934b Geográfica descripción. . . . AGN, *Publicaciones*, 25–26. 2 vols. Mexico. [For index to this edition, see Metcalfe, 1946b.]
BURRIEL, ANDRÉS MARCOS
1757   See Venegas, 1757.
BURRUS, ERNEST J., S.J.
1954   See Kino, 1954.
1956–60   See Alegre, 1956–60.
1961   See Kino, 1961a, 1961b, 1961c.
1962   See Píccolo, 1962.
1963   Misiones norteñas mexicanas de la Compañía de Jesús. *Bib. histórica mexicana de obras inéditas*, 25. Mexico. [Discussion of Jesuit establishments, 1751–57.]
1964   See Kino, 1964.
1965a   See Kino, 1965a.
1965b   Kino and the cartography of northwestern New Spain. Pioneers' Historical Society. Tucson, Arizona.

[Study of cartography of the Pimeria Alta, with reproduction of 17 maps.]
1966   Wenceslaus Linck's diary of his 1766 expedition to northern Baja California. *Baja California Travels Series*, 5. Los Angeles.
1967a La obra cartográfica de la Provincia Mexicana de la Compañía de Jesús, 1567–1967. 2 vols. Madrid.
1967b Ducrue's account of the expulsion of the Jesuits from Lower California, 1767–1769. Jesuit Institute of History, *Sources and Studies for the History of the Americas*, 2. Rome. [History of Lower California missions and missionaries, with letters of the latter.]
1967c Diario del Capitán Comandante Fernando de Rivera y Moncada, con un apéndice documental. 2 vols. *Col. Chimalistac*, 24–25. Madrid. [Complements Palou on Upper California at time of Serra (1774–77).]
1969   See Bandelier, 1969.
1971a Kino and Manje, explorers of Sonora and Arizona. Rome and St. Louis. [About 500 of the 800 pages are of original documents, nearly all on the Indians of Sonora and Arizona.]
1971b Juan María de Salvatierra, S.J. Selected Letters about Lower California. Los Angeles. [Translated and annotated by Burrus.]
1971c See Kino, 1971.
BUSTAMANTE, CARLOS M.
1826   See Beaumont, 1826.
1841–42   See Alegre, 1841–42.
CERVANTES, RAFAEL
1958   See Alcocer, 1958.
CHAPMAN, CHARLES E.
1921   A history of California: Spanish period. New York. Reprinted, 1949. [Discussion and evaluation of Francisco Palou (pp. 496–97).]
CHAVERO, ALFREDO
1904   Obras, 1. Mexico. [Work on Sahagún (1877), pp. 79–140. Vega collections of "Colección de Memorias de Nueva España . . . 1792," containing Beaumont Chronicle (vols. 7–11), discussed pp. 217–30.]
CHÁVEZ HAYHOE, SALVADOR
1941   See Benavente, 1941.
1945   See Mendieta, 1945a.
CIVEZZA, MARCELLINO DA
1879   Saggio di bibliografia . . . sanfrances-

cana. Prato. [Important survey of Franciscan sources.]

CLAVIGERO, FRANCISCO JAVIER, S.J.
1789 Storia della California. 2 vols. Venice. [Missions in Lower California, 1697–1768.]
1937 The history of [Lower] California. Translated from the Italian and edited by Sara E. Lake and A. A. Gray. Stanford. [Scholarly translation. Reprinted 1971 (Riverside, Calif.) with a new introduction by Homer Aschmann.]

CLINE, HOWARD F.
n.d. Sixteenth century Franciscan ethnohistorians. MS.

COGOLLUDO, DIEGO LÓPEZ DE, O.F.M.
1688 Historia de Yucatán. Madrid. [First of five editions of a fundamental work. For scholarly edition see 1957.]
1842–45 Historia de Yucatán. 2 vols. 2d ed. Campeche and Merida.
1867–68 Historia de Yucatán. 2 vols. 3d ed. Merida.
1955 Historia de Yucatan. 3 vols. 4th ed. Campeche and Mexico.
1957 Historia de Yucatán. 2 parts. 5th ed. [Edited by] Jorge Ignacio Rubio Mañé. Mexico. [Definitive scholarly edition. Biobibliographical notes, bibliography, with extended commentary. Facsimile of 1688 text.]

CORNEJO FRANCO, JOSÉ
1942 See Tello, 1942.
1945 See Tello, 1945.

DÁVILA GARIBI, JOSÉ IGNACIO
1945 See Espinosa, 1945.

DÁVILA PADILLA, AGUSTÍN, O.P.
1596 Historia de la fundación y discurso de la Provincia de Santiago de México de la Orden de Predicadores por las vidas de sus varones insignes y casos notables de Nueva España. Madrid. [First of three editions; for scholarly edition see 1955. Major chronicle.]
1625 Historia de la fundación y discurso de la Provincia de Santiago de México. . . . Mexico. [Reproduced in facsimile, 1955.]
1955 Historia de la fundación y discurso de la Provincia de Santiago de México. . . . [Edited by] Agustín Millares Carlo. Mexico. [Scholarly edition; facsimile text of 1625 edition with biobibliographical data, indexes.]

DÁVILA Y ARRILLAGA, JOSÉ MARIANO, S.J.
1888–89 Continuación de la historia de la Compañía de Jesús en Nueva España del P. Francisco Javier Alegre. 2 vols. Puebla.

DOMAYQUIA, JOAN DE
1945 See Mendieta, 1945a.

DONOHUE, JOHN AUGUSTINE, S.J.
1969 After Kino: Jesuit missions in northwestern New Spain, 1711–1767. Rome and St. Louis.

DUNNE, PETER MASTEN, S.J.
1951 Andrés Pérez de Ribas: pioneer Black Robe of the West Coast, administrator, historian. United States Catholic Historical Society. New York. [Scholarly biography, with full apparatus.]
1952 Black Robes in Lower California. Berkeley and Los Angeles. Reprinted 1968.

ECHARD, JACOBUS
1719–21 See Quétif and Echard, 1719–21.

EGUIARA Y EGUREN, JUAN JOSÉ DE
1755 Bibliotheca Mexicana; sive, Eriditorum historia virorum qui in America Boreali nati, vel alibi geniti, in ipsam domicilis aut studijs asciti, quavis lingua scripto aliquid tradiderunt . . . scriptis floruere editis aut ineditis. Tomus primus, exhibens litteras A B C. Mexico. [An early attempt to systematize Mexican bibliography, reaching only to letter C. The remainder of the MS, D to Juan de Ugarte, S.J. (unpublished), is at the University of Texas. See 1944 for Prologue.]
1944 Prólogo a la Bibliotheca Mexicana. Versión española anotada, con un estudio biográfico, por A. Millares Carlo. Fondo de Cultura Económica. Mexico. [Latin text and Spanish translation, first of its kind, of the important Prologue, virtually an intellectual history of Mexico to its date. Biobibliographical notes.]

ESCOBAR, MATÍAS DE, O.S.A.
1890 Americana Thebaida: Vitas patrum de los religiosos hermitaños de N. P. San Agustín de la Provincia de S. Nicolás Tolentino de Mechoacán. [Edited by] Nicolás León. Mexico. [Written ca. 1730, the complete work has never been published. This version was from an incomplete MS.]
1924 Americana Thebaida: Vitas patrum

. . . de Mechoacán. [Edited by] Nicolás León. Mexico. [Although the MS used by León for this version was complete, he arbitrarily shortened it for publication.]

ESPINOSA, ISIDRO FÉLIX DE, O.F.M.

1746 Chrónica apostólica y seráphica de todos los colegios de Propaganda Fide de esta Nueva España de missioneros franciscanos observantes, erigidos con autoridad pontificia y regia, para la reformación de los fieles y conversión de los gentiles. . . . Part 1. Mexico. [Only first of three parts published. Especially useful for Guatemala and "Gentilidad de Talamanca." See 1964 for best scholarly edition.]

1899 Crónica de la Provincia Franciscana de los Apóstoles San Pedro y San Pablo de Michoacán. La publica por vez primera el Dr. Nicolás León. Mexico. [Written ca. 1752, it was first printed in very limited edition, on poor paper, by León. He provided "Apuntamientos bio-bibliográficos." The 1945 edition is more satisfactory.]

1945 Crónica de la Provincia Franciscana de los Apóstoles San Pedro y San Pablo de Michoacán. Ampliamente mejorada e ilustrada. Apuntamientos bio-bibliográficos por Nicolás León. Prólogo y notas de José Ignacio Dávila Garibi. 2d ed. Mexico. [Reissue of 1899, with valuable notes, corrections, plates, and a new preface. Best scholarly edition.]

1964 Crónica de los Colegios de Propaganda Fide de la Nueva España. New edition, with notes and introduction by Lino G[ómez] Canedo, O.F.M. Academy of American Franciscan History, *Franciscan Historical Classics*, 2. Washington. [Scholarly reedition.]

FERNÁNDEZ DEL CASTILLO, FRANCISCO

1913–22 *See* Kino, 1913–22.

1920 Fray Antonio de Remesal. BNMex, *Boletín*, 12/9:151–73 (July–Dec.).

1925 Fray Agustín Dávila Padilla, Arzobispo de Santo Domingo. MNA, *Anales*, 3/4:448–53.

FLORENCIA, FRANCISCO, S.J.

1694 Historia de la Provincia de la Compañía de Jesús de Nueva España. . . .

Mexico. [Only one published of three planned volumes. First published history of Jesuits, covering years 1566–82.]

1955 Historia de la Provincia de la Compañía de Jesús de Nueva España. [Edited by] Francisco González de Cossío. Mexico. [Facsimile, with biobibliographical study and index of proper names.]

FLUVIÁ, FRANCISCO, S.J.

1754 *See* Ortega, 1754.

FORRESTAL, PETER F.

1954 *See* Benavides, 1954.

FOSTER, ELIZABETH ANDROS

1950 *See* Benavente, 1950.

FRANCO Y ORTEGA, ALONSO, O.P.

1900 Segunda parte de la historia de la Provincia de Santiago de México, Orden de Predicadores en la Nueva España, año de 1645 en México. [Edited by] José María de Agreda y Sánchez. MNA. Mexico. [Continuation (i.e., second part) of Dávila Padilla. Covers years 1591–1607.]

GÁLVEZ, ANTONIO, O.F.M.

1827 *See* Arlegui, 1851.

GARCÍA, ESTEBAN, O.S.A.

1918 Crónica de la Provincia agustiniana del Santísimo Nombre de Jesús de Mexico, Libro Quinto. [Edited by] Gregorio de Santiago Vela. Madrid. [Written ca. 1675 as continuation of Grijalva and hence "Libro Quinto." The monographic introduction by Santiago Vela was also published separately (1918a).]

GARCÍA ICAZBALCETA, JOAQUÍN

1858 *See* Benavente, 1858.

1866 *See* Tello, 1866.

1870 *See* Mendieta, 1870, 1945a.

1898 Fray Toribio de Benavente (Motolinía). Obras, 9:309–13. Mexico.

GARCÍA MÉNDEZ Y DESGARDIN, RAQUEL

1930 Los cronistas religiosos del siglo XVI. Mexico.

GARCÍA PIMENTEL, LUIS

1903 *See* Benavente, 1903.

GARIBAY K., ANGEL MARÍA

1947 *See* Ricard, 1947.

1959 *See* Landa, 1959.

GATES, WILLIAM E.

1937 *See* Landa, 1937.

GEIGER, MAYNARD, O.F.M.

1959 The life and times of Fray Junípero Serra, O.F.M. Academy of American Franciscan History, *Monograph Series*, 5–6. 2 vols. Washington. [Detailed coverage of late 18th-century Franciscan matters on the northern frontier, especially California.]

GENET, JEAN
1928–29 *See* Landa, 1928–29.

GÓMEZ, JOSÉ, O. Merc.
1770 *See* Aldana, 1770.

GÓMEZ CANEDO, LINO, O.F.M.
1959 Nuevos datos acerca del cronista Fray Antonio Tello. *Estudios históricos*, 1:117–21. Guadalajara, Mexico. [From AGI documents. Indicates earlier biographical data incorrect. Clarifies ambiguities and errors.]
1964 *See* Espinosa, 1964.

GÓMEZ DE OROZCO, FEDERICO
1924 *See* Grijalva, 1924, appendices.
1929 *See* Aldana, 1929.

GONZÁLEZ, JOSEPH, O.F.M.
1714–16 *See* Vásquez, 1714–16.

GONZÁLEZ, LUIS
1949 Fray Jerónimo de Mendieta. PAIGH, *Revista de la Historia de América*, 28:331–76 (Dec.). [Mendieta's ideas, Indians in the *History*, biobibliographical data.]

GONZÁLEZ DE COSSÍO, FRANCISCO
1945 *See* Villerías, 1945.
1955 *See* Florencia, 1955.
1957 Crónicas de la Compañía de Jesús en la Nueva España. Prólogo y selección de . . . Mexico. UNAM, *Bib. estudiante universitario*, 73. [Excerpts from Juan Sánchez Baquero, Andrés Pérez de Ribas, Francisco Javier Alegre.]

GONZÁLEZ DE LA PUENTE, JUAN, O.S.A.
1624 Primera parte de la chorónica augustiana de Mechoacán en que se tratan y excriven las vidas de nueve varones apostólicos augustinianos. Mexico.
1909 Crónica de la Orden de S. Agustín en Michoacán. [Biobibliographical notes by] Nicolás León. *In* Francisco Plancarte y Navarrete, ed., *Col. documentos inéditos y raros para la historia eclesiástica mexicana*, 1. Mexico. [Reissue of 1624, under variant title.]

GRAY, A. A.
1937 *See* Clavigero, 1937.

GRIJALVA, JUAN DE, O.S.A.
1624 Crónica de la Orden de N. P. S. Augustín en las provincias de la Nueva

España en quatro edades desde el año de 1533 hasta el de 1592. Mexico. [First published and most important Augustinian chronicle.]
1924 Crónica de la Orden de N. P. S. Augustín. . . . [Edited by] Federico Gómez de Orozco. Mexico. [Reissue of 1624, preserving original spelling. Documentary appendices, and bibliography on Augustinians in New Spain.]

GURRÍA LACROIX, JORGE
1953 *See* Aldana, 1953.

HABIG, MARION A., O.F.M.
1944–45 The Franciscan provinces of Spanish North America. *Americas*, 1:88–96, 215–30, 330–44. [Monographic treatment. A basic coverage.]

HAMMOND, G. P.
1945 *See* Benavides, 1945.

HANDBOOK OF LATIN AMERICAN STUDIES
1936– A selective and annotated guide to recent publications, prepared in the Hispanic Foundation, Library of Congress. 33 vols. to date. Cambridge, Mass., and Gainesville, Fla.

HENDRICHS, PEDRO R.
1942 *See* Baegert, 1942.

HODGE, FREDERICK WEBB
1916 *See* Benavides, 1916.
1919 Bibliography of Fray Alonso de Benavides. Heye Foundation, Museum of the American Indian, *Indian Notes and Monographs*, 3/1. New York.
1945 *See* Benavides, 1945.

IGLESIA, RAMÓN
1945 Invitación al estudio de fray Jerónimo de Mendieta. *Cuadernos americanos*, 22/4:156–72 (July–Aug.). [Outlines a vast study which Iglesias never completed.]

IGUÍNIZ, JUAN B.
1917 La crónica miscelánea de la Provincia de Santiago de Jalisco. BNMex, *Boletín*, 12/5:189–211 (Apr.–Sept.). Mexico. [Discussion of Antonio Tello.]
1944 *See* Ortega, 1944.
1945 *See* Mendieta, 1945b.

JESUITS, LETTERS FROM MISSIONS
1585 Annuae litterae societatis Iesu. Anni MDLXXXV. . . . [1587] Rome.
1586 Litterae societatis Iesv. Duorum Annorum MDLXXXVI et MDLXXXVII. . . . Romae in Collegio eiusdem societatis. [1589.]

1610–[1618] Annuae litterae societatis Iesv. Anni MDCX. . . . Dilingae, Apud Viduam Ioannis Mayer, 1610 [1618].

KINGSBOROUGH, LORD (Edward King)

JIMÉNEZ, FRANCISCO, O.P.

1929–31 Historia de la Provincia de San Vicente de Chiapa y Guatemala de la Orden de Predicadores. Prólogo del Lic. J. Antonio Villacorta C. Sociedad de Geografía e Historia, *Bib. Goathemala*, 1–3. 3 vols. Guatemala. [Written 1721-22. Some materials omitted from this version.]

KINGSBOROUGH, LORD (Edward King)

1848 *See* Benavente, 1848.

KINO, EUSEBIO FRANCISCO, S.J.

1913–22 Las misiones de Sonora y Arizona. Versión paleográfica e índice por Francisco Fernández del Castillo. AGN, *Publicaciones*, 8. Mexico. [Diary and chronicle, 1683–1711, on Pimería Alta.]

1919 Kino's historical memoir of Pimería Alta: A contemporary account of the beginnings of California, Sonora and Arizona. Translated into English and annotated by Herbert E. Bolton. 2 vols. Cleveland. [Standard scholarly translation. See 1948.]

1948 Kino's historical memoir . . . Translated into English and annotated by Herbert E. Bolton. 2 vols. in 1. Berkeley. [Reissue of Kino, 1919.]

1954 Kino reports to headquarters: Correspondence of Eusebio F. Kino, S.J., from New Spain with Rome. English translation [with original text] and notes by Ernest J. Burrus, S.J. Rome.

1961a Correspondencia del P. Kino con los Generales de la Compañía de Jesús, 1682–1707. Prólogo y notas de Ernest J. Burrus, S.J. Mexico.

1961b Kino's plan for the development of the Pimería Alta, Arizona and Upper California: A report to the Mexican viceroy. Translated and edited by Ernest J. Burrus, S.J. Tucson.

1961c Vida del P. Francisco J. Saeta, S.J. Prólogo y notas de Ernest J. Burrus, S.J. Mexico. [See 2d ed., 1971.]

1964 Kino escribe a la Duquesa Editado con notas por Ernest J. Burrus, S.J. *Col. Chimalistac*, 18. Madrid. [Letters containing many details on Indians of Lower California.]

1965a Kino writes to the Duchess. Translated and edited by Ernest J. Burrus, S.J. Jesuit Institute of History, *Sources and Studies for the History of the Americas*, 1. Rome. [English version of Kino, 1964.]

1965b *See* Burrus, 1965b.

1971 Kino's biography of Saeta. Translated with an epilogue by Charles W. Polzer, S.J. Spanish text edited by Ernest J. Burrus, S.J. Rome and St. Louis. [Second edition of 1961c.]

KIRCHHOFF, PAUL

1942 *See* Baegert, 1942.

KNOROSOV, Y. V.

1955 *See* Landa, 1955.

LAKE, SARA E.

1937 *See* Clavigero, 1937.

LAMARID, LÁZARO

1938–44 *See* Vásquez, 1938–44.

LANDA, DIEGO DE, O.F.M.

1864 Relation des choses de Yucatan de Diego de Landa. [Edited and translated by] Charles Etienne Brasseur de Bourbourg. Paris. [First edition, in French translation, of a major work written ca. 1566. The version is incomplete and arbitrarily divided; for critique, see Brinton, 1887. See Landa, 1938b, 1941, and 1969 for standard scholarly editions. See also Lizana, 1864.]

1881 Manuscrito de Diego de Landa tomado directamente del único ejemplar que se conoce y se conserva en la Academia de Historia. [Edited by] Juan de Dios de la Rada y Delgado. Madrid. [Second edition, first Spanish version. Preceded by Spanish translation of Léon de Rosny, 1876. First complete edition, but lacks maps.]

1900 Relación de las cosas de Yucatán. *Relaciones de Yucatán*. *In* DIU, 13:265–411. [Third edition, incomplete, fols. 28–46 omitted. One map, DIU, 11: after p. xl.]

1928–29 Relation des choses de Yucatan. Texte espagnol et traduction française en regard [par] Jean Genet. 2 vols. Paris. [Fourth edition, incomplete. Proposed vol. 3 never published; vol. 2 ends at fol. 45. Many useful notes; excellent introduction.]

1937 Yucatan before and after the Conquest by Friar Diego de Landa, with other related documents, maps and illustrations. Translated with notes [by William E. Gates]. *Maya Society*, Pub. 20. Baltimore. [Fifth edition, first English version, no Spanish text. Free translation. A variant edition for students has a preface, uncolored map.]

1938a Relación de las cosas de Yucatán sacada de lo que escribió el Padre Diego de Landa de la Orden de San Francisco MDLXVI. Primera edición yucateca. Precedida de una "Nota sobre la vida y la obra de Fr. Diego de Landa," escrita por el Profr. don Alfredo Barrera Vásquez, y seguida un apéndice que contiene la reimpresión de diez relaciones de las escritas por los encomenderos de Yucatán en los años 1579 y 1581."
[Edited by] José E. Rosado Escalante and Fávila Ontiveros. Merida, Yucatan. [Sixth edition. Excellent biobibliographical notes. Complete except for drawings of day signs in yearly calendar.]

1938b Relación de las cosas de Yucatán por el P. Fray Diego de Landa, Obispo de esa diócesis. Introducción y notas [por] Héctor Pérez Martínez. Con un apéndice en el cual se publica por primera vez varios documentos importantes y cartas del autor. Mexico. [Seventh edition. Complete MS, with additional documents, map of the chiefdoms (provinces), indexes of Maya terms, proper names. Standard Spanish language edition.]

1941 Landa's Relación de las Cosas de Yucatán. A translation, edited with notes by Alfred M. Tozzer. Peabody Museum, Harvard University, *Papers*, 18. Cambridge. [Eighth edition. Standard scholarly English translation, with massive analytical and bibliographical apparatus by a major authority. Contains additional documents.]

1955 Diego de Landa: Soobshchenie o delakh v Iukatani, 1566 [Relación de las Cosas de Yucatan]. Ak. Nauk SSSR. Moscow. [Ninth edition. Russian translation by Y. V. Knorosov from Genet and DIU (1900); notes based chiefly on Tozzer. Introductory matter outdated and propagandistic.]

1959 Relación de las cosas de Yucatan. Introducción por Angel M. Garibay K. 8 ed. *Bib. Porrúa*, 13. Mexi-

co. [Tenth edition, incorrectly labeled eighth on title page. Essentially a reissue of Landa, 1938b, without notes, but with new introductory materials. New edition, 1966.]

1968 Relación de las cosas de Yucatan: a translation. Edited with notes by Alfred M. Tozzer. Kraus reprint. New York. [Reprint of 1941 edition.]

LARRAIÑAGA, JUAN R.
1914–15 Fray Jerónimo de Mendieta, historiador de Nueva España (1525–1604). Apuntes bibliográficos. *Archivo Ibero-americano*, 1:290–300, 488–99; 2:188–201, 387–404; 4:341–73. Madrid.

LECINA, MARIANO, S.J.
1925–30 *See* Uriarte and Lecina, 1925–30.

LEJEAL, LUIS
1906 Les memoriales de Fray Toribio "Motolinia." XIV Internationalen Amerikanisten-Kongress (Stuttgart, 1904), [*Verhandlungen*], 1:193–221.

1907 Los memoriales de Fray Toribio Motolinía. *In* Benavente, 1903, appendix [separately paged], pp. 10–45. [Also apparently issued separately, with illustrations. Detailed analysis and comparison with Benavente's *Historia*.]

LEÓN, NICOLÁS
1890 *See* Escobar, 1890.
1898 *See* Beristáin de Souza, 1898.
1899 *See* Espinosa, 1899.
1909 *See* González de la Puente, 1909.
1924 *See* Escobar, 1924.
1945 *See* Espinosa, 1945.

LEÓN PINELO, ANTONIO RODRÍGUEZ DE
1629 El epítome de biblioteca oriental i occidental, náutica i geográfica. Madrid.

1958 El epítome de Pinelo, primero bibliografía del Nuevo Mundo. Estudio preliminar de Agustín Millares Carlo. Pan American Union. Washington. [A facsimile of the *Epítome de biblioteca oriental i occidental, náutica i geográfica* (Madrid, González, 1629) with extensive and valuable biobibliographical notes. The original has long been nearly unobtainable in the book markets and even the facsimile published in Buenos Aires in 1919 has become uncommon.]

1968 *See* Quiñones Melgoza, 1968.

LIZANA, BERNARDO DE, O.F.M.
1633 Historia de Yucatán. Valladolid, Spain.
1864 Historia de Yucatán. *In* Landa, 1864, pp. 348–65. [French translation of portions of part 1, I–IV.]
1893 Historia de Yucatán. Devocionario de Nuestra Señora de Izamal y conquista espiritual. MNA. Mexico.

LOOMIS, C. F.
1916 *See* Benavides, 1916.

LÓPEZ, ATANASIO, O.F.M.
1915–17 Fr. Toribio de Motolinía. *El Eco Fransciscano*, 32:713–17 (1915); 33: 14–18 (1916); 34:65–68 (1917).
1922 Misiones o doctrinas de Michoacán y Jalisco (Mejico) en el siglo XVI: 1525–1585. *Archivo Ibero-americano*, 9:340–425. [Important data; pp. 383–425 published for the first time the chronicle by Diego Muñoz, 1922.]
1925 Cuestenario historico. ¿Escribío Fr. Toribio Motolinía una obra intitulada "Guerra de los Indios de la Nueva España o Historia de la Conquista de México"? *Archivo Ibero-americano*, 12:221–47. (Mar.–Apr.). [Discusses relationships between Motolinía and Mendieta.]
1931 Fray Toribio Motolinía, misionero e historiador de Méjico en el siglo XVI. *Iluminaire* (Jan.–Feb.).

LÓPEZ, JUAN FRANCISCO, S.J.
1754 *See* Ortega, 1754.

LÓPEZ, RAFAEL
1932 *See* Beaumont, 1932.

LÓPEZ DE COGOLLUDO, DIEGO
See Cogolludo, Diego López de.

LÓPEZ PORTILLO Y ROJAS, JOSÉ
1891 *See* Tello, 1891.

LÓPEZ-VELARDE LÓPEZ, BENITO
1964 Expansión geográfica franciscana en el hoy norte central y oriental de México. Univ. Pontificia Urbana de Propagande Fide, *Cultura missional*, 12. Mexico. [Summary account of Franciscan expansion in northern Mexico with tables of mission areas.]
1916 *See* Benavides, 1916.

LYNCH, CYPRIAN J.
1954 *See* Benavides, 1954.

MCCARTY, KIERAN R.
1962 Los franciscanos en la frontera chichimeca. *Historia mexicana*, 11/3:321–60 (Jan.–Mar.). [Survey of Franciscan activities in northern New Spain.]

MARTÍNEZ, HÉCTOR PÉREZ
1938 *See* Landa, 1938b.

MEADE, JOAQUÍN
1962 Semblanza de Fray Joseph Arlegui. *Humanitas: Anuario del Centro de Estudios Humanisticos* (U. de Nuevo León), 3:441–62. [Biobibliographical data.]

MEDINA, BALTASAR DE, O.F.M.
1682 Chrónica de la Santa Provincia de San Diego de México de Religiosos descalzos de N. S. P. S. Francisco en la Nueva España; vidas de ilustres y venerables varones que le han edificado con excelentes virtudes. Mexico. [Sole Franciscan chronicle of this large province.]

MEDINA, JOSÉ TORIBIO
1897 *See* Beristáin de Souza, 1897.
1898–1907 Biblioteca hispano-americana (1493–1810). 7 vols. Santiago de Chile. [Standard bibliography; books published in Europe concerning colonial Spanish America.]
1904 La imprenta en Guadalajara de México, 1793–1821. Santiago de Chile. [Reissued by N. Israel, Amsterdam, 1966.]
1909–11 La imprenta en México (1539–1821). 8 vols. Santiago de Chile. [Indispensable work on colonial bibliography; this lists titles published in Mexico City. There are separate parallel treatments for provincial imprints: Puebla (1908), Merida de Yucatan (1904), Oaxaca (1904), Veracruz (1904), of less importance. Reissued by N. Israel, Amsterdam, 1965. See 1904.]

MENDIETA, GERÓNIMO DE, O.F.M.
1870 Historia eclesiástica indiana. [Edited by] Joaquín García Icazbalceta. Mexico. [Major chronicle, written 1596. Discussed in detail by Phelan, 1956, 1970.]
1945a Historia eclesiástica indiana. Con algunas advertencias de Joan de Domayquia. Sacadas de cartas y otras borradores del autor. Ed. Salvador Chávez Hayhoe. 4 vols. Mexico. [Reprint of Mendieta, 1870, including introductory material by García Icazbalceta. Additional indexes.]
1945b Vidas Franciscanas. Prólogo y selección de Juan B. Iguíniz. UNAM, *Bib. estudiante universitario*, 52. Mexico. [Selections from *Historia*

eclesiástica, with biobibliographical notes.]

MENDOZA, EUFEMIO
1871 *See* Tello, 1871.

METCALFE, GRACE
1946a Indice de la Palestra Historial. AGN, *Boletín*, 17 (no. 4), paged separately, pp. 1–22. [Index to Burgoa, 1934a.]
1946b Indice de la Geográfica Descripción. AGN, *Boletín*, 17 (no. 4, paged separately, pp.1–31. [Index to Burgoa, 1934b.]

MILLARES CARLO, AGUSTÍN
1944 *See* Eguiara y Eguren, 1944.
1955 *See* Dávila Padilla, 1955.
1958 *See* León Pinelo, 1958.

MONASTERIO, IGNACIO, O.S.A.
1928 El P. Mtro. Diego Basalenque, O.S.A. (1577–1651). *Archivo Agustiniano*, 29:406–17 (June).

MORENO, DIONISIO VICTORIA
1966 Los Carmelitas Descalzos y la conquista espiritual de México, 1585–1612. Mexico City.

MOTOLINÍA, [TORIBIO DE]
See Benavente, Toribio de.

MUÑOZ, DIEGO, O.F.M.
1922 Descripción de la Provincia de los Apóstoles San Pedro y San Pablo y de la milicia, habitación, costumbres y manera de vivir de los indios infieles chichimecas, en cuya conversión han entendido y entienden religiosos de nuestra Orden. *In* Atanasio López, 1922, pp. 383–425. [Data to about 1583, for Michoacan and Jalisco. An early, important chronicle.]
1951 Descripción de la provincia de San Pedro y San Pablo de Michoacán, en las Indias de la Nueva España. Crónica del siglo XVI. Introducción de José Ramírez Flores. Junta Auxiliar Jalisciense de la Sociedad Mexicana de Geografía y Estadística, 1950 [i.e., 1951]. Guadalajara, Mexico. [Limited edition. From printed sources are included six documents concerning Jalisco and adjacent areas.]

NICHOLS, ROY F.
1929 *Review of* Palou, 1926. *HAHR*, 9:230–31 (May).
See Palou, 1926.

NICOLAU D'OLWER, LUIS
1956 *See* Benavente, 1956b.

OCARANZA, FERNANDO
1933–34 Capítulo de la historia franciscana. 2 vols. Mexico. [Listing of principal works written in 16th and 17th centuries (2:67–78) by Franciscans in New Spain, according to Vetancurt, and in 19th century (2:239–44). Bibliography (1:517–20; 2:323).]

O'GORMAN, EDMUNDO
1969 *See* Benavente, 1969.
1971 *See* Benavente, 1971.

OJEA, HERNANDO, O.P.
1897 Libro tercero de la historia religiosa de la Provincia de México de la Orden de Sto. Domingo. [Edited by] José M. de Agreda y Sánchez. MNA. Mexico. [Continuation of Dávila Padilla, written 1608. Introductory materials give data on all official Dominican chroniclers of the province.]

ONTIVEROS, FÁVILA
1938 *See* Landa, 1938a.

ORNELAS MENDOZA Y VALDIVIA, NICOLÁS DE, O.F.M.
1962 Crónica de la Provincia de Santiago de Xalisco . . . 1719–1722. [Edited by Fr. Luis del Refugio de Palacio]. Instituto Jalisciense de Antropología e Historia, *Serie de Historia*, 2. Guadalajara. [There is also a 1941 edition (not seen). This one contains biobibliographical notes and indexes.]

OROZCO Y BERRA, MANUEL
1857 *See* Palou, 1857.

ORTEGA, JOSÉ, S.J.
1754 Apostólicos afanes de la Compañía de Jésus, escritos por un padre de la misma sagrada religión de su Provincia de México. Barcelona. [Beristáin first attributed this to Juan Francisco López, S.J., then to José Ortega, which is largely correct. Volume prepared for the press by Francisco Fluviá, S.J. Part 1, by Ortega, on Nayarit is especially valuable; the other two parts are now attributed to Johann Anton Balthasar, S.J. New editions appeared in 1877 and 1944.]
1887 Historia del Nayarit, Sonora, Sinaloa y Ambas Californias. Mexico.
1944 Apostólicos afanes de la Compañía de Jesús en su Provincia de México. Prólogo [por]Juan B. Iguínez. Mexico. [Part 1 (by Ortega): Maravillosa reducción y conquista de la Provincia de S. Joseph del Gran Nayar.

Parts 2, 3 (by Baltasar): De los principios, progresos y descaecimiento de lo espiritual conquista de la Provincia de Pimería Alta por la muerte del P. Eusebio Francisco Kino. De nuevos progresos, varios descubriemientos y estado presente de la Pimería Alta.]

PALACIO Y VALOIS, LUIS DEL REFUGIO DE, O.F.M.

1935 Un estudio sobre el Muy Reverendo Padre Fray Antonio Tello, Padre y Cronista de la Provincia de Santiago de Xalisco. Sociedad de Geografía y Estadística, Junta Auxiliar Jalisciense, *Boletín*. Guadalajara. [Biobibliographical notes, especially regarding authorship of various books. Appears as part 1 of Introduction in Tello, 1945, with added part 2 by same author.]

1939 *See* Torres, 1939.

1960 *See* Torres, 1960.

1962 *See* Ornelas Mendoza y Valdivia, 1962.

1965 *See* Torres, 1965.

PALOU, FRANCISCO, O.F.M.

1857 Noticias de la Nueva California. *In* M. Orozco y Berra, ed., *Documentos para la historia de Méjico*, 4 ser., v–vii. 3 vols. Mexico. [First printing of what amounts to a source book used by Palou for his *Vida* of Junípero Serra (Mexico, 1787). Abounds in useful information, somewhat unconnected. The Palou-Serra period is exhaustively noted in Geiger, 1959.]

1874 Noticias de la Nueva California. 4 vols. San Francisco.

1926 Noticias de la Nueva California. Historical Memoirs of New California. Translated and edited by Herbert E. Bolton. 4 vols. Berkeley. [For critical review of translation see Nichols, 1929.]

PAREJA, FRANCISCO DE, O.Merc.

1882–83 Crónica de la Provincia de la Visitación de Ntra. Sra. de la Merced, redención de cautivos de la Nueva España. Escrita en 1688. 1st ed. 2 vols. Mexico. [Pareja's manuscript was finished Nov. 4, 1687. There are 140 pages of documentary appendices, giving information on the Order through 1844. See Aldana, ca. 1770.]

PÉREZ ARRILUCEA, DIEGO, O.S.A.

1913–14 Trabajos apostólicos de los primeros misioneros Agustinos de Méjico. *La Ciudad de Dios* (El Escorial), 92:298–310 (Feb. 1913), 420–28 (Mar. 1913); 94:335–43 (Sept. 1913); 95:5–16 (Oct. 1913), 241–51 (Nov. 1913); 96:111–19 (Jan. 1914); 97:113–26 (Apr. 1914); 98:265–76 (Aug. 1914), 363–72 (Sept. 1914); 99:253–61 (Nov. 1914). [General coverage for colonial Mexico.]

PÉREZ DE RIBAS, ANDRÉS, S.J.

1645 Historia de los triumphos de Nuestra Santa Fee entre gentes las más bárbaras y fieras del Nuevo Orbe. Conseguidos por los soldados de la milicia de la Compañía de Jesús en las misiones de la Provincia de Nueva España. Madrid. [Major source on Sinaloa, Sonora. Stress on ethnohistory seen in subtitle: Refiérense asimismo las costumbres, ritos y supersticiones que usaban estas gentes; sus puestos y temples; las victorias. . . .]

1896 Corónica y historia religiosa de la Provincia de la Compañía de Jesús de México en Nueva España. 2 vols. in 1. Mexico. [Incomplete version of a general history of Jesuits, to 1654. This publication omits many chapters on Indians (49 in vol. 1, 9 in vol. 2), available in Manuscripts Division, Library of Congress. The complete work from the LC MS is being prepared for publication in Madrid, by Ernest J. Burrus, S.J., and Félix Zubillaga, S.J. The author purposely scanted work in northern missions, which he covered in detail in his 1645.]

1944 Historia de los triunfos . . . . Reimpreso por L. Alvarez y Alvarez de la Cadena. 3 vols. [Reissue of 1645, with Alvar Núñez Cabeza de la Vaca's "Los naufragios" included (1:1–74).]

1957 *See* González de Cossío, 1957.

PÉREZ MARTÍNEZ, HÉCTOR

1938 *See* Landa, 1938b, 1959.

PFEFFERKORN, IGNAZ, S.J.

1794–95 Beschreibung der Landschaft Sonora samst andern merkwürdigen Nachrichten von den innern Theilen Neu-Spaniens und Reise aus Amerika bis in Deutschlands. 2 vols. Cologne. [Includes materials also furnished by Jakob Sedelmayr, S.J. Important source on Sonora. Intended vol. 3 not known.]

1949 Sonora: A description of the Province. Translated and annotated by Theodore E. Treutlein. University of New Mexico, *Coronado Cuatro Centennial Publications*, 12. Albuquerque. [Scholarly translation, with valuable brief notes, reprint of map, and excellent biobibliographical data.]

PHELAN, JOHN LEDDY
1956 The Millennial Kingdom of the Franciscans in the New World: A study of the writings of Gerónimo de Mendieta (1525–1604). University of California, *Publications in History*, 52. Berkeley and Los Angeles. [Intellectual history, with considerable biobibliographical discussion of Mendieta, especially relations to Torquemada and others. Well indexed.]

1970 The Millennial Kingdom of the Franciscans in the New World. University of California Press. Berkeley. [Revised edition of 1956.]

PÍCCOLO, FRANCISCO M., S.J.
1962 Informe del estado de la nueva cristiandad de California. [Edited by Ernest J. Burrus, S.J.]. *Col. Chimalistac*, 14. Madrid. [Some 500 pages of original documents on Lower California Indians.]

PILLING, JAMES CONSTANTINE
1895 The writings of Padre Andrés de Olmos in the languages of Mexico. *American Anthropologist*, 8:43–60. [Also issued separately, Washington, 1895.]

PLANCARTE Y NAVARRETE [Bishop of Cuernavaca]
1909 *See* González de la Puente, 1909.

POLZER, CHARLES W.
1971 *See* Kino, 1971.

PUENTE, JUAN GONZÁLEZ DE LA
See González de la Puente, Juan.

QUÉTIF, JACOBUS, O.P., AND JACOBUS ECHARD, O.P.
1719–21 Scriptores Ordinis Praedicatorum recensiti, notisque historicis et criticis illustrati. . . . 2 vols. Paris. [Extensive bibliography of Dominicans.]

QUIÑONES MELGOZA, JOSÉ
1968 Los cronistas de órdenes religiosas mencionados en el *Epítome* de León Pinelo. BNMex, *Boletín*, 2a ep.,

17/3–4, pp. 17–40. [Biobibliographical notes on chroniclers in the 1629 listing, with data on editions, and studies arranged by Orders.]

RADA Y DELGADO, JUAN DE DIOS DE LA
1881 *See* Landa, 1881.

RAMÍREZ, JOSÉ FERNANDO
n.d. Indice biográfico por orden alfabético de los nombres que cita Antonio Remesal en la obra Historia de la Provincia de S. Vicente de Chyapa y Guatemala de la Orden de nro. glorioso padre Sancto Domingo. MS. [Name index to Remesal, 1619. A 218-page MS in Rare Book Division, Library of Congress.]

1858 Noticias de la vida y escritos de Fray Toribio de Benavente, ó Motolinía. *In* Benavente, 1858, pp. xlv–cliii.

1898 *See* Beristáin de Souza, 1898.

RAMÍREZ FLORES, JOSÉ
1951 *See* Muñoz, 1950 [i.e., 1951].

REA, ALONSO DE LA, O.F.M.
1643 Crónica de la Orden de N. Seráfico P. S. San Francisco, Provincia de San Pedro y San Pablo de Michoacán en la Nueva España. Año de 1639. Mexico.

1882 Crónica de la Orden. . . . Mexico. [Reprint of 1643 edition, with added documentary appendices and table of contents. No index.]

REMESAL, ANTONIO DE, O.P.
1619 Historia de la Provincia de S. Vicente de Chyapa y Guatemala de la Orden de nuestro glorioso Padre Sancto Domingo: escrívense juntamente los principios de las demás provincias desta religión de las Yndias Occidentales de la governación de Guatemala. . . . Madrid. [An extensive, important chronicle on Guatemala and Chiapas.]

1932 Historia general de las Indias Occidentales y particular de la gobernación de Chiapa y Guatemala: escríbese [*sic*] juntamente los principios de la religión de nuestro glorioso Padre Santo Domingo y de las demás religiones. Sociedad de Geografía e Historia, *Bib. Goathemala*, 4–5, 2 vols. Guatemala. [A reissue of 1619, with additional introductory materials.]

1964 Historia general de las Indias Occidentales y particular de la Gobernación de Chiapa y Guatemala. vol. 1. Edición y estudio preliminar de Carmelo Sáenz de Santa María. *Bib. autores españoles*, 175. Madrid. [Contains the first six books of the *Historia*. Very good preliminary study.]

REY, A.
1945 *See* Benavides, 1945.

RICARD, ROBERT
1923 Note sur Fr. Pedro Malgarejo, évangélisateur du Mexique. *Bulletin Hispanique*, 25:253–56 (July–Sept.). [See his additional note, 1924, pp. 68–69.]

1924 Notes sur les éditions et le manuscrit de la "Historia de los Indios de la Nueva España" de Fr. Toribio de Motolinía. *Revue d'Histoire Franciscaine*, 1:493–500 (Oct.).

1933a La "Conquête spirituelle" du Mexique. Essai sur l'apostolat et les méthodes missionaires des Ordres Mendiants en Nouvelle-Espagne de 1523–24 à 1572. Université de Paris, *Travaux et Mémoires de l'Institut d'Ethnologie*, 20. Paris. [Especially useful for bibliographical and critical notes on Franciscans, Dominicans, and Augustinians, to 1572.]

1933b Remarques bibliographiques sur les ouvrages de Fr. Toribio Motolinía. Société des Américanistes, *Journal*, n.s., 25:139–51. Paris. [Revisionist views on relations between the *Memoriales* and the *Historia de los Indios*.]

1947 La conquista espiritual de Mexico. Ensayo sobre el apostolado y los métodos misioneros de las órdenes mendicantes en la Nueva España de 1523–1524 a 1572. Traducción de Ángel María Garibay K. Mexico. [A few references not in 1933a.]

1966 The spiritual conquest of Mexico: An essay on the apostolate and the evangelizing methods of the mendicant orders in New Spain, 1523–1572. Translated by Lesley Byrd Simpson. University of California Press. Berkeley. [Review by Fintan B. Warren (HAHR, 47:562–64) points out numerous errors of translation.]

RODRÍGUEZ CABAL, JUAN, O.P.
1961 Catálogo de escritores dominicos en la Capitanía General de Guatemala. Sociedad de Geografía e Historia, *Anales*, 34:106–67. Guatemala. [Al-phabetical listings, with biobibliographical data, of Dominican writers in colonial Guatemala.]

ROSADO ESCALANTE, JOSÉ E.
1938 *See* Landa, 1938a.

ROSNY, LÉON DE
1876 Essai sur le déchiffrement de l'écriture hiératique Maya. Archives de la Société Américaine de France, n.s. 2, pt. 1, pp. 5–108 (part one of article).

ROZE, MARIE AUGUSTIN
1878 Les dominicains en Amérique; ou Aperçu historique sur la fondation des diverses provinces de l'Ordre des frères prêcheurs dans le nouveau monde. Paris.

RUBIO MAÑÉ, JORGE IGNACIO
1957 *See* Cogolludo, 1957.

SÁENZ DE SANTA MARÍA, CARMELO
1964 *See* Remesal, 1964.

SÁNCHEZ BAQUERO, JUAN, S.J.
1945 Fundación de la Compañía de Jesús en Nueva España, 1571–1580. [Introduction by Féliz Ayuso, S.J.] Mexico. [Incomplete version of a major work. Padre Ayuso published the incomplete MS of the Jesuit Central Archives in Rome. Introductory matter, dated 1927, includes biobibliographical data; notes and biobibliographical data on Jesuits mentioned by Sánchez Baquero.]

1957 *See* González de Cossío, 1957.

SÁNCHEZ GARCÍA, DANIEL
1914 *See* Benavente, 1914.

SANTIAGO VELA, GREGORIO DE, O.S.A.
1913–31 Ensayo de una bibliografía Ibero-americana de la Orden de San Agustín. 8 vols. El Escorial and Madrid. [Scholarly bibliography. Vols. 1-3 (Madrid), 1913–17; vols. 5, 6 (Madrid), 1920–22; vols. 7, 8 (El Escorial), 1925–31.]

1918a Historiadores de la Provincia Agustina de México en los siglos XVI y XVII. In *Archivo histórico hispano-agustiniano*, pp. 241–55. Madrid. [Also serves as introduction to García, 1918.]

1918b *See* García, 1918.

1923 La provincia agustina de Michoacán y su historia. *Archivo histórico hispano-agustiniano*, pp. 129–44, 266–79 (Mar.–Apr., May–June). Madrid.

SBARALEA, JOANNES HYACINTHUS, O.F.M.
1906– Bibliotheca historico-bibliographica.

Rome. [Continuation of Wadding, 1806, on Franciscan writings.]

SEDELMAYR, JAKOB, S.J.
1794–95   *See* Pfefferkorn, 1794–95.

SHELBY, CHARMION
1949   The cronistas and their contemporaries: Recent editions of works of the sixteenth and seventeenth centuries. *HAHR*, 29:295–317 (May). [A bibliographical list of reissues of standard or long out-of-print volumes, 1937–48, on both secular and religious chronicles.]

SIMPSON, LESLEY BYRD
1966   *See* Ricard, 1966.

SOMMERVOGEL, CARLOS, S.J.
1890–1930   Bibliothèque de la Compagnie de Jesús.   11 vols.   Brussels and Paris. [Standard Jesuit biobibliographical work. See 1960.]
1960   Bibliothèque de la Compagnie de Jesús.   12 vols.   Louvain. [Reissue of 1890–1930.]

SOTOMAYOR, JOSÉ FRANCISCO
1889   Historia del Apostólico Colegio de Nuestra Señor de Guadalupe de Zacatecas, desde su fundación hasta nuestros días.   2d ed.   2 vols.   Zacatecas.

STECK, FRANCIS BORGIA
1951   *See* Benavente, 1951.

STREIT, ROBERT
1916–67   Bibliotheca missionum.   24 vols. Vol. 1, Grundlegender und Allgemeiner Teil (Münster, 1916); vol. 2, Amerikanische Missionsliteratur, 1493–1699(Aachen, 1924); vol. 3, *idem*, 1700–1909 (Aachen, 1927); vol. 22 [supplement to vol. 1] (1963); vol. 23 (1964); vol 24, Amerika, 1910–24 (1967).   Aachen and Münster. [Basic point of departure: lists systematically biobibliographies of missionaries and their writings, with bibliographical notes on publication. Several supplementary volumes are being prepared. Earlier out-of-print volumes are also being reissued.]

TELLO, ANTONIO, O.F.M.
1866   Fragmento de una historia de la Nueva Galicia escrita hacia 1650.   *In* García Icazbalceta, *Col. documentos para la historia de México*, 2:343–438.   Mexico. [Part of book 2 of *Crónica miscelánea de la Sancta Provincia de Xalisco*. See 1891.]
1871   Fragmentos de la crónica de Xalisco.

[Edited by] Eufemio Mendoza.   *In* García Icazbalceta, *Col. documentos para la historia de México*, 3.   Mexico. [Portion of book 4, from corrupt and incomplete copy, from MS in Biblioteca pública, Guadalajara. Seemingly Mendoza had copied 36 chapters of book 4 and 27 of book 5.]
1891   Libro segundo de la crónica miscelánea, en que se trata de la conquista espiritual y temporal de la Santa Provincia de Xalisco en el Nuevo Reino de la Galicia y Nueva Vizcaya y descubrimiento del Nuevo México. [Edited, with bibliographical introduction, by] José López Portillo y Rojas.   Guadalajara. [Book 2 in its entirety. Editor states that book 3 was not by Tello, and was not worth publishing.]
1942   Crónica miscelánea de la Sancta Provincia de Xalisco.   Book 3. [Edited, with introduction, by] José Cornejo Franco.   Guadalajara. [Cornejo Franco shows book 3 is by Tello (denied in Tello, 1891). Volume is a series of clerical biographies.]
1945   Crónica miscelánea de la Sancta Provincia de Xalisco.   Book 4. [Edited by] José Cornejo Franco.   Guadalajara. [From original MS in Biblioteca Pública, Guadalajara. Included is a biography of Tello, and notes by Luis del Refugio de Palacio, published separately in 1935.]

TORRES, FRANCISCO MARIANO DE, O.F.M.
1939   Fragmento de la crónica de la Sancta Provincia de Xalisco.   Junta Auxiliar Jalisciense de la Sociedad Mexicana de Geografía y Estadística, *Folletines*.   Guadalajara. [Fragmentary 18th-century continuation of Tello, from MS in Biblioteca Pública, Guadalajara, Mexico, preceded by brief note signed J. C. F., and with biobibliographical notes (pp. 83–96) by Luis del Refugio de Palacio. Table of contents (pp. 99–100).]
1960   Crónica de la Sancta Provincia de Xalisco.   Notas de Fray Luis del Refugio de Palacio.   *Colección siglo XVI*, 8.   Guadalajara.
1965   Crónica de la Sancta Provincia de Xalisco . . . 1755.   Instituto Jalisciense de Antropología e Historia, *Serie de Historia*, 7.   Guadalajara. [Biobibliographical notes made by Luis del

Refugio de Palacio in 1931 (pp. 155–78). Indexes. Contains book 2, chaps. 8–13; book 3, chaps. 1–24.]

TOZZER, ALFRED M.
1941   See Landa, 1941.
TREUTLEIN, THEODORE E.
1949   See Pfefferkorn, 1949.
URIARTE, JOSÉ E. DE, S.J.
1904–16   Catálogo razonado de obras anónimas y seudónimas de autores de la Compañía de Jesús pertenecientes a la antigua asistencia española. 5 vols. Madrid. [Standard source of biobibliographical information on Jesuit writers.]
—— AND MARIANO LECINA, S.J.
1925–30   Biblioteca de escritores de la Compañía de Jesús pertenecientes a la antigua asistencia de España. 2 vols. Madrid. [Incomplete (from A through Ferrusola), but useful biobibliographical data on Jesuits.]
VÁSQUEZ, FRANCISCO, O.F.M.
1714–16   Chrónica de la Provincia del Santíssimo Nombre de Jesús de Guatemala de el Orden de N. Seráphico Padre San Francisco en el Reyno de la Nueva España, dividida en dos tomos. [Published by] Joseph González, O.F.M. Guatemala. [Each book has long subtitle. Book 1, 1524–65; book 2, 1565–1600.]
1938–44   Crónica de la Provincia del Santisimo Nombre de Jesús de Guatemala. 2d ed. [Edited by] J. Antonio Villacorta C. Sociedad de Geografía e Historia, Bib. Goathemala, 14–17. 4 vols. Guatemala. [With full scholarly apparatus, supplants 1714–16. Biobibliographical introduction by Lázaro Lamarid, O.F.M.]
VEGA, MANUEL DE LA
1826   See Beaumont, 1826.
VELA, GREGORIO DE SANTIAGO
    See Santiago Vela, Gregorio de.
VENEGAS, MIGUEL, S.J.
1757   Noticia de la California y de su conquista temporal y espiritual hasta el tiempo presente sacada de la historia manuscrita, formada en México año de 1739. 3 vols. Madrid. [The original MS by Venegas was entitled "Empressas Apostólicos" (1739). Complete MS version in Bancroft Library; contemporary copy in Academia de Historia, Madrid. It has not been published in full. Andrés Mar-

cos Burriel, S.J., edited and published it in part under the title above. There have been two re-editions of the Burriel version. The more recent is 1944.]
1944   Noticia de la California. . . . [Edited by] L. Alvarez y Alvarez de la Cadena. 3 vols. Mexico. [Text from 1757 edition. Maps, illustrations.]
VERA, FORTINO HIPÓLITO
1883   See Beristáin de Souza, 1883.
VETANCURT, AGUSTÍN DE, O.F.M.
1698   Teatro mexicano. Descripción breve de los sucesos ejemplares, históricos, políticos, militares y religiosos del Nuevo Mundo de las Indias. Mexico. [A continuation of earlier works (Benavente, Mendieta), on which Vetancurt leans heavily, adding many data. His chronicle is part 4 of this large work, to which was added a Menologio Franciscano (lives of missionaries). A major work.]
1870–71   Teatro mexicano. . . . Bib. histórica de la Iberia, 7–10. 4 vols. Mexico. [Vol. 1 prefaced by a biobibliographical notice; vol. 4, Menologio Franciscano. Superseded by 1960–61.]
1960–61   Teatro mexicano. . . . Col. Chimalistac, 8–11. 4 vols. Madrid. [Most accessible and useful edition. Vol. 1, Sucesos naturales, Sucesos políticos; vol. 2, Sucesos militares, Tratado de México, Tratado de Puebla; vol. 3, Crónica de la Provincia del Santo Evangelio; vol. 4, Menologio. Detailed analytic index.]
VILLACORTA C., J. ANTONIO
1929–31   See Jiménez, 1929–31.
1938–44   See Vásquez, 1938–44.
VILLERÍAS, GASPAR DE, S.J.
1945   Relación breve de la venida de los de la Compañía de Jesús a la Nueva España, año de 1602, manuscrito anónimo del Archivo Histórico de la Secretaría de Hacienda. Versión paleográfica del original [por] Francisco González de Cossío. Mexico. [Summary of a larger, yet unpublished work by the first official historian of the Jesuits in Mexico. This edition has seven photographic facsimiles of the Relación breve, and documentary appendices.]
WADDING, LUKE, O.F.M.
1650   Scriptores ordinis Minorum. Quibus accessit syllabus illorum, qui ex eo-

dem ordine pro fide Christi fortiter occubuerent. Priores atramento, posteriores sanguine christianum religionem asserverunt. Recensuit Fr. Lucas Wadding. Rome.

1806 Scriptores ordinis minorum. . . . Rome. [General standard biobibliographical coverage for Franciscans. For supplementary volumes see Sbaralea, 1906–. They have been appearing in Rome since 1906 under the title *Bibliotheca historico-bibliographica.*]

WAGNER, HENRY R.
1937 The Spanish Southwest, 1542–1794. 2 parts [continuously paged]. Albuquerque. [Standard work on biobibliography.]

WARREN, FINTAN B.
1962 Jesuit historians of Sinaloa-Sonora. *Americas,* 18:329–39 (Apr.). [Short descriptive bibliography.]

XIMÉNEZ, FRANCISCO
See Jiménez, Francisco.

ZAMBRANO, FRANCISCO
1961 Diccionario bio-bibliográfico de la Compañía de Jesús en México. Mexico City. [Massive compilation of 16th–18th-century Jesuits, 10 vols. of which had appeared by 1970 (last entry "Páez, Melchor F.").]

ZUBILLAGA, FÉLIX, S.J.
1956–60 *See* Alegre, 1956–60.
1956–71 *See* Annuae Litterae, 1956–71.

ZULAICA GÁRATE, ROMÁN
1939 Los Franciscanos y la imprenta en México en el siglo XVI. Mexico. [Biobibliographical study, with exhaustive descriptions of books published by Franciscans.]

14. Bernardino de Sahagún, 1499–1590

A. SAHAGÚN AND HIS WORKS

LUIS NICOLAU D'OLWER and
HOWARD F. CLINE

Bᴇʀɴᴀʀᴅɪɴᴏ ᴅᴇ Sᴀʜᴀɢ́ᴜɴ was born in Sahagun de Campos, Leon, Spain, about 1499. Little is known of his early life. He died in Mexico City in 1590.[1]

In 1529 Fray Bernardino de Sahagún began his apostolate with 19 others on the voyage from Spain led by Fray Antonio de Ciudad Rodrigo. Upon weighing anchor at Cadiz there remained behind Sahagún his childhood at Leon on the banks of the Cea River under the ancient walls of the Benedictine abbey which gave name to his birthplace, an adolescence at the University of Salamanca, and in the same city his religious training to wear the sackcloth of the "poverello." Thirty years of his life dissolved in the wake of memory while he sailed across the ocean, impelled by his zeal as a propagator of the Faith. On landing at Villa Rica de la Vera Cruz, 60 years of missionary life awaited him in New Spain.

When Sahagún arrived in the Valley of Mexico the construction of the city destined to eclipse the splendor of Tenochtitlan was in full apogee, a constructive, as well as destructive, fever. From the ruins that still remained Sahagún learned of the greatness, beauty, and splendor of Aztec culture. He describes the pagan Templo Mayor and its adjuncts with mixed feelings of enthusiasm and amazement. Thus, from the very first moment Sahagún appreciated the value of native culture. He also realized the difficult task ahead of replacing, in the hearts of such people, the gods in whose honor they had erected such impressive buildings.

---

[1] Ed. note: The late Luis Nicolau d'Olwer, before his death in 1963, submitted this article in Spanish. It was then translated by Howard F. Cline, whose minor editorial changes were approved by the author. It was essentially a summary of Nicolau d'Olwer, 1952. Later review of it disclosed flaws and major omissions. Drawing heavily on generous information and critical comments supplied by Charles Dibble, John B. Glass, and H. B. Nicholson, as well as on unpublished personal research, the Volume Editor has rewritten a number of pages. These changes from the original are noted. He also supplied the section "Evolution of the *Historia*." Cline has examined the Tolosa MS in Madrid, and has extensively used a microfilm of the Florentine Codex deposited in the Library of Congress. Throughout Article 14, FC = Florentine Codex, its books cited in Roman numerals, chapters in Arabic; HG = *Historia general*, cited in the same manner; PM = *Primeros memoriales*.

But Sahagún was of a reflective nature. He was not satisfied with a superficial evangelizing or with the spectacle of mass baptism. He wanted a true conversion. This could be achieved only through the profound understanding of Indian personality, reflected in native traditions and language.

The activities of Sahagún in New Spain were varied, intense, and fruitful: missionary activity in Tlalmanalco (1530–32), whence he climbed Popocatepetl; Xochimilco (1535); pedagogic work in the school for sons of Indian nobility at Santa Cruz de Tlatelolco (1536–40); return to mission life in the valley of Puebla and in Huexotzingo and Cholula, where he climbed Iztaccihuatl, and perhaps again Popocatepetl. He saw the eruption of Poyauhtecatl (Orizaba Peak) and had a second lengthy residence in Tlatelolco (1542–58), interrupted by his visits to Michoacan and Tula, whose ruins stirred great admiration in him. Reputed master without peer of the Nahuatl language, Sahagún wrote sermons and translated the Epistles and the Gospel, undoubtedly earlier but certainly during residence in Tepepulco (1558–61).

Submerged in Tlatelolco, where pre-Conquest native environment was better conserved than in reconstructed Mexico City, Sahagún became interested in the Indians not only as potential converts but equally as bearers of a high culture and rich historical past. He believed that Mexican antiquities should be preserved in their own language. Thus was born the *Tratado de la retórica y filosofía moral y teología de la gente mexicana*, compiled in Nahuatl about 1547.

Also in Tlatelolco (1550–55, perhaps even earlier) Sahagún developed the most historical of his various works, an account of the Conquest that later became book XII of his *Historia general*. Since the *Cartas de relación* by Cortés, much had been written about the Conquest, but all from the point of view of the victors and in Spanish. Sahagún had the singular idea of reversing the

FIG. 1—FRAY BERNARDINO DE SAHAGÚN. From Seler, 1922.

coin, to obtain data from native informants —contemporaries and participants of that drama—and to write the narrative in Nahuatl, the language of the recently conquered Aztecs.

Sahagún's persistent desire to preserve pagan beliefs in the Nahuatl language aroused great hostility, among his own Order, and in the Holy Office (Inquisition) and Council of the Indies in Madrid. This was temporarily abated by administrative directives. A provincial of the Franciscans in Mexico, Fray Francisco de Toral (elected in 1558) ordered Sahagún (ca. 1559) "to write in the *Mexican language* all that which may seem useful for the indoctrination, culture, and religious conversion to

187

Christianity among the natives of New Spain, to aid the workers and missionaries toward their indoctrination." On receiving the command, Sahagún drafted a memorandum (in Spanish) of all the subjects that he must deal with, "that which is written," he says, "in the 'Doce libros,' the 'Postilla,' and 'Cánticos'" (HG, II, Prol.).[2] He spent the following 32 years carrying out his plan, often in face of considerable obstacles.

The last years of Sahagún's long life were disappointing, but he continued to revise earlier works, even plan new ones. Gravely ill in Tlatelolco, where he had resided since 1571, Sahagún was moved to the convent of San Francisco de México. There he died October 28, 1590, according to a Spanish source, or February 5, 1590, according to the native *Anales mexicanos*, no. 4 (see Article 23, Item 206).

PLANS AND METHODS

Sahagún conceived a master threefold project: (1) a Mexican encyclopedia for training of missionaries; (2) an aid for preachers, with translated versions of the sacred texts, homilies, and explanatory sermons; and (3) books of songs and prayers for the converts. All these elements were to be in pure, elegant Nahuatl, a rich and expressive aboriginal language that was spoken widely in early colonial Mexico, and almost universally understood there (see Article 7).

The encyclopedia that Sahagún evolved is his major work. It is often cited as *Historia general*.[3] The only manuscript (PAL, fol. 1) with a complete title page calls it "Historia universal de las cosas de la nueva españa; repartida en doce libros, en lengua mexicana y española. . . ." The HG contains only a little political history, much more natural history, but mostly "moral history," or descriptions of beliefs, usages, and customs. An exhaustive treasury of the Nahuatl language, the HG was modeled on medieval European encyclopedias.[4] It is not, then, a "history" in a modern sense of the term.

Rather it stands unrivaled as a massive work on Aztec ethnography and linguistics.

Sahagún's initial motive was to absorb the language and beliefs of the native Mexicans in order to evangelize them effectively. Slowly he became interested in Indian things for their own sake. He observed how, on contact with the European culture, the native one disappeared or became hybridized and how language changed. He even feared that the Indian population stood on the verge of extinction.

Fray Bernardino wanted to describe and to inventory a ship he felt was going down. To do so he must obtain the information from the natives themselves, preferably by letting them speak in their own fashion about matters which affected their lives. In such a manner the linguistic aspects of his work aligned themselves with the ethnographic and folkloristic.

First Sahagún designed a strikingly modern questionnaire (now lost) dealing with major topics on many aspects of the Aztec culture as a base for the enterprise he wished to undertake; then he carefully selected the best-equipped informants. In general, they were upright old men who

[2] Citations to the *Historia* follow the 1956 Garibay edition. Various statements not otherwise documented rest on materials published in the Nicolau d'Olwer 1952 biography of Sahagún, which contains extended detailed references, omitted here for economy of space. [Ed. note: Sahagún's original memorandum ("minuta") is lost. The Prologue to book II that was written about 1570 details the history of the work to that time; it is reproduced and translated in Cline, 1971a.]

[3] This and the following sentence added by H. F. Cline.

[4] Ed. note: Garibay (1953–54, 2:70–71; 1956, 3:89) suggested Pliny's *Historia naturalis* as a model for the Sahagún HG; it is known that a copy of Pliny was in the library of the College at Tlatelolco. Robertson (1959, pp. 169–72; 1966, pp. 622–26), taking Garibay's suggestion into account, argues rather for a late medieval encyclopedia (itself modeled on Pliny), *De proprietatibus rerum*, by Bartholmaeus Anglicus (or de Glanville) as the actual European prototype, especially for the original Sahagún plans, before he added books VI and XII, not relevant topics for medieval European authors.

had matured and lived their best years under the Triple Alliance, who were able to recall the old traditions and could recount them without embellishment.

He sought their answers in the easiest attainable manner, one to which they were accustomed: interpretation of native pictorial documents. Through such stimulation he evoked old concepts, couched often in highly symbolic terms, sometimes in obscure language. Finally he crosschecked his data, "in such a manner," he says, "that the first sieve through which my work was sifted was Tepepulco, the second Tlatelolco, and the third Mexico" (II, Prol.). The interpretations of the paintings, for example, were recorded in Nahuatl. At all these stages there were attempts at grammatical concordances.

In this manner our author empirically used a rigorous method of ethnographical research, a method that might be called interview/roundtable agreement. Consequently, the role played by native informants and advisors in the gestation of the HG is quite important, if as yet by no means fully known or evaluated.[5]

As expected, the method produced an extremely objective, even impersonal work. Is that enough, however, for us to place our absolute faith in the HG? García Icazbalceta raised this question in 1886 (1954, p. 375), and partially answered it along the following lines, here clarified and extended.

There is one objection based precisely on what seems its best guarantee: the triple sieve through which the work was sifted. Insofar as the three places—Tepepulco, Tlatelolco, and Mexico-Tenochtitlan—represented one and the same tradition, the data for it became purer on emergence from the sieves. But what happened when they recorded parallel but markedly different local traditions? Does the last revision prevail? Or has a kind of amalgam, an enforced and artificial *koine* of common Aztec tradition, been formed? The circumstances suggest a certain caution in overgeneralizing from the Sahagún text alone, especially if comparative materials are available. Nicholson shows (Section B) that surprisingly few of the Tepepulco data made their way into the final HG (1569).[6]

Ethnographically, Sahagún attempted to fix Indian tradition at the moment that it was interrupted by the Conquest. He did not propose to "excavate" it to its earlier sources in more primitive substrata. His objective was to establish not "absolute" historical truth but merely versions of the past which the living natives of his day believed were true.

To establish even that image Sahagún also consulted old pictorial documents. He affirms, "These books and writings were mostly burned when the pagan things were destroyed, but *many remained hidden, which we have seen and are still kept, from which we have learned their ancient lore*" (HG, X, Relación 32).

EVOLUTION OF HISTORIA GENERAL *by Howard F. Cline*

The elaboration of the Nahuatl text of the HG and then its Spanish paraphrase was a long and complicated process, as much because of its inherent difficulties as on account of various outside obstacles, of which Sahagún speaks in detail[7] (HG, Dedicatory letter, Prologue; To the sincere reader; II, Prol.; IX, Prol.; X, Prol.; X, chap. 27). Essentially there are three interdependent parts of the final product: (1) a Nahuatl text, (2) a Spanish text, and (3) a pictorial account. His evolving work underwent numerous revisions and recombinations, which makes the total corpus a fascinating, com-

---

[5] Ed. note: Garibay (1953–54, 2:29–30) and León-Portilla (1961b, pp. xviii–xix, xxii) emphasize that Sahagún adopted the approach that Fr. Andrés de Olmos had earlier developed. Motolinía also employed it. In book II, Prologue, Sahagún details names of scribes and his ex-students, the *latinos*, Indians expert in Latin, Spanish, and Nahuatl, who reviewed the HG in its various states.

[6] Ed. note: This sentence added by H. F. Cline.

[7] Ed. note: Section 3 rewritten by H. F. Cline.

plex puzzle, as yet unraveled only in part. For many nonspecialized purposes it suffices to say that a complete scholarly edition of this final Nahuatl text is published with an English translation (Anderson and Dibble, 1950–70). Other editions are discussed in Section C.

Nahuatl Documentation and Drafts[8]

The preliminary native texts appear in the "Codices Matritenses" or Madrid Codices. These have been described in detail (Ballesteros Gaibrois and others, 1964). One group is in the Royal Palace Library, another in the Royal Academy of History. Folios from each are intermixed. Both codices, Palace and Academy, were reproduced photographically by Paso y Troncoso, 1905–07 (see Article 21, app. F). In very reduced form their pictorial elements are reproduced in color by Ballesteros Gaibrois (1964, vol. 2). Even now only partial transcriptions and translations of Nahuatl texts are available (see Section C). Mexican texts were written between 1559 and 1565 in Tepepulco and Tlatelolco, with subsequent revisions and reorganizations by Sahagún in Mexico.

PRIMEROS MEMORIALES, 1559–61. Sahagún's two-year stay in Tepepulco, where he had been transferred by Toral (1559–61), produced the so-called *Primeros memoriales*, abundantly illustrated (Paso y Troncoso, 1905b, vol. 6). They consist of four sections grouped into large chapters: (1) Gods, (2) Celestial and Underworld Affairs, (3) Lordship, and (4) Human Affairs. These later were subdivided into books (Table 1). More detailed consideration of this initial documentation is given by Nicholson in Section B. In 1576 Sahagún reported that he still had material from the Tepepulco period (II, Prol.).

In 1561 Sahagún moved "with his manuscripts" to the Convent of Santiago Tlatelolco, where he spent "a little over a year." A subsequent period appears to have been spent at the nearby Colegio de Santa Cruz

de Tlatelolco (1563–65). There his Tepepulco work was revised, corrected, expanded, and essentially replaced. Three series of documents belong to this period (1561–65): "Segundos memoriales," "Memoriales en tres columnas," and "Memoriales con escolios." In all of them there are only two illustrations. Sahagún and his *latino* aides experimented with various formats and arrangements of materials while in Tlatelolco.

SEGUNDOS MEMORIALES, ca. 1561–62.[9] Two fragments in which the Nahuatl text occupies the full width of the page are known as the "Segundos memoriales" (or "Primer manuscrito de Tlatelolco" or "Memoriales complementarios"). These are in chapter 1 of the Palace manuscript (fols. 49–52) and another in chapter 3 of the Academy manuscript (fols. 2–5). Added glosses by Sahagún on the latter concerning Aztec rulers contain information attributed by him to materials which Tenochtitlan Aztecs had provided in the form of pictures and writings to Canon Juan González, a protégé of Bishop Juan de Zumárraga, according to Torquemada (MI, 3:72–78). Not incorporated in the Florentine Codex, these additions (transcribed by Ballesteros-Gaibrois and others, 1964, 1:86–88) show slight resemblance to the Codex Mendoza (Jiménez Moreno, 1938b, p. 39), but this is probably coincidental.

MEMORIALES EN TRES COLUMNAS, ca. 1563–65. The "Memoriales en tres columnas" or "Segundo manuscrito de Tlatelolco" is organized in three columns and five large chapters, but for the most part only the central column in Nahuatl is completed. Chapters 1 and 2 are in the Palace manuscript (fols. 33–48, 54–159, 178–249) and chapters

---

[8] Ed. note: The chronology of the Nahuatl texts given by Nicolau d'Olwer revised and rewritten by H. F. Cline.

[9] Ed. note: Subsections on the "Segundos memoriales," "Memoriales en tres columnas," and "Memoriales con escolios" revised by J. B. Glass, September, 1971.

TABLE 1—DEVELOPMENT AND REORGANIZATIONS OF
SAHAGÚN'S *HISTORIA GENERAL,* 1559–69

	TEPEPULCO 1559–61	TLATELOLCO 1561–65		MEXICO 1565–69	
	Primeros Memoriales 1559–61 (Chapter)	(Chapter)	First (Book)	Second (Book)	Final 1569 (Book)
1. Gods (Dioses; Teteo)	Primero		I II III	I II III	I II III
2. Heaven and Underworld (Cielo e infierno; Ilhuicáyotl iuan Mictlancáyotl)	Segundo		IV	IV V VI	VII IV V
3. Polity (Señorío; Tlatocáyotl)	Tercero		VIII	VIII IX	VIII IX
4. Human Things (Cosas Humanas; Tlacáyotl)	Cuarto		V	X	X
	Quinto Natural Things (Cosas Naturales: Tlalticpac- cáyotl)		VI	XI	XI
		IX Conquest (Conquista)	XII		XII
		VII Rhetoric & Philosophy (Retórica y Filosofía Moral)	VII		VI

SOURCE: After Jiménez Moreno, 1938b, p. 33, adapted by H. F. Cline.

3–5 are in the Academy manuscript (fols. 6–50, 104–342). In two short sections (PAL, fols. 178–83; ACAD, fols. 104–11) all three columns are completed with the Spanish paraphrase in the left column and a glossary (scholia) of some text terms on the right. One leaf (PAL, fol. 243) bears the date 1564.

MEMORIALES CON ESCOLIOS, ca. 1565. The "Memoriales con escolios" are a clean and slightly revised copy of those two sections of the "Memoriales en tres columnas" in which all three columns are completed. They correspond to final book VII, chapters 1–5 (PAL, fols. 160–70) and book X, chapters 1, 2 and part of 3 (ACAD, fols. 88–96).

This manuscript is a model for the three-column manuscript which Sahagún projected but never completed.

The "Segundos memoriales," the "Memoriales en tres columnas," and the "Memoriales con escolios" together comprise the "Manuscrito de Tlatelolco" (1561–65). It represents a vast expansion of the Tepepulco material and most of it appears, sometimes verbatim, in the later Florentine Codex. This is the manuscript which Sahagún said had been copied in "ruinous hand" and on which he based his final organization of HG. The subject of chapter 5, Natural History, later designated as book VI and finally as book XI, first appears in this manu-

191

TABLE 2—FINAL 1569 ORGANIZATION OF SAHAGÚN'S *HISTORIA GENERAL*
COMPARED WITH EARLIER VERSIONS

Final 1569 (Book)	Short Title	Mexico 1565–68 (Book)	Mexico I (Book)	Tlatelolco 1562–65 (Chapter)	Tepepulco *Primeros Memoriales* 1559–61 (Chapter)
I	*Gods* 22 chapters, appendix	I	I	I	1
II	*Ceremonies & Feasts* 38 chapters, 6 appendixes	II	II	I	1
III	*Origin of the Gods* 14 chapters, appendix, 9 chapters	III	III	I	1
IV	*Soothsayers* 40 chapters, appendix	V	IV	II	2
V	*Omens* 13 chapters, appendix	VI	IV	II	2
VI	*Rhetoric* 43 chapters, 3 additions	VII	VII	—	—
VII	*Sun, Moon, Stars, Binding the Years* 13 chapters	IV	IV	II	2
VIII	*Kings and Lords* 22 chapters	VIII	VIII	III	3
IX	*Merchants* 22 chapters, 4 additions	IX	VIII	III	3
X	*The People* 29 chapters	X	V	IV	4
XI	*Earthly Things* 12 chapters, appendix	XI	VI	V	—
XII	*Conquest of Mexico* 41 chapters (1569), 42 chapters (1585)	XII	IX	—	—

SOURCE: Prepared by H. F. Cline, from Jiménez Moreno, 1938b.

script and may not have been part of the 1559 plan.

Later Sahagún divided the five large chapters into smaller books and chapters. This reorganization, discussed below, is reflected by glosses in Sahagún's handwriting on the "Manuscrito de Tlatelolco."

Historia general: Nahuatl

ORGANIZATION AND REORGANIZATION, 1565–68. Transferred to San Francisco de Mexico in 1565, Sahagún for three years himself reviewed and rearranged the draft "Memoriales" he had brought from Tlatelolco. He gave them three successive organizations (Jiménez Moreno, 1938b, pp. 39–40) and broadened the scope of the whole work by annexing to it the "Retórica" and the "Conquista," written earlier in 1547 and ca. 1555, respectively. The latter may possibly also have been drafted as early as 1547 (see Tables 1 and 2).

The final reorganization, ca. 1568, ended with 12 books, each divided into chapters and some into paragraphs, often with appendixes. By 1569 they were copied in final form, following the three-column division. Only the central column—the Nahuatl text —was fully completed. Sahagún noted that "The Mexicans added and amended many things in the twelve books as they were being copied" (HG, II, Prol.). The 1569 Nahuatl manuscript is lost.

MANUSCRITO DE 1569. The lost "Manuscrito de 1569" seemingly represents a final Nahuatl version of the HG, subsequently copied in the later bilingual ones, of which only one copy, the FC, survives. It is worth noting that additions and corrections were inserted by scribes in Mexico, changing matters recorded in Tlatelolco (II, Prol.).

In the "Manuscrito de 1569" the columns for the Spanish text and for the linguistic glossary or scholia were left blank, ". . . not having been able [to complete it] for lack of support and help." (HG, To the sincere reader). Aid and support for his scribes that Sahagún had requested from the provincial Chapter in 1570 were not received, notwithstanding the favorable opinions of the Censors of the Chapter: "esteemed writings, whose completion should be favored." The Chapter claimed lack of funds and ordered Sahagún to discharge his clerks and finish the work himself. But Sahagún ". . . being over 70 years of age and having a shaky hand," was unable to do so (HG, II, Prol.). For about five years (ca. 1571–75) the HG was interrupted and the individual books were dispersed throughout the province, as a result of the hostility of the General Commissary toward works written by friars in native languages. The arrival of a new General Commissary, Fr. Rodrigo de Sequera (Torrubia, 1756, pp. 196–97), on September 4, 1575, revitalized the preparation of the HG and expanded it to include full Spanish texts, which to that time had been only fragmentary.

RECAPITULATION.[10] By 1569 Sahagún had arranged the HG in its final form, and had prepared (with native aides) a complete Nahuatl text of it that seemingly remained unchanged thereafter. At that time he also proposed to provide equivalent Spanish texts, which were just beginning to be written, and explanatory notes (escolios, scholia) in Nahuatl. The Spanish texts were

being prepared, 1570–71 (see next subsection); but the scholia, so far as is known, were never finished.

The evolution of the HG to 1569 had been slow, utilizing materials prepared as early as 1547 (bk. VI) and gradually expanding. Many Nahuatl materials in the drafts were not included in the final text. Its main outlines were shown in a diagram by Jiménez Moreno (1938b, p. 33). His scheme appears here as Table 1.

Table 2 rearranges the data of Table 1 to indicate where in earlier native drafts all or portions of the present books of the HG may be found. Further research may well refine and alter these general outlines in detail. They present a state of knowledge some four centuries after Sahagún completed the Manuscrito de 1569.

Historia general: Spanish and Bilingual Texts, 1570–85[11]

Sahagún's intention of accompanying the Nahuatl with a Spanish text is clear from the three-column division of the "Memoriales con escolios," "Memoriales en tres columnas," and statements he made about the 1569 manuscript (To the sincere reader). Only brief samples of Spanish text appear in the "Memoriales con escolios." In 1569 Sahagún stated that the Spanish texts had not been prepared, hence nearly all materials in Spanish must postdate completion of the Nahuatl Manuscrito de 1569.

MEMORIALES EN ESPAÑOL (Castellano), ca. 1569–71. The initial draft of a Spanish text seems to be a document named "Memoriales en Español" by Paso y Troncoso, who reproduced it; Nicolau d'Olwer and others call it "Memoriales en Castellano." Entitled "Historia universal de las cosas de la Nueva España repartida en doze libros . . . ," it is found in the Palace manuscript (fols. 1–24; Paso y Troncoso, 1906, 7:401–

[10] Ed. note: Subsection "Recapitulation" inserted by H. F. Cline.

[11] Ed. note: This subsection rewritten by H. F. Cline.

193

48). It contains only books I and V, Spanish translations and paraphrases, without prefaces or appendices.

Dibble (*in litt.*, Mar. 26, 1968) reports that when the Spanish of this fragment is compared with that in extant copies of the HG (the Tolosano and Florentino, discussed below), the Spanish text of "the Florentino is nearest [to "Memoriales en Español"], to a point of being almost identical, whereas the Rich and Panes [copies of Tolosano] differ, including omission." This identity has bearing on a matter discussed below, the relationship of the Tolosano Spanish text (from which the Panes and Rich copies derived) to that in the Florentino. In anticipation it can be said that Dibble and Cline now believe the Tolosano to be a slightly later, edited copy of the Florentino, whose Spanish has been corrected and made more elegant.

SUMARIO, 1570. To circumvent Chapter orders in Mexico denying him clerical aid, Sahagún sought support in Europe. One of these attempts was reflected in the *Sumario*, seemingly dated May 20, 1570, apparently in Spanish and now lost. It contained, according to Sahagún, "a summary [table of contents] of all the books and of all the chapters of each book, and the Prologues, where briefly is stated what the books contained" (HG, Prol.). The *Sumario* was taken to Spain by his co-religionists, Miguel Navarro and Gerónimo de Mendieta, and given ca. 1571 to Juan de Ovando, President of the Council of the Indies, who had long been a correspondent of Mendieta (Nicolau d'Olwer, 1952, pp. 76–78).

BREVE CONPENDIO, 1570. Dated and signed December 25, 1570, Sahagún prepared a "Breve Conpendio de los rytos ydolatricos que los yndios desta Nueva España usavan en el tiempo de su infidelidad," which survives (Vatican Archives) and has been published incompletely by Schmidt (1906) and in full by Oliger (1942). This summary was directed to Pope Pius V in Rome. In Spanish, the *Conpendio* extracted portions of

book I, chapters 3, 4, 7, 8, and 9, included the Prologue to book II, with variant (from later) texts of book II, chapters 1–19, and extracts from chapter 24, as well as scattered materials from books III, IV, VIII, and IX. Sahagún reported to His Holiness that for the HG more than 1,000 pesos had already been spent on ink, paper, and clerical help, but if all the labor had been recompensed, it would have exceeded 10,000 pesos (Oliger, 1942, p. 39). He was seeking funds to have all the Spanish paraphrases and scholia prepared. The Pope ignored the appeal.

MANUSCRIPT OF 1576–77 (Enríquez). In the General Prologue, in the book II prologue, and in two dedications (one preceding bk. I, the other before bk. VI), Sahagún records his gratitude to Fray Rodrigo de Sequera, General Commissary of the Franciscan Order in New Spain. Sahagún named him the protector and "father" of the HG. Sahagún said it was he who brought it from neglect into full realization. Sequera did indeed play a critical role (Baudot, 1969).

Ovando, then engaged (with Juan López de Velasco) in a program of collecting historical and geographical data on the Indies (Cline, 1964, pp. 344–46), was interested by Sahagún's 1570 *Sumario*. To carry out Ovando's program, the Council of the Indies in the king's name ordered various colonial authorities to provide histories of their areas. One such directive went to Archbishop Pedro Moya de Contreras in Mexico. In his reply (Mar. 28, 1576) Moya reported he had learned that Sahagún had written such a work, and as it would be difficult to have others do it, thought "this history of all the things of New Spain" would meet the royal requirement. He said he had already ordered Sequera to arrange for its translation into Spanish and Mexican, and that the latter had agreed to do this. However, to assure that the work would be completed soon, Moya suggested that the Council issue a royal order to that effect. The

TABLE 3—DATES OF PROBABLE COMPOSITION,
SPANISH TEXT OF FLORENTINE CODEX

Book	Chapter	Text	Date	Folio
I	Prologue	Este año de mill e quinientos sesenta y nueve años	1569	verso, unfoliated, first folio
I	Prologue	Fin deste año de 1579	1579	ibid.
I	Conf. [par. A, 4th ser.]	Este año pasado de 1569	1570	40v
IV	Appendix	Este año de mjll y qujnientos y setenta y seis	1576	80v
VI	Dedication	[Vale to Sequera, 1579–80?]	1579–80?	unfoliated
VI	[end note]	Este año de mjll y qujnjentos y setēta y siete. Fin del libro sesto	1577	215v
VIII	5	Hasta este año de mjll y qujnjentos y setenta y vno	1571	10v
X	27, par. 8	Deste año de mjll y qujnjentos, y setenta y seys	1576	82
XI	12, par. 6, Note	Año de mjll y quiniētos y setenta este año de mill y qujnjentos y setenta y seis	1576	233v
XI	12, par. 8*	Agora este año de mjll y qujnjentos y setenta y seys: en el mes de agosto	1576	238v
		Ocho de noujembre [same year]	1576	ibid.
	12, par. 9*	En esta año de mjll y qujnjentos y setēta y seys	1576	240

NOTE: Prepared by H. F. Cline.

* Florentino differs here in numeration from Tolosano (via Panes copy); latter omits some material in Florentino referring to Nahuatl column. In Tolosano these are pars. 7, 8. No dates of composition or "current" dates in the Nahuatl text appear, except bk. VIII, chap. 5, where it reads 1565.

marginal note to this letter says "Send an order that this be done as soon as possible." That cedula is lost. It was the major authorization that Sahagún had been seeking. His gamble on the *Sumario* had paid off.

Baudot, who reproduces this Moya material from an original document, believes (1969, pp. 62–64) that in fact Sequera had initially urged Moya to this action. Sahagún reports that after Sequera's arrival in New Spain (Sept. 4, 1575), he became much interested in the HG and made possible re-copying the Nahuatl and preparation of the Spanish text, to fulfill the order by Juan de Ovando (HG, Prol.; II, Prol.). Unfortunately the latter died (Sept. 8, 1575) shortly after Sequera's arrival, and royal policies changed.

Various dates which Sahagún placed in the Spanish text indicate that the copy that Sequera ordered "de buen letra" was prepared 1576–77 (see Table 3). There seems to be only a single date of composition in the Nahuatl text, 1565; the parallel date in the Spanish text is 1571 (bk. VIII, chap. 5). The latest date in manuscript versions of the HG seems to come in the FC, Spanish, book I, Prologue. There it appears to read 1579.

Defective copying by those who prepared the Tolosa manuscript has incorrectly rendered one of these Spanish text dates (bk. IV, App.) as 1566 rather than the correct 1576 in the Florentine manuscript. The Tolosa date appears in some editions (Bustamante, Kingsborough, Acosta Saignes) and thus has led scholars like Nicolau d'Olwer (1952, pp. 66–68) and Robertson

(1959, p. 173) to erroneous conclusions about dating Sahagún materials (Glass, 1960). Sahagún described the manuscript "as in Spanish as well as in the Mexican language," 12 books, written in clean letter, the Spanish in one column, the Nahuatl in another (II, Prol.). He does not mention scholia or illustrations.

Just at a point when Sahagún (and Sequera) believed that auguries were favorable, the Spanish government changed a major policy. In Madrid the Council of the Indies (after Ovando's death) and the Holy Office (Inquisition) decided to ban future and suppress extant works in native tongues by missionaries, as possibly heretical and dangerous to true conversion. A series of orders on these matters came to the viceroy and the archbishop, among them a cedula of April 22, 1577, commanding that all Sahagún's works be sent immediately to Spain, and interdicting all similar productions. Sahagún wrote the king March 26, 1578, that he had already turned over the manuscript (i.e., his HG) to Sequera for transmittal. Later (1585) Sahagún repeated that the 1576–77 manuscript had been given to Viceroy Enríquez (via Sequera) for transmittal. In 1585 Sahagún did not know what had become of it, nor to this day is it known surely whether or not it was transmitted. For convenience this can be called the Enríquez copy.

A flurry of 1578 communications was specifically generated in part by Sahagún's March 26 letter to the king (i.e., Council of the Indies). What he had offered to do contravened the recent major policy change in Spain, proscribing works in native tongues by missionaries. In it he said that the viceroy had received the April, 1577, cedula and that when it arrived, Sahagún had already turned over to Sequera the fair copy of the HG made in 1577, but now (1578) he understood that Viceroy Enríquez and the Commissary had remitted the HG on the recent (i.e., February, 1578) *flota*. Sahagún described it as a version of 12 books in four

volumes and then rather naïvely informed the king that if the 1578 shipment did not arrive, please to notify him, "so that once again they can be copied," implying that he had retained copies. When the Council received this notice, the irritated officials made a marginal notation to "Send a cedula ordering the Viceroy to take anything that is left, drafts and originals, and send them all so that no draft remains" (Baudot, 1969, p. 65, n. 32, reproducing letter from original).

The cedula is dated September 18, 1578. In answer to it Archbishop Moya in December, 1578, reported that the Sahagún HG had been transmitted on a previous flota, ambiguously adding, "according to what its author told me" (Nicolau d'Olwer, 1952, p. 99). There seem to be no further exchanges.

The 1576–77 Enríquez bilingual version of the HG which Sahagún thought had been sent on the 1578 flota is lost. No acknowledgement of its receipt in Spain, or other trace, now remains. The fact that Sahagún later used his own earlier drafts, and that they were available to Mendieta, Torquemada, and others after his death implies that the order of September, 1578, was not carried out.

SEQUERA MANUSCRIPT, 1578–79 (Florentine Codex). Among his other duties, Sequera was at first informally, then in 1579 officially, appointed censor for the Holy Office in Mexico, a post uniquely concerned with manuscript works in native languages by missionaries. He consistently although respectfully opposed various orders from Madrid banning them, joined in this in one instance by heads of the Dominican and Augustinian Orders in Mexico, who following earlier appeals negated in Spain, jointly signed a petition of September 16, 1579, for relaxation of these edicts (Baudot, 1969, pp. 81–82). Seemingly while these pleas were pending, Sequera encouraged Sahagún to prepare a second complete copy of the HG, the only complete one that survives.

Sahagún reported in 1585 that earlier he had prepared 12 books in four volumes "in Spanish and Mexican, lavishly illustrated" (Bustamante, 1840, p. 334 [i.e., p. 234]) after he had previously given a copy of the same work to Viceroy Enríquez to transmit to the king. Sahagún further stated in 1585 that Sequera took this second copy to Spain, but had never written him about its fate.

The so-called Sequera Manuscript can now be firmly equated with the Florentine Codex on a number of grounds, several of which are new to the literature discussing this critical matter. As early as 1886, García Icazbalceta (1954, p. 360) suggested the equation, although he had never seen the Florentino. His hypothesis has remained a matter of scholarly controversy, accepted by Jiménez Moreno (1938b, pp. 35, 40). Garibay (1956, 1:11), for instance, did not agree to this identification but gives no good reasons, as pointed out by Nicolau d'Olwer (1957), who also accepted the identification.

The Spanish text of the Florentino has never been published in full. Dating of various matters has rested on defective published versions of modern copies from another 16th-century Spanish copy (Tolosano, discussed below). In copying and publishing, intervening editors and scribes have introduced errors.

A serious one appears in the General Prologue, where Sahagún reported that "to the end of this year" his work had not been available because those who should have favored it had not, until Sequera did. The published date has been 1575, spelled out. The FC clearly reads "1579," in numerals. Hence it postdates the 1578 flota remission. What he might have originally written in 1575 about the help Sequera had provided was even more true in 1579, when seemingly Sahagún thought that the 1576–77 manuscript had been lost or had fallen into hostile hands.

To express his gratitude to Sequera for rescuing the HG from oblivion, Sahagún in letters of transmittal dedicated the work to him. The first "Dedicatory letter," in Spanish, was to Sequera as Commissary General of New Spain, a post in which he served to about December, 1579. It is not in the FC but it precedes the Prologue and first volume of the HG, books I–V. A second "Dedication" to Sequera, in Latin, accompanied book VI, a volume in itself, with a report that it was the longest and strongest of the 12 books, a work "worthy of royal regard" in four volumes. Here Sahagún addressed Sequera as "Commissary General of the Indies (except Peru)," apparently merely a rhetorical flourish which indicates no change of status. In both dedications Sahagún bids Sequera goodby ("Vale"), and the second one especially wishes him well on his new endeavors. Although the "Vale" seemingly was cliché in such Latin dedications of the time, the added material suggests a late 1579 or early 1580 date. This second dedication is omitted from most published editions of the HG (Kingsborough has a garbled version), although it appears in Bandini (1793), from which it was reprinted by García Icazbalceta in 1886 (1954, p. 358). This and other missing and garbled pieces were recently published (Cline, 1971a). Thus both probably date not earlier than 1579, the second one certainly before February 26, 1580, when Sequera left Mexico, according to the native *Anales de Tecamachalco* (1892, p. 277).

From these data it seems clear that Sahagún in late 1579 or early 1580 gave to Sequera as he was departing from Mexico the copy of the two-column bilingual, "lavishly illustrated" HG that he mentions in 1585, for transmittal to the king. In light of the circumstances there is now no reasonable doubt that the Sequera Manuscript of 1578–79 is the Florentine Codex.

Indisputably the FC was prepared directly under Sahagún's supervision, and some is in his handwriting. His signature appears in book IV, Appendix, folio 81. In book X, chapter 27, a long "Relación del autor," some in his own handwriting, is substituted for a Spanish translation of body parts listed in the Nahuatl columns. The "Relación" sets forth the virtues of ancient and modern Mexican Indians, and defends missionary works written in native languages against charges of heresy or danger to native conversion. The long digression (which does not appear in the Nahuatl text) was dated by Sahagún's statements at November 8, 1576. We do not know, of course, whether the Enríquez copy contained a Spanish translation of the body parts, or whether Sahagún substituted this personal memoir in 1579 to substantiate and support the pleas he and others were making to allow trained Indians to aid them in writing missionary works in native tongues.

Physical features of the FC manuscript also fit a conclusion that it probably was in final stages of preparation when Sequera was about to leave Mexico. Book XII, like most of the others, is "profusely illustrated." The native illustrations are frequent as far as folio 62v of the 88 folios, but thereafter the scribes left numerous "windows" or blank spaces (on fols. 72, 73v, 74, 75, 75v, 79, 82, 83, 83v, 84v, and 88) for later inclusion of illustrations that were not completed, probably because of the pressure of time. Numerous egregious copyists' errors late in the manuscript similarly suggest a task performed under similar pressures. It is wholly likely that some otherwise unexplained disorder and confusion that Garibay noted in the Nahuatl text stems from the same cause (Garibay, 1953–54, 2:252).

The FC is in the Mediceo-Laurentian Library, Florence, Italy, in the Palatine Collection, MSS 218–20. In 1793 Bandini included it in a description of that collection. Paso y Troncoso (1896) also described it, and demonstrated by extant vestiges of the original four volumes that in a later rebinding these four volumes had been reduced to the present three. The Spanish text has not been published, but nearly all the Nahuatl text and the illustrations have appeared (see Section C, and Article 21, app. F).

The FC lacks a title page and the initial "Dedicatory letter." The Spanish text is in the left column, the Nahuatl in the right. It contains approximately 1,850 illustrations and numerous native ornamental designs (many of which have not been reproduced); some pictures have Nahuatl captions or numbers, and the drawings appear in one or another of the two columns. The blank spaces in book XII indicate that the Nahuatl text was copied first, then the Spanish, leaving designated areas for subsequent native drawings, all of which thus postdate 1577 and most likely were prepared in 1579.[12]

Verified information is lacking on when or how the FC was acquired by its present repository. Nuttall (1921, pp. 89–90) suggested that the FC, together with Codex Magliabecchiano, had been referred by Spanish authorities to Rome for papal judgment about the materials on pagan Mexican native rites. She implies that before the death of the Medici Pope Leo XI in 1605 "these two most important MSS. dealing with the subject" went to the private Medici family collection, of which the bibliophile Magliabecchi was librarian. Fortunately both manuscripts survived.

TOLOSA MANUSCRIPT, post–1580-ante–1588? There exists, as Muñoz Collection manuscript volume 50 (33 of the 1954–56 catalog) in the Royal Academy of History, Madrid, another nearly complete version of

[12] In 1939 Lansing Bloom secured in Italy a negative microfilm of the FC, which was deposited in the School of American Research at the Museum of New Mexico, Santa Fe. From it photographic enlargements were made, one set for the proposed Anderson and Dibble translation, with an insurance set deposited at the University of New Mexico. Later four additional sets were distributed to unnamed institutions in the United States, and one was sent to the Mexican government, all under the stipulation that none of these (except the Anderson-Dibble) was to be published for a period of five years (Olpin and Long, 1950). In 1960 the Mediceo-Laurentian Library itself commissioned a negative microfilm, a positive copy of which was purchased in 1968 by the Library of Congress, where it is available for reference use.

the Spanish text of the HG. All the present evidence (outlined below) points clearly to its being a slightly later but contemporary copy of the Spanish text of the FC. It was acquired by Juan Bautista Muñoz from the Franciscan Convent of Tolosa in Navarre, Spain (1783), hence its designation as the Tolosa Manuscript or Tolosano.

It has been several times described, first by Ramírez (1867b, not published until 1885) and most recently by Ballesteros Gaibrois and others (1964). With a defective title page, it is a single folio volume of 682 pages, in 16th-century hand, unillustrated except for a calendar wheel at page 396, a variant of one of the two drawings in the Tlatelolco "Memoriales in tres columnas" (1564–65), but seemingly nearer the same drawing in FC. The Spanish text has not been directly published. Since 1829–30 Tolosano has been known indirectly through publications from various defective copies, which differ slightly from one another (see Table 9).

The text, with some differences, is generally the same as FC. These differences are significant. Copyists who produced Tolosano corrected the misspellings of Florentino and added connectives, such as "que" and "el cual," to smooth out syntax and grammar. As noted above, the Spanish of "Memoriales en Español" is nearly identical with that of the FC but the Tolosano differs and contains omissions. Hence all published Spanish versions of the HG are partial texts from a defective copy.

Most significant, however, are the important editorial changes that have been made in parallel passages of the Tolosano. These are in the interest of readability, and omission of what at its time of copying might be considered controversial matters. Thus in book VI, chapter 42, more than half the riddles which appear in the FC have been omitted, with an editorial statement that they would be disgusting and boring; similar statements come at the end of chapter 43 to account for other omissions (Dibble,

in litt.). Comparison of the two texts of book XII by Cline reveals that the Tolosa text omits such things as lists of native objects (names of mantles, for instance) and of Mexican leaders carefully preserved in both Spanish and Nahuatl texts of the FC.

Garbled native words in published editions taken from later copies of the Tolosano led to earlier speculation that it was copied by persons familiar with Spanish but not with Nahuatl. Examination of the Madrid manuscript by Dibble indicates that in it the Nahuatl is correct. Hence the published errors can be attributed to later copyists and editors. After preliminary studies of these matters, both Dibble and Cline at present feel that what is known of the two manuscripts indicates that the Tolosano is a nearly contemporary but edited copy of the Florentine Spanish text. Both urge full scholarly publication of the two Spanish texts, so that further comparisons can be undertaken on a sound basis and the complete data from FC become available to scholars.

Baudot (1969, pp. 67–68) recently propounded an interesting and probably correct explanation of how Tolosano came into being, which takes into account the established data. He believes that on return to Spain in 1580, Sequera himself ordered a copy made of the Spanish portion of the text which Sahagún had handed him before leaving. Given the climate of official opinion against missionary writings in native tongues (which did not change until after 1582), he thus "sanitized" the HG by omitting all elements that would arouse suspicion, but made generally accessible the main body of a work that he had protected so long, minus a few unessential details of little interest to Spaniards.

If this hypothesis is correct, the Tolosa manuscript postdates 1580, and may have been copied before about 1583, when the earlier prohibitions against missionary works in native languages were relaxed. It quite likely predates 1588, when Sequera departs from present historical view after serving five years as provincial (1583–88) of the Franciscan Chapter of Valladolid, Spain (Baudot, 1969, p. 70).

Nothing now is known about how the manuscript reached the Franciscans of Tolosa. It came to notice there through Juan de San Antonio, Franciscan bibliographer who in 1732 mentioned a four-volume "Universal History of New Spain" in that convent, a note then reprinted by Eguiara and Clavigero. García Icazbalceta in 1886 (1954, pp. 352–53) probably correctly concluded that Father San Antonio had not personally seen the work, but had taken his bibliographical information from a title furnished him from Tolosa, as the extant manuscript is a single-volume folio work. The original title page is now defective, reading ". . . de las cosas de la Nueva . . . libros y quarto volumenes en lengua española. Compuesta por el muy Rdo. Pe. Fr. Bernardino de saagun de la orden de los Frayles menores de obseruancia" (Ballesteros Gaibrois and others, 1964, 1:181). The equivalent title, on which reconstructed ones rely, in the Sahagún materials of the Royal Palace manuscript (fol. 1) is "Historia universal, de las cosas de la nueua españa: repartida en doze libros, en lengua mexicana y española fecha por el muy reuerendo padre fray bernardino de sahagun: frayle de sant. francisco, de obseruancia." The latter is the only complete title page, ca. 1570, and therefore it is not known precisely what Sahagún may have called the later versions.

Juan Bautista Muñoz, alerted by various bibliographical notices, personally procured the manuscript on loan from the Tolosa convent April 30, 1783. He had earlier been commanded as Royal Cosmographer to prepare an extensive history of the Spanish Indies, and was empowered by the king to get from Spanish repositories the numerous sources he needed. Armed with a special order from the President of the Secretariat

of the Indies (dated Apr. 6, 1783), Muñoz obtained what he described as "one volume in folio, which contained the original history of New Spain." He kept it until his death in 1799, when with other Muñoz papers it passed to the secretariat. In 1800 the Franciscan friars of Tolosa requested its return but, at the suggestion of the king, voluntarily donated it to him in exchange for a literal copy prepared for them in 1802–04. The Tolosa manuscript then was deposited in the private library of the king. Under a donation authorized in September, 1815, most of the Muñoz Collection, including this manuscript, was deposited in March, 1816, in the Royal Academy of History, where it has since remained as volume 50 of the Muñoz Collection (García Icazbalceta, 1954, pp. 352–53).[13]

TOLOSANO COPIES, 1793–1816. Various handcopies of it were made after 1793. All printed versions derive from one or another of these and all are defective or inaccurate in varying degrees. Ramírez (1867b, 1885b, 1903), García Icazbalceta (1954, pp. 352, 360–67), Jiménez Moreno (1938b, pp. 42–45), and Nicolau d'Olwer (1952, pp. 181–88) discuss details of these copies and their publication. None seems complete or accurate. Summary data on them have been tabulated in Table 9. Generally speaking, the four-volume edition of the HG edited by Garibay (Mexico, 1956, 1969) has fewer defects than most earlier editions. A careful, scholarly edition of the Tolosa manuscript is a *sine qua non* for studies of Sahagún and colonial and precolonial New Spain.

LATER FRAGMENTS, 1584–85. Years later, when Sahagún was already in his eighties and believed his work lost, he reacted by returning to his task with serene tenacity. Despite repeated orders from the court and

[13] The Tolosa MS now has on its spine "A77. Colección de Muñoz. Sahagún Historia. 50. 9–4812." The Ramírez study (MS C-103) has an old number, 9–25–5 C103, no. 2; and a new number, 9–28–4/5524/2. It contains 100 numbered folios (i.e., 200 pages).

reported shipment of his proscribed works to Spain, there remained enough material in Mexico (rough drafts, partial transcriptions, notes) to allow him to recompile (under another guise) some parts of his HG—those he felt were indispensable for the training of missionaries. Above all, he produced two works (both in manuscript, preserved at the National Library of Mexico) destined to give the missionaries the means whereby they could uncover and recognize the persistence of idolatry.

Kalendario, ca. 1585. In a miscellaneous volume of manuscripts in the National Library of Mexico are two fragments which have been attributed to Sahagún. One is "Kalendario mexicano, latino y castellano," partially published by García Icazbalceta (1886, pp. 314–23) and completely by Iguíniz (1917 [i.e. 1918]). The copy is an early 17th-century one, probably made by Martín de León, who utilized these materials in his *Camino de cielo* (1611). He rearranged the Aztec calendar material found in Sahagún's "Conpendio" by confecting a calendar that began January 1 (11th day of the month Tititl), and suppressed the five "useless" days at the end of the native year by distributing them among five native months, making them 21 rather than 20 days. The Sahagún text in the center column varies from the "Conpendio" and similar materials in book II, chapters 1–19. García Icazbalceta (1954, pp. 364–69), in discussing the Gregorian reform of the Christian calendar, thought that perhaps Sahagún had attempted to make similar changes in the native one; Nicolau d'Olwer (1952, pp. 113–15) follows him in this, but the notion is highly dubious.

In 1576 Sahagún attached as an appendix to book IV a long polemic treatise (only in Spanish) directed at showing that Motolinía and early friars had not fully understood the native calendar. He was especially concerned with errors in one that Motolinía and others had confected for use in Tlaxca-la. The text of the 1585 "To the reader" introduction to the "Kalendario" renewed the polemic and extended it by listing the numerous ways that the colonial Indians had hoodwinked the early missionaries, whose mass baptisms had, according to Sahagún, left idolatry basically untouched. In this context it is highly unlikely that Sahagún himself would confect a native calendar after having violently criticized Motolinía for his confutation.[14]

Arte adivinatoria, 1585. The other fragment, "Arte adivinatoria" (or "Breve confutación de la idolatria" ["Prologue," "To the reader," chap. 1, García Icazbalceta, 1886, pp. 314–23]) is a companion piece to the "Kalendario," in which Sahagún made known his intention to translate it into Spanish. It presents new material only in the first chapter. The second chapter coincides with the first chapter of book IV of the HG, and thus successively to chapter 32 (same as HG, bk. IV, chap. 31) ending about halfway. It seems that Sahagún was writing it in 1585 from a Nahuatl text.

Relación de la conquista, 1585. The "Relación de la conquista," first written in Nahuatl not later than 1555, was translated into Spanish by 1577 and was finally incorporated as the last book (XII) of the HG, and so it appears in all editions. In 1585 Sahagún says that he corrected the Nahuatl text and accompanied it with a completely new Spanish version, together with scholia in Nahuatl (Leal, 1955, 1956; Cline, 1969). The original bilingual text, with scholia, is lost. A copy was apparently taken to Spain in 1697. A Spanish text of uncertain origin, presumably taken from it, returned to Mexico in 1832 and was there published by Bustamante (1840). The manuscript used by Bustamante thereafter was returned to Spain. In 1935 it was still in the hands of a Barcelona bookdealer (Jiménez Moreno, 1938b, pp. 42, 72, no. 101) but in 1968 was

[14] Based on unpublished research in Cline, 1971b.

reported by his successor as lost or in unknown private hands (Cline, 1969). Fortunately a copy, made for W. H. Prescott, is now in the Boston Public Library.[15]

Codex Ixtlilxochitl, Part 3 [1570?] 1585? In the National Library of Paris a Spanish manuscript (BNP, 65–71, fols. 113–22) corresponds, with additions and variations, to book II, chapters 1–19, of the Spanish text of the HG. Its dating and relationships are uncertain. It is most likely that this document is a 17th-century copy of a lost original, and may belong to the complex groups of documents (including other Sahagún materials) available to Torquemada and Alva Ixtlilxochitl. It passed through the Sigüenza, Boturini, and Aubin collections. Lehmann (1908) published the portion equivalent to chapters 1–18. Parts 1 and 2 of Codex Ixtlilxochitl are treated in the Census of pictorial materials (Article 23, Item 171).

RECAPITULATION AND COMMENTS. Following the completion of the 1569 manuscript in Nahuatl, Sahagún was chiefly engaged in preparing Spanish texts to accompany it. After a hiatus, when his Chapter withdrew support and dispersed his manuscripts, work was resumed in 1576 under the protection and encouragement of Rodrigo de Sequera. A complete bilingual manuscript was finished 1576–77, and Sahagún thought it had been sent to Spain on the February, 1578, flota. Since policy changes (1577–78) banned such works in native tongues, Sahagún feared that the 1576–77 manuscript was lost. He therefore prepared another copy, bilingual and profusely illustrated,[16] which Sequera took to Spain in 1580.

An edited version of the Spanish text, seemingly post–1580 and also probably made by Sequera's orders, was copied in Spain. By unknown means it was taken to the Spanish convent of Franciscans in Tolosa, where it was personally obtained in 1783 by Juan Bautista Muñoz, and eventually (1816) passed (via the Biblioteca Real) to its present location in the Royal

Academy of History in Madrid. It was subsequently handcopied, from 1793 onward; from these copies have come various substandard published versions, starting with Bustamante (1829–30). Neither the Spanish text of FC nor the direct publication of the Tolosano is yet available. Such scholarly publication of these two basic texts is a major desideratum.

Comparison of the Nahuatl texts with the Spanish texts indicates that the latter are not usually direct translations of the former. They are summaries and paraphrases. As Sahagún himself occasionally noted, the Nahuatl text ("la letra" in the author's phrase) is usually fuller, with details briefly paraphrased or even omitted in Spanish. Seldom does the Spanish text (so far as provisional examinations reveal) contain extensive data not in the Nahuatl, a generalization that does not apply to the later 1584–85 fragments or to dates of composition, of which only one appears in the native text. The long "Relación del autor" (X, 27), is another major exception. When the Spanish texts of FC are compared with equivalent passages in Tolosano, the latter at several points omits "boring" material, notably in books VI, XI, and XII, the only ones which seemingly have undergone even preliminary scholarly scrutiny.

[15] Cline has in preparation for publication by the Academy of American Franciscan History transcriptions and translation of book XII from FC and from the 1585 version from the Boston Public Library manuscript.

[16] Toro (1924, p. 14) suggested that the drawings were made by Agustín de la Fuente, described by Vetancurt as "natural de Tlatilulco . . . [que] hacía con la pluma, una estampa con tanta propriedad que parecía impresa." A brief biography of de la Fuente (d. 1610), who aided Sahagún, Oroz, Bautista, and other Franciscans, appears in Garibay, 1953–54, 2:225. No corroboration of Toro's hypothesis has appeared. Robertson (1959, p. 176) wrote that the initial "A" on a drawing in book IX (his pl. 71) was by de la Fuente, "one of the artists of the *Historia*." Although he refers readers to p. 47 "for the names of other artists" (ibid., n. 29), these turn out to be the *latino* aides and scribes. At present no one knows who made the Florentine drawings; all postdate 1577 (probably 1578–79).

About 1583 Sahagún began to rewrite earlier materials for a work he called "Vocabulario trilingüe (discussed below). The only surviving texts of it are the "Kalendario," the "Arte adivinatoria," and the "Relación de la conquista." It is not known with certainty when Sahagún composed materials in Codex Ixtlilxochitl (part 3) which parallel the 1570 "Conpendio," the HG (bk. II, chaps. 1–19), and the "Kalendario." No detailed comparisons of these related texts have been published.

WORKS ABOUT THE NAHUATL LANGUAGE[17]

Arte, 1569, 1585

The "Arte de la lengua Mexicana con su vocabulario apendiz" was twice edited. One edition was already completed in 1569 (HG, II, Preface). Sahagún was working on the other in 1585 (HG, XII, Preface, 2d version). Nothing seemingly is now preserved of these (possibly?) elementary grammars and dictionaries.

Historia general, 1569

The great linguistic work of Sahagún is the HG itself. He graphically described it as "a sweeping net to bring to light all the terms of this language, with their regular and metaphorical meanings, and ways of saying things." One thing has many synonyms, he noted, and a particular sentence might be said in many ways. This variation was done purposely, "for we know the terms for each thing and all the ways of saying something" (HG, I, Preface; bk. VII, To the reader). Some (like Mendieta and Torquemada) called the manuscript of 1569 the "Calepino" of the Mexican language.

Sahagún himself took notice of that fact.[18] In the 1569 passages of "To the sincere reader" (preceding bk. I) he remarked that many persons were asking about it, as they thought he was producing a great dictionary such as Ambrosio Calepino had prepared for the Latin language, giving all the various uses of given words. Sahagún said that it had been impossible for him to emulate Calepino's work, which was based on many Latin poems and orations, because there were at Sahagún's disposal no comparable written works in Nahuatl. He said, however, that he thought that the HG might well be used in the future by others who wanted to compile or extract a Nahuatl Calepino, because he provided in the 12 books a wide variety of words and usages in Nahuatl. Seemingly later in his life he began such a work, the "Vocabulario trilingüe."

Vocabulario trilingüe (Calepino?) 1584?

The exclusion of the third column in the final editions (1576–77, Florentino) possibly can in some measure be explained, apart from pressure of time, by a new undertaking of the indefatigable Sahagún: his "Vocabulario trilingüe" in Nahuatl-Latin-Spanish.[19] We know it was to be a major work. At times it apparently resembled a dictionary of Mexican antiquities utilizing elements from the HG, as for example his inclusion of the "superstitions" of book V, and description of the "secular feasts" in book VII, chapter 9. Sahagún was working on the "Vocabulario" in 1584. According to Torquemada (1723, bk. 20, chap. 46), he seemed to have finished it, but if so, it is lost.[20]

Ramírez (1898–1904, 2:119) and Chavero (1877a, pp. 5, 11) each once possessed a manuscript now in the Newberry Library, Ayer Collection (MS 1478). Both identified it as the famous "Vocabulario." It is indeed a work by Sahagún—his signature is on the first page and Martin Jacobita was the

[17] Ed. note: Nicolau d'Olwer's text resumes.
[18] Ed. note: This paragraph added by H. F. Cline.
[19] Ed. note: Nicolau d'Olwer's text resumes.
[20] Ed. note: García Icazbalceta (1954, pp. 371–72) concluded that the "Vocabulario trilingüe" was unfinished, but that variant citations in Torquemada and others to various books indicated something of its proposed structure.

scribe—but it is *not* the great 1584–85 "Vocabulario trilingüe."

The description given by Chavero better fits an elementary work. "In each line the first word is in Spanish followed by its Latin translation and the Mexican word above, in red ink, although in some places this latter one is missing." Perhaps it is a preliminary work, a copy of Nebrija's Spanish-Latin dictionary whose Nahuatl equivalents were being written in. The Ayer manuscript Vocabulary should be studied. It is available on microfilm (Aztec Manuscript Dictionary, 1957).

POSTILLA, OR DOCTRINAL ENCYCLOPEDIA, ca. 1540–79

The "Postilla" was to be the *instrumentum praedicationis* and be also the history of the Franciscan missionary efforts. Taken together, its contents would comprise a doctrinal encyclopedia, a vast plan outlined in the preface to the "Coloquios."[21] Sahagún seemingly conceived it in four parts.

Coloquios and Doctrina, 1564

The first would be the "Coloquios" (in 30 chapters), the second the "Doctrina cristiana," used by the first twelve Franciscan missionaries who "converted the Indians of New Spain." They were elaborated by Sahagún and his co-workers in Tlatelolco (1564), who put "in the Mexican language, fitting and polished" the records of the first missionaries. Its publication, authorized in 1583 (García Icazbalceta, 1886, p. 248), was frustrated, perhaps for the same reason (opposition by the Inquisition) that the manuscript preserved in the secret archives of the Vatican was mutilated (Pou y Martí, 1924; Nuttall, 1927; Lehmann, 1949). The manuscript of the "Coloquios" has been published. For the "Doctrina" see subsection "Apéndice, 1579."

Chronicle, 1564

The third part of the "Postilla" was to be a chronicle to deal with the "event of the

conversions by the Twelve Fathers and those who came after them during the next six years, among whom I came." But Sahagún stopped writing it in 1564, as "one of the Twelve" (Motolinía) had already provided this material (Coloquios, "To the cautious reader").

Postilla, 1540, 1563

The fourth part was a true "Postilla" (or Apostilla) of all the Epistles and Gospel Feasts of the year. It perhaps included the "Evangelios" and "Epistolas" and the "Sermones" since 1540, "not translated from any collection of sermons, but composed anew scaled to meet Indian capacity for understanding, short topics in simple language, solemn and general, easy to remember by all who heard them, high and low, principals and commoners, men and women." Thus says the manuscript once owned by Ramírez, by Chavero, by Fernández del Castillo, and now MS 1485 of the Ayer Collection in Chicago.[22]

Epistolas, pre–1540?

A manuscript of "Epistolas y Evangelios Dominicales," perhaps the earliest one by our author, also successively belonged to

[21] Ed. note: The "Postilla" was subject to a controversy between Nicolau d'Olwer opposing Barrera Vásquez and Jiménez Moreno, concerning the plan, contents, and dating. Here Nicolau d'Olwer repeats his convictions, set forth at greater length in 1952 (pp. 106–11). The tripartite nature of the "Postilla" proposed by Jiménez Moreno is set forth in his 1938b (pp. 16–17, 51–52, 74–76). Although all parties to the disputed matters lean more or less on García Icazbalceta, it seems clear that his 1886 discussions are outmoded; details of the controversy latter (1954, p. 339, n. 49).

[22] Ed. note: García Icazbalceta (1954, p. 335) are summarized in Millares Carlo's re-edition of the described and provided a transcription of the title of MS 1485, which reads (in part) "composed in 1540 and now beginning to be corrected and augmented this year of 1563, in this month of July." Sahagún here stated he was submitting the sermons, together with "all other works composed in Mexican language" for correction by the Holy Roman Mother Church. See Dibble and Mikkelsen, 1971, for a preliminary study of this large and important manuscript.

the Mexicans mentioned above. Its whereabouts is now unknown. Another is the magnificent codex discovered by Beltrami and published by Biondelli (1858). Perhaps yet other manuscripts preserve for us Nahuatl texts by Sahagún.[23]

Adiciones, 1568?

Some "Adiciones" exist to the "Postilla," with the alternative title "Declaración breve de las tres virtudes teologales." These were written many years after the "Postilla" (perhaps when its fair copy was made, 1568–69).

Apéndice, 1579

Finally, an "Apéndice" of 1579 terminates the work. The "Adiciones" and part of the "Apéndice," under the general title of "Doctrina cristiana en Mexicano," are found as MS 1468 of the Ayer Collection, also formerly belonging to Ramírez and Chavero.

Comments

The total work of the "Postilla" was close to publication in 1583. But after viceregal permission was granted, powerful obstacles interposed, like the earlier suppression of works in native tongues, and it never appeared. Sahagún apparently also planned a yet more restricted doctrinal encyclopedia. This is discussed by Nicolau d'Olwer (1952, pp. 61–62).

The intimate relationship of the "Postilla" with the HG is pointed out by Sahagún himself. In the preface of the "Apéndice" he says it is "A treatise which includes seven collations in the Mexican language that contain many secrets about customs of these natives and also many secrets and matters of this Mexican language" (Jiménez Moreno, 1938b, p. 82).

BOOKS OF SONGS AND PRAYERS
Cantares, 1564–83

The final part of Sahagún's main trilogy is the "Psalmodio cristiano" (or Cantares)

". . . for the Indians to sing in their ceremonies which they conduct in the churches." This was a collection of religious hymns aimed to substitute for music by which the Indians had adored their gods in their temples and chapels, with chorus and dances. They were written, therefore, according to the traditional rhythms and meter. These are quite distinct from the "Cantares a los dioses" in Nahuatl, found in the PM and the FC (bk. II), not paraphrased or translated into Spanish by Sahagún.

Finished in Tepepulco, the manuscripts were circulated among the Indians under authority granted ca. 1564 by Viceroy Velasco ("Psalmodio," Prol.). This was the only one of his works that Sahagún saw published in his lifetime, in Mexico by Pedro Ocharte in 1583 (Prologue to the reader, García Icazbalceta, 1886, p. 248). Although its distribution was originally recommended by the Third Mexican Council (1585), it was persecuted by the Holy Office (Jiménez Moreno, 1938b, pp. 26–28).

Manual del cristiano, ca. 1578

Sahagún also wrote a "Manual del cristiano" for use by converts. It never saw press, despite the permission to publish granted in 1578, at the height of the controversies over such works. The "Manual" contained the "Regla" or "Mandamiento de los casados" (with the "Impedimentos del matrimonio") and perhaps also the Ejercicios cuotidianos" (1574)—preserved in the Ayer Collection, MS 1484 (formerly Ramírez 764).

Sahagún's preoccupation with the purity

[23] Ed. note: Apparently from the Ugarte Collection. But now in the Library of the Instituto Tecnológico y de Estudios Superiores (Monterrey, Mexico) there is an unstudied volume of Sahagún texts (seen by Cline). From a microfilm copy of it graciously furnished by Eugenio del Hoyo, Dibble reports it to be translations into Nahuatl of parts of the Bible. From the Nicolás León Collection there is a *Doctrina, evangelios, y epístolas en lengua nahuatl* attributed to Sahagún in the John Carter Brown Library, Providence, Rhode Island.

TABLE 4—SAHAGÚN, *HISTORIA GENERAL*, MANUSCRIPTS AND THEIR PUBLICATION

Manuscript	Volumes	Probable Date	Present Location	Principal Publication
FLORENTINO	3	1578–79	Biblioteca Medicea-Laurenziana, Florence, Italy. Palat. Col. Cod. 218–220 [reduced from 4 vols.]	See Table 9
			Spanish text	None
			Nahuatl text	Anderson and Dibble, 1950–70
			Pictorials	Paso y Troncoso, vol. 5 (1905a; i.e., ca. 1923)
a. Paso y Troncoso,[1] bks. I–IX	3	1893–98	INAH/AH	Acosta Saignes?, 1946
bks. X–XII	1	1893–98	Unknown	
b. Italian translation, bks. I–V	1	17thC	Hispanic Society of America (ex-Phillipps 21041)	—
TOLOSANO	1	Post-1580– ante 1588?	RAH, Muñoz Coll., vol. 50	—
Copies:				
a. Muñoz (partial)	1	ca. 1799	RAH, Muñoz Coll., vol. 51	—
b. García Panes, bks. I–XI	3	1793	BNMex, MSS 1510–12	Bustamante, 1829–30
c. García Panes, bk. XII	1	1793	Unknown since 1886	Bustamante, 1829a
d. Tolosa replacement[2]	2?	1802–04	Unknown; destroyed 1808?	—
e. Bauzá[3]	?	?	Unidentified	
f. Kingsborough 541	2	?	Unidentified	One of these was published by Kingsborough, 1831[4]
g. Kingsborough 542	2	?	Hispanic Society of America (ex-Phillipps 11646)	
h. Rich MS 21	2	?	NYPL, Rich MS 55	
i. Hiersemann	2	?	Hispanic Society of America	
j. Rich MS 22 (partial)	1	?	NYPL, Rich MS 20	—
k. Kingsborough (partial)	1	?	NYPL (ex-Phillipps 16190)	—
BOOK XII (revised)	?	1585	Unknown	—
a. Montemayor	1?	1585?	Unknown	—
b. Cortina	1	?	Unknown since 1935	Bustamante, 1840
c. Prescott	1	1839	Boston Public Library	—

NOTE: Prepared by H. F. Cline; revised by J. B. Glass.

[1] It is not yet certain whether the Spanish text of this copy derives from the Florentino or Tolosano manuscripts.

[2] Nicolau d'Olwer (1952, p. 182) speculated, without evidence, that this copy was NYPL, Rich MS 55.

[3] The date of post-1816 proposed by García Icazbalceta (1954, p. 362) cannot be supported.

[4] Kingsborough (6:265–66) claimed that he used a copy in Muñoz' handwriting.

of the Nahuatl language dominates all these works, aside from their religious feeling.

EVALUATION

With Sahagún's deep understanding of the Mexican Indians also came an identification with them. He was not being vaguely philanthropic, nor was he moved solely by Christian charity—even less by paternalistic protection, distant and disdainful. Rather he displayed genuine Franciscan affection and sincere friendship, intermixed with respect for native talents and sympathy for Indian suffering.

With scientific honesty he made use of native collaboration and publicly acknowledged his gratitude for indigenous help in his work. He admired Indian art, crafts, and intellect. Above all, he esteemed their systems of government and organization, in which he says ". . . they are ahead of many other nations that presume to be civilized" (HG, I, Prol.).

A spirit free from ethnic, cultural, or patriotic prejudice, Fray Bernardino de Sahagún was not moved to seek Crown favor or advance his own personal interests. Before being a subject of his emperor (Charles V) or of the "Prudent King" (Philip II), he was first of all a member of universal society, of the Christian Republic whose limits he tried to broaden by converting the pagan. Converting them, yes; assimilating them, no. Our missionary, Fray Bernardino de Sahagún, remained convinced that the conquest of the New World brought only one unarguable gain: religion. For him, apart from this, native cultures were not inferior in anything substantial, and in some points were even superior to imported European cultures.

B. SAHAGÚN'S *PRIMEROS MEMORIALES*, TEPEPOLCO, 1559–1561

H. B. NICHOLSON

Sahagún himself (Garibay, 1956, 1:27–31, 105–07; Cline, 1971a, pp. 242–44, 247–49), in his general prologue and, above all, in that to book II of his *Historia general* (*universal*) *de las cosas de* (*la*) *Nueva España*, tells us most of what we know about the Tepepolco phase of the project. After receiving an order from his provincial, Fray Francisco de Toral, to compile in Nahuatl what would be useful in furthering the Christianization of the natives, Sahagún moved to Tepepolco. There, with the aid of a "minuta o memoria," he began a systematic interrogation of a group of informants consisting of the "señor del pueblo," Don Diego de Mendoza, and 10 or 12 "principales ancianos." He was aided by four of his trilingual ex-students of the Tlatelolco Colegio de Santa Cruz, also *principales*. For close to two years he pursued his questioning, following the order of his *minuta*. His informants supplied him with pictorial materials in response to his queries, and the trilingual students wrote the explanations below them.

Sahagún mentions no dates, but there is good evidence (Nicolau d'Olwer, 1952, pp. 51, 55) that this Tepepolco investigation took place between January 5, 1558, and September 6, 1561, most probably during 1559–61. In this latter year Sahagún was transferred to Tlatelolco, where he conducted the same type of investigation with another group of elderly, high-born, native informants, discussing with them the data he had gathered in Tepepolco and obtaining much new information on similar and other topics.

One of the very interesting aspects of the *Primeros memoriales* is that most of its data were supplied by informants hailing not from one of the great native power centers of central Mexico but from a populous but relatively obscure community. Aside from the invaluable *Relaciones geográficas* of the 1579–85 series, the lesser communities of Mesoamerica are rarely well represented in the 16th-century sources. The fact that the PM provide a view of late pre-Hispanic culture from the standpoint of a subordinate community lends them special ethnographic value.

PRIMEROS MEMORIALES: PASO Y TRONCOSO RECONSTRUCTION

Paso y Troncoso, after a careful examination of the Códices Matritenses, selected 88 folios which he believed belonged to materials Sahagún had collected in Tepepolco and which he baptized with the title "Primeros memoriales." Of these 54 were from the Códice Matritense de la Biblioteca del Real Palacio and 34 from the Códice Matritense de la Real Academia de la Historia. Paso y Troncoso's reconstruction resulted in a continuous, virtually complete manuscript containing four chapters divided into 49 paragraphs (I:14; II:7; III:17; IV:11; see Tables 5–8).[24] Some of the paragraphs are further subdivided into sections, to which Paso y Troncoso often applied alphabetical designations. Photographic reproductions of these folios, labeled according to subject matter by Paso y Troncoso, were published by the Mexican government (Paso y Troncoso, 1905b; see Article 21, app. F). The same volume contains color lithographs of the pictorial representations of the PM (cf. Ballesteros Gaibrois and others, 1964, vol. 2, pls. 2–53 [color photoreproductions]).

Data for each of the four chapters of the PM are summarized in Tables 5–8, respec-

tively. These include Paso y Troncoso's designation of the subject of each paragraph, the pagination in Paso y Troncoso (1905b), the foliation in either the Royal Palace (PAL) manuscript or in the Royal Academy of History (RAH) manuscript, the section in the FC in which the PM material is now found, and finally, references to the major modern paleographies and translations. As these provide page citations, this detail is omitted below in a description of the contents.

DESCRIPTIONS

Chapter I (Table 5)

Paragraph 1 of chapter I is missing. The Nahuatl title of this chapter, therefore, is unknown. Paso y Troncoso labeled it "Ritos, Dioses," while Jiménez Moreno (1938b, table) assigned to it the Nahuatl title "Teteo." It is intriguing to speculate with what par. 1 might have been concerned. If it was utilized anywhere in the final HG, it is difficult to identify. Sahagún later in Tlatelolco gathered some mythic-traditional materials involving Huitzilopochtli, Tezcatlipoca, and Topiltzin Quetzalcoatl, to which he devoted much of HG, III, and it is possible that this first paragraph of the PM was devoted to another treatment of these same themes. HG, III, also included sections con-

---

[24] Cline in an unpublished study has suggested that a possible Sahaguntine "cuaderno viejo en folio" owned in 1762 by Antonio Sanz, a Madrid printer, which the Real Academia de la Historia unsuccessfully sought to purchase and which has since been unreported, indicates that the PM might originally have included a fifth chapter devoted to "natural history" (*tlalticnaccayotl*), a section which Jiménez Moreno (1938b, pp. 31–32, table) and others have assumed was added only in the post-Tepepolco period. It is described (Ramírez, 1885, pp. 89–90 [1903, p. 5]; García Icazbalceta, 1886, pp. 286–88 [1954, pp. 355–56]) as containing Nahuatl text in columnar format, with "muchas pinturas de esas cosas de la historia natural" (animals, birds, etc.). In any case, it does not seem unlikely that Sahagún included a "natural history" section (final HG, XI) in his original "minuta" or "memoria" prepared at the outset of his Tepepolco investigations.

TABLE 5—SAHAGÚN, *PRIMEROS MEMORIALES* (TEPEPOLCO, 1559–61)
Chapter I: Ritos, Dioses

Para-graph	Subject	FPT 1905b (pages)	Codices Matritenses (PAL)	Florentine Codex	Major Modern Translations
1	Missing	—	—	—	—
2A*	Las 18 fiestas del año	1–7	250r–253r	—	Seler, 1899 [no. 119] (part), 1927 [no. 268], pp. 54–251, passim [N-G]. Garibay, 1948, pp. 291–312 [N-S]. Aguirre, 1950–51, v. 1 [N-S]
B*	Fiesta cada 8 años	8–9	253v–254r	II, app. 2	Seler, 1893 [no. 61a] [N-G-E]; 1927 [no. 268], pp. 248–51 [N-G]. Garibay, 1948, pp. 317–20 [N-G]. Aguirre, 1950–51, v. 1 [N-S]
3A*	Servicios a los dioses: Ofrendas	10	254v	II, app. 4	Aguirre, 1950–51, v. 2 [N-S]. León-Portilla, 1958b, pp. 46–52 [N-S]
B*	Sacrificios cruentos	11	255r	II, app. 5	Aguirre, 1950–51, v. 2 [N-S]. León-Portilla, 1958b, pp. 52–56 [N-S]
C*	Votos, devociones	12–13	255v–256r	II, app. 5	Aguirre, 1950–51, v. 2 [N-S]. León-Portilla, 1958b, pp. 56–60 [N-S]
D*	Ceremonias en ciertas fiestas	13–14	256r–256v	II, app. 6	Aguirre, 1950–51, v. 3 [N-S]. León Portilla, 1958b, pp. 60–64 [N-S]
E	Otras varias ceremonias	14–16	256v–257v	II, app. 7	Aguirre, 1950–51, v. 3 [N-S]. León-Portilla, 1958b, pp. 64–70 [N-S]
4	Ministros de los dioses	18–22	258v–260v	II, app. 8	Aguirre, 1950–51, v. 4 (incomplete) [N-S]. Schultze Jena, 1952, pp. 82–93 [N-G]. León-Portilla, 1958b, pp. 86–109 [N-S]
5A*	Atavios de los dioses	23–35	261r–267	Some derived illus., I	Seler, 1890 [no. 30], passim; 1902–23, 2:420–508, passim; 1927 [no. 268], pp. 33–58 [N-G]. Garibay, 1956, 4, pp. 279–90 [S]. León-Portilla, 1958b, pp. 111–54 [N-S]
B*	Atavios de los ministros de los dioses (2 illus. only)	36	267v	—	—
6	Objetos que servían	37	268r	—	León-Portilla, 1958b, pp. 79–80 [N-S]

KEY:
* Section illustrated
E, English
G, German
N, Nahuatl
S, Spanish
FPT, Francisco del Paso y Troncoso
PAL, MS in Biblioteca de la Palacio Real, Madrid
Seler numbers in square brackets refer to entries listed in Article 20, Appendix

(*Table 5, continued*)

Para-graph	Subject	FPT 1905b (pages)	Codices Matritenses (PAL)	Florentine Codex	Major Modern Translations
	para los ritos en el templo				
7°	Edificios del templo	38–39	268v–269r	—	Seler, 1901 [no. 129], pp. 116–17; 1902–23, 2:771–72 [N-G]. Alcocer, 1935, p. 25 [N-S]. León-Portilla, 1958b, pp. 80–82 [N-S]
8	Deservicios a los dioses (title only)	40	269v	—	—
9	Ministros principales de los dioses	41	270r	—	León-Portilla, 1958b, pp. 108–09 [N-S]
10	Funciones de los dioses	42–43	270v–271r	—	León-Portilla, 1958b, pp. 154–59 [N-S]
11	Ritos diarios a horas fijas	44–45	271v–272r	II, app. 9	León-Portilla, 1958b, pp. 70–75 [N-S]
12	Ejercicios en el templo	46	272v	II, app. 10	León-Portilla, 1958b, pp. 74–79 [N-S]
13	Votos y juramentos	47	273r	II, app. 11	León-Portilla, 1958b, pp. 78–79 [N-S]
14	Cantares a los dioses	48–64	273v–281v	II, app. 12 (explanatory notes omitted)	Brinton, 1890 [N-E]. Seler, 1902–23 [no. 165], 2:961–1107 [N-G]. Garibay, 1940, pp. 3–30 (part) [S]; 1956, 4:291–306 [S]; 1958 [N-S]

cerned with the afterworlds, and this subject is another possibility. However, other than the obvious fact that it must have been concerned with some aspect of religion, unless the folios containing this first paragraph are discovered it will probably never be known specifically to what topic it was devoted.

Paragraph 2 contains pictorial and textual résumés of the 18 *veintena* ceremonies, plus a special ceremony held every eight years (Atamalcualiztli). Sahagún compiled much more detailed textual accounts of the 18 veintenas subsequently in Tlatelolco, which he incorporated in HG, II. These briefer, unused Tepepolco versions were unknown, therefore, until discovered by modern scholarship; they were not made completely available until publication by Paso y Troncoso (1905b). Their paleography and first complete translation (German) were not published until 1927, by Seler (the Atamalcualiztli section [illustrated] was published by him much earlier in 1893 [no. 61a]); the first five veintenas only were published by him in 1899 [no. 119]. Garibay in 1948 published the first Spanish version, also with the paleography.[25] Brief as they are, these 19 summaries provide the most detailed textual accounts and illustrations of the versions of these fundamental rituals as performed in a major Acolhuacan community. This section, consequently, is one of the most important in the PM. A direct translation into English is an obvious desideratum.

Paragraph 3 is a long annotated list of terms for various ritual exercises, the first portion of which contains pictorial representations of each. Sahagún included this

[25] Aguirre (1950–51) contains the paleography and Spanish translation of this paragraph, plus the other PM sections indicated in Table 5. His paleography and translation, however, largely derived from that of Garibay, cannot be recommended.

paragraph in HG, II, Appendix, 4–7, dividing it into four titled sections (Paso y Troncoso divided it into five sections, labeled A–E). Paragraph 4, which Sahagún included in HG, II, Appendix, 8, is devoted to a lengthy annotated list of sacerdotal titles. León-Portilla (1958b) published paleographies and Spanish translations of both paragraphs; Schultze Jena (1952) published par. 4 (Nahuatl-German).

Paragraph 5 is probably the best-known section of the PM. Together with the twin pictorials, Telleriano-Remensis and Vaticanus A [Rios], it was the principal Rosetta Stone used by Seler partially to decipher the ritual-divinatory screenfolds of the "Codex Borgia group," the Tonalamatl Aubin, the Codex Borbonicus, etc. It consists of 37 pictorial representations of deities (or deity impersonators), with an itemization of the details of the costume and insignia of each —plus two sketchy (one unfinished) drawings of priests on the verso of the last folio of the paragraph (which Paso y Troncoso assigned to a separate [B] section, under its own title).

Subsequently in Tlatelolco Sahagún compiled similar data, often with additional information, on 23 of these same deities (adding two [Tezcatzoncatl and Tlazolteotl] not included in the Tepepolco list), and it was these Tlatelolco data that he included in HG, I, rather than those obtained in Tepepolco. However, 20 of the deity representations were copied as illustrations for the FC in a more Europeanized style (Peñafiel, 1890, vol. 1, pls. 90–100 [Seler tracings]; Paso y Troncoso, 1905a, pls. 1–4 [republished in Dibble and Anderson, 1950–70, pt. 2]). As indicated, Seler recognized at once the great iconographic importance of this section of the PM as soon as he first had the opportunity to examine it (1889) and published copies of the deity representations and paleographies of the Nahuatl texts, with German translation (Seler, 1890 [no. 30], 1902–23, 2 [1904], 1927 [no. 268]). Another paleography and first direct Spanish

translation was published by León-Portilla (1958b), with new copies of the illustrations by Alberto Beltrán.

Paragraph 6 is an unannotated list of 24 items connected with ritual exercises, a paleography and Spanish translation of which was included in León-Portilla, 1958b. Paragraph 7 is the well-known pictorial representation of a walled temple precinct and textual list of sacred structures in it (usually identified with the Templo Mayor of Tenochtitlan). Both the text (with German translation) and illustration were first published by Seler (1901), new paleographies and translations by Alcocer (1935) and León-Portilla (1958b), while the illustration has been subsequently reproduced innumerable times. Paragraph 8, "evils of the gods," consists of the title only. Paragraph 9 consists only of five unannotated sacerdotal titles, all of which contain the words "Mexico" or "Mexicatl" in them (León-Portilla, 1958b). Paragraph 10 treats "that attributed" to various of the deities listed in par. 5. Although frequently cited by Seler, the first complete paleography, with Spanish translation, was not published until 1958 by León-Portilla.

Paragraphs 11, 12, and 13, respectively, dealing with the solar cult and daily ritual associated with it, various ritual activities in the temples, and vows and oaths, were included in HG, II, Appendix, 9–11. All three paragraphs were also first paleographized and translated into Spanish by León-Portilla (1958b).

Paragraph 14, after par. 5, is probably the best-known PM section. It consists of 20 sacred chants dedicated to as many deities or groups of deities, with explanatory glosses. Sahagún also included them (adding five illustrations) in the FC version of the HG (II, Appendix, 12) but without the glosses or the usual paraphrastic Spanish translation. They are in an archaic form of Nahuatl, some in an extremely obscure and archaic idiom. Their accurate translation, therefore, poses great difficulties; their cor-

TABLE 6—SAHAGÚN, *PRIMEROS MEMORIALES* (TEPEPOLCO, 1559–61)
Chapter II: Cielo y Infierno

Para-graph	Subject	FPT 1905b (pages)	Codices Matritenses	Florentine Codex	Major Modern Translations
1*	Cuerpos que resplande-cen	65–66	PAL 282r–282v	—	Schultze Jena, 1950, pp. 54–59 [N-G]
2*	Cuerpos formado en el aire	66–67	PAL 282v–283r	—	Schultze Jena, 1950, pp. 58–61 [N-G]
3*	Cuenta de los años	67–73	PAL 283r–286r	—	Schultze Jena, 1950, pp. 78–83 [N-G]
4*	Cuenta de los signos	73–107	PAL 286r–303r	—	Schultze Jena, 1950, pp. 88-97 [N-G]
5A	Agüeros	108–109	PAL 303v–RAH 85r	—	Garibay, 1944, pp. 307–11 [N-S]. Schultze Jena, 1950, pp. 2–3 [N-G]. López Austin, 1969a, pp. 98–100 [N-S]
B	Sueños	110	RAH 85v	—	Garibay, 1944, pp. 311–13 [N-S]. Schultze Jena, 1950, pp. 28–29 [N-G]. López Austin, 1969a, pp. 100–03 [N-S]
6	Lo que pasaba en la otra vida	111–112	RAH 84r–84v	—	Seler, 1919 [no. 252], p. 30; 1927 [no. 268], pp. 302–04 (part) [N-G]
7	Exequias	112	RAH 84v	—	Seler, 1919 [no. 252], p. 31; 1927 [no. 268], pp. 304–05 [N-G]

KEY:

* Section illustrated
E, English
G, German
N, Nahuatl
S, Spanish
FPT, Francisco del Paso y Troncoso
PAL, MS in Biblioteca de la Palacio Real, Madrid
RAH, MS in Academia Real de la Historia, Madrid
Seler numbers in square brackets refer to entries listed in Article 20, Appendix

rect interpretation, even more. Brinton, using both the PM and FC versions, first attempted a paleography and English "translation" in 1890, the latter effort essentially a failure. Seler, in 1904 [no. 165], published a paleography and German translations—far more successful than those of Brinton—with copious notes. Garibay (1940, 1956) published some preliminary Spanish translations, then, in 1958, a major monograph including the paleography, Spanish translations, and extensive notes. His effort is to some extent an improvement over that of Seler published 54 years before, but sometimes the versions and interpretations of his German predecessor are still to be preferred.

Chapter II (Table 6)

This chapter covers "in ilhuicacaiutl yoā ȳ mictlancaiutl," "the realm of the celestial and the underworld" (Paso y Troncoso's "Cielo y Infierno"). It is the shortest of the PM chapters, containing only seven paragraphs. None was used in the HG, although quite similar materials, collected later in Tlatelolco, are found in HG, III, Appendix, IV, V, and VII. The paragraphs are concerned with: (1) annotated illustrations of the sun, moon, constellations, and comets; (2) the same for the wind, rain, and other celestial phenomena; (3) the 52-year cycle (annotated year signs); (4) the 260-day divinatory cycle (*tonalpohualli*; annotated day signs and short texts); (5) capsule descriptions of various omens and dream prognostications; (6) the nature of the underworld (Mictlan); (7) the funerary rites for rulers. In addition, in the right column of the last two paragraphs was added a "historia mylagrosa," as Sahagún's annotation calls it, which supposedly occurred 10 or 12 years before the Conquest. Paragraphs 1–4 were paleographized and translated into German by Schultze Jena (1950); the paleography and Spanish translation of par. 5 was published by Garibay (1944–47) and López Austin (1969a). Seler (1919 [no. 252], 1927 [no. 268]) published the paleography and German translation of pars. 6 and 7.

Chapter III (Table 7)

This chapter is entitled "in tlatocayutl," "rulership." Only parts of one paragraph of this chapter (par. 1, B, C) were incorporated in the HG (VIII, 3, 4) by Sahagún. As was so frequently the case, he apparently preferred the similar, usually lengthier materials obtained later in Tlatelolco. This chapter contains the most paragraphs, but some are quite brief. The first paragraph contains illustrations of the sequence of rulers of Tenochtitlan, Tetzcoco, and Huexotla, with concise textual summaries of their reigns. Sahagún obtained a similar, purely textual listing for Tenochtitlan and a new one for Tlatelolco, both of which he used, adding illustrations, in the FC version of the HG (VIII, 1, 2).[26] The PM Tenochtitlan list was not made available until publication by Paso y Troncoso (1905b). The PM Tetzcoco and Huexotla dynastic lists, on the other hand, were incorporated in HG, VIII, 3, 4, with illustrations copied from those in the PM. Kutscher (1961) published the paleography and German translation of the Tetzcoco list.

Paragraph 2 is an illustrated list of titles of high functionaries who aided the rulers and priests. Paragraph 3 is an unillustrated list of activities and duties of the rulers, plus a concise expository text in the right column. Similar texts were collected in Tlatelolco and appear in HG, VIII. Neither of the PM paragraphs seemingly has been paleographized and translated into a modern language.

Paragraph 4 is a list of various items in the cuisine of the nobility, the wealthy, and the commoners. Sahagún compiled a somewhat similar but considerably longer list in Tlatelolco and included it in HG, VIII, 13. Alcocer (1938) paleographized and translated this paragraph into Spanish. Paragraph 5 is a list of garments and hair styles worn by both sexes of the nobility, with illustrations of richly attired male and female nobles. Paragraph 6 is a list of articles of adornment worn by rulers when they danced. Similar Tlatelolco-derived listings appear in HG, VIII, 8, 9, 15. These two paragraphs, together with par. 8 of chapter

---

[26] HG, VIII, 1 and 2, are clearly derived from a listing, with brief historical notes, of the rulers of Tenochtitlan and Tlatelolco (interdigitated here, separated as chaps. 1 and 2 in the HG) which comprises RAH, fols. 2–5, whose script and format differ from the rest of the Manuscrito de Tlatelolco original Nahuatl version (RAH, fols. 6–23) of what became HG, VIII. They appear to have been composed earlier, in 1560, as can be inferred from the stated duration of the reigns of the last listed Tenochca and Tlatelolca rulers and which is made explicit in the HG titles of these chapters. Nicolau d'Olwer (1952, pp 56–57) grouped these folios with PAL, fols. 49–52 (Paso y Troncoso's [1905b, pp. 38–41] "Memoriales complementarias," which Jiménez Moreno [1938b, pp. 37, 66–67] called "Segundos Memoriales" or "Primer Manuscrito de Tlatelolco") and expressed his doubt whether they were composed in Tepepolco or Tlatelolco. If a 1560 date for RAH, fols. 2–5, is accepted, this dynastic list was probably produced in the former community (perhaps by one of the four trilingual graduates of the Tlatelolco Colegio de Santa Cruz), for it can be demonstrated that Sahagún was working on his ethnographic-linguistic project in Tepepolco during this year. However, it clearly stands apart from the organizational structure of the PM as here defined.

TABLE 7—SAHAGÚN, *PRIMEROS MEMORIALES* (TEPEPOLCO, 1559–61)
Chapter III: Señorío

Paragraph	Subject	FPT 1905b (pages)	Codices Matritenses (RAH)	Florentine Codex	Major Modern Translations
1A*	Señores de Mexico	113–14	51r–51v	—	—
B*	Señores de Tetzcoco	115–16	52r–53r	VIII, 3	Kutscher, 1961, pp. 254–62 [N-G]
C*	Señores de Uexutla	117–18	53r–53v	VIII, 4	—
2*	Auxiliares de los señores	118–19	53v–54r	—	—
3*	Negocios que trataban los señores	119–20	54r–54v	—	—
4	Manjares y bebidas	120–21	54v–55r	—	Alcocer, 1938 [N-S]
5*	Vestido y compostura de señores y señoras	122–23	55v–56r	—	Seler, 1902–23, 2: 515, 518–20 [N-G]
6	Adornos para el baile	123–24	56r–56v	—	Seler, 1902–23, 2: 535–36 [N-G]
7	Pasatiempos varoniles	124	56v–57r	—	—
8	Utensilios de labor, mujeriles	124–25	56v–57r	—	—
9	Edificios	125–26	57r–57v	—	—
10	Muebles y enseres	126	57v	—	—
11	Nómina de hombres malos	127–28	58r–58v	—	Seler, 1899, [no. 118], passim; 1927 [no. 268], pp. 356–64 (part) [N-G]. Garibay, 1946–47, pp. 167–74, 235–40 [N-S]; 1956, 4:307–12 [S]
12	Nómina de malas mujeres	129	59r	—	Seler, 1899 [no. 118], passim; 1927 [no. 268], pp. 364–67 [N-G]. Garibay, 1946–47, pp. 240–43 [N-S]; 1956, 4:312–14 (part) [S]
13	Crianza de mancebos y doncellas	130	59v	—	—
14	Origen de los chichimecos y poderío de los señores	131–33	60r–61r	—	—
15*	Amonestaciones de los magistrados al pueblo	134–40	61v–64v	—	—
16*	Motivos para el enojo del señor	141–42	65r–65v	—	—
17*	Motivos para la tristeza del señor	142–43	65v–66r	—	—

KEY:
* Section illustrated
E, English
G, German
N, Nahuatl
S, Spanish
FPT, Francisco del Paso y Troncoso
RAH, MS in Academia Real de la Historia, Madrid
Seler numbers in square brackets refer to entries listed in Article 20, Appendix

IV, were paleographized and translated (German) by Seler in 1904.

Paragraph 7 consists of a very brief list of terms for the pastimes of the rulers, plus one article of adornment seemingly out of place (and included by Seler in his 1904 study, cited above). A much longer account of the same topic was obtained in Tlatelolco and appears in HG, VIII, 10. Paragraph 8 is an unannotated listing of feminine (nobility and commoners) utensils. A somewhat similar compilation, focusing on the weaving tools, was obtained in Tlatelolco and included in HG, VIII, 16. Paragraph 9 is a brief list of terms for various types of administrative and religious structures; HG, VIII, 14, deals with the same general theme. Paragraph 10 is a list of terms for various furnishings and other items used in these structures, particularly different types of thrones, seats, and mats; HG, VIII, 11, contains a somewhat more extensive list of royal seats and mats. No paleographies or translations of pars. 7–10 have been noted.

Paragraphs 11 and 12 contain annotated lists of terms for various types of magicians and sorcerers, both male and female. This is a well-known section, most of which was paleographized and translated into German by Seler (1899 [no. 119], 1927 [no. 268]) and all of which was paleographized and translated into Spanish by Garibay (1944–47; Spanish only and par. 12 incomplete, 1956). It contains extremely valuable data on the shamanistic side of the religious system.

The last five paragraphs have yet to be paleographized and translated. Paragraph 13 is a concise account of the education of boys and girls. More extensive Tlatelolcan materials dealing with this same general theme were included in HG, III, Appendix, 4–8, and VIII, 20, 21. Paragraph 14 is an important one which provides the only significantly historical portion of the PM other than the dynastic lists of par. 1. It deals with the migration from Chicomoztoc of seven leading central Mexican groups, then provides a fairly extensive account of the privileges and prerogatives of the ruling class. There is nothing closely comparable to it in the HG. Paragraphs 15, 16, and 17 are illustrated texts, respectively dealing with the admonitions addressed to their people by the lords, the reasons for a lord's anger, and the reasons for a lord's sorrow. Although the theme of par. 15 is somewhat similar to some of the discourses included in HG, VI, apart from this there is no really comparable material in the HG.

Chapter IV (Table 8)

This chapter is entitled "yn tlacayutl," "human affairs," and contains 11 paragraphs. Paso y Troncoso also inserted, after the folio containing most of the eighth paragraph, folios 72–80 of the RAH MS, which contain numerous pictorial representations of leaders and warriors wearing elaborate military costumes and devices and these attires and insignia alone, plus brief texts and single labels. He also inserted, after the folio containing par. 9 (apparently on the basis of identity of subject matter) the next folio (81) of the RAH MS, although the handwriting is quite distinct and it contains a chapter heading at the end which does not fit the PM sequence. None of the paragraphs of this chapter appear in the HG.

The first paragraph is a brief enumeration of basic kinship terms. Paragraph 2 provides a similar list of terms for sex and age categories, briefly annotated. These topics are extensively covered by Tlatelolcan data in HG, X, 1–3. Paragraphs 3 and 4, respectively, contain lists of names for men and women, plus brief texts explaining the naming system. There is nothing comparable in the HG. These four paragraphs were paleographized and translated into German by Schultze Jena (1952). Paragraphs 5 and 6, respectively, contain lists of the exterior and interior organs of the body, briefly an-

TABLE 8—SAHAGÚN, *PRIMEROS MEMORIALES* (TEPEPOLCO, 1559–61)
Chapter IV: Cosas Humanas

Para-graph	Subject	FPT 1905b (pages)	Codices Matritenses (RAH)	Florentine Codex	Major Modern Translations
1	Parentesco	145	82r	—	Schultze Jena, 1952, pp. 4–5 [N-G]
2	Sexo y edad	145	82r	—	Schultze Jena, 1952, pp. 4–7 [N-G]
3	Nombres de varón	145–46	82r–82v	—	Schultze Jena, 1952, pp. 6–7 [N-G]
4	Nombres de mujer	146	82v	—	Schultze Jena, 1952, pp. 6–7 [N-G]
5	Organos exteriores del cuerpo	146–47	82v–83r	—	Gall, 1940, pp. 90–92 [N-G]. López Austin, 1972, pp. 132–34 [N-S]
6	Organos interiores	148	83v	—	Gall, 1940, pp. 92–93 [N-G]. López Austin, 1972, pp. 134–36 [N-S]
7	Nómina de condiciones y oficios	148	83v	—	Schultze Jena, 1952, p. 30 [N-G]
8A	Nómina de armas e insignias de los señores	149	68r	—	Seler, 1891 [no. 40a], passim (part); 1902–23, 2:546–75 [N-G]. Sullivan, 1972, pp. 158–73 [N-E]
8B	Nómina de armas e insignias de los capitanes	150, 169	68v–69r	—	Seler, 1891 [no. 40a], passim (part); 1902–23, 2:575–94 [N-G]. Sullivan, 1972, pp. 172–89 [N-E]
(8)°	Illustrations: insignia of lords and captains (short texts, single labels)	151–67	72r–80r	—	Seler, 1891 [no. 40a], passim (part); 1902–23, 2:549–73, passim (part) [N-G]. Sullivan, 1972, pp. 188–91 [N-E]
9	Nómina de las dolencias y sus remedios	169–72	69r–69v (81r–81v)	—	Gall, 1940, pp. 93–118 [N-G]. López Austin, 1972, pp. 136–47 [N-S]
10	Modos de cortesía y de vituperio entre nobles	173	70r	—	Schultze Jena, 1952, pp. 62–65 [N-G]
11	Modos de cortesía y de vituperio entre plebeyos	174–75	70v–71r	—	Schultze Jena, 1952, pp. 64–67 [N-G]

KEY:
° Section illustrated
E, English
G, German
N, Nahuatl
S, Spanish
FPT, Francisco del Paso y Troncoso
RAH, MS in Academia Real de la Historia, Madrid
Seler numbers in square brackets refer to entries listed in Article 20, Appendix

notated. HG, X, 27, contains a much lengthier account, compiled in Tlatelolco, of the same topic. Freiherr von Gall (1940) published the paleography and German translation of these two paragraphs; López Austin has recently (1972) produced the first Spanish translation. Paragraph 7 contains a list, briefly annotated, of terms for various categories of persons according to status, office, age, etc. Similar material, much extended, is in HG, X. Schultze Jena (1952) published this paragraph (Nahuatl-German).

Paragraph 8 is another of the better-known sections of PM. It consists of a long, annotated list of the war costumes, equipment, and devices of the rulers and captains. As mentioned, Paso y Troncoso included here nine folios containing glossed illustrations of many of the items mentioned in this list (plus a few not mentioned), whose exact relation to this paragraph of the PM is not certain. HG, VIII, 8, 9, 12, also contain lists of items of this type, gathered in Tlatelolco. This paragraph (plus the illustrated folios) was paleographized and translated into German by Seler (1904); latterly, Sullivan (1972) has published its first direct English translation.

Paragraph 9 (to which, as indicated above, Paso y Troncoso added an isolated folio in another handwriting dealing with the same topic) contains a list of names of diseases, each briefly annotated with a description of the cure. HG, X, 28, contains much more extensive data on the same subject, compiled in Tlatelolco and "confirmed" by eight named Tenochca physicians. Freiherr von Gall (1940) published this paragraph (Nahuatl-German) and, more recently, López Austin (1972; Nahuatl-Spanish). Paragraphs 10 and 11 are short texts dealing with the forms of courteous and discourteous address respectively between nobles and commoners. The HG contains nothing really comparable. Both paragraphs were paleographized and translated into German by Schultze Jena (1952).

Discussion

Tables 5–8 and the preceding analysis reveal several matters of interest. One is that the bibliography of the PM is complex. Most of the PM has been paleographized and translated into German, Spanish, or English, in widely scattered publications. Translations of all of chapters I, II, and IV are now available. On the other hand, 11 of the 17 paragraphs of chapter III have not been translated (and only one portion of the first paragraph). Most of these untranslated paragraphs are brief listings, essentially in the nature of annotated vocabularies. The last five, however, are running texts, one of which (par. 14) is quite substantial and contains important traditional material. Certainly in any specification of priorities within the current upsurge of interest and activity in more adequate publication and analysis of the Sahaguntine corpus, paleographies and translations (preferably into Spanish, the *lingua franca* of Mesoamerican studies) of these paragraphs should be placed high on the list.

One other thing the tables make very clear: very little of the ethnographic information collected by Sahagún in Tepepolco at the outset of his ambitious project actually ended up, as such, in the final 12 books of the HG. It amounts to only five full paragraphs and parts of two others, out of a total of 47 (excluding pars. 1 and 8). And all, with only one exception (Tetzcoco and Huexotla dynasties in chap. III, par. 1), are confined to HG, II, Appendix. Even the fairly extensive illustrative material was virtually ignored in the final work, the only certain exceptions being the 20 deity representations derived from those in chapter I, par. 5, which illustrate the FC version of HG, I, and the Tetzcoco and Huexotla dynastic lists of the FC version of HG, VIII, 3, 4, derived from the pictures of chapter III, par. 1.

Whatever the reasons—perhaps because his Tlatelolco information was generally

more copious than that compiled in Tepepolco, because he knew the former community more intimately, and because some
of his best native assistants originated there
—when drawing up the HG, Sahagún consistently preferred his Tlatelolco to his Tepepolco data, especially when they covered
about the same ground. This fact has not
been sufficiently appreciated. One reason,
perhaps, is that Sahagún's own phrasing of
the relation of his Tepepolco to his Tlatelolco information in his prologue to HG, II, is
somewhat ambiguous and appears to place
greater emphasis on the Tepepolco materials than on those from Tlatelolco, when the
exact opposite was clearly the case. Sahagún thus did not just revise and expand his
Tepepolco data in Tlatelolco. Although obviously still guided by his Tepepolco *minuta*, he gathered a great amount of new and
independent information, most of which
passed into the final HG whereas most of
the PM did not.

The full implication of this circumstance
is that the PM can generally stand on its
own as a separate document and should be
handled as such rather than merely as a
brief, preparatory stage in the compilation
of the HG.

Certainly the publication of paleographies of all its texts and their translations
into a current major language, as a unit,
with notes, indexes, and all other normal
apparatus of modern critical scholarship,
would seem to be one of the most obvious
needs of Sahaguntine studies. Although the
tables show that most of the PM has been
paleographized and translated, they also
indicate that such publications are widely
scattered throughout the literature and in
different languages—aside from being somewhat uneven in quality. Merely to assemble
in one place all of the significant PM translations requires the acquisition of a great
number of separate, often scarce publications. The great desirability, therefore, of
the unitary publication of the paleography
and translation of the *Primeros memoriales*
is evident. It is to be hoped that this task
will be taken up by Sahagún scholars in the
not too distant future.

C. SAHAGÚN MATERIALS AND STUDIES, 1948–1971

HOWARD F. CLINE

This section provides bibliographical information on publications of Sahagún texts,
and indicates the principal directions which
studies of Sahagún have taken since the late
Nicolau d'Olwer submitted Section A in
1962. In general that treatment rests on his
own excellent biography (Nicolau d'Olwer,
1952), with only minor later bibliographical
additions, to about 1956. From 1948 to 1971
Sahaguntine studies have flourished, a recent development not fully reflected in Section A. These pages, therefore, are basically
a bibliographical epilogue to it, treating
general studies and trends, and discussing
translations and studies of the HG.

PUBLICATIONS, 1829–1947

Table 9 summarizes the mass of material
previously noted by Nicolau d'Olwer (1952,
pp. 183–88) illustrating the gradual publication of Sahagún texts from the first
(Bustamante, 1829a) through 1947, when

218

TABLE 9—SELECTIVE LIST OF PUBLISHED WORKS AND TRANSLATIONS
OF SAHAGÚN, 1829–1947

Editor/Translator	Manuscript Source	Materials	Comment
		1829:	
Bustamante	Tolosano-Panes	HG, XII	Early (1576) text; Bustamante, 1829a
		1829–30:	
Bustamante	Tolosano-Panes	HG, vol. 1, I–IV vol. 2, V–IX vol. 3, X–XI	3 vols. Lacks I, Appendix (see García Icazbalceta, 1886); III, 3; VI, 25, 27, altered and mutilated; other defects (see Ramírez, 1867b [1885b])
		1830: °	
Kingsborough	Tolosano-Bauzá	HG, vol. 5, VI, 1–40 (1830); VI, 41 ff.; VII–XII (1831) vol. 7, I–V	Various omissions; see Ramírez, 1867b [1885b], pp. 115–16
		1840:	
Bustamante	[Montemayor?]- Cortina	HG, XII	Revised 1585 text, with irrelevant additional materials. Only extant version of this text
		1843:	
Bustamante [C]	Tolosano-Panes, Montemayor- Cortina	HG, XII, 23	Reprints 1576 and 1585 text; other irrelevant material
		1880:	
Jourdanet and Simeón	[Tolosano-Panes]	HG, I–XII	F trans. of Bustamante, 1829a, 1829–30
		1886:	
García Icazbalceta	Tolosano-Panes	HG, I, Appendix	Omitted from Bustamante, 1829–30; Kingsborough, 1830; Jourdanet and Simeón, 1880
		1890:	
Brinton	Florentino [N], PM	HG, II, Appendix [20 hymns]	PM, I, 14, N-E trans.
Peñafiel	Florentino	HG, I, illus. [Imágenes de los Dioses]	Based on tracings by Seler
Seler	PM, Mem. 3 col.	PM, I, 5; HG, I [Como los Dioses van adornados]	N-G trans., illus., discussion (Seler, no. 30)
		1890–95:	
Paz	[Tolosano-Panes]	HG, I–XII	4 vols., re-edition, Bustamante, 1829a, 1829–30

° There is also an edition dated 1831 in the Library of Congress.

KEY:

E, English	N, Nahuatl
F, French	S, Spanish
G, German	HG, *Historia general*

PAL, MS in Biblioteca de la Palacio Real, Madrid
PM, *Primeros memoriales*
RAH, MS in Real Academia de la Historia, Madrid
Mem. 3 col., Memoriales en tres columnas
Mem. escolios, Memoriales con escolios
Mem. Español, Memoriales en Español

(*Table 9, continued*)

Editor/Translator	Manuscript Source	Materials	Comment
		1892:	
Seler	Mem. 3 col.	HG, IX, 16, 17 (2d part), 20, 21 [Orfebrería, etc.]	N-F trans., notes (Seler, no. 36)
		1893:	
Seler [G]	PM	PM, I, 2B	N-G trans., 1 illus. in color (Seler, no. 61a)
		1899:	
Seler [N]	PM	PM, I, 2; HG, II, 20–38	N-G trans., discussion (Seler, no. 119–3)
		1904:	
Seler	PM, Florentino [N]	PM, I, 14; HG, II, Appendix [20 hymns]	N-G trans., notes, illus. from Florentino (Seler, no. 165)
		1905:	
Seler	PM, Florentino [N]	PM, I, 14; HG, II, Appendix	E trans. of Hymn XV to Xipe from Seler, 1904; notes (Seler, no. 141)
		1905–07:	
Paso y Troncoso	Florentino	vol. 5, illus.	Paso y Troncoso, 1905a
	Matritenses	vol. 6, PM; Mem. escolios; illus.	Paso y Troncoso, 1905b
	Matritenses, PAL	vol. 7. Mem. 3 col., I, II [HG, I–III, VII, IV, V]; Mem. Español [HG, II, V]	Paso y Troncoso, 1906
	Matritenses, RAH	vol. 8. Mem. 3 col., III–IV [HG, VIII–XI]	Paso y Troncoso, 1907
		1906:	
Schmidt [N]	Vatican	Breve conpendio	Summaries of HG, I–II; complete text only of I
		1922:	
Kunike [C]	[Tolosano-Panes]	HG, III, VII, X, (selected chaps.)	Selections from Bustamante, G trans. Reprinted 1961
		1924:	
Pou y Martí	Vatican	Coloquios	N and S incomplete MS
		1927:	
Mazari	PM, Florentino [N]	PM, I, 14; HG, II, Appendix	Hymn VIII to Xochipilli; from text in Paso y Troncoso, 1907, adapted to modern N, S trans., melody
		1927:	
Nuttall	Vatican	Coloquios	S-N text [from Pou y Martí, 1924]
Seler-Sachs (Seler)	Florentino, Matritenses	PM, II, 2; II, 6–7; III, 11 (part), 12; Mem. 3 col., VIII, 15; HG, I, 1–29; II, 20–38, App. 2; III, 1–14, App. 1–9; IV, 29; V, 27; IX, 16, 17 (2d part), 20–21; X, 29; XII (complete)	N-G trans. by E. Seler; illus., notes by Lehmann, Krickeberg. Trans. 1890 ff. (Seler, no. 268)
		1929:	
Chávez Orozco [C]	[Tolosano-Panes]	HG, XII	Reissue, Bustamante, 1829a
		1932:	
Bandelier	[Tolosano-Panes]	HG, I–IV	E trans. of Bustamante, 1829–30, incomplete

(*Table 9, continued*)

Editor/Translator	Manuscript Source	Materials	Comment
		1936:	
Campos	[Tolosano-Panes]	HG, VI	Reprint, Bustamante, 1829–30, includes 3 of the 20 hymns trans. by Vigil into S from Brinton, 1890
		1937:	
Garibay K. [C]	PM, Florentino [N]	PM, I, 14; HG, II, Appendix [hymns]	N-S trans. (partial) of hymns
		1938:	
Ramírez Cabañas	Tolosano-Panes	HG, I–XII,	5 vols. with added material. Bustamante, 1829a; Seler-Sachs (Seler, no. 268), trans. into S by Heinrich Berlin; S trans. of Seler, 1892 (no. 36) and 1904 (no. 165) by Gott
		vol. 1, Jiménez Moreno, 1938a; HG, I–IV	
		vol. 2, HG, V–IX	
		vol. 3, HG, X–XI, N. León, 1938; Alcocer, 1938	
		vol. 4, HG, XII	
		vol. 5, Cantares; Orfebreria	
		1940:	
Gall [N]	PM, Mem. 3 col.	HG, X, 27, 28; PM, IV, 5, 6, 9	N-G trans., discussion
		1942:	
Oliger [N]	Vatican	Breve conpendio	Complete text; summaries of HG, I, II
		1944:	
Vargas Rea [C]	Vatican	Coloquios	Garbled reissue of Nuttall, 1927
		1944–47:	
Garibay [N]	PM	PM, II, 5; III, 11–12	N-S trans., notes
		1946:	
Acosta Saignes	Florentino? [S]†	HG, I–XII,	3 vols., notes, guide to study, bibliography
		vol. 1, Intro., HG, I–VI	Paso y Troncoso MS (INAH)
		vol. 2, HG, VII–IX	Paso y Troncoso MS (INAH)
	Tolosano-Panes (bks. X, XI)	vol. 3, HG, X–XII	Paso y Troncoso MS (INAH), bks. X–XI Tolosano-Panes (INAH); bk. XII Nuttall MS Florentino (S) (INAH)
		1956:	
Garibay K. [C]	Tolosano-Panes		4 vols. Some subdivision of paragraphs, glossary of N terms in S text
		1969:	
Garibay K. [C]	Tolosano-Panes		New edition of 1956

SOURCE: Nicolau d'Olwer, 1952, pp. 183–88, rearranged and tabulated by H. F. Cline. Additions by Cline [C], by Nicholson [N], by Glass [G]. Citations to Seler numbers refer to Article 20, Appendix.

† Ed. note: There are numerous discrepancies between published text and the manuscript version.

Nicolau more or less closed his comprehensive bibliographical treatment. Until 1938 students had relatively untrustworthy and incomplete versions of the basic HG with which to work.[27] The principal one through the years had been Bustamante (1829–30), based on the Tolosano-Panes copy, variously translated and edited.

Even the five-volume Ramírez Cabañas (1938) version was essentially a reissue of that derivative manuscript, freed from some of Bustamante's more glaring errata and omissions. The 1938 edition took into some account various translations earlier made directly from Nahuatl by Seler and others, as well as a Paso y Troncoso copy of the Spanish text of books I–VI. This, however, is merely a late copy of Tolosa. Jiménez Moreno's (1938a, 1938b) discussion of Sahagún and his work in the Ramírez Cabaña edition remains useful.

The three-volume edition of HG (1946) edited by Acosta Saignes provides a slightly variant Spanish text. After his death in 1916, when parts of the Francisco Paso y Troncoso collection came from Europe to Mexico, only books I–VI (vols. 1, 2) were received. In 1940 the Mexican Government purchased books VII–IX (vol. 3) from a dealer; Paso y Troncoso's copies of books X–XII (vol. 4) continue to be lost (Article 21). Acosta Saignes to some degree utilized the Paso y Troncoso copy for books I–IX, and the García Panes copy for books X–XI. For book XII he said that he had used a hand-copy of the Florentine text made ca. 1895 (?) by Zelia Nuttall, owned by the MNA. Thus although parts of the 1946 edition include materials from FC, it does not reproduce the whole manuscript.

Without advising the reader, Acosta Saignes prefaced this 1578–79 text of book XII with an introduction not found in Flo-

rentino or Tolosano but prepared by Sahagún in 1585 to precede a quite variant revision in which he had changed markedly his interpretation of the Conquest. As noted above, this confusion of texts, plus Acosta Saignes' reprinting an erroneous date (1566 for 1576) in book IV, Appendix, has led even careful scholars like Robertson (1959, p. 173; Glass, 1960, p. 126) to the erroneous conclusion that HG was composed 1566–85. We have seen that it was completed in Nahuatl in 1569, with the illustrated, bilingual FC coming in 1578–79, and with the Tolosano copy of the latter following 1580.

Below we discuss the Garibay (1956) edition. It formed part of a general Mexican plan for studies of Sahagún.

GENERAL PLANS, 1867–1964

Generally speaking, the state of affairs about 20 years ago had seen the HG only incompletely published, from more or less corrupt texts. Since that time, a number of voices have repeated the earlier calls for full scholarly publication of a reliable total corpus of original Sahagún material and critical studies. Such a pressing need was stated clearly a century ago by Ramírez (1867b [1885b]). His own efforts to replace the unsatisfactory editions of Bustamante and Kingsborough were never completed (Article 21).

Interest in publication of the Sahagún corpus was revived at the Fourth International Congress of Americanists in Madrid, 1881, largely as a result of a paper presented by Bonifacio Montejo y Robredo on smallpox in America (Montejo y Robredo, 1882). Although much of the material was plagiarized from another work (Nicolau d'Olwer, 1952, p. 193), Montejo y Robredo had consulted the Tolosa Manuscript and transcribed book VII, chapter 2, and discussed at length Sahagún texts and the need for their publication. This suggestion plus the "discovery" of the 1867 Ramírez study he had mentioned apparently spurred another Americanist in the Royal Academy,

[27] The author gratefully acknowledges substantial aid from H. B. Nicholson, who provided valuable critical reviews of earlier drafts and added important data. Charles E. Dibble has also been very helpful.

Antonio M. Fabié, to propose on August 27, 1882, that it undertake to publish in full a critical scholarly edition of the Sahagún corpus (Madrazo, 1885, p. 684). A committee was named, headed by Cayetano Rosell, to prepare it; on November 23, 1882, it drew up a plan, including a proposal to publish the FC and other codices at government expense, with an erudite discussion of the manuscripts (Rosell, 1882). The death of Rosell, the prime mover, on March 26, 1883, seemingly terminated Spanish interest in the project.

The Rosell report was given wider circulation in 1882 by a Spanish journalist, whose account was reproduced in the *Anales* of the National Museum (Mexico) in 1886 (Llanos, 1882). In that year García Icazbalceta also published his massive *Bibliografía mexicana del siglo XVI*, which contained a basic study of the texts (García Icazbalceta, 1954, pp. 327–76). It terminated with a eulogistic footnote for the work on Sahagún undertaken by Paso y Troncoso, with the expressed hope that he would conclude and publish it (ibid., p. 376, n. 165).

The vast plan developed by Paso y Troncoso for publication of Sahagún materials is discussed in Article 21. Since his day the pressing need for full publication of the corpus has been reiterated. Charency voiced it (1899, pp. 2–3) early, repeated by Jiménez Moreno (1938b), Nicolau d'Olwer (1952, pp. 191–98), and restated by Mengin (1964). A list of desiderata was drawn up by McQuown (1958) in a review of the Anderson-Dibble efforts.

The agreed need for publication remains, and the recommended coverage is broad. It envisages facsimiles of all of Sahagún's works, historical and other; transliterations and translation of all these; a complete glossary of linguistic items; critical history of each manuscript with pedigree and family tree; identification of all informants and scribes, with relevant data about their background and qualifications; identification of the varieties of Nahuatl and their present

offshoots; grammar of the language; content index of all of Sahagún's work; and, finally, critical evaluations of the content. At this writing (1971) this ideal has not been reached, but visible if uneven progress toward it has been made since 1948 in the publications noted below.

NATIONAL AND INTERNATIONAL TRENDS, 1938–67

Germany

In Germany just before, during, and after World War II various older scholars trained in the Seler school devoted themselves to publishing native sources in German translation. In addition to the several items by Seler listed in Table 9, he had used Sahagún extensively, and numerous, if fragmentary, translations into German appear in his collected works, and in his classic studies of codices (Article 20). His work on the Borgia, for instance, has a translation of a substantial portion of book VI, chapter 29 (Seler, 1904–09 [no. 154], 2:87–88). His students followed similar paths.

Their major work appeared in a series of seven *Quellenwerke zur alten Geschichte Amerikas aufgezeichnet in den Sprachen der Eingeboren*, edited in large part by Gerdt Kutscher at the then Lateinamerikanischen Bibliothek (later Iberoamerikanische Institut) in (West) Berlin (Kutscher, 1959; Bock, 1959; Comas, 1954, pp. lxii–lxiii). Three numbers were devoted to Sahagún materials, translated by Lehmann (1949) and Schultze Jena (1950, 1952) from Nahuatl, published with German in parallel columns, with glossaries and other scholarly apparatus in the great Germanic tradition of scholarly presentation of documentary texts. Other numbers, although not exclusively Sahaguntine, provide helpful versions from native writers of Middle America.[28]

[28] The series included: 1, *Die Geschichte der Königreiche von Colhuacan und Mexiko* (1938), edited by Walter Lehmann; 2, *Popol Vuh. Das Heilige Buch der Quiché Indianer von Guatemala* (1944) edited by Leonhard Schultze Jena; 3, *Sterb-*

Seemingly unconnected with this scholarly enterprise was Jahn's (1962) free adaptation, without the Nahuatl paleography of the Seler translations of Sahagún from Nahautl to German earlier published by his widow (Seler-Sachs, 1927 [no. 268]) in collaboration with Walter Lehmann and Walter Krickeberg.

France

Recent French students have not been active in studies of Sahagún. Apart from Jacques Soustelle's use of Sahagún (along with numerous other sources) in his popular accounts of Aztec life, only two other specifically Sahagún items have come to notice. Utilizing the 1938 Mexican publication of HG, Jacques Donvez (1957) compiled a small anthology for teachers of Spanish in French secondary schools, using especially chapters from book VI, with notes, from standard authorities. Noted below (book VI) is Forest's (1960) French translation of a Sahagún chapter.

---

ende *Götter und christliche Heilsbotschaft* [Sahagún Colloquios] (1949), edited by Walter Lehmann; 4, *Wahrsagerei, Himmelskunde und Kalendar der alten Azteken* (1950), edited by Leonhard Schultze Jena; 5, *Gliederung des alt-aztekischen Volks in Familie, Stand, und Beruf* (1952), edited by Leonhard Schultze Jena; 6, *Alt-aztekische Gesänge* [Cantares Mexicanos, National Library, Mexico] (1957), edited by Leonhard Schultze Jena; 7, Don Domingo Francisco de San Anton Munon Chimalpahin Quauhtlehuanitzin aus Amequemecan (Amecameca): *Memorial Breve acerca de la fundación de la ciudad de Culhuacan* (1958), edited by Walter Lehmann and Gerdt Kutscher.

Citations to Seler numbers refer to Article 20, Appendix.

[29] George T. Smisor (1943) reported that the Office of Coordinator of Inter-American Affairs (U.S. Government) had granted Fisk University funds to permit Gabriel S. Yorke to complete the translation of HG left unfinished by the death of Fanny Bandelier in 1932. Yorke proposed to utilize the Ramírez Cabañas (1938) text. Nothing further is known of this project.

[30] "The English translation of the Nahuatl was to parallel, in a sense, the late Renaissance feeling of Sahagún's Spanish through the employment of occasional archaisms which might give it something of the atmosphere of the King James version of the Bible" (Olpin and Long, 1950).

224

United States

One major undertaking in the United States illustrates the enormous investment of time and effort required to flesh out even a small segment of the desirable general translation and publication scheme.[29] In 1950 Arthur J. O. Anderson and Charles E. Dibble began a direct translation of HG into English from the Nahuatl version of the Florentine manuscript (Olpin and Long, 1950).[30] Their goal has been to transliterate and translate as accurately as possible, taking into account (and crediting) other editors and translators. They also provide pithy, accurate notes on botany, mythology, persons, places, and other topics. They reproduce the pictorial portion, usually grouped at the middle of each volume, using the lithographs published by Paso y Troncoso, plus a few photographs taken directly from the original manuscript. Color photos of FC have not been fully published by anyone.

The massive Anderson and Dibble enterprise, after nearly two decades, has drawn to a close with the publication (1969) of book VI. For various reasons their translations did not appear chronologically in the numerical order of the books. Table 10 indicates the publication dates. They propose, as part 1 of the 13-part monograph, later to provide introductory materials, table of contents, bibliography, and general index. When it appears, that bibliography will undoubtedly supersede the present effort.

Mexico

The dean of Nahuatlatos in Mexico, the late Father Angel María Garibay K., and his students, around 1950 also independently envisaged an elaborate undertaking, only partially completed at Garibay's death in 1967. Essentially it was to provide many, if not all, the primary desiderata for Sahaguntine studies sketched above. Garibay noted that it was "So grand an enterprise, and so beyond the forces of a single person that, if

TABLE 10—*HISTORIA GENERAL*: TRANSLATION OF FLORENTINO
BY ANDERSON AND DIBBLE°

Book	Short Title	Publication Date	Part
	Preface, introduction, table of contents, bibliography, general index		1
I	The Gods (2d rev. ed., 1970)	1950	2
II	Ceremonies	1951	3
III	The Origin of the Gods	1952	4
IV	The Soothsayers	1957	5
V	The Omens	1957	6
VI	Rhetoric	1969	7
VII	The Sun, Moon, and Stars, and the Binding of the Years	1953	8
VIII	Kings and Lords	1954	9
IX	The Merchants	1959	10
X	The People	1961	11
XI	Earthly Things	1963	12
XII	The Conquest of Mexico	1955	13

° General History of the Things of New Spain. Florentine Codex. Translated from the Aztec into English, with notes and illustrations, by Arthur J. O. Anderson and Charles E. Dibble. School of American Research, Monograph 14. Santa Fe, New Mexico.

it is beautiful to dream about it, it is nearly impossible to bring it to completion" (Garibay, 1956, 1:9–10, 19–20). However, certain important elements have appeared.

In 1956 Garibay himself edited a four-volume version of HG, with a useful general introduction that noted his own earlier work of biographizing Sahagún's informants (Garibay, 1953–54, 2:209–26) and some other specialized studies. However, although the 1956 Garibay edition has become generally standard in the Spanish language, it does not compare in stature with the Anderson-Dibble effort.

Garibay leaves the text virtually unannotated, although he precedes each book with a useful introduction. The text itself was taken from the 1938 edition (Tolosano-Panes), against which Garibay said he had (occasionally?) collated photographic versions of the FC (Spanish), making several minor and a few major emendations of the 1938 text, itself primarily based on Bustamante (1829a, 1829–30).[31] It is clear when the FC text is read against the Garibay edi-

tion that he did little more than use its version of Nahuatl words, but did not restore passages omitted in the Tolosano. A novel feature of the 1956 edition is that Garibay, while retaining the customary division of books and chapters, has attempted to add numbers to paragraphs into which he has broken the text, to facilitate citation. With minor exceptions, the only direct translations from Nahuatl, claimed in the work's subtitle, appear in appendixes to volume 4. In volume 3, at the end of book VI, Garibay added some Spanish text, and some translation from Nahuatl not included in Bustamante; in volume 4, in addition to reproducing the Spanish from Bustamante (1829), Garibay essayed a translation of book XII from the Nahuatl of the FC. His edition also includes a glossary of Nahuatl terms Sahagún used in his Spanish text.

Nicolau d'Olwer (1957) discussed the Garibay edition in detail. He praised the appendix material, direct translations from

[31] In preparation by Cline is a transcription and English translation of FC, bk. XII.

Nahuatl rather than via German, as generally in the 1938 Mexican edition. He also felt the introductory statements Garibay placed at the head of each book were quite helpful, noting especially the new ideas concerning book X. He urged publication of the Tolosano text rather than copies like the Panes. Nicolau d'Olwer rebutted Garibay's iconoclastic views about dates of the FC, and pointed out Garibay's error in thinking that Motolinía (1548–51) as provincial of the Order rather than Toral had ordered Sahagún to write HG. Nicolau d'Olwer stated that the Garibay handling of book XII (Conquest) caused confusion. Garibay, as did Acosta Saignes, includes the 1585 Introduction (not found in Florentino or Tolosano) but does not advise the reader that it preceded a quite variant text, which he does not reproduce. He publishes the earlier (1576?) Spanish text, and also provides his own Spanish translation of the Nahuatl (Florentino).

To place Nahuatl studies, especially those related to Sahagún, on a firm institutional basis in Mexico, the National University established (within its Institute of History) a Seminar of Nahuatl Culture (1957), headed by Garibay and largely directed by one of his students, Miguel León-Portilla. The seminar's publication program sponsors three series: *Fuentes indígenas de la cultura nahuatl*, with a subseries, *Textos de los informantes de Sahagún*; *Monografías*; and a journal, *Estudios de Cultura Nahuatl* (Nicholson, 1960, pp. 31–32). Individual titles are briefly discussed below. The *Estudios* continue to appear annually. Items in them (and in the two other series) are generally carefully and extensively noted by Nicholson in his continuing comprehensive coverage of pre-Hispanic and Contact period ethnohistory of Mesoamerica for the *Handbook of Latin American Studies* (Nicholson, 1960–70).

Spain

Yet another national group effort pro-

duced important, if less voluminous, results. Under Manuel Ballesteros Gaibrois, the Seminar of Americanist Studies in the University of Madrid (Spain) undertook an elaborate description and analysis of the Sahagún manuscripts in the Palace and in the Academy of History in Madrid (Ballesteros Gaibrois and others, 1962). The results were published in 1964 as a two-volume work (Ballesteros Gaibrois and others, 1964).

The first volume contains disparate materials. There is an incomplete history of the manuscripts and of the gradual publication of the Sahagún corpus. It is followed by detailed descriptions of the Palace manuscript, then those in the Academy, including a generalized summary of the Tolosano. There is then an extended but generalized attempt to correlate similar materials from the Palace manuscript, the Tolosano, and the Spanish of the Florentino, chiefly by reproduction of chapter headings. Linguistic materials in the "Memoriales con escolios" (PAL, bk. VII, fols. 160–70, 178–83; ACAD, bk. X, fols. 88–96, 104–111) form a substantial section. A catalog of the 70 illustrations (with many more drawings) in the Palace and Academy manuscripts and their correspondence to illustrative material in the FC is provided. Unfortunately a final discussion of watermarks is highly derivative and fails to provide identifying data that would aid in fixing more clearly chronological sequences and other inferences which such detail can often support.

The second volume, in reality a small portfolio, reproduces in color the illustrations of the Madrid manuscripts, except the single drawing in the Tolosa. The very reduced scale of reproduction makes these separate plates quite inconvenient for specialized scholarly purposes. Students will necessarily continue to rely on the earlier Paso y Troncoso facsimiles for details.

International

Sahaguntine studies have informally always been international. More formally they became institutionalized at the 36th International Congress of Americanists held in Spain in 1964. Leading specialists like Jiménez Moreno and León-Portilla (Mexico), Dibble and Anderson (United States), Kutscher (Germany), Ballesteros Gaibrois and Alcina Franch (Spain), Rudolf van Zantwijk (Holland), among others, formed an International Association of Nahuatlatos (Asociación, 1967, p. 1). In September, 1966, the 37th International Congress of Americanists (Argentina) recognized the body, and authorized it to seek funds to publish regularly a news and bibliographical bulletin, and to foster studies on Aztec history, culture, language, and related aspects of Mexican native history. "Now," its first *Report* states, "it remains to us only to function effectively, to carry out the cooperative and common goals that were our prime objective."

TOPICAL WRITINGS AND GENERAL STUDIES, 1950–66

Sahagún's role as protagonist of Indian views, relations between native and European culture, and the evangelization enterprise of the Franciscans form a continuing complex of recent writings. Luis Villoro (1950, pp. 29–77) analyzes Sahagún's providential views of natives and philosophy of history, among other matters, in a long chapter in a volume on *indigenismo*. Based chiefly (though not exclusively) on Sahagún materials, León-Portilla (1967) reconstructed the Aztec "world view" at Contact. To this general synthesis he has added several shorter essays, some of the more important of which appeared in a collected work (León-Portilla, 1958a). Arthur J. O. Anderson (1960), using Sahagún materials, discusses transculturation, especially through the Franciscan missionary efforts, concluding that it was generally successful because of their sympathetic understanding of native patterns, and willingness to preserve all that did not contravene Christian teachings.

Nicolau d'Olwer (1958) contributed an interesting and important essay to this theme, discussing convergences of native and Christian practices. He stressed Sahagún's criticisms of the first missionaries for their utopian outlook, which permitted pagan practices to lurk under Christian guises.

The problem of relationships between native and European is also analyzed by those working with the documentary materials. Dibble (1962) outlines Sahagún's ethnographic contribution, with special attention to relative degrees of European and aboriginal influences in the various parts of the HG, providing an estimate for each book. Among other similar inquiries are Garibay's (1953) discussion of Sahagún's methods of work and various texts which he did not utilize in the final work; the relations between the pictorial and text elements in the earlier and final versions were investigated by Dibble (1963). At the 37th International Congress of Americanists (Argentina) he presented a paper, "The role of the informants and the pictorial documents in Fray Sahagún's *Historia*," which was published (Dibble, 1968).

An historian of art, Donald Robertson, has also concerned himself with such relationships. He devoted a chapter of a book (Robertson, 1959, pp. 167–78) to detailed examination of pictorial elements in both PM and FC, distinguishing the native from the European traditions in the latter (the PM are all native), book by book. In a later article (1966) he recapitulates much well-known material about the Sahagún HG, and to some greater degree documents his thesis that it took for its general model Bartholomaeus [de Glanville] Anglicus' 13th-century encyclopedia, *De proprietatibus rerum* (generally based on Pliny) with some divergences from it because of peculiarly local problems in summarizing an exotic culture that had undergone conquest. Robertson's conclusions in both works are identical, that HG is in the tradition of late medieval encyclopedias (modified by Renaissance learning) and native culture, fusing these in a new way (Robertson, 1959, pp. 162–72; 1966, p. 626).

Despite manifest advance along many fronts in the publication of texts and special studies of Sahagún materials, one topic has received but small notice. Little or no important new information has recently been contributed to clarify various obscurities in the biography of Sahagún. Apart from the Nicolau d'Olwer volume (1952), other biographical publications have been based on well-known sources (Hedrick, 1959, 1969; León-Portilla, 1966c; Thompson, 1962). Charles E. Dibble (*in litt.*) has indicated that when the Anderson-Dibble translation program has been completed, he hopes to seek out further biographical data.

HISTORIA GENERAL: TRANSLATIONS AND STUDIES

Sahagún's major work is the *Historia general*, to which many other of his writings contributed. H. B. Nicholson discusses in Section B in detail the PM, among the first of these earlier approaches, with the important and surprising discovery that their connection with the final HG is much less direct and evolutionary than had previously been assumed. Here we shall omit paleographical and translation publications exclusively concerned with draft materials like the PM, treated above, in favor of providing an inventory of such materials and specialized studies related directly to the HG. The order of the books themselves provides a suitable subject index.[32]

The massive Anderson-Dibble enterprise outlined in Table 10 has, of course, dominated the field of translations. Not only has it provided a careful English version, but publication of the Nahuatl text has provided opportunities for independent translations of it into Spanish. For several books, notably III, VIII, and XI, there has been

[32] Much of the information summarize here is taken from Nicholson, 1960–70.

228

little or no translation and study beyond that by Anderson and Dibble.

Book I: The Gods

Burland's (1963) examination of the goddess Chalchiuhtlicue (chap. 11), comparing Sahagún with other sources, is only peripherally a Sahaguntine item. Thompson (1966a) does the same for Ayopechtle, blue-chinned goddess of maguey. A similar approach is also used by Fernández (1963) for Huitzilopochtli (bk. II, app. 1), in which León-Portilla translates into Spanish the relevant portion from the Nuttall copy of the Nahuatl Florentino. Merchants' gods are mentioned below (bk. IV).

Book II: Ceremonies

Sahagún's appendix 2 to book II, which lists the structures of the Tenochtitlan Templo Mayor, was translated from Nahuatl into Spanish (parallel columns), with introductory remarks and explanatory notes by López Austin (1966a). In 1958 Garibay provided translations, with important introductory materials, notes, and related materials from other manuscripts, of the 20 hymns which Sahagún included from PM as appendix 12, in Nahuatl only and without annotations. Less important is the posthumous publication of Barlow's remarks on Hymn 15, to Xipe Totec, following closely the 1905 Seler translation (Barlow, 1963). Rather speculative is Mendoza's attempt to deduce the rhythmic and tonal patterns of these cantos (Mendoza, 1958).

Book III: The Origin of the Gods

In 1960 López Austin published the paleography of the Nahuatl text, Spanish translation, and an analysis of the appendix. In it are described the three most important afterworlds of the native system of belief.

Book IV: The Soothsayers

A scholarly translation of the Royal Palace Library materials (Codices Matritenses) into German with full apparatus is provided by Schultze Jena (1950) as the final portion.

Considerable scholarly attention has been paid to the rituals of the merchants, found in chapters 16–19 (see below, bk. IX, for other aspects). Utilizing Schultze Jena's 1950 and 1952 translations, Lanczkowski (1962) studied them in detail. Garibay (1961) gives a Spanish translation of the Royal Palace Library manuscript version of chapters 16–19 as an appendix to his translations of other materials on merchants found in book IX. López Austin (1966b) provides Nahuatl-Spanish translations of chapters 31–32 (part), along with materials from book X, in a somewhat confused publication on magic and shamanism.

Book V: The Omens

Schultze Jena's volume in the *Quellenwerke* series gives a complete translation from Nahuatl of the Royal Palace manuscript to German, with Nahuatl text, glossary, and other apparatus (Schultze Jena, 1950, pp. 1–29), but he omits the important appendix found in FC. From the Nahuatl published by Anderson and Dibble (1957), López Austin (1969a) gives a Spanish translation, preceded by a scholarly introduction and followed by an illuminating commentary on the text.

Book VI: Rhetoric

In a series of works Thelma D. Sullivan (1963, 1965, 1966) partially closed the gap left by Anderson and Dibble, until their translation of book VI was published in 1969. Her English translation from Nahuatl covers prayer to Tlaloc (chap. 8), pregnancy, childbirth, deification of women who died in childbirth (chaps. 27–29) as well as proverbs, riddles, and figures of speech (chaps. 41–43). She provides the FC Nahuatl text and English translation in parallel columns, with notes. García Quintana (1969) discusses ritual bathing after childbirth, followed by the paleography of the Nahuatl (chaps. 36–38) and a Spanish translation with notes.

Anderson (1966) describes a manuscript in Bancroft Library (M–M 464) which contains Mexican sayings virtually identical to 40 in these same chapters 41 and 43, raising the question of whether the Bancroft version is a copy of the other, or whether both derive from a common (lost?) original. To these can be added translations into Spanish of the moral homilies of parents to children (chaps. 17–20) by León-Portilla (1960, 1961a), and Forest (1960). The latter gives Nahuatl paleography and French translation of chapter 19, a mother's exhortation to her daughter. Sahagún scanted these in the Spanish of FC. These and related materials of book VI are basic to reconstruction of Aztec value systems, as well as linguistic usages.

Book VII: Sun, Moon, Stars, and Binding the Year

The middle portion of Schultze Jena, 1950, gives Nahuatl-German translation of the entire book. Using the Anderson-Dibble paleography of the Nahuatl version of FC, López Austin (1963) translated into Spanish chapters 9–12, dealing with the New Fire ceremony held at 52-year intervals, adding explanatory notes.

Book VIII: Kings and Lords

Anderson (1948b) excerpted some parts of chapter 10 in an article on home diversions of Aztec nobles.

Book IX: The Merchants and Craftsmen

This book, dealing with economic life within the Aztec empire and with manufacture of luxury articles in metals, gems, and feathers, has always been of direct major concern to archaeologists from at least the time of Seler (1892 [no. 36]).

Schultze Jena (1952) translated from the Nahuatl of the Royal Academy manuscript those chapters (17 [1st part], 18, 19) of this section left untranslated by Seler. Garibay and McAfee (1956) translated chapters 15–

21 into Spanish. Schultze Jena (1952) and Garibay (1961) translated chapters 1–14, dealing with the merchants, from the Nahuatl of the Royal Academy manuscript respectively into German and Spanish, the latter adding extensive notes. Thompson (1966b) analyzes the merchants' gods listed in chapter 3, comparing with similar materials in book I, chapter 19, and with merchant god representations in Mesoamerican codices and archaeological remains. Dibble and Anderson (1967b) reprinted the English translation of chapters 16 and 17 in a well-illustrated article, companion piece to a similar reprint of chapters 18–21 (Dibble and Anderson, 1967a). Sahagún provided only the Nahuatl (no Spanish) of chapters 16, 17 (second half), 20, 21, and hence these various translations are of special importance.

Chapter 16, on goldworking, has been critically examined by several persons. Easby (1957) tested the descriptions against present knowledge and concluded that Sahagún and his informants were acute observers of processes not even now fully understood. The "lost wax" process therein described was also reviewed in detail by Anderson (1959). Utilizing the Sahagún description, Long (1964) reports that he was able successfully to produce copper bells, and suggests that the described method was probably the same for gold and copper. Emmerich (1965, pp. 177–83) reproduces in his survey of pre-Hispanic ornamental metallurgy the Anderson and Dibble translation of chapters 15 and 16. Of minor interest is the fact that chapter 16 even found its way into a handsome catalog of the famous collection of pre-Contact gold objects owned by the National Bank of Colombia (Acuña, 1950).

Book X: The People

Many topics occupy this book. It covers kinship, social structure, crafts, markets, anatomy, medical practices, and terminates

with an origin legend. Translations and studies of these various aspects have appeared. Chapter 11, treating of sorcerers and other "vicious folk," was translated into Spanish from the FC Nahuatl by López Austin (1966b). Aztec foods as reported by Sahagún was a topic investigated by Ramos Espinosa (1944).

Rivera (1941) made botanical identification of foods and herbs sold in markets (chaps 18, 19, 21, 22, 24–26), many of which also recur in book XI. She used and cited the Paso y Troncoso 1905 plates of the latter for her work.

Chapters 27 and 28, concerning anatomy, diseases, and cures, translated into German by Gall (1940), have also been investigated, especially by Dibble, Anderson, and the latter's colleague Spencer L. Rogers. General treatments of Aztec medicine are based on Sahagún and related texts by Vargas Castelazo (1954–55) and Guerra (1966). Dibble (1959) examined Aztec nomenclature for body parts (chap. 27) and noted some of the difficulties in translating them properly. Two articles by Rogers and Anderson (1965, 1966) pursued the theme by comparing data in chapter 27 with contemporary European knowledge of anatomy at the time of Sahagún, recording some 890 terms. Their conclusions were that Aztecs emphasized extremities, sensory and reproductive apparatus, and bones, but had an underdeveloped terminology for internal organs and trunk. Rivera (1941) botanically identified medicinal plants in chapter 28 (pars. 2–6). Dibble (1966) made a special study of the effectiveness of 11 herbs prescribed in chapter 28 to relieve fevers, with chemical analysis of them and their actual therapeutic value. In his study of this same chapter, Anderson (1961) concluded that despite the imputed importance of magic, the Aztecs had in fact developed a large body of useful empirical lore for curing, particularly related to herbs, setting of bones, emollients, and care of teeth. López Austin (1969b), comparing the same chapter with Códice Matritense (fols. 163–72v), gives copious notes to Nahuatl and Spanish versions and an etymological analysis of terms for medicinal plants. His second study (1971) is a continuation, using other portions of the Sahagún text.

Chapter 29, devoted to the ethnography of late pre-Hispanic central Mexico, is the subject of a doctoral thesis by Piña Chan (1970) and two inquiries by León-Portilla. In one León-Portilla (1963) translates from Nahuatl to Spanish the Aztec origin legend that also seeks to explain how the calendar and divinatory systems came into being. In the other (1966a) he discusses the value and importance of the ethnographic sketches of non-Aztec peoples. He concludes that Sahagún apparently utilized a standard questionnaire (which León-Portilla reconstructs) to give them a uniform format, but the data elicited probably represented the real basic attitudes of his Nahuatl informants toward their neighbors. To illustrate, León-Portilla translates (parallel columns of Nahuatl-Spanish) material on the Huastecs from the Royal Academy manuscript (fols. 187r–188r, 193v–194v).

Book XI: The Earthly Things

Book XI is a long summary of zoology, botany, and related topics of natural history. In a series of articles Martín del Campo (1938–41) made zoological identifications of animals, birds, and reptiles described in chapters 1–5. These have been included, modified, and extended in the Dibble-Anderson translation of this book.

No extended parallel botanical identifications of plants and herbs have yet been published for the following chapters. As previously mentioned in book X, many of those identified by Rivera (1941) also reappear here. Emily W. Emmaert (Trueblood), building on similar data she earlier published on the Badianus herbal, is identifying plants in book XI, utilizing comparative materials from Hernández and others.

The psychogenic drugs mentioned in chapter 7 are the special subject of continuing technical investigation on an international basis. Two short, illuminating articles were published by the Swedish anthropologist S. Henry Wassén (1960, 1961), especially discussing pharmacological findings on ololiuqui (Rivea corymbosa) by the Swiss scientist Albert Hoffman. This drug had earlier been the subject of a pioneer inquiry by Shultes (1941) and Osmond (1955). For 16th-century data Shultes relies heavily on Hernández, who took much of this material from Sahagún. López Austin (1965) also translated chapter 7 from FC Nahuatl into Spanish, with summary identification of the various drugs. The Italian Manganotti (1966) treated the most important hallucigens—peyotl, ololiuqui, teonanacatl—and translates various relevant passages from Sahagún into Italian. With replete bibliography R. Gordon Wasson (1966) discusses these, as well as other native hallucigens, with a supporting article by Albert Hoffman (1966) providing further pharmacological information than Wassén had earlier reported.

Anderson published twice (1948a, 1963) on materials in chapter 11, colors and pigments. The earlier is a popular treatment with some translation of text, but the more recent is a scholarly discussion which lists systematically colors named by Sahagún, with scientific determination of their sources. Castillo Farreras (1969) translates into Spanish and discusses chapter 12, par. 8, dealing with various types of roads.

Book XII: The Conquest of Mexico

As a transition from historical ethnology to the more formal Europeanized historiography of colonial Mexico, book XII has always been of special interest to historians as well as to anthropologists and archaeologists. It is the subject of a summary article by Luis Leal (1955, 1956) and another by Cline (1969). Large portions were excerpted and, with other related materials giving native views of the Conquest from Indian prose and pictorial sources, appeared under the editorship of León-Portilla and Garibay as a teaching anthology for university students (León-Portilla and Garibay, 1959). A useful English translation of this work by Lysander Kemp appeared in English as *The Broken Spears* (León-Portilla and Garibay, 1962). The scholarly edition of Sahagún's 1578 Nahuatl text in English remains Anderson and Dibble, 1955. Garibay, in his 1956 edition of HG (vol. 4), gives his Spanish translation of the same Nahuatl of FC. Cline has completed the transcription and translation of the Spanish text of FC (which differs from texts published on the basis of copies of the Madrid manuscript) and translation of the 1585 revision published by Bustamante (1840).

MINOR TEXTS

Properly, main scholarly attention has emphasized the HG and its prototypes in the PM and the *Manuscrito de Tlatelolco*. In addition there has been a small increment of minor texts. Lehmann's 1938 translation from Nahuatl to German of the "Colloquios," previously known only in Nahuatl and Spanish (Pou y Martí, 1924; Nuttall, 1927) appeared posthumously, delayed by World War II (Lehmann, 1949). The trilingual vocabulary (Nahuatl-Latin-Spanish) of about 1580 in the Newberry Library (Ayer MS 1478), attributed to Sahagún, was made available on microfilm in 1957 by the University of Chicago, without commentary (Aztec Manuscript Dictionary, 1957).

REFERENCES

ACOSTA SAIGNES, M., ed.
1946   Fray Bernardino de Sahagún: Historia general de las cosas de Nueva España. Noticia preliminar, bibliografía, notas, revisión y guía para estudiar a Sahagún. 3 vols. Mexico.

ACUÑA, LUIS ALBERTO
1950   El trabajo indígena del oro. *In* El Museo de Oro. Banco de la República, Ediciones conmemorativas de la fundación del Banco de la República en su XXV aniversario, 1923–48, 1948 [i.e., 1950], pp. 29–37. Bogota.

AGUIRRE, PORFIRIO, trans.
1950–51   Primeros memoriales de Tepepulco. Anónimos indígenas. Traducidos del nahuatl al español por Porfirio Aguirre. Vols. 1–4, unpaged. Vargas Rea, Col. Amatlacuilotl. Mexico.

ALCOCER, IGNACIO
1935   Apuntes sobre la antigua México-Tenochtitlan. PAIGH, Pub. 14. Tacubaya, D.F.
1938   Dos estudios sobre Sahagún: 1, Las comidas de los antiguos mexicanos; 2, Consideraciones sobre la medicina azteca. *In* Ramírez Cabañas, 1938, 3:365–82.

ANALES DE TECAMACHALCO
1892   Anales de Tecamachalco. *In* J. García Icazbalceta, *Nueva colección de documentos para la historia de México*, 5:272–77.

ANDERSON, ARTHUR J. O.
1948a   Pre-Hispanic Aztec colorists. *El Palacio*, 55:20–27.
1948b   Home diversions of the Aztec chief. *El Palacio*, 55:125–27.
1959   Sahagún's informants on the waste wax gold-casting process. *El Palacio*, 66:155–58.
1960   Sahagún's Náhuatl texts as indigenist documents. *ECN*, 2:31–42.
1961   Medical practices of the Aztecs. *El Palacio*, 68:113–18.
1963   Materiales colorantes prehispánicos. *ECN*, 4:73–83.
1966   Refranes en un santoral en mexicano. *ECN*, 6:55–61.

—— AND CHARLES E. DIBBLE
1950–70　See Article 14C, Table 10.

ASOCIACIÓN
1967　Informe. Asociación internacional de Nahuatlatos. Mexico City and Madrid.

AZTEC MANUSCRIPT DICTIONARY
1957　Sahagún, Bernardino. Aztec manuscript dictionary. [Ca. 1590. Newberry Library, Ayer MS 1478.] University of Chicago Library, *Microfilm collection of manuscripts on Middle American cultural anthropology*, no. 37. Chicago. See Butler, 1937.

BALLESTEROS GAIBROIS, MANUEL, AND OTHERS
1962　Los manuscritos matritenses de Sahagún. XXXIV International Congress of Americanists (Vienna, 1960), *Proceedings*, pp. 226–43.

1964　Códices matritenses de la *Historia general de las cosas de la Nueva España*. Trabajo realizado por el Seminario de Estudios Americanistas, bajo la dirección de Manuel Ballesteros Gaibrois. 2 vols. *Col. Chimalistac de libros y documentos acerca de la Nueva España*, 19/20. Madrid.

BANDELIER, FANNY, trans.
1932　Bernardino de Sahagún, a history of ancient Mexico, 1547–1577, translated by . . . from the Spanish version of Carlos María Bustamante. Vol. 1 [bks. 1–4; no more published.] Fisk University Social Science Series. Nashville, Tenn.

BANDINI, A. M.
1793　Catalogus manuscriptorum qui nuper in Laurentianam translati sunt. Tomus 3 et ultimus. Florence.

BARLOW, ROBERT H.
1963　Remarks on a Náhuatl hymn. *Tlalocan*, 4/2:185–92.

BAUDOT, GEORGES
1969　Fray Rodrigo de Sequera, avocat du diable pour une histoire interdite. *Caravelle*, 12:47–82. Toulouse.

BIBLIOTHECA INLUSTRIS
1842　Bibliotheca inlustris ac praehonorabilis domini Edvardi Vicecomte de Kingsborough. . . . Catalogue of the rare and valuable library. . . . Dublin.

BIONDELLI, B., ed.
1858　Evangeliarium, epistolarium et lectionarium aztecum sive mexicanum ex antiquo codice mexicano nuper reper-
to depromtum cum praefatione, interpretatione admonitionibus, glossario edidit. Milan.

BOCK, HANS-JOACHIM
1959　La Biblioteca Iberoamericana. *In* Thiele, 1959, pp. 38–41.

BRINTON, D. G.
1890　Rig-Veda americanus. Sacred songs of the ancient Mexicans with a gloss in Nahuatl. Ed. with a paraphrase, note and vocabulary. *Library of Aboriginal American Literature*, 8. Philadelphia.

BURLAND, COTTIE A.
1963　The goddess Chalchihuitlicue as an expression of an archetype in ancient Mexican religion. VI Congrès International des Sciences Anthropologiques et Ethnologiques (Paris, 1960), *Compte rendu*, 2:373–76.

BUSTAMANTE, CARLOS M.
See Article 21, Appendix A.

BUTLER, R. L.
1937　A check list of manuscripts in the Edward E. Ayer collection. Chicago.

CAMPOS, RUBEN M.
1936　La producción literaria de los Aztecas. Tall. Graf del Museo de Arqueología, Historia e Etnografía, XI. Mexico.

CASTILLO FARRERAS, VICTOR M.
1969　Caminos del mundo Nahuatl. *ECN*, 8:175–87.

CHARENCEY, H. DE
1899　L'historien Sahagún et les migrations mexicaines. Louvain.

CHAVERO, ALFREDO
See Article 21, Appendix E.

CHAVEZ OROZCO, LUIS, ed.
1929　[Bernardino de Sahagún.] La conquista. Sec. de Relaciones Exteriores, *Cuadernos populares*, ser. 3, nos. 1–2. Mexico.

CLINE, HOWARD F.
1964　The *Relaciones Geográficas* of the Spanish Indies, 1577–1586. HAHR, 44:341–74.

1969　Notes on Sahagún's History of the Conquest: *General History*, Book XII. *In* Homenaje á José Miranda, Colegio de México. Mexico. In press.

1971a　Missing and variant prologues and dedications in Sahagún's *Historia General*: texts and English translations. *ECN*, 9:237–51.

1971b　[with Mary W. Cline] Ancient calendars and early historical chronologies of Mexico: critical and revisionist ethnohistorical studies. In preparation.

COMAS, JUAN
1954 Los Congresos Internacionales de Americanistas: síntesis histórica e índice bibliográfico general, 1875–1952. Instituto Indigenista Interamericano, Ediciones especiales. Mexico.

DIBBLE, CHARLES E.
1959 Nahuatl names for body parts. *ECN*, 1:27–30.
1962 Spanish influence on the Náhuatl text of Sahagún's "Historia." XXXIV International Congress of Americanists (Vienna, 1960), *Proceedings*, pp. 244–47.
1963 Glifos fonéticos del Códice Florentino. *ECN*, 4:5–60.
1966 La base científica para el estudio de las yerbas medicinales de los aztecas. XXXVI Congreso Internacional de Americanistas (Seville, 1964), *Actas y Memorias*, 2:63–67.
1968 Sahagún and his informants. XXXVII International Congress of Americanists (Argentina, 1966), *Actas y Memorias*, 3:145–53.

—— AND ARTHUR J. O. ANDERSON
1950–70 *See* Article 14C, Table 10.
1967a The feather merchants, translated by Charles E. Dibble and Arthur J. O. Anderson from the 16th century Aztec manuscript by Fray Bernardino de Sahagún. *Craft Horizons*, 27/2:18–23.
1967b The goldworkers and lapidaries, translated by Charles E. Dibble and Arthur J. O. Anderson from the 16th century Aztec manuscript by Fray Bernardino de Sahagún. *Craft Horizons*, 27/5:16–21.

—— AND NORMA B. MIKKELSEN
1971 La olografía de Fray Bernardino de Sahagún. *ECN*, 9:231–36.

DONVEZ, JACQUES
1957 Tenochtitlan México descrito por Fray Bernardino de Sahagún. Collection Ibero-Americaine. Paris.

EASBY, DUDLEY T., JR.
1957 Sahagún y los orfebres precolombinos de México. INAH, *Anales*, 9:85–117.

EMMERICH, ANDRE
1965 Sweat of the sun and tears of the moon: Gold and silver in pre-Columbian art. University of Washington. Seattle.

FERNÁNDEZ, JUSTINO
1963 Una aproximación a Coyolxauhqui. *ECN*, 4:37–53.

FERNÁNDEZ DEL CASTILLO, FRANCISCO
1964 La medicina de Tlatelolco y Fray Bernardino de Sahagún. *Gaceta Medica de México*, 94:217–29.

FOREST, JACQUELINE
1960 Discours de la mére Aztèque à sa petite fille. *ECN*, 2:149–61.

GALL, AUGUST F. VON
1940 Medizinische Bücher (tici-amatl) der alten Azteken in der ersten Zeit der Conquista. *Quellen und Studien zur Geschichte der Naturwissenschaft und Medizin*, 7:4–5, 81–299.

GARCÍA ICAZBALCETA, JOAQUÍN
See Article 21, Appendix D.

GARCÍA QUINTANA, JOSEFINA
1969 El baño ritual entre los nahuas según el Códice Florentino. *ECN*, 8:189–213.

GARIBAY K., ANGEL M.
1937 La poesía lírica azteca, esbozo de síntesis crítica. Mexico.
1940 Llave de Náhuatl. Colección de trozos clásicos, con gramática y vocabulario para utilidad de los principantes. Otumba, Mexico.
1944–47 Paralipómenos de Sahagún. *Tlalocan*, 1/4:307–13 (1944) [Agüeros y Suenos], 2/2:167–74 (1946) [Hombres malos], 2/3: 235–54 (1947) [Hombres malos y mujeres malas].
1948 [ed.] Relación breve de las fiestas de los dioses: Fray Bernardino de Sahagún. *Tlalocan*, 2:289–320.
1952 Versiones discutibles del texto náhuatl de Sahagún. *Tlalocan* 3:187–90.
1953 Fray Bernardino de Sahagún: Relación de los textos que no aprovechó un su obra. Su método de investigación. Sociedad Folklórica de México. Aportaciones a la investigación folklórica de México. *Cultura mexicana*, 2. Mexico.
1953–54 Historia de la literatura Nahuatl. 2 vols. Mexico.
1956 [ed.] Historia general de las cosas de Nueva España, escrita por Fr. Bernardino de Sahagún Franciscano y fundada en la documentación en lengua mexicana recogida por los mismos naturales. La dispuso para la prensa

en esta nueva edición, con numeración, anotaciones y apéndices [por] Angel María Garibay K. 4 vols. Biblioteca Porrúa, 8, 9, 10, 11. Mexico.

1958 [ed. and trans.] Veinte himnos sacros de los nahuas (Fray Bernardino de Sahagún). *Fuentes indígenas de la cultura náhuatl; informantes de Sahagún*, 2. Mexico.

1961 [ed. and trans.] Vida económica de Tenochtitlan. 1. Pochtecayotl (Arte de Traficar) por Bernardino de Sahagún. *Fuentes indígenas de la cultura náhuatl; informantes de Sahagún*, 3. Mexico.

1969 Historia general de las cosas de Nueva España. Numeración, anotaciones y apéndices de Angel María Garibay K. 4 vols. Biblioteca Porrúa, 8, 9, 10, 11. Mexico. Re-issue of Garibay, 1956.

—— AND BYRON MCAFEE
1956 Translation of Caps. I–XXII of Book XII. *In* Garibay, 1956, 3:65–86. [Translated from original Nahuatl, 1950.]

GLASS, JOHN B.
1960 *Review of* Robertson, 1959. *American Antiquity*, 26:128–29.

GUERRA, FRANCISCO
1966 Aztec medicine. *Medical History*, 10/4:315–38. London.

HEDRICK, BASIL C.
1959 Bernardino de Sahagún (ca. 1499–1590). School of Inter-American Studies, *Grandes Figuras de América*, 4. University of Florida. Gainesville, Florida.

1969 Fray Bernardino de Sahagún: historian and ethnologist of the New World. Latin American Institute, *Specialia*, 1:50–56. Southern Illinois University. Carbondale.

HELLBROM, ANNA-BRITTA
1967 La participación cultural de las mujeres: indias y mestizas en el México precortesiano y postrevolucionario. Ethnografiska Museet. Stockholm.

HOFFMAN, ALBERT
1966 The active principles of the seed of *Rivea corymbosa* (L.) Hall F. (ololiuhqui, badoh) and *Ipomoea Tricolor* Cav. (badoh negro). *In* Pompa y Pompa, 1966, pp. 349–57.

IGUÍNIZ, J. B.
1917 [i.e. 1918] El calendario mexicano atribuído a Fray Bernardino de Saha-

gún. BNMex, *Boletín*, 6:189–222.

JAHN, JANHEINZ, ed.
1962 Das Herz auf dem Opferstein; Aztekentexte. Aus der Ursprache übertragen von Eduard Seler ausgewählt und mit einem Vorwort verschen von Janheinz Jahn. Dusseldorf.

JIMÉNEZ MORENO, W.
1938a Fray Bernardino de Sahagún y su obra. *In* Ramírez Cabañas, 1938, 1:xiii–lxxxi.

1938b Fray Bernardino de Sahagún y su obra. [Separate reprint from Ramírez Cabañas, 1938, paged in arabic.] Mexico.

JOURDANET, D., AND RÉMI SIMÉON, eds.
1880 Histoire générale des choses de la Nouvelle Espagne, par le R. P. Fray Bernardino de Sahagún. Traduite et annotée. . . . Paris.

KINGSBOROUGH, LORD [EDWARD KING], ed.
1830–48 [Sahagún]. Historia universal de las cosas de Nueva España. *In* Antiquities of Mexico, 9 vols.: 5:345–493 [bk. 6, chaps. 1–40], 7:i–vii, 1–447 [bks. 1–5; bk. 6, chaps. 41–43; bks. 7–12]. London. [See Bibliotheca inlustris, 1842. LC also has an 1831 ed.]

KUNIKE, HUGO
1922 Aztekische märchen nach deno Spanishdren deo Sahagún. Spitzbogen verlag. Berlin.

1961 Aztekische märchen nach deno Spanishdren deo Sahagún. [New edition of 1922.] Spitzbogen verlag. Berlin.

KUTSCHER, GERDT
1959 Los estudios americanos en Berlin. *In* Thiele, 1959:34–37.

1961 Ein Stammbaum des königlichen Geschichtes von Tetzcoco. *Baessler-Archiv*, n.s., 9 (2):233–63.

LANCZKOWSKI, GÜNTER
1962 Die religöse Stellung der aztekischen Grosskaufleute. *Saeculum: Jahrbuch für Universalgeschichte*, 13:346–62. München, Germany.

LEAL, LUIS
1955 El libro XII de Sahagún. *Historia mexicana*, 5:184–210.

1956 El libro XII de Sahagún: una rectificación. *Historia mexicana*, 5:623.

LEHMANN, WALTER
1908 Der sogenannte Kalendar Ixtlilxochitls. Ein Beitrag zur Kenntnis der achtzehn Jahresfeste der Mexikaner.

Anthropos, 3:988–1004. Vienna.

1938 Die Geschichte der Königreiche von Colhuacan und Mexico. Ibero-amerikanisches institut, Berlin, *Quellenwerke zur alten Geschichte Amerikas*, vol. 1. Stuttgart and Berlin.

1949 [ed.] Sterbende Götter und christlische Heilsbotikschaft. Wechselreden indianischer Vornehmer und spanischer Glaubenapostel in Mexiko 1524, "Colloquios y doctrina Christiana," des Fray Bernardino de Sahagún aus dem Jahre 1564. *Quellenwerke zur alten Geschichte Amerikas*, vol. 3. Stuttgart and Berlin.

LEÓN, MARTÍN DE

1611 Camino del cielo en lengva mexicana. . . . Cõpuesta por el P. F. Martín de Leõ, de la ordẽ de Predicadores. . . . Mexico.

LEÓN, NICOLAS

1938 Ensayo de nomenclatura e identificación de las láminas 98 a 138 del Libro II de la "Historia de las cosas de Nueva España." *In* Ramírez Cabañas, 1938, 3: 327–64.

LEÓN-PORTILLA, MIGUEL

1956 La filosofía nahuatl. Instituto Indigenista Interamericano. Mexico.

1958a Siete ensayos sobre cultura náhuatl. UNAM, *Ediciones filosofía y letras*, 31. Mexico.

1958b [ed. and trans.] Textos de los informantes de Sahagún: Ritos, sacerdotes y atavíos de los dioses. Introducción, paleografía, traducción y notas. UNAM, Instituto de Historia, Pub. 42. Mexico.

1960 La educación del niño entre los nahuas: consejos a una niña náhuatl. *Nicaragua Indígena*, 2/31:14–18 (Organo del Instituto Indigenista Nacional). Managua.

1961a Consejos de un padre náhuatl a su hija. *América Indígena*, 21:339–43.

1961b [i.e. 1964] Visión de los vencidos: relaciones indígenas de la conquista. . . . 3d ed. UNAM. Mexico.

1963 El mito náhuatl de los orígenes de la cultura. UNAM, *Universidad de México*, 18/1:35–377.

1966a Los huaxtecos según los informantes de Sahagún. *ECN*, 5:15–29.

1966b La filosofía náhuatl estudiada en sus fuentes. Prólogo de Angel María Garibay K. UNAM, Seminario de Cultura Náhuatl, Monog. 10. Mexico.

1966c Significación de la obra de Fray Bernardino de Sahagún. *ECN*, 1:13–27.

1967 La institución de la familia náhuatl prehispánica: un antecedente cultural. *Cuadernos americanos*, 26(5):143–61.

1968 [ed. and trans.] Ritos, sacerdotes y atavíos de los dioses. UNAM, Instituto de Historia, Seminario de Cultura Nahuatl [Guadalajara, Mexico, Edmundo Aviña Levy, ed.]. (Fuentes indígenas de la cultura nahuatl. Textos de los informantes de Sahagún, 1. Instituto de Historia, Pub. 42.) Reissue of León-Portilla, 1958b.

—— AND ANGEL MARÍA GARIBAY K., eds. and trans.

1959 Visión de los vencidos: relaciones indígenas de la conquista. Introducciones, selección y notas: Miguel León-Portilla; versión de textos nahuas: Angel M. Garibay K.; ilustraciones de los códices: Alberto Beltrán. UNAM, *Bib. estudiante universitario*, 81. Mexico.

1962 The broken spears: The Aztec account of the conquest of Mexico. Translated from Nahuatl by Angel María Garibay K.; English translation by Lysander Kemp. [Translation of León-Portilla and Garibay, 1959.] Boston.

LLANOS, ADOLFO

1882 Sahagún y su historia de México. *El Día* (Madrid, Dec. 11), reprinted in MNA, *Anales*, 3:71–76 (1886) [*See* Nicolau d'Olwer, 1952, p. 195, n. 61.]

LONG, STANLEY

1964 *Cire-perdue* copper casting in pre-Columbian Mexico: an experimental approach. *American Antiquity*, 30:189–92.

LÓPEZ AUSTIN, ALFREDO

1960 Los caminos de los muertos. *ECN*, 2:141–48.

1963 Fiesta del fuego nuevo, según el Códice Florentino. UNAM, *Anuario de Historia*, 3:73–91.

1965 Descripción de estupefacientes en el Códice Florentino. UNAM, *Universidad de México*, 19/5:17–18.

1966a El Templo Mayor de Mexico Tenochtitlan según los informantes indígenas. *ECN*, 5:75–102.

1966b Los temacpalitotique: brujos, profanadores, ladrones y violadores. *ECN*, 6:97–117.

1969a Augurios y abusiones: Introducción, versión, y notas. UNAM, *Cultura Nahuatl: Fuentes*, 7 (Textos de los informantes de Sahagún, 4). Mexico.

1969b De las enfermedades del cuerpo humano y de las medicinas contra ellas. *ECN*, 8:51–121.

1971 De las plantas medicinales y de otras cosas medicinales. *ECN*, 9:125–230.

1972 Textos acerca de las partes del cuerpo humano y de las enfermedades medicinas en los Primeros Memoriales de Sahagún. *ECN*, 10:129–53.

McQUOWN, NORMAN A.
1958 The *General History of the Things of New Spain*, by Bernardino de Sahagún. *HAHR*, 38:235–38.

MADRAZO, PEDRO DE
1885 Resumen de los acuerdos y tareas de la Real Academia de la Historia desde 30 de abril de 1882 hasta igual día de 1884. RAH, *Memorias*, 10.

MANGANOTTI, DONATELLA
1966 La triade sacra degli antichi Aztechi. *L'Universo: Rivista bimestrale dell' Istituto Geográfico Militare*, 46:501–36. Firenze, Italy.

MARTÍN DEL CAMPO, RAFAEL
1938–41 Ensayo de interpretación del libro undécimo de la *Historia general de las cosas de Nueva España* de Fray Bernardino de Sahagún. UNAM, Instituto de Biología, *Anales*, 9:379–91 (reptiles); 11:385–408 (birds); 12:489–506 (mammals).

MAZARI, IGNACIO
1927 Un canto arcaico. MNA, *Anales*, ep. 4, 5:55–59.

MENDOZA, VINCENTE T.
1958 El ritmo de los *Cantares mexicanos* recolectados por Sahagún. XXXI Congreso Internacional de Americanistas, *Miscellanea Paul Rivet Dictata*, 2:777–86. Mexico.

MENGIN, ERNST
1964 Los resultados principales y fines de la filología azteca. XXXV Congreso Internacional de Americanistas (Mexico, 1962), *Actas y Memorias*, 3:451–78.

MONTEJO Y ROBREDO, BONIFACIO
1882 Procedencia americana de las bubas. IV Congreso Internacional de Americanistas (Madrid, 1881), *Actas*, 1:334–416. Madrid.

NICHOLSON, H. B.
1960–70 Handbook of Latin American Studies, 1960, pp. 30–42; 1961, pp. 57–70; 1962, pp. 56–66; 1963, pp. 50–61; 1965, pp. 75–96; 1967, pp. 156–99; 1970, pp. 60–103. [Ethnohistory: Mesoamerica section.]

NICOLAU D'OLWER, L.
1952 Historiadores de América. Fray Bernardino de Sahagún (1499–1590). PAIGH, Comisión de Historia, Pub. 142. Mexico.

1957 De nuevo Sahagún. *Historia mexicana*, 6:615–19.

1958 Comments on the evangelization of the New World. *The Americas*, 14:399–410.

NUTTALL, ZELIA
1921 Francisco Cervantes de Salazar: biographical notes. *Journal de la Société des Américanistes de Paris* (n.s.), 13:59–90.

1927 [ed.] El libro perdido de los pláticas o coloquios de los doce misioneros de México. *RMEH*, 1, supplement, pp. 101–55. [Reissue of Pou y Martí, 1924]

OLIGER, LIVARIO
1936 Sahagún, O.F.M. e una sua vita di S. Bernardino in lengua nahuatl. Estratto dal *Bullettino di studi bernardiniani*, anno 2, no. 3. Siena.

1942 [ed.] Breve compendio de los ritos idolátricos de Nueva España, auctore Bernardino de Sahagún, O.F.M. Rome.

OLPIN, A. RAY, AND BOAZ LONG
[1950] Temporary Foreword [to Anderson and Dibble, 1950]. n.p. Santa Fe.

OSMOND, HUMPHREY
1955 Ololiuqui, the ancient Aztec narcotic: Remarks on the effects of *Rivea corymbosa* (ololiuqui). *Journal of Mental Science*, 101:526–37.

PASO Y TRONCOSO, F. DEL
See Article 21, Appendix F.

PAZ, I., ed.
1890–95 Historia general de las cosas de Nueva España. *Bib. mexicana*, 22–25. Mexico.

PEÑAFIEL, A.
1890 Monumentos del arte mexicano antiguo: Ornamentación, mitología, atributos y monumentos. 3 vols. Berlin.

PIÑA CHAN, ROMÁN
1970 Arqueología y tradición histórica: un testimonio de los informantes de Sahagún. UNAM, Tesis de Doctorado, 1970 (136 pp., illus.). Mexico.

POMPA Y POMPA, ANTONIO, ed.
1966 Summa anthropologica: En homenaje a Roberto J. Weitlaner. Mexico.

POU Y MARTÍ, J., ed.
1924 El libro perdido de las pláticas y coloquios de los doce primeros misioneros de México. *Miscelanea Fr. Ehrle*, 3:281–335. Biblioteca Vaticana. Rome.

RAMÍREZ, JOSÉ F.
See Article 21, Appendix B.

RAMÍREZ CABAÑAS, J., ed.
1938 Fray Bernardino de Sahagún: Historia general de las cosas de Nueva España. 5 vols. Mexico.

RAMOS ESPINOSA, A.
1944 Las cosas de la alimentación en la Historia de Fray Bernardino de Sahagún. SMGE, *Boletín*, 59:5–17.

RIVERA M., IRENE
1941 Ensayo de interpretación botánica del Libro X de la Historia de Sahagún. UNAM, Instituto de Biología, *Anales*, 12:439–88.

ROBERTSON, DONALD
1959 Mexican manuscript painting of the early colonial period: the Metropolitan Schools. Yale University Press. New Haven.
1966 The sixteenth century Mexican encyclopedia of Fray Bernardino de Sahagún. *Cahiers d'Histoire Mondiale*, 9:617–27. Neuchatel, Switzerland.

ROGERS, SPENCER L., AND ARTHUR J. O. ANDERSON
1965 El inventario anatómico Sahaguntino. *ECN*, 5:115–22.
1966 La terminología anatómica de los mexicas precolombinos. XXXVI Congreso Internacional de Americanistas (Seville, 1964), *Actas y Memorias*, 2:69–76.

ROSELL, CAYETANO
1882 Informe. Historia universal de las cosas de la Nueva España por el R. P. Fr. Bernardino de Sahagún. Academia Real de la Historia, *Boletín*, 2:181–85.

SCHMIDT, P. W., ed.
1906 Fray Bernardino de Sahagún, O.F.M. "Un breve compendio de los ritos idolátricos que los yndios desta Nueva España usaban en el tiempo de su infidelidad" nach dem vaticanischen Geheimarchiv aufbewahrten Original zum ersten Mal herausgegeben. *Anthropos, Ephemeris internacionalis ethnologica et linguistica*, 1:320–38. Salzburg.

SCHULTES, RICHARD EVANS
1941 A contribution to our knowledge of *Rivea corymbosa*, the narcotic ololiuqui of the Aztecs. Harvard University, Botanical Museum. Cambridge, Mass.

SCHULTZE JENA, LEONHARD, ed.
1950 Wahrsagerei, Himmelskunde und Kalender der alten Azteken, sus dem aztekischen Urtext B. de Sahagún's. *Quellenwerke zur alten Geschichte Amerikas*, 4. Stuttgart and Berlin.
1952 Gliederung des alt-Aztekischen Volks in Familie, Stand und Beruf. Aus dem Aztekischen Urtext Bernardino de Sahagún's. *Quellenwerke zur alten Geschichte Amerikas*, 5.

SELER, EDUARD G.
1901 Die Ausgrabungen am Orte des Haupttempels in Mexiko. *Mittheilungen der Anthropologischen in Wien*, 31 (3d ser., 1):113–37. Reprinted (much enlarged) in Seler, 1902–23, 2:767–904.
See Article 20, Appendix.

SELER-SACHS, CAECILIE
See Article 20, Appendix, no. 268.

SMISOR, GEORGE T.
1943 New translation of Sahagún. *Tlalocan*, 1/2:164.

SULLIVAN, THELMA D.
1963 Nahuatl proverbs, conundrums, and metaphors, collected by Sahagún. *ECN*, 4:93–177.
1965 A prayer to Tlaloc. *ECN*, 5:39–55.
1966 Pregnancy, childbirth and the deification of the women who died in childbirth: texts from the Florentine Codex, Book VI, Folios 128v–143v. *ECN*, 6:63–95.
1972 The arms and insignia of the Mexica. *ECN*, 10:155–93.

THIELE, ALBERT, ed.
1959 Berlin: Piedra de Toque del Mundo Libre, textos documentos. Hamburg.

THOMPSON, J. ERIC S.
1962 Sahagún, first ethnologist of the New World. *El Palacio*, 69:65–68.
1966a Ayopechtli, an aspect of the Nahua goddess of the maguey. XXXVI

Congreso Internacional Americanistas (Seville, 1964), *Actas y Memorias*, 2:103–06.

1966b Merchant gods of Middle America. *In* Pompa y Pompa, 1966, pp. 159–85.

TORO, A.
1922 Importancia etnográfica y linguistica de la obra del P. Fray Bernardino de Sahagún. XX Congreso Internacional de Americanistas (Rio de Janeiro, 1922), *Annaes*, 2/2:263–77 (1928). [Also in MNA, *Anales*, ep. 4, 2:1–18 (1924).]

TORQUEMADA, JUAN DE
See Article 17, Appendix A.

TORRUBIA, JOSEPH
1756 Chrónica de la seraphica religión del glorioso patriarcha San Francisco de Assis. . . . Novena parte. Rome.

VARGAS CASTELAZO, MANUEL
1954–55 La patología y la medicina entre la mexica. *Revista Mexicana de Estudios Antropológicos*, 14:119–43.

VARGAS REA, LUIS, ed.
1944 Colloquios y doctrina christiana con que los doze frailes de San Francisco embiados por el papa Adriano sesto y por el emperador Carlos quinto convertieron a los indios de la Nueva España, por Fray Bernardino de Sahagún. [Reprinted in Nuttall, 1927.] Mexico.

VILLORO, LUIS
1950 Los grandes momentos del indigenismo en México. El Colegio de México. Mexico.

WASSÉN, S. HENRY
1960 Glimtar av aztekisk medicin. Medicinhistoriska Museet, *Medicinhistorisk Arsbok*, pp. 1–16. Stockholm.
1961 Fran de gamla aztekerns och moderna cunaindianernas medicinska värld. *Särtryck ur Farmacevtisk Revy*, 60/132:1–10. Stockholm.

WASSON, R. GORDON
1966 Ololiuhqui and other hallucigens of Mexico. *In* Pompa y Pompa, 1966, pp. 329–48.

15. Antonio de Herrera, 1549-1625

MANUEL BALLESTEROS GAIBROIS

Son of Rodrigo de Tordesillas and Inés de Herrera, Antonio de Herrera y Tordesillas was born in Cuellar, in the present province of Segovia, Spain. The exact date of his birth is not known, but since the time of Nicolás Antonio (1783), who said Herrera was 76 years old at his death in 1625, it is generally fixed at 1549. Little is known of his youth.[1]

As secretary and later as agent for Príncipe Vespasiano Gonzaga, Duke of Sabionetta, Herrera accompanied him to Italy in 1570. Until Gonzaga's death, Herrera aided him in various posts in Italy and Spain, at the same time developing a wide network of friendships among Spanish grandees and at the court. In 1581 he married a wealthy Navarrese, Juana de Esparza y Artieda, whose family funds permitted Herrera to begin acquisition of properties in Madrid. Doña Juana died in 1584; two years later their daughter Juana also died.

On recommendations from Gonzaga, before his death in 1586, Herrera entered royal service, where he spent the remaining years of his life. Given various posts, he engaged in writing a rather wide variety of histories and chronicles and translating works from Italian. Finally, in 1596 he achieved a main ambition when he was named Major Chronicler of the Indies of the Royal and Supreme Council of the Indies. In the same year he was remarried, to María de Torres. To his title of Chronicler of the Indies was added that of Chronicler of Castile in 1598. For a short time he moved with the court to Valladolid (1601–05) but thereafter returned and remained in Madrid.

Herrera was involved in a number of political intrigues, especially those related to Italian-Spanish politics. In one instance these activities led to his being exiled and jailed (1609–11), but his various posts and salaries, of much importance to him, were not affected. Although his major work, *Hi-*

[1] Ed. note: This is a much reduced version of an article in Spanish which Dr. Ballesteros Gaibrois contracted to write at an early stage in the development of this Guide. Later changes in editorial plans and in available space made this reduction necessary. The English summary has been made by the Volume Editor. Dr. Ballesteros Gaibrois expects to publish the fully documented original in Spanish.

Fɪɢ. 1—PORTRAIT OF ANTONIO DE HERRE-RA Y TORDESILLAS ON TITLE PAGE OF *DESCRIPCIÓN DE LAS INDIAS* (1601)

storia general de los hechos . . . , appeared between 1601 and 1615, he continued to write until his death March 27, 1625.[2]

Wᴏʀᴋs (see app. A)

Most of the many works written by Antonio de Herrera y Tordesillas have no relevance to the ethnohistory of Middle America. As we shall see, even his major publication on America, *Historia general de los hechos* . . . , makes only a very small contribution to it.

One body of his published materials included translations from Italian. Thus in 1588 appeared his Spanish version of Juan Tomás Minandoy's *History of the Turco-Persian Wars*, and in 1592 a similar translation from Italian of Juan Botero, *Ten Books on the Basis of the State*. In 1607 he also translated from Italian Cardinal de Fermo's *Spiritual Battle and Art of Serving God*.

His own historical works began with his publication in 1589 of a history of Scotland and England during the life of Mary Stuart,

followed in 1591 by a history of Portugal and the conquest of the Azores, 1582–83. In 1598 appeared his history of France, 1585–94, and also a memoir on jurisdictional disputes in Milan, 1595–98.

Years 1601–12 witnessed appearance of a large three-part "General History of the World" during the reign of Philip II. The first part covered the years 1553–70; the second, 1571–85; and the third, 1585–98. In effect continuing what for him was contemporary history he wrote a treatise on Aragon and its political problems in 1591–92 that was published in 1612. A Latin work appeared (1622a), a description of the American Indies, to which were appended descriptions of voyages by Jacob le Maire and Magellan. His final work, published in 1624 (a year before his death), was a set of commentaries on Spanish, French, Venetian and other Italian explorers and sailors from 1281 to 1559.

Posthumously appeared a Spanish translation of his 1622 description of the Indies (1728–30) at the hands of Nicolás Rodríguez Franco, the same editor-printer who had reissued Torquemada in 1725. In 1804 various writings by Herrera, especially eulogizing Cristóbal Vaca de Castro, a member of the Council of the Indies and Governor of Peru, were partially published by Antonio de Zamácola, reprinted in 1918. Herrera also left unpublished various historical works, none of which is related to Middle American ethnohistory.

Hɪsᴛᴏʀɪᴀ Gᴇɴᴇʀᴀʟ ᴅᴇ ʟᴏs Hᴇᴄʜᴏs ᴅᴇ ʟᴏs Cᴀsᴛᴇʟʟᴀɴᴏs

Coverage

Between 1601 and 1615, Herrera pub-

[2] Ed. note: The biographical note above is summarized from the detailed original. The single best sketch of Herrera is by Ballesteros y Beretta (1934), on which the summary essentially rests. See also Antonio, 1783; Baeza y González, 1877; Ballester y Castell, 1927; Catalina García, 1897; Domínguez Bordona, 1935; Esteva Barba, 1964; Fernández Duro, 1890; Morel-Fatio, 1905; Pérez Pastor, 1891–1907; 1894.

lished four folio tomes (eight volumes) entitled *Historia general de los hechos de los Castellanos en las Islas y Tierra Firme del Mar Océano*, issued by the royal printing establishment in Madrid. Because of his scheme of organization these volumes are called the "Decades." The work was the first attempt to provide a comprehensive, systematic history of the Spanish empire in America, from Discovery to 1554.

Apparently using Livy or other classical historians as models, Herrera divided his materials at approximately ten-year intervals, with a total of eight such Decades. With a slavish adherence to chronology, Herrera thus grouped widely scattered topical and geographical books and chapters within each decade, abruptly breaking off the narrative until it is resumed some distance away in the following decade. Cortés and Magellan, Spain and America, all are juxtaposed within the narrow chronological limit. There is no clear criterion for division among books or chapters within books; they are of unequal length, and there is repetition between contiguous chapters.

Appendix B provides a selective summary of the decades, books, and chapters that cover New Spain, Guatemala, Yucatan, Nicaragua, Honduras, and some areas of northern Mexico. The long chapter titles in the work itself provide an index to their contents.

Sources

As official Chronicler of the Indies, Herrera had at his disposal the vast documentation that had been accumulated by royal officials and others for a variety of purposes. Many such works he knew appear in a manuscript, "Indice general de los papeles o registros del Consejo de Indias para la Historia General de las Indias," in the Royal Academy of History, Madrid (formerly MS D–95); they were used by Herrera, as well as later by León Pinelo (Paso y Troncoso, 1905, 4:38–39, n. 1).

Herrera himself, in a much-quoted pas-

sage (dec. VI, bk. 3, chap. 19), tells about materials. He said that when the king ordered him to write his general history he also ordered that all papers in various files of government, as well as those held by the king's secretary, be given him. These, stated Herrera, included reports sent to Spain by Bishop Sebastián Ramírez (de Fuenleal) and the viceroys Antonio de Mendoza and Francisco de Toledo. Among them were the "relaciones" of Bishop Juan de Zumárraga, the "memoriales" by Diego Muñoz Camargo and Fray Toribio de Benevente, "and many others." He also had Juan de Ovando bring together the *Relaciones geográficas* which provided data on pre-Spanish life of the Indians, and the founding of towns and other activities of the Spaniards. Moreover, he records seeing 32 additional manuscripts and books by authors like Bartolomé de las Casas and José de Acosta, as well as the *Memoriales* by Cervantes de Salazar.

In part this listing of materials by Herrera was made to rebut what he felt was a criticism of his work by Torquemada. He concludes the list with the statement, ". . . these, I know for certain, were not seen by the author who has published a *Monarquía indiana* and in addition to preferring the Padres Olmos, Sahagún, and Mendieta, who have no authority, to the aforesaid [works], he understands that one cannot write History without having been in the Indies, as if Tacitus would have had to visit the Levant in order to write its history" (ibid.).

As with Torquemada, one of the great values of Herrera is his eclecticism. The various 19th-century charges of "plagiarism" are essentially irrelevant in Herrera's case. This would be an anachronistic imposition of later scholarly standards on normal historiographical practices of the day, especially among official chroniclers and historians. The more proper scientific question, to which no definitive answer can yet be given, is What sources did Herrera use (with or without credit), and of these which of ethnohistorical value are now uniquely preserved in his work? The publication since his time of many of the then unpublished materials utilized by Herrera has permitted modern scholars to trace in detail his usages for given parts of the *Historia general de los hechos.*

Of direct relevance to Middle America is a detailed examination by Bosch García (1945) of the sources Herrera employed for his narrative of the conquest of Mexico in decade II, and part of decade III. Torre Revello (1941) provides general information on sources. These are complemented by identifications made by the various editors of the Academy of History (Madrid) edition of the *Historia general,* listed on Table 2. Much remains to be done.

Bosch García (1945) was startled at the results of his investigations of Herrera's sources for the conquest narrative of New Spain.[3] He found that Herrera at the start of the undertaking had prepared a general bibliography, and at the beginning of the narrative interwove chapters from four main writers: Bernal Díaz, Cervantes de Salazar, Francisco López de Gómara, and Bartolomé de las Casas (see Article 12, Items 12, 44, 54, 56). As writing proceeded, however, one after another of these was dropped. The first to be eliminated was López de Gómara, whose last appearance was decade II, book 5, chap. 8. Las Casas suffered the same fate, terminally used in book 6, chap. 12 of the same decade, according to Bosch García. Bernal Díaz lasted slightly longer, through Cortés' confrontation with Narvaez, book 9, chap. 20 of that decade.

Throughout the remainder of decade II (to chap. 22) and all of decade III (through chap. 8), Herrera placed his primary reliance on Cervantes de Salazar. The latter include portions of decade II, chaps. 11, 13, 15, which give descriptions of Tlaxcalan matters not found in chroniclers directly named by Herrera.[4] Again in chap. 18 is unidentified material concerning Indian allies. A small portion of chap. 7 and all of chap. 8, book 9, similarly are not covered by

sources identified by Bosch García. A small section of chap. 18, book 10, probably comes directly from Cortés material available to Herrera, listing Cortés Indian allied towns, but attributed by Bosch García to Herrera as a digest of the preceding sections. Again concerning the rites and customs of Tepeaca, chaps. 21–22, book 10, Herrera was using sources not then identified by Bosch García. As seen below, these come from the *Relaciones geográficas.*

If Cervantes de Salazar himself was a wholly original source, the matter of Herrera's narrative base would be simplified. A full investigation of Cervantes de Salazar remains to be done, despite a useful but very preliminary study by Díaz-Thomé (1945). The latter concluded, "Whatever be the place and narrated event in the work of Cervantes de Salazar it always appears as a copy of that by López de Gómara" (ibid., p. 28), a finding that is overgeneralized. Díaz-Thomé does point out the former's use of a now lost *Memorias o comentarios de la conquista de México* by Alonso de Ojeda, also used by Torquemada and Herrera, but he notes the minor nature and limited value of the data this probanza provides (ibid., pp. 32–33).

Previously Atanasio López (1925) had examined Cervantes de Salazar in connection with an exhaustive investigation of a now lost work by Toribio de Benavente (Motolinía; see Article 13) on the conquest of Mexico, in an important revisionist article of which Díaz-Thomé was apparently unaware. López states that Cervantes de Salazar, who used both works, often citing them jointly, sharply accused López de Gó-

---

[3] This and the following paragraphs, including Table 1, inserted by Volume Editor.

[4] Note by J. B. Glass: Despite implications and statements to the contrary, by Bosch García (1945), parts of decade II, bk. 6, chaps. 11B–18 (chaps. 12–19 of the Paraguayan edition) concerning Tlaxcala are paraphrased or digested from the *Historia de Tlaxcala* by Diego Muñoz Camargo (see Article 27B, Item 1072). This source is cited by Herrera in chap. 18 and is included in his list of sources.

TABLE 1—RELACIONES GEOGRÁFICAS UTILIZED BY HERRERA

Census Number[°]	Relacion geográfica	Herrera	Paso y Troncoso (1905) Citation
57	Ixtepexic	III, 3–15	4:11, 12, 18
73	Nexapa	III, 3–14	4:31
138	Usila	III, 3–15	4:48, 49
21	Miahuatlan	III, 4–14	4:128, 132, 139
11	Atlatlauca	III, 3–14	4:168, 170
109	Teozapotlan	III, 3–14	4:193
46	Guaxilotitlan	III, 3–15	4:199
107	Teotitlan del Camino	III, 3–15	4:218
110	Tepeaca	II, 10–21	5:19, 31, 38, 43, 44
		II, 10–22	

NOTE: Prepared by H. F. Cline.
[°] See Article 8.

mara of plagiarism because of his heavy reliance on Motolinía without proper credit (López, 1925, p. 228; Cervantes de Salazar, 1914, p. 174). He noted how on the basis of Cortés' letters and other now lost accounts by conquistadores, Cervantes de Salazar occasionally corrected Motolinía and López de Gómara (who followed him), and where the two differed, preferred Motolinía. Cervantes de Salazar also used another lost work by Motolinía, a later writing that included materials now found in both his surviving *Historia* and *Memoriales*, from which several chapters of his book 1 were taken (Ricard, 1933b; López, 1925, p. 246). López (ibid., pp. 235–37) also found that Bernal Díaz similarly had made use of the lost Motolinía chronicle of the Conquest. López was favorably impressed with Cervantes de Salazar's careful and critical use of the several sources at his disposal. Thus when Herrera was copying Bernal Díaz, López de Gómara, and, above all, Cervantes de Salazar, he was also indirectly including much material from Motolinía.

In editing his *Papeles de Nueva España* (see Article 21), Francisco del Paso y Troncoso noted various sections of the *Relaciones geográficas* that Herrera had excerpted at greater or shorter length for the *Historia general*. We are not sure that Paso y Troncoso systematically collated all the latter with the former, which he knew only in part. From those he did indicate it would seem clear that Herrera used them highly selectively, both among the RG corpus as a whole, and for passages within a given document. Various *relaciones* are annotated, probably by Herrera, according to Paso y Troncoso (1905, 4:11–12, n. 4). Table 1 summarizes the places Paso y Troncoso noted where Herrera used these materials. It is probably incomplete. Further such investigations could improve our knowledge. This tabulation, for example, does clarify the source of data for Tlaxcalan materials of decade II, book 10, chaps. 21–22, not identified earlier by Bosch García (1945).

It would thus seem that decade III, book 3, chaps. 14–15, treatment of Oaxaca, was drawn primarily from *Relaciones geográficas*. Paso y Troncoso does not note similar use of them by Herrera for matters within the archbishopric of Mexico. It is not clear whether this means merely that Paso y Troncoso did not attempt a similar collation or that Herrera did not utilize those from that jurisdiction.

In addition to the available sources already listed and identified by Herrera with particular sections of the *General history*, he mentions others whose precise contribution has not been established.[5] He talks, for

[5] Author's text resumes.

244

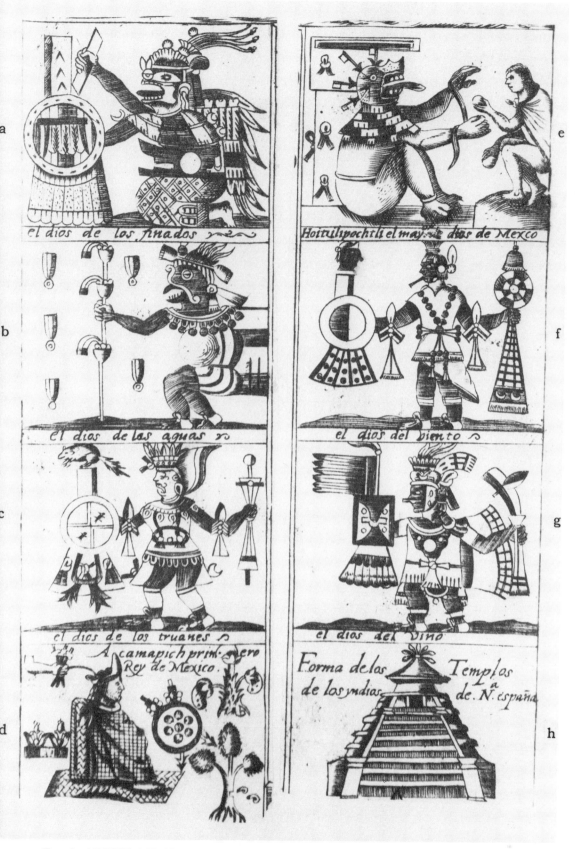

Labels within the figure:

- el dios de los finados
- Hoitulipochsli el may... dios de Mexco
- el dios de las aguas
- el dios del viento
- el dios de los truanes
- el dios del vino
- Acamapich prim...ero Rey de Mexico.
- Forma de las de los yndias — Templos de N.ª españa

FIG. 2—NATIVE MEXICAN DRAWINGS FROM HERRERA, *DESCRIPCIÓN DE LAS INDIAS*, TITLE PAGE (1601). See Table 2 for explanations.

Fıɢ. 3—NATIVE MEXICAN DRAWINGS FROM HERRERA, *HISTORIA GENERAL*, DE-
CADA 2, TITLE PAGE (1601). See Table 2 for explanations.

TABLE 2—SOURCES OF HERRERA'S TITLE-PAGE VIGNETTES

Figure	Herrera	Códice del Museo	Códice Magliabecchiano	Lost Unknown Magliabecchiano Group	Other
2	*Descripción de las Indias*				
a	El dios de los finados	27	45N	—	—
b	El dios de las aguas	26	*44N	—	—
c	El dios de los truanes	[45]	*64N	—	—
d	Acampichtli, primero Rey de Mexico	—	—	—	G
e	Hoitzilpochtli, el mayor dios de México	[64]G	73N; [79] S	S, G	—
f	El dios del viento	56	*65N	—	—
g	El dios del vino	31, 34, 36, 39	49, 51, 56N, 54S	—	—
h	Forma de los templos de los indios	—	—	—	G
3	*Historia general*, dec. II				
a	Guerreros	—	—	—	G
b	Uno de los ydolos	—	—	—	G
c	Fiesta para matar	*12	[30]N	—	—
d	Guerreros	—	—	—	G
e	Motezuma va al templo	[17]	[35]	S; (?)G	(?)G
f	Van a ser sacrificado	*53	[70]N	—	—

NOTE: Prepared by H. F. Cline.
KEY:
Asterisk means nearly identical; square brackets indicate significantly variant details.
G, identified by J. B. Glass (*in litt.*).
N, identified by Nuttall, 1903, with her page numbers.
S, identified by Simpson, 1968.

example, of the *relación* de Nuño de Guzmán, and "Memoriales de cosas de Nueva España," by Alonso de Mota, as well as a versified treatment of Cortés by de Lasso y Vega. Intriguingly he reports access to a volume by a "Franciscan padre of Yucatán," which might well have been the long lost original Diego de Landa *relación*, now known only in copy (see Article 13).

Ramírez (1867b [1885b, p. 112; 1903, p. 21]) attempted to show that despite statements by Prescott and others that Herrera had not known Sahagún's *Historia general*, he had in fact used its book 12, the conquest of Mexico.[6] This seems to be the only specific use of Sahagún that has been attributed to Herrera and it has been accepted by Nicolau d'Olwer (1952, p. 176) although it is contrary to the findings of Bosch García (1945). According to Ramírez, a passage in decade II, book 10, chap. 12, contained in-

formation that could derive only from Sahagún's book 12, chap. 26. Ramírez also noted that Torquemada (bk. 4, chap. 72) had refuted this passage by citing Sahagún's *revised* (1585) account of the Conquest in which the information differed. Unfortunately, the conclusion which Ramírez drew cannot be sustained since the passage in question was taken by Herrera from Cervantes de Salazar (bk. 4, chap. 127), a work which was unknown to Ramírez. In view of Herrera's reference, in his list of authorities, to Sahagún as a work "without authority" cited by Torquemada, it appears that Herrera did not use Sahagún. If he did, it was not in the passage cited by Ramírez.

On two of the elaborately illustrated title pages of the 1601 volumes of the *Gen-*

[6] This paragraph written by John B. Glass.

247

eral history appear 14 vignettes, taken from such native Mexican pictorials. Eight of these are on the title page of the *Descripción de las Indias Occidentales* (fig. 1) and six appear on the title page of decade II (fig. 2).

As early as 1903 Zelia Nuttall (p. vii) identified seven of these vignettes with scenes in the Codex Magliabecchiano. Later Robertson (1959, pp. 125–33, 201–02) discussed the complex relationships of various other texts and pictorial materials related to Codex Magliabecchiano, especially noting the parallels between it and the unpublished Códice del Museo de América (Madrid), and suggesting that both in fact derived from a now lost prototype. In preparing the census of pictorial documents (Article 23, Magliabecchiano Group; Herrera), Glass reviewed these materials.

Simpson, a student of Robertson's, in a recent unpublished paper specifically analyzed the 14 Herrera vignettes on the title pages (Simpson, 1968, pp. 19–24). He contends that rather than utilizing two separate manuscripts (Museo de América, Magliabecchiano), Herrera probably took 11 of the vignettes from the now lost prototype. Some scenes are close to those in one or the other extant document, but at least three differ significantly or cannot be found in either.

Glass's findings differ slightly.[7] Of the eight vignettes on the *Descripción*, six are attributable to the Magliabecchiano group, with two from it represented on decade II. He notes some resemblance between the litter scene (fig. 2, *e*) and the Magliabecchiano group, but attributes the otherwise unidentified vignettes to one or more lost manuscripts distinct from the lost Magliabecchiano prototype posited by Robertson and Simpson. Glass discusses this fully in Article 23, Item 133. Table 2 attempts to synthesize this information.

In summary, it may be said that although Herrera had available to him a wide variety of materials, which he listed with pride, for

Middle America he placed main reliance on a relatively reduced number. Cervantes de Salazar led Bernal Díaz, López de Gómara, Las Casas, and Muñoz Camargo for the period of early contact between Europeans and natives in central Mexico. Detailed studies of other portions of the *Historia general's* sources for other Middle American areas and periods are presently lacking.

Methods

Herrera's constant preoccupation with money perhaps helps explain some of his work habits. His reliance on clerical assistance was also a factor. He was a professional writer, long accustomed to producing translations and commissioned works to meet deadlines, and he did it rather well.

By order of Philip II the Royal Chronicler could not be paid the final third of his annual salary until his historical production of the year had been submitted for review. This perhaps clarifies why, almost upon his appointment in 1596, Herrera immediately began work on the *Historia general*, and seemingly for the next 19 years labored faithfully on it, interrupted (as we have seen) by his arrest and exile and by other publications.

Herrera was assigned a copyist who was to provide designated texts and maps which he wanted (Medina, 1898–1907, 2:9–10). One of the earliest texts copied for him was the Cervantes de Salazar *Crónica*, in 1597.

In the same year he ordered a manuscript copy made of Las Casas' *Historia*, but apparently it did not reach his hands until 1599. Bancroft, in an otherwise generally favorable critique of Herrera, noted that there were many evidences in the *Historia general* that his clerical assistance had been incompetent. He pointed out that when many sources used by Herrera were later printed "we can see that his notes were badly extracted . . . the cause being simply carelessness" (Bancroft, *Works*, 6:317).

[7] This and two following paragraphs inserted by Volume Editor.

TABLE 3—HERRERA'S *HISTORIA GENERAL*,
ROYAL ACADEMY EDITION, 1934–57

Volume	Decade	Books	Publication Date	Editorial Notes
1	Descripción de las Indias		1934	Antonio Ballesteros y Beretta
2	I	1–5	1934	Angel Altolaguirre y Duvale
3	I	6–11	1935	*Idem*
4	II	1–5	1936	Antonio Ballesteros y Beretta
5	II	6–10	1936	*Idem*
6	III	1–4	1947	Angel González Palencia
7	III	5–10	1947	Miguel Gómez del Campillo
8	IV	1–6	n.d.	*Idem*
9	IV	7–10	n.d.	*Idem*
10	V	1–5	n.d.	*Idem*
11	V	6–10	1950	*Idem*
12	VI	1–5	1953	*Idem*
13	VI	6	1954	*Idem*
14	VII	1–6	1955	*Idem*
15	VII	7–10	1956	*Idem*
16	VIII	1–5	1956	*Idem*
17	VIII	6	1957	*Idem*

NOTE: Prepared by H. F. Cline.

In addition to paying the copyists, the Council of the Indies gave other fiscal support to Herrera's enterprise. On September 3, 1597, for instance, it paid for 14 copperplates, presumably maps or the elaborate title pages. There is record of a payment on April 17, 1608, for getting a fair copy of the *Historia general*.

Apparently under the economic pressure to produce, Herrera preferred to utilize works already elaborated rather than building his own from scattered documents. Thus as the geographical portion of the *Historia general* he employed, with only a few minor additions, the *Geografía y descripción de las Indias* written earlier by Juan López de Velasco, then unpublished (Altolaguirre y Duvale, 1930). Juan Bautista Muñoz (1793, p. xxii) noted Herrera's use of work by Ferdinand Columbus (Article 12, Item 2) and Las Casas for decade I. Similarly for Peru, Herrera leaned heavily on Pedro de Cieza de León's *Crónica de Quito*, according to Marcos Jiménez de la

Espada (1877, pp. xiii–xxi). Herrera's main sources were few but well selected. Bosch García's findings that Herrera started out using four major authors and finally narrowed them to one (Cervantes de Salazar) for the conquest of Mexico, underlines what seemingly was Herrera's general method.

Editions

The first volumes of Herrera's *Historia general de los hechos de los Castellanos en las Islas i Tierra Firme del Mar Océano* (4 vols. in 2) were printed in Madrid in 1601. They were reprinted in Valladolid in 1606. The title page of volume I indicates that the work would cover four decades, from 1492 to 1531, one decade per volume. In this edition the Juan de Velasco description of the Indies, with maps, is an appendix in the second volume. The remaining volumes (4 vols. in 2) appeared in Madrid in 1615, decades V–VIII bringing events to 1554. For many years the standard edition was a Spanish reissue in eight volumes (Madrid,

1728–30), under the editorship of Barcia, who placed the description of the Indies as an introduction, and provided important notes, corrections, and an index. The standard scholarly edition now is that issued in 17 volumes (1934–57) by the Royal Academy of History in Madrid. Table 3 lists contents and dates of publication, which was interrupted from 1936 through 1947. The 10-volume set (1944–46), with prologue by J. Natalicio González, published in Asunción, Paraguay, has illustrations, but otherwise is inferior to the Academy version.

Herrera's work has been freely translated into several languages. Most foreign editions are defective. The principal ones are French (1659–60, 1671), and a poor English translation by John Stevens (6 vols., London) in 1725–26, reprinted in 1740 and 1743. A Spanish reprint of 1728 (Antwerp) lacks maps and is otherwise faulty. Volume 1 of the Academy edition discusses these and other editions, as does Wagner (1924).

Conclusions

Antonio de Herrera y Tordesillas, as major Royal Chronicler of the Indies, performed well the task his king had set for him. He provided a sweeping and trustworthy account of the discovery and conquest of the Spanish New World, although it is difficult at times to connect the threads of that great and complex adventure in his treatment. For the years he covers, 1492–1554, his work is not only one of the most complete, but also the most reliable. Although sometimes few, he chose his sources well. As might well be expected from his background, training, and outlook, Herrera was nearly exclusively concerned with Spaniards, not with Indians.

The American natives in his narrative are foils for the European actions, not actors. Torquemada delighted in pointing out the numerous minor and some major errors he had found in Herrera's treatments of Indian affairs. In fact, Herrera makes no original contribution to Middle American ethnohistory, as such. He does, however, provide the major context of it, and for this we agree with Bancroft that Herrera "merits the gratitude not alone of his countrymen but of the world" (*Works*, 6:317).

Appendix A. HERRERA SELECTED WORKS, *by Howard F. Cline*

Historia general
1601–15 Historia general de los hechos de los castellanos en las islas y Tierra Firme del Mar Océano. 8 tomes in 4 vols. Emprenta Real. Madrid. [Each tome separately paginated; elaborately illustrated title pages. Maps from the then unpublished Juan López de Velasco's 1574 *Geografía y descripción de las Indias*, which in this edition follows decade IV; later editors usually place it before decade I; it has been issued separately under Herrera's authorship. The original manuscript of the *Descripción* was first published in 1880 (Article 12, Item 6).]

1606 Historia general. . . . 2 vols. Valladolid. [Reissue of decades I–IV and *Descripción* from Madrid 1601 edition.]

1659–71 Histoire general des voyages et conquêtes des Castillans dans les Iles et Terre-Firme des Indes Occidentale, traduit de L'espagnol par N. de las Coste. 3 vols. Paris. [French translation.]

1707 Drie verscheyde togten ter zee en te land in de West-Indien gedaan in 't jaar 1523 en vervolgens. . . . *In* Pieter van der Aa, *Naankeurige versameling*, 10 deel, no. 2. Leyden. [Partial Dutch translation.]

1725–26 The general history of the vast

continent and islands of America, commonly call'd the West Indies . . . by Antonio de Herrera, translated into English by Capt. John Stevens. 6 vols. London. [Abridged inaccurate English translation of whole work, (not just decades I–III as stated by Sabin), arbitrarily divided into six decades. Reissued, with new title pages, 1740.]

1727? De gedenkwaaridige en al- om beroemde voyagien der Spanjaarden na West-Indien. . . . *In* Pieter van de Aa, *De aanmerkenswaardigste en alomberoemde zee-en land reizen.* 2 vols. Stuck 3–4. Leyden. [Partial Dutch translation, 1492–1526.]

1728 Historia general. . . . 4 vols. Antwerp. [Spanish reissue, whose errors and defects were noted by Nicholás Rodríguez Franco, printer of the following edition.]

[1726?] 1728–30 Historia general. . . . A. González de Barcia y Zúñiga, ed. 8 vols. Imprenta Real de Nicolás Rodríguez Franco. Madrid. [For many years the standard Spanish ꞌedition. Barcia placed the *Geografía y descripción* before the text of the *Historia* and also issued it separately (Madrid, 1728). There seem to be variant editions, showing dates from 1726, one set having 9 vols. in 5. There is also a separately issued *Tabla general de las cosas notables y personas contenidas* (Madrid, 1728).]

1732 General observations and an account of the first discovery of America by Christopher Columbus from the History of the West Indies, written in Spanish by Antonio de Herrera. *In* A. Churchill, *A collection of voyages,* 5:591–640. London. [Partial English translation.]

1934–57 Historia general. . . . Antonio Ballesteros y Beretta, Angel Altolaguirre, et al., eds. 17 vols. Academia Real de Historia. Madrid. [Standard modern scholarly edition. For further details, see Table 3 in text of this article.]

1944–46 Historia general. . . . Prólogo de Juan Natalicio González. 10 vols. Asuncion, Paraguay. [Reissue of defective Spanish text from 1728 Antwerp edition, with pagination of that edition in margins. Useful illustrations, but otherwise not recommended for scholarly use.]

GEOGRAFÍA Y DESCRIPCIÓN DE LAS INDIAS

1601 [See comment under *Historia general,* 1601 and 1606.]

1622a Novus Orbus sive descriptio Indiae Occidentalis, auctore . . . Supremo Castellae & Indiarum athoritate Philippi III Hispaniarum Regis Historiographo. Accesserunt & aliorum Indiae Occidentalis descriptiones & navigationes nuperae Australis "Jacobi le Maire" Historia, uti & navigatorum Omnium per Fretum Magellanicus succinta narratio. Amsterdam. [Latin translation of *Descripción,* with added materials; 6 maps.]

1622b Nievv vverelt, anders ghenaempt Vvest Indien. Amsterdam. [Dutch translation.]

1622c Description des Indes Occidentales, qu'on appelle aujourdhuy le Nouveau-Monde. Amsterdam. [French translation of first 103 pages; remainder is miscellaneous material. Another 1622 edition has slightly variant imprint.]

1623 T. de Bry [ed.]. America. Zwölfter Theil der Newen Welt, das ist: Grundliche volkommene Entdeckung aller der West indianischen Landschafften, Insuln und Königreichen. . . . Frankfurt. [German translation.]

1624 T. de Bry [ed.]. Novi Orbis pars duodecima. Sive Descriptio Indiae Occidentalis. . . . Frankfurt. [Latin translation.]

1625 A description of the West Indies. *In* Samuel Purchas, *Purchas his pilgrimage,* vol. 3, bk. 5, pp. 855–917. London. [English translation.]

1730 Descripción. . . . La Oficina Real de Nicolás Rodríguez Franco. Madrid. [Separately issued from *Historia general* by same printer.]

OTHER PUBLISHED WORKS

1588 Historia de la guerra de Turcos y Persanos, escrita por Juan Tomás Minandoy en quatro libros, comenzando del año de 1576 que fueron los primeros motibos della, hasta el año de 1585 . . . traduzida de italiano por Antonio de Herrera. Madrid.

1589 Historia de lo sucedido en Escocia e Inglatierra, en quarenta y quatro años que bivió María Esuardo, Reyna de Escocia, escrita por . . . criado del Rey Nuestro Sr. Madrid.

1591 Cinco libros . . . la historia de Portugal, y conquista de las Islas de los Azores, en los años de 1582 y 1583. Madrid.

1592 Diez libros de la razón del estado. Con tres libros de las causas de la grandeza y magnificencia de las ciudades [por Juan Botero]. Traducido de italiano en castellano, por mandado del Rey, nuestro señor, por Antonio de Herrera, su criado. Madrid.

1598a Historia . . . de los sucessos de Francia, desde el año de 1585, que comenzó la Liga Católica, hasta el fin del año 1594. Madrid.

1598b Información en hecho y relación de los que passó en Milán, con las competencias entre las jurisdicciones Eclesiastica y seglar, desde el año de 1595 hasta el de 1598. Madrid.

1601–12 Primera [segunda, tercera] parte de la historia general del mundo, de XVII años del tiempo del Señor don Felipe II, el Prudente, desde el año el de [1570, 1571–85, 1585–98]. 3 vols. Madrid (vols. 1, 3) and Valladolid (vol. 2).

1607 Battalla espiritual y arte de servir a Dios, con la Corona y Ledanía de la Virgin Maria por Cardenal de Fermo. Traduzida del italiano por Antonio de Herrera, cronista de Su Magestad. Emprinta [sic] Real. Juan Flamenco. Madrid.

1612 Tratado, relación y discurso histórico de los movimientos de Aragón, sucedidos en los años de mil y quinientos y noventa y uno, y de mil y quinientos y noventa y dos: y de su origen y principio, hasta que la Magestad de D. Felipe II, el Prudente . . . compuso y quietó las cosas de aquel Reyno. Imprenta Real. Madrid.

1624 Comentarios de los hechos de los españoles, franceses, y venecianos en Italia, y de otras repúblicas, potentados, príncipes, y capitanes famosos yta-

lianos, desde el año de 1281 hasta el de 1559. Madrid.

POSTHUMOUS PUBLICATIONS

1804 De las varias epistolas, discursos y tractados de . . . a diuersos claros varones las cuales contienen muchas materiales útiles para el gouierno político y militar, con un elogio de el Licenciado Xpoual Vaca de Castro, del Consejo Supremo y Gouernador de los Reynos del Pirú, iten resumen de lo que passo nel descobrimiento de las reliquias del Monte de Granada. MS E75.1035, Biblioteca Nacional. Madrid. [Published by Juan Antonio de Zamácola under title *Discursos morales, políticos e históricos de don Antonio de Herrera, cronista del Rey don Felipe II, autor de las Décadas de Indias y de otras muchas obras,* Tomo I (all published), Madrid. Of the 25 discursos only 16 are here published.]

1918 Elogio de [Cristóbal] Vaca de Castro. Ed. Juan Francisco V. Silva. Madrid.

UNPUBLISHED WORKS (SELECTIVE LISTING)

? De las varias epistolas, discursos y tractados. . . . [Nine discursos left unpublished by Zamácola, 1804.]
De los provechos de la Historia, qué cosas y de quantas maneras del officio del historiador y de cómo se ha de inquirir, la fé y la verdad y cómo se ha de escribir. MS. Biblioteca Nacional. Madrid.
Carta original sobre las circunstancias de los principales personajes de la Corte. MS J106–311, Biblioteca Nacional. Madrid.
Letra original . . . en dos relaciones del estado de la Plaza de Sabionetta y mercedes hechas a la casa de Mántua. MS, Biblioteca Nacional. Madrid. [Currently missing.]

1601 Discurso sobre la muerte del Rey de Francia. MS 1149–2347, Biblioteca Nacional. Madrid.
Historia de los sucesos de Francia. MS S, 26–6437, Biblioteca Nacional. Madrid. [Copy of a printed work suppressed by royal order for diplomatic reasons.]

Decade	Date	Book	Chapter	Topic
II	1510–20	2	17, 18	Córdoba expedition to Yucatan
		3	1, 3, 9–13	Grijalva expedition; Cortés in Cuba
		4	6–8, 11, 12	Cortés in Yucatan, Tabasco
		5	4–14	Cortés en route to Mexico from Veracruz
		6	1–19	Cortés and Tlaxcalans
		7	1–18	Cortés enters Tenochtitlan; description of city and customs
		8	1–8	Cortés and Montezuma; Montezuma imprisoned
		9	1–6, 18–21	Spaniards in Tenochtitlan; Narvaez expedition
		10	1–4, 8–22	Narvaez vs. Cortés; Noche Triste; Aztecs vs. Spaniards; Customs of Tepeaca (chaps. 21–22)
III	1521–30	1	1, 2, 5–8, 12, 13, 17–22	Conquest; siege of Tenochtitlan
		2	1–2, 6–19	Spanish victory; origin of Mexicans; native history; religion and culture of Mexicans
		3	1–18	Pacification of Michoacan, Culiacan, Oaxaca, Mixteca, Zapoteca, Pacific Ocean, Panuco
		4	8, 15–19	Cortés' government; customs of New Spain, Matlazingo, Utatlan, Otomis, Xilotepec
		5	1–3, 6–14	Cortés' government; expedition to Honduras; Alvarado in Guatemala; customs of Guatemala, Zapotecas
		6	2, 10–12	Cortés' enemies; Honduras expedition
		7	3, 8, 9	Pacification of Tabasco
		8	1–7, 14, 15	Honduras expedition continued; Cortés' problems in New Spain
		9	7, 9, 10	Cortés' return to Mexico; exploration of Spice Islands; Spaniards in Honduras and Nicaragua
		10	1, 7, 8	Government of Honduras, New Spain
IV	1521–30	1	6–9	Spice Islands expedition; events in Nicaragua
		2	1–3	Government of New Spain; Zumárraga; expeditions of Alvarado, Narvaez, Montejo
		3	2–4, 7–10	Montejo in Yucatan; Guzmán in Panuco; First Audiencia
		4	2, 3	Estrada vs. Guzmán; government of Indians in New Spain
		6	3, 4	Salcedo in Honduras; royal government of New Spain
		7	2–5	Chichimec wars; Honduras, Nicaragua, Yucatan, Guatemala
		8	1–11	Chichimecs; Indian customs of Honduras; Nicaragua; Guatemala; cochineal
		9	5–16	Archbishopric of Mexico; bishopric of Veracruz; Indian customs; epidemics; depopulation; Guzmán and Nueva Galicia; events in Yucatan
		10	1–4, 11–12	Yucatan and abandonment of province; customs, rites, antiquities of Yucatan; Chiapas

(*Appendix B, continued*)

Decade	Date	Book	Chapter	Topic
V	1531–40	1	6–10	Ordinances re Indians; Culiacan; Honduras
		7	2–4	Nicaragua
		8	9, 10	Pacific Ocean expeditions
		9	1–2, 8, 9	Mendoza and Second Audiencia; Yucatan, Honduras
VI	1540–50	1	8–10	Contreras in Nicaragua; Alvarado and Montejo in Honduras; Michoacan; royal ordinances re Indians
		3	19	Montejo in Honduras
		7	6–8	Alvarado in Guatemala; Vázquez de Coronado in Culiacan; Marcos de Niza and Cibola
		9	11–15	Vázquez de Coronado, Cibola, Quivira; Mendoza's ordinances re discoveries, lands

Note: Prepared by Ballesteros Gaibrois; tabulated by H. F. Cline.

REFERENCES

Altolaguirre y Duvale, Angel
1930 El atlas de Juan López de Velasco. Informe leido en el congreso de historia de la geografía de Bruselas de 1930.

Antonio, Nicolás
1783 Bibliotheca Hispano Nova. Madrid.

Baeza y González, Tomás
1877 Apuntes biográficos de escritores segovianos. Sociedad Económica Segoviana de Amigos del Pais. Segovia, Spain.

Ballester y Castell, Rafael
1927 Las fuentes narrativas de la historia de España durante la edad moderna (1474–1808). Fasciculo I: Los Reyes Católicos, Carlos I, Felipe II. Valladolid.

Ballesteros y Beretta, Antonio
1934 Proemio. *In* Herrera, 1934–57, 1:ix–lxxxviii.

Bancroft, Hubert Howe
See Article 19, Appendix A.

Bosch García, Carlos
1945 La conquista de la Nueva España en las *Décadas* de Antonio de Herrera y Tordesillas. *In* Estudios de Historiografía, 1945, pp. 143–202.

Catalina García, Juan
1897 La fecha de la muerte del cronista Herrera. RAH, *Boletín*, 30:328–32.

Cervantes de Salazar, Francisco
1914 Crónica de la Nueva España que escribió el Dr. D. Francisco Cervantes de Salazar, cronista de la imperial ciudad de México. [Prologue by M. Magallón.] Hispanic Society of America. Madrid.

Díaz-Thomé, Jorge Hugo
1945 Francisco Cervantes de Salazar y su crónica de la conquista de la Nueva España. *In* Estudios de Historiografía, 1945, pp. 15–47.

Domínguez Bordona, Jesús
1935 Manuscritos de América. Biblioteca de Palacio. Madrid.

Esteva Barba, Francisco
1964 Historiografía indiana. Madrid.

Estudios de historiografía
1945 Estudios de historiografía de la Nueva España por Hugo Díaz-Thomé, Fernando Sandoval, Manuel Carrera Stampa, Carlos Bosch García, Ernesto de la Torre, Enriqueta López Lira, Julio Le Riverend Brusone, con una introducción de Ramón Iglesia. Mexico.

Fernández Duro, Cesáreo
1890 Epitafio de Antonio de Herrera, cronista mayor de Indias, y noticias rela-

tivas a la publicación de sus *Décadas.*
RAH, *Boletín,* 16:173–77.

HERRERA Y TORDESILLAS, ANTONIO DE
See Article 15, Appendix A.

JIMÉNEZ DE LA ESPADA, MARCOS
1877 Tercero libro de las guerras civiles del Perú, el cual se llama la guerra de Quito, hecho por Pedro de Cieza de León. *Bib. hispano-ultramarina,* 2. Madrid.

LEAL, LUIS
1955 El libro XII de Sahagún. *Historia mexicana,* 5:184–210.

LÓPEZ, ATANASIO
1925 Cuestionario histórico, ¿Escribio Fr. Toribio Motolinia una obra entitulada "Guerra de los Indios de la Nueva España o Historia de la conquista de México? *Archivo Ibero-Americano,* 23:221–47. Madrid.

MEDINA, JOSÉ TORIBIO
1898–1907 Biblioteca hispano-americana (1493–1810). 7 vols. Santiago, Chile.

MOREL-FATIO, ALFREDO
1905 El cronista Antonio de Herrera y el Archiduque Alberto. *Revista de Archivos, Bibliotecas y Museos,* 12:55–57. Madrid.

MUÑOZ, JUAN BAUTISTA
1793 Historia del Nuevo-mundo, escribíala D. Juan Bautista Muñoz. Vol. 1. Madrid.

NICOLAU D'OLWER, LUIS
1952 Historiadores de America: Fray Bernardino de Sahagún (1499–1590). PAIGH, Comisión de Historia, Pub. 40. Mexico.

NUTTALL, ZELIA, trans.
1903 The book of life of the ancient Mexicans. Univ. of California Press. Berkeley.

PASO Y TRONCOSO, FRANCISCO DEL
See Article 21, Appendix F, PNE, second series.

PÉREZ PASTOR, CRISTÓBAL
1891–1907 Bibliografía madrileña o descripción de las obras impresas en Madrid. 3 vols. Madrid.
1894 Testamento de Antonio de Herrera. RAH, *Boletín,* 25:305–12.

RAMÍREZ, JOSÉ FERNANDO
See Article 21, Appendix B.

RICARD, ROBERT
1933a La "conquête spirituelle" du Mexique: Essai sur l'apostolat et les méthodes missionaires des ordres mendiants en Nouvelle-Espagne de 1523–24 à 1572. *Travaux et Mémoires de l'Institut d'Ethnologie,* 20. Paris.
1933b Remarques bibliographiques sur les ouvrages de Fr. Toribio Motolinia. *Journal de la Société des Américanistes,* n.s. 25:139–51. Paris.

ROBERTSON, DONALD
1959 Mexican manuscript painting of the early colonial period: The metropolitan schools. Yale Historical Publications, *History of Art,* 12. Yale University Press. New Haven.

SIMPSON, JON J.
1968 The full-page standing figures in Codex Tudela. MS, copy in Hispanic Foundation, Library of Congress.

TORRE REVELLO, JOSÉ
1941 La expedición de Don Pedro de Mendoza y las fuentes informativas del cronista . . . Herrera y Tordesillas. *In* Homenaje al Dr. D. Emilio Ravigniani, pp. 605–29. Buenos Aires.

WAGNER, HENRY R.
1924 Antonio de Herrera, *Historia general de las Indias Occidentales.* (Repaginated reprint from his *Spanish Southwest*). Berkeley.

16. Juan de Torquemada, 1564-1624

JOSÉ ALCINA FRANCH

onarquía indiana, written and published in the early 17th century by Fray Juan de Torquemada, stands as one of the great colonial monuments in the ethnohistory of Middle America. Paradoxically, as its usefulness becomes increasingly clearer with the growth of historical studies of pre-Hispanic and post-Contact Indian cultures and societies, the more obvious becomes the fact that we know surprisingly little about the author or the sources of this major work. Here we shall try to summarize the relatively meager information presently available, with the hope that in due course future investigations will clarify many aspects of the man and his work now only very imperfectly known.[1]

Few indeed are the confirmed data on the life of Juan de Torquemada. There is no extended account of his life and works. Nineteenth-century scholars like Ramírez (1858–66; 1:1–109; 1944; 1957) and García Icazbalceta (1870; pp. xvii–xlv; 1886, 1886–92, 4:vii–xvi; 1896–99, vol. 4, Biografías, 2; 1954) pioneered investigations of Torquemada, followed later by Ballesteros y Beretta (1954) and Phelan (1956). Recent revisionists are Moreno Toscano (1963a, 1963b), and León-Portilla (1964). In general, however, much of what is known about Torquemada comes from his own work, or notices by the editor-printer of the second (1723) edition of the Monarquía indiana, Nicolás Rodríguez Franco.

Even a basic date in Torquemada's life is not fully established. Apparently he was born in Torquemada (Palencia, Spain), from which his name within the Franciscan Order was taken, following the practice of the times (González Obregón, 1899, p. 4; Ramírez, 1944, p. 201; García Icazbalceta, 1886–92, 4:xii; Valle Arizpe, 1946, p. 154). Various students have placed his date of

[1] Ed. note: Translated from the Spanish and edited by Howard F. Cline, who expresses appreciation for critical review and important information from John L. Phelan and especially from H. B. Nicholson. In the text the *Monarquía indiana* is abbreviated MI, with citations to the second (1723) edition.

256

birth between 1550 and 1565, with the earliest possible seemingly at 1559[2]. Until the matter can be settled by further documentation, perhaps the best that can be said at this time is that probably Torquemada was born in 1564, plus or minus a year.

As a child he came to New Spain at an unknown date. He says (MI, 1:302) that he grew up in Mexico City. There is a blank in his biography until he took vows in the Franciscan Order in the Convent of San Francisco of Mexico. Nor is that date fully fixed as between 1579 or 1583. The earlier is based on Padre Figueroa's *Libro becerro*, but Ramírez and García Icazbalceta (who discuss the matter) also argue for the later (Ramírez, 1944, p. 201; García Icazbalceta, 1886–92, 4:xii; 1896–99, 4:223). Without adding new evidence, various later secondary and derivative writings stress the 1583 date.

There is one portrait, date and painter unknown, from the colonial period (fig. 1). Curiously enough, its label states that Torquemada was Mexican born. The picture shows him as a young man standing before a high table writing a book in a library. The painting was previously in the Colegio de Santiago Tlatelolco but it now hangs in the Mexican National Museum of Anthropology (Alamán, 1942, 2:139, 160; Pijoan, 1964, p. 4, fig. 3).

Two famous masters of the era directed Torquemada's studies: Antonio Valeriano and Fray Juan Bautista. The former, an alumnus of the Indian Colegio de Santa

Fig. 1—PORTRAIT OF JUAN DE TORQUEMADA, NOW IN MUSEO NACIONAL DE ANTROPOLOGÍA, MEXICO. From Pijoan, 1946, fig. 3.

[2] The 1559 date is based on his presumed entrance into the Franciscan Order in 1579, at age 20, itself not certain; Ramírez (1854, pp. 864–66) says he took his vows at age 18 or 20; a suspect cedula the latter published allegedly granting privileges to descendants of Ixtlilxochitl, mentioning Torquemada, with a 1551 date, does not appear valid, according to García Icazbalceta (1886–92, 4:xii–xiii; 1896–99, 4:223–25), who did not believe Torquemada was then born. On the same grounds the 1550 date given by Wilgus (1942, p. 23) without further authority seems improbable. Moreno Toscano (1963a, p. 13) indicates 1565 as most probable. León-Portilla (1964, p. xiv) argues for 1557.

Cruz Tlatelolco, was an Indian leader and teacher in Azcapotzalco, praised by Torquemada himself, who acknowledged indebtedness to him as his instructor of "lengua mexicana" (MI, 3:114–15). When he died he left Torquemada his manuscripts, including a translation of Cato into Nahuatl, which Torquemada thought of publishing (MI, 3:114). Later hands have suggested that Valeriano also taught him Latin, logic, and philosophy (Alamán, 1942, 1:226; Beristáin de Souza, 1947, 5:37; González Obregón, 1899, p. 4; Steck, 1944, pp. 83–84). Torquemada also tells us that Fray Juan Bautista taught him theology (MI, 3:581), to which secondary accounts like Bancroft have added philosophy, native language, and antiquities (Bancroft, 1886, *Works*, 10:786–88).

Scattered passages in MI provide an unsystematic and sometimes ambiguous account of Torquemada's travels and knowledge of various areas. Probably before 1581 he had visited Guatemala, where he knew a bastard daughter of Pedro de Alvarado and met the aged Bernal Díaz, who died in 1584 (MI, 1:324, 327, 351). Seemingly this journey took him to Honduras, where Torquemada reported drinking unwittingly "as a youth" a concoction made from lice (MI, 1:335). At about that time Torquemada apparently resided in the Convent of Chiauhtla (MI, 3:105), and in 1582 he lived in the Convent of Zacatlan (MI, 1:280; 3:219). Although García Icazbalceta (1886–92, 4:xiv) casts doubt on the assertion, Torquemada said he was in the Convent of Perihua, Michoacan, in 1584.

He tells us that he shared administration of Indians with Gerónimo de Zarate in the Chapel of San Joseph (Convent of Santiago Tlatelolco) in 1590–92, when Torquemada tried to have Indian tribute lowered (MI, 1:653). In 1608 he reported he had spent more than 22 years preaching to Indians, i.e., since 1586 (MI, 3:232). The title page of his *Vida y milagros* (1602) indicates that in 1602 he was Guardian of the Convent of Tulancingo, following a stay in the Huasteca, where he collected materials on the Totonac (MI, 1:280–81). From 1604 through 1611 he similarly served in the Convent of Santiago Tlatelolco, with added responsibility for the famous Colegio de Santa Cruz for instruction of Indian youths, sadly decayed from its earlier prosperity (MI, 3:113, 115, 582). During those years he also journeyed elsewhere in New Spain: 1604, Zacatecas (MI, 2:337; 3:342); 1606, Jalisco

(MI, 1:388); 1610, Veracruz (MI, 1:411). According to his own statement, Torquemada in his last years (1612–22) visited northern areas, including the Conchos, Tepehuanes, and others (García Icazbalceta, 1886–92, 4:xiii–xiv, quoting Torquemada, 1622).

There has been some confusion about these journeys, caused in part by García Icazbalceta's misreading (1886–92, 4:xii–xiv) of a passage in MI, Prólogo General, and followed by others.[3] In it Torquemada stated he had not visited the other Franciscan provinces of "Mechoacan, Jalisco, Zacatecas, Huasteca, Yucatan, Guatemala, and Nicaragua," which García Icazbalceta construed to mean he had not left his own of Santo Evangelio. What Torquemada said was that he had not gone to those places "to inquire into them" (*para inquirirlas*), referring to the "ecclesiastical matters" that he was discussing. In omitting the latter phrase García Icazbalceta distorted the meaning, which implies that although Torquemada may have been in those places (as we see above he had), it was not as an official visitor of the Franciscan Order.

The years which Torquemada served as Guardian of the Convent of Tlatelolco (1604–11) were especially important. The Franciscan Comisario General de las Indias, Fray Bernardo de Salva named Torquemada (April 6, 1609) "Chronicler of the Order of San Francisco of New Spain." He was directed to write a history that would treat not only Franciscan missionary labors but also the most notable native traditions (MI, Carta Nuncupatoria). Seemingly as early as 1592–93 he had begun gathering materials for this enterprise, which became in final form the *Monarquía indiana* (MI, General Prologue).

During these years Torquemada added the responsibilities of architect and engineer to his ecclesiastical and chronicler's duties. Directing native Indian workmen,

[3] Ed note: This paragraph, based on data from H. B. Nicholson, inserted by Volume Editor.

he erected a vaulted church for the Convent of Santiago Tlatelolco, and with help from Baltasar de Echave and an Indian woodcarver named Miguel Mauricio (who also did the paintings) he created an altarpiece (retablo) which Torquemada modestly states was "among the best which may be found in New Spain" (MI, Prólogo General; 2:488; cf. Chimalpahin, *Diario*, quoted by McAfee and Barlow, 1948, p. 179). In 1604 the viceroy, Conde de Monterrey, charged him with renovation of the *calzada* of Guadalupe after a disastrous flood, and with his Indian workmen Torquemada aided reconstruction of the Chapultepec causeway (MI, 1:728–29). About 1605 Torquemada organized a theatrical presentation of the life of the Apostle St. James, in Latin, Nahuatl, and Spanish, which the viceroy attended. The Indian who played the part of Santiago, Diego de San Juan, became so enthusiastic that he departed from the script with an eloquent sermon Torquemada hardly recognized (MI, 3:44–45).

During 1612–13 Torquemada was Guardian of the Convent of Tlaxcala (MI, Permits and Approvals). At the Chapter meeting held in Xochimilco his fellow Franciscan friars elected him to succeed Hernando Durán as provincial of the Provincia de Santo Evangelio de la Nueva España, a post Torquemada assumed January 18, 1614 (Vetancurt, 1960–61, 4:395–96). In turn at the end of his three-year term he was succeeded by Fray Juan López, who had been provincial of Michoacan.

Torquemada died suddenly on Tuesday, January 1, 1624. "Help me, unloose my chest where my heart is," he cried as he was felled by what apparently was a cardiac attack, without previous warning as he climbed into the pulpit to say Matins at midnight, according to an anonymous Nahuatl account by an Indian eyewitness (Unos anales coloniales, 1948, pp. 182–84). In the presence of the other religious Fray Juan de Torquemada died at the Convent of San Francisco (Mexico City), of which

possibly he was Guardian at that time (García Icazbalceta, 1886–92, 4:xiii; 1896–99, 4:225; Ballesteros y Beretta, 1954, p. 35).

His unexpected demise was profoundly felt by fellow religious, the Indian alumni of the Tlatelolco school, and natives who had worked with him. During the funeral, responses were said for him at six places[4] and on entering San Francisco, where he was buried "on the right hand of the main altar" (Unos anales coloniales, 1948, p. 183).

WORKS (Listed in app. A)

Monarquía indiana

Above all Fray Juan de Torquemada is remembered as a major figure for his *Monarquía indiana*, the common short title for *Los veinte y un libros rituales y monarquía indiana, con el origen y guerras de los yndios occidentales, de sus poblaciones, descubrimientos, conquista, conversion y otras cosas maravillosas. . . .* Its translation outlines the general scope of the three-volume work: The twenty-one ritual books and Indian monarchy, with the origin and wars of the western Indians, their peoples, discovery, conquest, conversion, and other marvellous matters. Torquemada also penned other, lesser works which we shall briefly notice below.

The *Monarquía indiana* twice appeared in printed editions, much later followed by modern facsimiles of the second edition. The four editions appeared respectively in 1615, 1723, 1943–44, and 1969.

Torquemada says that since 1592 or 1593 he had been gathering materials before he was directed in 1609 to write the chronicle ordered by Fray Bernardo de Salva (MI, General Prologue). Seemingly he finished his work in 1613, four years after his charge and 20 or 21 years after he started the project.

Passing references in the text reveal that

---

[4] Alcoticpac, Atezcapan, again in Alcoticpac, Santa María la Redonda, La Concepción, and Santa Isabel.

Torquemada had been completing various books of the work since 1604, and that he did not write them in the chronological sequence in which they appear in the final manuscript.[5] Here are dates he provided: book 1, 1610 (MI, 1:54); book 2, October, 1607 (MI, 1:85); book 3, 1604–05 (MI, 1:309); book 4, 1610 (MI, 1:411); book 5, 1609, 1612 (MI, 1:758, 768); book 10, 1605, 1611 (MI, 2:246, 307); book 12, 1604 (MI, 2:395); book 13, 1607 (MI, 2:487).

Figure 2 shows the title page of the first edition. The original Torquemada volume was printed by Matías Calvijo in Seville in 1615. It is extremely rare, as apparently the greater part of the edition was lost in a shipwreck (MI, Preface). This helps explain why even early in the 18th century the work was so scarce that Antonio de Solís, Pedro Fernández del Pulgar, and Gabriel Alvarez de Toledo could scarcely obtain copies, "even though they offered 24 doubloons for the three volumes" (MI, Preface).

The rarity of the 1615 edition may also account for the various and frequently contradictory descriptions given it in standard bibliographical literature. Few persons have actually seen the volumes, and so there is often confusion about printer, place, and date of issue.[6]

Figure 3 gives the title page of the second, now standard, edition of 1723. The second edition of MI is based on a text prepared and edited by its printer, Nicolás Rodríguez Franco, who provides information about it in a "Proemio." He based his version on the original manuscript by Torquemada, then to be found "in the library of Señor don Andrés González de Barcia, of the Supreme Councils of Castile and of War." Rodríguez Franco collated the manuscript with copies of the 1615 edition he found in the Royal Library and the Imperial College of the Company of Jesus. He stated that he had found "that in the first printing there were more omissions and errors than are common in most works, as in it some paragraphs were lacking, and with many erroneous and misspelled names in the body of the History; in the margins there were innumerable mistakes." Therefore, he "corrected some and added others."

The book was not actually published until 1725, despite the date 1723 on the title page. The "Fe de Erratas" sheet for volumes 2 and 3 are dated November 24, 1724. The Printer's Proemio has January 20, 1725, as the date.

No detailed examination has yet been undertaken of differences between the 1615 and 1723 printed versions, or their relationship to the original Torquemada manuscript. Apparently no one has even attempted to ascertain the fate of the latter since it was reported in 1723. A scholarly, critical edition of the irreplaceable *Monarquía indiana* is a major desideratum for ethnohistorical investigations.

The third edition adds nothing to the second. It was issued by Salvador Chávez Hayhoe in Mexico (1943–44) as a facsimile in offset printing. The fourth (1969) edition is a reduced facsimile of the 1723 text, preceded by introductory remarks by León-Portilla.

The *Monarquía indiana* is both history and religious chronicle in the traditions outlined by Burrus in Article 13.[7] As Moreno Toscano has shown (1963a, pp. 23–42), Torquemada from an early age had been

---

[5] Ed. note: Paragraph added by Volume Editor.

[6] Correctly described by Antonio (1783–88, 1:787–88), Ballesteros y Beretta (1954, p. 37), Bancroft (1886, *Works*, 10:787), Beristáin de Souza (1947, 5:37–38), González Obregón (1899, p. 7), León Pinelo (1958, p. 102), Medina (1898–1907, 2:149–50), Peral (1944), Phelan (1956, p. 106), and Wilgus (1942, p. 23) who provides without comment alternative incorrect date and place. Clavigero (1844, p. 303) dated 1614 at Madrid. Madrid, 1613, is incorrectly given by Leclerc (1878, no. 570), Sánchez Alonso (1944, 2:249) and Wilgus (1942, p. 23).

[7] Ed. note: This and the following four paragraphs prepared by the Volume Editor.

FIG. 2—*MONARQUÍA INDIANA*, TITLE PAGE OF FIRST EDITION (1615)

Fig. 3—*MONARQUÍA INDIANA*, TITLE PAGE OF SECOND EDITION (1723)

interested in historiography, and developed a theory of history that derived in part from the chroniclers' usages of the past, in part from a deep knowledge of classics, and in part from his own views. He was not writing a personal memoir, but rather viewed his work as a systematic and critical summing up of what had already been written about Mexican history, which later hands could utilize as time passed. He intended to emphasize the history of evangelization (MI, 1:574), which he thought would be his main contribution, even though previous persons had treated it and others would (MI, 1:16; 2:619). He wished to bring earlier writings up-to-date, and hence stressed the founding of new religious establishments since others had written about the earlier ones (MI, 3:360).

A second main motive underlay his work, one that gives it special value for ethnohistory. He purposely aimed to revindicate native culture, and demonstrate that its disparagement by Spaniards was unjust and historically incorrect (MI, 1:16, 175; 2:558–59; 3:360). Many of the long and complex digressions, utilizing biblical and classical references and allusions, were designed to show not only that aboriginal Indian cultures followed universal laws of history concerning development of peoples, but that the cultures and societies of Mexico equaled if they did not surpass ancient and classical civilizations. At the same time he had to point out how such New World peoples were improved by missionaries who taught them Christianity (Moreno Toscano, 1963a, pp. 46–47). He also wanted a certain literary immortality, stating, "I was moved not only to read, but also to write, to have a part in this enterprise, in the glory that those who write are accustomed to have" (MI, General Prologue).

The *Monarquía indiana* is divided into three large volumes, and these into books and chapters. Volume I is "Natural history." He gives information on lands and early peopling of New Spain (bks. 1–2), sum- marizes the dynastic histories of major Mexican aboriginal populations (bk. 3), and tells how they were conquered by the Spanish (bk. 4). Book 5, terminating volume 1, provides an annalistic record of the civil and ecclesiastical administration of New Spain to his day, records Spanish entradas in northern New Spain, and makes mention of noteworthy happenings in the Philippines, China, and Japan.

Volume 2 is very important for ethnohistory. Torquemada in it treats native religion (bks. 6–10), government (bk. 11), laws (bk. 12), institutions (bk. 13), and social and military life (bk. 14). In a vast comparative undertaking, Torquemada in this volume shows parallels between Indian usages and those recorded in biblical and classical sources. Further, Mexican Indian institutions are compared with those of the Caribbean, North and South America, even including Brazil.

Volume 3 is essentially a religious chronicle, almost exclusively devoted to the history of evangelization of the Indians of New Spain. As noted below, Torquemada contributed little original to books 15–21, which make up volume 3, essentially reprinting an edited version of Mendieta's *Historia eclesiástica indiana*, then in manuscript. Book 15 relates the arrival of monks in New Spain, followed by an account of ecclesiastical administration, devotion of the Indians, and miracles (bk. 16). The benefits of evangelization to natives and various favors conceded by the Spanish monarchs, executions by the Inquisition, establishment of monasteries, and mission efforts, especially by Franciscans, in Florida, Philippines, and Japan follow (bks. 17–19). Book 19 ends with a list of Franciscans who wrote on Indian history. Book 20 includes biographies of notable Franciscans who led exemplary lives, especially from the Province of Santo Evangelio. Moreno Toscano (1963a, pp. 97–98) lists these biographies. Finally, book 21 discusses Franciscan martyrs of the mission effort in New Spain.

Minor Works[8]

Nearly all standard authorities note a work of hagiography mentioned by Torquemada, *Vida de Fray Sebastián de Aparicio* (MI, 1:315). As appendix A indicates, two editions of it (1602 and 1605) are known, one from the press of Diego López Dávalos in Santiago Tlatelolco, the other from that of Pedro Passo, Valladolid, Spain (Andrade, 1899, pp. 2–3; Cuevas, 1946, 3:503; González Obregón, 1899, pp. 6–7; Medina, 1898–1907, 2:73).

Two works written by Torquemada in 1622 remained unpublished until issued by García Icazbalceta in 1892 (Torquemada, 1892a, 1892b; see app. A below). These tracts defended the independence of friars (regulars) from episcopal (secular) jurisdiction, stressing the services rendered, especially to Indians, by the Orders of Santo Domingo, San Francisco, and San Agustín.

González Obregón (1899, p. 7) and Valle Arizpe (1946, p. 155), among others, mention manuscript works by Torquemada which now seem lost, although no intensive bibliographical or archival research has been undertaken to verify the titles or locate the originals. These are supposed to include other lives of saints, various comedies in Nahuatl, and the play in Spanish, Latin, and Nahuatl mentioned above.

SOURCES[9]

For other aspects of Torquemada we still lack anything more than partial investigation of the sources he utilized in compiling the *Monarquía indiana.* Unfortunately most of the small scholarly attention paid such matters has been directed to a moral rather than a scientific issue, whether or not Torquemada was a plagiarist and, if so, to what degree.

We shall discuss that matter below, but here we can note that little has been done since 1870, when in raising this issue García Icazbalceta (1870, pp. xxxvii–xlv) made

detailed comparisons between the works of Mendieta and Torquemada. Paso y Troncoso is said to have collated passages from Sahagún with those of Torquemada, but his results remained unpublished (García Icazbalceta, 1886, pp. 271–72; Nicolau d'Olwer, 1952, pp. 175–76). Without entering into details, León-Portilla (1964, pp. xiii–xxxiii) has surveyed the problem of Torquemada's sources.

One of Torquemada's chief claims to continued and growing recognition is his inclusion of data from sources now lost and his free borrowing from predecessors who had access to such materials. To date, however, only minor examination of such sources and Torquemada's use of them has appeared in print. A very small start was made by Moreno Toscano (1963a), who partially lists his citations. A thoroughgoing review and analysis of Torquemada's sources is a major desideratum. The sketch below aims at summarizing some problems, not solving all of them.

Native Sources

Torquemada was proud that he knew, utilized, even owned Mexican Indian native sources. Examination of his text by Cline (1969) substantiates the claim he made concerning his use of them (MI, 1:289) but also reveals that in many instances Torquemada is irritatingly vague in citations. Hence it is hazardous in the extreme to equate his general descriptions of such native documents to any particular ones that have survived, except in a handful of cases. He delighted in pointing out that his own work corrected errors found in Herrera, López de Gómara, Acosta, and others who did not utilize the native materials he employed (MI, 1:295).

Torquemada divided such native sources by the Indian groups whose history or culture they treated, rather than by format.

---

[8] Ed. note: Author's text resumes.
[9] Ed. note: This section, inserted by Volume Editor, summarizes material in Cline, 1969.

For him "pinturas" were obviously pictorial items, with "relación" or "memorial" usually denoting prose. "Historia" was a general term he employed, covering either or mixed formats. He makes numerous references to the corpus of native writings, and to his own diligent exploitation of the surviving items, which he said were very incomplete because many native sources had been burned by Bishop Juan de Zumárraga (MI, 1:140, 159, 234, 239, 253, etc.).

In scattered passages Torquemada reported using native sources from a wide variety of groups in central Mexico. These included "Tulteca, Chichimeca, Alculhua, Tepaneca and Mexicana" (MI, 1:295), "three Mexican and one Texcocan history" (MI, 1:172), Tlatelolco (MI, 1:294), and material from Olmos based on such histories from "Mexico, Texcoco, Tlaxcala, Huexocingo, Cholula, Tepeaca, Tlalmanalco and other principal towns" (MI, 2:76). He cited annals from Azcapotzalco (MI, 1:252) but data on that community seemingly came from BNP 254, a manuscript in Nahuatl "relatifs aux Toltèques" which also treats Tlaxcalan matters (Hasler, 1958). Diego Muñoz Camargo also used the same document (Gibson, 1952, pp. 261–63). For Tlaxcala Torquemada placed heavy reliance on two works by Muñoz Camargo, his *Historia de Tlaxcala* (MI, 1:498, 531, etc.) as well as the separate *Historia natural* (MI, 2:617), also providing a brief biography of this Mestizo historian (MI, 1:523). Presumably Torquemada had access to these and perhaps other manuscripts through the historian's son (Gibson, 1952, p. 239), including pinturas "that I have seen" (MI, 2:366).

Torquemada's close friendship with Texcocan Indians and Mestizos also provided him with native sources from that important community. Notably he used what must have been a manuscript, the same as or much like the *Matrícula de tributos*, called by him "Libro de Pinturas," owned by the grandson of Nezahualpilli, Don Antonio Pimentel, "who was very curious about these and other things" (MI, 2:544). He also furnished Torquemada with a document giving fiscal accounts of Nezahualpilli's household (MI, 1:166); Clavigero apparently used this minor document (León-Portilla, 1964, p. xiv; Burrus, 1959, pp. 67–68). Notably, however, Torquemada had nothing but scorn for the "Relación del orígen de los indios . . ." (Codex Ramírez) written about 1579 by Juan de Tovar, a Jesuit born in Texcoco. Torquemada claimed to own the document, which he characterized as a "bad and false" account that had misled Acosta, Herrera, and others (MI, 1:97, 171, 172).

Fernando de Alva Ixtlilxochitl, another descendant of Nezahualpilli, also furnished native materials. In fact, Torquemada and he shared use of such sources, but there remain several puzzling questions concerning these sources and the variant accounts of the same episodes written by these two men (Le Riverend Brusone, 1945, pp. 311–12). Both employed Codex Xolotl (MI, 1:32, 38, 39, 44, 79, 252, 253). Probably the "ancient painting" Torquemada cites which showed the palace of Nezahualpilli is Codex Quinatzin, also used by Alva Ixtlilxochitl; it survives in the National Library in Paris. The latter repository also has an anthology of colonial copies of five native histories in Nahuatl (BNP 22, 22bis) whose originals (or similar copies) were available to both Torquemada and Alva Ixtlilxochitl. Torquemada reported that he owned a Texcocan document on which were depicted the 15 ancient divisions of the realm (MI, 1:176).

Torquemada also said he owned an "Historia Antigua" from Tlatelolco (MI, 1:294), and cites others he had seen (MI, 1:94). The former seems to differ from another used by him, which he described as being a history in the Mexican language, written by an Indian who had become Christianized, and who wrote an account of the Conquest which contained "many things from which I have benefited for this History"

(MI, 1:491); he cites it again concerning details of the Noche Triste not found in Spanish sources (MI, 1:509). This is probably "Historia de Tlatelolco desde los tiempos mas remotos, manuscrito de 1528," surviving in a colonial copy (BNP 22, 22bis) now available in facsimile and various translations.

Torquemada is far from precise in describing native sources from Tenochtitlan. He refers to a number of them, but in very generalized terms (e.g., MI, 1:234, 254, 269, 283, 340; 2:78–79). He said he owned one that showed Montezuma's palace (MI, 2:436).

Torquemada distinguished between the "ancient histories" and certain post-Contact accounts written by natives, such as the "Annales" (BNP 22, 22bis) mentioned above. He noted that there were various native accounts of the Conquest, some of which he had in his possession, and said that he wanted to translate and publish them, as they recorded the Indian side (MI, 1:379–80). In a similar vein he refers to post-Conquest materials from Tlaxcala, painted shortly after the Conversion, as well as to Tlaxcalan "memoriales y relaciones" of the Conquest that he had used (MI, 1:419, 523).

Torquemada also stressed that many historical data were to be found in native songs. He used one from Coatlinchan for Aculhuacan history (MI, 1:126), as well as others for Tlaxcala (MI, 1:268, 468), and Tenochtitlan (MI, 1:291). He warned readers that this class of sources did not follow exact chronologies, but did contain information not found elsewhere (MI, 1:258).

Similar was his use of homilies which Aztec parents used for guidance of their children, two of which he reproduced in extenso. These had first been translated by Olmos, had passed into the hands of Bartolomé de las Casas and thence to Torquemada, who confessed that there were still metaphorical meanings that had escaped them all(MI, 2:498–99). Torquemada also used native poems as sources. From one such passage

(MI, 1:80) Garibay reconstructed an epic poem of Quilaztli (Garibay, 1953–54, 1:138, 295, 307; 2:46).

As an historian and avid student of native religions and fiestas, Torquemada was especially concerned with native calendrical documents. He said he owned three or four of these, some in figuras (historical), others in cifras (symbols). In addition he owned the calendar wheel drawn by his fellow Franciscan, Fr. Toribio Motolinía (MI, 2:301). The latter is the so-called Motolinía Calendar Wheel in UTX (see Veytia Calendar Wheel no. 2, Article 23, Item 388). Torquemada drew attention to a problem recurrent in study of these matters, that different central Mexican groups, while using the same basic system, apparently varied among themselves on the day which started their new year (MI, 2:302). As noted in Article 17, Clavigero later tried to impose a more rational system on Torquemada's calendrical material than the original Torquemada data permitted.

In a well-established Franciscan tradition pioneered by Olmos and Sahagún, Torquemada supplemented his written native sources by direct interrogation of native informants. Thus when two native written sources were in disagreement about Chimalpopoca, he turned to living Indians, among them a descendant of that ruler (MI, 1:126) to resolve the problem. He gives the names of similar native informants in Tlatelolco: Melchor de Soto (MI, 1:94–95), Juan de Tovar (MI, 1:573)—not the historian—and Melchor de Mendoza (MI, 2:476–77), among others. For the Tenochca he named Antonio Calmecahua, a surviving war captain of the Conquest who lived to age 130, according to Torquemada (MI, 1:509).

Perhaps the most extended and most significant use of these direct oral ethnohistorical inquiries by Torquemada related to the Totonac Indians. He tells us that in 1600 he gathered data on the ancient realm from don Luis, a cacique born in 1520, whose father had transmitted this lore to him. Torquemada reported his own skepticism about the exact 80-year cycles in the 800-year history he recorded, but said that further inquiries among other Totonacs seemingly corroborated don Luis' account (MI, 1:278–81).[10]

Although for most Central American ancient history Torquemada leaned heavily on Motolinía, he did add original ethnohistorical materials for Honduras. These were based on "questioning the ancients," and Torquemada apologizes for the relatively small amount of new information he was able to elicit (MI, 1:330).

From this cursory review certain broad generalizations appear, subject to later refinement and much elaboration when more detailed examinations are made. Torquemada made extensive and important use of native materials. These included prose, historical poems and songs, calendrical documents, and pictorial sources. They came from various native communities, the greater number being confined to Nahuatl-speaking areas of central Mexico. He supplemented written sources by direct inquiry of knowledgeable native and Mestizo informants, and here made important original contributions to our knowledge of the Totonac, and a minor contribution for Honduras. Seemingly he had no firsthand native materials for Oaxaca, western Mexico, northern Mexico, and most of the Maya regions.

Spanish Language Sources[11]

Torquemada leaned more heavily on sources in the Spanish language than he did on native productions. Until more detailed analyses of all Torquemada's sources are published, the degree he relied on one or another still remains conjectural. Certain very broad generalizations can be made from data at hand.

Torquemada loved and respected Fray Bernardino de Sahagún and his work. He also utilized him extensively. In addition to employing the revised book 12 (1585) of Sahagún's *Historia general* dealing with the Spanish conquest (MI, 1:491), Torquemada cites him frequently. Paso y Troncoso concluded that Torquemada copied passages from at least nine of the 12 books (García Icazbalceta, 1886, pp. 271–72 [1954, p. 343]; Nicolau d'Olwer, 1952, pp. 175–76).

Demonstrably the author whom Torquemada used even more was Fray Gerónimo de Mendieta, most of whose *Historia eclesiástica indiana* (1870) (see Article 13) was included in *Monarquía indiana*. This was conclusively shown by García Icazbalceta (1870, pp. xxxvii–xlv), who provides a detailed listing which we need not repeat here. Torquemada himself thus contributed little original to books 15–21 (MI, vol. 3), as noted by Ricard (1947, p. 58). For discussion of charges of plagiarism later leveled against him it is worth noting important changes which Torquemada made in Mendieta's manuscript. Phelan (1956, p. 107) states that "Torquemada made a radical revision in the spirit and significance of Mendieta's material by means of careful use of the scissors," deleting and suppressing all that seemed offensive and critical of Spanish action in America, abounding in the *Historia eclesiástica indiana*.[12]

Ramírez, who investigated Torquemada's references to Motolinía (Ramírez, 1944, pp. 164–65), another Franciscan source of the

---

[10] Torquemada's own statements do not bear out the suggestions that Torquemada used pictorial sources now lost, or lost works by Olmos, for the Totonacs (Krickeberg, 1933, p. 8; Pijoan, 1946, pp. 171–72). Torquemada reported that formerly Totonac priests wrote histories, but his own account is based on what the natives say (MI, 1:278–81; 2:134, 181).

[11] Ed. note: Author's text resumes.

[12] Fr. P. A. López (1931) has suggested, without further evidence, that Mendieta and Torquemada drew on a common source, a presumably lost work of Fray Toribio Motolinía (quoted in Ricard, 1947, p. 58). Ed. note: This possibility rests on relationships of various works by Benavente (1858) ("Motolinía"), whose own productions are not clearly related as yet, as discussed in Article 13.

Monarquía indiana, found that Torquemada cited 66 passages. Of these Ramírez was able to locate 36. He concluded that more or less textually copied from Motolinía were 3/23, 11/27, 16/22, and 17/9.[13] Again this topic is not exhausted, as when Ramírez undertook his comparisons the Motolinía *Memoriales* had not been published; he worked only with the *Historia*.

Curiously enough, although Herrera and Torquemada demonstrated bitter enmity toward one another in their contemporary published works, the latter borrowed from the former. Torquemada, for instance, related how at the request of the royal chronicler the viceroy had sequestered and sent to him in Spain the *Historia general* by Sahagún (MI, 3:387); Torquemada, as did Mendieta, wrote that these volumes would be of small use to *him*, because he could not read Nahuatl (MI, 3:387; Leal, 1955, p. 192). Torquemada accused Herrera of adding things that neither he nor Sahagún had said (MI, 1:379–80). Torquemada, who had in fact freely borrowed (with credit) from the first two volumes of Herrera, published in 1601, placed other strictures on him (MI, 1:347, 349, 354, 361, 379, 409, 411, 416, etc.). Herrera repaid in kind when his final two volumes appeared in 1615 (Herrera, 1728, 2:280–81, dec. 6, bk. 3, chap. 19; dec. 5, bk. 2, chap. 4).

The degree of Torquemada's borrowings from Herrera, as in other cases, rests on informed guesses by secondary authorities who have not stated the evidence and comparisons in full. Bancroft (1886, *Works*, 10:787), followed by Phelan (1956, p. 108), avers that Torquemada's book 4, chronicle of the Conquest, was in large part taken from Herrera. He had seemingly based his account chiefly on Cervantes de Salazar who, on his part, had apparently literally copied large parts of López de Gómara (Phelan, 1956, p. 108). As Article 13 has shown, many of these broad generalizations about reliance of one Spanish author on another are being narrowed and shaded as

research on the historiography of the Conquest continues. For the moment we shall leave open, until other avenues have been explored, the matter of whether or not Torquemada's narrative is third hand from López de Gómara, via Cervantes de Salazar, as is current opinion.

Fray Andrés de Olmos also served Torquemada, probably to a lesser degree than Mendieta, Sahagún, or others mentioned. Olmos had written an important work on the aboriginal Indian cultures of New Spain, a work now unfortunately lost. He later made a summary or compendium of it. It has been assumed that Torquemada used the latter for passages related to native cultures, but García Icazbalceta expressed doubts about that possibility. He felt (1870, p. xxvii) that Torquemada indirectly knew Olmos' work only through those parts of it which had been included by Mendieta. Torquemada specifically states he had manuscripts by Olmos, whom he ranked as a major authority. Whether Torquemada's "Conversations of the Ancients" (*huehuetlatolli*) (MI, 13:36) came directly from an Olmos manuscript or from a version of Olmos that Fray Juan Bautista had published in 1600 is still disputed (Garibay, 1953–54, 1:403; Medina, 1907–12, 2:6; Zulaica Gárate, 1939, p. 225).

Torquemada himself mentions numerous other primary and secondary sources in Spanish. Some of these are listed by Moreno Toscano (1963a).

THE PROBLEM OF PLAGIARISM[14]

The problem of whether Torquemada's inclusion of nearly all of Mendieta's *Historia eclesiástica indiana* in his own *Monarquía indiana* without sufficient academic credit has not only obscured the significant virtues of the latter work but has tended to bias various judgments about Torquemada. In

---

[13] Ed. note: Books/chapters.
[14] Ed. note: This section added by Volume Editor.

view of the many substantive but yet un-answered questions about the man and his work, a relatively inordinate amount of scholarly concern has centered on discussing this nearly scientifically irrelevant question.

The issue did not come to the fore until the late 19th century, although it harked back to 1698 statements by Padre Vetancurt (1871, p. 146). In it he had attributed all the *Monarquía indiana* to Mendieta, whose works remained unpublished until 1870. In that year García Icazbalceta issued the *Historia eclesiástica indiana*, with an extensive introduction denouncing Torquemada as an unexcusable plagiarist, appending a table showing passages he had lifted nearly verbatim from Mendieta (García Icazbalceta, 1870, pp. xvii–xlv). Various subsequent students have followed this "plagiarist" line, Ballesteros y Beretta (1954, pp. 35, 37) and Nicolau d'Olwer (1952, p. 115), among others.

The defense also had roots in the colonial period. Rodríguez Franco, editor-printer of the 1723 edition, explained that Torquemada had openly cited Mendieta (MI, Preface), and hence "guilt" was only a matter of degree, if at all. Later apologists like Valle-Arizpe (1946, p. 153) and León-Portilla (1964, p. xxi) invoke the general lack of scruples in earlier centuries about extensive use of original materials without precise citations, pointing out that nearly all writers of history followed the practice. Official chroniclers of Orders like Herrera and Torquemada were especially prone; Herrera freely lifted portions from Cervantes de Salazar, Bernal Díaz, Hernán Cortés, and many others.

The problem was given sharp refocus by Phelan (1956) in his extended study of Mendieta. Phelan points out that Mendieta was a character euphemistically called "intrepid," or "vigorous," and more directly "violent." His work reflected these qualities. He launched strong charges against the secular clergy (non-friars) and laymen. In

normal practice when he finished the work, it would have been sent to Spain for review by the Council of the Indies for permission to publish it; whether this step was taken, and permission refused, is not established. Phelan argues that probably in anticipation of such refusal, or even submittal to the Council, local Franciscan authorities in New Spain decided that in its original form the work could not appear in print, and thus bring censure on Mendieta and them. In any case, the unpublishable Mendieta manuscript was turned over to Torquemada, a member of the moderate Franciscans, to exploit whatever might be exploitable in it (Phelan, 1956, p. 107).

Phelan tells us (ibid., p. 107) that Torquemada proceeded to prune all statements that "might offend the sensibilities of laymen or secular clergy." If so, the desire to mask the identity of Mendieta as author of various books of the *Monarquía indiana* was less a case of common plagiarism than of carrying out the wishes of the Franciscan Order to have published a suitably edited version of Mendieta's work that would not draw criticism from the Council of the Indies or others. We might add to these considerations the consistently depersonalized or institutional view which religious Orders and their chroniclers held concerning individual works by their members (Article 13; Phelan, 1956, p. 106; Valenzuela Rodarte, 1959, p. 43).

It would seem that perhaps the matter might now rest by stating that Torquemada did incorporate most of the best of Mendieta into his *Monarquía indiana*, as he included important parts of other works, cited and uncited. Whatever the final moral judgments, it was precisely this eclecticism that gives Torquemada's work its enduring value.

Evaluation[15]

Judgments passed on the *Monarquía indiana*, like the volumes themselves, have been

[15] Author's text resumes.

diverse, contradictory, often ponderous. There seems to be general agreement, however, that Torquemada amassed an astounding number of facts about aboriginal and post-Contact Indians of Middle America, however obtained and prolixly presented.

Eighteenth-century students appreciated the wealth of information in this great compendium, disordered and difficult as it now is to read or use. Ronan shows (Article 17) that it served Clavigero as his principal source, and that in fact Clavigero's own work is more an attempt to introduce 18th-century order and reason into Torquemada's materials than an original Clavigero contribution, even to the point of creating a more rational calendar than Torquemada's sources would permit. Cavo, too, was a warm admirer and exploiter of Torquemada, labeling him "Father of ancient and modern Mexican history" (Cavo, 1949, pp. 88, 250). Eulogists also numbered Echevarría y Veytia in their ranks (Veytia, 1944, 2:249).

Proponents in the 19th and 20th centuries are several. Samples would be Alamán (1942, 2:139), Ortega (Veytia, 1944, 2:194), Orozco y Berra (1878, p. 193), Bancroft (1886, *Works*, 10:786), González Obregón (1899, p. 7), Reyes (1948, p. 53), and Rico González (1949, p. 42). The line extends to Phelan (1956, p. 111), for whom the *Monarquía indiana* is one of the classic works of colonial Mexican historiography, and to Moreno Toscano (1963b, pp. 43–45) and León-Portilla (1964, p. xxxiii) who were similarly impressed. These latter two young scholars have taken leadership in "revindicating" Torquemada against disparagement by the 19th-century Mexican Positivist and Hispanist historians.

Apart from those who have belabored Torquemada on the plagiarism issue are others who find the *Monarquía indiana* less than enchanting. Ballesteros y Beretta (1954, p. 37) thought that the moral homilies and various digressions "make insufferable" the reading of it. He suggested, as did Father Garibay (1953–54, 2:47), that a version be edited to eliminate these obstacles, partially if not totally. Such counsel might have merit for the ethnohistorian who, with a given narrow interest, penetrates the volumes only in search of specific concrete facts, but would have less appeal for the historian of ideas and colonial academic culture. It is exactly Torquemada's asides, comparisons, and commentaries of a classic or biblical nature which provide clues to the understanding or misunderstanding of the work's "internal unity and its not insignificant place in colonial historiography" (Phelan, 1956, p. 109).

Torquemada's work indeed contains also innumerable contradictions and confusions, partly as a result of his eclecticism. Orozco y Berra (1878, p. 194) and García Icazbalceta (1886–92, 4:xiii–xiv; 1896–99, 4:225–26) have pointed out some of these. The long overdue critical analysis of the massive Torquemada text undoubtedly would reveal many more. But it is equally likely to reveal unknown and hidden treasures and strengths.

The known faults should not obscure the high value of Torquemada's *Monarquía indiana*. He provided an extraordinary, almost unmatched, body of utilizable materials from early times to the close of the 16th-century, tracing the ancient and (for him) modern history of Mexico. Inadvertently, if not involuntarily, he saved ancient sources, reports, oral traditions, and other data which without Torquemada would have been irretrievably lost.[16]

---

[16] Other references consulted but not cited are Chavero, [1887], and Réville, 1885.

APPENDIX A. TORQUEMADA, WORKS

1602 Vida y milagros del sancto confessor de Christo F. Sebastian de Aparicio frayle lego de la orden del Seraphico P.S. Francisco, de la Prouincia del sancto Euangelio. Recopilada por el P. —— predicador, guardian del conuento de Tullantzinco. En Mexico. Con privilegio. En el colegio Real de Sanctiago Tlatilulco: En la emprenta de Diego Lopez Daualos. Por C.

1605 Vida y milagros del sancto confessor de Christo, Fray Sebastian de Aparicio frayle lego de la orden del Serafico padre san Francisco, de la Prouincia del santo Euangelio. Recopilada por el P. F. Iuan de —— predicador, guardian del conuento de Tullantzinco. Con privilegio. En Valladolid. En casa de Pedro Lasso.

1615 Ia [IIa, IIIa] Parte de Los Veynte y un libros rituales y Monarchia Yndiana con el origen y guerras de los Yndios Occidentales. De sus poblacones descubrimiento conquista conuersion y otras cosas Marauillosas de la mesma tierra distribuydos en tres tomos compuesto por ministro prouincial de la orden de Nuestro Seraphico Padre S. Francisco en la Prouincia del Sancto Euangelio de Mexico en la Nueba Espana. Con privilegio. En Seuilla por Matthias Clauijo Año 1615. [Three vols. of 15 fols. + 844 pp. + 11 fols.; 5 fols. + 665 pp. + ? fols.; 7 fols. + 713 pp. + 9 fols.]

1622 See 1892a, 1892b.

1723 [1725] Primera [Segund, Tercera] Parte de los Veinte i un libros rituales i Monarchia indiana con el origen y guerras de los Indios Ocidentales de sus poblacones, descubrimiento, conquista, conuersion y otras cosas marauillosas de la mesma tierra distribuydos en tres tomos. Compuesto por —— ministro prouincial de la orden de Nuestro Serafico Padre. San Francisco en la prouincia del Santo Evangelio de Mexico en la Nueba España. Con privilegio. En Madrid en la Oficina y a costa de Nicolás Rodriguez

Franco. Año de 1723. [Three vols. of 20 fols. + 768 pp. + 36 fols.; 7 fols. + 623 pp. + 28 fols.; 8 fols. + 634 pp. + 21 fols., n.d.]

1892a Razones informativas que las tres ordenes mendicantes, es a saber, la de Sancto Domingo, San Francisco y San Agustín, dan por donde no les conviene subjectar sus religiosos al examen de los obispos; y puesto que esto se haya de ejecutar inviolablemente, les conviene mas dejar la doctrina y administracion de los indios que tienen a su cargo y recogerse en sus conventos a la sola guarda y observancia de su religion y regla; y otras cosas concernientes a la administracion de los indio y cosas dignas de saber en esta materia; donde tambien se trata que tener la dicha doctrina los religiosos no es en agravio de los obispos, y del provecho que de tenerla a los dichos indios se les sigue, y servicio que a Dios en esto se hace y a la Corona de Castilla. Recopiladas por Fray —— (1622). Mexico. In Joaquín García Icazbalceta, ed., Nueva colección de documentos para la historia de México, 5:125–80.

1892b Servicios que las tres ordenes han hecho a la Corona de Castilla en estas tierras de la Nueva España desde que entraron a su conversion hasta estos presentes tiempos; y que los clérigos no se ocupan en esto; del número de ellos; del número de las lenguas y agravios del arzobispo y otras cosas concernientes al otro memorial informativo. Por Fray —— Minorita de la Provincia del Santo Evangelio de México (1622). Mexico. Ibid., 5:180–240.

1943–44 Monarquía indiana. Reimpresión facsimilar de la 2ª edición por S. Chavez Hayhoe. 3 vols. Mexico. [See 1723.]

1969 Monarquía indiana. Introducción por Miguel León-Portilla. 3 vols. Biblioteca Porrúa, 41–43 [reduced facsimile of 1723 ed.]. Mexico.

APPENDIX B. TENTATIVE CHRONOLOGICAL OUTLINE OF THE
BIOGRAPHY OF TORQUEMADA

By Howard F. Cline

Date	Event	Approximate Age	Source
1564?	Birth in Spain	—	Various
1577	Youth in Mexico City	13	MI, 1:301–02; 2:146
1579?	Entrance into Franciscan Order	15	Figueroa; García Icazbalceta, 1886–92, 4:xii; 1896–99, 4:223
1581?	Acquaintance with Bernal Diaz and others in Guatemala	17	MI, 1:324, 327, 351
1581?	In Honduras as a "youth"	17	MI, 1:335
1582	Residence in Convent to Tacuba	18	MI, 2:604
1583?	Final vows in Franciscan Order	19	García Icazbalceta
1590–92	Indian administrator, Chapel of San Jose, Tlatelolco	26–28	MI, 1:653
1592	Gathering of historical data	28	MI, Prólogo general
1595	Acquaintance with Mendieta and talk with him about *Historia eclesiástica indiana*	31	MI, 3:82
1600–01	Guardian, Convent of Zacatlan; learning of Totonac; collection of data	36–37	MI, 1:281; 3:203, 219
1602	Guardian, Convent of Tulancingo	38	*Vida y milagros*
1602	*Vida y milagros* published	38	Appendix A above
1604–11	Guardian, Convent of Santiago Tlatelolco; administrator of Colegio de Santa Cruz	40–51	MI, 3:113, 115, 582
1604	Writing of MI, bks. 3 and 12	40	MI, 1:309; 2:395
1604	Journey to Zacatecas with Fr. Pedro de la Cruz	40	MI, 2:337; 3:342
1604	Renovation of causeways and calzadas; supervision of native labor	40	MI, 1:728–29
1605	Theatrical presentation in Latin, Spanish, and Nahuatl	41	MI, 3:44–45
1606	Journey to Jalisco	42	MI, 1:388; 2:582
1609	Church of Santiago Tlatelolco finished under his supervision	45	MI, 2:307; 3:215
1609	Named Chronicler of Franciscans, April 6	45	MI, Carta
1610	On viceregal orders, reestablishment of native market of Tlatelolco	46	MI, 2:555
1610	Journey to Veracruz	46	MI, 1:411
1610–11	Agitation at having "voladores" ceremony prohibited	46–47	MI, 2:306–07
1612	Permission received to publish MI	48	MI, Lic. y Ap.
1612–13	Guardian, Convent of Tlaxcala	48–49	MI, Lic. y Ap.
1612–22	Journeys to northern Mexico	48–58	Torquemada, 1622
1614–17	Provincial of Province of Santo Evangelio	50–53	Vetancurt, 1871
1615	MI published; edition lost at sea	51	MI, title page to Proemio, 1723
1624	Death and burial at Convent of San Francisco	60	Unos Annales, 1948

REFERENCES

ALAMÁN, LUCAS
1942 Disertaciones sobre la historia de la República Mejicana desde la época de la conquista que los españoles hicieron a fines del siglo XV y principios del XVI de las islas y continente americano hasta la independencia. *Col. grandes autores mejicanos*, vols. 6, 7, 8. Mexico.

ALTOLAGUIRRE Y DUVALE, ANGEL DE
1954 Descubrimiento y conquista de México con una introducción sobre fuentes por Antonio Ballesteros y Beretta. Salvat. *Historia de América y de los pueblos americanos*, 7. Barcelona.

ALVARADO TEZOZOMOC, HERNANDO
1878 Crónica mexicana. Mexico.

ANDRADE, VICENTE DE P.
1899 Ensayo bibliográfico mexicano del siglo XVII. 2d ed. Imprenta del Museo Nacional. Mexico.

ANTONIO, NICOLÁS
1783–88 Bibliotheca Hispana Nova. 2 vols. Madrid.

BALLESTEROS Y BERETTA, ANTONIO
1954 Introducción (sobre fuentes). *In* Altolaguirre y Duvale, 1954.

BANCROFT, HUBERT HOWE
See Article 19, Appendix A.

BENAVENTE, TORIBIO DE [MOTOLINÍA]
See Article 13, Bibliography.

BERISTÁIN DE SOUZA, J. M.
1947 Biblioteca Hispano Americana Septentrional (1521–1825). Ediciones Fuente Cultural. 5 vols. Mexico.

BURRUS, ERNEST J., S.J.
1949 See Cavo, 1949.
1959 Clavigero and the lost Sigüenza y Góngora manuscripts. *ECN*, 1:59–90.

CAVO, P. ANDRÉS
1949 Historia de México. Paleografía de E. J. Burrus. Prólogo de Mariano J. Cuevas. Mexico.

CHAVERO, ALFREDO
See Article 21, Appendix E.

CLAVIGERO, FRANCISCO J.
See Article 17, Appendix.

CLINE, HOWARD F.
1969 A note on Torquemada's native sources and historiographical methods. *The Americas*, 25:372–86.

CUEVAS, MARIANO J.
1946 Historia de la iglesia en México. 5 vols. Mexico.
1949 See Cavo, 1949.

ECHEVERRÍA Y VEYTIA, MARIANO FERNÁNDEZ DE
See Veytia, Mariano.

ESTUDIOS DE HISTORIOGRAFÍA
1945 Estudios de historiografía de la Nueva España por Hugo Díaz-Thomé, Fernando Sandoval, Manuel Carrera Stampa, Carlos Bosch García, Ernesto de la Torre, Enriqueta López Lira, Julio Le Riverend Brusone, con una introducción de Ramón Iglesia. Mexico.

GARCÍA ICAZBALCETA, JOAQUÍN
See Article 21, Appendix D.

GARIBAY K., ANGEL MARÍA
1953–54 Historia de la literatura nahuatl. 2 vols. Mexico.

GIBSON, CHARLES
1952 Tlaxcala in the sixteenth century. New Haven.

GONZÁLEZ OBREGÓN, LUIS
1899 Elogio de Fray Juan de Torquemada. *In* Andrade, 1899, pp. 3–9.

HASLER, JUAN A., ed.
1958 Anónimo mexicano: paleografía. *Archivos Nahuas*, tomo 1, fasc. 2, pp. 303–23. Jalapa.

HERRERA DE TORDESILLAS, ANTONIO DE
See Article 15, Appendix.

KRICKEBERG, WALTER
1933 Los Totonaca. Publicaciones del Museo Nacional. Mexico.

LEAL, LUIS
1955 El libro XII de Sahagún. *Historia mexicana*, 5:184–210.

LECLERC, CHARLES
1878 Bibliotheca Americana. Paris.

LEÓN PINELO, ANTONIO DE
1958 Epítome de la Biblioteca Oriental i Occidental, Náutica i Geográfica. Introducción de A. Millares Carlo. Facsimile ed. Pan American Union. Washington.

LEÓN-PORTILLA, MIGUEL
1964 *Introduction to*: Juan de Torquemada, *Monarquía indiana . . .* selección.

UNAM, *Bib. estudiante universitario*, 84. Mexico.

LE RIVEREND BRUSONE, JULIO
1945 *La historia antigua de México* del Padre Francisco Javier Clavijero. *In* Estudios de Historiografía de la Nueva España, pp. 293–323. Mexico.

LÓPEZ, P. ATANASIO
1931 Fray Toribio Motolinía, misionero e historiador de México en el siglo XVI. *Illuminare* (Feb.). Madrid.

MCAFEE, BYRON, AND R. H. BARLOW, trans. and eds.
1948 Unos anales coloniales de Tlatelolco, 1519–1633. Academia Mexicana de la Historia, *Memorias*, 7:152–87.

MEDINA, JOSÉ TORIBIO
1898–1907 Biblioteca Hispano-Americana (1493–1810). Santiago, Chile.
1907–12 La Imprenta en México. 8 vols. Santiago, Chile.

MILLARES CARLO, A.
1958 *See* León Pinelo, 1958.

MORENO TOSCANO, ALEJANDRA
1963a Fray Juan de Torquemada y su *Monarquia indiana*. Universidad Veracruzana-México, Facultad de Filosofía, Letras, y Ciencias, *Cuadernos*, 19. Jalapa.
1963b Vindicación de Torquemada. *Historia mexicana*, 12:497–515.

NICOLAU D'OLWER, LUIS
1952 Fray Bernardino de Sahagún (1499–1590). PAIGH, Comisión de Historia, Pub. 142. Mexico.

OROZCO Y BERRA, M.
See Article 21, Appendix C.

PERAL, MIGUEL ANGEL
1944 Diccionario biográfico mexicano. 2 vols. Mexico.

PHELAN, JOHN LEDDY
1956 The millennial kingdom of the Franciscans in the New World: A study of the writings of Gerónimo de Mendieta (1525–1604). Univ. California, Publications in History, vol. 42. Berkeley-Los Angeles. [Revised ed., 1970.]
1960 Neo-Aztecism in the eighteenth century and the genesis of Mexican nationalism. *In* Culture in History: Essays in honor of Paul Radin, Stanley Diamond, ed., pp. 760–70. Columbia University Press. New York.

PIJOAN, JOSÉ
1946 Arte precolombiano mexicano y maya. *In* his Summa Artis: Historia General del Arte, vol. 10. Madrid.

RAMÍREZ, JOSÉ F.
See Article 21, Appendix B.

RÉVILLE, A.
1885 Les Religions du Mexique, de l'Amérique Centrale et du Pérou. Paris.

REYES, ALFONSO
1948 Letras de la Nueva España. Fondo de Cultura Económica, *Col. Tierra Firme*, 40. Mexico.

RICARD, ROBERT
1947 La conquista espiritual de México. [Translation of French ed., 1933.] Mexico.

RICO GONZÁLEZ, VÍCTOR
1949 Historiadores mexicanos del siglo XVIII: Estudios historiográficos sobre Clavijero, Veytia, Cavo y Alegre. UNAM, Instituto de Historia.

SÁNCHEZ ALONSO, BENITO
1944 Historia de la historiografía española: Ensayo de un examen de conjunto. 3 vols. Madrid.

STECK, FRANCISCO DE B.
1944 El primer colegio de América: Santa Cruz de Tlatelolco. Mexico.

TORQUEMADA, JUAN DE
See Article 16, Appendix A.

UNOS ANALES COLONIALES
1948 Unos anales coloniales de Tlatelolco, 1519–1633. Byron McAfee and R. H. Barlow, trans. and eds. Academia Mexicana de la Historia, *Memorias*, 7:152–87.

VALADÉS, DIEGO
1579 Rhetorica Christiana ad concionandi et orandi usum accommodata, utriusque facultatis exemplis suo loco insertis, quae quidem ex indorum macime deptompta sunt historiis, unde praeter doctrinam summa quoque delectatio comparabitur. Perugia.

VALENZUELA RODARTE, ALBERTO
1959 Capítulos para una historia de la literatura mexicana. Capítulos IX–XI. Biblioteca Nacional, *Boletín*, 10(4):25–43. Mexico.

VALLE-ARIZPE, ARTEMIO DE
1946 Historia de la ciudad de México según los relatos de sus cronistas. 4th ed. Mexico.

VETANCURT, AGUSTÍN DE
1871 Menologío franciscano de los varones más señalados que con sus vidas exemplares ilustraron la provincia de

el Santo Evangelio de México. Mexico.

1960–61 Teatro mexicano. . . . 4 vols. *Col. Chimalistac*, 8–11. Madrid.

VEYTIA, MARIANO FERNÁNDEZ DE ECHEVERRÍA Y

1944 Historia antigua de México. Reproducción de la edición de C. F. Ortega de 1836. Mexico.

WILGUS, A. CURTIS

1942 Histories and historians of Hispanic America. New York.

ZULAICA GÁRATE, ROMÁN

1939 Los Franciscanos y la imprenta en México en el siglo XVI. Mexico.

17. Francisco Javier Clavigero, 1731-1787

CHARLES E. RONAN, S.J.

THE NAME CLAVIGERO would have meant little or nothing in Mexican history had it not been for Francisco Javier (Mariano) Clavigero, the third of eleven children.[1] Born in Veracruz, September 9, 1731, he was thus a creole.[2] His parents were María Isabel Echegaray and Blas Clavigero. Doña María, also a creole, had been born in Veracruz around the turn of the century, the daughter of Juan de Echegaray and María Fernández Marín.[3]

Don Blas, his father, was a *peninsular*. Born in "Melgar de Arriba in the bishopric of León in Old Castile" near Valladolid on February 15, 1699, he was the son of Isabel Molaguero and Bartolomé Clavigero, deputy corregidor of the district in which he lived.[4] After completing his early education at the University of Paris, Blas returned to Spain, where he continued his studies and entered the service of the Duke of Medinaceli, but after a time quit this post and emigrated to Mexico. There for seven years (August, 1720–September, 1727) he served as an official in the comptroller's office in Veracruz and, during the absence of the comptroller himself, don Juan de Echegaray,

his father-in-law, he filled this position temporarily also.[5] On April 26, 1726, he married doña María (Romero Flores, 1939, p. 316).

Desiring to improve his status, he re-

[1] The author gratefully acknowledges a grant-in-aid from the American Philosophical Society for research on Clavigero in Europe. The Volume Editor expresses appreciation to Charles Gibson, John B. Glass, Peggy Korn, Henry B. Nicholson, and John L. Phelan for their critical review and aid on earlier versions of this article.

This article was completed in February, 1969, and has now been revised by the author to include pertinent material which has appeared since that date. He has just completed a full-length biography of Clavigero.

[2] MS, Libro de admisiones, Tepotzotlan, Gabinete de manuscritos, BNMex, MS 1115 (67), fol. 15. Unless otherwise indicated, all the biographical data contained in this article are from Maneiro, 1791–92, 3:28–78. Maneiro, a Mexican Jesuit, was Clavigero's principal biographer. See Maneiro, 1941, 1956, for translations.

[3] MS, Testamento de María Isabel Echegaray, Sept. 15, 1740. Registro de Testamentos del año 1740, ANP, 4, fols. 105–06.

[4] MS, Testamento de don Blas Clavigero, July 5, 1740. Registro de Testamentos del año 1740, ANP, 4, fols. 82–83; also Libro de Bautismos, 1630 hasta 1724. Archivo de la parroquia de San Miguel Archangel, Melgar de Arriba, Valladolid, Spain.

[5] Relazión de Servizios de Don Blas Clabijero, AGI, Indiferente General, leg. 163, fol. 1.

1—FRANCISCO JAVIER CLAVIGERO. From
Scott, 1944.

turned to Spain in January, 1730 (Rubio Mañé, 1969, pp. 506–07) with highest recommendations from the royal officials in Veracruz, to seek the king's favor. This resulted in his being appointed to the highly prized post of *alcalde mayor* of the province of Xicayan in the Mixteca Baja, located on the southwest coast in the present state of Oaxaca.[6] Back in Veracruz in the late summer of 1730, he did not go immediately to his new post, as his predecessor had not yet finished his term of office. In the interim, he was named alcalde mayor and *capitán a guerra* of Teziutlan y Atempa, a district in the northeastern part of the present-day state of Puebla. Remaining there a year (September, 1732–September, 1733), he then moved to the Mixteca Baja, where he assumed his duties, establishing residence in Jamiltepeque. Leaving office as alcalde mayor in 1739, he moved to Puebla where he was assigned as administrator of the royal *alcabalas* (sales tax) and *familiar* (agent)

of the Inquisition (Castro Morales, 1970, pp. 11–12; Rubio Mañé, 1969, pp. 510–12).

In these provincial regions, Francisco Javier Clavigero passed his earliest years, a very impressionable period that saw him develop into a bright, alert lad, intellectually inquisitive, possessed of a superb memory. About 1740, Francisco entered the Jesuit Colegio de San Jerónimo in Puebla. There he studied Latin grammar, syntax, and other subjects, followed by the liberal arts program in the Colegio de San Ignacio in the same city. An excellent student, he was not content to pursue only the required subjects, but also read in the secular and religious literature of Spain and Spanish America and displayed a certain interest in mathematics and the mechanical arts. In 1746 he was graduated as a "bachiller de Artes."[7]

The first big step in Clavigero's life was his entrance into the Jesuit Order on February 13, 1748, at Tepotzotlan, a small village about 15 miles north of Mexico City, where he began his two-year period of noviceship.[8] Upon its completion, he pronounced his vows of poverty, chastity, and obedience February 22, 1750, thereby joining the ranks of the Society and now ready to begin his studies for the priesthood.[9] Entering the college department of the seminary, he read further in the Latin humanities, mastered French, pursued Spanish literature more widely, and made his first acquaintance with Greek and Hebrew under the tutelage of a German Jesuit residing at Tepotzotlan. From here, he moved on to Puebla to study

[6] MS, Don Blas Clavigero. Traslado del título de Alcalde Mayor de la Provincia de Xicaian en la Nueva España para el dicho Don Blas residente en dicho reino, y en el caso que se expresa para Don Juan de Rementería, 14 de junio de 1730. AGI, Audiencia de México, leg. 1219, fol. 1.

[7] Grados de Bach[s] e Artes de 1740 a 1759, AGN, Universidad 167, fol. 85.

[8] Ibid.

[9] MS, Supplementum 1[i] et 2[i] Catalogi Provinciae Mexicanae a die 15 Junii anni 1749 usque diem 1[m] Aprilis anni 1750 die 22 Februarii, ARSJ, Mexico 7, fol. 338.

scholastic philosophy at the Colegio de San Ildefonso. There he also became better acquainted with the new currents of thought by reading the works of the noted Spanish Benedictine, Benito Feijóo, who whetted his appetite for what the 18th century called "modern philosophy." For Clavigero this meant a modified Aristotelianism familiar with and strongly influenced by 18th-century science, with heavy emphasis on inductive critical analysis. He also read about Descartes, Newton, and von Leibnitz. He had to pursue these studies with a certain caution, given some of his colleagues' suspicion of such authors.

Terminating his philosophical studies, Clavigero returned to Mexico City where he began a four-year course of theology at the Colegio de San Pedro y San Pablo, commonly known as the Colegio Máximo.[10] Theological studies apart, this was another very formative period in Clavigero's life. During this time he continued the study of Nahuatl, which he had begun as a novice, with a view to working among the Indians, a desire he had nourished since his noviceship when he made the acquaintance of several noted Jesuit missionaries of Lower California who were living out their last days at the novitiate in Tepotzotlan. At this juncture, through Father Rafael Campoy, a Jesuit colleague, he was introduced to what remained of the books and pictorial documents related to Mexican antiquities which the 17th-century savant, Carlos Sigüenza y Góngora, had collected and bequeathed to the Colegio Máximo on his death in 1700. Clavigero's enthusiasm for Mexican antiquities grew apace. The study of the Sigüenza Collection would serve him in later years when he would write in defense of Aztec Mexico.

As a theological student, Clavigero also acted as a dormitory prefect or disciplinarian for a short while. This is a point worth stressing. This modest appointment has been up to now misinterpreted and construed as prefect (headmaster) of the entire

Colegio de San Pedro y San Pablo.[11] That he held the position in a dormitory we know both from Clavigero himself and from a short biographical sketch of the latter, written by an admirer, Felix Sebastián, S.J. (n.d.).[12] This and other misrepresentations of events in Clavigero's life—such as the many Indian languages he allegedly spoke when, in reality, he knew only Nahuatl—have created a species of "Clavigero myth" that has given a somewhat distorted picture of the man. No service is done history by its continuance.

Ordinarily, Jesuits are ordained to the priesthood after the completion of their third year of theological studies. Not having reached the canonical age of 23 by the end of his third year (1753), Clavigero had to wait another 12 months. During the interval, he taught rhetoric at the Colegio de San Ildefonso, where he gained a reputation as a severe critic of the traditional methods of preaching—a result, undoubtedly, of the "new approach" he felt should be taken toward many traditional practices in Mexico. It was at this time also that Clavigero made his first request to be sent to the Indian mis-

[10] MS, Catalogus 1us Provinciae Mexicanae a P. Johanne Antonio Balthasar Provinciali confectus et ad R. admodum P.N. Generalem missus die 1 Decembris anno 1751, ARSJ, Mexico 8, fol. 6. This catalog shows Clavigero as a second-year theologian.

[11] Such an erroneous conclusion was based on a faulty translation by Mariano Beristáin of a passage in Maneiro's Latin biography (1791–92) of Clavigero, in which it was stated that the latter was "praefectus alumnorum." The Mexican bibliophile, Beristáin, translated it as "prefect of the Colegio" instead of "student prefect" (or disciplinarian).

[12] MS, Filiación que se hace de los Regulares de la Comp^a con el nre. de JHS. pertenectes de la provincia de México venido en diferentes embarcaciones. AHN, Sección Clero, Jesuítas, leg. 826, 5. Also Felix Sebastián, S.J., MS, "Memorias de los Padres y Hermanos de la Compañía de Jesús de la Provincia de Nueva España, difuntes después del arresto acaecido en la Capital de México, el día 25 de Junio del año 1767. Escritas por Felix de Sebastián, sacerdote de la misma Provincia, Misionero que era de la nación Tubara." BCA, Cartaggio XVI, A531, A532.

sions.[13] Finally, on October 13, 1754, he was raised to the priesthood by the archbishop of Mexico City, don Manuel Rubio y Salinas.[14] He then completed the required remaining two years of Jesuit seminary training, one year being devoted to further theological studies at the Colegio de San Ildefonso in Puebla, followed by a year of third probation at the Colegio de Espiritu Santo in the same city. This was a period of final testing of his vocation and further study of the Jesuit rules and constitutions.

By the end of 1756 Clavigero was ready for his first assignment as a priest. He was sent to the *Casa Profesa* in Mexico City, where he worked for a short time as a parish priest until he was transferred to the Colegio de San Ildefonso in the same city and was made moderator of the theological academy.[15] This did not last for long, however. On December 23, 1757, he received a letter from Father Provincial Agustín Carta informing him that he was to go to Guadalajara to teach liberal arts. Disturbed very much by the appointment, the young Jesuit besought his superior to send him to the Indian missions, as he had already requested on several occasions. The provincial compromised and sent him to the Colegio de San Gregorio in Mexico City, a school for the education of natives, adjoining the Colegio de San Pedro y San Pablo.[16]

Arriving at his new post sometime during the early summer of 1758, Clavigero plunged into a more intense study of Nahuatl. Before long he was hearing confessions in that tongue, preaching and administering to the spiritual and temporal needs of the natives.[17] He was also made chaplain of the city's Indian prisons. Living only a step away from Colegio Máximo, whose library housed the Sigüenza Collection, Clavigero continued his historical studies. And, according to Maneiro, it was during these years, between 1756 and 1762, that he made the acquaintance of a group of intellectually inquisitive students whose interest in "modern philosophy" and history he helped kindle. Among them were Lino Gómez, later to become an important ecclesiastical figure; Ignacio Borunda, whom William Hickling Prescott extravagantly calls "Mexico's Champollion" (Prescott, n.d., p. 62); Juan Maneiro, Clavigero's biographer; Manuel Lardizabal, future lawyer of the Council of Castile and friend of Clavigero at the Spanish court; Juan Benito Díaz de Gamarra, the future Oratorian and "modern philosopher"; and finally, José Alzate, the future priest-scientist.

In the spring of 1762 Clavigero was moved to the Colegio de San Francisco de Javier in Puebla, another school for the Indians, where he taught while acting as itinerant missionary to the Indian villages of the area. He perfected his knowledge of Nahuatl and, as time permitted, continued his study of Mexican history (Clavigero, 1945, 1:75; Echeverría y Veytia, 1931, 2:429–33). For him this was a delightful pastime. The period in Puebla, however, ended Clavigero's work with the Indians.

In December, 1762, the provincial, feeling that the young missionary could be used more effectively in the classroom, informed him that he was to go to Valladolid, Morelia, to teach liberal arts.[18] The assignment was a heavy blow, but he reluctantly obeyed.

[13] MS, Aposento del Padre Francisco Xavier Clavixero. Cartas de correspondencia con los superiores y otros Padres sobre various Particulares, AGN, Archivo de Hacienda, leg. 1955, fol. 256.

[14] MS, Supplementum 1[i] et 2[i] Catalogi Provinciae Mexicanae a die 15 Junii anni 1749 usque ad diem 1[m] Aprilis anni 1750, ARSJ, Mexico 7, fol. 338.

[15] MS, Filiación que se hace de los Regulares, AHN, Sección Clero, Jesuítas, leg. 826, 5.

[16] MS, Papeles Jesuítas, Libro IV de las consultas de la Provincia, Agosto, 1756, MNA/AH, MS antiguo, XII (23).

[17] MS, Noticias del Colegio de San Gregorio de México a cargo de los Padres de la Compañia de Jesús, 1695 at 1763, Colección Cuevas, Colección Histórica Americanista, Mexico City, 91.3.

[18] MS, Catalogus 1[us] Provinciae Mexicanae a P. Franc[o] Zevallos Provinciali confectus et ad admodum P. N. Generalem missus die 28 Decembris 1764, ARSJ, Mexico 8, fol. 190.

Clavigero's love for missionary work should give pause to those fomenters of the "Clavigero myth" who have been promoting the idea that Clavigero from the very start was a flaming evangel of "modern philosophy," straining at the leash to get into the classroom to announce the "good news." The evidence simply does not bear this out. That he was deeply interested in the "new learning" there can be no doubt (Villoro, 1963); when put to teach it, he did a fine job. But his primary interest, at least in the beginning of his priestly life, was work among the Indians. If he could not get to the California missions, then he was content with the home missions. It must be recalled that the 18th century was not an age of specialization or departmentalization. It was not out of the ordinary, in a century when a learned man took all knowledge for his field, for a missionary to be well acquainted with and interested in the new intellectual trends or for the intellectual also to be a devoted missionary. Eusebio Kino, the well-known Jesuit missionary of the Pimeria Alta, was a perfect example of this. So also was Clavigero.

With a sad heart Clavigero arrived in Valladolid in the summer of 1763.[19] There he carved a niche for himself in Mexican history by teaching the first complete course in "modern philosophy" to be given in the viceroyalty (Navarro, 1948, pp. 174–94). He thus inaugurated a modest but significant reform which undoubtedly would have taken hold in all Jesuit colegios in New Spain had it not been for the expulsion of the Order just a few years later (1767). In April, 1766, Clavigero was very abruptly transferred to Guadalajara to take over the philosophy classes of a Jesuit colleague who had been dismissed from the Society.[20] Having come to love teaching in Valladolid, his reaction to the change was quite severe. He found the work most distasteful (he compared himself to a cobbler mending an old pair of shoes) but completed the course successfully, having used the opportunity to

introduce the students of Guadalajara to "modern philosophy" also.

During the ensuing academic year (1766–67), he was assigned to apostolic labors in the colegio, where he also studied history and wrote two works.[21] One was *Diálogo entre Filáletes y Paleófilo*, in which he argued that "in the study of Physics one should endeavor to search out the truth and by no means propagate some already established judgment that conforms with the opinion of the ancients." The other was a *Vejamen* entitled "Un Banquete de la Philosophia" [sic], a clever defense of inductive critical analysis.[22]

Clavigero was in Guadalajara only a year when Charles III expelled the Jesuits from the Spanish Empire. The decree was executed in New Spain in June, 1767. After a long arduous journey, the exiled clerics were allowed to settle in the papal states toward the end of 1768. After a year's residence in Ferrara, Clavigero was assigned to Bologna, where he witnessed the suppression of the Order in 1773. He lived on thereafter as a diocesan priest under the jurisdiction of the local bishop, supporting himself on the very meager pension granted all the Jesuit exiles by the Spanish government.

The last four years of his life were troubled by broken health. Kidney and gall bladder disorders began to manifest themselves late in 1783 and became progressively worse. Endeavoring to continue his studies despite excruciating pain, he was finally forced to submit to painful surgery

[19] MS, Catalogus perpetuus domorum, collegiorum missionum, personarum, at munerum provinciae mexicanae Societatis Jesu (1704–1763), MNA/AH, MS Jesuítas, no. 39.

[20] MS, Aposento del Padre Clavigero, AGN, Archivo de Hacienda, leg. 1955, fol. 226.

[21] MS, Colegio de Guadalajara. Año de 1767. Primero visita día 11 de Abril de dicho año. Cerrada día 20 de dho. mes y año. P. Provincial Salvador Gandara, AGN, Archivo de Hacienda, leg. 547–2.

[22] Vexamen 2º que hizo el P. Marriano [sic] Clavigero y dixo en el Colegio de la Compañía de Jesús de la Ciudad de Guadalaxara el día (no date given). BNMA, MS 12467.

from which he never fully recovered. The end came April 2, 1787.

He was buried in the crypt of the former Jesuit Church of Santa Lucía in Bologna. To the resounding credit of the Mexican government, however, Clavigero's remains were repatriated and buried (August 6, 1970) in Mexico's Pantheon of Illustrious Men in the nation's capital. A noble gesture, indeed, overwhelmingly acclaimed by the people, in recognition of the Jesuit's patriotic services to his fatherland (*Excelsior*, 1970; *Hoy*, 1970; *El Dia*, 1970). Both Italian and Spanish newspapers carried news of his death and spoke of him in highly eulogistic terms (Gaceta, 1787; Gazzetta Universale, 1787). Even Spain's royal agent, Luís de Gneco, living in Bologna, sang his praises in a letter to the Spanish ambassador to the Holy See, Nicolás de Azara.[23]

When the Jesuits were expelled from the king's domains, their activities, both as priests and educators, were very much restricted by royal and papal decrees. As a result, many of them turned to intellectual pursuits, like writing, to fill up their many leisure hours. Such was the case with Clavigero.

It was to Mexican history that he directed his principal attention. The major end result of all such activity was the *Storia antica*, although other projects also occupied his time. These included such works as the *Storia della California* (see Article 13, bibliography), a lengthy correspondence with the Spanish Jesuit philologist, Lorenzo Hervás y Panduro on Mexican antiquities (Clark, 1937), the composition of an ecclesiastical history of New Spain which, although begun, was never completed (Clavigero, 1780–81, 2:76), and other works of lesser importance. Our main interest, however, is the *Storia antica*.

[23] MS, Carta de Luís de Gneco a Nicolás de Azara, 13 de Maio de 1786, Archivo de la embajada de España, Ministerio de Asuntos Exteriores, Madrid, leg. 579.

STORIA ANTICA: PUBLISHING HISTORY

When Clavigero took up the pen, his plan was to edit a sort of encyclopedia of Mexican antiquities to preserve for posterity a record of the notable achievements of that native civilization. A friend, however, impressed by the amount of material he had collected, urged him to write a history of ancient Mexico, pointing out that it would be more useful to the public than an encyclopedia. At first appalled by the size of the task, he finally acquiesced and began to gather materials. This brought him into contact with European writers like William Robertson, Count de Buffon, Abbé Raynal, and, above all, the Dutch savant, Corneille de Pauw, all of whom had written about America and her inhabitants. His creole Mexican patriotism was wounded by what they said (Navarro, 1954). He now had further reason for writing a history of Mexico to refute the misinformation these authors had spread and to acquaint Europe with the truth about the New World.

The ensuing polemic resulted in his bringing together under one cover the first complete history of ancient Mexico. Even though he states that his principal purpose in writing was for the benefit of his countrymen, it is quite obvious that polemical reasons were also uppermost in his mind. He engaged in one of the famous disputes of the 18th century, touching on the relative merits of the Old World versus the New World (Gerbi, 1960). As a foremost protagonist of the latter, he can rightfully be called the 18th century's "Voice of America."

Some time after 1771 Clavigero began the composition of the *Historia antigua* (Clavigero, 1780–81, 4:13). Writing in Spanish, he completed the volumes by 1778. This is clear from his famous letter of March 25, 1778, to Echeverría y Veytia in which he states: "To the three volumes of the *Historia*, another of interesting and, for the most part, relevant Dissertations will be added.

These Dissertations, which I have finished, are eight." Since there is every reason to assume that the author was speaking about his *Spanish* manuscript, this information also clears up a hitherto obscure point as to whether the Dissertations were ever written in Spanish. Until now, it has been gratuitously assumed that they were written only in Italian because, unlike the *Historia* proper, the Spanish manuscript containing them has never been found. This letter proves otherwise.

In 1780 Clavigero published the first three volumes, and in 1781 the fourth. This was not a Spanish edition as might be expected, but one in Italian, entitled *Storia antica del Messico*. What had happened?

Clavigero is not too clear on the point. In one place he wrote: "urged on . . . by some Italian friends who were most desirous to read it in their own language, I took upon myself the new and fatiguing task of translating it into Tuscan" (Clavigero, 1780–81, 1:26). In another place he said, "It was published in Italian because there was no other alternative" (ibid., pp. 8–9). A further reason, quite possibly, for an Italian edition, was financial. Realizing that there would be little market for a Spanish edition in Italy, Clavigero was easily persuaded to translate it into Italian, thereby attracting Italian subscribers whose purchase of the history would guarantee funds for its publication. The view is supported by the list of a hundred subscribers to the Italian edition, appended to volume 2 of the *Storia antica*.

There is not the slightest evidence, however, as some have contended, that Clavigero was forced to publish his history in Italian because his attempts to bring out a Spanish edition were thwarted by the Spanish government. There is no indication that he made any effort whatsoever prior to 1783 to publish such a Spanish edition. After that date, the story was different, as has been proved (Ronan, 1970).

In keeping with 18th-century custom, the

Storia antica carried a dedication. The first three volumes were dedicated by the author to the Royal and Pontifical University of Mexico. Owing to insurmountable difficulties, Clavigero was unable to forward copies of the work to Mexico until early 1784. They were received by the university authorities with great satisfaction (ibid.). The viceroy, don Bernardo Gálvez, to whom a copy had also been given, urged that an honorarium, to which he contributed, be sent the author. Others urged that Clavigero be numbered among the university's doctors with a right to a proper remuneration should he ever return to New Spain (Clavigero, 1789b, 1:4). The fourth volume was dedicated to Count Giovanni Renaldo Carli, an Italian student of Mexican antiquities and a government official in the Austrian possessions in northern Italy. Clavigero had unwittingly but deeply offended him by critical remarks on the count's *Lettere Americane*, dealing with pre-Hispanic Mexico, which had appeared anonymously in the *Magazzino Letterario* of Florence (Clavigero, 1780–81, 1:8–9). On learning of the importance of the author and how hurt he was, Clavigero was persuaded to dedicate his fourth volume to the nobleman to assuage his feelings. There followed an exchange of letters in the *Gazzetta di Cremona* on the disputed matters between the two historians, in which each one defended his original position (*Gazzetta di Cremona*, 1782).

To his very pleasant surprise, our author received a letter in the late spring of 1783 from Manuel Lardizabal y Uribe, Mexican-born attorney to the Council of Castile, urging him to send the Spanish original of his History to Madrid for publication. Delighted with the idea, he spent the next six months polishing and revising the first two manuscript volumes, which he forwarded in December, 1783, to the Madrid publisher, Antonio de Sancha.[24] On receiving them

[24] MS, Letter of Clavigero to Hervás y Panduro, Dec. 20, 1783, Vatican Library, MS Vaticana Latina, codex 9802, fol. 203. *Catalogus Provinciae*

the following summer, Sancha wrote to the secretary of the Council of the Indies, Francisco Cerdá y Rico, informing him of their arrival and of his desire to publish them; he said that Lardizabal, to whom, at Clavigero's request, the volumes had been turned over for a critical reading, found them quite satisfactory and favored publication.[25]

Since permission for publication in 18th-century Spain had to be given by both the Council of Castile and the Council of the Indies, Sancha, in September, 1784, sought the required permission from the former Council. It referred the two volumes to the Royal Academy for censorship. Clavigero never sent the remaining two volumes to Madrid, and (as stated below) the first two are lost. In Madrid their knowledge about the final two volumes was based on the Italian edition. We may also note that one change Clavigero made in the Spanish volumes he sent to Madrid was the addition of Fernández de Echeverría y Veytia to his "Noticia de los escritores . . . ," referring to

him as an "habil y docto caballero mexicano" who had written a history of Mexico which lack of funds had kept him from publishing, and which was probably buried "in some obscure archive." This note is absent from all published editions of Clavigero's work.[26]

Happily, the Academy appointed Pedro de Luxan, Duque de Almodovar, as censor. Within a short time, he returned a favorable vote. In November, 1784, the Council of Castile granted permission for publication.[27]

The following April (1785) Sancha then approached the Council of the Indies.[28] There the story was quite different. In September, 1784, several months prior to Sancha's visit, the Council had been ordered by José de Gálvez, Minister of the Indies, to examine the *Historia antigua* very carefully when it was brought before them. Charles III was personally interested in the matter, and had recently been informed that the work was derogatory to Spain and her conquest of America.[29]

What had occasioned the king's interest and Gálvez' message to the Council was a letter the latter had received in September, 1784, from Ramón Diosdado Caballero, a Spanish Jesuit exile living in Rome who had read the *Storia antica*. Highly incensed at what he felt was Clavigero's hispanophobia and exaggerated descriptions of Mexican culture, he wrote to the Spanish Minister warning him of the scandalous nature of the work.[30] He also told him about a partially completed refutation he was writing to counteract the evil influence of the Mexican Jesuit's history and stated that he would most willingly forward the manuscript, which he hoped to publish, to Madrid if Gálvez cared to read it. Entitled *Observaciones americanas y suplemento crítico a la historia del ex-Jesuíta Don Francisco Xavier Clavigero*, it was a bitter criticism of the *Storia antica*.

Hence, when Sancha appeared before the alerted Council of the Indies with Clavigero's manuscript, they immediately turned it

---

Mexicanae Societatis Jesu in quo singulorum nomen, cognomen, patria, aetas, atque ingressus in eandem continetur, anno Domini, 1758.

[25] MS, Letter of Antonio de Sancha to José Cerdá y Rico (n.d.), AHN, Madrid, Cartas de Indias, no. 468.

[26] MS, Letter of the Council of the Indies to José de Gálvez, Oct. 19, 1784, AGI, Indiferente General, exp. año 1784, leg. 398; also Dn. Antonio Sancha impresor en esta Corte: sobre que se le concede licencia para imprimir la traducción que se ha hecho del Toscano de la obra titulada Historia antigua de México, AHN, Sección Consejos suprimidos, Consejo de Castilla, Año 1784, leg. 5548, no. 10. El Consejo de las Indias pleno de tres salas, Madrid, 21 de Octubre de 1789, AGI, Indiferente General, 38, fol. 44.

[27] MS, Continuación de las censuras. Años del 1784 y 1785. Censura de la Historia Antigua de México de Clavigero, Madrid y Novre. 4 de 1785, RAH, leg. 7, no. 17.

[28] MS, Sobre la historia de Clavigero. El Consejo de las Indias pleno de tres salas, Madrid, 21 de Octubre de 1785, AGI, Patronato 196, fol. 46v.

[29] MS, Letter of José de Gálvez to the Council of the Indies, Sept. 21, 1783, AGI, Indiferente General, exp. año 1784, leg. 398.

[30] MS, Letter of Ramón Diosdado Caballero to José de Gálvez, Aug. 5, 1784, AHN, Cartas de Indias, no. 491.

over to two censors for diligent perusal.[31] After a lengthy examination, the latter returned a favorable verdict (in November, 1785), urging publication. Sancha was delighted with the news and made ready to publish the work. But in January, 1786, Gálvez intervened again and ordered, at the king's behest, another examination of the History and further informed the Council that to aid the censors to form a solid judgment on the merits of the work he was forwarding to them the manuscript copy of Diosdado's *Observaciones* which he had received since he had last written them in September, 1784. He also added the criticism which Juan Bautista Muñoz, to whom the *Observaciones* had been submitted for censorship, had made of them. Gálvez carefully called the Council's attention to the fact that Muñoz, in his critique, had not only made some pertinent comments on Clavigero and his History but had also considered a number of Diosdado's criticisms of the *Storia antica* quite valid. Accordingly, the censors subjected the Clavigero work to another examination. Their note submitted in September, 1786, was the same. They added, however, that, if the Council felt that the reading public would profit by a number of critical emendations and explanatory notes placed in the text, then they suggested that the publisher Sancha be appointed to make them, in keeping with those recommended by Muñoz.

The Council in March, 1787, fully approved the censor's main recommendations, just a month before Clavigero's death. The Council (disregarding the recommendation of appointing Sancha to correct the manuscript) agreed that the following additions, suggested by Muñoz, be made to the history before it was presented for royal approval:

[31] MS, Sobre la historia de Clavigero. El Consejo de las Indias pleno de tres salas, 21 de Octubre de 1789, AGI, Patronato 196, fols. 46–73. The rest of the material in this paragraph and the following two are from the same reference.

Volume I. A footnote should be added calling the reader's attention to the injustice of the exaggerated comparison Clavigero made between the Turkish oppression of the Greeks and the Spanish oppression of the New World Indians. However, the review should explain that the comparison has a certain justification but should not be overdrawn as was done by the translator of the recent French edition of Count Carli's *Lettere Americane*. At the beginning of the volume, a footnote should tell the readers about the author's background and outlook and judgment of the book's value should be included. Pertinent footnotes should also rectify some of the judgments and censures Clavigero made of certain authors in his bibliography.

Volume II. In this volume, a preface should be added, based on the valid criticism found in Diosdado Caballero's *Observaciones*, pointing out how the natives under Spanish rule have, relative to their ancestors, progressed in the field of law and government and in the liberal and mechanical arts. Some comment should also be made on Mexico's ancient population and on the true causes of population decline in the Americas so as to refute the exaggerated claims of Clavigero.

Volume III. In view of the fact that Diosdado Caballero made more observations on this volume, which treats of the Conquest, than on any other because of its frequent unjust attacks on Cortés and the conquistadores, special attention should be given to the explanatory and corrective notes that are to be added.

Volume IV. On the supposition that this volume, which contains the dissertations, does not treat of objectionable matter, and since Diosdado Caballero made no observations on it, it seems wise to publish it first; for although the author considered it his fourth volume, nonetheless, to satisfy the great public desire to read Clavigero's history, this volume could be published first while the other three are being emended for simultaneous publication.

The Council now looked for an "intelligent, wise person" capable of making the necessary revisions in the shortest time possible. Their choice was don Francisco Cerdá y Rico, a secretary of the Council of the Indies and a prominent figure in 18th-century

284

Spanish literary circles. With royal approval, the Council, in late November, 1789, turned over Clavigero's two-volume manuscript to Cerda y Rico. To guide him in his revision, they added the manuscript copy of Diosdado's *Observaciones* and the dossier containing Muñoz's evaluation of both the latter works.

Once again it looked as though the disputed history would appear soon. Incredible as it now may seem, and for reasons not at all clear, Cerda y Rico did nothing to the manuscript. On his death in January, 1800, the Clavigero work was found untouched. All manuscripts and the dossier, however, were returned to the Council of the Indies by the dead reviser's heirs. One more attempt was made to find another person to make the desired revisions. Despite suggestions, the endeavor came to naught. Thus ended all attempts to publish the two-volume Spanish manuscript which Clavigero had sent to Madrid in December, 1783. This important manuscript, after its return to the Council of the Indies, was lost. Efforts were made by some of Clavigero's admirers to find it, all in vain (Uriarte, 1904, 4:579).

Fortunately Clavigero retained a copy of the Spanish manuscript of the 10 books which compose the *Historia antigua* proper. On his death in 1787, his brother Ignacio kept the work until his own demise in 1826. It then came into the hands of the Jesuits, who were returning to Mexico after the restoration of the Society by Pope Pius VII in 1814. The manuscript was placed in the archives of the Jesuit province, where it was lost to view, and even Clavigero's authorship of it was forgotten. Early in the present century, it was identified by Manuel Díaz Rayón, S.J. It then disappeared from sight and reappeared in the hands of a dealer in the United States.

To re-purchase it, Carlos María Heredia, S.J., raised a considerable sum. His brother, Vicente, turned it over to Mariano Cuevas, S.J., the well-known Mexican scholar, who

published, though defectively, the Spanish holograph in 1945. To make it as complete as the Italian edition (*Storia antica del Messico*), which contains not only the history proper but also the 1780 Clavigero letter to the Royal University of Mexico, maps, illustrations, genealogical charts, a preface, an invaluable introduction, and a series of dissertations, Cuevas added these to his Spanish manuscript, from the 1853 Vásquez Spanish translation of the original Italian edition. He also added a 1784 Clavigero letter to the Royal University of Mexico.

In 1958, however, Editorial Porrúa of Mexico City brought out a revised edition of the 1945 Cuevas publication, the most important difference being inclusion of the ninth dissertation on the origin of syphilis, which Cuevas had omitted in 1945. This, along with other helpful minor revisions, makes the 1958 edition more complete than the 1945 edition, although it is most unfortunate that the editors omitted from this publication the 1784 Clavigero letter. The 1962, 1964, and editions of the *Historia antigua* merely reprint the 1958 text, which will soon be superseded by the critical edition of the latter work which the Guatemalan Jesuit, Manuel Ignacio Pérez Alonso, is preparing for publication.

The traditional explanation for Clavigero's *Historia antigua* not being published in Spanish in the 18th century has been the alleged opposition of the Spanish government and the "bloody criticism" contained in Diosdado's *Observaciones*. On the basis of the evidence presented, such a view must be set aside. The Council of the Indies, as we have seen, officially approved publication under certain stipulated conditions.

What, then, actually did happen? A possible explanation is that despite official approval for publication, a small group at court of the same mind as Diosdado's were determined to prevent publication or to do all in their power, at least, to put it off as long as possible. The reviser Cerda was of this cabal, and we have seen the results of his delaying tactics. When royal inquiries regarding the fate of the manuscript were made in 1800, interest in it had died off. No one of influence cared any longer, and the manuscript sank from sight and still awaits discovery. On the other hand, it is possible that Cerda may have intended to make the revisions but was prevented from doing so because of poor health; and when the untouched document was returned to the Council of the Indies on his death in 1800, no one could be found to undertake the formidable task of revision. However, until more conclusive evidence is forthcoming, the question remains quite open.

Storia antica: Description of the Work

The Italian edition was the first to appear and is the fullest and most complete version written directly by Clavigero. It seems best to describe it. The appendix below lists later editions and translations. The *Storia antica* comprises four well-illustrated volumes, with a table of contents in each and an index of the complete work at the end of volume 3.

Volume 1 is made up of five books. The first contains a short, though defective, treatise on the geography and natural history of Mexico and a brief study of the character of the pre-Hispanic Indian groups of central Mexico. The four remaining books treat not only the history of the Aztecs and their contemporaries down to the coming of the Spaniards but also their predecessors in the Valley of Mexico. Included also is a map embracing the Mexican empire and kingdoms of Acolhuacan and Michoacan (fig. 2) and a genealogical chart of the kings of Mexico from Ilhuicatl to Quauhtemotzin (fig. 3).

Of special value, however, is Clavigero's letter to the University of Mexico dedicating the first three volumes of the history to the rector and faculty of the university, missing from his Spanish manuscript. In addition there are: the author's prologue explaining how and why the history was written; a very useful bibliographical essay on writers on the ancient history of Mexico of the 16th, 17th, and 18th centuries; and a list of some of the famous collections of Mexican picture writings, such as the Mendoza Collection (usually known as the Codex Mendoza; see Article 23, Item 196), the Vatican Collection, the Vienna Collection, the Sigüenza Collection, and the Boturini Collection, the last two of which Clavigero had studied in Mexico City.[32]

Volume 2 embraces books 6 and 7. Book 6 is devoted to Aztec religion and its manifold practices. Book 7 takes up the political, economic, military, artistic, intellectual, domestic, and judicial life of the Aztecs as well as their agriculture, medicine, forms of recreation, dress, commerce, and other occupations of everyday life. Appended to this volume is a list of notables, mostly Italian, the "Signori Associati" who subscribed to the *Storia antica*. There are also six "Additions" designed to clarify various points: the first four deal with the Mexican century, the Mexican year, and the Mexican calendar. The fifth is a reprint of a letter to Clavigero dealing with the Mexican computation of time written by the Jesuit philologist, the Abbé Lorenzo Hervás y Panduro. The sixth contains Clavigero's criticism of Count Carli's *Lettere Americane*, mentioned above.

Volume 3, containing books 8, 9, and 10, deals exclusively with the conquest of Mexico from the arrival of the Spaniards in 1517 to the fall of Tenochtitlan in 1521. Also added are two charts: the first lists the descendants of Cortés to the end of the 18th century; the second lists the descendants of Montezuma, ninth king of Mexico.

Volume 4, which carries a very florid dedication to Count Carli, is made up of nine dissertations "on the land, animals, and inhabitants of the Kingdom of Mexico in which the Ancient History of that Country is confirmed, many Points of Natural His-

---

[32] Ed. note: Burrus (1959, pp. 78–80) published a Clavigero MS concerned with the Boturini and Sigüenza collections.

Fig. 2—MAP OF THE MEXICAN EMPIRE AS OF 1521, FROM CLAVIGERO'S STORIA ANTICA (1780). From Brittle Book Microfilm, Colección de Libros, 9:xciv (Madrid).

GENEALOGIA DEI RE MESSICANI

DEDOTTA INSIN DAL COMINCIAMENTO DEL SECOLO XIII.

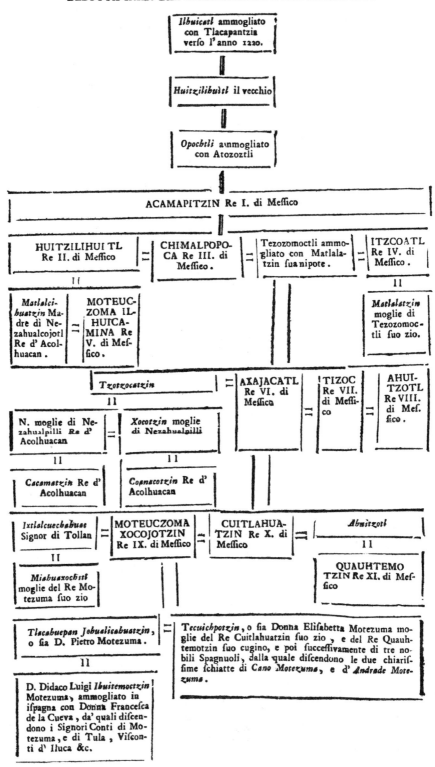

Fig. 3—GENEALOGY OF MEXICAN KINGS TRACED FROM BEGINNING OF 13TH CENTURY, FROM CLAVIGERO'S *STORIA ANTICA* (1780). From Brittle Book Microfilm, Colección de Libros, 9:xciv (Madrid).

tory illustrated, and numerous Errors refuted, which have been published concerning America by some celebrated authors."
The dissertations are:

I. On the inhabitants of America and particularly of the kingdom of Mexico.
1. Who were the first inhabitants of America?
2. How and from what area did these first
inhabitants pass over to America?
II. On the principal epochs in the history of the
kingdom of Mexico.
1. Correspondence between the Mexican
years and ours and on the date of the
foundation of Mexico.
2. On the chronology of the Mexican kings.
3. On the chronology of the Conquest.
III. On the land in the kingdom of Mexico.
1. On the supposed inundation of America.
2. On the climate of the kingdom of Mexico.
3. On the quality of the land of the kingdom
of Mexico.
IV. On the animals of the kingdom of Mexico.
1. On the animals proper to the kingdom of
Mexico.
2. Quadrupeds of the Old Continent with a
tail [and] of America.
3. On European animals brought to America:
camels, oxen, sheep, goats, pigs, horses,
mules, dogs, and cats.
4. Catalog of American quadrupeds:
a. species known and acknowledged by
Count de Buffon.
b. species confused by Count de Buffon
with others.
c. species unjustly ignored by Count de
Buffon.
V. On the physical and moral constitution of
the Mexicans.
1. On the physical qualities of the Mexicans.
2. On the spiritual qualities of the Mexicans.
VI. On the culture of the Mexicans.
1. On the lack of money.
2. On the use of iron.
3. On the art of building ships, bridges, and
making lime.
4. On the lack of learning.
5. On the art of the Mexicans.
6. On Mexican languages [with a list of]
authors of grammars and dictionaries in
native languages.
7. On Mexican laws.

8. Catalog of European and creole authors
of Christian and moral doctrine written in
the [native] tongues of New Spain.
9. [Catalog of] authors of grammars and dictionaries in the [native] languages.
VII. On the boundaries and inhabitants of the
kingdoms of Anahuac.
1. On the boundaries of the kingdom of Anahuac.
2. On the inhabitants of Anahuac.
VIII. On the religion of the Mexicans.
IX. On the origin of the French evil.
1. Opinion of the doctors of antiquity.
2. The French evil and the possibility of its
having reached Europe from other countries of the ancient world.
3. The French evil and the possibility of its
having reached Europe other than
through contact.
4. The French evil and its non-provenance
from America.

One interesting item which Clavigero
prepared for the *Historia* but did not use
was a brief key to the pronunciation of the
Nahuatl language.[33]

CLAVIGERO'S SOURCES

For a clear understanding of Clavigero's
sources, it is advisable to divide the *Historia
antigua* into four parts: (1) geography and
natural history; (2) history of the Aztecs
and other pre-Hispanic peoples; (3) history
of the Conquest; (4) the dissertations. The

[33] Advertencia, opúsculo manoscritto. BCA, Colección Mezzofanti, Cartaggio XII, no. 10. Aunque
cualquiera Lector es libre para pronunciar las palabras mexicanas como quisiere, no será unútil el no-
tar aquí su legítima pronunciación. Los Mexicanos
no pronuncian jamás la *X* como nuestra *J*, sino como
la *CH* de los Franceses. Tampoco pronuncian las
LL como nosotros sino como los Latinos. Pronuncian si la *ch* como nosotros en las voces *chinche,
chuya, muchacho*. El *Hua, hue, hui* suena casi si
Gua, gue, gui, y el *uh* como si fuera *uj*. Los Mexicanos dan terminación aguda a nunguna de las
voces de su lengua, que se leen en esta Historia, ni
menos hacen algun esdruxulo: y assi no dicen Méjico como nosotros, sino Mexico. Puede, pues, darse
por regla general para las palabras mexicanas desta
obra, que todas tienen la penúltima sílaba larga,
salvo que sea *u* antes de vocal, como en Acólhua
(no Acolúa como decían nuestros Españoles) Anáhuac, Coatlícue etc.

sources of each section, discussed elsewhere in more detail by Ronan (1958), are:

Part 1. (A) *Geography*: (1) Clavigero's own knowledge of Mexico's geography and information he acquired from Jesuit colleagues, all of which he acknowledged as inexact; (2) maps of Mexico also acknowledged as inexact; (3) other authors, such as Boturini, Solís, Bernal Díaz, Bomare, and others. (B) *Natural history*: (1) author's own knowledge and information he acquired from Jesuit colleagues; (2) other writers, such as Buffon, Ulloa, Bomare, Pliny, and the noted *protomédico* Francisco de Hernández, on whom the Jesuit relied very heavily for his material on the vegetable and mineral kingdoms of Mexico.

Part 2. *History of the Aztecs and other pre-Hispanic peoples*: as is well known, Clavigero drew very heavily on Juan de Torquemada's *Monarquía indiana*. A detailed comparison of the latter work with the *Historia antigua* (Flusche, 1966), clearly proves that Clavigero quarried most of his material, by far, from this source. Recasting, revising, and synthesizing his data, he presented it to the public in one book, but Torquemada shines through every page. The sections dealing with native Mexican history are nothing more than an orderly compendium of the *Monarquía indiana*. Clavigero did not, however, follow the latter work slavishly; he corrected many errors, unraveled chronological problems, and rejected much of Torquemada's miraculous interpretation of history. Additional authors consulted and sprinkled about in the pages of the *Historia antigua* were Gómara, Acosta, Gemelli Carreri, Boturini, and others.[34]

Part 3. *History of the Conquest*: this section

also shows a heavy dependence on Torquemada although not to the same extent as the other part. Again, comparison of the two histories proves this. Other authors and works cited are Lorenzana's edition of Cortes' letters, Solís, Acosta, Vetancurt, the Conquistador anónimo, Herrera, and the *Colección de Ramusio*.

Part 4. *Dissertations*: easily the most original part of the entire history, these are based on wide reading in French, Spanish, English, and Latin authors. Often expository but largely polemical in nature, they were written to refute such European writers as de Pauw, Buffon, and others and also to elucidate and clarify a number of points on Mexican antiquities which could not be dealt with fully in the history proper. Space does not allow a listing of all authorities consulted, but some of the more important are Torquemada, who is cited more than any other single author; Boturini, Sigüenza y Góngora, the *protomédico* Hernández, Vetancurt, Montesquieu, Feijóo, Bomare, Eguiara y Eguren, Buffon, Bernal Díaz, Acosta, the Codex Mendoza, and others.

EVALUATION

When Clavigero took up the historian's pen, he came to the field well prepared. In addition to having an excellent training in the humanities, he also possessed an understanding of the native Mexicans, had acquired a fluency in Nahuatl, and knew well the story of Mexico's Aztec past. The Jesuit historian's background eminently fitted him to try his hand at historical writing, which in the 18th century was "a species of literature, a humane study, an art, rather than a science."

Like all historians, however, he had his strong points and his weak ones. His greatest merit lies in the fact that he was the first to write a separate work devoted solely to the history of ancient Mexico. Ferreting out the facts of ancient Mexican history from Torquemada's very prolix *Monarquía indiana*, he presented an excellent synthesis, giving careful attention to chronology and clothing it in what was most important in the 18th century, a pleasant, smooth literary style. His sentimental interest in ancient

---

[34] Ed. note: Clavigero knew the works of Sahagún, now basic to studies of ancient Mexican history, only indirectly through the liberal use which Torquemada had made of them (Articles 14 and 16). Clavigero's incorrect statements about Sahagún were seemingly taken from Vetancurt, who originally confused the name of the viceroy who sequestered Sahagún's MSS, errors repeated by Clavigero. The latter's mentioning a note by Fray Juan de San Antonio, *Bibliotheca universal franciscana* (1732, 1:213) that a four-volume MS of the *General history* could be found in the Franciscan convent, Tolosa, Navarre, Spain, seemingly led to eventual exhumation of the great Sahaguntine corpus (Nicolau d'Olwer, 1952, pp. 177–78).

Mexico helped create wide interest in the subject (Villoro, 1950). As Adolph Bandelier (1908, p. 9) points out, his history controlled popular opinion for many decades. It has also been argued that the *Storia antica* played a part in stirring in the hearts of many creoles a feeling of unity with Mexico's Aztec civilization and culture, a growing spirit of nationalism, a conviction that their country's ancient past had placed a stamp of individuality on them that set them apart from Spain and hence justified their seeking independence from the mother country (Phelan, 1960; Grajales, 1961).

Moreover, the able role that Clavigero played in the lively polemics of his time over the relative merits of the Old World versus the New gave added prestige to his history. It vaulted him to international fame, and made him the outstanding "Voice of America" of the 18th century. Not only did he defend America, and especially Mexico, against calumnious writers but he also left Europe much more enlightened about the New World and with a higher regard for Mexican creole intellectual achievement. His history has always been held in high esteem by historians. Even today it is looked upon as an important secondary source, despite its weaknesses. These relate especially to its anthropological shortcomings, and the fact that marked advances have been made since Clavigero's time in the study of Mexican antiquities.

Regarding other weak points, it is to be noted that Clavigero wrote in an environment still "saturated with theology," to use a phrase of Jacques Maritain, and in a rational century that was mounting continuing attacks against Christianity. His writings reflected this environment and age. He tended to evaluate everything—especially if it touched on religion in any way—against a theological background, using Scripture and theology as his norms for judgment. Such a method, understandable though it might be, was obviously biased and subjective and worked at times against the objectivity of the *Storia antica*.

However, the gravest accusation against Clavigero is plagiarism. Undoubtedly, it was not looked upon with the same degree of disfavor in the 18th century as it is today. Even then students like Juan Bautista Muñoz and William Robertson did not fail to comment on it. As indicated, the substance of Clavigero's history is drawn from the *Monarquía indiana*, but is supplemented with a sizable amount of material whose source is Gómara, Acosta, Gemelli Carreri, Boturini, and several others. Generally speaking, apart from Clavigero's attempt to reconstruct Aztec chronology, it can rightfully be called a compendium of Torquemada's work. But it is more than that. For, although the facts were quarried from the *Monarquía indiana*, the author placed his own personal interpretation on them. Otherwise, how explain Diosdado Caballero's reaction to the history or the charges that Clavigero was anti-Spanish? Hence, the *Storia antica* is more than just a compendium, it is a reworked digest with an unmistakable Clavigero stamp.

There is no denying the fact, however, that, despite his occasional avowal of dependence on Torquemada, at no time does the Jesuit ever acknowledge his exceedingly heavy dependence on him. Rather, he leaves the reader under the impression that his own History has been culled from a wide variety of sources, as its full title would lead one to believe. He often cites the *Monarquía indiana* in the footnotes in the very act of synthesizing a section of the latter, thus giving the impression that it was just one of many sources consulted. In reality, it was almost the only one for that passage. He simulates a knowledge of authors, of archives, of documentation, and of many bits of knowledge that he knew chiefly through Torquemada. But the reader, unaware of this, is overwhelmed and is led to view the author as a man of much vaster erudition than he really was.

Moreover, he assumes an air of originality

that he did not actually possess. He speaks of his 36 years in Mexico as though he had passed them all studying Mexican antiquities and doing research. As a matter of fact, Clavigero was only 36 years of age when he left Mexico for Italy and he spent relatively few of those years in the study of Mexican history. In a word, plagiarism and a sort of masquerade are quite clear.

However, one must judge cautiously. It would seem unfair to measure nearly any 18th-century writer according to the norms that are used for plagiarism today. Practices to which Clavigero resorted were not uncommon in his time and were not looked upon then as they are in the 20th century.

Clavigero, even in plagiarism, was in the general tradition of colonial writings about ancient Mexico. To some degree this actually strengthens and gives continued limited importance to his *Storia antica*. Other articles in this volume of the *Handbook* show the partial reliance of Sahagún on Olmos, Mendieta on them both, and Torquemada on these earlier sources, both through direct use of Sahagún and through his own heavy borrowings from Mendieta. Through his own summaries and reordering of Torquemada, Clavigero thus unwittingly

but still effectively was transmitting a considerable body of original ethnographic data derived from Olmos' and Sahagún's informants and other 16th-century sources, some now lost.

One final word. Although all agree that Clavigero was a learned man and an able historian, there is no denying the fact that, as a result of the exaggerated merits that have been attributed to him and to the *Storia antica*, an out-of-focus picture has been handed down over the past century and a half. Even a sort of "Clavigero myth" has developed. Hence, it is hoped that this article will help explode the myth and put our picture of him back in proper focus. No service is done history by endowing him with merits beyond his due.[35]

[35] In addition to specific references in text and footnotes, the following contain minor materials related to Clavigero and his times: Alzate y Ramírez, 1831; Bancroft, 1883; Batllori, 1953; Beristáin de Souza, 1816–21; Burrus, 1953, 1954; Contreras, 1954; Dávila y Arrillaga, 1888; Decorme, 1914–59; Diosdado Caballero, 1814; García, 1931; García Granados, 1931; González Casanova, 1948; González de Cossío, 1946; González Obregón, 1939; Le Riverend Brusone, 1945, 1953; Macías, 1883; Medina, 1914; Miranda, 1946; Navarro, 1948, 1953, 1956; Phelan, 1948, 1956; Rico González, 1949; Robertson, 1788; Uriarte and Lecina, 1925–30; Zelis, 1871.

Appendix. CLAVIGERO, HISTORICAL WORKS

The listing here of works by Clavigero has purposely omitted several fragmentary items of minor bibliographical and historiographical interest. One of these is Julio Jiménez Rueda's *Capítulos de historia y disertaciones de Francisco Javier Clavigero* (Bibl. estudiante universitario, 44). Another, which embraced book 1 of the "Historia antigua de Mexico," appeared anonymously (until p. 450) in *Memorias de la Sociedad Económica de la Habana*, vol. 18 (1844), pp. 127–41 (no. 104, May), 176–92 (no. 105, June), 242–62 (no. 106, Aug.), 415–24 (no. 107, Sept.), 437–50 (no. 108, Oct.). This fragment was labeled "la quinta edición castellana" by Cuevas (1944, pp. 13–14) with incomplete citation.

Other items are listed in García Granados, 1937, pp. 299–304. His descriptions have not been verified. He notes an 1846 single volume excerpt (vol. 2 of the 1844 Lara ed.), published in Philadelphia, as well as an 1803 Mexican version of an earlier very faulty Italian summary (1782) that Clavigero himself noticed (*Storia della California*, pp. 25–27) had appeared in a Florentine periodical. He also lists a one-volume Mexican summary of 1877 and a 1930 reprint of the first dissertation.

Known to García Granados only through secondhand notices were two minor publications of Clavigero's work on Lower California. One of these, an extract (copy in the Bancroft Library), was published in California in the

1860s. The other was a serialized version of the work first appearing during 1931 in *El Mexicano*, a military newspaper of Lower California. According to a brief notice in the *Boletín bibliográfico mexicano* (Librería de Porrúa, Apr. 30, 1947), it appears that the serialized version was completed by 1947. Another serialized version of the work, translated into English, appeared in the San Diego *Herald*. It ran from April 17, 1858, to September 10, 1859.

1780–81 Storia antica del Messico cavata da' Migliori storici Spagnuoli, e da' manoscritti, e dalle pitture antiche degl' Indiani: divisa in dieci libri, e corredata di carte geografiche, e di varie figure; e dissertazioni sulla terra, sugli animali, e sugli abitatori del Messico. Per Gregorio Biasini All' Insegna di Pallade. Con Licenza de' Superiori. 4 vols. [vol. 4, 1781]. Cesena.

1787 The history of Mexico, collected from Spanish and Mexican historians, from manuscripts, and ancient paintings of the Indians illustrated by charts and other copper plates. To which are added, critical dissertations on the land, the animals, and inhabitants of Mexico. Translated from the original Italian by Charles Cullen. 2 vols. London.

1789a Geschichte von Mexico aus Spanishchen und mexicanischen Geschichte schreiben, Handsschriften und gemalden der Indianer zusamenmengetragen und durch Karten und Kupferstiche erlautert nebst einigen cristischen abhandlungen über die Beschaffenheit des Landes, der Thiere und Ein Wohner von Mexico Ausdem Italienischen des Abts, . . . der Ritter Carl Cullen ins Englische, und aus diesen mins Deutsche überstat. Im Schwickerstschen Verlage (1789–1790). 2 vols. Leipzig.

1789b Storia della California. Opera postuma del Nob. Sig. Apresso Modesto Fenzo. Con licenza de' Superiori, e privilegio. 2 vols. Venice.

1804 The history of Mexico. Collected from Spanish and Mexican historians, from manuscripts, and ancient paintings of the Indians. Illustrated by charts, and other copper plates. To which are added, critical dissertations on the land, the animals, and inhabitants of Mexico. Translated from the original Italian by Charles Cullen. 3 vols. Philadelphia.

1806 The history of Mexico, collected from Spanish and Mexican historians, from manuscripts and ancient paintings of the Indians illustrated by charts and other copper plates. To which are added, critical dissertations on the land, the animals, and inhabitants of Mexico. By Charles Cullen. 3 vols. Richmond, Va.

1807 The history of Mexico, collected from Spanish and Mexican historians, from manuscripts, and ancient paintings of the Indians illustrated by charts, and other copper plates. To which are added, critical dissertations on the land, the animals, and inhabitants of Mexico. Translated from the original Italian by Charles Cullen. 2d ed. London.

1817 The history of Mexico, collected from Spanish and Mexican historians, from manuscripts, and ancient paintings of the Indians illustrated by charts, and other copper plates. To which are added, critical dissertations on the land, the animals, and inhabitants of Mexico. Translated from the original Italian by Charles Cullen. 3 vols. Philadelphia.

1826 Historia antigua de Megico: sacada de los mejores historiadores espanoles, y de los manuscritos, y de las pinturas antiguas de los indios; dividida en diez libros: adornada con mapas y estampas, e ilustrada con disertaciones sobre la tierra, los animales, y los habitantes de Megico, . . . traducida del Italiano por José Joaquín de Mora. Le publica R. Ackermann, Strand, y en su Establecimiento en Megico: asi mismo en Colombia, en Buenos Aires, Chile, Peru y Guatemala. 2 vols. London.

1844 Historia antigua de Mexico y de su conquista, sacada de los mejores historiadores espanoles, y de los manuscritos y pinturas de los indios. Dividida en diez libros: adornada con mapas y estampas, e ilustrada con disertaciones sobre la tierra, los animales y los habitantes de Mexico. . . . traducida del Italiano por J. Joaquín de Mora. 2 vols. Mexico.

1852 Historia de la antigua o Baja California. . . . traducida del italiano por el presbitero don Nicolás García de San Vicente. Mexico.

1853 Historia antigua de Mejico, sacada de los mejores historiadores espanoles, y de manuscritos y pinturas antiguas de los indios. Dividida en diez libros. Adornada de cartas geográficas y litografías; con disertaciones sobre la tierra, animales y habitantes de Mejico. Traducida por el Dr. D. Francisco Pablo Vásquez, Colegial Antiguo del Eximio de San Pablo de Puebla y Maestre-Escuelas Dignidad de la Santa Iglesia de dicha Ciudad. Mexico.

1861 Historia antigua de Mejico, sacada de los mejores historiadores españoles, y de manuscritos y pinturas antiguas de los indios. Dividida en diez libros. Adornada de cartas geográficas y litografías; con disertaciones sobre la tierra, animales y habitantes de Mejico. Traducida por el Dr. D. Francisco Pablo Vásquez, Colegial Antiguo del Eximio de San Pablo de Puebla y Maestre-Escuelas Dignidad de la Santa Iglesia de dicha Ciudad. 4 vols., publicada en el folletin de "El Constitucional." Mexico.

1868 Historia antigua de Mexico y de su conquista, sacada de los mejores historiadores españoles, y de los manuscritos y pinturas de los indios. Dividida en diez libros: adornada con mapas y estampas, e ilustrada con disertaciones sobre la tierra, los animales y los habitantes de México. . . . traducida del Italiano por J. Joaquín de Mora. Publicada por Antonio Ruiz, Jalapa.

1883 Historia antigua de Mexico y de su conquista, sacada de los mejores historiadores españoles, y de los manuscritos y pinturas de los indios. Dividida en diez libros: adornada con mapas y estampas, e ilustrada con disertaciones sobre la tierra, los animales y los habitantes de México. . . . traducida del Italiano por J. Joaquín de Mora. Publicada por Dublan. 2 vols. Mexico.

1917 Historia antigua de Mexico y de su conquista, sacada de los mejores historiadores espanoles, y de los manuscritos y pinturas de los indios. Dividida en diez libros. Adornada con mapas y estampas, e ilustrada con disertaciones sobre la tierra, los animales y los habitantes de

Mexico. . . . traducida del Italiano por J. Joaquín de Mora, y precedida de notas bio-bibliográficas del autor, por Luis González Obregón. 2 vols., publicada por la Dirección General de Bellas Artes. Mexico.

1933 Historia de la antigua o Baja California. Traducida del italiano por el presbitero don Nicolás García de San Vicente. Imprenta del Museo Nacional de Arqueología, Historia y Etnografía. Mexico.

1937 The history of (Lower) California. Trans. and ed. by S. E. Lake and A. A. Gray. Stanford University Press.

1944 Historia antigua de Mexico. Traducción de José Joaquín de Mora (publicada por primera vez en Londres, 1826). Prefacio de Julio Le Riverend Brusone. Estudio biográfico de Rafael García Granados. Editorial Delfin, 2 vols. Mexico.

1945 Historia antigua de Mexico, primera edición del original escrito en castellano por el autor. 4 vols. Ed. Mariano Cuevas, S.J. Porrúa, *Col. Escritores mexicanos*, 7–10. Mexico.

1958 Historia antigua de Mexico. 4 vols. Ed. Mariano Cuevas, S.J. Mexico. [This is an amplified edition of the 1945 ed. published by Editorial Porrúa.]

1962 Historia antigua de México por Francisco Javier Clavigero. 4 vols. Ed. Mariano Cuevas, S.J. Mexico. [Reprint of 1958 ed.]

1964 Historia antigua de México por Francisco Javier Clavigero. Edición y prólogo del R. P. Mariano Cuevas. Porrúa, *Col. "Sepan cuantos,"* 29. Mexico. [Also reprint of 1958 ed.]

1968 Historia antigua de Mexico por Francisco Javier Clavijero. Edición y prólogo de Mariano Cuevas. Porrua, *Col. "Sepan cuantos,"* 29. Mexico. [Also reprint of 1958 ed.]

REFERENCES

ALZATE Y RAMÍREZ, JOSÉ ANTONIO, ed.
1831 Gacetas de literatura de México. 4 vols. Mexico.

BANCROFT, HUBERT HOWE
See Article 19, Appendix.

BANDELIER, ADOLPH F.
1908 Francisco Saverio [sic] Clavigero. In The Catholic Encyclopedia, 4:9. New York.

BATLLORI, MIGUEL, S.J.
1953 El abate Viscaro: historia y mito de la intervención de los jesuítas en la independencia de hispanoamérica. PAIGH. Caracas.

BERISTÁIN DE SOUZA, MARIANO, ed.
1816–21 Biblioteca hispano-americana septentrional; o catálogo y noticia de los literatos, que ó nacidos, ó educados, ó florencientes en la America Septentrional española, han dado a luz algún escrito, ó lo han dexado preparado para la prensa. 3 vols. Mexico.

BURRUS, ERNEST, S.J.
1953 Francisco Javier Alegre, historian of the Jesuits in New Spain, 1729–1788. Archivum Historicum Societatis Jesu, 22:439–509 (Jan.–June).
1954 Jesuit exiles, precursors of Mexican independence? Mid-America, 36: 161–75 (July). Loyola University. Chicago.
1959 Clavigero and the lost Sigüenza y Góngora manuscripts. ECN, 1:59–90.

CASTRO MORALES, EFRAÍN
1970 Documentos relativos al historiador Francisco Javier Clavijero y su familia. Puebla.

CLARK, CHARLES UPSON
1937 Jesuit letters to Hervás, on American languages and customs. Journal de la Société des Américanistes, n.s. (XXIX, fasc.), 1:97–145. Paris.

CLAVIGERO, FRANCISCO JAVIER
See Article 17, Appendix.

CONTRERAS, DORIS M.
1954 Clavigero: un estudio de su Historia antigua de México, sus fuentes históricas, con índice analítico de la obra.

MS, unpublished M.S. thesis, University of the Americas. Mexico.

CUEVAS, MARIANO, ed.
1944 Tesoros documentales de México, siglo XVIII: Priego, Zelis, Clavigero. Mexico.

DÁVILA Y ARRILLAGA, JOSÉ MARIANO
1888 Continuación de la historia de la Compañía de Jesús en Nueva España del P. Francisco Javier Alegre. Puebla.

DECORME, GERARDO, S.J.
1914–59 Historia de la Compañía de Jesús en la República Mexicana durante el siglo XIX. 3 vols. Guadalajara.

DIOSDADO CABALLERO, RAMÓN, S.J., ed.
1814 Bibliothecae Scriptorum Societatis Jesu Suplementa. Rome.

ECHEVERRÍA Y VEYTIA, MARIANO, FERNÁNDEZ DE
1931 Historia de la ciudad de la Puebla de los Angeles en la Nueva España. 2 vols. 2d ed. Puebla.

EL DIA
1970 El Dia, pp. 1, 3 (6 de agosto). Mexico City.

ESTUDIOS DE HISTORIOGRAFÍA
1945 Estudios de historiografía de la Nueva España por Hugo Díaz-Thomé, Fernando Sandoval, Manuel Carrera Stampa, Carlos Bosch García, Ernesto de la Torre, Enriqueta López Lira, Julio Le Riverend Brusone, con una introducción de Ramón Iglesia. Mexico.

EXCELSIOR
1970 Excelsior, p. 23 (4 de agosto); pp. 1, 13 (5 de agosto); p. 1 (6 de agosto). Mexico City.

FLUSCHE, DELLA
1966 Francisco Javier Clavigero: A Source Analysis. Seminar paper written for Seminar given by Charles Ronan, S.J., Loyola University, Chicago, Illinois.

GACETA
1787 Gaceta de Madrid, April.

GARCÍA, RUBÉN
1931 Bibliografía del historiador Francisco Javier Clavijero. Mexico.

GARCÍA GRANADOS, RAFAEL
1931 Noticia bibliográfica de las obras del abate Francisco Clavigero. MNA, Anales, ep. 4, 7:407–17.

1937 Clavijero: estudio bibliográfico. *In* his Filias y Fobias (Opúsculos Históricos), pp. 279–309. Mexico.

GAZZETTA DI CREMONA
1782 *Gazzetta di Cremona*, pp. 1–8. Cesena.

GAZZETTA UNIVERSALE
1787 *Gazzetta Universale*, 22:222-23 (Apr. 7). Florence.

GERBI, ANTONELLO
1960 La disputa del Nuevo Mundo. Mexico.

GONZÁLEZ CASANOVA, PABLO
1948 El misioneismo y la modernidad cristiana en el siglo XVIII. Mexico.

GONZÁLEZ DE COSSÍO, FRANCISCO
1946 Autógrafos de los PP. Clavigero y Landívar. AGN, *Boletín*, 17:173-86.

GONZÁLEZ OBREGON, LUÍS
1939 Cronistas e historiadores. Mexico.

GRAJALES, GLORIA
1961 Nacionalismo incipiente en los historiadores coloniales: estudio historiográfico. UNAM, Instituto de Historia, Pub. 1/65, Cuadernos Serie Histórica, 4. Mexico.

HERVÁS Y PANDURO, LORENZO
1793 Biblioteca jesuitica española de escritores que han florecido por siete lustros: estos empiezan desde el año 1759, principio del reinado del augusto rey católico Carlos III y acaban en el año 1793. MS, 2 vols. [Owned by Jesuit Novitiate of San Ignacio de Loyola, Loyola, Spain.]

HOY
1970 Hoy, p. 26 (29 de agosto). Mexico City.

JIMÉNEZ RUEDA, JULIO, ed.
1944 [Francisco Xavier Clavigero.] Capítulos de historia y disertaciones. Prólogo y selección por. . . . UNAM, *Bib. estudiante universitario*, 44. Mexico.

LE RIVEREND BRUSONE, JULIO
1945 La *"Historia antigua de México"* del padre Francisco Javier Clavigero. *In* Estudios de Historiografía, pp. 295–323. Mexico.
1953 Problemas de historiografía. *Historia mexicana*, 3:52–68 (July–Aug.).

MACÍAS, JOSÉ MIGUEL
1883 Biografía de egregio historiador, naturalista, poligloto, Francisco X. Clavigero. Veracruz.

MANEIRO, JUAN LUÍS, S.J. [JOANNIS ALOYSII MANEIRI VERACRUCENSIS]
1791–92 De vitis aliquot mexicanorum aliorumque qui sive virtute sive litteris Mexici imprimis floruerunt. 3 vols., especially 3:28–78 (Clavigero). Bologna.
1941 [Clavigero.] *In* Gabriel Méndez Plancarte, Humanistas del siglo XVIII. UNAM, *Bib. estudiante universitario*, 24:1–39. [Partial Spanish translation of Maneiro, 1791–92.] Mexico.
1956 [Clavigero.] *In* Navarro, 1956, pp. 119–79. [Complete Spanish translation of Maneiro, 1791–92.]

MEDINA, JOSÉ TORIBIO
1914 Noticias bio-bibliográficas de los jesuítas expulsos de América en 1767. Santiago, Chile.

MIRANDA, JOSÉ
1946 Clavigero en la ilustración mexicana. *Cuadernos americanos*, 3/4:180–96 (May–Aug.).

NAVARRO, BERNABÉ
1948 La introducción de la filosofía moderna en México. Mexico.
1953 Los jesuítas y la independencia. *Abside*, 16:43–62. Mexico.
1954 La cultura mexicana frente a Europea. *Historia mexicana*, 3:547–61.
1956 Vidas de mexicanos ilustres del siglo XVIII. *Bib. estudiante universitario*, 74:119–79. Mexico.

NICOLAU D'OLWER, LUIS
1952 Historiadores de América: Fray Bernardino de Sahagún (1499–1590). PAIGH, Comisión de Historia, Pub. 40. Mexico.

PHELAN, JOHN LEDDY
1948 The political and philosophical thoughts of Francisco Xavier Clavigero, 1731–1787. MS, unpublished M.A. thesis, University of California, Berkeley.
1956 The millennial kingdom of the Franciscans in the New World: A study of the writings of Gerónimo de Mendieta (1525–1604). Berkeley. [Revised ed. 1970.]
1960 Neo-Aztecism in the eighteenth century and the genesis of Mexican nationalism. *In* Culture in History: Essays in honor of Paul Radin, Stanley Diamond, ed., pp. 760–70. Columbia University Press. New York.

PRESCOTT, WILLIAM HICKLING
n.d. History of the conquest of Mexico

and history of the conquest of Peru. Modern Library. New York.

1944 Historia de la conquista de Méjico; con un basquejo preliminar de la civilización de las antiguos Mejicanos, y la vida de conquistador Hernando Cortés; traducida al castellano por d. José María González de la Vega . . . y anotada por d. Lucas Alamán. Buenos Aires. [Reproduces 1844 Mexican edition.]

RICO GONZÁLEZ, VÍCTOR
1949 Francisco Javier Clavigero. *In* his Historiadores mexicanos del siglo XVIII: Estudios historiográficos sobre Clavijero, Veytia, Cavo y Alegre, pp. 13–75. UNAM, Instituto de Historia.

ROBERTSON, WILLIAM
1788 History of America. [Contains added material not in Robertson, 1775.] Edinburgh, Scotland.

ROMERO FLORES, JESÚS
1939 Documentos para la bibliografía del historiador Clavigero. INAH, *Anales*, 1:307–35.

RONAN, CHARLES, S.J.
1958 Francisco Javier Mariano Clavigero: A study in Mexican historiography. MS, unpublished Ph.D. dissertation, University of Texas.

1970 Clavigero: The Fate of a Manuscript. *The Americas*, XXVII:113–36 (October).

RUBIO MAÑÉ, IGNACIO
1969 Noticias biograficas del padre Clavigero, 1731–1787. AGN, Boletin, 10 (2a serie):497–558.

SEBASTIÁN, FELIX, S.J.
n.d. Vita Patris Francisi Xaverii Clavigero. *In* his Memorias de los padres y hermanos de la Compañía de Jesús del arresto acaecido en la capital de México el día 25 de junio del año 1767. . . . MS, 2 vols. Biblioteca del Archigimnasio, MSS 531–32, 1:62–68. Bologna.

URIARTE, EUGENIO DE, S.J.
1904 Catálogo razonado de obras anónimas y suedónimas de autores de la Compañía de Jesús pertenecientes a la antigua asistencia española, con un apéndice de otras de los mismos, dignos de especial estudio bibliográfico (28 sept. 1540–16 ag. 1773). 4 vols. Madrid.

——, AND MARIANO LECIMA, S.J.
1925–30 Biblioteca de escritores de la Compañía de Jesús pertenecientes a la antigua asistencia de España desde sus orígenes hasta el año de 1773. 2 vols. Madrid.

VEYTIA, MARIANO
See Echeverría y Veytia, Mariano.

VILLORO, LUIS
1950 Los grandes momentos del indigenismo en México. *El Colegio de México*, pp. 89–122. Mexico.

1963 La naturaleza americana en Clavijero. *La Palabra y El Hombre*, 28:543–50. Universidad Veracruzana. Jalapa.

ZELIS, RAFAEL DE, S.J., ed.
1871 Catálogo de los sujetos de la Compañía de Jesús que formaban la provincia de México el día del arresto, 25 de junio de 1767. Mexico.

18. Charles Etienne Brasseur de Bourbourg, 1814–1874

CARROLL EDWARD MACE

CHARLES ETIENNE BRASSEUR de Bourbourg was called the founder of Maya research by William Gates (1932, p. 1). Brasseur's discovery of the Landa manuscript in 1863, his unusual ability to acquire manuscripts, and the impetus his enthusiasm gave to Maya studies possibly earned him that title. He was justly criticized, however, for his use of the materials he found. Basing his work on the confused accounts of Spanish and Indian chronicles, he set out to write a complete history of native Middle America. In his eagerness to bring order into a chaos of myth and tradition, he took excessive liberties with his sources and relied on unacceptable linguistic analogies. His final synthesis proclaimed that all Indian manuscripts described geological upheavals which had transformed the world. He belongs to a group whose dubious theories have pushed them to the margin of the main course of ethnohistorical studies (Wauchope, 1963, pp. 41–49).

Brasseur was mainly interested in proving that intercontinental communication had existed in the remote past, and in describing where and how it had taken place. From 1850 until 1861 he believed that migrations had moved from the east and north to the west, but after 1862 he believed instead that the survivors of an American Atlantis had colonized the rest of the world. Rosny and others called this second period absurd. At the same time—perhaps to salvage something of his friend's work—Rosny overrated the value of his first period (Rosny, 1876, p. 38). A careful reading of Brasseur's vast production reveals that the first period is scarcely more dependable than the second. A relatively comprehensive listing of his writings forms Appendix A.

His work was often directed to proving fanciful and preconceived ideas. Instead of describing accurately what he saw, he transformed reality to make it fit his convictions. This unfortunate tendency may have been related to his talent for fiction. Between 1843 and 1855 he produced 13 successful novels, and it was with the attitude of a romantic novelist that he approached Americanist studies. The ethnographic descriptions he made are undependable and surprisingly uninteresting. On the other hand,

Fɪɢ. 1—CHARLES ETIENNE BRASSEUR DE BOURBOURG. From Winsor, 1889–92.

his descriptions of ancient events he had not seen, but could imagine, are frequently written with elegance and power. Raynaud (1925, p. xxvii) described his work as a "tres mauvais roman," but Marcel Bataillon (1954, p. 425) made a better evaluation when he called it a "grande aventure de l'imagination."

Today there is little of value in Brasseur for the student, but because of the manuscripts he made known and the contemporary interest he generated his life and work are still of interest. His name appears in almost every book on the Middle American Indian. Despite all shortcomings he was influential in establishing ethnohistorical studies and hence takes a recognized place in the evolution of that specialty. Since much that has been written about him is sketchy or incorrect—partly because of his own carelessness—this article will give a summary of his life and principal works.[1]

Brasseur was born in 1814 in the town of Bourbourg in northern France. The account of the supposed discovery of a Phoenician

sword in Brazil and the Del Río report on Palenque, which he read as an adolescent, appear to have inspired his historical vocation: "Un vague pressentément me montra, dans le lointain, je ne sais quels voiles mystérieux qu'un instinct secret me poussait à soulever" (Brasseur, 1857c, p. iii). At the age of 20 he went to Paris, where he worked as a journalist for *Temps* and *Monde*, and wrote novels, three of them with the pseudonym of Ravensburg. Some of these novels were still being reprinted as late as 1880. Their success supplied the funds for his travels and the publication of several of his works on America.

His family moved to Ghent in 1838 (Arriola, 1967). Brasseur there began to study for the priesthood, motivated more by the opportunity for study than by a real vocation. In 1873 he told Herbert B. Adams: "My ecclesiastical duties have always rested very lightly on me" (Adams, 1891, p. 284). He was ordained in Rome in 1845, and the same year went to Canada, the first of several trips to the New World. There he taught Church history and composed his *Histoire du Canada, de son église et de ses missions.* Brasseur (1857c, p. iv) wrote that he had difficulty in obtaining manuscripts, ". . . que des précautions jalouses s'efforçaient de dérober à ma connaissance." The book was not successful. According to Winsor (1889–92, 8:172), "The wrath of the Church in Quebec was visited upon the Abbé. . . . Ferland wrote his excellent and fair *Cours d'Histoire du Canada* largely to correct the French abbé's errors."

Brasseur's historical method was never to improve. In the 20th century his studies on America have suffered the same fate as his early history of Canada. Walter Lehmann wrote (1909, p. 34), ". . . it has been by no

[1] Ed. note: Because of space limitations the Volume Editor substantially reduced the length of the author's original contribution. He wishes to indicate that only works in English, Spanish, and French were consulted in preparation of the article. Titles by Brasseur to which references are made will be found in Appendix A.

means an easy task to get rid of all the quaint ideas his bulky publications have made popular in Europe."

Brasseur resigned from the University of Quebec in May, 1846, and journeyed to Boston. There he read Prescott, whose work revived his youthful enthusiasm for Americanist studies. The abbé then returned to Rome, where for two years he studied Kingsborough and the manuscripts in the Vatican Library. He went to France in February of 1848, left for America in July, and in October sailed from New Orleans to Mexico.

On the ship Brasseur had the good fortune to meet M. le Vasseur, Minister of France to Mexico, who made him chaplain of the French Legation. This opened to him the libraries of the city, and in the museum he copied a manuscript by Ordóñez, a priest who had lived near the ruins of Palenque. This strange work contained some fragments from Ximénez and a confused account of Votan, culture hero of the Tzeltal Indians, who, according to Ordóñez, had built Palenque. Fantastic details described Votan's four trips back to the Middle East. Another manuscript Brasseur "discovered" was the one he called the Codex Chimalpopoca in honor of his Nahuatl teacher, Faustino Chimalpopoca. It was hardly a new find, since Aubin already had two copies and a translation, but for Brasseur it was one of the most important discoveries of his life. At first he found what he believed to be historical fact veiled in its myths, but in 1867 he imagined that it revealed to him a secret system of sacred writing. The abbé copied a translation made by his teacher, but wrote later that he himself had translated it (Brasseur, 1857c, p. xiv).

In 1851 Brasseur published in Mexico his first study of Middle American Indian history, a badly organized and barely readable little book called *Lettres pour servir d'introduction à l'histoire primitive des nations civilisées de l'Amérique septentrionale*, which was by his own admission only a su-

perficial account of his studies. In it he stated that according to Ordóñez, Votan was born in Cuba of Phoenician parents. Votan built Palenque and made four trips to the Middle East, where on one occasion he saw the temple of Solomon. Ordóñez believed that Votan had led the Quiche from Chaldea to America. Brasseur's opinion is not clear, but it appears that he shared this belief until 1855, when he gave the Quiche a Scandinavian origin. The abbé's book also included fragments of the work he would later call the Popol Vuh. For that reason he later insisted that he, not Scherzer, had first brought Ximénez to the attention of scholars (Brasseur, 1861b, p. xiv), a claim not honored by present students. Brasseur mailed copies of the book to Europe and the United States, and with it attracted the interest of Aubin and Squier. Larrainzar (1876, pp. 325–37) has studied the inconsistencies in Brasseur's use of the Votan myth.

The abbé returned to Paris in October, 1851, where Aubin made his library available to him. Longpérier had opened an American museum in the Louvre in 1848, and Brasseur assumed an important role in the small but active group of French Americanists. He suggested (1852a, p. 421) that the government send a scientific expedition to Mexico. The idea was premature, but some credit for its final realization in 1863 should go to him.

After writing more novels and studying in Rome, the abbé sailed again to the United States in the winter of 1854. He saw Squier in New York, and in Washington spent some time taking notes from Las Casas, Durán, and other manuscript copies in the library of Colonel Peter Force (now in the Library of Congress).

Brasseur sailed from New York in October, 1854. After spending three months in Nicaragua and San Salvador, he reached Guatemala City on February 1, 1855. He had missed Scherzer by only three months.

The abbé moved into the house of a diplomat friend. As in Mexico, his personal charm and clerical status opened all doors. Mariano Padilla was his guide around the city, and the young Gavarrete lent him the Cakchiquel manuscript that Brasseur was to use much but never publish. Brasseur wrote that it was a gift, but, according to Brinton (1885, p. 54), it was only a loan which the abbé never returned. Brasseur was fascinated by Guatemala, and felt on the verge of a great discovery. He wrote to Alfred Maury that he was astonished to find the Indians using words of Germanic origin, like the Quiche word for book, *vuh*. Was it possible, he wondered (1855g, p. 157), that the Quiche were from northern Europe? By August 7 he was so convinced that they were that he sent letters with this information to the *New York Tribune* (Brasseur, 1855e) and to Squier, who published it in the *Athenaeum* (Brasseur, 1855f). His statements attracted much attention.

Squier, writing to Maury on December 8, 1855, leveled devastating criticism at Brasseur's tendencies to make hasty and ill-informed generalizations on wholly inadequate, even absurd grounds. He contrasted the abbé's brief sojourn and superficial acquaintance with Central America with his own two years of systematic research, which had failed to reveal any real evidence of extra-American origins, attacking Brasseur's use of myth and art as lacking any probative value of common origins. He correctly characterized Brasseur as having a desire to produce an effect by unfounded assertions and incorrect facts (Squier, 1855b). Although prone to take to the press to retaliate against his critics, Brasseur seemingly never retorted to Squier's scathing critique. But it did not deter him from his ways.

The archbishop, García Palaéz, took an interest in the 40-year-old traveler and in April, 1855, offered him the parish of Rabinal. The abbé left Guatemala City with an Indian escort on May 15. During the trip, avid for corroboration of all that he had read in the chronicles, Brasseur concluded that some boulders he saw in the hacienda of Carrizal were the ruins of a city of the pre-Votan race of Quinames (Brasseur, 1860, Dec. 2). This observation was recorded by Bancroft (1875–76, 4:118), whose writer (Henry L. Oak) complained of Brasseur's lack of method, but nevertheless accepted many of the observations and conclusions of his first period. From a pass overlooking Rabinal, the traveler saw the ruins he called Nim-Pokom and Cakyup,[2] both of which he was the first to describe. They remained his only archaeological discoveries. The Indians welcomed him with a procession, and, according to Brasseur, he at once excited their devotion with his manner and a sermon he preached in the church: "Je commençai à penser que je devenai reéllement un personage" (Brasseur, 1859a, p. 279).

The abbé wrote later that this (1855) was the happiest year of his life. Yet his statements about what happened are so undependable that it is difficult to sift truth from fancy. It is certain at least that he wrote a great deal. He had all of his manuscripts, and it was in Rabinal that he wrote most of the first two volumes of the *Histoire des nations civilisées*. He also worked on translations of the Popol Vuh, the Cakchiquel manuscript, and the Rabinal Achí, an aboriginal drama. According to Brasseur (1861c, p. xiv; 1871, p. 156), the Popol Vuh was one of several manuscripts he obtained from a local Indian named Ignacio Coloche. Adrián Recinos (1950, p. 44) has suggested that Brasseur brought it with him from the capital, but Munro Edmonson (1971, p. viii) believes that the abbé did indeed find another copy of the Popol Vuh in Rabinal, and that this copy is now in the Newberry Library.

Brasseur pursued archaeological interests, but his descriptions were exaggerated and frequently inaccurate. Of a round altar on a peak to the north of Cakyup—now partially

---

[2] Variously spelled.

destroyed by a local search for gold—he wrote that it was a pyramid, but this novelistic transformation of reality kept him from recording an interesting discovery. According to A. Ledyard Smith (1955, p. 44), it is precisely the round shape that makes it "a most unusual construction." Brasseur (1860, Dec. 31) described the hilltop ruins of Cakyup with much exaggeration and concluded that Cakyup was the ancient city of Rabinal. Either dominated by this idea or eager to support it, the abbé wrote in his *Histoire des nationes civilisées* (1858b, p. 550) that according to Remesal, Cakyup had been one of the last strongholds of the Rabinal Indians. According to Brasseur (1859c, p. 795), Remesal had written that the king of Rabinal ruled at Zamaneb while his younger brother ruled at Cakyup, but this is not true. Remesal did not mention Cakyup; of the younger brother, he wrote (1964, p. 229) only that a younger brother of the cacique accompanied the Indian traders to fetch Father Cáncer. Furthermore, the Rabinal Indians were brought not from Cakyup but from mountains about 26 miles to the west between Joyabaj and the present town of Cubulco (Ximénez, 1929, 1:195–96). The abbé also wrote (1862b, 2:22) that Cakyup was an ancient city, that the Quiche occupied it in the 11th century, and that the Rabinal Achí commemorated an event that had occurred there in the 13th century. According to Smith (1955, p. 48), however, the ruins at Cakyup are dated to the period of the Spanish conquest. Other liberties taken by Brasseur, other discrepancies and even contradictions that appear in this hastily written and probably unrevised work might be listed but to go further would serve no purpose. It is already apparent that he was not greatly concerned with historical accuracy, a fact now known to later investigators but not apparent to the audience of the later 19th century.

During the year in Rabinal, Brasseur traveled over much of Verapaz, and also

seems to have taken his ecclesiastical duties with some seriousness. Letters now preserved in the National Archives of Guatemala reveal an interest in local affairs.[3] He failed, however, to obtain dialogues of the town's other dance-dramas or to write ethnographic information of any interest. Statements in the *Grammaire de la langue quichée* (1862) and footnotes scattered throughout his works record such trivia as the fact that the corn grew high in the garden and that the *tun* could be heard for a mile. He left Rabinal about May 17, 1856, and finished the second volume of the *Histoire des nations civilisées* during the two months he spent in San Juan Sacatepequez. In that town he probably polished his translation of the Cakchiquel manuscript, on which Brinton (1885, p. v) relied in the preparation of his own translation, The Annals of the Cakchiquels. Brasseur spent the next five months in Escuintla and Guatemala City, and left Guatemala for France on January 11, 1857.

On July 16, 1857, he, Aubin, Léon de Rosny, and other scholars in Paris founded the Société Américaine de France, the first learned society dedicated exclusively to Americanist studies (Rosny, 1904, p. 6). In 1859 it was absorbed by the Société d'Ethnographie, but in 1873 it was revived as a separate group. Brasseur deserves much of the credit for its formation.

In 1859, after finishing his major four-volume work *Histoire des nations civilisées du Mexique et de l'Amérique-Central* (1857–59), discussed below, he was sent back to America on a mission of exploration by the Ministry of Education. He reached Mexico about May 15, and traveled across the peninsula of Tehuantepec, using the miserable accommodations of the Louisiana Society of Tehuantepec. The abbé described the journey in an entertaining book called *Voyage*

---

[3] These letters were seen in 1958 in the provincial archives in Salama. Brasseur also recorded financial information (of minor interest) about *cofradías* in each Libro de Cofradía.

sur l'isthme de Tehuantepec dans l'état de Chiapas et la République de Guatémala (1861d), but it contained an account only of the trip across Tehuantepec. He never published a projected second volume which was to describe his adventures in Chiapas and Guatemala. Information about that part of the trip appears only in the introduction to *Recherches sur les ruines de Palenqué* (1866a) and scattered footnotes. Brasseur saw much of Chiapas, and in Ciudad Real (the present San Cristobal de las Casas) the governor, Angel Corso, gave him some manuscripts. Political unrest kept him from going to Palenque, so from Ococingo he journeyed up into the Cuchumatanes, where in October he visited Zaculeu and Huehuetenango. During the following months the abbé lived among the Mam and Quiche, and finished his translation of the Popol Vuh. In June he copied the Título de los señores de Totonicapan. After spending some weeks in Guatemala City, he returned to the Mam country, went from there to Coban, and by October of 1860 was again in Paris. Apparently he did not return to Rabinal.

Early in 1861 he became a member of the Société de Géographie de Paris, and in February of that year read a paper on the illfated *Manuscrit pictographique américain* of Domenech, calling it "le plus complet des premiers pas des indigènes sauvages pour exprimer leurs idées" (Brasseur, 1861b, p. 151). When a few months later the German scholar Petzholdt deduced that it was only a collection of drawings scribbled by the son of a German immigrant, the European press had a holiday at the expense of Domenech and Brasseur (Barros Arana, 1910, p. 465). It was the abbé's first public humiliation, but because of earlier triumphs and the approaching publication of his Popol Vuh, he remained undaunted and plunged ahead with his work.

From April through December of 1861 his name appears frequently in the *Comptes-rendus* of the Société d'Ethno-graphie. He served as chairman on July 15 and August 27, and on December 16 gave a talk about the deplorable condition of the American Museum of the Louvre. It had been closed for six months, and the abbé and Aubin were chosen to write an official protest. From 1861 through 1863 he completed various works, notably the Popol Vuh and *Grammaire de la langue quichée*, noted below.

By the summer of 1863 he was again in America, but the only thing known about this fifth trip is that he explored the ruins of Copan and Quirigua. On his way back to France, he stopped in Madrid, where in December, 1863, with astonishing ease, he found the manuscript of a copy of Landa in the Library of the Academy of History. According to Brasseur (1869c, p. 36), it was the first manuscript he picked up. He copied it in Madrid, and on January 20, 1864, notified the French Académie des Inscriptions et Belles Lettres of his remarkable discovery. Brasseur returned to Paris in March, where his edition of Landa, hastily and carelessly prepared, was published in July (see below).

The Commission Scientifique du Mexique was formed in 1863. Having read in Landa that Maya books were buried with their priests, Brasseur was eager to join the expedition. He wanted to excavate in Yucatan to find more codices, but this hope was frustrated when the governor, Salazar Ilarregui, refused to allow it. There was a dispute, and when a local newspaper, *El monitor*, championed the cause of the abbé, Salazar forced it to close (Aldana Rivas, 1865, Jan. 21). Brasseur (1866, p. 10) retaliated by writing that Salazar had been motivated only by envy. He was unable to visit either Chichen Itza or Tulum because of an Indian uprising, but he did spend some time in Mayapan, Uxmal, and Izamal. The illness of his artist companion kept him from traveling on to Palenque. In Yucatan the abbé found only the Buenaventura *Arte de la lengua maya* and a few other vocabularies and manuscripts. He had reached Merida on November 12, 1864, and journeyed on to Mexico City about January 24, 1865.

Maximilian asked him to remain in Mexico as Supervisor of Museums and Libraries as well as Minister of Education, but Brasseur (1871, p. iv) declined, explaining that he needed freedom to continue his research. Sailing from Veracruz on April 25, 1865, he proceeded to Omoa and Copan, from where he traveled for the third time to Guatemala City. In France César Daly suggested to the Commission Scientifique that the abbé might have Fuentes y Guzmán copy and check the manuscript of Bernal Díaz del Castillo, but instead Brasseur visited friends and planned a Quiche-Cakchiquel dictionary, which was never published. He returned to Madrid early in 1866. The letters and essays he wrote on the trip were published in the three-volume *Archives de la Commission Scientifique du Mexique*.

With astonishing good fortune, the abbé found in Madrid what he had vainly sought in Yucatan—a Maya codex. It belonged to Juan Tro y Ortolano, who allowed Brasseur to take it to Paris. The abbé named it the Codex Troano in his honor, and on April 19, 1866, the Commission Scientifique du Mexique decided to publish it along with a study by Brasseur and the materials he had brought from Yucatan.

The Waldeck drawings of Palenque which the French government had purchased (Cline, 1947) were finally published in 1866. Brasseur's introduction was called "Recherches sur les ruines de Palenqué et sur les origines de la civilisation du Mexique," but he wrote little about Palenque, which he still had not seen. He did have the good judgment to include earlier descriptions of Palenque, but his own introduction is without value, and in the words of Bandelier (1880, p. 99) is, ". . . a confused and disorderly jumble, barely readable."

Since 1859 Brasseur had been increasingly annoyed by the lack of interest shown

Americanist studies by the majority of his colleagues in the Société d'Ethnographie. Sarcastic comments on his ideas about Atlantis, to which he referred several times, must have disturbed him deeply, but not as much perhaps as the disdainful critical silence that followed the publication of *Quatre lettres sur le Mexique* (Brasseur, 1868). "J'y renversais d'un coup les idoles caressées par les germanistes de l'Institut. Et cependant, il ne s'en est pas trouvé un seul qui ait ouvert la bouche pour me réfuter, si j'avais tort, ou m'aplaudit si j'avais raison. Ils ne m'en ont pas lu, je le sais. . . ." (Brasseur, 1871, p. xxvii). This increasingly hostile situation took its toll on Brasseur. A symptom of growing paranoia was revealed in his statement (1868, p. 318) that the Louvre refused to buy Indian gold objects in order to keep it secret that the ancient Americans had been the world's finest goldsmiths.

Brasseur finally saw Palenque in January, 1871, where he claimed to have discovered an additional temple, the Sanctuary of the Mystic Tree. He wrote (1871, p. xxvii) that research in the temple had convinced him that he had read the Codex Troano backwards, and that each page of the codex should be read from the top down and from left to right. With that melancholy note his study (described below) of the codex ended.

In October of 1871 the catalog of Brasseur's library was ready for publication. The defiant and bitter introduction attacked his critics, calling them "Lilliputians" (1871, p. xviii), and ended with a declaration of faith in his doctrines: "A l'aide de la science mexicaine, j'ai levé le voile bleu du sanctuaire d'Isis. . . ." (p. xlviii).

His last article was based on a talk of May 6, 1872, called "Chronologie historique des Mexicains," and published in the *Actes* of the Société d'Ethnographie. Surprisingly, it is the clearest and best-organized piece he ever wrote. Relying for a last time on the Codex Chimalpopoca, he concluded (1873a,

p. 82) that beginning about 10,500 B.C., four periods of cataclysms had changed the world, and each had been caused by a temporary shifting of the earth's axis.

In 1872 the Ministry of Education sent him to Spain to begin work on a catalog of all the American manuscripts in Spanish libraries. Political unrest and his own declining health forced him to return to France. He visited Rome for the last time in December, 1873, where Herbert Adams met him and remarked on the extraordinary charm of his personality (Adams, 1891, p. 283). Three weeks later (January, 1874) Brasseur died at Nice.

PRINCIPAL MONOGRAPHIC WORKS

Few modern scholars read Brasseur de Bourbourg's monographs. Those who may occasionally dip into them generally do not realize the importance they held among readers of the mid-19th century. It was an era when European, British, North American, and Mexican scholars were slowly rediscovering ancient Indian Mexico, a generally prescientific age. When the abbé wrote, the exhumation of the great Sahagún corpus had yet to be made. Pioneer scientific studies by Seler and Tozzer and their students were more than a generation away in the future. Prescott's craftsmanlike works on Mexico and Peru were popular, but unlike Brasseur, whose disordered productions stand in stark contrast, Prescott was primarily concerned with the Spanish conquest, with minimum attention to the pre-Contact civilizations as stage setting for this great drama. Brasseur's special place in the development of ethnohistorical writings is his nearly exclusive concern with aboriginal history. Even the polemics of his day which were stirred by his attempt to provide a broad theoretical framework drew popular and scholarly attention to the importance of aboriginal American Indian civilizations.

Here we shall note in chronological order his principal monographic works. We separate them from his publication of sources,

although his introductions and notes to the latter often repeat and change his erratic thinking also embodied in the longer works.

Between 1857 and 1859 Brasseur de Bourbourg published the four-volume *Histoire des nations civilisées du Mexique et de l'Amérique-Central*, his major original work. For it his most important sources were Torquemada, what was then known of Sahagún, Veytía, Las Casas, Alva Ixtlilxochitl, the Codex Chimalpopoca, the Popol Vuh, and the Cakchiquel manuscript. Some 22 per cent of the citations are from Torquemada alone.

In the first volume the abbé conceded that the primitive Americans might have come from Asia via the Bering Strait, and that there may have been some Jewish and even Chinese influence, but because of their analogies with Egypt, he was certain that Palenque and other great American centers had been inspired by great men from the east, "legislateurs," who had brought monotheism, law, and art to the primitive natives. In this way he also reconciled conflicting theories of northern and eastern migrations. To trace the migrations and activities of these "legislateurs" and their descendants, he needed only a suitable historical approach.

He found it in the statement of Humboldt that history is sometimes present in myth. Supported by this authority, Brasseur began to see historical fact in all American myths. By interpreting them as he wished, he constructed a changing history of ancient America. It is important to point out that in this work he rejected the notion of Atlantis, which figures largely after 1861.

The first of the leaders, according to Brasseur, was the Phoenician, Votan, who defeated a native race called the Quiname, built Palenque, and founded the empire of Xibalba. Brasseur (1857c, p. 119) wrote that he had reasons to believe that at one time Xibalba covered all of Mexico and a part of the present United States. Zamna reached Yucatan a few years later, where he built

Mayapan and introduced an alphabet. Their work was symbolized for Brasseur by the last creation myth of the Popol Vuh. He wrote (ibid., p. 15) that the Quiche might have come from Scandinavia and moved south through the present United States, where they might have built the mounds of the Mississippi Valley.

Following these broad lines, the abbé traced migrations of Nahua-Toltec west from Asia via Europe in the first century B.C. and their migrations through Middle America under their culture hero Quetzal-coatl and other leaders. For him the word *nahual* was analogous to English "know all," possibly implying a British sojourn (ibid., p. 102). These Nahua folk settled around Palenque, and founded other Central American city-states which warred with each other.

According to Brasseur (ibid., p. 126), the Nahuas began to migrate all over North and South America in the second century A.D. He described their supposed movements with elaborate care. One group went south into Nicaragua; another, the Tutul Xiu, journeyed into Yucatan. The abbé devoted special attention to the group called Toltec. After pushing far to the north and then returning south into Mexico, they founded a kingdom at Tula. With this northern swing, Brasseur tried to reconcile conflicting traditions of northern and southern migrations; he was followed in this solution by Bancroft (Winsor, 1889, 1:138). The Toltec developed the highest pre-Conquest culture, and allegedly wrote the sacred book called the Teo-Amoxtli, which Brasseur saw reflected in every important Indian manuscript he found. They grew decadent, however, and were defeated in the 11th century by the Teo-Chichimec, who swept upon them from the north. Some of the most dramatic pages of this volume 1 (ibid., p. 411) contain Brasseur's vision of the destruction of Tula.

Volume 2, a history of what Brasseur called the Middle Ages, is devoted especial-

ly to the rise of the Guatemalan and Mexican kingdoms. His documentation for Yucatan was still too scanty for much development. Volume 3 contains much ethnographic information, but the student would be wise to consult the abbé's sources. Volume 4 describes the Spanish conquest.

Some critics of the day were suspicious of the work's detailed and facile explanations and its liberal and undisciplined use of myth as a source for history. An article in the *Atlantic Monthly* heaped praise on Brasseur, but the editor, James Russell Lowell, warned that the traditions and manuscripts had "been considerably modified in passing through the lively fancy of the abbé" (Lowell, 1858, p. 776), a view shared in France by Charencey (1859a, p. 31). Bancroft accepted some of Brasseur's ideas, but Brinton (1885, p. 44) called this kind of history "valueless." Whereas Brasseur read too much history into myth, Brinton could see none at all, and insisted that Votan, Quetzalcoatl, and even the Toltec were nothing but solar myths, which ". . . have no business in the pages of sober history" (ibid., p. 11). According to Brasseur (1859c, p. i) the work enjoyed a great popular success, especially in England, America, and Russia.

His *Grammaire de la langue quichée* was ready for publication in March of 1862. It included a grammar, based mainly on that of Ximénez, an essay on Indian poetry and drama, and the Rabinal Achí. In this work the abbé offered further evidence for the affinities of American languages to those of Europe. Whereas he had written earlier that many American words were of Germanic origin, he now affirmed that the reverse was true, and that the etymologies of many European and even Persian words were to be found in America. Reversing his position of 1857, he wrote here for the first time that Atlantis had existed, and that it had possessed a high culture long before Europe or Asia. In his opinion the east and west had been in constant communication, and the only question left to answer was why communication had ceased. His answer, he stated, would appear in a future publication.

The Rabinal Achí had been his most important discovery in Rabinal (1855). He deserves much credit for bringing this material to light, but again little of what he wrote about it can be believed. Brasseur (1940, p. 302) first wrote to Padilla on June 2 that he had found a manuscript of the native drama, but on August 7 he wrote in letters to the *New York Tribune* and to Squier that he had obtained it from the dictation of a grateful Indian whose life he had saved (Brasseur, 1855e, 1855f). The abbé never abandoned the second story but, inexplicably, in the *Grammaire de la langue quichée* (1862b, 2:25) he included a statement of the Indian, Bartolo Ziz, that he himself had written it down in 1850. This has caused much confusion among historians (Mace, 1967a, p. 13).

He was also deliberately inaccurate in describing the drama, probably to give it greater interest for his European readers. The cast includes only two Eagle and Jaguar Warriors, but he wrote (1862b, 2:22) that 12 warriors performed in his presence —which is doubtful—and that before the Conquest entire battalions had taken part. A more serious mistake was a change he made in the ending. In actual performance the two warriors pretend to execute Quiché-Achí by touching his head with their hatchets, but Brasseur (ibid., 2:19) made it more grandiose by writing that they place Quiché-Achí on a stone and sacrifice him. Writers who have not witnessed it have taken this to mean that the Indians imitate an Aztec sacrifice. At least one modern critic used this invention of Brasseur to prove an Aztec origin for the drama (Balmori, 1955, p. 593).[4]

As a major native drama that has survived, the Rabinal Achí continues to be of growing interest to students of literature as well as to ethnohistorians. It is important to note that Brasseur's novelistic imagination

seemingly makes his 1862 version undependable. It is an expansion of his first translation (1859a, pp. 293–99), from which it differs. Bandelier (1880, p. 111) early recognized the unsatisfactory nature of the Brasseur text, stating that Brasseur had "disfigured it," and "that a new and accurate translation was absolutely requisite." But none has been made to date. All modern versions, even that of the critical Raynaud (1929a, 1929b, 1930, 1953) either have relied too heavily on Brasseur's dubious work or have simply translated it.

In 1913 an Indian named Manuel Pérez copied the Quiche version that Brasseur had published in the *Grammaire de la langue quichée*. The Pérez text, with numerous changes he made in it, serves as the base for present Indian performances. Pérez utilized two letters invented in the 16th century by La Parra. A direct translation from Quiche, taking into account the Pérez modifications, is a desideratum, perhaps for the first time giving an accurate version of this remarkable survival.

On January 8, 1863, at a meeting of the Société d'Ethnographie, Pruner-Bey (1863, pp. 8–17) read a favorable criticism of the *Grammaire*, but rejected the abbé's theory that Quiche and European languages were related. He ignored Brasseur's statements about Atlantis; nor does it appear that they were mentioned by the abbé's colleagues during the discussion. They may have hoped to discourage his new theory by passing over it in silence. Remembering this meeting, Brasseur (1871, p. xxii) called Pruner-Bey "malicieux." The work received an Honorable Mention from the Académie des

---

[4] In August of 1970 the Rabinal-Achí was altered by the organizers of a Folklore Festival in Coban, who insisted that Quiché Achí should be executed according to Brasseur's "description." Initially opposed to this change, the Rabinal Indians have accepted it, and the alteration appears to be permanent. Quiché Achí is now stretched across a gilded bench or a mat, and Rabinal Achí pretends to cut open his chest. Other changes were the addition of two more princesses and the creation of new costumes.

Inscriptions et Belles Lettres, and the abbé was asked by the Ministry of Education to write an introduction for a sumptuous edition of Waldeck's equally misleading drawings of Palenque.

In 1866, Brasseur de Bourbourg published this introductory essay as "Recherches." Again it is full of mytho-historical speculations, altering some of his previous theories. He believed now that the Nahua had migrated from the Appalachian region. The religious ideas built around Quetzalcoatl and Tezcatlipoca no longer represented the deification of Nahua leaders, as he had stated earlier, but instead commemorated events of the cataclysm that destroyed Atlantis. The abbé now rejected all of the Votan myth, but offered no new explanation for the origin of Palenque. He was no longer even certain that Palenque had been the capital of Xibalba, and suggested that the capital may have been Mayapan or Chichen Itza. He was smarting under the criticism of his colleagues, especially that of Vivien de Saint-Martin, and wrote bitterly (1866a, p. xv) that their opinions were incorrect and unjust: "On semble nous faire un crime, néanmoins, de nos recherches. . . ." It was Brasseur's opinion that his introduction to Landa (see below) had not contradicted but only expanded his earlier work.

Brasseur's next major publication was the equally chaotic *Quatre lettres sur le Mexique* in 1868. As with several of his books, he paid for the publication himself. The myths of the Nahua and the Toltec had now lost all human reality for him, and instead had become the veiled accounts of geological phenomena. He was more than ever convinced of the existence of Atlantis and of its destruction. He needed only the proper tools to construct a history of it. One was the elaborate system of double meanings which, to his joy, occurred to him in the winter of 1867. While studying yet again his beloved Codex Chimalpopoca, he came to imagine that it had been written so that each word would have two or more meanings, depending on the rhythm and the caesura. In this way the priests had concealed accounts of the cataclysm in language that to the uninitiated would appear to describe only historical events or to be religious poetry. For example, by changing *Xi-bal-ba* to *Xib-al-ba*, the abbé believed that he had discovered a secret geological meaning: "l'embryon qui se remue dans les entrailles . . . le feu couvant en bas" (Brasseur, 1868, p. 228). Xibalba was not, therefore, an ancient empire, the enemy of the Nahua, but was revealed as a symbol of the subterranean volcanic power that destroyed Atlantis. By writing Quetzalcoatl as *Quetz-alco-atl*, he was able to find five new geological meanings. This meant that, like Humpty Dumpty, Brasseur could make a word mean anything he wanted. With this ingenious device he set out to make a new translation of the Codex Chimalpopoca and to write a new history of the world. Other "revelations" provided equally aberrant conclusions about Atlantis and cataclysms, affinities of languages, hieroglyphic meanings, and similar native matters that make the *Quatre lettres* chiefly a literary curiosity.[5] He included a fragment of a new translation of the Codex Chimalpopoca based on this theory of a movable caesura. It is clear that he never took it any further. His history of Atlantis was built on a new interpretation of myth and Maya hieroglyphs, rather than on a tedious new translation of manuscripts.

Brasseur (1871, p. xxvii) wrote that *Quatre lettres sur le Mexique* had outsold any of his other books. His obituary notice in the *Annuaire* of the Société Américaine reluctantly pointed out the widespread interest in his "errors," saying "elles ont porté vers l'archéologie américaine toutes les ima-

---

[5] Brasseur concluded, for example, that the four cornerposts of an Indian house symbolized the four islands on which the survivors of Atlantis sought refuge, and that with the white feathers in the procession of St. Paul, the Indians of Rabinal sought to preserve the tradition of the glaciers which had covered the Caribbean region after the cataclysm.

ginations avides de nouveauté" (Madier de Montjau, 1875b, p. 90). According to Rosny (1875, p. 55), however, not a single scholar accepted Brasseur's views on Atlantis. Among American archaeologists, only Le Plongeon (1879) agreed with him.

DISCOVERY AND PUBLICATION OF SOURCES

Brasseur de Bourbourg's chief claim on posterity is that he found and published sources of continuing interest to ethnohistory. In an era when these were deficient, they were epoch-making, in spite of the fact that we now know him as a suspect editor whose introductory materials and notes are filled with the same wild fancies that appear in his own monographic writings.

As seen, Brasseur disputed Scherzer's primacy in publishing the Popol Vuh, which owes its common name to Brasseur's French translation. There is no question of the importance of the manuscript (discussed in Articles 21 and 22). There are grave doubts about Brasseur's handling of it, and certainly about his interpretations of its meaning.

The last work of his first or pre-Atlantis period, the Popol Vuh, was published in the fall of 1861. In the long preface he wrote that Ximénez' translation was subjective and inaccurate, and that the Dominican had not understood the Indian mentality. He especially criticized Ximénez for having identified Xibalba with a mythical underworld, but nevertheless admitted that his own translation owed much to him. Brasseur's interpretation of myth in the Popol Vuh was similar to that of 1857, but richer in details. For example, according to the abbé, only seven of the Nahua leaders survived the floods and winds at Xicalanco, and hence the sacred number seven of American religions. The nine trials in Xibalba represented nine different battles, and the ball game heard overhead by the lords of Xibalba indicated that the Nahua had settled in the mountains of Verapaz (Brasseur, 1861c, p. cxxxvi). He suggested a Scandinavian origin rather than an Asian for

the Nahua and retained his belief that Votan had founded Palenque, but now rejected some of the more fantastic details of his voyages.

It was in the Popol Vuh that Brasseur (1861c, p. xxxii) first quoted the idea of Humboldt that primitive cultures were sometimes the debris of higher civilizations destroyed by natural catastrophes. This concept was to be of crucial importance in his later work, where he would use it to support his theories about an American Atlantis.

In a review in *Nouvelles annales des voyages*, Cressonière (1862, pp. 87–116) praised the work and could find no fault with either the translation or the interpretation. Max Müller wrote that Brasseur had erred in naming it the Popol Vuh and had called it *Le livre sacré* only to have a "fine sounding title" (Müller, 1907, p. 326). He refused to accept the abbé's statement that it was the original of the Teo-Amoxtli, and disagreed with the historical interpretation of its myths. Brinton did not like the translation, and of the interpretation he wrote (1883, p. 33) that Brasseur was "a Euhemerist of the most advanced type and saw in every myth the statement of historical fact." Stoll (1938, p. 133) has pointed out that certain of Brasseur's translations were designed only to support his preconceived ideas about Xibalba. It was the opinion of Recinos (1950, pp. 53–56) that Ximénez had understood the Indian mentality much better than the abbé, and that Brasseur's translation owed much to Ximénez. On the positive side he pointed out that it was a notable work despite its many errors.

Without dispute, Brasseur's discovery and first publication (1864d) of Bishop Landa's *Relación de las cosas de Yucatán* (discussed in Article 13) was a major contribution to Middle American ethnohistorical studies. But, as in other cases, one must note its significant imperfections, which have made this edition chiefly of antiquarian rather than current scholarly interest.

Valentini (1880, p. 35) pointed out that

the abbé had given neither the date of his discovery nor a description of the manuscript. The Madrid edition of 1884 revealed that Brasseur had indeed been unusually careless. Brinton compared the two editions and concluded (1887, p. 2) that the abbé had omitted about one-sixth of the text, made a faulty translation, and even "did not hesitate occasionally to alter the original when he could not get at its meaning conveniently."

The introduction contained a detailed explanation of Brasseur's theories about Atlantis and the cataclysm that destroyed it around 6000 B.C. For the first time he quoted (1864d, p. xvi) the opinion of Eckstein that early migrations were frequently caused by comets, volcanos, and other catastrophes; Eckstein joined Humboldt in Brasseur's hierarchy of authority. The abbé wrote that all American religions, rites, and dance-dramas commemorated the catastrophes which the Codex Chimalpopoca and the Popol Vuh now seemed to him to describe.

According to Tayac (1867a, p. 66), the Landa caused numerous polemics in France. Several professors of the Collège de France remarked that Brasseur had set back the study of history by 300 years (Brasseur, 1871, p. xxv). In Mexico, however, Larrainzar (1865, p. 24) wrote that it was at least a praiseworthy attempt to find the truth in an area where others had given up.

Another major coup was Brasseur's discovery in 1866 of the Codex Troano, a basic document for Maya studies (see Article 23, Item 187). He published it in two volumes, with the now standard introductory theorizing. Subsequent editions have replaced his for scholarly use.

The first volume of the Manuscrit Troano appeared in 1869. It included the abbé's study and an excellent reproduction of the codex. Volume 2 was published the following year with another introduction, a Maya grammar, a chrestomathy, and a Maya-French vocabulary of about 7,600 words. Scholars agreed that it was the most com-

plete vocabulary available, but insisted that it be used with caution as "the derivations and analogies proposed are of a character unknown to the science of language" (Brinton, 1882b, pp. 75–76).

Brasseur wrote in the introduction that for nearly a year he had made no progress in interpreting the codex. He thought at first that it might be a rural almanac, but was not certain if it was phonetic or even Maya. According to the abbé (1869c, p. v), it was only after two years of fruitless conjectures that his sudden insights of 1868 gave him the key to its meaning: "je pénétrai peu à peu le mystère de ces images bizarres; enfin, les derniers voiles s'écartèrent et je commençai à lire d'un bout à l'autre les inscriptions." He informed Rosny before the publication of the book that he had completely mastered all of the glyphs (Brasseur, 1869b, p. 79), and Rosny (1875, p. 55) wrote that he had often heard Brasseur say that he could read Maya books as easily as books written in English. As usual, however, the abbé's enthusiasm was premature. His ingenious approach to the problems of Maya writing reveals some interesting insights, which, had he been psychologically capable of combining his vast knowledge of American languages with careful scholarship, might have led him to important discoveries. But he was determined to relate every glyph to the upheavals that had destroyed Atlantis; and that led his work far astray.[6]

The few critics who ventured to publish their opinions about the Troano all disagreed with its conclusions. Leoncio Angrand, who had worked with the abbé for several months, mailed a circular to the learned societies of Europe and America, disclaiming any responsibility for it (Haven, 1870, p. 57; Angrand, 1870). A review

[6] Ed. note: Appendix B gives further detail on Brasseur's attempt to use the Landa alphabet to "read" Maya signs. A series of publications by the Russian Y. V. Knorozov in the 1950s revived some interest in efforts to solve these riddles, but to date results are inconclusive or negative.

(signed only "R.S.") in the *Revue archéologique* justly praised the abbé's devotion to American studies, but totally rejected his ideas about the Manuscrit Troano (R.S., 1870, pp. 213, 257). In his dismay Brinton (1870, p. 7) wrote the strongest statement: "It is painful not to be able to say a single word in favor of his views. . . . They are so utterly wild that we are almost afraid to state them."

It appears that during the three years between 1870 and Brasseur's death there was no other written criticism of the work. Scholars ignored it, and Brasseur was more hurt by this than he would have been by a clamorous reaction. He complained bitterly to Rosny about what he called "la conspiration du silence" (Rosny, 1876, p. 39), and apparently saw a plot to discredit him. It is probable that paranoia had begun to gain control of his judgment. Rosny (ibid., p. 40) deplored the ideas in the introduction, but attacked the scholars who had been too disdainful to comment on them. As usual, Rosny found something good to say about his friend's work, and pointed out that the catalogue of glyphs would be of use to scholars. Bancroft (1874–75, 2:780) rejected the abbé's ideas, but also condemned his sneering critics, many of whom Bancroft felt were "utterly incompetent to understand them."

EVALUATION

Most of Abbé Brasseur de Bourbourg's ethnohistorical work is no longer of value, but critics have been unanimous in their praise of his untiring efforts to collect manuscripts and to interest the world in Americanist studies.[7] Brinton (1868b, p. 40), his most severe critic, paid him the highest tribute: "But while thus regretting the use he has made of them, all interested in American antiquity cannot thank too much this indefatigable explorer for the priceless materials he has unearthed in the neglected libraries of Spain and Central America and laid before the public."

[7] In addition to specific citations and references given above, the following works were used in preparation of this article: Acuña, 1968; Aldana Rivas, 1864; Baer, 1911; Benoist, 1865; Bernal, 1962; Boban, 1886; Bollaert, 1863, 1866; Brinton, 1868a, 1882a, 1884, 1890; Carrillo y Ancona, 1865, 1869; Catin, 1927; Charencey, 1859b, 1874; Chavero, n.d. [1939?]; Chávez Zelaya, 1955; Cortambert, 1867; Daly, 1867; Diéguez Flores, 1888, 1923; Duchateau, 1875; Ferland, 1854; Field, 1873; Gatschet, 1879; Haven, 1878; Howitt, 1856; Labarthe, 1870; Leclerc, 1878; Leinaweaver, 1968; Lejeal, 1903; Le Plongeon, 1879; Lorenz, 1867; Mace, 1967b; Madier de Montjau, 1875a, 1876; Mitre, 1909, 1911; Molé, 1945; Pinart, 1883; Recinos, 1953, 1956; Rice, 1888; Rosny, 1887; R.S., 1871; Sabin, 1869; Saenz de Santa María, 1959; Saint-Martin, 1866, 1867; Salisbury, 1876; Schoebel, 1874; Soustelle, 1967; Squier, 1855a; Tayac, 1867b; Thomas, 1882; Trübner, 1856a, 1856b; Vandegehuchte, 1860; Villacorta, 1929.

APPENDIX A. BRASSEUR DE BOURBOURG, WRITINGS

Manuscripts:
n.d.   Basseta, Domingo, Vocabulario quiché; [compiled by] Basseta, [with additions by] Brasseur de Bourbourg. 3 vols. In BNP. [Copy in Peabody Museum, Harvard University.]
n.d.   Notice historique sur l'origine des peuples du Mexique et la puissance de ses rois. [Unpublished manuscript of 24 pages. Listed by Pinart, 1883, p. 25. Present location unknown.]
n.d.   Quelques faits et découvertes qui

tendent à trouver l'ancienne civilisation de l'Amerique. [Unpublished manuscript. Listed by Léon de Rosny as no. 1 in the collection of Lucien de Rosny, Documents relatifs à l'archéologie de l'Amèrique ancienne. Present location unknown.]
n.d.   Vocabulario de las lenguas quiche y cakchiquel. [Manuscript of 148 pages; first pages typewritten. Photographic reproduction by William E. Gates of the original manuscript in BNP.

Manuscript undated and never published. Gates copy available in Peabody Museum, Harvard University.]

1859–65 Lettres et mémoires de Brasseur de Bourbourg, 1859 à 1865. Accompagnés de photographies. MSS Angrand 4. 1 vol. Papier. XIXe siècle. 270 mm x 220 mm, 70 feuillets. BNP, Léonce Angrand Collection. [Poorly reproduced photostatic copies, LC, Manuscripts Division. Seemingly all later published, but not examined in detail.]

Published, 1851–73:[8]

1851 Lettres pour servir d'introduction à l'histoire primitive des nations civilisées de l'Amérique septentrionale adresées à Monsieur le Duc de Valmy. Cartas para servir de introducción á la historia primitiva de las naciones civilizadas de la América setentrional. Mexico. [Double columns, French and Spanish. Treats myth of Votan and parts of Popol Vuh. Published again in SMGE, *Boletín*, 8:309–36 (1860); 10:319–44 (1863).]

1851? Nagualism, or Sketches of the Mexican superstition since the Conquest. Read October 16 before the National Institute. [From E. G. Squier's Scrapbook; formerly owned by Gates. Now in Peabody Museum, Harvard University. 17 typed pages. Published in *Weekly National Intelligencer*, probably between 1850 and 1855. Most of the information in this paper also appears in Brasseur's *Voyage sur l'Isthme de Tehuantepec.* See 1861d.]

1852a Des antiquités mexicaines. A propos du *Mémoire sur la peinture didactique et l'écriture figurative des anciens mexicains*, adressé à l'Académie des Sciences, par M. J. M. A. Aubin, ancien professeur de l'Université. *Revue archéologique ou recueil de documents et de mémoires relatifs a l'étude des monuments, et à la philologie de l'antiquité et du moyen age*, IX année: 408–21 (Sept.). [Reviews research of Aubin. Recommends a scientific expedition to Mexico.]

1852b Histoire du Canada, de son église et de ses missions, depuis la découverte de l'Amérique jusqu'à nos jours, écrite sur des documents inédits compulsés dans les archives de l'archevêché et de la ville de Québec, etc. Paris.

1855a Antigüedades guatemaltecas. Correspondencia particular del señor Abate Brasseur de Bourbourg al señor redactor de la Gaceta de Guatemala. *Gaceta de Guatemala*, 7, nos. 67 and 68: (July 20 and July 27). [Letter dated Rabinal, July 9, 1855.]

1855b Carta al Sr. Redactor de la Gaceta de Guatemala. *Gaceta de Guatemala*, 7, no. 56: May 18. [Dated Guatemala City, May 14. Written one day before departure for Rabinal. Expresses gratitude to city. Has not been published elsewhere.]

1855c Variedades. Una carta del Abate Brasseur de Bourbourg al Sr. Conde Enrique de la Motte-Thoy. Rabinal en la Verapaz, Julio 25 de 1855. *Gaceta de Guatemala*, 7, nos. 85–88: (Nov. 23–Dec. 14). [Describes Antigua and Guatemala City.]

1855d Curious discoveries in Guatemala: The remains of antique cities. *Pennsylvania Inquirer*, 53, no. 123: Nov. 22. [The same letters had been published the day before in the *New York Tribune* (see 1855e). An editorial note in the *Inquirer* stated: "This is all curious indeed, if true." Paragraphs from both letters were published under the same title in *Weekly National Intelligencer* Dec. 1, 1855, no. 1,046. The editorial note from the *Inquirer* was included. Brasseur saw a copy of the *Intelligencer* in Rabinal.]

1855e Interesting discoveries in Guatemala: Ruins of unknown ancient cities; Traces of early migrations from the north. *New York Tribune*, 15, No. 4,552: (Nov. 21, 1855). [Two letters, the first a translation of one July 9, 1855, published in *Gaceta de Guatemala* July 20 and 27. The second letter published here for the first time. Dated Verapaz, Aug. 7, it gives at length information about the dictation of the Rabinal Achí by Bartolo Ziz, in almost the same words of the letter he wrote to Squier on the same day. This letter contains his first statement that the Quiche had come south through the United States in their migration from Denmark and Norway, and has not been published again.]

---

[8] Ed. note: The author has made every effort to make this section comprehensive.

1855f A letter from Brasseur to E. G. Squier, dated Rabinal, August 7, 1855. *The Athenaeum*, no. 1467: 1435–1436 (Dec. 8). [A paraphrase of the second letter published in *New York Tribune* Nov. 21, 1855. [See 1855e.]

1855g Notes d'un voyage dans l'Amérique Centrale. Lettres à M. Alfred Maury, bibliothécaire de l'Institut. *Nouvelles annales des voyages*, 147:129–58 (Aug.). [Two letters. First dated Guatemala, Mar. 28; second, Apr. 28. Both treat trip through Nicaragua. Second describes linguistic "discoveries" and suggests Scandinavian origin for the Quiche.]

1856a Antigüedades de Centro-America. Artículo remitido por el Abate Brasseur de Bourbourg al editor de la Gaceta. [Dated Sept. 17, 1856. Does not appear in *Gaceta de Guatemala* for 1856 or 1857. A typewritten copy, 4 pages, "copied from Squier's scrap book" available in Peabody Museum, Harvard University. Contains only historical generalizations of little interest. States that he began to collect works on America before age of 15.]

1856b Antigüedades guatemaltecas. [Three letters addressed to the editor.] *Gaceta de Guatemala*, 8, nos. 23, 36, 41: (Apr. 5, May 21, June 7). [(1) Rabinal, Feb. 23. Attacks editor of *Pennsylvania Inquirer*. Contradicts statement of Scherzer that Brasseur had sought Popol Vuh in Mexico. Preliminary statement on double meaning in Popol Vuh. Mention of dictation of Rabinal-Achí. (2) Rabinal, Apr. 12. Interpretation of Popol Vuh later used in *Histoire des nations civilisées du Mexique et de l'Amérique-Centrale*. (3) Guatemala City, June 2. Traditions in Ximénez and Cakchiquel manuscripts appear to prove system of Ordóñez. Northern origin for the Quiche also indicated. In this letter he favors neither system over the other, although in letter of Aug. 7 he had stated flatly that they had come from Scandinavia and passed through the United States.]

1857a Aperçu d'un voyage dans les états de San Salvador et de Guatemala. *Bulletin de la Société de Géographie de Paris*, 13:272–93 (Apr., May). [Read

by Brasseur in a public meeting Apr. 17, 1857.]

1857b Archives des indigènes. Paris. [Described by Sabin as a book of 66 pages. Not examined.]

1857c Histoire des nations civilisées du Mexique et de l'Amérique-Centrale, durant les siècles antérieurs à Christophe Colomb, écrite sur des documents originaux et entièrement inédits, puisés aux anciennes archives des indigènes. Tome Premier, comprenant les temps héroïques et l'histoire de l'empire des toltèques. Paris. [A major work. See text discussion. For other vols. see 1858b, 1858c, 1859c.]

1857d Nociones de un viaje a los Estados de San Salvador y Guatemala, leidas en la sesion pública anual del 17 de Abril de 1857 por M. el Abate Brasseur de Bourbourg. *El museo guatemalteco*, 1, Sept. 2, Sept. 12, nos. 41, 42. [Translated by Manuel Diéguez from "Aperçu d'un voyage dans les états de San Salvador et de Guatemala." See 1857a.]

1857e Nociones de un viaje a los Estados de San Salvador y Guatemala, leídas en la sesión pública anual del 17 de abril de 1857. *Gaceta del Salvador*, 6, Sept. 16, Sept. 26, nos. 41, 44. [Taken from *El museo guatemalteco*. See 1857d.]

1857f Resumen histórico y cronolójico de los Reyes de Guatemala antes de la Conquista. Estractado de los documentos orijinales y compilado por el abate C. E. Brasseur de Bourbourg. *El museo guatemalteco*, 1: no. 29 (May 14). [Dated Rabinal, Dec. 19, 1855. Historical information from the Popol Vuh and the Cakchiquel manuscript.]

1858a [and Victor Adolphe Malte-Brun] Carte des états du Mexique au temps de la conquête en 1521; dressée sous la direction de M. l'abbé Brasseur de Bourbourg, d'après les anciens documents de la Vice-Royauté, les cartes de la Société de Géographie et de Statistique de Mexico, . . . par V. A. Malte-Brun. Paris.

1858b Histoire des nations civilisées du Mexique et de l'Amérique-Centrale, durant les siècles antérieurs à Christophe Colomb, écrit sur des documents originaux et entièrement inédits, puisés aux anciennes archives des indigènes. Tome Second, comprenant l'histoire de l'Yucatan et du Guatémala; avec celle de l'Anahuac, durant le moyen age aztèque, jusqu'à la fondation de la royauté à Mexico. Paris. [See 1857c, 1858c, 1859c.]

1858c Histoire des nations civilisées du Mexique et de l'Amérique-Centrale, durant les siècles antérieurs à Christophe Colomb, écrite sur des documents originaux et entièrement inédits, puisés aux anciennes archives des indigènes. Tome Troisième, comprenant l'histoire des états du Michoacan et d'Oaxaca et de l'empire de l'Anahuac jusqu'a l'arrivée des espagnols. Astronomie, religion, sciences et arts des aztèques, etc. Paris. [See 1857c, 1858b, 1859c.]

1858d Histoire du commerce et de l'industrie chez les nations aztèques avant la découverte de l'Amérique par Christophe Colomb, extrait de l'Histoire des nations civilisées du Mexique et de l'Amérique Centrale. *Nouvelles annales des voyages*, 158:257–321; 159:45–84 (June, July). [With only a few changes this reprints *Histoire des nations civilisées du Mexique et de l'Amérique Centrale*, 3:605–54.]

1858e Quelques traces d'une émigration de l'Europe septentrionale en Amérique dans les traditions et les langues de l'Amérique Centrale. Lettre addressée à M.C.C. Rafn, secrétaire de la Société Royal des Antiquaires du Nord à Copenhague. *Nouvelles annales des voyages*, 160:261–92 (Dec.). [Contains list of supposed analogies between European and Quiche words.]

1859a De Guatémala à Rabinal. Episode d'un séjour dans l'Amérique Centrale pendant les années 1855 et 1856. *La revue européenne*, 1:46–74, 275–301 (Feb. 1, 15).

1859b Essai historique sur les sources de la philologie mexicaine et sur l'ethnographie de l'Amérique Centrale. *Revue orientale et américaine*, 1:354–80, 2:64–75 (Feb., April?). [Treats early writers, distribution of languages, and lists books and manuscripts not yet mentioned in other bibliographies.]

1859c Histoire des nations civilisées du Mexique et de l'Amérique-Centrale, durant les siècles antérieurs à Christophe Colomb, écrite sur des documents originaux et entièrement inédits, puisés aux anciennes archives des indigènes. Tome Quatrième, conquête des états du Mexique et du Guatémala, etc. Etablissement du gouvernement espagnol et de l'Eglise Catholique. Ruine de l'idolatrie, déclin et abaissement de la race indigène. Paris. [See 1857c, 1858b, 1858c.]

1860 De Guatemala a Rabinal. Episodio de un viaje en la América del Centro en los años de 55 y 56. *Gaceta de Guatemala*, 11, nos. 69–81 (Dec. 2, 1859–Jan. 27, 1860). [Translated from *La revue européenne*. See 1859a.]

1861a Coup d'oeil sur la nation et la langue des Wabis, population maritime de la côte de Tehuantepec (Mexique). *La revue orientale et américaine*, 5:261–71. [Objective scholarly article with short Huave vocabulary.]

1861b Manuscrit pictographique américain, précédé d'une notice sur l'idéographie des peaux-rouges, par M. l'abbé Em. Domenech. *Bulletin de la Société de Géographie de Paris*, 5 ser., 1:146–56 (Feb.). [Suggests a 17th-century origin for the manuscript. Describes it as "un monument unique probablement dans son genre," but considers Domenech's interpretation "arbitraire." Much of the article is a defense of Aubin.]

1861c Popol Vuh. Le livre sacré et les mythes de l'antiquité américaine, avec les livres héroïques et historiques des quichés. Ouvrage original des indigènes de Guatémala, texte quiché et traduction française en regard, accompagnée de notes philologiques et d'un commentaire sur la mythologie et les migrations des peuples anciens de l'Amérique, etc., composé sur des documents originaux et inédits. Paris. Collection de documents dans les langues indigènes, pour servir à l'étude de l'histoire et de la philologie de l'Amérique ancienne, 1. [A major work. See text. According to Montalbán (1929, p. 30), the Popol Vuh had to that time been published six times, first by Karl Scherzer (1857), then Brasseur (1861). Juan Gavarrete translated into Spanish the latter (1871), several times reprinted.]

1861d Voyage sur l'isthme de Tehuantepec dans l'état de Chiapas et la République de Guatémala, exécuté dans les années 1859 et 1860. *Nouvelles annales des voyages,* 172:129–96 (Nov.). [Describes only trip through Tehuantepec. Second part never published. First part republished, 1862.]

1862a Documents sur le Mexique. *Bulletin de la Société d'Anthropologie de Paris,* 3:248–50. [Observations on goiter and alcoholism among the Indians of Guatemala.]

1862b Grammaire de la langue quichée suivie d'un vocabulaire et du drame de Rabinal Achi. Gramatica de la lengua quiche. Grammaire de la langue quichée, espagnole-française, mise en parallèle avec ses deux dialectes, cakchiquel et tzutuhil, tirée des manuscrits des meilleurs auteurs guatémaliens. Ouvrage accompagné de notes philologiques avec un vocabulaire comprenant les sources principales du quiché comparées aux langues germaniques et suivi d'un essai sur la poésie, la musique, la danse et l'art dramatique chez les mexicains et les guatémaltèques avant la conquête; servant d'introduction au Rabinal-Achi, drame indigène avec sa musique originale, texte quiché et traduction française en regard. Paris. *Collection de documents dans les langues indigènes, pour servir a l'étude de l'histoire de la philologie de l'Amérique ancienne,* 2. [A major publication.]

1862c Sommaire des voyages scientifiques et des travaux de géographie, d'histoire, d'archéologie et de philologie américaines, publiés par M. l'abbé Brasseur de Bourbourg. Saint-Cloud. [14 pp.]

1864a Archéologie américaine. Cours de M. l'abbé Brasseur de Bourbourg (Soirées littéraires de la Sorbonne). Antiquités du Mexique et de l'Amérique Centrale, etc. *La revue des cours littéraires de la France et de l'étranger,* 1:337–46 (May 28). [Talk at the Sorbonne, illustrated with photographic slides, legends, personal reminiscences.]

1864b Esquisses d'histoire, d'archéologie, d'ethnographie et de linguistique, pouvant servir d'instructions générales, *Nouvelles annales des voyages,* 183:5–68 (July). [Also appeared in *Archives de la Commission Scientifique du Mexique,* 1:85–136 (1865).]

1864c Lettre de M. l'abbé Brasseur. Académie des Inscriptions et Belles Lettres. *Comptes Rendus,* 8:70–71. [Dated Madrid, Jan. 20, 1864, describing Copan and his discovery of Landa.]

1864d Relation des choses de Yucatan de Diego de Landa. Texte espagnol et traduction français en regard, comprenant les signes du calendrier et de l'alphabet hiéroglyphique de la langue maya accompagné de documents divers, historiques et chronologiques, avec une *Grammaire* et un *Vocabulaire* abrégés français-maya précédés d'un essai sur les sources de l'histoire primitive du Mexique et de l'Amérique Centrale, etc., d'après les monuments égyptiens et de l'histoire primitive de l'Egypte d'après les monuments américains. Paris. *Collection de documents dans les langues indigènes pour servir a l'étude de l'histoire et de la philologie de l'Amérique ancienne,* 3. [A major publication. Also contains part of *Historia de Nuestra Señora de Itzamal* (pp. 348–65), Pío Pérez (pp. 366–419), Maya history (pp. 420–29), Frère Romain Pane (pp. 431–58), grammar based on Beltrán and Ruz (pp. 459–79), Maya-French vocabulary (pp. 480–506), and a vocabulary of words from Haiti (pp. 507–12).]

1864e S'il existe des sources de l'histoire primitive du Mexique dans les monuments égyptiens et de l'histoire primitive de l'ancien monde dans les monuments américains. Paris. [Offprint from *Relation des choses de Yucatan.* Identical, except for first sentence and a note on p. 6.]

1865a Esquisses d'histoire, d'archéologie, d'ethnographie et de linguistique pouvant servir d'instructions générales. *Archives de la Commission Scientifique du Mexique* 1:85–136. 3 vols. Paris. [First published in *Nouvelles annales des voyages,* 183:5–68 (July, 1864). A few fragments published in 1925 in *L'Echo du Méxique,* 5, nos. 50 and 51:5–6, 5–6. Not examined.]

1865b Lettres de M. Brasseur de Bourbourg, datées de Mérida et de Mexico, au sujet de la Péninsule Yucatèque. *Archives de la Commission Scientifique de Mexique,* 1:454–60. 3 vols. Paris. [Describe Yucatan, Merida, Uxmal.]

1866a Monuments anciens du Mexique. Palenqué et autres ruines de l'ancienne civilisation du Mexique, collection de vues, bas-reliefs, morceau d'architecture, coupes, vases, terres cuites, cartes et plans, dessinés d'après nature et relevés par M. de Waldeck. Texte rédigé par M. Brasseur de Bourbourg, Membre de la Commission Scientifique du Mexique, etc., Ouvrage publié sous les auspices de S.E. le Ministre de L'Instruction Publique. [on p. 3] Recherches sur les ruines de Palenqué et sur les origines de la civilisation du Mexique. Paris.

n.d. [1866b] Monuments anciens du Mexique. Recherches sur les ruines de Palenqué et sur les origines de la civilisation du Mexique. Texte publié sous les auspices de S.E.M. le Ministre de l'Instruction Publique. Paris. [Text published without drawings or explanations of Waldeck. No date given in volume.]

1867a Essai historique sur le Yucatan et description des ruines de Ti-Hoo (Mérida) et d'Izamal, etc. Rapport adressé à son Excellence M. le Ministre de l'Instruction Publique. *Archives de la Commission Scientifique du Mexique,* 2:18–64. 3 vols. Paris. [Dated Mexico City, Feb. 24, 1865.]

1867b Extraits de deux lettres écrites à S. Exc. le Ministre de l'Instruction Publique, par M. l'abbé Brasseur de Bourbourg, l'une de Guatemala, à la date du 15 juillet 1865, l'autre de la Véra-Cruz, à la date du 2 décembre de la même année. *Archives de la Commission Scientifique du Mexique,* 2:298–311. 3 vols. Paris. [Describes trip through Honduras to Copan, and trip in Guatemala.]

1867c Rapport sur les ruines de Mayapan et d'Uxmal au Yucatan (Mexique), adressé à son Excellence M. le Ministre de l'Instruction Publique. *Archives de la Commission Scientifique du Mexique,* 2:234–88. 3 vols. Paris. [Uses much information from Stephens. Dated Mexico, Mar. 25, 1865.]

1868 Quatre lettres sur le Mexique. Exposition absolue du système hiéroglyphi-

que mexicain. La fin de l'âge de pierre. Epoque glaciaire temporaire. Commencement de l'âge de bronze. Origines de la civilisation et des religions de l'antiquité, d'après le Teo-Amoxtli et autre documents mexicains. Paris. *Collection de documents dans les langues indigènes pour servir à l'étude de l'histoire et de la philologie de l'Amérique ancienne,* 4.

1869a Catalogue des caractères mayas (fondus à l'imprimerie impériale pour la publication du Manuscrit Troano. Etudes sur le système graphique et la langue des Mayas). Paris. [Listed by Brasseur: "Ce catalogue, extrait des Etudes sur le système graphique et la langue des Mayas, n'a été tiré à part que pour l'usage de l'Imprimerie Impériale."]

1869b Lettre à M. Léon de Rosny sur la découverte de documents relatifs à la haute antiquité américaine et sur le déchiffrement et l'interprétation de l'écriture phonétique et figurative de la langue maya. (Extrait des *Mémoires de la Société d'Ethnographie*). 20 pp., 2 pls. Paris. [Offprint from *Mémoires de la Société d'Ethnographie,* vol. 11 (second series, vol. 1), Paris, 1871, pp. 78–95, 2 pls. Cover of this volume, dated 1872, also bears the words *Revue Ethnographique.* This volume may also have been issued as *Revue Ethnographique,* vol. 1; its first installments appear to have been dated 1869. The volume is the equivalent of *Revue Orientale et Américaine,* vol. 11 (1869?–) but it is uncertain if any copies bear this title page.]

1869c Manuscrit Troano. Etudes sur le système graphique et la langue des mayas. Mission Scientifique au Mexique et dans l'Amérique Centrale, ouvrage publié par ordre de S.M. l'Empereur et par les soins du Ministre de l'Instruction Publique. Linguistique. Tome Premier. Paris. [Contains study of Maya writing, supplementary study, and chromolothographic reproduction of codex.]

1869d [Note on the word *papa* in Iceland and America, on page 200 of Explicación del Codex Telleriano-Remensis]. *Archives paléographiques de l'orient et de l'Amérique,* 1:190–232 (edited by Léon de Rosny; only one volume).

[Brasseur suggests early American colonization of Iceland.]

1870a Manuscrit Troano. Etudes sur le système graphique et la langue des mayas. Mission scientifique au Mexique et dans l'Amérique Centrale. Ouvrage publié par ordre de S. M. l'Empereur et par les soins du Ministre de l'Instruction Publique. Linguistique. Tome Second. Paris. [Contains introduction, grammar, chrestomathy, and a Maya, French, and Spanish vocabulary.]

1870b Prehistoric America. *New York World*, 11, no. 3257: July 18. [Enthusiastic letter from L. Harper, dated Brussels, June 30. Translation of a letter of Brasseur of June 8, Ghent. Much on Atlantis and Brasseur's geologic theory of history.]

1870c Le mystère de l'Ile de Pâques, communication de M.V.A. Malte Brun à M. Brasseur de Bourbourg et réponse y relative, du 12 janvier 1870. *Annales des voyages de la géographie de l'histoire et de l'archéologie*, pp. 107–19. [Elaboration of theories: Man first appeared in plateaus of Asia. All Indian documents are geological history from 10,000 B.C., etc.]

1871 Bibliothèque mexico-guatémalienne, précédée d'un coup d'oeil sur les études américaines dans leurs rapports avec les études classiques et suivie du tableau par ordre alphabétique des ouvrages de linguistique américaine contenus dans le même volume, rédigée et mise en ordre d'après les documents de sa collection américaine. Paris.

1872 Dictionnaire, grammaire et chrestomathie de la langue maya, précédés d'une étude sur le système graphique des indigènes du Yucatan (Mexique). 2 vols. in 1. Paris. [Same as Manuscrit Troano, but without reproduction of codex. Binder's title: *La langue maya*.]

1873a Chronologie historique des mexicains. *Actes de la Société d'Ethnographie*, s. 2, t. 3 (t. 7 de la collection): 77–85 (meeting of May 6, 1872).

1873b Memorial de Tecpan Atitlán. *Boletín de la Sociedad Económica de Guatemala*, nos. 29–43. [A translation by Gavarrete from the unpublished French version of Brasseur, which

passed to Pinart and thence to Brinton. Listed by Brinton. Not examined.]

Posthumous Publications, 1875–1967:

1875 Coup d'oeil sur la nation et la langue des Wabis, population maritime de la côte de Tehuantepec (Mexique). *Archives de la Société Américaine de France*, N.S., 1:131–42. [Published previously. See 1861a.]

1894 Popol Vuh. Versión española por Juan Gavarrete de la traducción francesa de Brasseur. *El educacionista*, 1894–1896 (Guatemala). [See 1861c. Listed by Saenz de Santa María, 1959, p. 258. Not examined.]

1906–07 El Popol-Vuh ó libro sagrado de los antiguos votánides. *Revista del Archivo de la Biblioteca Nacional de Honduras*, 3, nos. 2–16: (Nov. 25, 1906–June 25, 1907). [The Spanish version of Gavarrete. See 1894. Gavarrete version of Brasseur's translation also published by Arturo Ambrogi in vol. 6 of the Biblioteca Centroamericana.]

1906b Resumen histórico y cronológico de los reyes de Guatemala, antes de la conquista, extractado de los documentos originales y compilado por el abate E. C. Brasseur de Bourbourg. *Revista del Archivo de la Biblioteca Nacional de Honduras*, 2:609–13, 642–46 (Aug. 25, Sept. 10). [Published previously in *El museo guatemalteco*. See 1857f.]

1925 Nociones de un viaje a los estados de San Salvador y Guatemala. *Anales de la Sociedad de Geografía e Historia*, 1:203–13 (Jan.). [Published previously. See 1857a, 1857d, 1857e.]

1926 Popol Vuh; libro sagrado del quiché; version española del texto francés del abate Carlos Esteban Brasseur de Bourbourg. Ediciones de la Biblioteca Nacional. Bajo los auspicios del Señor Presidente de la República de el Salvador. El Salvador, (Sección de linotipía de la Imprenta Nacional). [Not examined.]

1928 Le Popol-Vuh. *Cahiers de la république des lettres, des sciences, et des arts*, 11:47–49. Paris. [A fragment of Brasseur's translation of the creation myth.]

1929 Arquelogía guatemalteca. *Anales de*

la Sociedad de Geografía e Historia de Guatemala, 6:52–71 (Sept.). [An article by Villacorta containing most of the letter of July 9, 1855. See 1855a, 1855e, and 1855d.]

1940   Dos cartas inéditas del abate Brasseur de Bourbourg, dirigidas al doctor José Mariano Padilla, fechadas en Rabinal el 23 de mayo y el 3 de junio de 1855. Anales de la Sociedad de Geografía e Historia de Guatemala, 16:298–303 (Dec.). [States that Qahuyu Cakyup is "el antiguo Rabinal" and also that he had found a manuscript of the Rabinal Achí in the possession of his servant's uncle.]

1943   Estampas del Popol Vuh by Carlos Mérida. Mexico. [Fragments of Gavarrete's translation of Brasseur accompany paintings.]

1945a   Antigüedades guatemaltecas. Tres cartas del Abate Brasseur de Bourbourg. Anales de la Sociedad de Geografía e Historia, 20:7–17 (Mar.). [Letters dated Rabinal, Feb. 23, 1856; Rabinal, Apr. 12, 1856; Guatemala City, June 2, 1856. [Published previously in Gaceta de Guatemala. See 1856b.]

1945b   De Guatemala a Rabinal. Episodio de un viaje en la América del Centro en los años de 1855 y 1856. Anales de la Sociedad de Geografía e Historia, 20:113–18, 232–35, 296–99 (June, Sept., Dec.). [Published previously in La revue européene and Gaceta de Guatemala. See 1859a, 1860.]

1946   De Guatemala a Rabinal. Episodio de un viaje en la América del Centro en los años de 1855 y 1856 (conclusion). Anales de la Sociedad de Geografía e Historia, 21:157–71 (June). [Published previously in La revue européene and Gaceta de Guatemala. See 1859a, 1860.]

1947   Antigüedades guatemaltecas. Anales de la Sociedad de Geografía e Historia, 22:99–104 (March, June). [See also 1929. Letter dated Rabinal,

July 9, 1855. Published previously in Gaceta de Guatemala (1855a) and New York Tribune (1855e). Some paragraphs were published in the Weekly National Intelligencer (see 1855d).]

1949   Antigüedades guatemaltecas. Correspondencia del señor Abate Brasseur de Bourbourg. Anales de la Sociedad de Geografía e Historia, 24:164–73 (March, June). [Published previously in Gaceta de Guatemala with the title: "Una carta del Abate Brasseur de Bourbourg al Sr. Conde Enrique de la Motte-Thoy." See 1855c.]

1952   Informe acerca de las ruinas de Mayapán y de Uxmal. Yikal Maya Than, 13:19–41; 96:119–21, 143–46, 161–65, 185–88, 199–200, 212–14, 216–20. Merida. [Translated from article in vol. 2 of Archives de la Commission Scientifique du Mexique. See 1867c. Not examined.]

1961   Gramática de la lengua quiché según manuscritos de los mejores autores guatemaltecos; acompañada de anotaciones filológicas y un vocabulario. Editorial del Ministerio de Educación Pública "José de Pineda Ibarra." Guatemala. Instituto Indigenista Nacional. Publicaciones Especiales, 18. [Does not include "Essai sur le poésie, . . ." or the Rabinal Achí. See 1862b.]

1967   Hojas sueltas relativas al Lacandón. Antropología e historia de Guatemala, 19:87–93 (Dec.). [Historical essay based especially on Remesal. Listed in Archivo General del Gobierno as Relaciones históricas. Títulos indígenas. Extractos tomados de los cronistas de la época colonial sobre el Lacandón, por el Abate Brasseur de Bourbourg (Al-18, exp. 54882, leg. 6074). Published for the first time by Pedro Tobar Cruz in Papeles históricos del abate Brasseur de Bourbourg. Antropología e historia de Guatemala, 19:84–93 (Dec., 1967).]

Appendix B. BRASSEUR DE BOURBOURG'S TRANSLATIONS OF MAYA SIGNS

Brasseur was the first to state that calendar glyphs could serve as phonetic signs (Brasseur, 1869c, p. 41; Rosny, 1878). Had he used this insight with more scholarly caution and objectivity he might have made a contribution toward interpreting Maya writing, still mysterious.[9] Instead he was interested only in seeking proof for his theories concerning Atlantis. Maya codices treat to some degree the natural calamities that occur frequently in Middle American myth and history (Sánchez de Aguilar, 1900, p. 95; Rosny, 1902, p. 20), but the abbé was determined to relate every glyph to ancient upheavals of nature. His interpretations are difficult, a capricious and sometimes contradictory labyrinth of erudition. Nevertheless, as this was the first attempt to read a Maya codex, his method may be of interest to the long history of Maya studies.

A typical example of how he interpreted Maya writing is his explanation of the Landa glyphs for "t" and ti. By comparing the Landa alphabet with the sentence that Landa wrote, "Ma in Kati," Brasseur concluded that a little figure, a "germe," at the bottom of the circular glyph Landa gave for the letter "t" was a variant of the phonetic glyph for the word ti in the sentence. In his geological fixation, the glyph for ti looked like a rising hill or peak. He reasoned, therefore, that the figure at the bottom of the round glyph for "t" was also a hill, and that the circular form surrounding it represented a layer of ice. As the ice melted, the hill would appear ". . . à l'éclat du soleil du premier printemps" (Brasseur, 1870a, p. xxviii). The abbé reasoned that the survivors of Atlantis had probably exclaimed "t" on seeing peaks rise again above the ice, and therefore that glyph, a representation of a rocky peak, was chosen by the Maya to represent the word ti in a phonetic alphabet. With this symbolic glyph a tradition of the cataclysm was preserved, and the glyph could serve both as a phonetic sign and an ideograph (1870a, p. xxviii): ". . . l'idée qu'on donne l'image se reproduit dans le nom" (1869c, p. 34).

[9] Ed. note: For a modern summary of Maya "rebus writing," see Thompson, 1965, pp. 653–57. Problems of the so-called "Landa alphabet" are also discussed (ibid., pp. 652–54).

Since, according to Brasseur, the modern word ti meant "place," the round glyph for the letter "t" and the phonetic glyph for ti could also mean "place" and he sought additional justification for this interpretation (or perhaps found the first suggestion for it) in the similarity of the round glyph for "t" to an Egyptian hieroglyph for city (1868, p. 34). In his interpretation of the Codex Troano he therefore translated the glyph for "t" and all of its variants —which are now called kin and are thought to mean sun or day—as "place." Of course, for him it invariably appeared in a geological context as flooded land or a rising mountain. Another ingenious explanation was for Imix, which he managed to translate as "profond foyer" or "mamelle du foyer volcanique" (1869c, p. 93).

The Landa alphabet glyphs for "p" and "pp" looked to Brasseur like heads with the lips tightly closed. He reasoned that they served as phonetic letters by showing lips as they are held before an explosive pronunciation of "p" and that as ideographs they represented volcanos about to erupt. A head with an open mouth meant for him that the volcano was erupting or had already erupted, and closed eyes meant that it was extinct. The glyph he saw as a bee symbolized for him lava or hot gas working in the earth. Red number bars represented land covered with molten lava, and black bars represented land in a normal state.

Armed with these and other ideas, Brasseur set out to translate several pages of the Codex Troano, reading from the bottom up and from right to left, because the figures faced left, and also because—according to him—it made sense only when read in that direction (1869c, pp. 224, 225). The translations he pieced together were such subjective accounts of eruptions and catastrophes that they failed to satisfy even him. Instead of revising the introduction and translations to accommodate new "discoveries," he let them stand as they were and simply added a supplement with new and contradictory interpretations. Tollan, for example, became the lacustrine region which covered a part of the globe after a glacial epoch (1869c, p. 225), and the 20 day glyphs symbolized the 20 principal countries of that region (1869c, p. 226).

319

Another new interpretation of crucial importance for his last period was the one he gave to the calendar glyph *chuen*. He had first translated it as "lieux soulevés" (1869c, pp. 81, 149), but in the supplement he wrote that it meant "ice" (1869c, pp. 231–33). This new conviction led him to a different translation of line 3 of what he called the summary page of the Codex Troano. Instead of mountains rising out of the sea, it now seemed to him to describe mountains emerging from ice (1869c, p. 235). This in turn produced new interpretations of the cataclysm.

In *Quatre lettres sur le Mexique*, Brasseur had written (1868, p. 280) that a very short glacial period had followed the eruptions, but in the introduction to the Manuscrit Troano he wrote that glaciers were present before the eruptions (1869c, pp. 115, 158). To clarify the enigma he turned again to the Codex Chimal-

popoca. Further study of that work convinced him that several cataclysms instead of only one had transformed the world (1869c, p. 223).

In volume 2 of the Manuscrit Troano he wrote that the glacial epoch had been followed by a lacustrine period. Volcanic eruptions brought that to an end, and were followed 2000 years later by a final period of volcanic activity (1870a, p. xlvi). Glaciers covering the Mediterranean region were melted by the newly formed Gulf Stream after the final eruptions and the disappearance of Atlantis (1871, p. xxxvi). His last statement was that beginning about 10,500 B.C., four periods of cataclysms, each caused by a temporary shifting of the earth's axis, had changed the world (1873a, p. 82). The abbé was now lost in geological speculation; the survivors of Atlantis followed the Toltecs into the limbo of his discarded enthusiasms.

REFERENCES

Acuña, René
   1968 Título de los Señores de Sacapulas. *Folklore américas*, 38:1–45 (June).

Adams, Herbert B.
   1891 The Abbé Brasseur de Bourbourg. *Proceedings of the American Antiquarian Society*, n.s., 7:274–90 (April).

Aldana Rivas, Manuel
   1864–65 [Articles describing Brasseur's activities in Yucatan and the dispute of Brasseur and Aldana Rivas with Salazar.] *El Monitor*, nos. 2–11 (Nov. 16, 1864–Jan. 21, 1865).

Angrand, Leoncio
   1870 Antigüedades mexicanas: Rectificaciones importantes. SMGE, *Boletín*, 2(2):712–13.

Arriola, Jorge Luis
   1967 El abate Charles Etienne Brasseur de Bourbourg, un ilustre americanista. *El Imparcial*, July 27, 28, 31; August 1–4.

Baer, Joseph, and Company
   1911 Americana . . . including scarce and precious books, manuscripts and engravings from the collections of Emperor Maximilian of Mexico and Charles Et. Brasseur de Bourbourg, the library of Edward Salomon, late governor of the state of Wisconsin, and other important collections, of-

fered for sale by Joseph Baker [*sic*] and Co. Frankfort am Main.

Balmori, Clemente H.
   1955 Teatro aborigen americano. *Estudios americanos*, 9:577–601 (June).

Bancroft, Hubert Howe
   See Article 19, Appendix A.

Bandelier, Adolph Francis Alphonse
   1880 Notes on the bibliography of Yucatan and Central America. *Proceedings of the American Antiquarian Society*, n.s., pt. 3, 1:82–118.

Barros Arana, Diego
   1910 Necrología americana: M. Brasseur de Bourbourg. *Obras completas*, 9: 459–69. Santiago, Chile.

Bataillon, Marcel
   1954 Mérimée et l'américanisme d'il y a cent ans. *Bulletin hispanique*, 56: 424–30.

Benoist, J. H.
   1865 Questions sur les origines et les antiquités américaines. (1st article.) *Actes de la Société d'Ethnographie Américaine et Orientale*, 4:348–56.

Bernal, Ignacio
   1962 Bibliografía de arqueología y etnografía: Mesoamérica y norte de México, 1514–1960. INAH, *Memorias*, VII. Mexico.

Boban, Eugène
   1886 The Boban collection of antiquities,

curios and coins, also books, manuscript and printed. New York.

BOLLAERT, WILLIAM

1863 Observations on the "Popol Vuh," or the Books of the National History of Guatemala; also remarks on the commentary. *Transactions of the Royal Society of Literature of the United Kingdom*, 2d ser., 7:421–40.

1866 Examination of Central American hieroglyphs: Of Yucatan, including the Dresden Codex, the Guatémalien of Paris, and the Troano of Madrid; the hieroglyphs of Palenqué, Copan, Nicaragua, Veraguas, and New Granada; by the recently discovered Maya alphabet. *Memoirs of the Anthropological Society of London*, 3:288–314. [Contains short letter of Brasseur suggesting that codex was a calendar.]

BRASSEUR DE BOURBOURG, CHARLES ETIENNE
See Article 18, Appendix.

BRINTON, DANIEL GARRISON

1868a The Abbé Brasseur and his labors. *Lippincott's Magazine*, 1:79–86 (January).

1868b The myths of the New World: A treatise on the symbolism and mythology of the red race of America. New York.

1870 The ancient phonetic alphabet of Yucatan. New York. [8 pages of sharp criticism of Brasseur's interpretation of Manuscrit Troano.]

1882a American hero-myths: A study in the native religions of the western continent. Philadelphia.

1882b The Maya chronicles. *Library of Aboriginal American Literature*, 1. Philadelphia.

1883 Aboriginal American authors and their productions, especially those in the native languages: A chapter in the history of literature. Philadelphia.

1884 Memoire of Dr. C. H. Berendt. *Proceedings of the American Antiquarian Society*, n.s., pt. 3, 2:205–10 (April).

1885 The Annals of the Cakchiquels. The original text, with a translation, notes, and introduction. *Library of Aboriginal American Literature*, 6. Philadelphia.

1887 Critical remarks on the editions of Diego de Landa's writings. *Proceed-*

ings of the American Philosophical Society, 24:1–8 (Jan.–June).

1890 Essays of an Americanist. Philadelphia.

CARRILLO Y ANCONA, CRESCENCIO

1865 La historia de Yucatán. *El Monitor*, no. 9 (Jan. 4). [Reprinted as "El Abate Brasseur y la arqueología," *Revista de Mérida*, 1:104–09 (1869).] Merida.

1869 El Abate Brasseur y la arqueología. *Revista de Mérida*, 1:104–09.

[CATIN, PAUL]

1927 Catalogue général des livres imprimés de la Bibliothèque Nationale. 196 vols. Paris. [Bibliography of Brasseur, 18:1115–22. Novels also listed in vol. 16 of the Larousse Grand Dictionnaire Universel du XIXᵉ Siècle.]

CHARENCEY, HYACINTHE DE

1859a Traditions des peuples: Histoire des nations civilisées du Mexique et de l'Amérique Centrale, durant les siècles antérieurs à Christophe Colomb, écrite sur des documents originaux et entièrement inédits, puisés aux anciennes archives des indigènes, par M. l'abbé Brasseur de Bourbourg. 1st article. *Annales de philosophie chrétienne*, 4th ser., 19:22–31 (vol. 58 of the collection).

1859b Traditions des peuples: Histoire des nations civilisées du Mexique et de l'Amérique Centrale, durant les siècles antérieurs à Christophe Colomb, écrite sur des documents originaux et entièrement inédits, puisés aux anciennes archives des indigènes, par M. l'abbé Brasseur de Bourbourg. 2d article. *Annales de philosophie chrétienne*, 4th ser., 19:113–26.

1874 Note sur M. l'Abbé Brasseur de Bourbourg. *Bulletin de la Société de Géographie de Paris*, 7:508–10 (May).

CHAVERO, ALFREDO
See Article 21, Appendix E.

CHÁVEZ ZELAYA, M. ENRIQUE

1955 A 100 años de Carlos Esteban Brasseur de Bourbourg. *Diario de Centro América*, no. 21924 (Aug. 10). [Contains "Los antropófagos de Tesulutlán" by Manuel Diéguez Flores.]

CLINE, HOWARD F.

1947 The apocryphal early career of J. F.

Waldeck, pioneer Americanist. *Acta Americana*, 5:278–300 (Oct.–Dec.).

CORTAMBERT, RICHARD
1867 Séance générale du 23 décembre 1866. Rapport annuel par M. Richard Cortambert. *Actes de la Société Américaine de France*, 2:66–80.

CRESSONIÈRE, L. DE LA
1862 Popol Vuh: Le livre sacré et les mythes de l'antiquité américaine, etc. *Nouvelles annales des voyages*, 174:87–116 (April).

DALY, CÉSAR
1867 Extraits des procès-verbaux des séances de la Commission Scientifique du Mexique. *Archives de la Commission Scientifique du Mexique*. 3 vols. Paris. [Vol. 2: Séance du 22 juin 1865, pp. 176–81.]

DIÉGUEZ FLORES, MANUEL
1888 Tradiciones guatemaltecas: Los antropófagos de Tesulutlán. *La Revista*, 1st ser., 8:120–23 (Aug. 16). Organo de la Academia Guatemalteca, Correspondiente de la Academia Española.
1923 Tradiciones: Artículos literarios; estudios de derecho. ["Los antropófagos de Tesulutlán," pp. 25–32.] Guatemala.

DUCHATEAU, JULIEN
1875 Sur l'écriture calculiforme des Mayas. *Archives de la Société Américaine de France*, 2d ser., 1:31–33.

EDMONSON, MUNRO S.
1971 The Book of Counsel: The Popol Vuh of the Quiche Maya of Guatemala. Tulane University, Middle American Research Institute, Pub. 35. New Orleans.

FERLAND, JEAN BAPTISTE ANTOINE
1854 Observations sur un ouvrage intitulé Histoire du Canada par M. l'abbé Brasseur de Bourbourg. Paris.

FIELD, THOMAS WARREN
1873 An essay towards an Indian bibliography, being a catalogue of books relating to the history, antiquities, languages, customs, religion, wars, literature, and origin of the American Indians. New York. [Critical bibliography of Brasseur, pp. 42–45.]

GATES, WILLIAM
1932 The Dresden Codex. Maya Society, Pub. 2. Baltimore.

GATSCHET, ALBERT S.
1879 Perez' Maya-Spanish dictionary.

American Antiquarian, 2:30–32.

HAVEN, SAMUEL F.
1870 Report of the librarian. *Proceedings of the American Antiquarian Society*, no. 55, pp. 42–60 (Oct.). [Quotes at length from Brasseur's letter to Rosny in 1869 and from his letter to Harper in 1870.]
1878 Report of the librarian. *Proceedings of the American Antiquarian Society*, no. 70, pp. 89–100 (meeting of Oct. 22, 1877).

HOWITT, MARY
1856 Supposed traces of ancient Scandinavians in South America. *The Athenaeum*, no. 1473, p. 75 (Jan. 19).

LABARTHE, CHARLES DE
1870 Note sur le Manuscrit Troano. *Revue Orientale*, 2:142–43. [Also called in same publication *Bulletin de l' Athénée Orientale* and *Mémoirs de l'Athénée Orientale*.]

LARRAINZAR, MANUEL
1865 Dictamen presentado a la Sociedad de Geografía y Estadística de Mexico por el Sr. Lic. D. Manuel Larrainzar, sobre la obra del Sr. Abate C. Carlos Brasseur de Bourbourg, cuyo título es el siguiente: "Si ecsiste el origen de la historia primitiva de México en los monumentos egipcios, y el de la historia primitiva del Antiguo Mundo en los monumentos americanos." SMGE. Mexico.
1876 Estudios sobre la historia de América, sus ruinas y antigüedades, comparadas con lo más notable que se conoce del otro continente en los tiempos más remotos, y sobre el origen de sus habitantes. 5 vols. in 2 parts [especially 4:325–57]. Mexico.

LECLERC, CHARLES
1878 Bibliotheca americana: Histoire, géographie, voyages, archéologie et linguistique des deux Amériques et des Isles Philippines. Paris.

LEHMANN, WALTER
1909 Methods and results in Mexican research. Paris.

LEINAWEAVER, RICHARD E.
1968 Rabinal Achí, commentary. *Latin American Theatre Review*, 1–2:3–53 (spring). University of Kansas, Center of Latin American Studies.

LEJEAL, LÉON
1903 L'archéologie américaine et les études

américanistes en France. *Revue internationale de l'enseignement*, 45: 215–32 (Mar. 15).

LE PLONGEON, AUGUSTUS

1879 Archaeological communication on Yucatán. *Proceedings of the American Antiquarian Society*, no. 72, pp. 65–75 (meeting held Oct. 1878).

LORENZ, OTTO

1867 Catalogue général de la librairie française pendant 25 ans (1840–1865). 32 vols. Paris. [Bibliography for Brasseur, 1:363, 5:201.]

LOWELL, JAMES RUSSELL

1858 [Editorial note following] "American Antiquity." *Atlantic Monthly*, 1: 769–76 (May).

MACE, CARROLL EDWARD

1967a New information about dance-dramas of Rabinal and the "Rabinal-Achí." *Xavier University Studies*, 6:1–19 (Feb.).

1967b Nueva y más reciente información sobre los bailes-drama de Rabinal y del descubrimiento del Rabinal Achí. *Antropología e historia de Guatemala*, 19:20–37 (Dec.). [Expanded Spanish version of 1967a.]

MADIER DE MONTJAU, EDUARD

1875a Discours sur les études américaines. *Annuaire de la Société Américaine de France*, 3:5–30 (séance du 18 février, 1873).

1875b Nécrologie: Brasseur de Bourbourg. *Annuaire de la Société Américaine de France*, 3:90.

1876 Notice historique sur Brasseur de Bourbourg. *Actes de la Société d' Ethnographie*, n.s., 1:138–43 (séance du 5 juin, 1876). [Title page dated 1875.]

MITRE, BARTOLOMÉ

1909 La obra de Brasseur de Bourbourg. *Museo Mitre: Catálogo razonado de la sección lenguas americanas*, pp. 19–24. Buenos Aires. [Previously published in *La biblioteca*, 1:34–39 (1896), Buenos Aires.]

1911 Brasseur de Bourbourg. *In* Obras completas de Diego Barros Arana, 9: 305–10. Santiago, Chile. [Previously published in *La revista chilena*, 1876.]

MOLÉ, HARVEY E.

1945 The abbé Brasseur de Bourbourg. A paper read May 21, 1945, for the Monday Night Club of Summit, New Jersey. [Typewritten copy in NYPL.]

MONTALBÁN, LEONARDO

1929 Historia de la literatura de la América Central. San Salvador.

MÜLLER, FRIEDRICH MAX

1907 Chips from a German workshop. 5 vols. Vol. 1: Essays on the science of religion. ["Popol Vuh," pp. 309–36, March, 1862.] New York.

PINART, ALPHONSE

1883 Catalogue de livres rares et précieux, manuscrits et imprimés, principalement sur l'Amérique et sur les langues du monde entier composant la bibliothèque de M. Alphonse L. Pinart et comprenant en totalité la bibliothèque Mexico-Guatémalienne de M. l'abbé Brasseur de Bourbourg. Paris. [Bibliography for Brasseur, pp. 22–26.]

PRUNER-BEY, FRANZ

1863 Rapport sur l'ouvrage de M. Brasseur de Bourbourg: Grammaire de la langue quiché et vocabulaire. Drame quiché "Rabinal Achí," musique du Guatemala. *Bulletin de la Société d'Anthropologie de Paris*, 4:8–17.

R. S.

1870 *Review of* Manuscrit Troano: Etudes sur le système graphique et la langue des Mayas, par M. Brasseur de Bourbourg. Vol. 1 printed 1869. *Revue archéologique*, 21:213–16 (Mar.). Paris.

1871 *Review of* Manuscrit Troano: Etudes sur le système graphique et la langue des Mayas, par M. Brasseur de Bourbourg. Vol. 2 printed 1869. *Revue archéologique*, 22:257–60 (Oct.). Paris.

RAYNAUD, GEORGES

1925 Les dieux, les héros et les hommes de l'ancien Guatemala d'après le Livre du Conseil. Paris.

1929a Descubrimiento del Rabinal Achi, según el abate Brasseur de Bourbourg. *Anales de la Sociedad de Geografía e Historia*, 6:197–201 (Dec.). [Translated by Luis Cardoza y Aragón.]

1929b El varón de Rabinal. Preface: Un solitario. *Anales de la Sociedad de Geografía e Historia*, 6:45–51 (Sept.). [Translated by Luis Cardoza y Aragón. Preface published again by Francisco Monterde *in* Teatro indígena prehispánico: Rabinal Achí, pp.

123–39 (1955). *Bib. estudiante universitario.* Ediciones de la Universidad Nacional Autónoma.]

1930 El varón de Rabinal. Text. *Anales de la Sociedad de Geografía e Historia,* 6:347–70 (Mar.). Notes to text, 6:481–91 (June). [Translated by Luis Cardoza y Aragón.]

1953 Rabinal-Achí: Ballet-drama de los indios quichés de Guatemala, con la música indígena. [Translated from the unpublished French version of Raynaud by Luis Cardoza y Aragón.] Editorial del Ministerio de Educación Pública, vol. 43. (See 1929a, 1929b, and 1930.) Guatemala.

RECINOS, ADRIÁN
1950 Popol Vuh: The sacred book of the ancient Quiché Maya. English version by Delia Goetz and Sylvanus G. Morley. University of Oklahoma Press. Norman.

1953 The Annals of the Cakchiquels. Translated from the Cakchiquel Maya by Adrián Recinos and Delia Goetz. Title of the Lords of Totonicapán. Translated from the Quiché text into Spanish by Dionisio José Chonay. English version by Delia Goetz. University of Oklahoma Press. Norman.

1956 Cien años de la llegada del abate Brasseur de Bourbourg a Guatemala. *Anales de la Sociedad de Geografía e Historia,* 29:12–17 (Jan.–Dec.).

REMESAL, ANTONIO DE
1964 *See* Article 13, Bibliography.

RICE, ALLEN THORNDIKE
1888 *Introduction to* The ancient cities of the New World, being voyages and explorations in Mexico and Central America from 1857–1882, by Désiré Charnay. Translated from the French by J. Gonino and Helen S. Conant. New York.

ROSNY, LÉON DE
1875 L'interpretation des anciens textes mayas. *Archives de la Société Américaine de France,* 2d ser., 1:53–118.

1876 Essai sur le déchiffrement de l'écriture hiératique maya. *Archives de la Société Américaine de France,* n.s., 2:5–108 (part one of article).

1878 De la formation des mots dans l'écriture hiératique du Yucatan. *Actes de la Société Américaine de France,* n.s., 3?:1–4 (séance du 11 février).

1887 Discours d'overture de M. Léon de

Rosny. *Archives de la Société Américaine de France,* n.s., 5:178–88 (part 4, Dec.).

1902 L'Atlantide historique: Etudes d'ethnographie de d'archéologie américaines. Bibliothèque Américaine A. Lesouef. Supplément au Bulletin des Livres Américains, vol. I.

1904 L'Amérique pré-colombienne: Etudes d'histoire, de linguistique et de paléographie sur les anciens temps du Nouveau Monde. Paris.

SABIN, JOSEPH
1869 Bibliotheca Americana: Dictionary of books relating to America (1868–1936). 29 vols. New York. [Bibliography for Brasseur, 2:418–21.]

SAENZ DE SANTA MARÍA, CARMELO, S.J.
1959 Una ojeada a la bibliografía lingüística guatemalteca. *Revista de Indias,* 19:255–71 (Apr.–June).

SAINT-MARTIN, VIVIEN DE
1866 La carte du Mexique. *L'Année géographique,* 4:326–27.

1867 Généralités américaines. *L'Année géographique,* 5:289–96.

SALISBURY, STEPHEN
1876 Report of the council. *Proceedings of the American Antiquarian Society,* no. 66, pp. 11–61 (Apr.). [Treats Brasseur, pp. 38–45.]

SÁNCHEZ DE AGUILAR, PEDRO
1900 Informe contra idolorum cultores del obispado de Yucatán [1615]. MNA, *Anales,* 6:14–122.

SCHOEBEL, CHARLES
1874 Rapports et communications: "Relation des choses de Yucatan," de Diego de Landa, . . . par l'abbé Brasseur de Bourbourg. *Actes de la Société d' Ethnographie,* 3:249–53 (séance du 21 juillet, 1864).

SMITH, A. LEDYARD
1955 Archaeological reconnaissance in Central America. Carnegie Institution of Washington, Pub. 608. Washington.

SOUSTELLE, JACQUES
1967 Mexico. Translated from the French by James Hogarth. Archaeologia Mundi: Series prepared under the direction of Jean Marcadé, Professor of Archaeology at the University of Bordeaux. Cleveland and New York.

SQUIER, EPHRAIM GEORGE
1855a Letter from Mr. E. G. Squier about a letter from Brasseur de Bourbourg. *The Athenaeum,* no. 1467, p. 1435

(Dec. 8). [Concerns Brasseur's letter dated Rabinal, Aug. 7, 1855.]

1855b Lettre de M. E. G. Squier a M. Alfred Maury [à propos de la lettre de M. Brasseur de Bourbourg] insérée au cahier des annales d'août 1855. *Nouvelles annales des voyages,* 3:273–85. [Concerns Brasseur's letters to Maury, March 28 and April 28, 1855.]

STOLL, OTTO

1938 Etnografía de la República de Guatemala [1884]. [Translated by Antonio Goubaud Carrera.] Guatemala.

TAYAC, GASTON DE

1867a Séance du 20 novembre 1866. *Annuaire du Comité d'Archéologie Américaine,* 2:65–66.

1867b [Critical remarks on] S'il existe des sources de l'histoire primitive du Mexique dans les monuments égyptiens. *Annuaire du Comité d'Archéologie Américaine,* 2:83–85 (séance du 29 janvier).

THOMAS, CYRUS

1882 A study of the Manuscript Troano. [Introduction by Brinton.] *In* J. W. Powell, ed., Geographical and geological survey of the Rocky Mountain region, vol. 5, pt. 3. Contributions to North American Ethnology. 9 vols. Washington.

THOMPSON, J. ERIC S.

1965 Maya hieroglyphic writing. *In* Handbook of Middle American Indians, vol. 3, art. 25.

TOBAR CRUZ, PEDRO

1967 Papeles históricos del abate Brasseur de Bourbourg. *Antropología e historia de Guatemala,* 19:84–93 (Dec.).

TRÜBNER, NICOLAUS

1856a The new discoveries in Guatemala. *The Athenaeum,* no. 1472, pp. 42–43 (Jan. 12).

1856b Central American archaeology. *The Athenaeum,* no. 1492, pp. 683–85 (May 31).

VALENTINI, PHILIPP J. J.

1880 The Landa alphabet: A Spanish fabrication. *Proceedings of the American Antiquarian Society,* no. 75, pp. 59–91. [Also issued separately.]

VANDEGEHUCHTE, M.

1860 Voyage de M. l'abbé Brasseur de Bourbourg à Tehuantepec, dans l'état de Chiapas, et son arrivée à Guatemala. *Nouvelles annales des voyages,* 6th ser., I, 165:5–24. [Favorable review of *Voyage sur l'Isthme de Tehuantepec.*]

VILLACORTA C., J. ANTONIO

1929 Arqueología guatemalteca. *Anales de la Sociedad de Geografía e Historia de Guatemala,* 6:52–71 (Sept.).

WAUCHOPE, ROBERT

1963 Lost tribes and sunken continents. University of Chicago Press. Chicago.

WINSOR, JUSTIN

1889–92 Narrative and critical history of America. 8 vols. Cambridge. [Treats Brasseur, 1:170–72; 8:172.]

XIMÉNEZ, FRANCISCO

1929 Historia de la Provincia de San Vicente de Chiapa y Guatemala de la Orden de Predicadores. 3 vols. *Biblioteca "Goathemala" de la Sociedad de Geografía e Historia,* 1–3. Guatemala.

19. Hubert Howe Bancroft, 1832-1918

HOWARD F. CLINE

Hubert Howe Bancroft's main historiographical interests lay in his adopted state of California, but in pursuing them he contributed much to knowledge of related areas, including Middle America. Of 39 volumes comprising his massive historical series on the Pacific states, the first 16 relate directly to it. The initial five tomes, *Native Races* (*Works*, 1–5), have special relevance to ethnohistory; the volume *Primitive History* (*Works*, 5), not only was a pioneering contribution when it was first published in 1875, but even today it still remains nearly unique as a major synthesis of many pre-Hispanic developments. It is supplemented by important materials in the companion volume *Civilized Nations* (*Works*, 2), which summarized much of what had been published on Aztecs and Maya to 1874. His subsequent treatments of the history of Central America (*Works*, 6–8), Mexico (*Works*, 9–14), and of the north Mexican states and Texas (*Works*, 15, 16), although focussed on colonial Spanish American and national topics, constitute great mines of important data. They are the usual point of departure for

further investigations, because of the replete information and bibliographical apparatus they contain.

Main sources of biographical information on Bancroft are his own published works, and a modern sympathetic treatment of him by John Caughey (1946),[1] who makes minor additions, chiefly from manuscripts in the Bancroft Library at the University of California, Berkeley. Bancroft's *Literary Industries* (*Works*, 39) gives much detail on his life to 1890, supplemented by *Retrospection* (1912), less detailed and less accurate, with an octogenarian's outspoken and polemical views on current events. Considerable autobiographical elements are also found in his *California Inter Pocula* ["California in her cups," i.e., intoxicated with gold] (*Works*, 35), dealing with Gold Rush days, and in *Essays and Miscellany* (*Works*, 38).

Bancroft was descended from British stock, directly from one John Bancroft who sailed to America in 1632, settling in New England, as did another 17th-century ma-

[1] Citations may be found in Appendix A.

326

3. 1—HUBERT HOWE BANCROFT. From Caughey, 46.

ternal ancestor, John Howe. Hubert's parents, Azariah Ashley Bancroft and Lucy Howe, born respectively in Massachusetts and Vermont, were neighbors on adjoining farms to which their families had emigrated shortly after Granville, Ohio, was established in 1806 by a religious colony from New England.

Fourth of six children, Hubert Howe Bancroft was born there May 5, 1832. He was brought up in the transplanted rural village Puritanism of the day, receiving an elementary education. In 1847 he began to prepare himself for college, perhaps to take up law as a career, but soon abandoned the idea in favor of making himself financially independent as soon as possible. In August, 1848, at age 16 he left home, work-ing his way on a canal boat to Buffalo, New York, where George H. Denby, a brother-in-law, had invited him to work in his bookstore. Although relations with his employer were often troubled, Bancroft learned much about book merchandizing. Discovery of gold in California indirectly interrupted this apprenticeship. Determined to expand his business by shipping to the risky but lucrative new market, Denby persuaded Bancroft to handle a $5,000 stock for retail sale there.

In February, 1852, Bancroft sailed from New York via Panama for San Francisco. While waiting in California for the arrival of the consigned books, he joined his father and a brother in various unsuccessful enterprises in the gold fields. On arrival of the book shipment, Bancroft arranged for their sale by others, and on his own earned a good living selling books and stationery (obtained on credit), until he was persuaded by his sister on the death of Denby to return east in November, 1855. Unsatisfied with life in Buffalo, Bancroft returned to California in April, 1856, with a grubstake of $5,000 loaned him by his sister. Thereafter his home and career were in the West.

His life during the next 10 years was a traditional business success story. Even the Civil War was a boon to the young book merchant, who received payments in local gold, and paid eastern suppliers in depreciated money, gaining 25 per cent on the transactions. By 1870 Bancroft's company was the largest west of Chicago. It wholesaled and retailed stationery and books, sold sheet music, pianos, organs, and musical instruments. In that year he added manufacturing facilities—printing, engraving, lithographing, and bookbinding. These activities were organized by separate departments, all under the general management of A. L. Bancroft, Hubert's younger brother. In a large building housing the Bancroft enterprises, the fifth floor was reserved to Hubert Howe Bancroft, for his library and burgeoning scholarly activities, that formed

327

"Literary Industries," a ninth department of the business.

Happily married and now financially independent, Bancroft traveled to Europe. There he became convinced that his own career should fall somewhere between that of the idle aristocracy he saw in Europe, who scorned work, and that of his fellow Americans, who were obsessed with amassing material wealth. An accidental development of his business enterprise led him to historiography, an interest that grew as he became a diligent book collector.

The original impulse to build a collection had a practical origin, as did many of Bancroft's enterprises. For commerical purposes he had published a Pacific Coast handbook, edited by William H. Knight. To make proposed revisions, Bancroft thought it more efficient to group reference and other works around Knight's desk. He was surprised to learn that his own retail book stock yielded some 75 titles on California. He then had the other shops of San Francisco ransacked. As the collecting fever mounted, he haunted shops on trips to New York, Boston, and Philadelphia to pick up titles on western America. By 1862 he had accumulated about a thousand volumes.

In that year, Bancroft first visited London, where he saw books by the hundreds in secondhand shops. His short visit did not permit him to purchase more than a dozen boxes, but it did turn his mind to a more efficient policy of acquisition. He decided that rather than selecting individual volumes with California references he would obtain all possible titles related to its general area, Panama to Alaska. With his wife, he returned in 1866 to Europe where he spent nearly two years touring and purchasing. By 1868 the collection had grown to 10,000 titles.

Bancroft thought he had about completed the task of building his collection when the José Maria Andrade Library (7,000 Mexican items) came on the market in 1869. Unable to attend the sale personally, Bancroft commissioned a London agent, who obtained 3,000 important pieces. In June, 1869, when the Fischer Library was similarly auctioned, Bancroft through his agent acquired about one-third of the 2,962 Mexican works. Both these collections had been part of the ill-fated Imperial Mexican Library planned by Maximilian; in 1880 the collection of another Maximilianist exile, José Fernando Ramírez, was offered for sale in London. Here for $30,000 Bancroft's agent obtained most of the works in which Bancroft was interested. He also (1876) purchased the books and manuscripts on Central America accumulated by E. G. Squier. Although the Bancroft collection continued to grow through individual purchases, its main Middle American elements had been acquired by about 1880. Thereafter the notable accretions were newspapers and manuscript materials, chiefly related to local California and state history.[2] Ultimately the collection amounted to around 60,000 volumes; it has been described several times.

Bancroft's gradual metamorphosis from bookseller to collector to author was a logical evolution. With his strong insistence on utility and useful knowledge, he pondered how all the factual information in his vast collection could best be systematized and exploited. Around 1870 a dozen projects flitted through his mind, as he decided possible subjects of books or series: a history of gold, interoceanic communications, railways, voyages and travels, ethnology of western America. He stumbled into his final plan largely by accident.

Tugged by various alternatives, he determined in 1871 to compile a Pacific states encyclopedia. The relatively small volumes he envisaged were to be comprised of book-

[2] Oak (1893, p. 26) stated that through 1869 most purchasing for the library had been done personally by Bancroft, after which (1870–80) he as librarian had principal responsibility. He pointed out, "The manuscript archives of Spain and Mexico were practically not searched; and in this respect only has the completeness of the collection been exaggerated."

length and shorter articles contributed by specialists. He began to round up collaborators, all enthusiastic, but nearly all expectant that from his collection Bancroft would provide them with the raw factual material for their commissioned pieces. When it became apparent that in addition to the burdens of editing, he would have also to provide basic information, Bancroft abandoned the project. His lack of characteristic drive can partially be explained by the recent death of his beloved wife.

"Listless and purposeless," he passed a summer in the east, until roused by a direct question from a close friend. She said, "The next ten years will be the best of your life; what are you going to do with them?" After rejecting various alternatives, he decided to produce a comprehensive history of the Pacific states, a complete and detailed exposition. He felt that this goal, for which his collecting activities had provided materials, would challenge his best efforts. Once the decision was made, he returned to San Francisco and in December, 1871, began to survey his collection and formulate plans for its utilization to carry out the gigantic scheme.

Without going into details, some of which appear below, we can say that Bancroft applied to his historiographical enterprise many of the practices that had made him successful enough in business at age 39 to retire and decide to write the complete history of one-twelfth the world's surface. He recruited and trained a staff of specialists numbering all told nearly 600; he devised an indexing system, and an assembly-line technique which brought the various parts of the history he had outlined to complete manuscript, then to manufacture and distribution. Skilled in management and merchandizing, he even arranged for advance publicity of the early volumes by making a trip east to solicit favorable reviews and testimonials from the literary Titans of the times—Whittier, Charles Francis Adams, Parkman, and others (Lewis, 1936). Mark

Twain was said to have gotten up at 2 A.M., encased in a fur overcoat, to read the prepublished first volume of *Native Races* until daylight (*Works*, 39:363).

Under a driving sales manager, Bancroft's canvassers corralled prospects who were cajoled into committing themselves to buy complete sets of the *Works*, ranging in price from $175.50 to $390, depending on bindings. Like Leland Stanford (who subscribed for 40 sets), prospective purchasers did not always realize the extent of their commitment (Clark, 1933). It is estimated that about 6,000 sets, at least 234,000 volumes, were sold, with a gross return of more than $1,000,000. Bancroft's biographer notes that he "managed to recoup on his great investment and did not sustain a loss. Considering the length, weight, and solidity of the set, this outcome is nothing short of remarkable" (Caughey, 1946, p. 300). This accomplishment is even more startling when it is realized that in 1886 Bancroft had to replace his main store and plant after it was burned to the ground; fortunately the library had been moved to a separate building and was thus unscathed.

No sooner had the last of the 39 volumes of *Works* been completed and distributed in 1890 than Bancroft fed into his hungry presses a seven-volume biographical sequel, entitled *Chronicles of the Builders of the Commonwealth: Historical Character Study* (1891–92). The sale of *Works* had identified a market susceptible to his sales blandishments; in addition, Bancroft made certain of minimum commercial risk by charging fees to those whose biographies were to be included among "these men of strength and influence" who had shaped the American West. Subscriptions and fees amounted to $219,225, "several times the cost of preparation and manufacture" (Caughey, 1946, p. 322). Benito Juárez and Junípero Serra were included without fee.

Somewhat similar in aim was yet another five-volume set. It was "an exaction of tribute from purchasers such as had shown by their support of the *Chronicles of the Builders* that they could be counted on to order a work of this sort" (Caughey, 1946, p. 328). This was *The Book of the Fair* (1893), a profusely illustrated coverage of the Columbian Exposition in Chicago, issued in a deluxe limited edition (400 sets). Bancroft continued to exploit this status-symbol-conscious clientele by offering them a parallel (subscriptions limited to 950) 10-volume folio set of a work with a prolix title, *Achievements of Civilization: The Book of Wealth* . . . (1896–1908), a superficial historical survey from ancient Chaldea to the United States of his day.

By 1890, however, the major historiographical work of Bancroft had been published. The above subscription volumes and the miscellaneous later publications have relatively minor scholarly merit. In his final quarter-century, Bancroft issued minor writings as the spirit moved him. His writings are listed in Appendix A.

During his later years Bancroft was subject to much adverse critical notice, notably by the superpatriotic Society of California Pioneers. They publicly stripped him of honorary membership because of the disparaging remarks in his histories about their friends and relatives—John C. Frémont, the hero of the Bear Flag revolt, and Johann A. Sutter. He likewise gained unwanted notoriety in a libel suit brought by an ungrateful nephew. Ex-employees also took to the press with claims that they had unjustly been denied recognition for their authorship of great parts of the *Works*. Thus for much of the remainder of his life, his earlier historical work fell under a cloud. The overemphasis on the questionable methods of the subscription series and the sharp commercial practices in marketing the *Works* obscured the many solid merits of the latter.

One notable event of this last period was the sale of the Bancroft Collection to the University of California. Once the *Works* and the *Chronicles* were out of the way by 1892, Bancroft tried to get the state legis-

lature to appropriate $250,000 to purchase his library. But though the proposed legislation was supported by many impressive names, its opponents, especially newspapers, were able to rally sufficient opposition to kill the effort. The transfer by purchase was revived in 1898, then thwarted when the university librarian set its value at $116,000, less than half the asking price. Within the university a group of scholars, headed by Henry Morse Stephens, professor of history, and a close adviser of the institution's new president, Benjamin Ide Wheeler, continued to agitate for the purchase.

Prolonged negotiations culminated in a proposal by Bancroft to sell the collection for $250,000. He agreed to contribute $100,000 of this sum, on condition that the university would keep the collection intact, call it the Bancroft Library, and suitably house and maintain it. Another stipulation that was dropped in the final settlement was that when sufficient funds were available, the university would establish a chair, "Bancroft Professorship of Pacific Coast History." Before the university regents would accept this offer, they invited a well-known historian, Reuben Gold Thwaites, to appraise the Bancroft collection. He placed a minimum market value of $315,000 on it, not counting the indexes, catalogs, notes, and original narratives dictated to Bancroft's agents. With this favorable report in hand, and fiscal arrangements finally agreed to, the university purchased the collection for $150,000, net, the formalities of transfer taking place November 25, 1905. Bancroft accepted a note for $250,000, but gave the university a certified check for $100,000 (Caughey, 1946, p. 363).

On March 2, 1918, Bancroft died at home of acute peritonitis after a 26-hour illness. His mature career had spanned a fecund era of American life from the War with Mexico through World War I. In a generation of self-made men, he had made his mark, in business and in scholarship, largely through a rare combination of intelligence, acumen, managerial talent, and a willingness to envision large undertakings and then mobilize the means to accomplish them.

PLANS AND METHODS

Bancroft's specific plans for a comprehensive history of the Pacific states developed relatively slowly until the massive enterprise was well under way. In similar fashion the methods that he employed evolved by trial and error over a decade from 1871. At the outset at least, Bancroft was not aware of the degree to which he would necessarily rely on others for actual authorship, or that his final role would be that of coordinator of a cooperative research team.

To some degree both plan and scope of the volumes emerged from what Bancroft always considered the key to the vast literary plant: the index and abstracts of the collection. When the idea of his work was (in 1871) largely to gather data on travels and voyages, Bancroft, hiring clerical assistance, tried experiments in abstracting and minutely indexing printed works. Neither proved satisfactory.

The final classification system was a pragmatic solution to a complicated problem. Bancroft and staff selected about 50 major topics which they felt would embrace all real knowledge, and cover the contents of the whole collection. These main headings were then subdivided. Once the list of subject headings and their subdivisions had been determined, each was assigned an abbreviation. The whole collection was then strained through that sieve; only information applicable to the Pacific states was retained, and basically only factual data were noted. "These forty or fifty subjects," wrote Bancroft, "formed the basis of the index, while excluding tons of trash, with which every author seems bound in a greater or less degree to dilute his writings" (*Works*, 39:238–39).

Copies of the classification scheme were

```
Ind.  Tehuan.  Zapotecs.  1847.

Macgregor, J.  Progress of America.  London, 1847.
     Vol. I., pp. 848–9.

Location, Character, Dress, Manufactures.
```

FIG. 2—SAMPLE INDEX SLIP. From Bancroft, *Works*, 39:240.

given to each of numerous clerical assistants, who were also assigned a book to index by it. He then prepared a 3-by-5-inch slip in a prescribed format: top line was main subject, subdivision(s) and date; second line, bibliographical data, with pages cited; third line, topical notes. Figure 2 illustrates such a slip.

Bancroft not only tells about the difficulty of training indexers, but relates further details, including the special cupboards he invented to hold the thousands of slips. He notes that indexing work, which went on for years, cost him $35,000, and was supervised by William Nemos.[3] The index was expected to place before any writer a complete review of the literature of the subject on which he was engaged. It also permitted him to order further notes on those works and pages of principal interest. Thus at the base of the system were indexers; just above were the notetakers.

These two categories constituted the semi-menial clerical staff, working under the direction of Nemos or the general supervisor, Henry L. Oak. Bancroft estimated that this portion of the labor for the *Works* cost him $80,000. Caughey says the uniformity of the surviving notes resides only in that each is clearly labeled as to source and subject: the notes are quite disparate in format, each being the part of a foolscap sheet cut up to form the individual notes.

[3] Oak (1893, p. 27) doubted the figure of $35,000, and objected to Bancroft's naming Nemos, rather than himself, as the one in charge. Oak also claimed that the index was less important than abstracting, and had been used mostly for *Native Races*.

Table 1—BANCROFT'S *WORKS*: SUMMARY

History Pacific States (volume)	Works (volume)	Title	Vol.	Subtitle	Date	Pages
	1	NATIVE RACES	1	Wild Tribes	1882	797
	2		2	Civilized Nations	1882	805
	3		3	Myths & Languages	1882	796
	4		4	Antiquities	1882	807
	5		5	Primitive History	1882	796
					SUBTOTAL	4,001
1	6	HISTORY OF CENTRAL AMERICA	1	1516–1521	1882	704
2	7		2	1530–1800	1883	766
3	8		3	1801–1887	1887	776
					SUBTOTAL	2,246
4	9	HISTORY OF MEXICO	1	1516–1521	1883	702
5	10		2	1521–1600	1883	790
6	11		3	1600–1803	1883	780
7	12		4	1804–1824	1885	829
8	13		5	1824–1861	1885	812
9	14		6	1861–1887	1888	760
					SUBTOTAL	4,673
10	15	HISTORY OF NORTH MEXICAN STATES & TEXAS	1	1531–1800	1883	773
11	16		2	1801–1889	1889	814
					SUBTOTAL	1,587
				MIDDLE AMERICA	SUBTOTAL	12,507
12	17	HISTORY OF ARIZONA & NEW MEXICO, 1530–1888			1888	829
13	18	HISTORY OF CALIFORNIA	1	1542–1800	1884	744
14	19		2	1801–1824	1884	795
15	20		3	1825–1840	1885	792
16	21		4	1841–1845	1886	726
17	22		5	1846–1848	1886	784
18	23		6	1848–1859	1888	787
19	24		7	1860–1890	1890	826
					SUBTOTAL	5,454
20	25	HISTORY OF NEVADA, COLORADO & WYOMING, 1540–1888			1890	828
21	26	HISTORY OF UTAH			1890	808
22	27	HISTORY OF THE NORTHWEST COAST	1	1543–1800	1884	735
23	28		2	1800–1846	1884	768
					SUBTOTAL	1,503
24	29	HISTORY OF OREGON	1	1834–1848	1886	789
25	30		2	1848–1888	1888	808
					SUBTOTAL	1,597
26	31	HISTORY OF WASHINGTON, IDAHO & MONTANA			1890	836
27	32	HISTORY OF BRITISH COLUMBIA, 1792–1885			1887	792
28	33	HISTORY OF ALASKA, 1730–1885			1886	775
29	34	CALIFORNIA PASTORAL			1888	808
30	35	CALIFORNIA INTER POCULA			1888	828
31	36	POPULAR TRIBUNALS	1		1887	789
32	37		2		1887	808
					SUBTOTAL	1,597
33	38	ESSAYS & MISCELLANY			1890	764
34	39	LITERARY INDUSTRIES			1890	808
				TOTAL PAGES,	Works	30,734

Even more curious were the filing procedures; the topical slips were placed by subject in paper bags (like grocery bags), which were fastened by clothespins on clotheslines, awaiting the writer's need of those materials.

Finally, the writing process completed the manuscript, which then proceeded through the normal manufacturing steps. A critical question that we shall defer is that of group authorship. Writers, like indexers and abstractors, in Bancroft's view were employees expected to work from 7:15 A.M. to 6:00 P.M. all days except Sunday (half-hour for lunch). Bancroft records that many of the indexing and abstracting staff were "of Spanish and Mexican origin, not half of whose names I ever knew. Month after month they plodded more or less diligently along, as part of the great combination, directed perhaps by Savage, Oak, or Nemos, and drawing their pay every Saturday" (*Works*, 39:274).[4]

Thus to Bancroft's historiography were applied most of the classical elements of mass production: specializations, uniformity of procedures, scheduled and integrated work flow, even quality controls. Some concept of the quantity that the system produced may be deduced from Bancroft's calculation that production time for the five volumes of *Native Races* was "equivalent to the well-directed efforts of one man, every day, Sundays excepted, from eight o'clock in the morning till six at night, for a period of fifty years" (*Works*, 39:305).

Both plans and procedures evolved from initial efforts on *Native Races*. Bancroft recites how he first started his History by writing a long dissertation on voyages to 1540, and a 300-page introduction, to which was appended an account of the conquests of Darien and Peru. In drafting the Spanish

materials, he reluctantly came to the conclusion that he would have to do something about the natives, who seemingly intruded at every point, throwing colonial history into disarray. His own words about Indians are graphic: "Wherever I touched the continent with my Spaniards they were there, a dusky disgusting subject. I did not fancy them. I would gladly have avoided them. I was no archaeologist, ethnologist, or antiquary, and had no desire to become such. My tastes in the matter, however, did not dispose of the subject. The savages were there, and there was no help for me; I must write them up to get rid of them" (*Works*, 39:295).

He relates that he had planned to put all needful information in two volumes. As writing proceeded, however, these expanded to five. Bancroft admitted that "whatever I take up is almost sure to overrun first calculations as to space" (*Works*, 39:303). So with the rest of the History.

As late as 1878, after having produced the five unwanted and unexpected tomes on Indians, Bancroft thought the History proper could be encompassed within 14 volumes. By 1882 the plan had expanded, but it was not until 1884 that the fixed number of 39 volumes for the *Works* was finally decided. This decision was partially in response to the need to know in advance the scope of each set and subset, for scheduling purposes, both in production and in manufacturing. Once the rigid framework was established, later volumes were tailored in coverage and format to fit it (Caughey, 1946, pp. 254–55). The final product consisted of the *Native Races*, plus histories of areas (28 volumes), completed by four topical volumes and two of personal essays and of autobiography.

Table 1 summarizes basic physical data about the *Works*. From it can be seen that in any given year volumes from various parts of the History might appear, to the bafflement of subscribers, most of whom apparently were not at first aware (nor was

---

[4] Oak (1893, pp. 63–64) was highest paid of the staff; he rose from $75 monthly to $200, plus room rent, twice the next highest; he got no vacation pay or pension, and even had to buy from his own funds a personal set of the *Works*.

Bancroft) how large the total number would be. A second induction is the appalling magnitude of the final outcome. Apart from end-matter paginated in Roman numerals, the *Works* cover a total of 30,734 closely printed pages. At an average of between 600 and 700 words a page, they represent about 20 *million* words, a staggering average output of a million words a year from 1871.

For purposes here we note that only the first 16 volumes directly touch Middle American areas. They occupy about 40 per cent of the printed space of the *Works*, their 12,500 pages providing perhaps the largest connected coverage of the history of the area from pre-Contact times to late 19th century.

FORMAT

Here we also note that each volume of the *Works* is well made, and that the set is attractive and well designed for scholarly use. Individual volumes are remarkably free of typographical errors, contain clear maps and diagrams, and are sturdily bound. Each contains a detailed table of contents, whose subtopics are repeated at the top of text pages in running heads. In the case of multivolume series, an impressive list of principal authorities is found at the beginning and the final volume contains an extensive and generally reliable index; the pattern is repeated for single-volume state histories, none of which covers our area. The most characteristic feature of all volumes is the extensive use of footnotes and endnotes, many of which are long detailed topical bibliographies or critical reviews of topics. Equally or more useful are such notes which discuss individual sources; generally these provide biographical data, bibliographical history, and evaluations.

Because such data are conveniently summarized in Bancroft to the date of publication of his *Works*, and represent much of the continuing value of his efforts, Appendix B to this article lists such materials. Although many of his discussions have been

supplemented, and works known to him only in manuscript or corrupt texts in the 1880s have since been published, for many purposes the Bancroft notes provide a handy ready reference point to launch further inquiries.

AUTHORSHIP

Description of Bancroft's general system has already suggested that his role was primarily that of entrepreneur, planner, and general editor rather than actual author of works whose title pages exclusively bore the name of Hubert Howe Bancroft. Unlike the problems of borrowing and plagiarism with which companion articles in this volume of the *Handbook* on Torquemada, Herrera, and Clavigero are concerned, the authorship issue in the case of Bancroft is essentially whether he was morally correct in denying credit to his collaborators, by failing to identify them and their contributions. Controversies over these matters have merged with other polemical aspects of Bancroft's activities—an acrimonious debate with Lewis Morgan and followers on the nature of native society, alleged denigration of Establishment authors like Washington Irving and Prescott, overzealous efforts of the sales staff, the mercenary nature of the Bancroft subscription volumes following *Works*, treatment of Californian and Mormon pioneers, charges of stealing personal papers and public records, among others. Many of the problems have been discussed at length by Caughey (1946), and are irrelevant when we narrow treatment to the specific Bancroft volumes related to Middle America.

The first main indictment of Bancroft's monopolizing credits for authorship was sparked by the appearance in 1890 of the final volume of the *Works*, an autobiographical summary entitled *Literary Industries* (*Works*, 39). Like others in the series, it was partially staff-written. It not only gave the life and times of H. H. Bancroft, but also outlined the complicated system of authorship that Bancroft had devised. It mentioned numerous helpers, but Bancroft did not indicate to what degree they had actually been the final authors of the printed texts. To correct what he thought were unjust charges against Bancroft and his methods, but more to obtain personal recognition, his long-time aide Henry L. Oak began in 1891 to prepare what he thought was a more correct statement of what went on in Bancroft's literary workshop. It was published as a pamphlet in 1893 (Oak, 1893), after a most curious exchange of views, also included in the Oak publication.

Henry L. Oak was a New Englander, born in Maine (1844) of Welsh, English and Scotch stock who had early emigrated to America. He started his college years at Bowdoin, but was graduated from Dartmouth in 1865. After teaching school in various places, he edited a religious paper put out by Bancroft's company, and in 1869 became the latter's librarian and "superintendent of that wide range of intricate detail essential to extracting material in the Bancroft library" (*Works*, 39:246–49).

Oak for 18 years was the chief assistant to Bancroft, who called him "first among my collaborators" (*Works*, 39:246). Bancroft's views seemingly were shared by co-workers (*Works*, 39:250–51; Morris, 1903a, p. 308), certainly by himself (Oak, 1893). Because of ill health, Oak retired in 1887 on completion of the *History of Arizona and New Mexico* (*Works*, 17).

As the person who had been primarily responsible for operations of the system that produced the *Works*, Oak had a stake in refuting what he considered unjust charges against their reliability, but at the same time thought that he and others who had actually written large parts of them should not have been so slighted in *Literary Industries*. Brooding in hermit-like seclusion, Oak wrote Bancroft that before he died he would like to be known for "the only piece of literary work he has ever done, or is ever likely to do" (Oak to Ban-

croft, April 3, 1892, in Oak, 1893, p. 8). But he included a curious proposal in the same communication: "And even now if you are willing to give me for past services, say $20,000 . . . I should still feel myself so bound, destroying my statement and all memoranda, and whenever I could not conscientiously speak in your favor, keeping strict silence."

In reply Bancroft said, "I doubt if authors are in the habit of giving their employees any credit at all." He added, "In regard to the threat you make that if I don't give you $20,000, you will publish something against me, I say, 'Proceed'" (Oak, 1893, pp. 67–68). Oak did, but seemingly his relatively mild pamphlet had little circulation; references to it are few, and it is now a rare fugitive piece. Almost equally futile was Oak's gesture of presenting Dartmouth College, his alma mater, with a set of 10 Bancroft volumes with his name inserted as author (Caughey, 1946, p. 266).

More effective were the efforts of another collaborator, Mrs. Frances Fuller Victor. Bancroft, who generally would have nothing to do with female employees, testified in *Literary Industries* to her ability, "if for no other reason than to deliver me from the charge of prejudice." He noted she was "a lady of cultivated mind, of ability and singular application; likewise her physical endurance was remarkable" (*Works*, 39:237–38). This was not enough for an authoress who before joining the Bancroft factory had been a literary figure in her own right. In various Oregon and Utah newspapers she set forth her claims as author of various Bancroft *Histories*, and in 1893 at the winter fair in San Francisco she exhibited four volumes with a special preface inserted and her name displayed as author (Morris, 1903a, pp. 344–45; Morris, 1903b). In the long run, however, her most devastating actions against Bancroft consisted in supplying William A. Morris with detailed notes on Bancroft's literary workshop.

Morris was a professional historian, a

specialist on British history. He was also an Oregonian and a good friend of Mrs. Victor. Partly to redress what he considered lack of appropriate academic credit for her, and to provide historical scholars with some notion of who had prepared the *Works*, he utilized Mrs. Victor's *ex parte* testimony as the main basis of a long detailed article, "The origin and authorship of the Bancroft Pacific States publications: a history of a history," that appeared in the *Oregon Historical Quarterly* in 1903. Interestingly enough, Morris reported that for this exposé, "Mr. Oak himself refuses to give testimony, doubtless on account of his former intimate personal connection with Mr. Bancroft and his acquiescence in the plan followed," as well as poor health (Morris, 1903a, p. 305). It seems also that Morris talked with other Bancroft collaborators, and had access to an unpublished autobiography of Thomas Savage. Even unsophisticated users of the Bancroft *Works* are still directed to this Morris exposé by its repeated citation on Library of Congress printed cards relating to Bancroft. Morris also prepared the short sketch of Bancroft in the standard *American Dictionary of Biography* (Morris, 1928).

Another hostile article on Bancroft entered professional historical literature in 1911, entitled "Hubert Howe Bancroft: his work and method," by Rockwell D. Hunt. Published by the Historical Society of Southern California, it seemingly starts to pay homage to Bancroft, who had in 1911 been elected President of the Pacific Coast Branch of the American Historical Association, and to honor him on his forthcoming 80th birthday. Based primarily on Bancroft's own *Literary Industries* and supplemented by data from the Morris article, Hunt's effort sought to destroy the myth of Bancroft as historian. Moreover, the tenor of the argument is that the real authors were inept and, by extension, the *Works* suspect. "It would be extremely difficult to find one man who wrote on Bancroft's works whose name would carry the real authority of a

history specialist," he noted and then added, "The real writers are for the most part unknown people—I will not call them, with one critic, 'a horde of hack writers'" (Hunt, 1911, p. 168). Apparently without himself having worked in the fields tilled by Bancroft and staff, he states, "If the work were thoroughly reliable the historical student would possess an inexhaustible fund of historical data; unfortunately, this has not been established" (ibid., p. 171). After comparing Bancroft unfavorably with Justin Winsor and Lord Acton, he concluded, "Bancroft was a plain business man who had never entered college and who erroneously conceived that a vast library could be reduced to a finished history by an elaborate machinery and mere division of labor" (ibid., p. 172).

Bancroft's own justifications for his egoistic procedures reveal ignorance and insensitivity but not chicanery. He consistently held that to clutter the title pages of a set of *Works* with numerous names would handicap the sales campaigns.[5] In scholarly circles he was at first as unknown as his assistants, but not so in the publishing world, especially the West. Above this clearly practical consideration was a related one, that the essential unity of his plan to cover the vast Pacific states areas would best be conveyed by using only his name as sole author (Caughey, 1946, p. 257).

There seems to be no question that Bancroft conceived of himself as author, and of his assistants as paid employees who were hired to aid him in various degrees. As such they were to utilize the resources he placed at their disposal, under his supervision and the authority he delegated to Oak and others. In his view, the assistants had no rights in the product of their labors, for

---

[5] Oak (1893, p. 12), in his essentially fair and scholarly assessment, noted of Bancroft, "His commercial instincts were always stronger than his aspirations for legitimate literary reputation, though the latter also seemed, for some years at least, a powerful incentive."

TABLE 2—AUTHORSHIP OF BANCROFT'S *WORKS*, VOLUMES 1–16

Works	Series	Volume	Subtitle	Authors
1	*NATIVE RACES*	1	Wild Tribes	Bancroft ($\frac{1}{3}$), Harcourt ($\frac{1}{6}$), Fisher ($\frac{1}{6}$), Oak ($\frac{1}{6}$), Nemos ($\frac{1}{6}$)
2		2	Civilized Nations	Harcourt (all)
3		3	Myths & Languages	Fisher ($\frac{11}{16}$), Goldschmidt ($\frac{5}{16}$)
4		4	Antiquities	Oak (all)
5		5	Primitive History	Oak (all)
6	*HISTORY OF CENTRAL AMERICA*	1	1516–1521	Bancroft ($\frac{1}{2}$), Oak ($\frac{1}{6}$), Nemos ($\frac{1}{3}$) rewritten by Kuhn, Kuhn ($\frac{1}{3}$)
7		2	1530–1800	Bancroft ($\frac{1}{18}$), Nemos ($\frac{1}{2}$), Bates ($\frac{1}{4}$), Peatfield ($\frac{1}{12}$), Kuhn ($\frac{1}{5}$) rewritten by Nemos
8		3	1801–1887	Savage (all)
9	*HISTORY OF MEXICO*	1	1516–1521	Bancroft ($\frac{1}{5}$–$\frac{1}{4}$), Nemos ($\frac{3}{4}$–$\frac{4}{5}$)
10		2	1521–1600	Nemos ($\frac{2}{3}$), Peatfield ($\frac{1}{12}$), Savage ($\frac{1}{4}$)
11		3	1600–1803	Nemos ($\frac{1}{3}$–$\frac{1}{2}$), Peatfield ($\frac{1}{12}$), Savage ($\frac{1}{3}$), Griffin ($\frac{1}{12}$)
12		4	1804–1824	Bancroft ($\frac{1}{12}$), Nemos ($\frac{1}{4}$), Peatfield ($\frac{1}{4}$), Savage ($\frac{1}{3}$)
13		5	1824–1861	Nemos ($\frac{1}{4}$), Peatfield ($\frac{1}{12}$), Savage ($\frac{2}{3}$)
14		6	1861–1887	Nemos ($\frac{2}{3}$), Peatfield ($\frac{1}{12}$), Savage ($\frac{1}{4}$)
15	*HISTORY OF NORTH MEXICAN STATES*	1	1531–1800	Oak (all)
16		2	1801–1889	Nemos ($\frac{1}{4}$) using an earlier MS by Harcourt, Peatfield ($\frac{3}{4}$)

SOURCE: Caughey, 1946, pp. 262–63 (adapted).

which he believed he paid them adequately. Such basic attitudes are clearly revealed in a letter he wrote to Mrs. Victor in 1878 when she was joining the Bancroft employ (Morris, 1903a, p. 340):

The work is wholly mine. I do what I can myself, and pay for what I have done over that; but I father the whole of it and it goes out under my name. All who work in the library do so simply as my assistants. Their work is mine to print, scratch, or throw in the fire. I have no secrets; yet I do not tell everybody just what each does. I do not pretend to do all the work myself, that is, to prepare for the printer all that goes out under my name. I have three or four now who can write for the printer after a fashion; none of them can suit me as well as I can suit myself. One or two only will write with

very little change from me. All the rest require sometimes almost rewriting.

At age 80 Bancroft still wrote, "My men used also to complain that I was not fair to myself in giving them credit for so much that they were not entitled to. I assured them it gave me pleasure to make such acknowledgement both verbally and in my *Literary Industries*" (Bancroft, 1912, p. 338). Posterity has not wholly agreed with him.

It is clear that Bancroft neither understood nor followed normal canons developed by gentlemen-scholars in which there is perhaps overemphasis on bestowing specific credits for intellectual assistance. Even Caughey, a sympathetic biographer, considers that Bancroft was much less than

TABLE 3—AUTHORSHIP OF BANCROFT'S *WORKS*, BY AUTHORS

Works		Bancroft	Bates	Fisher	Goldschmidt	Griffin	Harcourt	Kuhn	Nemos	Oak	Peatfield	Savage	Total
1	NATIVE RACES	.33	—	.17	—	—	.17	—	.17	.17	—	—	1.01
2		—	—	—	—	—	1.00	—	—	—	—	—	1.00
3		—	—	.78	.22	—	—	—	—	—	—	—	1.00
4		—	—	—	—	—	—	—	—	1.00	—	—	1.00
5		—	—	—	—	—	—	—	—	1.00	—	—	1.00
	SUBTOTAL	.33	—	.95	.22	—	1.17	—	.17	2.17	—	—	5.01
6	CENTRAL AMERICA	.50	—	—	—	—	—	.33	.33	.17	—	—	1.30
7		.06	.25	—	—	—	—	.20	.50	.08	—	—	1.09
8		—	—	—	—	—	—	—	—	—	—	1.00	1.00
	SUBTOTAL	.56	.25	—	—	—	—	.55	.83	.25	—	1.00	3.39
9	MEXICO	.25	—	—	—	—	—	—	.75	—	—	—	1.00
10		—	—	—	—	—	—	—	.67	—	.08	.25	1.00
11		—	—	—	—	.08	—	—	.51	—	.08	.33	1.00
12		.08	—	—	—	—	—	—	.25	—	.25	.33	.91
13		—	—	—	—	—	—	—	.25	—	.08	.67	1.00
14		—	—	—	—	—	—	—	.67	—	.08	.25	1.00
	SUBTOTAL	.33	—	—	—	.08	—	—	3.10	—	.57	1.83	5.91
15	NORTH MEXICAN STATES	—	—	—	—	—	—	—	—	1.00	—	—	1.00
16		—	—	—	—	—	—	—	.25	—	.75	—	1.00
	SUBTOTAL	—	—	—	—	—	—	—	.25	1.00	.75	—	2.00
	TOTAL	1.22	.25	.95	.22	.08	1.17	.53	4.35	4.22	1.22	2.83	16.31

frank by maintaining so strenuously that he was personally responsible for the *Works*, and that even by the ethic of his day should have made more explicit and precise acknowledgment of what his major assistants had done. Failure to take such action constituted, says Caughey, a "fundamental error of his procedure, which was indeed his tragic flaw" (Caughey, 1946, pp. 257, 336).

Once that moral issue has been settled, attention may now turn to the actual authors who wrote selected volumes of direct concern to us. In advance it may be noted that many of the general charges against Bancroft do not apply to them. As there was

little or no market in Mexico and Central America for his sets, no tendency to ameliorate or change judgments about persons or institutions for greater sales is evident in the volumes for those areas. Most of them were, especially for colonial times, completed well before the rigid scheme and advancing deadlines imposed special strains on the later state histories. The group was compiled under the meticulous supervision of Oak and Bancroft, before the retirement of the former and the dilution of the latter's attention when his energies were turned to recouping losses from the 1886 fire.

From available sources, manuscript and

printed, Caughey constructed a chart of authorship for the *Works*. He also correctly indicates the necessary imprecision and difficulties of pinning neatly creative or editorial responsibilities in the face of imperfect evidence and the complex nature of the processes in the Bancroft literary factory (Caughey, 1946, pp. 258–65). Table 2 reproduces an adapted version of his scheme.

The same information, based on a chart published by Caughey (1946, pp. 262–63) is rearranged in Table 3. Contradictory or deficient data account for the fact that the sum of proportions attributed to various authors in any given volume does not always equal 100 per cent. The conclusion seems clear that Bancroft himself actually wrote only a small part of the Middle American portion of his *Works*.[6]

The Corps of Writers and their Contributions to "Native Races"

Table 3 also reveals that of those who actually penned the Middle American parts of Bancroft's *Works*, Nemos and Oak between them wrote nearly half, with only Savage otherwise credited with the equivalent of more than two volumes. In a brief analysis of the volumes we can bear in mind that for ethnohistory some are of more direct interest than others, and their authors therefore of higher concern. Fortunately in addition to the published material itself we have available a fairly extensive group of biographies of the contributors, in Bancroft's *Literary Industries*.[7] We shall confine our analysis to the volumes of *Native Races* (*Works*, 1–5), which are of continuing interest to ethnohistorians.

One of the few places that Bancroft specified particular credits was in the preface to *Native Races* (*Works*, 1:xi) where he rendered "just acknowledgment" to his helpers in carrying out the plan: "to Mr. T. Arundel-Harcourt, in the researches on the manners and customs of the Civilized Nations; to Mr. Walter M. Fisher, in the investigation

of Mythology; to Mr. Albert Goldschmidt in the treatise on Language; and to Mr. Henry L. Oak, in the subject of Antiquities and Aboriginal History." This roster is essentially correct, but it is incomplete.

Wild Tribes, initiating the series (*Works*, 1), contains seven long chapters. Starting with Alaskan aborigines, they work southward, with chapters 6 ("Wild Tribes of Mexico," *Works*, 1:615–83) and 7 ("Wild Tribes of Central America," 1:684–797) of special relevance here. For each group the authors systematically attempt to cover a broad range of comparable information, gleaned from a wide variety of sources: physical types, clothing and costume, dwellings, food and agriculture, weapons, war and slavery, crafts, arts, trade, marriage and life cycle, amusements, disease and medicine, and some notes on general character. Each chapter closes with a long endnote that draws on various authorities to establish tribal boundaries within the cultural area of the chapter. At the beginning of each chapter is a detailed map based on such notes.

Differing slightly from Caughey's chart, Morris (1903a, p. 307) says that nearly all the volume was written by a man who called himself William Nemos (1848–?), *nom de plume* of a polyglot Finn, a minor nobleman's son, who was trained in Moscow, Vienna, Stockholm, and Uppsala. He had resided in India, London, Australia, and Hawaii before drifting to San Francisco and

---

[6] Oak reverses the common view of Bancroft, by saying that Bancroft was an excellent writer, and that some of the best literary parts of the *Works* came from his pen. Oak said Bancroft really was very lax as a compiler and was too impatient to be a researcher; rather than use the famous abstracts, he would get a half ton or so of books around him, dip into them, and dash off his prose without checking the major sources. As he could not readily read Spanish or French, this caused certain difficulties which it was Oak's chore to smooth out (Oak, 1893, pp. 34–36).

[7] "Some of My Assistants" is the title of chap. 11 (*Works*, 39:245–76). A popular edition of *Literary Industries* (N.Y., 1891) omits this chapter. Morris (1903a) supplements biographies in minor detail.

entering Bancroft's employ in 1871 (*Works*, 39:251–55). To Oak, Morris attributes chapter 3 ("Columbians," 1:150–321), and to Harcourt chapter 4 ("Californians," 1:322–470). Oak (1893) agrees.

In Bancroft's plan, various groups that subsequent research has shown to be parallel in development with the Aztecs and Maya were grouped under "Wild Tribes." Among others there are included the Tarascans, Zapotecs, Mixtecs, and various other smaller Mexican and Central American societies. From the printed sources, Nemos brought together a vast body of data for each of the topics he systematically covered. His work is still the most extensive comparative ethnohistorical synthesis of the Middle American area. The ethnological maps, prepared by Albert Goldschmidt, are comprehensive and generally accurate.

Volume 2, "Civilized Nations," is devoted nearly exclusively to an extended treatment of the Aztecs, followed by a shorter but parallel coverage of the Maya. After two general introductory chapters, there come lengthy chapters on Aztec government, palaces and households, classes (one on the privileged, another on middle and lower), life cycle, feasts and amusements, public festivals, food and agriculture, dress, commerce, war, laws and courts, arts and manufactures, the Aztec calendar, picture writing, architecture and dwellings, medicine and funeral rites. The Maya are treated in six chapters: government, classes, laws; education and family; feasts and amusements; food, dress, commerce, war; arts, calendar, and hieroglyphics; and buildings, medicine, burials, character.

Bancroft penned the first chapter, setting forth his theory of differences between savagism and civilization (*Works*, 2:1–80); Oak provided chapter two, a general view of the Nahua peoples and the Maya (2:81–132). Oak, according to his own account (1893), was also responsible for two chapters of direct continuing concern to ethnohistorians, chapter 17 on Aztec picture writing (2:523–

52) and chapter 24 on the Maya calendar and hieroglyphics (2:748–82). His endnote to chapter 2, providing the etymologies of tribal names (2:125–32), gives data not readily summarized elsewhere. Notable for the time are his discussions of the pictorial document collections, and reproductions of several historical codices (2:529–30, 539, 544–45, 548–49, 772, 774).

The remaining 21 chapters of the volume seemingly were almost exclusively the work of T. Arundel-Harcourt (Morris, 1903a, p. 306). Like Nemos, this young man preferred to work under a pseudonym. He claimed to have been born in 1851, son of a British gentleman, educated in classics. He ran away to India, then did a term at Heidelburg in Germany before drifting to Montana and thence to California, where he joined Bancroft's group in November, 1872. He left for a while in 1874 to edit the *Overland Monthly* but returned to the library. Later he transferred into newspaper work, and died in San Francisco in 1884 (*Works*, 39:264–65; Morris, 1903a, pp. 303–04). Morris considered him "the most able of the library corps. But while he was brilliant, handsome, and witty, he was at the same time erratic and unreliable" (Morris, 1903a, p. 304).

It was thus Harcourt's statements, rather than Bancroft's own, which generated a now forgotten polemic between Bancroft and Lewis Henry Morgan over the nature of Aztec society. Generalizing from his own studies of the Iroquois, Morgan had elaborated a theory of native societies that appeared in extended form in 1877. It was partially adumbrated in Morgan's 1876 article entitled "Montezuma's Dinner," an attack on Bancroft's treatment, in the *North American Review*. Based largely on material furnished him by Bandelier (which he only partly understood), Morgan indicated that it was (according to his theory) impossible that the Aztecs had as advanced a civilization as the chroniclers reported; he averred they had no empire, and in short were in what he called "Middle Status of Barbarism" (Morgan, 1877, pp. 186–88). Modern historical scholars (Gibson, 1947) find the Morgan contentions a "strained accommodation of Aztec society to the general plan for all society . . . his most important statements were never substantiated by any citation to authority."

But at the time, the Morgan views were taken up by others, especially when *Native Races* was reissued as volumes 1–5 of *Works* (Caughey, 1946, p. 139). To vindicate the reliability of contemporary evidence, on which volume 2 of *Native Races* rested, Bancroft issued (1883) a rather violent pamphlet against Morgan and his followers entitled "Early American Chroniclers." This essay was later included in *Essays and Miscellany* (*Works*, 38:1–38). Winsor, who summarizes the issues, noted that the "ungracious tone" of Bancroft's rebuttals helped produce "a divided reception for his new venture [the *Works*]" and that "the manner of this rejoinder is more offensive than that of the volumes which it defends" (Winsor, 1889, 1:ix). Winsor adds that the solid merits of the Bancroft volumes were really their own best defense, and that the polemic was unnecessary.

Civilized Nations still forms a useful introduction to the complexities of Aztec and Maya societies. Largely because the Maya society was skimped in the volume, and has been the subject of considerably more sustained modern research, its treatment now seems less satisfactory than that of the Nahuas. Many particular details of the latter have undergone correction or expansion, but the general framework remains valid.

Little consulted, and less valuable, is volume 3, *Myths and Languages*. About two-thirds (*Works*, 3:1–550) is concerned with mythology; the remainder deals with aboriginal languages (3:551–796).

In contrast to previous portions, mythology is at first divided according to topics and themes rather than geographical units subdivided by topics. It thus has the scat-

tered and almost antiquarian aspect of Frazier's *Golden Bough* through chapter 4. At that point (chaps. 5–11) gods and worship are approached by areas and cultures: Eskimo (chap. 5), northern Mexico (chap. 6), Aztecs (chaps. 7–10), and Maya (chap. 11), with a final general chapter on aboriginal beliefs concerning the hereafter. Authorship seems to have been a complicated matter. Morris attributes to Walter M. Fisher the main portion of the work.[8] However, Fisher obtained much help from Nemos, who completed the treatment when in October, 1874, Fisher left the manuscript "half-finished" to accept editorship of the *Overland Monthly*. Harcourt then revised the contributions of both Fisher and Nemos (Morris, 1903a, p. 307).

The language portion tends to be of more interest to the historian than to the linguist. It is chiefly remarkable for a cautious sifting of the then known facts in a sphere where conservatism about likenesses and affiliations was at that time more remarkable than common. Basically the treatment is geographical, with discussion moving from north to south. A general scheme, with mention of the languages to be treated, appears in the opening chapter of the language section (*Works*, 3:562–73). In each instance in the discussion of a tongue there are notes on peculiarities, grammar, and often comparative vocabularies. Chapters 8–11 (*Works*, 3:706–81), dealing with northern Mexican, Aztec and Otomi, central and southern Mexican, and the Maya-Quiche languages, provide data on groups within our Principal Area, (defined in Article 1, fig. 1). Perhaps the chief value of these pages lies in their extensive citations from historical sources describing the linguistic habits of Indians, many of whose dialects early became ex-

[8] Walter M. Fisher (1849–1919), Anglo-Irish from Ulster, was well educated, chiefly in literature. He joined the library in 1872, and toward the close of 1875 returned to London. He wrote *The Californians* (1876), mentioning in passing the Bancroft group with whom he worked (*Works* 39:261–63).

tinct. The body of language data in the *Relaciones geográficas*, analyzed in Article 9, was not available in Bancroft's day, but his treatment contains much information from contemporary colonial sources not found in them.

Compilation of the treatise was done by Albert Goldschmidt, and seemingly in part revised and rewritten by Bancroft himself (Morris, 1903a, p. 307). His companions remembered Goldschmidt as "a linguist of great ability, and [he] was able to translate almost any language which he encountered, but was inclined to fritter away his time" (ibid., p. 304). Bancroft called him a "pleasant social man, of no very pronounced parts, in age about thirty-five, given to ease and quietness rather than to physical exertion or hard study," and also praised his mastery of languages (*Works*, 39:264).[9]

Extensive, intensive, and increasingly sophisticated archaeological work over the past century has made *Antiquities*, fourth volume of *Native Races*, almost completely obsolete. It deals primarily with Central America, Mexico, Southwestern United States, with less attention to the northwest, and moundbuilders. A final chapter deals with Peruvian antiquities. The chief value to present research is to provide information on pre-scientific expeditions and a baseline from which to note development of knowledge since 1870. Various sources agree that Oak wrote the entire volume (Morris, 1903a; Caughey, 1946, p. 262).

Oak also was the principal author of *Primitive History*, fifth and final volume of *Native Races*. It begins with a lengthy chapter that reviews various theories of American Indian origins—Hebrew, Egyptian, Welsh, and others—as a prelude to an important chapter, "Introductory to Aboriginal

History," that outlines the hazards of ethnohistory and discusses types of sources and their reliability. In sequence then come chronological treatments, divided into pre-Toltec (chap. 3), Toltec (chap. 4), Chichimec (chaps. 5–7), and Aztec (chaps. 8, 9). Appended finally are treatments of the marginal areas: eastern Plateau, Michoacan, Oaxaca (chap. 10), Quiche-Cakchiquel empire of Guatemala (chap. 11), miscellaneous Central American groups (chap. 12), and finally a single chapter (13) on the pre-Conquest Maya of Yucatan. In many ways the volume remains the most enduring of the series, which is perhaps merely to say that specialized studies (apart from archaeological investigations) and general historical syntheses have been less pursued over the past century.

Bancroft apparently wrote the detailed treatise of origins (*Works*, 5:1–132; Morris, 1903a, p. 306). Nemos is credited with the three final chapters of Guatemalan and Yucatecan annals (*Works*, 5:540–634; Morris, 1903a, p. 306). The main body (chaps. 3–10) was written by Oak.

Both the original composition and subsequent developments in knowledge have left *Native Races* quite uneven in utility for current use. "Different parts of the Native Races," noted Morris, "differ greatly in value. Oak was habitually scholarly and always made an effort at honest research. Nemos was likewise thoroughly reliable. Goldschmidt was noted for his shiftlessness, and Fisher and Harcourt are charged with such uncritical methods as the incorporation in their writings of statements found in magazine articles which were nowhere verified" (Morris, 1903a, p. 308). After pointing out that the series was in effect a vast though unified factual compilation of what was known in the 1870s, Caughey summarizes by saying, "Correspondingly, any work such as *Native Races* . . . was bound gradually to go out of date. As intimated above, this aging has not been uniform, because stu-

[9] Albert Goldschmidt, son of a Jewish clothing dealer from Hamburg, had been a sailor, loved music, but primarily was interested in languages. According to Nemos he was "the most systematic idler in the library" (Morris, 1903a, p. 304).

dents of the Indian have made more progress along some lines than along others . . ." (Caughey, 1946, p. 138). It is not uncommon, however, for modern investigators to use parts of seemingly "obsolete" volumes as a starting point for review of developments (Tozzer, 1941).

EVALUATION

The professional reputation of Hubert Howe Bancroft over the years has undergone various changes. He still remains a controversial figure on several scores.

Even before the completion of Bancroft's *Works* and the appearance in them of the autobiographical *Literary Industries,* Justin Winsor essayed a biobibliographical sketch and professional evaluation of the historiography (Winsor, 1889, 1:viii–ix). Without particularly stressing the point, Winsor mentioned that at least half the texts had been written by others than Bancroft, whom he termed "the organizer of an extensive series of books." Noting that publication of *Native Races* indicated that a new force had been brought to bear on historical research —"the force of organized labor from many hands; and this implied competent administrative direction and ungrudged expenditure of money"—and despite drawbacks, Bancroft had produced a useful work. He felt the factory method had revealed "a want of uniform discrimination, and . . . that promiscuous avidity of search which marks rather an eagerness to amass than a judgment to select, and give literary perspective."

Winsor was less happy with the *History of the Pacific States*, criticizing its style, and "a want of knowledge on points where the system of indexing employed by his staff had been deficient," among other points. He especially deplored the aggressive tactics Bancroft used to defend his work against critics, and stated "his important work needs no such adventitious support." Winsor concluded by stating that the wide range of sources used, full citations employed, and discussion of authorities "make the work pre-eminent for its bibliographical extent." With only small differences in emphasis, this acute early view tends to be the present one, although subsequent critics have varied widely from time to time.

As already discussed, extended critical statements from 1893 through 1911 by Oak, Mrs. Victor, then Morris and Hunt, attacked the Bancroft historiographical enterprise on much the same grounds, without giving many offsetting favorable judgments. In this same vein Charles V. Langlois, a leading French historian, wrote an extended exposition and critique of Bancroft's methods, but like others he drew his information chiefly from *Literary Industries*, without having actually read the histories (Langlois, 1902, p. 252, n. 1, "Je n'ai jamais eu l'occasion de consulter les 39 volumes"). Langlois did not wholly reject what he termed Bancroft's "sweatshop system" but tried to show that both its novelty and value were overexaggerated; he thought it perhaps suited "new lands" like western America, where inadequate previous documentary publications and monographic historical studies were available (Langlois, 1902, pp. 267–73).

At Bancroft's death in 1918, the professional historical journals were generally quite cautious and restrained in their judgments. Caughey summarizes the mixed attitudes by pointing out that on the one hand, fellow historians were willing to credit him with a magnificent contribution, the Bancroft Library, to Pacific slope historiography, "and with a substantial and enduring contribution in his published volumes. On the other, they were ready to inject into memorial notices bits of the hostile criticism that had become endemic" (Caughey, 1946, p. 385).

Caughey also records a gradual rehabilitation of Bancroft's repute by specialists of regional, especially Western, history. Authors like Charles E. Chapman, Eugene C. Barker, Bernard De Voto, and Caughey himself (Caughey, 1945; 1946, pp. 386–90) in retraversing topics and areas Bancroft covered generally emerge with a high respect for his work. They all tend to agree with De Voto's statement that "I have found that you had better not decide that Bancroft was wrong until you have rigorously tested what you think you know" (De Voto, 1943, p. 525). Along such revisionist lines, another historian recently wrote, "In courses on historiography it is now fashionable to disparage Bancroft because of some obvious limitations. The novice, however, ignores

him only at real peril. . . . His volumes are the point of departure for the areas he touched" (Cline, 1967, p. 7).

Possibly the most appropriate evaluation was inadvertently written by Bancroft himself. The words he applied to Herrera in large part almost equally fit his own work, at least that part related to Middle America: "Even today he may be called chief among historians of Spanish-American affairs; not for his style, bald and accurately prolix; nor for his method, slavishly chronological, and miserably failing in the attempt to do several things at once; but because of his massed material" (*Works*, 6:317).

Appendix A. BANCROFT, PRINCIPAL WORKS

1874–75 The native races. 5 vols. New York. [Reissued, 1882, as *Works*, 1–5.]

1882–90 Works. 39 vols. San Francisco. [For details, see Table 1.]

1883 The early American chroniclers. San Francisco. [Diatribe against Lewis Henry Morgan and followers; first 38 pages, somewhat less violent, were reprinted in *Essays and Miscellany* (*Works*, 38:1–38). Defends reliability of colonial eyewitness sources.]

1887a Vida de Porfirio Díaz. San Francisco. [Sympathetic biography.]

1887b A popular history of Mexico. San Francisco.

1891–92 Chronicles of the builders of the commonwealth: Historical character study. 7 vols. San Francisco. [Originally scheduled to be "Kings of the Commonwealth," historical summaries are followed by extensive biographies, often included on a fee basis; the set was sold on a subscription basis.]

1893a The Book of the Fair: An historical and descriptive presentation of the world's science, art, and industry, as viewed through the Columbian Exposition at Chicago in 1893. . . . 5 vols. Chicago and San Francisco. [Limited to 400 deluxe subscription sets.]

1893b Resources and development of Mexico. San Francisco.

1896–1908 Achievements of civilization: the Book of Wealth: Wealth in relation to material and intellectual progress and achievement; being an inquiry into the nature and distribution of the world's resources and riches, and a history of the origin and influence of property, its possession, accumulation, and disposition in all ages and among all nations, as a factor in human accomplishment, an agency of human refinement, and in the evolution of Civilization from the earliest to the present era. 10 vols. New York. [Deluxe subscription set, limited to 950 copies, a "companion and consort" to Book of the Fair (1893a).]

1899 The new Pacific. New York.

1912 Retrospection: Political and personal. New York. [Autobiographical and subjective views. Chaps. 17–18 summarize development of the Bancroft library and methods of writing history.]

1914 History of Mexico. New York.

1917 In these latter days. Chicago.

APPENDIX B. SELECTED REFERENCES TO BIOBIBLIOGRAPHIES, TOPICAL
BIBLIOGRAPHIES, AND EXTENDED NOTES IN BANCROFT'S *WORKS*

REFERENCES

CAUGHEY, JOHN WALTON
1945 Hubert Howe Bancroft, historian of western America. *American Historical Review*, 50:461–70 (Apr.).
1946 Hubert Howe Bancroft, Historian of the West. Berkeley and Los Angeles.

CLARK, GEORGE T.
1933 Leland Stanford and H. H. Bancroft's "History," a bibliographical curiosity. Bibliographical Society of America, *Papers*, 27:12–23.

CLINE, HOWARD F.
1967 Latin American history: development of its study and teaching in the United States since 1898. *In* H. F. Cline, ed., Latin American history: Essays on its study and teaching, 1898–1965, 1:6–16. Austin.

DE VOTO, BERNARD
1943 The year of decision 1846. Boston.

GIBSON, CHARLES
1947 Lewis Henry Morgan and the Aztec "Monarchy." *Southwestern Journal of Anthropology*, 3:78–84.

HUNT, ROCKWELL D.
1911 Hubert Howe Bancroft: his work and method. Historical Society of Southern California, *Publications*, 8:158–73.

LANGLOIS, CHARLES V.
1902 H. H. Bancroft et cie. *In* his Questions d'Histoire et d'Enseignement, pp. 243–73. Paris.

LEWIS, OSCAR [b. 1893]
1936 The launching of Bancroft's "Native Races." *Colophon*, n.s., 1:323–32.

MORGAN, LEWIS HENRY
1876 Montezuma's dinner. *North American Review*, 122:265–308 (Apr.).
1877 Ancient society, or researches in the lines of human progress from savagery through barbarism to civilization. New York.

MORRIS, WILLIAM ALFRED
1903a The origin and authorship of the Bancroft Pacific States publications: a history of a history. Oregon Historical Society, *Quarterly*, 4:287–364 (Dec.).
1903b A woman who loved Oregon. *Book-Lover*, 4:277–79.
1928 Hubert Howe Bancroft. *Dictionary of American Biography*, 1:570–71.

OAK, HENRY L.
1893 "Literary Industries" in a new light: a statement on the authorship of Bancroft's "Native Races" and "History of the Pacific States," with comments on these works and the system by which they were written. . . . San Francisco.

TOZZER, ALFRED M.
1941 Stephens and Prescott, [H. H.] Bancroft and others. *In* Los Mayas Antiguos, César Lizardi Ramos, ed., pp. 33–60. Mexico.

WINSOR, JUSTIN
1889–92 Narrative and critical history of America. 8 vols. Boston.

20. Eduard Georg Seler, 1849-1922

H. B. NICHOLSON

Eduard Georg Seler was one of the most influential and productive Americanists during the three and a half decades between 1885 and 1920. His interests and talents were broad and varied. He made fundamental contributions to aboriginal American linguistics, archaeology, native history, and ethnography. This article is concerned with only one aspect of his monumental published contribution, that which can be characterized today as Mesoamerican ethnohistory: his investigations into the documentary and native-tradition pictorial sources which provide data on the indigenous cultures of this area co-tradition.[1]

Seler was born December 5, 1849, in Crossen an der Oder (then in Prussia, presently in Poland), the third of four children. His father, Gottlieb Robert Seler, was a teacher, of modest means, in the local municipal school. Of somewhat delicate constitution in his youth, Seler nevertheless was an exceptional student, and his outstanding academic record earned him a fellowship for the children of teachers to the Joachimsthalsche Gymnasium in Berlin, which he at-

tended from 1863 to 1869. In the latter year, after receiving his bachelor's degree, he began attendance at the University of Breslau, majoring in mathematics and natural science, with particular attention to botany (which continued as a lifelong interest). He

[1] Seler's bibliography up to 1922 was compiled by his principal student, Lehmann, and published in his *Festschrift* (1922). Although it contained various errors and was not entirely complete, it comprised the great majority of his publications. It was reprinted, with Spanish translations of the titles and with the articles of vol. 4 of the *Gesammelte Abhandlungen* added, in the 1949 *El México Antiguo* homenaje. This work, issued at the suggestion of Jiménez Moreno as a special volume (7) of *El México Antiguo* on the 100th anniversary of Seler's birth, includes the most important biographical notices of Seler and discussions of his scholarly career by Linga, Termer, Jiménez Moreno, Martínez del Río, Caso, and Höpfner. In a review of the Akademische's 1960–61 re-edition of the *Gesammelte Abhandlungen*, I included a brief appraisal of Seler's contribution to Mesoamerican studies (Nicholson, 1962). Seler's bibliography was published a third time, with some corrections and updating, by Anders in his 1967 *Wort- und Sachregister*. The appendix to the present article excerpts entries of most of Seler's works on ethnohistory, retaining Anders' numbers, to which references are made in the text. Anders also gives an excellent concise summary of Seler's life and work and a list of published Seler obituaries.

348

FIG. 1—EDUARD SELER. From *Journal de la Société des Américanistes de Paris*, n.s., vol. 15 (1923).

served about a year of military duty in 1870–71 during the Franco-Prussian War, participating in the siege of Paris; with the cessation of hostilities in the spring of 1871, he returned to his studies, but now at the University of Berlin. During this period, because of his limited financial resources, Seler was obliged to accept tutorial posts in the houses of wealthy and prominent Berlin families.

In the spring of 1875 Seler passed his Oberlehrer examination, and the following year he accepted a teaching post in natural science and mathematics at the Dorothenstädtischen Realgymnasium in Berlin. However, in 1879 poor health forced him to abandon his position and return to his aged mother in Crossen. His doctor (the father of his future wife) advised moving to a

warmer climate, so he moved to Trieste, joining his sister who was a teacher there in the German College. He now turned increasingly to linguistic studies, especially of the Indogermanic languages including Russian and Sanskrit, and became well grounded in general comparative linguistics. Out of these studies there emerged an interest in ethnography-archaeology which soon became focused on the New World, especially that area today often referred to as Nuclear America: the central portion of the Western Hemisphere where genuine civilizations flourished in pre-European times.

In 1881 the Marquis de Nadaillac published *Les premiers hommes et les temps préhistoriques* and in 1883 *L'Amérique préhistorique*. The following year Seler's first publication appeared, ostensibly a German translation, with W. Schlösser, of both of Nadaillac's works in a single volume, but actually a much modified and improved version in which Seler already displayed an extensive knowledge of the documentary sources on the Middle and South American native cultures (no. 1).[2]

In 1884 Seler definitely committed himself to a professional Americanist career when he joined the group around Adolf Bastian then building the new Königlichen Museum für Völkerkunde in Berlin, beginning as an assistant and ultimately becoming director (1904–22) of the American Division. About this time Seler also seems to have begun his first major scholarly work, a study, based on available documentary sources, of the conjugation systems of the Mayance languages, which was published in 1887 and for which he received his doctorate at the University of Leipzig (no. 6).

In 1885 Seler married Caecilie Sachs, the daughter of his physician. This was a great turning point in his career; his bride came from a wealthy family, and henceforth Seler's economic self-sufficiency was assured.

[2] Ed. note: Numerical references are to Seler's writings listed in the Appendix.

Caecilie became his faithful companion and helper in his researches, particularly as a photographer in the field, and eventually became a significant author in her own right. In his marital year Seler also published his first original scholarly contribution: a brief treatment of the language of the Colorados of coastal Ecuador (1885 [1902–23, 1:3–64, with two substantial supplements]). The following year he published his first study in Mesoamerican ethnohistory (no. 5). From that date until his death 36 years later hardly a year went by without the appearance of at least one significant contribution to this theme. A selected list of these appears in the Appendix.

MESOAMERICAN ETHNOHISTORICAL INVESTI-GATIONS, 1886–1922

For convenience, Seler's ethnohistorical writings can be grouped into a few major categories: (1) translations of and commentaries on native-language texts; (2) interpretations of western Mesoamerican native-tradition pictorials; (3) Mayanist researches; and (4) ethnographic and culture-historical syntheses derived all or in part from ethnohistorical sources. Before discussing each category, however, a general summary of the development of Seler's Mesoamerican ethnohistorical researches is in order.

Seler's 1886 paper, *Maya-Handschriften und Maya-Götter* (no. 5), was, significantly, concerned with two of his greatest lifelong interests: Mesoamerican native religion and writing systems. He also clearly affirmed therein his position regarding the essential nature of lowland Maya hieroglyphic writing, holding that it was fundamentally ideographic (pictographic-"logographic"), a position from which he never deviated. The fact that it dealt with a Mayanist rather than a strictly Mexicanist theme should occasion no surprise. Seler was one of the greatest pioneer Mayanists, although his important contribution to this field has often been insufficiently recognized. Partly, perhaps, this is because his Mayanist researches

were much overshadowed in bulk by his Mexicanist investigations, partly also because his contemporary countryman, Ernst Förstemann, was more actively engaged in, and made more basic overall contributions to, the hieroglyphic-calendric aspect of Mayanist research.

Maya–Handschriften und Maya–Götter was inspired by the first article (1886) of another important early German Mayanist, Paul Schellhas, on Codex Dresden, with special emphasis on the deity representations and their hieroglyphs. In the same year Förstemann published his classic original commentary on Dresden (having published its first accurate facsimile six years previously). Seler entered the field, then, at a time when German scholarship, in its finest and most influential period, was first seriously moving into Mayanist research, which hitherto had been dominated by pioneer French and United States students. It is hardly surprising, therefore, that Seler's earliest ethnohistorical researches should be particularly directed to Mayanist themes. However, even in this article (no. 5) ostensibly devoted to a strictly Mayanist problem, Seler's technique—which became so typical of all his investigations—was to employ central Mexican data to aid in the interpretation of Maya area data, in this case deity identifications in the most important of the three surviving lowland Maya books.

The following year (1887) saw a veritable outburst of Selerian publications, which quickly established him as an Americanist of major stature. Four of these were concerned again with Mayanist themes, three of them directly following up his first paper (nos. 7, 10, 11). However, the most important was his article on the Codex Borgia group (no. 8), the first he ever published on a purely Mexicanist topic. This landmark paper staked out a research field that he was to dominate completely for the next three decades. In the same year he undertook his first trip to Mexico, during which he conducted his first archaeological field investigations. His ethnohistorical interests and publications, however, did not diminish as a result. On the contrary, in 1888 two of his most important papers in this category appeared: his detailed, seminal analysis of the 20 day signs of central Mexican and Maya area 260-day divinatory cycles (no. 14)—displaying a remarkable erudition and analytic skill so early in his scholarly career —and his interpretation of the Tonalamatl Aubin (first published complete in Mexico the year before), presented to the seventh International Congress of Americanists in Berlin and published in 1890 (no. 18). The latter was the first really thorough and basically successful analysis of a Mexican ritual-divinatory pictorial.

To the 1888 Berlin congress a prominent pioneer United States Americanist, Daniel Brinton (with whom Seler had stayed the year before near Philadelphia and who had aided his German colleague by making available to him various unpublished manuscripts in his library), sent a brief paper describing the Sahaguntine *Códice Matritense de la Biblioteca del Real Palacio*. A short comment to this paper by Seler was also published following it in the proceedings of the congress, wherein he mentioned that he had worked with the Florentine Codex and went on to discuss particularly its illustrative aspect (Brinton, 1890a). This was the first published contribution by Seler to what was to become one of his greatest achievements, his translations of and commentaries on Sahagún-collected Nahuatl texts. Possibly further stimulated by Brinton's report,[3] Seler the following spring (1889) traveled to Madrid to inspect the Códices Matritenses for himself, an event which constituted another of the major turning points in his scholarly career. For he quickly recognized the fundamental ethnographic and linguistic importance of these lengthy Nahuatl texts—as well as the priceless value of the illustrative material they contained—and he was to devote considerable effort over the years to their careful translation and annotation.

As early as the summer of the following year he was able to publish the paleography and translation of the sections on the costume and insignia of the deities in the *Primeros memoriales* (Tepepolco) and the *Manuscrito de Tlatelolco*, with extensive commentary (no. 30). In the fall of the same year he presented (published in 1892) to the eighth Americanist Congress in Paris the paleography and French translation, also extensively annotated, of the chapters (omitted, even in paraphrastic Spanish translation, by Sahagún in the *Historia general*) of the *Manuscrito de Tlatelolco* devoted to a description of the techniques employed by the native metallurgists, lapidaries, and featherworkers (no. 36). Both contributions were of fundamental importance. They were the first direct, essentially accurate translations into modern European languages of Sahagún-collected Nahuatl texts ever published.[4] The section on deity

---

[3] The Códices Matritenses had been exhibited during the fourth Americanist Congress in Madrid in 1881 and were mentioned in a published catalog of all MSS exhibited at the congress (Exposición, 1881). Cayetano Rosell's proposal to the Real Academia de la Historia (Madrid) that the Spanish government underwrite the cost of a critical edition of the Códices Matritenses was published in the Academy's bulletin (Rosell, 1882). Madrazo's report on the sessions of the Academy during which Rosell's proposal was discussed was published in the Academy's *Memorias* (Madrazo, 1885). The same year a detailed description of the *Códice Matritense del Real Academia de la Historia*, written by Ramírez in 1867, was published in the Academy's bulletin (Ramírez, 1885b). García Icazbalceta also paid considerable attention to the Códices Matritenses in his classic article on Sahagún in his *Bibliografía Mexicana del Siglo XVI* (1886). If Seler had access to some or all of these publications, therefore, he must have been well aware of the existence of the Códices Matritenses long before the submission of Brinton's report. See Article 14C in this volume of the *Handbook*.

[4] Brinton's 1890b publication of the Nahuatl versions of the 20 *Primeros memoriales* chants was accompanied by an attempted English translation. All competent students have agreed, however—Seler most of all—that this attempt was essentially a failure.

351

costume-insignia was of particular value, for these illustrations and texts provided Seler and other scholars with invaluable keys to the identification and interpretation of the deity representations in the native traditional pictorials. He immediately used them to excellent advantage in his Tonalamatl Aubin study, which was published this same year (no. 18).

Undoubtedly stimulated by his Sahaguntine discoveries, Seler now turned his attention increasingly to the Mexican pictorials. In 1891 he published an important pioneer study on the insignia and costume of the Mexican nobility and warrior elite (no. 40a), in which he incorporated relevant textual and pictorial data from the Códices Matritenses—and of which he published a greatly expanded version in the second volume of his Collected Works (1904), fully incorporating all of the pertinent Sahagún material in both the *Primeros memoriales* and the *Manuscrito de Tlatelolco*. In 1893 appeared his classic commentaries to the "Humboldt Fragments," 16 (really 10) post-Conquest Mexican pictorials in the Königlichen Bibliothek zu Berlin (no. 58). Although, not unexpectedly in a pioneer work, Seler made various errors in his interpretations, these were the first genuinely thorough critical analyses of nonritual Mexican pictorials, bringing all relevant material to bear, and established a model for all subsequent commentaries of this type. He also incorporated in his analysis of the first piece (whose Guerrero provenience was revealed only in 1940 by the discovery of an additional section of the screenfold and other related items in Azoyú) an important discussion of the late pre-Hispanic central Mexican calendar, including the most successful attempt to correlate it on a day-to-day basis with the Christian calendar which had been made up to that time.[5]

In 1895 Seler published his well-known study of the wall paintings of Mitla, which, justifiably, he labeled "eine mexikanische Bilderschrift in Fresko" and carefully in-

terpreted with the aid of various Mixteca-Puebla pictorials (no. 88). After a long field trip to Middle America in 1895–97, he resumed his intensive investigations into the Mexican ritual-divinatory pictorials. In 1898 he published a fundamental study (no. 99) of the 260-day divinatory cycle (*tonalpohualli*; Seler always preferred to call this the *tonalamatl*, although this term, strictly speaking, referred to the book in which it was painted rather than to the cycle itself). In the same year appeared his important article on the "Venus calendar" (no. 110) in three members of the Borgia group (stimulated by Förstemann's earlier discovery of this cycle in Dresden) and a description of and capsule commentary on Codex Borgia (no. 112). In 1899 he published a study (no. 119 [2]) of the representations of the 18 annual *veintena* ceremonies in certain central Mexican pictorials, which superseded an 1887 paper on the same topic (no. 9). These studies helped solidify the firm foundation he had built for his detailed commentaries to various important western Mesoamerican native tradition pictorials, which were soon to appear.

During this same *fin de siècle* decade, although he was now increasingly concerned with archaeological studies, Seler continued to work on his translations and analyses of the Madrid and Florence Sahaguntine Nahuatl texts, long passages of which, with the aid of his wife, he had copied between 1889 and 1893. Two of the most important fruits of his Sahaguntine project appeared in 1899. The first (no. 118) was a study of sorcery and shamanism in late pre-Hispanic central Mexico, based largely on Sahaguntine Nahuatl textual materials, which he trans-

[5] The currently most accepted correlation, that of Caso (first presented in 1938 and published in 1939), differs by only one day from that of Seler. The difference is due to Seler's hypothesis that the year took its name from the first day of Toxcatl, the fifth *veintena* in the usual system, whereas Caso maintains that the year, which began with Izcalli, took its name from the last day of the last veintena, Tititl.

cribed paleographically and translated. The second was the first part (veintenas 1–5) of a projected complete paleography, translation, and discussion of Sahagún's two (Tepepolco, Tlatelolco) Nahuatl accounts of the 18 annual veintena ceremonies (no. 119 [3]). This last publication was of special value, for these lengthy descriptions represent some of the most detailed surviving accounts, in the original language, of the rituals of an early civilization ever compiled. They are of fundamental importance for students of the religious aspect of Mesoamerican culture. Unfortunately, Seler was not able to issue the second part of these translations in his lifetime.

Seler's Mayanist interests, both ethnohistorical and archaeological, were also vigorously pursued during these years. In an important group of papers published between 1891 and 1898 he continued his pioneer studies of the lowland Maya calendar; in a familiar 1891 paper (no. 40) he analyzed the Zapotec version as well. He also utilized a great amount of ethnohistorical evidence in interpreting different Maya area archaeological specimens and monuments in various publications between 1891 and 1900, especially a triad of well-known studies on the glyphic inscriptions of Copan, Quirigua, Palenque, and the Tikal wood lintels (Seler, 1902–23, 1:712–862). His interest in Maya religion continued, and in a significant 1898 paper (no. 104) he discussed the deities mentioned in the Popol Vuh. His work on the decipherment of the hieroglyphic texts of the screenfolds also did not slacken. In the year of the four-hundredth anniversary of the discovery of America he engaged in a spirited debate, principally in the pages of *Science*, with the leading United States student of the lowland Maya pictorials, Cyrus Thomas (nos. 43, 45, 46). This was over the question—which still rages today—of whether this system was essentially "ideographic" or "phonetic," Seler steadfastly continuing to hold the former view.

Late in the next-to-last decade of the cen-tury a remarkable Maecenas for Mexicanist research appeared, Joseph Florimond, the Duc de Loubat. He was particularly interested in financing accurate facsimilies and interpretations of the most important pre- and post-Conquest native-tradition pictorials. Loubat financially backed Seler's 1895–97 Mexico-Guatemala expedition, founded a chair for him at the University of Berlin in 1899, and between 1900 and 1909 published at his expense four lengthy monographic interpretations by Seler of as many Mexican ritual-divinatory screenfolds whose facsimilies he also published: Tonalamatl Aubin (nos. 121, 122), 1900 [1900–01]; Codex Fejérváry-Mayer (no. 131), 1901 [1901–02]; Codex Vaticanus B (nos. 138, 139), 1902 [1902–03]; Codex Borgia (nos. 154, 275), 1904–09 [1963]. These famous monographs, taken together, probably represent Seler's most significant single contribution to Mesoamerican studies, and on them rests his greatest reputation. Although each was ostensibly devoted to an analysis of a single pictorial specimen, to aid his analyses Seler employed a broadranging comparative technique with the result that they also constituted fairly thorough interpretations of many other pieces as well (especially Telleriano-Remensis/Vaticanus A, Laud, Cospi [to which he also devoted a special article (no. 123) in 1900], Borbonicus, and Magliabechiano), nor were relevant Maya area data omitted.

Seler also published during this period a few articles relating to his studies of the religious pictorials. The most important of these (1906, published in 1907 [no. 187]) was that in which he declared his adherence to the lunar school of mythological interpretation of Ernst Siecke, which strongly influenced—not always favorably—the second volume (1906) of his Borgia commentary and all his later writings on Mesoamerican religion. Seler also conducted during this period his most serious foray (no. 150) into the interpretative problems of the Mixteca group of pictorials (1903). The results were disastrous, however, for he attempted to apply astronomical explanations involving presumed corrective mechanisms of the "Venus calendar" to pictorial narratives of a genealogical-historical character in the Codex Zouche-Nuttall. This paper, in fact, can be considered the only complete failure of Seler's entire scholarly career.

In 1906 Seler published his first detailed interpretation of a nonritual pictorial (no. 185) since his 1893 study of the "Humboldt Fragments," the Lienzo de Guevea (from a small Zapotec-speaking community near Tehuantepec, dynastically linked to Zaachila). His earlier Zapotec studies pursued in connection with his monograph on the Mitla wall paintings had well prepared him for this paper. In 1909–10 appeared his thorough survey and analysis of the zoological representations in the Mesoamerican native tradition pictorials (no. 204), a monumental effort which continues to be of great value. The latter year his analyses of the name and place glyphs of the "Plano en Papel de Maguey" (native plan of part of Tenochtitlan-Tlatelolco) were published as a section in volume 3 of Maudslay's English translation of the Genaro García edition of Bernal Díaz del Castillo (no. 204a). His last significant publication (no. 213) on the pictorials was a brief discussion of Codex Kingsborough (Tepetlaoztoc; cf. Paso y Troncoso, 1913) as part of his summary of the eighteenth Americanist Congress, London, 1912 (1913).

During all this time Seler never ceased to work on his Sahaguntine Nahuatl translations, although he was unable to publish more than the 20 sacred chants of the *Primeros memoriales* (1904, no. 165) and two brief texts (no. 252) from the same source (1919). Fortunately, Seler's widow was able to publish, five years after his death, his most important unpublished paleographies and translations of the Sahagún-compiled Nahuatl texts they had copied in Madrid and Florence (no. 268). Seler would probably have concentrated more on his Saha-

gún translations and studies had he not been denied further access to both the Códices Matritenses and the Florentine Codex by Paso y Troncoso's "embargo," imposed after Seler's last copying stint in 1893, which lasted until his Mexican colleague's death in 1916. Seler's commentary to and paleography and partial translation of the 20 religious chants (no. 165)—of priceless value to the student of religion—constitute one of Seler's greatest achievements for they are in a very difficult and archaic idiom.

Seler's work on lowland Maya hieroglyphic writing tapered off after an important outburst of activity around the turn of the century. His last paper exclusively devoted to the hieroglyphic writing (no. 181) in the three screenfolds was published in 1906 (coincidentally the year of Förstemann's death), although his animal representations study (no. 204) of 1909–10 contained, passim, many important discussions of the hieroglyphs connected with the zoomorphic depictions. His publications on the archaeological aspect of Mayanist research, however, actually increased during the last two decades of his life, and in these contributions he characteristically incorporated considerable data derived from documentary and pictorial sources.

In addition to his commentaries and studies on Mexican and lowland Maya pictorials and his Sahagún-collected Nahuatl text translations, Seler continued to publish various other important studies on Mesoamerican ethnohistorical themes. Outstanding examples are: his discussion (no. 65) of the "Aztlan problem" (1894); his critical analysis (no. 66) of the terms "Anahuac" and "Nahuatl" (1897); his well-known study (no. 111) of Quetzalcoatl-Kukulcan in Yucatan (1898); his classic reconstruction (no. 171) of late pre-Hispanic Tarascan culture (1908); his discussion (no. 191) of central Mexican cosmogonical-legendary themes with particular emphasis on those concerned with Topiltzin Quetzalcoatl and the Toltecs (1910); his detailed description (no.

223) and discussion (1913) of the important early Nahuatl historical document usually called today the Anales de Tlatelolco (BNP/FM #22); and his concise summary (no. 243) of pre-Hispanic central Mexican religion in the Hastings *Encyclopedia of Religion and Ethics* (1916). In the posthumous fourth volume of his Collected Works (1923) there also appeared: the first part of an important synthesis of pre-Hispanic central Mexican mythology and religion (no. 254); a perceptive discussion of the "Toltec problem" (no. 261); and an unfinished article dealing with the end of the Toltec period (with a rather speculative "epilogue" by Lehmann [no. 262]).

Between 1902 and 1915 most of Seler's papers on Mesoamerican ethnohistory, archaeology, linguistics, and ethnography were reprinted, along with many papers on non-Mesoamerican themes, in four stout volumes. A fifth volume (fourth in the series) was published by his widow a year after his death. In many cases these reprinted articles were modified and updated, and additional illustrations were frequently added. Occasionally they were thoroughly rewritten. Various original articles also appeared in these volumes.[6]

Seler's last years were made difficult by the first World War and its aftermath. When he bade farewell to Mexican shores in the fall of 1911, it was his last glimpse of the land to the study of whose native cultures he had devoted much of his life. The eighteenth International Congress of Americanists held in London in the spring of 1912 was the last he attended, for European hostilities prevented his coming to the Washington, D.C., meeting of 1915. By the time of the next congress, in Rio de Janeiro, August, 1922, he was a dying man. He had played a leading role in every Americanist Congress since the Turin meeting in 1886 (he was president of the 1910 Mexico City meeting). His Festschrift appeared in his 73rd year and contained the first nearly complete bibliography of his writings, compiled by Lehmann, as well as a compact summary, assembled by his widow, of the itineraries of his six New World trips (Lehmann, 1922).

On November 23, 1922, the soul of Eduard Seler traveled at last to *in quenamican, temohuayan in huilohuayan*, the abode of the dead, the place of descent, the end of journeys. . . .

MAJOR PUBLICATIONS

Each of the principal categories of Seler's Mesoamerican ethnohistorical researches, mentioned above, will now be discussed in detail.

Native Language Texts: Translations and Commentaries

The great bulk of Seler's contribution here was devoted to Nahuatl texts collected by Sahagún. Although he also clearly controlled Yucatecan Maya and Quiche-Cakchiquel and had a good working knowledge of the other Mayance languages as well as Zapotec, Mixtec, Tarascan, and perhaps others, Seler only published various translations of individual words and short passages in connection with the discussion of specific problems. He had apparently translated much of the Popol Vuh, the Anales de los Cakchiqueles, and the Books of Chilam Balam, but only brief passages appear scattered throughout his writings.

[6] Nine of Seler's papers and monographs, originally published between 1891 and 1898, were translated into English under the direction of Charles P. Bowditch and published in 1904 in Bulletin 28 of the Bureau of American Ethnology (no. 156). These included his studies of the "Humboldt Fragments," his monograph on the Mitla wall paintings, his paper on the "Venus calendar" in Codices Borgia, Vaticanus B, and Cospi, his paper on Mesoamerican calendric systems which included the first significant treatment of the Zapotec system, and a paper which represented one of the first attempts to correlate the katun counts of the Books of Chilam Balam with the Christian calendar. The publication of these translations, together with the English versions of three of his four Loubat-financed "codex" commentaries, served to make Seler's researches much more widely known to English-speaking scholars.

The original times of appearance of all of Seler's Sahaguntine translations and commentaries were mentioned above. As indicated, five years after his death nearly all the Sahagún-compiled Nahuatl texts he had translated were published in a single volume (no. 268). Most of these were unpublished manuscripts Seler had left behind, but Caecilie Seler-Sachs, wanting to consolidate as many of these translations as possible, included all those previously published except the 20 sacred chants (no. 165) and the sections of the *Primeros memoriales* and the *Manuscrito de Tlatelolco* devoted to the costume and insignia of the nobility published in his 1891 and 1904 articles on this subject (no. 40a).

These 1927 texts were derived from three separate Sahagún manuscript compilations which represent three stages in the development of his great ethnographic project: the Nahuatl *Primeros memoriales* (Tepepolco, 1559–61), the Nahuatl *Manuscrito de Tlatelolco* (1561–65), and the Spanish-Nahuatl *Florentine Codex* (Tlatelolco, 1578–79). At the ninth Americanist Congress in Huelva in 1892 Seler had formally urged the complete publication of the Sahagún documentation in Madrid and Florence (no. 52). After his return to Berlin that fall he attempted, without success, to obtain support for this project from the Königliche Preussische Akademie der Wissenschaften zu Berlin. He desisted from further attempts to find support, contenting himself with copying as much more as he could in Madrid the following spring and hoping that the requisite financial aid would some day be forthcoming. When, years later, in 1906, he hoped to be able to resume the task of copying further sections, he ran head-on into the Mexican government's embargo. He therefore turned to translating, over the years, as much as he could of the material he had already copied (Seler-Sachs, 1927, preface).[7]

Even though the project was truncated by circumstances beyond Seler's control, his achievement in translating this much of the

Sahagún corpus of Nahuatl texts was an extraordinary one. No one previously had successfully translated any amount of Nahuatl texts dealing with ethnographic matters. Seler's 19th-century Nahuatlato predecessors (Galicia Chimalpopoca, Brasseur de Bourbourg, Aubin, Siméon, and others) had concerned themselves almost exclusively with historical texts. Seler was breaking new ground here, and the skill and thoroughness with which he performed his task is remarkable, particularly his translations and analyses of the metaphorically obscure and idiomatically quite archaic 20 sacred chants (no. 165). His publication of the *Primeros memoriales* and *Manuscrito de Tlatelolco* sections on the costumes, insignia, and attributes of the principal deities was also an important breakthrough. Together with the famous twin post-Conquest pictorials Telleriano-Remensis and Vaticanus A, they provided the most useful key for the decipherment of the western Mesoamerican ritual-divinatory pictorials.

Although Seler's greatest fame stemmed from his substantive researches, he made no more valuable contribution to Mesoamerican studies than these paleographies and translations of hitherto unpublished Saha-

[7] His widow's 1927 publication includes:
Primeros memoriales: chap. 1, par. 2 (18 veintena ceremonies plus Atamalcualiztli), 5 (costume and insignia of the gods); chap. 2, par. 6 (Mictlan), 7 (confirmation of rulers); chap. 3, par. 11 (male sorcerers), 12 (female sorcerers).
Manuscrito de Tlatelolco (in terms of later *Florentine Codex–Historia general* format): bk. 1:1–22 (costumes, insignia, and attributes of deities—adding sections on Amimitl and Atlahua not included in FC and HG but omitting section on Tlazolteotl); bk. 2:20–38 and Appendix (2) (18 veintenas and Atamalcualiztli); bk. 8:20–21 (rearing of sons of nobles and steps through which a young man must pass to become a judge [*tecuhtlato*]), plus a chapter (15 in the MT format), omitted in FC-HG, dealing with the upbringing and education of the children of the commoners; bk. 9:16, 17 (second part), 20–21 (techniques of metallurgists, lapidaries, and featherworkers).
Florentine Codex: bk. 3:1–14 (birth of Huitzilopochtli; annual penitents dedicated to Huitzilopochtli; Tezcatlipoca; Topiltzin Quetzalcoatl of

gún-compiled Nahuatl texts, particularly those which he annotated. His widow did not exaggerate when she wrote (Seler-Sachs, 1927, preface):

Es kann nicht überraschen, dass ein grosser Teil von Eduard Selers Arbeit dieser reinen und reichfliessenden Quelle galt. Von dem Augenblick an, als die Beschäftigung mit den Kulturvölkern Amerikas seine Lebensaufgabe wurde, hat der Sahagun ihn gefesselt, begleitet und geleitet.

Western Mesoamerican Native-Tradition Pictorials: Interpretations

Seler's labors here can conveniently be broken down into those studies concerned with the "secular" pictorials and those with the ritual-divinatory group. Seler thoroughly analyzed and interpreted 10 items (nos. 58, 185) in the first category (excluding the Testerian, *Humboldt Fragment 16*). He worked just with the name and place glyphs of one, the "Plano en Papel de Maguey" (no. 204a), commented briefly on two, Cuauhtlantzinco and Kingsborough (nos. 117, 213) and utilized limited data from a number of others. As mentioned, his studies of the nine "Humboldt Fragments" (no. 58) represented the first thorough, critical analyses of this type.

Tollan); bk. 3: Appendix (1–9) (afterworlds; *telpochcalli*; *calmecac*; high priests); bk. 4:29 (Cihuateteo); bk. 5:27 (warding off sorcerers); bk. 10:29 (ethnography of central Mexico); bk. 12 (Conquest, from Tlatelolcan standpoint).

In addition, a passage of Chimalpahin's seventh *Relación* (paleography and French translation published by Siméon in 1899) concerned with the Spanish conquest of Tenochtitlan-Tlatelolco was included in the section otherwise devoted to bk. 12.

[8] For example, apart from the revelation, occasioned by the Azoyú discoveries of 1940, that the first piece hails from Guerrero rather than the Chalco-Huexotzinco region, as Seler surmised, the discovery in 1965 of the "Oztoticpac Lands Map of Tetzcoco, 1540" (Cline, 1966, 1972) indicates that the sixth piece represents the old Oztoticpac palace of the ruling family of Tetzcoco rather than the whole city of Tetzcoco, as Seler assumed. He also mistook the symbols of lineal measurements for demographic tallies.

Considering the fact that Seler was again playing the role of pioneer, his interpretations of the members of this group have held up for the most part quite well, although later discoveries have vitiated some of his conclusions.[8]

His analysis of the Lienzo de Guevea (no. 185) is another excellent performance and still stands as the only thorough interpretation of an important pictorial certainly produced in a Zapotec-speaking community. As for his brief remarks on Codex Kingsborough (no. 213), it can only be regretted that Seler never was able to undertake a complete study of this very interesting 16th-century pictorial (photographic reproduction published in 1912 by Paso y Troncoso), for which an adequate published analysis is still lacking.

Seler's long commentaries to four of the most important ritual-divinatory pictorials, Tonalamatl Aubin (nos. 121, 122) and the Codices Féjérváry-Mayer (no. 131), Vaticanus B (nos. 138, 139), and Borgia (nos. 154, 275) constitute his best-known scholarly achievement. And it certainly was a major achievement if one considers what was known about the significance of the representations in these four screenfolds and others allied to them before Seler undertook his intensive studies. In his first article (no. 8) on the Borgia group (1887) he had indicated the methodology he was to follow —working systematically from the known to the unknown, from the annotated post-Conquest pictorials such as Telleriano-Remensis/Vaticanus A, carefully comparing each piece with every other, searching out equivalent representations and parallel passages—and he displayed this method to good advantage in his original study of the Tonalamatl Aubin, presented to the seventh Americanist Congress in Berlin only one year later (no. 18). His investigations in this area received a great stimulus the following year when he gained access in Madrid to the *Primeros memoriales* pictorial representations of 37 major deities, with detailed Nahuatl itemization of their costume and insignia. He was able to incorporate many of these data in the published version (no. 18) of his first Tonalamatl Aubin commentary (1890).

Seler had been forced to work with only a ca. 1851 Aubin-ordered lithograph of the Tonalamatl Aubin (of which just the last two sheets were colored) published in 1887 as part of the fourth volume of the *Anales del Museo Nacional de México*. Shortly thereafter the Duc de Loubat initiated his facsimile publication project, commencing with the Vaticanus B (1896) and continuing with Borgia (1898), Cospi (1898), Telleriano-Remensis (1899), Borbonicus (in part, 1899), and Vaticanus A (1900). Interested in publishing the first accurate reproduction of the Tonalamatl Aubin as well, Loubat commissioned Seler to write an expanded and updated version of his 1890 commentary to go with it. Seler complied; the monograph (nos. 121, 122) appeared in 1900 (English translation, 1900–01). In the meantime (1899) an aesthetically much more sophisticated but basically quite similar *tonalamatl*, that of Codex Borbonicus, had been published, with brief commentary by Hamy. Seler, in effect, wrote a commentary on this piece as well in his Tonalamatl Aubin interpretation (cf. Paso y Troncoso, 1898), illustrating a few scenes from it by line drawings. Principally because an extensively annotated 16th-century tonalamatl (Telleriano-Remensis/Vaticanus A) was available to him to use as a departure point—as well as highly relevant illustrative and textual data in the Sahagún documentation, Durán, Codex Magliabechiano, and other sources—Seler's interpretation was in general quite successful. Even today it requires only minor corrections and additions.

The Duc de Loubat also commissioned a Seler commentary to accompany his forthcoming facsimile of Codex Féjérváry-Mayer. Both appeared (no. 131) in 1901 (English translation, 1901–02). There is no "standard" tonalamatl in Féjérváry-Mayer, and

most of its sections are difficult to interpret although most of the deities can be identified. Seler's elucidation of this piece, therefore, was much less successful than his Tonalamatl Aubin commentary.

The next year saw the publication of another Loubat-financed Seler commentary (nos. 138, 139), this time on Codex Vaticanus B, the first facsimile in the Loubat series. This screenfold does contain two tonalamatl, one in the same format as Telleriano-Remensis/Vaticanus A–Aubin–Borbonicus, plus other sections related to the 260-day divinatory cycle in at least a partially understandable fashion. Much of Seler's interpretation, therefore, is solid and convincing. For the more obscure sections, however, his explanations are often quite speculative; some are certainly erroneous.

Seler's great Loubat-financed commentaries were capped by a particularly detailed commentary on the most spectacular member of the Borgia group, the Borgia itself (no. 154). It appeared in two parts, in 1904 and 1906 (with a brief added section, an index and errata, by Lehmann, in 1909). In this lengthy monograph Seler, in effect, interpreted the major sections of all members of the Borgia group and many related pieces outside the group. Again, it can be said that Seler's interpretations of the clearer, most obviously tonalpohualli-connected Borgia sections are generally sound, but for the more obscure sections, especially the unique long central section (sheets 29–46), they are often even more speculative than those advanced in his commentaries on the Codices Féjérváry-Mayer and Vaticanus B. Although the Borgia commentary was more important than the other three, no English translation was issued, and it consequently had a more restricted dissemination. Fortunately, in 1963 a reasonably accurate Spanish translation (no. 275) was published in Mexico, along with a new facsimile. In spite of its many imperfections, Seler's Codex Borgia commentary can be fairly characterized as probably the single most important treatise on pre-Hispanic Mesoamerican religion yet published.[9]

As indicated above, Seler published only a short article on Cospi (no. 123). However, since this piece is much briefer than the others and all sections of its obverse are cognate with sections in Borgia, Vaticanus B, and/or Féjérváry-Mayer, whereas its reverse is generally cognate with sections of the last named, he, in effect, also interpreted Cospi in his commentaries to the other three. Seler never devoted any article or monograph formally to Laud, Féjérváry-Mayer's "twin," but the few sections which are cognate with other members of the group were interpreted in the appropriate commentaries. Two other pictorials often classified with the Borgia group, Fonds Mexicain 20 and Porfirio Díaz Reverse, were also interpreted in part by Seler, particularly in his Borgia commentary. The first named, however, was the subject of a special study by his most prominent pupil, Lehmann, in 1905 (with brief comment by Seler [no. 172]).

As speculative as they frequently are— and rarely was Seler so speculative elsewhere, the result of his frequently trying to explain more than the limited data available to him would reasonably allow plus his earlier "Venusian" and later "lunar obsessions"—these long commentaries are remarkable displays of erudition and powers of analysis. They often display Seler's interpretational skills at their very best. They will probably never be entirely superseded. Certainly no serious student of pre-Hispanic Mesoamerican civilization can afford to ignore them.

[9] See Nicholson, 1966, for a brief comment on Seler's Borgia commentary, occasioned by the Mexican Spanish translation of 1963. Cf. Nowotny, 1961.

[10] In a recent survey of the history of the decipherment of lowland Maya hieroglyphic writing, Kelley (1962, p. 7), for example, stated, "The tremendous range of Seler's contributions to the study of the Maya hieroglyphs has been most inadequately recognized in the English and American literature of Mayan studies."

Mayanist Researches

As was pointed out above, Seler began his scholarly career as much, if not more, a Mayanist as a Mexicanist. This distinction, however, is essentially a recent one. At the time Seler initiated his researches it was scarcely recognized, certainly least of all by Seler himself, who more than any other major student of his period emphasized the essential unity of the higher cultures of Mesoamerica. However, for convenience, his investigations into the ethnohistory of the Mayance-speaking regions of Mesoamerica will be treated more or less separately here.

Between 1886 and 1910 Seler published a number of papers devoted wholly or in part to the problem of the decipherment of lowland Maya hieroglyphic writing. Most of them were much more concerned with the hieroglyphic texts in the three surviving screenfolds than with the inscriptions on the monuments, although three important turn-of-the-century contributions (1899–1900) dealt with the inscriptions of Copan, Quirigua, Palenque, and Tikal. In his commentaries on the Mexican pictorials he frequently discussed comparable passages in the three lowland Maya books. During this same period he also published important papers on Maya calendrics, utilizing both the three surviving screenfolds and various documentary sources, particularly Landa, the Books of Chilam Balam, and the highland Guatemala sources.

No Maya specialist, to my knowledge, has thoroughly appraised Seler's contributions to a greater understanding of the Maya writing system and calendar. It seems clear that English-speaking students, at least, have consistently tended to undervalue them.[10] Among Seler's most important contributions were: the identifications of the four color glyphs associated with the direction glyphs (no. 13); his recognition (no. 40) of the Akbal-Lamat-Ben-Etz'nab set of year bearers in Codex Dresden (contrasting with the Kan-Muluc-Ix-Cauac set current in northern Yucatan at Contact); his many significant discussions and identifications of the deity representations and their name and title hieroglyphs in the pictorials, which included various important corrections of the influential Schellhas alphabetical classification (e.g., nos. 5, 10, 11, 13, 14, 111, 154, 181, 204); his convincing demonstration (no. 82) of the true length (20 × 360 days) of the katun; his penetrating pioneer analysis (no. 14) of the 20 day signs and the terms for them in different Mayance languages and their relationships to the terms in other Mesoamerican languages; his tentative readings (nos. 5,7, 10, 11, 13, 14, 111, 154, 181, 204) of various glyphs and glyph groups in the three screenfolds, some of which have received wide acceptance if not always clear recognition of his priority of discovery (see, especially, Kelley, 1962, passim); and his near understanding (Seler, 1902–23, 1:851–62) of the significance of the controversial "seating of" glyph (see Thompson, 1950, pp. 119–21).

Seler quickly accepted and championed the important discoveries of Förstemann concerning the mechanism of the Long Count, with its "zero point," 4 Ahau 8 Cumku, and the Venus cycle. He also played a useful role as critic of the work of others. His corrections of the Schellhas deity classification scheme have been mentioned (a work later effectively carried on, above all, by Thompson and Zimmermann). His criticisms of Thomas and Goodman were often well taken and helped to discourage further perpetuation of their errors. Seler's firm conviction of the essentially "ideographic" nature of the script and his prestige and influence obviously played a significant role in causing the long eclipse of the "phonetic approach" after Thomas' famous "retraction" in 1904.

Seler's productivity as a student of the lowland Maya pictorials and the hieroglyphic writing fell off sharply during his last years. The reasons for this are not entirely clear. His increasing preoccupation with Mexicanist research in the narrower sense, his growing interest in archaeological description, the rapid rise of the United States school of calendric-astronomical epigraphers, led by Bowditch and Morley, and, perhaps most importantly, his conviction that major breakthroughs were simply impossible if the ideographic theory was accepted, all apparently combined to cause him to phase himself out of further productive research in a field to which he had made a number of significant pioneer contributions.[11]

Seler was also quite conversant with the Maya area documentary sources, both in Spanish and in the aboriginal languages. He used this background frequently to good advantage in his important study (no. 111) of Quetzalcoatl-Kukulcan in Yucatan (1898) and his later archaeological contributions (Chacula, 1901; Chichen Itza, 1910–15; Acanceh, 1911; Palenque, 1915; "Quetzalcoatl-Fassaden," 1916; Uxmal, 1917; and others). His overall contribution in this area, however, was not a major one. It remained for later scholars more intensively specialized in Maya research, above all, Roys, Barrera Vásquez, and Recinos, to make the more significant advances in this aspect of Maya ethnohistory.

Ethnographic and Culture-Historical Syntheses

Seler was obviously intellectually much more disposed to analysis than synthesis— or, to phrase it in more current parlance, he was strongly "problem-oriented"—but he did produce various general discussions and summaries which were of considerable value. It will be recalled that his first publication (no. 1) was a co-translation (with much revision and new material added by himself) of a general synthesis of American In-

[11] See his pessimistic and highly conservative statement at the end of his 1908 article analyzing the representations and hieroglyphs on a vessel from Nebaj, Guatemala (Seler, 1902–23, 3:729).

dian cultures. His first original effort along this line, a summary (nos. 32, 33) of late pre-Hispanic central Mexican religion in *Ausland* (1890–91), is little known and was superseded by his later work. At the time, however, it provided a more general audience with a convenient summary of the knowledge of the subject he had acquired up to that time. His compact summaries, both largely derived from documentary and pictorial sources, of Mesoamerican musical instruments and shamanism and witchcraft (nos. 113, 125) in *Globus* (1899, 1900) can also be considered to fall, in some sense, in this category. His remarkably comprehensive study (no. 204) of the animal representations in the Mexican and Maya pictorials (including much archaeological data), published in *Zeitschrift für Ethnologie* in 1909–10, also deserves mention here again, although its theme is somewhat specialized. His summary (no. 243) of late pre-Hispanic central Mexican religion in the Hastings *Encyclopedia of Religion and Ethics* (1916) represents the only concise overall synthesis he ever published on this subject he knew so well and effectively expresses his more mature views.

Toward the end of his life Seler was trying to produce some significant syntheses, but these efforts were cut short by his final illnesses and death. He had completed the first five chapters of an ambitious general account of central Mexican native religion and mythology, which were published posthumously in volume 4 (no. 254) of the Collected Works, as well as fragments (no. 266) of a popular book on Mexico based in part on ethnohistorical sources. Seler also published two interesting papers (1895, 1902) about midway through his career dealing with the always controversial question of the origins of Mesoamerican civilization, which utilized considerable documentary-pictorial data (nos. 86, 142). His resolute antidiffusionist position is strongly affirmed in both.

Worth special mention are his very useful summary (no. 88) of Zapotec history, religion, and calendar in his monograph on the Mitla wall paintings (1895) and, above all, his synthesis (no. 171) of late pre-Hispanic Tarascan culture (1908). The latter is remarkable because it represents the only attempt Seler, who was so well equipped for it, ever made to reconstruct more or less comprehensively a pre-Hispanic Mesoamerican culture (based largely on the *Relación de Michoacan*). It also represents his only serious excursion into the still poorly cultivated field of west Mexican ethnohistory. Its great value and utility cause regret only that Seler did not produce more syntheses of this character, particularly for the area he knew best, central Mexico.

EVALUATION

Seler's great contributions to sheer knowledge should be apparent enough from the foregoing discussion. Although he did not concern himself with all areas of Mesoamerican civilization as known from documentary and pictorial sources, those aspects which did stimulate his interest he characteristically investigated with thoroughness and perception. Seler's achievement, however, goes well beyond this. It can be argued (cf. Caso, 1949; Nicholson, 1962) that Seler's disciplined analytic methodology represents an even greater contribution to Mesoamerican studies. Although he occasionally violated his own principles in his anxiety to explain more than the limited evidence available to him would permit, his basically critical approach, his thoroughness and remarkable breadth of knowledge, lent nearly all his work special value.

Seler was very conscious of his pioneering role—he seems to have been quite attracted to it—and he felt strongly that a scholar, like any good explorer, should proceed cautiously, methodically, step by step as he moved into relatively unknown territory. The level of specificity and detail on which he customarily proceeded obviously somewhat intimidated and even sometimes frustrated fellow students. He himself on occasion felt obliged almost to apologize for his own thoroughness. Nevertheless, his conviction was firm, as he expressed it at the end of his meticulous study of the costume and insignia of the late pre-Hispanic central Mexican political and military elite (Seler, 1902–23, 2:619):

Mit Generalideen, Hineindeutungen und Auffassungen wird man nicht zur Klarheit gelangen. Das Erste ist die Feststellung des Thatsächlichen. Und dass das Verfolgen der Einzelheiten weitere Aublicke nicht ausschliesst, ja in vielen Fällen diese erst ermöglicht, das wird dem Leser auch in der obigen rein technischen Studie nicht entgangen sein.

In an appraisal and understanding of Seler's scholarly approach and methods he should, of course, be placed within the context of the intellectual atmosphere of his time, pre–World War I Germany. Thoroughness and critical positivism were then particular hallmarks of all high-level German scholarship at its best. Against the larger backdrop of turn-of-the-century Berlin, in whose leading scholarly and academic circles Seler and his wife so freely and successfully moved, his achievement does not perhaps seem so remarkable. Many of his contemporaries in other fields fully equaled or surpassed his productivity and knowledge. However, in the Middle American field even in Germany there was really no one to rival the overall scope of his erudition (the only serious candidate was Förstemann, but he was far more of a narrow specialist than Seler). Outside of Germany, only Paso y Troncoso even approached him in scholarly stature, but the Mexican student was considerably more specialized and made his greatest single contribution as a discoverer and editor of important unpublished documents (Article 21), a field in which Seler never seemed to be much interested apart from his Sahaguntine translation project.

After Seler, Middle American ethnohistory and archaeology could never really be quite the same—and never were quite the same. This is perhaps the most accurate measure of the impact of a scholar on the development of his particular specialty. In Germany and the rest of Europe his influence has been lasting and pervasive, his banner being carried forward most successfully by his students, Lehmann, Krickeberg, and Termer, and, in turn, their students and associates, Kutscher, Zimmermann, Nowotny, Barthel, Spranz, and others. A fellow countryman and indirect disciple, Hermann Beyer, introduced Seler's rigorous research methods into Mexico. Beyer's pupil, Alfonso Caso, carried on the Selerian tradition of superior scholarship with remarkable success commencing in the 1920s, while effectively transmitting it to the younger generation of Mexican ethnohistorians and archaeologists, in which task Jiménez Moreno and Kirchhoff have latterly also played major roles. In the English-speaking world Seler's impact seems to have been more gradual; perhaps Thompson has been most influenced by it and best exemplifies his thorough, broad, critical approach.

The comprehensive history of Mesoamerican studies remains to be written. When it is, Seler's entire scholarly career will finally receive the critical attention it has long deserved. Until then, it is hoped that this brief summary of only the ethnohistorical aspect of his broad-ranging Mesoamerican researches will be of some utility. As Thompson (1950, p. 28), speaking of Seler's brilliant countryman and colleague, Förstemann, remarked, "It is well to cite the record of this remarkable man, for with the recent progress in Maya archaeology the great contributions of the pioneers in the field are easily forgotten." Too easily, one might add. Without sufficient knowledge of the step-by-step development of any field of research one's perspective cannot be very sophisticated, entirely apart from the ever-present danger of needlessly repeating work done long before. An adequate knowledge of the career and accomplishments of this even more remarkable man, the Nestor of Middle American studies, therefore, would seem to be indispensable for any serious student of Mesoamerica's past.

APPENDIX. SELER, SELECTED WRITINGS OF ETHNOHISTORICAL INTEREST

These papers and monographs are listed chronologically. The majority are taken (with slight correction and modification) directly from Anders, 1967, whose numeration precedes the entry. GA refers to:

SELER, EDUARD
1902–23 *Gesammelte Abhandlungen zur Amerikanischen Sprach und Altertumskunde.* 5 vols. Berlin, Asher (vols. 1, 2) and Behrend (vols. 3–5). Offset reprint, by Akademische Druck- u. Verlagsanstalt, Graz, 1960–61. Mimeographed English translations of the majority of the German language articles, issued by Carnegie Institution of Washington (edited by J. Eric S. Thompson and Francis B. Richardson), Cambridge, 1939. Index (Wort- und Sachregister) to vols. 1–3, Berlin, Behrend, 1914.

* * *

1884

1. Die ersten Menschen und die prähistorischen Zeiten mit besonderer Berücksichtigung der Urbewohner Amerikas. Nach dem gleichnamigen Werke des Marquis de Nadaillac herausgegeben von W. Schlösser und Ed. Seler. Autorisierte Ausg. (Stuttgart, 1884, Ferd. Enke). 8°. XII und 527 S., Titelbild und 70 Textholzschnitte. Kap. VIII–XIII, Die Urbewohner Amerikas, 146–351.

1886

5. Maya-Handschriften und Maya-Götter. Ztschr. f. Ethn., XVIII (1886). Vdhlg. (416)–(420). GA, 1:357–66.

1887

6. Das Konjugationssystem der Maya-Sprachen. Inaug.–Dissert. 1887 (Berlin, 1887, Gebr. Unger). 8°. 51 S. und Lebenslauf. GA, 1:65–126.

7. Über die Bedeutung des Zahlzeichens 20 in der Maya-Schrift. Ztschr. f. Ethn., XIX (1887). Vhdlg. (237) bis (241), ill. GA, 1:400–06.

8. Der Codex Borgia und die verwandten aztekischen Bilderschriften. Ztschr. f. Ethn., XIX (1887). Vhdlg. (105) bis (114). GA, 1:133–44.

9. Eine Liste der mexikanischen Monatsfeste. Ztschr. f. Ethn., XIX (1887). Vhdlg. (172) bis (176). GA, 1:145–51.

10. Über die Namen der in der Dresdener Handschrift abgebildeten Maya-Götter. Ztschr. f. Ethn., XIX (1887). Vhdlg. (224) bis (231), ill. GA, 1:367–89.

11. Entzifferung der Maya-Handschriften. Ztschr. f. Ethn., XIX (1887). Vhdlg. (231) bis (237), ill. GA, 1:390–99.

1888

13. Der Charakter der aztekischen und Maya-Handschriften. Ztschr. f. Ethn., XX 1–38 und 41–97 (1888), ill. GA, 1:407–16.

14. Die Tageszeichen der aztekischen und der Maya-Handschriften und ihre Gottheiten. Ztschr. f. Ethn., XX 10–97 (1888), ill. Nachtrag 1.c. (16)–(18). GA, 1:417–503.

18. (see 121) Das Tonalamatl der Aubinschen Sammlung und die verwandten Kalenderbücher. VII Am. Kgr., Berlin, 521–735 (1888 [1890]), 173 Abb.

1889

19. Die Chronologie der Cakchiquel-Annalen. Ztschr. f. Ethn., XXI (1889). Vhdlg. (475) bis (476). GA, 1:504–06.

19a. Der altmexikanische Federschmuck des Wiener Hofmuseums und über mexikanische Rangabzeichen im Allgemeinen. Ztschr. f. Ethn., XXI (1889). Vhdlg. (63) bis (85), ill.

1890

30. (see 192, 268) Altmexikanische Studien I.

Ein Kapitel aus den in aztekischer Sprache geschriebenen, ungedruckten Materialien zu dem Geschichtswerk des Padre Sahagun (Göttertrachten und -attribute). Veröff. a. d. Kgl. Mus. f. V. I, Heft 4, 117–74 (Berlin, 1890), ill. GA, 2:420–508.

1890/91

32, 33. Religion und Kultus der alten Mexikaner. "Ausland": LXIII 781–86; 814–17 (1890); LXIV 81–85, 112–15, 776–80, 794–99, 814–20, 825–29, 861–69 (1891).

34. Uitzilopochtli, Dieu de la guerre des Aztèques. VIII Am. Kgr., Paris, 387–400, 3 Abb. (1890 [1892]).

35. (cf. 66) Sur le mot "Anauac." VIII Am. Kgr., Paris, 586–87 (1890 [1892]).

36. (see 268) L'orfèvrerie des anciens Mexicains et leur art de travailler la pierre et de faire des ornements en plumes. VIII Am. Kgr., Paris, 401–52 (1890 [1892]), ill. GA, 2:620–63.

39. ad Cod. Tro und Cod. Cortesianus. Zusammengehörigkeit beider Maya-Bilderhandschriften. VIII Am. Kgr., Paris, 653–54 (1890 [1892]).

1891

40. Zur mexikanischen Chronologie mit besonderer Berücksichtigung des Zapotekischen Kalenders. Ztschr. f. Ethn., XXIII, 89–133 (1891), ill. GA, 1:507–54 (1902). [Mexican chronology with special reference to the Zapotec calendar. Smithsonian Inst., Bull. 28, pp. 13–15, ill. Washington, 1904.]

40a. Altmexikanischer Schmuck und soziale und militärische Rangabzeichen. Ztschr. f. Ethn., XXIII (1891). Vhdlg. (114)–(144), ill. GA, 2:509–619 (greatly expanded).

1892

43. On Maya Chronology. Science, XX, no. 496. New York, 1892. GA, 1:557.

44. Neue Beiträge zur mexikanischen Chronologie. Ztschr. f. Ethn., XXIV (1892). Vhdlg. (311) bis (313).

45. Ein neuer Versuch zur Entzifferung der Maya-Schrift. Globus, LXII, 59–61 (1892), ill. GA, 1:558–61.

46. Does there really exist a phonetic key to the Maya hieroglyphic writing? Science, XX, no. 499. New York, 1892. GA, 1: 562–67.

52. Vorschlag, die aztek. Mss. Sahaguns herauszugeben mit der Übersetzung Sahaguns. IX Am. Kgr., Huelva, I, 108–11 (1892 [Madrid, 1894]).

52a. Sobre la escritura hierática del Yucatán. IX Am. Kgr., Huelva, I, 108–11 (1892 [Madrid, 1894]).

1893

54. Mexikanische Gemälde. Ztschr. f. Ethn., XXV (1893). Vhdlg. (178) bis (179). GA, 2:669–71.

57. Die Columbus-Festschriften der Kgl. Bibl. in Berlin und der mexikanischen Regierung. Vhdlg. d. Ges. f. Erdkd. Berlin, 1893, 511 bis 521. GA, 1:152–61.

58. Die mexikanischen Bilderhandscriften Alexander von Humboldts in d. Kgl. Bibl. zu Berlin (1893). I. A. d. Gen.-Verw. der Kgl. Bibl. Berlin, Fol. (1893). GA, 1:162–300. [Mexican picture writings of Alexander von Humboldt. Smithsonian Inst., Bull. 28, pp. 127–229, ill. Washington, 1904.]

60. Is the Maya hieroglyphic writing phonetic? Science, XXI, no. 518. New York, 1893. GA, 1:568–75.

61. Some additional remarks on Maya hieroglyphic writing. Science, XXI, no. 524. New York, 1893. GA, 1:576.

61a. Das Fest der (ungesalzenen, ungewürzten) Wasserkrapfen. (Paleography of Nahuatl text and German translation of account of Atamalcualiztli ritual in Códice Matritense del Real Palacio, fols. 253v–254r [Primeros memoriales, chap. 1, par. 2 (B)], plus color plate of depiction of ceremony.) In J. Walter Fewkes, "A Central American ceremony which suggests the Snake Dance of the Tusayan villagers," American Anthropologist, o.s., 6:285–306.

1894

65. Wo lag Aztlan, die Heimat der Azteken? Globus, LXV, 317–24 (1894), ill. GA, 2: 31–48.

66. (see 35) Über die Worte "Anauac" und "Nauatl." X Am. Kgr., Stockholm, 36–37, 211–44, ill. (1894 [1897]). GA, 2:49–77.

70. Förstemann, Kl. Abhdlg. Maya-Venusumlauf. X Am. Kgr., Stockholm, 141–42 (1894 [1897]).

1895

82. Die wirkliche Länge des Katuns der Maya-Chroniken und der Jahresanfang in der Dresdener Handschrift und auf den Copan-Stelen. Ztschr. f. Ethn., XXVII (1895). Vhdlg. (441) bis (449), ill. GA, 1:577–87.

83. Bedeutung des Maya-Kalenders für die historische Chronologie. Globus, LXVIII, Nr. 3, S. 37–41 (1895). GA, 1:588–99. [Significance of the Maya calendar in historic chronology. Smithsonian Inst., Bull. 28, pp. 327–37. Washington, 1904.]

84. Bespr. Brinton, A Primer of Maya hieroglyphics. Ztschr. f. Ethn., XXVII, 192 (1895).

86. (see 142) Über den Ursprung der altmexikanischen Kulturen. Habilitationsrede. Preussische Jahrbücher, LXXIX, 488–502 (1895). GA, 2:3–15.

88. Wandmalereien von Mitla. Eine mexikanische Bilderschrift in Fresko, nach eigenen, an Ort und Stelle aufgenommenen Zeichungen herausgegeben und erläutert. Fol., 58 S., 55 Abb., 13 Tafeln (in rot). Index 51–56 (Berlin, 1895, A. Asher & Co.). [Wall paintings of Mitla. Smithsonian Inst., Bull. 28, pp. 247–324. Washington, 1904.]

89. Wandmalereien von Mitla. XI Am. Kgr., México, 87, 274 (1895 [1897]).

90. Chicomoztoc; Geldsurrogate. XI Am. Kgr., México, 64–65 (1895 [1897]).

1897

98. Eine angeblich in Nordamerika gefundene Aztekenhandschrift. Globus, LXXII, 33, 1 Abb. (1897).

1898

99. Das Tonalamatl der alten Mexikaner. Ztschr. f. Ethn., XXX (1898). Vhdlg. (165) bis (177), ill. GA, 1:600–17.

100. Der Festkalendar der Tzeltal und der Maya von Yukatan. Ztschr. f. Ethn., XXX, 410–16 (1898). GA, 1:706–11.

104. Über die Herkunft einiger Gestalten der Qu'iché- und Cakchiquel-Mythen. Arch. f. Relig. Wiss., I, 91–97 (1898). GA, 3:573–77.

110. Die Venusperiode in den Bilderschriften der Codex Borgia-Gruppe. Ztschr. f. Ethn., XXX (1898). Vhdlg. (346) bis (383), ill. GA, 1:618–67. [Venus period in the picture writings of the Borgian Codex Group. Smithsonian Inst., Bull. 28, pp. 335–91. Washington, 1904.]

111. Quetzalcouatl-Kukulcan in Yucatán. Ztschr. f. Ethn., XXX, 377–416 (1898), ill. GA, 1: 668–705.

112. Der Codex Borgia. Globus, LXXIV, 297–302, 315–19 (1898), ill. GA, 1:301–40.

113. Mittelamerikanische Musikinstrumente. Globus, LXXVI, 109–12 (1899), ill. GA, 2:695–703.

1899

117. Die mexikanischen Gemälde von Cuauhtlantzinco. Globus, LXXV, 96–97 (1899). GA, 1:352–54.

118. Altmexikanische Studien II. (1) Zauberei und Zauberer im alten Mexico. Veröff. K. Mus. f. Völkerkunde, Berlin, VI, Heft 2–4, S. 29–57, ill.

119. (see 268) Altmexikanische Studien II. (2) Die bildlichen Darstellungen der mexikanischen Jahresfeste 58–66, ill. (3) Die achtzehn Jahresfeste der Mexikaner (1. Hälfte) 67–209, ill. Veröff. K. Mus. f. Völkerkd., Berlin, VI, Heft 2–4, S. 58–209. Nachtrag und Berichtigung 210–11, Index 212–24.

120. Widerlegung der Theorie vom asiatischen Ursprung der zentralamerikanischen Kulturen. Globus, LXXV, 166–67 (1899).

1900

121, 122. (see 18) Das Tonalamatl der Aubinschen Slg. Eine altmex. Bilderhandschr. der Bibl. Nat. in Paris (Mss. Mex. Nr. 18–19). Auf Kosten S. Exz. des Herzogs von Loubat hrsg. mit Einleitung und Erläuterungen. Fol. obl. (Berlin, 1900). (a) 2 S. Vorwort; 145 S., 51 Textabb.; (b) Tafel 3–20 (Codex), (Index 183–145), (Tageszeichenlisten: Mexiko, Nicaragua, Metztitlan, Guatemala, Cakchiquel, Zo'tzil, Maya, Zapoteken 6–8). Engl. Übers. von Keane (Berlin-London [Asher], 1900–01).

123. Codex Cospi, die mexikanische Bilderhandschrift von Bologna. Globus, LXXVII, 323–325 (1900), ill. GA, 1:341–51.

125. Zauberei im alten Mexiko. Globus, LXXVIII, 89–91 (1900), ill. (Kurzfassung in: Universum. Natur und Technik, 16 Jg. Heft 15/16, S. 436–438, 2 ill., Wien, 1961). GA, 2:78–86.

129. Die Ausgrabungen am Orte des Haupttempels in México. *Mittheilungen der An-*

thropologischen Gesellschaft in Wien. Vol. 31 (3d ser., vol. 1), pp. 113–37. Vienna. (Reprinted in his *Gesammelte Abhandlungen,* vol. 4, pp. 767–904, 1904.) Devoted almost entirely to archaeological matters.

1901

130. Pinturas jeroglíficas. Colección Chavero. (Fälschungen!) Ztschr. f. Ethn., XXXIII (1901). Vhdlg. (266).
131. Cod. Féjérváry-Mayer. Eine altmexikanische Bilderhandschrift des Free.-Public-Museums in Liverpool (12014/m) auf Kosten Sr. Exz. des Herzogs von Loubat herausgegeben, erläutert von Ed. Seler. 4°. VI und 230 S., 219 Textabb. und Tafeln. Index 213–230 (Codex in roten Konturen nebst Interpretation). (Berlin, 1901). Engl. Übers. von Keane (Berlin-London [Asher], 1901–1902).

1902

138. Codex Vaticanus Nr. 3773 (Cod. Vatic. B). Eine altmexikanische Bilderschrift der Vatikanischen Bibliothek, herausgegeben auf Kosten Sr. Exz. des Herzogs von Loubat. 4°. VI und 331 S., 585 Abb., Index 335–356, in 2 Hälften (Vorder- und Rückseite des Codex) mit Tafeln (Berlin, 1902).
139. Codex Vaticanus B. Im Auftrag des Herzogs von Loubat (1902–1903). Engl. Übers. von Keane (Berlin-London [Asher] 1902–1903).
141. (see 165) On ancient Mexican religious poetry. XIII Am. Kgr., New York, 171–74 (1902 [1905]).
142. (see 86) Über den Ursprung der mittelamerikanischen Kulturen. Ztschr. Ges. f. Erdkd., Berlin, XXXVII, 537–52 (1902). GA, 2:16–30.
143. On the present state of our knowledge of the Mexican and Central American hieroglyphic writing. XIII Am. Kgr., New York, 157–70 (1902 [1905]), ill.

1903

150. Die Korrekturen der Jahreslänge und die Länge der Venusperiode in den mexikanischen Bilderschriften. Ztschr. f. Ethn., XXXV, 27–49, 121–55 (1903), ill. GA, 3:199–220.

1904

152. Druck des diccionario de Motul. XIV Am. Kgr., Stuttgart, LXXV–LXXIX (1904 [1906]).
154. (see 275) Codex Borgia. Eine altmexik.

Bilderschrift d. Bibl. der Congregatio de Propaganda Fide [Rom]. Herausgegeben auf Kosten Sr. Exz. des Herzogs von Loubat. (I) (Tafel 1–28). 4°. IV und 353 S. 586 Abb. (Berlin, 1904). (II) (Tafel 29–76). 4°. Vorwort, 310 S. 304 Abb. (Berlin, 1906). (III) Nachtrag und Index (von Dr. W. Lehmann). 4°. Vorwort (Berlin, 1909). Nachtrag zu Kap. 21. [Analogie des Zapotek. od. Cuikatek. Cod. Porfirio Diaz 1–4 (5 Abb.)], Index 5–152, Druckfehlerverzeichnis 153–154.

156. see Beiträge in: Mexican and Central American Antiquities, Calendar Systems and History. Translated from the German under the supervision of Ch. P. Bowditch. Smithsonian Institution, Bureau of American Ethnology, Bull. 28, pp. 13–391, 651–64 (Washington, 1904), ill. Neben Arbeiten von Förstemann, Schellhas, Sapper und Dieseldorff sind in dem Sammelband folgende ethnohistorischen Publikationen Selers übersetzt: 40, 58, 83, 88 und 110. [Notes and emendations 667–70.]
162. Memoriales des Fray Toribio Motolinia. XIV Am. Kgr., Stuttgart, S. LIX–LX (1904 [1906]).
165. (see 141) Die religiösen Gesänge der alten Mexikaner. GA, 2:959–1107.

1905

171. Die alten Bewohner der Landschaft Michoacan. [Geschrieben Herbst 1905]. GA, 3:33–156.
172. ad Lehmann, Ms. Aubin 20. Ztschr. f. Ethn., XXXVII, 871 (1905). (Codex Vindob., Cod. Nuttall.)

1906

181. Parallelen in den Maya-Handschriften. Globus, XC, Nr. 12, S. 187–193, 14 Abb. (1906). GA, 3: 695–709.
185. Das Dorfbuch von Santiago Guevea. Ztschr. f. Ethn., XXXVIII, 121–155 (1906), ill. GA, 3:157–93.

1907

187. Einiges über die natürlichen Grundlagen der mexikanischen Mythen. Ztschr. f. Ethn., XXXIX, 1–41, 11 Abb. (1907). GA, 3:305–51.

1908

191. Die Sage von Quetzalcouatl und den Tolteken in den in neuerer Zeit bekanntgewordenen Quellen [W. Lehmann, Historia de Colhuacan y de México]. XVI Am. Kgr.,

Wien, 129–150, 9 Abb. (1908). GA, 5:178–96.

1908/09

192. (see 30, 268) Costumes et attributs des divinités du Mexique selon le P. Sahagun. Journal de la Soc. des Am. Paris, n.s. 5, S. 164–220 (1908), ill.; n.s. 6, S. 101–46 (1909), ill.

1909/10

204. Die Tierbilder der mexikanischen und Maya-Handschriften (mit Taf. IV und 1005 Abb.). Ztschr. f. Ethn. 1909/1910, XLI, 209–57, 301–451, 784–846 (1909); XLII, 31–97, 242–87 (1910), ill. GA, 4:453–758.

1910

204a. "Plan of Maguey Fiber": Identifications of place and name glyphs. In Alfred P. Maudslay, The true history of the conquest of New Spain by Bernal Diaz del Castillo, one of its conquerors, from the only extant copy made of the original manuscript edited and published by Genaro García. Printed for the Hakluyt Society. Vol. 3 (pamphlet), pp. 17–25. London.

1912

213. Bericht über die 18. Tagung des intern. XVIII, Am. Kgr., London, 27 Mai bis 1 Juni, 1912. Ztschr. f. Ethn., XLIV, 525–48, 19 Abb. (1912). GA, 5:152–67.

1913

222. Der Bedeutungswandel in den Mythen des Popol Vuh. Anthropos (1913). (Bespr. über Pohorilles.)

223. Das Manuscrit Mexicain Nr. 22 der Bibl. Nationale (Paris). Sitzber. K. P. Akd. d. Wiss. Berlin, LIII, phil.-hist. Cl., 1029–1050, 5 Abb. (1913).

1916

243. Mexicans (ancient). In William Hastings, ed., Encyclopedia of Religion and Ethics, vol. 8, pp. 612–17. New York.

1919

251. Tal von Mexiko. Deutsch-Mexikanische Rundschau, I, Nr. 1, S. 6–8; Nr. 2, S. 4–7 (1919).

252. (see 268) Kleinere mexikanische Texte. Fr. Bernardino de Sahagún, Ms. Acad. de la Hist. f. 84 (Madrid). (1) Bestattung des Königs. (2) Das Leben in der Unterwelt. Deutsch-mexikanische Rundschau, I, Nr.

3/4, S. 30–31 (Sept., Oct., 1919).

253. Der Einmarsch der Spanier in die Hauptstadt König Moctezumas. Zur Erinnerung an die Eroberung Mexikos vor 400 Jahren. Illustrierte Zeitung, Leipzig, CLIII, Nr. 3986, S. 623–624, mit 13 Abb. (20 Nov. 1919). GA, 4:445–52.

1920

254. (see 259, 272) Mythus und Religion der alten Mexikaner. (1) Das Weltbild der alten Mexikaner 3–38. (2) Entstehung der Welt und der Menschen, Geburt von Sonne und Mond 38–64. (3) Die ersten Menschen und die Sternenwelt 64–98. (4) Der Hauptmythus der mexikanischen Stämme und der Kulturheros von Tollan 98–156. (5) Uitzilopochli, der sprechende Kolibri (156–167). Erster Abschnitt der GA, 4:1–167.

1921

257. Cacao, Cacahuet, Cacavuete. Deutschmexikanische Rundschau, III, Nr. 1, S. 5–6.

1923

261. Zur Toltekenfrage (Vortrag, Historiker-Kongress, Liverpool, 1912. GA, 4:342–51.

262. Das Ende der Toltekenzeit (unvollendet, mit einem Nachwort von W. Lehmann). GA, 4:351–61.

264. Totemismus in Mittelamerika. GA, 4:384–88.

266. Bruchstücke einer allgemein verständlichen Darstellung des Landes Mexiko, seiner Bevölkerung und seiner Entdeckungsgeschichte [Das mexikanische Land. Die eingeborene Bevölkerung Mexiko's. Die alte und die neue Welt und ihre Beziehungen zueinander (Entdeckungsgeschichte). Im Angesichte der Opferinsel. Der Einmarsch der Spanier in die Hauptstadt König Motecuhçoma's (see 253)]. GA, 4:403–52.

1927

268. Fray Bernardino de Sahagún. Einige Kapitel aus dem Geschichtswerk des-. Aus dem Aztekischen übersetzt von Eduard Seler. Hsgg. von Cäcilie Seler-Sachs in Gemeinschaft mit Walter Lehmann und Walter Krickeberg. 4°, XI und 574, mit Abb. im Text und auf Tafeln (Stuttgart, Strecker und Schröder). An Stelle des im Vorwort zum IV. Band angekündigten VI. Bandes der GA, der Übersetzungen aus dem Sahagun und des Popol Vuh enthalten sollte, nachdem deren Aufnahme in den IV. Band wegen des zweisprachigen Satzes 1923 nicht

möglich war; Die Gründe für das Fehlen einer Gesamtübertragung der Werke Sahaguns sind im Vorwort S. VIII–X angeführt; das Werk enthält folgende Abschnitte:

1. Die Götter (Ms. der Biblioteca del Palacio, Madrid, Hdschr. a; Span. Ausg., Buch I, Kap. 1–22).
2. Tracht und Attribute der Gottheiten (Ms. de Biblioteca del Palacio, Madrid, Hdschr. b; mit ausführlichen Erläuterungen in GA, 2:420–508).
3. Die Jahresfeste (Ms. der Biblioteca del Palacio, Madrid, Hdschr. a und b; Span. Ausgabe, Buch II, Kap. 20–38 und App., Kap. II; Über die ersten fünf Feste siehe 119).
4. Uitzilopochtli und Tezcatlipoca (Biblioteca Laurenziana, Florenz; Span. Ausg., Buch III, Kap. 1 und 2).
5. Quetzalcouatl von Tula (Biblioteca Laurenziana, Florenz; Span. Ausg., Buch III, Kap. 3–14).
6. Die Wohnorte der Toten (Biblioteca Laurenziana, Florenz; Academia de la Historia, Madrid; Span. Ausgabe, Buch III, App., Kap. 1–3; vgl. 252).
7. Von den im Kindbett gestorbenen Frauen (Biblioteca Laurenziana, Florenz; Span. Ausgabe, Buch IV, Kap. 29).
8. Die Erziehung der Knaben (Academia de la Historia, Madrid; Span. Ausgabe,

Buch VIII, Kap. 36 und 37; Biblioteca Laurenziana, Florenz; Span. Ausgabe, Buch VIII, App. Kap. 4–9).
9. Zauberer, Gaukler, Wahrsager, schlechte Weiber (Academia de la Historia, Madrid; Biblioteca Laurenziana, Florenz).
10. Die Kunst der Goldschmiede, Steinschneider und Federarbeiter (Academia de la Historia, Madrid; siehe 36 mit zahlreichen Anm.).
11. Die Völker (Biblioteca Laurenziana, Florenz; Span. Ausgabe, Buch X, Kap. 29).
12. Die Eroberung der Stadt Mexiko (Biblioteca Laurenziana, Florenz; Span. Ausgabe, Buch XII; weiters p. 193–199 aus der 7. Relación Chimalpains). Eine freie Verwendung ohne den aztekischen Text erfolgte in 274.

1962

274. Das Herz auf dem Opferstein. Aztekentexte. Aus der Ursprache übertragen von Eduard Seler. Ausgewählt und mit einem Vorwort versehen von Janheinz Jahn. Vlg. Kiepenheuer & Witsch, Düsseldorf.

1963

275. (see 154) Comentarios al Códice Borgia, I und II; Códice Borgia. Fondo de Cultura Económica. México. (= Span. Ubers. von 154 + Faks. Ed.).

REFERENCES

ANDERS, FERDINAND
1967   Wort- und Sachregister zu Eduard Selers Gesammelte Abhandlungen zur Amerikanischen Sprach- und Altertumskunde. Akademische Druck- u. Verlagsanstalt. Graz.

BRINTON, DANIEL
1890a On the Nahuatl version of Sahagún's "Historia de Nueva España." Congrès International des Americanistes, *Compte rendu* (Berlin, 1888), pp. 83–89 (with comment by Seler and others).
1890b Rig Veda Americanus: Sacred songs of the ancient Mexicans, with a gloss in Nahuatl. *Library of Aboriginal American Literature*, 8. Philadelphia.

CASO, ALFONSO
1939   La correlación de los años azteca y cristiano. RMEA, 3:11–45. [Reprinted, with modifications in text and illustrations, in Caso, 1967, pp. 41–64.]
1949   Influencia de Seler en las ciencias antropológicas. *El México Antiguo*, 7:25–28.
1967   Los calendarios prehispánicos. UNAM, Instituto de Investigaciones Históricas, Serie de Cultura Náhuatl, Monogr. 6.

CHIMALPAHIN QUAUHTLEHUANITZIN, DOMINGO FRANCISCO DE SAN ANTÓN MUÑON
1889   Annales: Sixième et septième relations (1258–1612). Rémi Siméon, trans. and ed. *Bibliothèque linguistique americaine*, 12. Paris.

CLINE, HOWARD F.
1966   The Oztoticpac lands map of Texcoco, 1540. *Quarterly Journal of the*

Library of Congress, 23:75–115. Washington.

1972 Oztoticpac lands map of Texcoco, 1540. *In* Walter W. Ristow, comp., A la Carte: Selected papers on maps and atlases, pp. 5–33. Library of Congress. Washington.

EXPOSICIÓN

1881 Lista de los objetos que comprende la Exposición Americanista. M. Romero, ed. Madrid. [Catalog of MSS exhibited at the Fourth International Congress of Americanists, Madrid, 1881.]

FÖRSTEMANN, ERNST

1886 Erläuterung zur Mayahandschrift der Königlichen öffentlichen Bibliothek zu Dresden. Warnatz und Lehmann. Dresden.

GARCÍA ICAZBALCETA, JOAQUÍN

See Article 21, Appendix D.

HÖPFNER, LOTTE

1949 De la vida de Eduard Seler: recuerdos personales. *El México Antiguo*, 7:58–74.

JIMÉNEZ MORENO, WIGBERTO

1949 Seler y las lenguas indígenas de México. *El México Antiguo*, 7:16–21.

KELLEY, DAVID H.

1962 A history of the decipherment of Maya script. *Anthropological Linguistics*, 4(8):1–48. Bloomington, Ind.

LEHMANN, WALTER

1905 Die fünf im Kindbett gestorbenen Frauen des Westens und die fünf Götter des Südens in der mexikanischen Mythologie. *Zeitschrift für Ethnologie*, 37:848–71.

1922 Festschrift Eduard Seler; dargebracht zum 70. Geburtstag von Freunden, Schulern und Verehrern. Strecker und Schröder. Stuttgart.

LINGA, CARLOS R.

1949 Eduard Seler. *El México Antiguo*, 7:7–10.

MADRAZO, PEDRO DE

1885 Resumen de los acuerdos y tareas de la Academia Real de la Historia desde 30 de abril de 1882 hasta igual día de 1884. RAH, *Memorias*, 10:671–706.

MARTÍNEZ DEL RÍO, PABLO

1949 Lo que México debe a Eduardo Seler. *El México Antiguo*, 7:22–24.

NADAILLAC, MARQUIS DE

1881 Les premiers hommes et les temps préhistoriques. Paris.

1883 L'Amérique préhistorique. Paris.

NICHOLSON, H. B.

1962 *Review of* Eduard Seler, "Gesammelte Abhandlungen zur Amerikanischen Sprach- und Altertumskunde, 2d ed., Akademische Druck- u. Verlagsanstalt, Graz. *American Anthropologist*, 64:1097–1101.

1966 A note on "Comentarios al Códice Borgia." *Tlalocan*, 5:125–32.

NOWOTNY, KARL A.

1961 Tlacuilolli: die mexikanischen Bilderhandschriften, Stil und Inhalt; mit einem Katalog der Codex-Borgia-Gruppe. Monumenta Americana herausgegeben von der Ibero-Amerikanischen Bibliothek zu Berlin. Schriftleitung: Gerdt Kutscher, 3. Berlin.

PASO Y TRONCOSO, FRANCISCO DEL

See Article 21, Appendix F.

RAMÍREZ, JOSÉ F.

See Article 21, Appendix B.

RIVET, P.

1923 Obituary of Eduard Seler. *Journal de la Société des Americanistes de Paris*, 15:280–87.

ROSELL, CAYETANO

1882 "Historia universal de las cosas de la Nueva España" por el M. R. P. Bernardino de Sahagún. RAH, *Boletín*, 2:181–85.

SCHELLHAS, PAUL

1886 Die Maya-Handschrift der Kgl. Bibliothek in Dresden. *Zeitschrift für Ethnologie*, 18:12–84.

SELER, EDUARD

See Article 20, Appendix.

SELER-SACHS, CÄCILIE

See Article 20, Appendix, no. 268.

SIMÉON, RÉMI

1889 *See* Chimalpahin Quauhtlehuanitzin, 1889.

TERMER, FRANZ

1949a Eduard Seler. *El México Antiguo*, 7:29–57. [German and Spanish versions.]

1949b La importancia de Eduard Seler como investigador e impulsor de las ciencias americanistas. *El México Antiguo*, 7:11–15.

THOMPSON, J. ERIC S.

1950 Maya hieroglyphic writing: introduction. Carnegie Institution of Washington, Pub. 589. Washington.

21. Selected Nineteenth-Century Mexican Writers on Ethnohistory

HOWARD F. CLINE

URING THE 19TH CENTURY Mexican investigators provided a larger contribution to historical reconstruction of the Indian past than did any other national group. Foreigners like Brasseur de Bourbourg (Article 18) and Bancroft (Article 19), as well as a galaxy of Europeans like Seler (Article 20), Rosny, and others who concerned themselves with archaeology, ethnohistory, and the precolonial period, aided the Mexican effort to discover their national roots, but the main burden fell on Mexicans (see vol. 12, Introduction; Comas, 1950, pp. 99–100). Cumulatively the Mexican endeavors in the national period provided the modern student with an abundance of historical riches.

Among the many Mexican contributors of that era the names of José Fernando Ramírez, Manuel Orozco y Berra, Joaquín García Icazbalceta, and Francisco del Paso y Troncoso are familiar and outstanding. Of lesser stature, but near the top of a second echelon, is Alfredo Chavero. In the highly selective treatment of these writers here the name of Carlos M. Bustamante has been included, less for any lasting value of his work than as an early prototype of the group of national historians who helped establish important and continuing traditions of Mexican historiography.

These canons came into being largely to fulfill one general requirement of modern nationalism. It prescribes that a separate nationality or nation must consciously know and unconsciously share an historical legacy whose unique elements differentiate it from others. To provide such a shared sense of the past was the expressed or latent assumption underlying much historiographical activity in 19th-century Mexico. In this common aim after 1821 these writers of the national period differed from colonial writers, who shared no such single patriotic goal.

Although agreeing on the need for a better knowledge of the Mexican past, historians were divided in view on what it was and what it meant. A basic philosophical and political issue lay at the heart of their disagreements, and even today it continues to affect interpretations and emphasis. What the nature of Indian society was at the

G. 1—CARLOS MARÍA DE BUSTAMANTE. From lado Álvarez, 1933.

Some of these matters have already been touched upon in the Introduction (vol. 12) to this Guide.

Many new themes have attracted the attention of recent Mexican historians (Jiménez Moreno, 1952; Manrique, 1966). One theme to which, unfortunately, they still give only sparse attention is Mexican historiography of the 19th century. There is a continuing stream of useful general and monographic works on Mexican colonial writers (see Articles 12 and 13), but not even a single comparable general work on the many major and minor figures for the national period, let alone detailed studies of them (González, 1966, p. 51). Monographic biobibliographical treatments which do appear on 19th-century writers are more likely to be concerned with political or literary figures than with professed or amateur historians. Fortunately, however, there is a modest monographic base of description and analysis for the selected writers we have chosen here to discuss.

CARLOS MARÍA BUSTAMANTE, 1774–1848

Carlos María Bustamante typifies an early generation in Mexican national historiography. Born in Oaxaca November 4, 1774, he was educated there and took a law degree in the waning days of the viceroyalty. He played an increasingly active role in the Mexican independence movement, was captured and imprisoned by royalist forces, and, on his release, continued his agitations against the remaining Spanish and their defenders even after separation from Spain was an accomplished fact. During the first quarter of Mexico's independent existence after 1821 he intermingled his considerable talents as journalist, politician, and self-taught historian in a noteworthy and highly controversial career that ended with his death September 1, 1848.

Apart from dozens of periodical articles and political speeches, Bustamante during his life published more than 20,000 pages of history and left many works in manuscript.

coming of the Spaniards, and whether Spanish rule during the colonial period enriched or impoverished Mexico, are questions at the root of an ancient yet still vital controversy.

Generally speaking, those who stress Indian contributions are loosely grouped as "indigenistas." Others, who especially emphasize the importance of European colonial elements over the native in Mexico's national development, are classed as "Hispanistas." In presentation of materials, in selection of documents and research topics, the writers of one group tend to denigrate or at least understate the contributions of the other and to question the values they represent. Mexican history seen from an advanced indigenista point of view appears quite distinct from that presented by a dogmatic Hispanist (Velázquez, 1966, p. 483).

Until recently a mysterious labyrinth, this vast corpus was given some bibliographical control by a seminar under the direction of Edmundo O'Gorman (1967). Apart from an index of Bustamante's parliamentary effusions, their pioneering guide contains 487 general items, of which nos. 175–325 are Bustamante manuscripts found scattered in the United States and Mexico.

In an extended, almost unique analytical account of Bustamante, Ortega y Medina (1963) demonstrated how the contemporary and later reputation of the man clearly reveals the continuing ideological battles in Mexico between indigenistas, of whom Bustamante was an archetype, and the Hispanistas, equally symbolized by his contemporary and antithesis, Lucas Alamán (Velázquez, 1948). In addition to clashing directly in political forums, these two major historians of their era waged an early national battle of the books. Bustamante's *Cuadro histórico de la América mexicana . . .* (5 vols., 1821–27; augmented 2d ed., 1843–46) and Alamán's *Historia de México, con una noticia preliminar del sistema de gobierno que regía en 1808* (5 vols., 1849–52), drawing on many of the same sources and covering similar ground, could not be more opposed in interpretation. For Alamán, Spain was the great cultural mother, with Mexican independence an undeserved act of ingratitude by malcontent creoles like Bustamante; Indians and Indian history do not figure greatly in Alamán's various works. Bustamante, of course, rejected this cool analysis, with glorification of the Indian past, exaltation of the heroes of Independence, and application of the Black Legend to Spain's rule in Mexico.

By an ironic twist of fate many of the later 19th-century criticisms of Bustamante derive from a pamphlet which Alamán published anonymously in 1849, shortly after Bustamante's death, entitled *Noticias biográficas del licenciado don Carlos María Bustamante y juicio crítico de sus obras, escritas por un amigo de don Carlos y más*

amigo de la verdad (Alamán, 1849, 1946). The factual base of the "friend's" [!] treatment was a highly colored set of autobiographical notes that Bustamante himself had published anonymously in 1833 under the curious title *Hay tiempos de hablar, y tiempos de callar*, with a list of Bustamante's previous works appended (pp. 35–36). Alamán's harsh judgments formed an arsenal of critical remarks on which later conservative writers like García Icazbalceta (1853) drew heavily for inclusion in compilations like the *Diccionario universal de historia y geografía*. The sole book-length political biography of Bustamante, written by a Spaniard in the Alamán tradition, depicts him as a mediocre buffoon (Salado Alvarez, 1933, 1968). As might be expected, in view of Bustamante's strong interests in the precolonial Indian past and his passionate nationalism, he has been undergoing rapid rehabilitation in 20th-century Mexican indigenista intellectual circles (Ortega y Medina, 1963, pp. 47–58).

Works

Bustamante's own writings on ethnohistory have only minimal merit, beyond being clear indicators of the climate of opinion in his era. In them he penned highly politicized accounts to serve civic and patriotic ends, illustrating clearly his unquestioned belief that history should be an important weapon in the war of ideas. The Indian past for him was both a model of virtue that newly independent Mexican nationals should emulate, and a horrible example of the tyrannical and rapacious Spanish culture that had robbed them of their own culture and burdened Mexico with a colonial legacy that should be extirpated. His most extended ethnohistorical account, two volumes of ancient Mexican history, *Mañanas de la alameda de Mexico* (1835–36), a didactic text, expounds these views at length. So, too, his *Galería de antiguos príncipes mexicanos* (1821) shows the parallelism between the Aztec and European societies in the 15th century, to the marked advantage of the former. Bustamante's *Historia del emperador Moctheuzoma Xocoyotzin* (1829) portrays him as a model ruler. Yet another pamphlet was given a title which states its purpose: to show that perfidious Spaniards had subverted the Republic of Tlaxcala and had cunningly persuaded those hereditary enemies of the Aztecs to carry on the European conquest for them.[1]

His publication of ethnohistorical sources sprang from these same political urges, and they express the same themes in their titles. The work of Fernando de Alva Ixtlilxochitl, for instance, was baptized, "Horrible cruelties of the conquerors of Mexico, and of the Indians who helped them subjugate it for the Crown of Castile . . ." (Bustamante, 1829b). Appendix A lists selected works.

Bustamante's importance to us here is his first making such basic but heretofore unpublished sources like that known. In his zeal to create a patriotic history of Mexico, he issued first editions of the works of Alegre (1841–42), Cavo (1836–38), Beaumont (1826d), Veytia (1826c), Alva Ixtlilxochitl (1829b), and above all, Sahagún's *Historia* (1829a, 1829–30). He also published a long defense of his own work by León y Gama (1832) and manuscript works of Boturini (1821, 1822). These were historiographical landmarks at the beginning of a national tradition.

Evaluation

There has been universal criticism of Bustamante's editorial habits and methods. Even by mid-19th-century Mexican historiographical standards, García Icazbalceta's charge (1853, p. 758) that Bustamante had "committed all the faults an editor can incur" is not overly exaggerated. Careless transcription, omissions, insertion of editorial opinions without clear indications, and argumentative irrelevant notes unrelated to the text are but some characteristic features. Bustamante's own traits as a credulous and superficial historian further vitiate the works. Hence for modern scholarship his editions of sources are more literary curiosities than useful founts of data.[2]

Two considerations, however, must be kept in mind. First, Bustamante did not publish these sources to serve some abstract scientific goal of historical truth, but to serve avowed political purposes. Second, even had the former aim been paramount, it must also be remembered that modern canons of historical editing had not emerged clearly by Bustamante's time. In general they developed slowly in Germany, starting with the appearance of *Monumenta Germaniae Historica* (1826–), also originally stimulated by patriotic urges to provide Germans with a common history for political purposes. Knowledge of the newer editorial and historiographical standards diffused slowly to Mexico, chiefly through Ramírez' and García Icazbalceta's acquaintance with William H. Prescott and his works, long after Bustamante's several publications of sources had appeared. Bustamante was a child of his times, an age in which as distinguished a contemporary United States scholar and editor as Jared Sparks (1789–1866) could unconcernedly alter and change published documents of the American Revolution to serve patriotic and civic ends. These circumstances perhaps help explain Bustamante's serious scholarly lapses; they obviously do not condone or remove them.

For purposes here, Bustamante is significant. With all his scholarly defects and with all the drawbacks in his publications, his work early initiated an important Mexican national tradition of searching out and publishing basic materials on the Indian past and its fate in the colonial period. Later, more skilled hands refined and "purified" this early national tradition through appli-

---

[1] *Necesidad de la unión de todos los megicanos contra las asechanzas de la nación española y liga europea, comprobada con la historia de la antigua República de Tlaxcallan* (Mexico, 1826).

[2] Bustamante, 1840, is a possible exception.

cation of less subjective methods, but Bustamante serves as a transitional link in the transfer of ethnohistoriography from late colonial times (Clavigero and others) into the new national context, where it has since remained.[3]

José Fernando Ramírez, 1804–1871

"Without having written a history of Mexico," Alfredo Chavero ([1887], p. lx) said of his mentor and colleague, "Ramírez is, nevertheless, the foremost of our historians." This was an opinion widely shared in Mexico and abroad during the late 19th century.

Born May 5, 1804, in Hidalgo de Parral, Chihuahua, José Fernando Ramírez was the son of José María Ramírez and Josefa Alvarez. His father was a colonel in royal service and also a rich miner. The boy was educated in Durango, capital of the colonial intendancy of Nueva Vizcaya. He then took legal training in Zacatecas, Guadalajara, and Mexico City. Despite the death of his father in 1828, he continued studies of law, and in 1832 received his final professional degrees and was admitted to the bar. Throughout most of his life he practiced jurisprudence at state, national, and international levels, while simultaneously carving out diverse careers as public servant, historian, archaeologist, litterateur, essayist, and bibliophile. Ramírez corresponded extensively with William H. Prescott and other foreign historians.

He served as representative and senator in Congress. Among numerous other posts, in 1852–54 he was director and curator of the National Museum, which he reorganized along lines it followed for many years. In political exile 1855–56, he visited Europe to search in libraries and archives for documentary materials related to Mexican history (Gardiner, 1962, pp. 29–30). He was allowed to copy manuscripts, codices, and

Fig. 2—JOSÉ FERNANDO RAMÍREZ. From Ramí[?] 1898–1904, vol. 1, frontispiece.

other documents of prime importance. Only the Vatican failed to allow him to work in its collections. On this trip he visited Alexander von Humboldt in Potsdam (1855).

When Ramírez returned to Mexico in 1856 he again (1857) was appointed to the directorship of the National Museum, a post he held until 1864. Among other duties he headed the executive council of the Acad-

---

[3] Other references not cited in the text are: Martínez Baez, 1963; Gurría Lacroix, 1964, pp. 161–68.

emy of Fine Arts. As director of the embryonic National Library, he busied himself in collecting for it books and manuscripts from various religious houses which the Mexican Reform was extinguishing.

Ramírez became closely identified with conservative political groups which invited Emperor Maximilian to the ephemeral Mexican throne. Under him, Ramírez served as Imperial Minister of Relations and President of the Council (July, 1864–March, 1866). When French troops were withdrawn and it appeared that Maximilian's Empire was doomed, Ramírez returned to Europe to continue his unending quest for historical materials. He retired to join his family in Bonn, Germany, where he died March 4, 1871. Thus in sparse outline is Ramírez' rich and varied life, a more extended account of which is given by González Obregón (1898, pp. v–xxv).

The Ramírez Collections

Ramírez was an untiring collector of books and historical manuscripts. In 1851 his library in Durango contained, according to his own count, some 7,477 volumes; of these about 3,200 related to law, and another 2,800 to history. Unsuccessfully he attempted to donate to the Mexican government (which was then considering establishing its National Library) his collection as well as a property to house it, if he would be made life director, with a residence, salary, and staff paid from government funds. When forced to leave Durango for political reasons in 1851, Ramírez sold this library and his house to the state for 31,000 pesos, withholding some 20 boxes of materials, including manuscripts concerned with the history of Mexico. The first Ramírez collection formed the beginnings of the State Public Library.

At that time he resolved to acquire only the bare minimum of books he needed for his research, but by 1858 (after his European trip) his second library amounted to 8,178 volumes, chiefly on American, Asian, Egyptian, and Nubian antiquities. He had two copies (one an author's gift) of Kingsborough's enormous work, *Mexican Antiquities*, which Ramírez had corrected by comparing drawings of codices with the originals in Paris, Oxford, Berlin, Vienna, Dresden, Bologna, and Rome (González Obregón, 1898, pp. xiv–xx).

After Ramírez' death (1871) his collection was dispersed. It came first from Germany to Mexico, where a majority of the books and manuscripts were sold by Ramírez' heirs to Alfredo Chavero. While retaining some, the latter in turn resold most of the library to Manuel Fernández del Castillo on the express condition that it would not be sold abroad. Despite this condition, Fernández del Castillo placed all but a few on sale (1880) in London, where H. H. Bancroft purchased the bulk of the offerings (see Article 19; González Obregón, 1898, pp. xlv–xlvi). Other titles were obtained by collectors like E. E. Ayer and the Library of Congress. Some 20 volumes, entitled *Opúsculos históricos*, manuscripts of Ramírez' own works and his copies of documents remain with other similar materials in the Archivo Histórico del Instituto Nacional de Antropología e Historia (q.v., Article 28). Many of Ramírez' other compilations and papers are lost or in unknown private hands (González Obregón, 1898, pp. xliii–xliv).

Publications

In his 1898 introduction to the collected works of Ramírez, Luis González Obregón listed various of Ramírez' published and unpublished works (1898, pp. xvi–xliii). For our purposes those he categorized "Various Writings" and "Juridical Defenses and Cases" (pp. xxvi–xxx) are of little interest. Under the headings "Historical and Biographical Studies" and "Unpublished Writings and Compilations," however, appear useful summaries showing the wide range of Ramírez' investigations and the considerable body of information he published in the field of ethnohistory. A selected list of Ramírez' works of ethnohistorical interest appears in Appendix B.

From it will be seen that his first (1844) was a series of notes and essays relating to native sources, calendar, archaeological remains, details on Cortés, and other supplemental data to strengthen Prescott's treatments. Retired to his study while American troops were in Mexico City, Ramírez in 1847 published the residencia of Pedro de Alvarado, with biographic notices, and notes on pictorial documents; the latter, which were also issued separately, deal with the Manuscrito de Aperreamiento and Codex Ríos (Vaticanus A) (see Article 23, Items 9 and 270; Ramírez, 1847b). He contributed several important articles to the 10-volume encyclopedia on Mexican history and geography (Andrade and Escalante, 1853–56), in the field of jurisprudence and ancient Mexican history.

One result of his European exile was a detailed description (1855) of Mexican codices in the National Library of Paris (still unpublished). Seemingly while in Paris Ramírez arranged to have made and distributed lithographs of numerous codices in the Aubin Collection, prepared by Jules Desportes at the Imperial Institute for Deaf Mutes (Chavero, 1884, pp. 243–45; González Obregón, 1898, pp. xxxv–xxxvi).

On his return to Mexico, Ramírez in 1858 published lithographs of the Mapa Sigüenza and Códice Boturini, with commentary on each. Further comments on these which Ramírez made about 1860 on the basis of manuscript materials appeared much later (Ramírez, 1945, 1952, 1953). In 1859 Ramírez provided a long biobibliographical study of Motolinía, to precede García Icazbalceta's publication of the *Historia de los Indios* (see Article 13, Bibliography, Benavente, 1858).

Two items which Ramírez published in his lifetime related to an extensive plan he had developed to reissue major sources.

Neither was completed. In 1863 he wrote a long account of the baptism of Montezuma II, which was to form part of introductory material to projected publication of Diego Muñoz Camargo's *Historia de Tlaxcala*; Ramírez never published the latter, although apparently the edition issued by Chavero (1892b) was based on Ramírez' copy and utilized his notes, though not this published piece (González Obregón, 1898, p. xxxvii). In the dying days of Maximilian's Empire, Ramírez issued the first of three volumes reprinting Durán's *Historia* (1867a); later (1880) the remaining two volumes (one text and an atlas) appeared, with the plates copied earlier by Ramírez, and a somewhat confused commentary on Aztec religion and migration history by Chavero. In addition to Durán, Ramírez had projected editions of Alvarado Tezozomoc, Alva Ixtlilxochitl, and Tovar (Códice Ramírez). Again, some of these later appeared under Chavero's and Vigil's editorship from the Ramírez copies.

Of special interest is Ramírez' plan to reissue Sahagún. In collating the version which Bustamante had published (1829–30) against the text published by Kingsborough (1830–31), Ramírez had encountered innumerable errors and deficiencies in both versions which as early as 1850 he expected to correct. He proposed also to add materials from his study of various codices—Telleriano-Remensis, Vaticanus B, Mendocino—and to reproduce from these what he thought were the illustrations to the *Historia general*, unaware of the Florentino manuscript (González Obregón, 1898, pp. xxxvii–xxxviii). In 1867 Ramírez wrote a still useful history of the Sahagún manuscripts in Madrid, published posthumously (1885b, 1903), but his edited version of Sahagún seems to be among the lost Ramírez manuscripts.

Following Ramírez' death in 1871 various hands mined materials which he had left. We have seen that Chavero extended Ramírez' work by publishing his materials. At present it is not fully known how much of the relatively large body of materials published by Chavero represents his own work and how much of it derives rather directly from Ramírez, many of whose materials Chavero obtained following the latter's death.

Other posthumous publications of Ramírez materials (listed in Appendix B) derive from manuscripts presently in INAH. Among these is a contribution of bibliographical importance: Ramírez' additions to the basic Beristáin (1816–21) biobibliographical coverage, published in 1898. Earlier appeared Ramírez' Foreword to the two-volume manuscript collection known as "Anales antiguos de México y sus contornos" (Ramírez, 1885a). In the shoddy editions of Luis Vargas Rea, *Anales* 1–4 of that collection were published in 1948. The main corpus of the *Anales* still awaits a scholarly edition. Vargas Rea also issued in 1945 and 1952 Ramírez' commentaries on Códice Boturini, Telleriano-Remensis, Ríos (Vaticanus A), and the Anales de Cuauhtitlan.

As may be inferred, Ramírez marks a major advance over many of the same activities undertaken earlier by Bustamante. Ramírez was aware of many of the native pictorial and prose sources, as well as those in the European traditions related to ethnohistory, most of which he had examined in the original, and many of which he had copied. His own studies, while now generally superseded, lack the polemical tone of Bustamante, and his publications of texts are generally reliable. With contemporaries like Joaquín García Icazbalceta, with whom he corresponded (Teixidor, 1937), Ramírez was influential in improving and extending the

Fig. 3—MANUEL OROZCO Y BERRA. From Orozco y Berra, 1960.

national scholarly tradition in Mexico of gathering and publishing for scholarly use the basic native pictorial and written records from which reliable ethnohistory could be written.[4]

MANUEL OROZCO Y BERRA, 1810–1881

Manuel Orozco y Berra has many points of similarity with his intellectual master and political protector, José Fernando Ramírez. The biobibliography of Orozco y Berra reveals these.[5]

Born in Mexico City June 8, 1810, Manuel Orozco y Berra was the son of a minor military figure of Mexican independence, Captain Juan Nepomuceno Orozco (who fought with Mariano Matamoros) and María del Carmen Berra, a devout Catholic. Manuel went to school in Mexico City during the troubled days of the Independence

[4] Consulted but not cited in the text is a more recent study: Moreno, 1965.

[5] Incorporated into this treatment is material from a draft article on Orozco y Berra prepared in Spanish by Miguel León-Portilla at the invitation of the Volume Editor before volume 13 underwent editorial reorganization. Use of that manuscript, especially for its bibliography, is gratefully acknowledged.

revolution, entering the famous College of Mines in 1820, from which he received a degree in topographic engineering in 1834. Economic and political circumstances removed him in 1835 to Puebla, where he held various technical posts while studying law. In 1847 he earned his degree, with highest honors. During his stay there he began a literary career by writing for local journals. Ramírez, with whom he became a close friend, called him back to Mexico City in 1852 and obtained a post for him in the National Archives, of which he later became director.

Active in scientific circles, Orozco y Berra was named to rectify the official map of the Mexican Republic (1856). He was appointed chief administrative officer in the Ministry of Development in 1856, and in the following year he became minister. During these years he also contributed various articles to the Andrade and Escalante *Diccionario Universal* (1853–56). At the same time he edited and published four series (20 volumes) of documents on Mexican history (see Article 11). Various of his official reports from the Ministry of Development indicated a growing interest in historical geography, distributions of native tongues, and related ethnohistorical matters.

Apparently Orozco y Berra had previously been part of the Liberal republican faction headed by Benito Juárez, when Maximilian's Empire was established in Mexico through French collaboration with conservative Mexican political forces. Despite this association, he, from penury, remained in Mexico City and accepted various posts under the Empire. He became a member of the Council of State (headed by Ramírez) and director of the National Museum, a post refused by Brasseur de Bourbourg. Orozco y Berra (1864) prepared an elaborate administrative plan for the territorial reorganization of Mexico under the Empire (Bassols Batalla, 1963; O'Gorman, 1966, pp. 161–66).

When the Empire fell (1867), Orozco y Berra did not seek exile in Europe, as did Ramírez, probably because of lack of funds. The restored Republican government sentenced Orozco y Berra to four years in prison and fined him 4,000 pesos for his collaboration in the Intervention. Shortly thereafter he was released, and his fine halved. However, he never fully returned to public life, although he continued to be a major figure in the activities of the Mexican Society of Geography and Statistics. He accepted a post as minor functionary in the National Mint, and during the final decade of his life devoted himself quietly at home to historical studies, especially the preparation of his magnum opus, the *Historia antigua* (1880b), only two volumes of which had appeared by the time of his death January 27, 1881.

In the Introduction to the latter, after dutifully thanking his patrons for the small job in the Mint which cared for the pressing needs of his growing family, Orozco y Berra pathetically pointed out that this post had been essential to solve "the problem which has so preoccupied me during a lifetime, to have simultaneously both time and money" (Orozco y Berra, 1880b, 1:vi). This basic economic constraint made it necessary for him to use the libraries of others—especially Ramírez, García Icazbalceta, Andrade—as he could amass none of his own. Despite severe limitations of time and money, Orozco y Berra produced a respectable body of scholarly work. It has several times been detailed at length (Sosa, 1884; Sosa and others, 1890; Carreño, 1945b; Rico González, 1953). Appendix C lists a selection.

Our own attention now shifts to the two main works on which his reputation essentially rests, his *Historia antigua y de la conquista de México*, and *Historia de la dominación española en México*. These have been analyzed in detail by Susana Uribe Ortiz (1963) in a very useful monograph.

Historia antigua y de la conquista de México

The *Historia antigua* is a four-volume

work, to which is appended an unpaginated small folio volume of 18 numbered plates (on each of which are several items) and a foldout sketch map of Mexico City and environs at the time of Conquest. The plates reproduce numerous individual native place glyphs, calendrical signs, and other graphics which Orozco y Berra had found in searching the several native documents he utilized.

After having worked in the sources for many years, Orozco y Berra in the *Historia antigua* quite self-consciously aimed to provide a major synthesis of Indian Mexico at the coming of the Spaniards, and to give as circumstantial an account as possible of the Conquest. To complete these matters through the later colonial period, he had already written *Historia de la dominación española en México*, treating developments from 1522 through 1789 (see next section), which was not published in his lifetime. Thus one primary aim of his major works was to provide a synthesis, heretofore lacking, of Mexican history from precolonial times to the close of the 18th century, a time span longer than that embraced by colonial writers like Torquemada, Robertson, Clavigero, or even more modern ones of his own era like Prescott. At the time the *Historia antigua* was written, the major portion of Bancroft's work had not appeared (Article 19).

Orozco y Berra was a child of his times. Those times had seen a considerable advance over Bustamante, even Ramírez, in concepts of historiography, especially at the hands of the German historians who increasingly stressed the critical approach, use of firsthand sources, and psychological as well as sociological relationships of events, generally related if possible to "universal principles." Orozco y Berra was especially influenced by the great German historian Leopold von Ranke (1795–1886), whose method for preparation of his classic *Die römischen Päpste* (3 vols., 1834–36) Orozco y Berra sought to apply to Mexican history (Uribe Ortiz, 1963, pp. 16–17). Like von Ranke, he hoped consciously to free himself from subjective passions of race, religion, party, or patriotism, and to write dispassionate, "scientific" history, a goal at the polar extreme from that of Bustamante.

This intent appears in the introductory remarks to *Historia antigua* (1:v–vi), where Orozco y Berra notes that previous authors who had treated the themes he was covering could be divided into two main groups. One, for reasons of religion, race, or view of civilization, disregarded Indians and exalted Spaniards; the other, for patriotic or philosophical reasons, attributed more virtues to Indians than they really merited, and sought to denigrate Spanish heroes. He stated that he hoped to avoid these extremes, and would attempt to seek truth and justice as impartially as possible.

He proposed to do this on the basis of primary Spanish documents from archives of Spain and Mexico, various chronicles and other writings in Spanish or Nahuatl, and the native pictorial documents found in published works or still in manuscript. In the same Prologue, Orozco y Berra noted how in the course of the 13 years it took to prepare it the size of the work grew at an alarming rate, until finally he decided to cut it off at four reasonably sized volumes, the first of which was printed in June, 1880, on a subsidy of 8,000 pesos ordered by President Porfirio Díaz (ibid., pp. vii–viii).

Orozco divided his *Historia antigua* into four main parts and, within these, into books and chapters. Part 1 is Civilization; 2, Prehistoric Man in Mexico; 3, Ancient History; 4, The Conquest of Mexico. Part 1 occupies the first (580 pages) and some of the second published volume (to p. 253). The remainder of that tome is devoted to part 2 (pp. 255–492), a total of six chapters in two books, and to the beginning of part 3 (pp. 493–596). Volume 3 is wholly concerned with Ancient History (520 pages), as is volume 4 with the Conquest (683 pages).

Under part 1, Orozco distributed "Civilization" into five books. The first (9 chapters) covers mythology, religion, major and minor gods, and rites. The second (7 chapters) is concerned with social life, classes, economic matters, and political organization. Hieroglyphic writing and numeration occupy the 9 chapters of book 3, with discussions of the calendar systems forming 8 chapters in book 4. The final book 5 is a survey of cultural and political geography of the Aztec empire, the independent other Indian realms, and the Maya regions.

Although entitled Prehistoric Man, part 2 tends more to summarize archaeology and material culture than to discuss Paleo-Indians. Its purpose was to provide a baseline for Orozco y Berra to demonstrate the slow march of Man upward toward modern Progress. Book 2 examines the moot question of Asiatic or other origins of the Indians and Old World contacts. Orozco y Berra judiciously noted, after reviewing a vast amount of material, that insufficient evidence was then available to draw more than the most general conclusions (2:488–89).

Ancient History, part 3, is an attempt to provide a chronological account of native groups from earliest times to Conquest. It is divided into three books. The first (4 chapters) devotes two chapters each to the Maya and to groups in Michoacan, summarizing their cultures. The second book focuses more directly on the Valley of Mexico, its 10 chapters covering early "obscure times" through the defeat of the Tepanecs. Book 3 (11 chapters) is a detailed history of the Triple Alliance, with a final panorama of Mexico on the eve of the Conquest.

As its title suggests, part 4, The Conquest, is a minute annalistic account from first Spanish probings to the final fall of Tenochtitlan, closing with the capital being rebuilt. The Epilogue (4:677–83) is a summary recapitulation and Orozco y Berra's judgments. After agonizing about the matter, he concluded on balance that for civilization in general, the Spanish conquest of Mexico was a good and desirable accomplishment, and in the long run redounded to the benefit of the native populations.

Examination of sources used by Orozco y Berra supports the conclusion that he attempted to utilize a wide range of materials and that he analyzed them carefully. León-Portilla (1960, 4:583–603) and Uribe Ortiz (1963, pp. 87–106) have each reconstructed from Orozco y Berra's footnote citations the bibliography of his Historia antigua. In the more complete Uribe Ortiz study there are approximately 4,000 individual works listed, ranging from large printed collections to short technical articles cited by Orozco y Berra.

The following remarks on his sources are neither comprehensive nor necessarily definitive. They rest on casual examination of these reconstructed listings. The first main impression is that Orozco y Berra used a great amount of manuscript material. Many of the titles then in manuscript subsequently were published, but some yet remain unpublished. There are over 50 such entries for manuscripts. One class is Spanish administrative documents such as the Actas de Cabildo (Mexico City), and other reports in the National Archives, including parts of Cortés' Residencia. Various 16th-century materials, notably the "Libro de oro y tesoro índico," Las Casas' Historia apologética, Motolinía's Historia and his Memoriales, as well as later materials like those of Ordóñez y Aguiar, all figure in the Orozco y Berra bibliography, then in manuscript. He cited nearly all the Relaciones geográficas of the García Icazbalceta collection (now in Texas), as well as a few of the 18th-century reports. In manuscript he exploited Mestizo writers like Ixtlilxochitl, Muñoz Camargo, Tezozomoc, and Pomar's Relación de Texcoco. There is a long listing of native prose sources in manuscript, not the least of which were the Ramírez volumes of Anales antiguos de México y sus contornos; included are the Anales of Cuauhtitlan, Tecamachalco, Toltecas, Tolteca-Chichimeca,

Tepanecas, and Historia de los Mexicanos por sus Pinturas. Many of these had never been exploited before; they were omitted by Prescott and others in the 19th century like Bancroft, whose *Native Races* Orozco y Berra also utilized.

Scrutiny of the printed materials from which Orozco y Berra drew his information shows a similar wide range. He thoroughly exploited the collections of printed documents that gradually had begun to appear during the 19th century, and cited the now standard array of secular colonial writers and religious chroniclers. To these he added travel accounts, printed maps, and local histories which reprinted documents. Among secondary and monographic materials is a wide spectrum in English, French, and Spanish, with German only in Spanish translation.

For purposes here, one notable feature of the *Historia antigua* is Orozco y Berra's direct use of native pictorial documents, published and unpublished. He studied with care the codices published by Humboldt, Kingsborough, Ramírez, Rosny, and others. The results of these investigations generally are found in part 1, books 3 and 4, and in the fifth volume of plates. It might also be said that a number of important pictorial sources which subsequent scholars have had at their disposal for reconstruction of Aztec society and events of the Conquest—the Sahagún materials (especially Florentino), Lienzo de Tlaxcala, and others—were not used by Orozco y Berra.

Evaluations of Orozco y Berra's *Historia antigua* have tended to divide into two general classes, more or less along philosophical and ideological lines. On the one side were his contemporaries, García Icazbalceta (1896–99), Francisco Sosa (1884), José M. Vigil and others (1890), who had unreserved and unstinted praise; modern younger students like León-Portilla (1959; 1960, 4:xxx–xlvi) and Uribe Ortiz (1963), who has made the most penetrating study, have joined this laudatory band.

Adverse critics are modern: Alicia Huerta Castañeda (1942), Father Angel Garibay K., and Luis Villoro (1950), who devotes a chapter to Orozco y Berra. Garibay (Orozco y Berra, 1960, vol. 1) faults him for not knowing native culture from Nahuatl poems and other materials collected by Sahagún and his informants. Villoro, also an indigenista, on the other hand, in the most extended critique objects to the cold impersonal nature of the work, leaving the Indians dehumanized, the victims of a more or less mechanistic method which applies untested "universal principles" to their history. He provides various examples of Orozco y Berra's departure from "objectivity" to reveal personal prejudices in the Hispanista vein.[6]

Whatever defects the work may have, the major fact remains that Orozco y Berra's *Historia antigua* is an important and remarkable achievement of 19th-century historiography which cannot be overlooked. Not only is it the first, but it still remains nearly the only comprehensive coverage of its topic, outdated in many parts by superseding scholarly advances, but not yet replaced.

Historia de la dominación española en México

Compared with his *Historia antigua*, Orozco y Berra's *Historia de la dominación española en México* (1906, 1938b) is a markedly lesser work. In part this is explained by the fact that he wrote it at the beginning of his career, at age 33, when he was clearly less familiar with the primary sources than he was 30 years later. It therefore lacks maturity and complexity of structure. O'Gorman (1939a) demonstrated the heavy reliance which Orozco y Berra placed on Cavo's *Tres siglos*, published in 1836–38 by Bustamante (see Appendix A).

[6] Orozco y Berra is quoted as saying that the Indians were "a parasitic plant on the social tree of Mexico" (González y González, Cosío Villegas, and Monroy, 1957, pp. 151–52).

381

The treatise in four books is essentially the annals of the colonial period from 1522 through 1789. The first two deal with the years immediately following Conquest, and are written as though they were a continuation of the *Historia antigua* that he wrote much later. Book 3 treats "Civilization," and the final one is concerned with details of royal government. Orozco y Berra never fully explained why his terminal date is 1789 rather than 1810 or 1821, although perhaps he felt that the beginnings of Independence could be dated from that point.

Uribe Ortiz (1963, p. 62) suspects that much of the *Dominación española* was written in Puebla, where Orozco y Berra lacked the libraries and archives he could exploit when later he came to Mexico City. Rather than cite colonial legislation from direct and well-known sources, for instance, he takes summaries of cédulas from chroniclers and historians like Herrera. He places much reliance on the town records (Actas de Cabildo) of Mexico City, but relatively few other manuscript sources. Uribe Ortiz has listed his cited sources, about one-fourth the number for the *Historia antigua* (ibid., pp. 107–11).

In a wide-ranging view of the early years of the colony, with conquest and pacifications beyond the Valley of Mexico as themes, Cortés figures largely in Orozco y Berra's first two volumes. He is seen as a great administrator, explorer, organizer, and statesman, though not without faults. In general, native matters enter only peripherally into the *Dominación* volume, hence we can dismiss it shortly.

Although the volumes were written in 1849, they did not appear during Orozco y Berra's life. A plan to serialize it in the *Revista Literaria* produced only chapter 1 of book 1. Then the manuscript was forgotten. It formed part of the José María Lafragua Collection that was donated to the National Library in 1876 (Iguíniz, 1943, p. 280), as a seemingly anonymous manuscript whose author was identified as Orozco y Berra at

the turn of the century. The director of the National Library, José M. Vigil (1880–1909), strongly urged its publication; in 1906 the Mexican government appropriated funds. The printshop to which the work had been entrusted then went bankrupt; when a government representative sought to obtain the printed sheets for volumes 2–4, the new proprietor informed him that since no one had claimed them, he had sold them as wastepaper. Fortunately the library had retained the original manuscript and the printed pages of volume 1, which it issued in 1906. It was not until 1938, however, that the complete *Historia de la dominación española en México* appeared (Orozco y Berra, 1938b), with biobibliographical notes written earlier by Genaro Estrada and editorial notes by Silvio Zavala (Uribe Ortiz, 1963, p. 61). By then the *Historia* had little more than antiquarian value.

Other Writings

Space limitations restrict more than passing mention of other writings of ethnohistorical interest by Orozco y Berra. Most are discussed in the works listed under References at the end of this article.

More as pioneering works than as having present value, his *Geografía de las lenguas y carta etnográfica* (1864) and his *Historia de la geografía* (1880a) warrant notice. Various later classifications and linguistic maps have almost completely superseded the former (see Article 7). Less modern scholarship has been devoted to historical geography, hence the *Historia de la geografía* is still a point of departure (Cline, 1959, 1962). Many of the maps, including copies of native items discussed in it and an earlier publication (Orozco y Berra, 1871) remain in the Mapoteca Orozco y Berra of the Dirección de Geografía, Meteorología e Hidrología, Mexico City (see Article 28 for listings).

Finally, the three volumes of appendices to the *Diccionario universal de historia y geografía* (Andrade and Escalante, 1853–56) were edited, if not wholly written, by Orozco y Berra. The original publication, mentioned above under Ramírez, ran to seven volumes. In 1855–56 Orozco y Berra compiled these three additional volumes of reprints and original works. Susana Uribe Ortiz (1963, pp. 76–80) had described the many peculiarities of this hodgepodge, which among trivialities also contains unexpected solid studies and documents. These materials were reissued in 1938 (Orozco y Berra, 1938a).

Evaluation

In historical context, Orozco y Berra ranks as a major figure among 19th-century students of the Mexican Indian past. His major synthesis, *Historia antigua y de la conquista de México* in a sense closed an era, ushering in a long epoch, not even yet terminated, when micro- rather than macro-studies have predominated. That work, for its importance in the development of Mexican historiography and for its substance, still remains required reading, despite now visible limitations and drawbacks.[7]

JOAQUÍN GARCÍA ICAZBALCETA, 1825–1894

Joaquín García Icazbalceta defined his primary role as "writing nothing new but gathering materials that others might do so" (Martínez, 1951, p. 83). As a collector, bibliographer, and editor of historical and linguistic documents he received in his lifetime and afterwards much well-deserved acclaim for meticulously carrying out this important mission. His works have generally withstood the test of time, and are a modern point of departure for serious study of colonial Mexico.

Joaquín García Icazbalceta was born in Mexico City on August 21, 1825. His father was a well-to-do Spanish merchant, Eusebio

FIG. 4—JOAQUÍN GARCÍA ICAZBALCETA. From Winsor, 1889–92.

García Monasterio, and his mother a Mexican, Ana Ramona de Icazbalceta y Musitu. Because of the intense anti-Spanish atmosphere of the time, the family temporarily withdrew to Cadiz, Spain, when the boy was four years old, and did not return to Mexico until 1836. Joaquín was never enrolled in any school, but he was given a solid private education by tutors at home. He early turned to literary pursuits, even editing a small literary magazine (1836–40) in which he published essays. His father wished him to follow a mercantile career, and made him a partner in a business the family owned in Mexico City. Then, as later, Joaquín seemingly managed to combine well careers as a businessman and as a writer; he eventually became one of the most affluent *hacendados* in the rich state of Morelos, a solid pillar of the later Porfirian regime (González Navarro, 1957, p. 265). At

---

[7] Other references: Carreño, 1945b; García, 1934; García Cubas, 1890; Márquez Montiel, 1955; Martínez Ceballos, 1931; Martínez Torner, 1933; Navarro, 1954; O'Gorman, 1939b; Soto, 1935; Uribe Ortiz, 1953.

age 21 he was translating Shakespeare into Spanish, a task interrupted by his entrance into the Mexican army in 1847 to resist North American troops attacking Mexico City.

By the close of the war in 1848, García Icazbalceta seemingly had determined to devote his intellectual life to historical undertakings. He began to collect bibliography and amass documents. His first published historical work, in fact, stemmed from that latter urge. In order to obtain copies of the many historical documents which William Hickling Prescott had obtained, García Icazbalceta in 1847 purposely cultivated his friendship. Prescott was already in correspondence with many Mexican historians (Gardiner, 1959). García Icazbalceta approached him through their mutual friend, Alamán, who told Prescott the youth was translating into Spanish Prescott's *Conquest of Peru* (Gardiner, 1962; Teixidor, 1937, p. 8). Because he felt that the North American historian had left the narrative unfinished, García Icazbalceta (1849a) added four additional appendix chapters in the translation to cover the years 1549–81 (Gardiner, 1958, p. 158, Item p–10). That same year he also published a Spanish translation from Ramusio's Italian of a 16th-century "Account of the Conquest of Peru" by Pedro Sánchez (García Icazbalceta, 1849b).

The remaining 45 years of his life were devoted to Mexican bibliography and historiography. He formed part of the midcentury Mexican group, along with Alamán, Ramírez, Orozco y Berra, and others, who produced the pioneering multivolume *Diccionario universal de historia y de geografía* (Andrade and Escalante, 1853–56), for which he wrote 54 biographies, including that of Bustamante. He also prepared numerous articles that appeared in the *Boletín* of the Society of Geography and Statistics, and in the *Memorias* of the Mexican Academy of Language, of which he was a founder and director. In 1891 President Porfirio Díaz named him, as the leading Mexican historian, to head the Junta Colombina to prepare a large Mexican exhibit for Spain, but ill health forced him to resign from that post in favor of his friend and younger colleague, Paso y Troncoso (see section below). Joaquín García Icazbalceta was beginning to publish a large *Vocabulario de mexicanismos* (issued posthumously in 1899 by his son) when death overtook him in Mexico City on November 26, 1894, at age 69.

García Icazbalceta's devout Catholicism influenced his outlook and thus his selection and handling of sources, He set forth these firm religious convictions in a devotional volume, *El alma en el templo* (1863) published in Mexico by Librería del Portal de Agustinos. Many later testimonials to his strong faith were published by his grandson (García Pimentel y Elguero, 1944). Yet his rigid historical self-training made him skeptical of the appearance in Mexico of the Virgin of Guadalupe, as noted in a posthumously published *Carta acerca del origen de la imagen de Nuestra Señora de Guadalupe de México* (1896) for which clerical historians even now criticize him (Bravo Ugarte, 1946). His religion reinforced an economic and political conservatism that has made his works the archetype of Hispanism in the eyes of Mexican students of historiography (María del Carmel Velázquez, 1966, p. 483). Rather than being concerned with Indian life and civilization in the precolonial or later eras, García Icazbalceta's primary interests lay in the Europeanization of Mexico in the 16th century. Yet in pursuing those interests he provided many tools and data of value to ethnohistory.

García Icazbalceta's careful craftsmanship as bibliographer and editor developed a firm, if narrow, base for solid historiography. His collected works fill 10 volumes (1896–99), and his more important writings have been reissued, often with additional information to keep them current. His life and work have generated a relatively continuous stream of biobibliographical writings about him. Twice published is a standard if pedestrian biography by Manuel G. Martínez (1947, 1950). A selected list of works by García Icazbalceta appears in Appendix D.

The Collection

About 1849 García Icazbalceta began to form a "Collection of Documents for the History of America," which eventually grew to 87 large volumes, each containing one or more copies of original manuscripts, some of the highest importance. The first dated volume in the collection is volume 5, 1851. Those added between about 1849 and 1853 are largely transcripts of materials, many furnished him by William Hickling Prescott, mostly in volumes 7–11.[8] Details of these are found in their correspondence, 1850–57 (Gardiner, 1962). Through efforts of Francisco González de Vera, his friend and aide in Madrid, García Icazbalceta obtained in 1853 and later original manuscripts of major importance to ethnohistory and colonial Mexican history.

On November 29, 1853, García Icazbalceta excitedly wrote his friend Prescott that only shortly before he had received from Europe a collection of more than 60 original documents dating from the period 1524–80. It included autograph letters of Cortés, Las Casas, and the *Relaciones geográficas* now in the University of Texas Collection. All told, there were more than 1,500 pages of manuscript (Gardiner, 1962, p. 24).

Many came from the library of Bartolomé José Gallardo, a Spanish bibliographer, writer, and politician who died in 1853 (Cline, 1964, p. 356, n. 40). Of great importance from this source, for instance, was the "Libro de oro y tesoro índico," volume 31 of García Icazbalceta's collection, which contains 13 documents, six of which are

from the mid-16th century and related to ethnohistory: Orígen de los mexicanos; Memoriales of Motolinía; Relación de los Mexicanos por sus pinturas; Relación de genealogía y linaje de los señores; Leyes que tenían los indios de Nueva España; La gente de la Nueva España tributaba de aquellas cosas (see Article 27B, Item 1083, "Oro y tesoro índico"). García Icazbalceta obtained this item via his friend Andrade in 1861, but seems directly (through González de Vera) to have acquired a great number of other Gallardo manuscripts between 1853 and 1861 (Cline, 1964, p. 357, n. 41). As suggested earlier in this Guide (Article 5), that collection may have been the origin of the large collection of original 16th-century *Relaciones geográficas* acquired by García Icazbalceta in 1853, found in his volumes 20, 23, 24, and 25. From the Gallardo collection also came Gerónimo de Mendieta's *Historia eclesiástica indiana*, published by García Icazbalceta in 1870, with an erudite introduction discussing Torquemada's use of that manuscript (Article 16).

Fortunately, after García Icazbalceta's death his large manuscript collection and important library of 12,000 volumes remained relatively intact. Despite minor losses from it during the Mexican Revolution, the manuscript collection passed nearly complete by sale to the University of Texas Library in 1937, which also purchased some of the more important rare printed books. The manuscripts have been listed and described (Gómez de Orozco, 1927; Catálogo, 1936), most completely by Castañeda and Dabbs (1939). Many of the ex-García Icazbalceta manuscripts remain unpublished.

Works

Possibly García Icazbalceta's most enduring contribution lies in bibliography, where his publications remain models. His master work was *Bibliografía mexicana del siglo XVI*, which he began to develop in 1846, but did not publish until 1886. It is a

---

[8] These included such important works as Motolinía, Muñoz Camargo, and Fernández de Oviedo.

descriptive catalog of books printed in Mexico 1539–1600, with extensive scholarly notes on contents, authors, and editions, with an important introductory monograph on early printing in Mexico. Of fundamental importance, this volume was updated and reissued in 1954 by Millares Carlo.

A lesser but still important bibliographical monument is *Apuntes para un catálogo de escritores en lenguas indígenas de América*, which García Icazbalceta published in 1866. Its introduction tells us that he designed it as a specialized bibliography, a necessary antecedent to more general bibliographical works, which he believed should be based on them, to avoid perpetuation of bibliographical errors. Later hands have added many titles not known to García Icazbalceta, but his volume still warrants attention.

As an editor of historical materials, García Icazbalceta also significantly aided scholarship. He is especially notable for initiating in Mexico the publication of collected historical documents, with his pioneer two-volume *Colección de documentos para la historia de México*, of which the first appeared in 1858, the second in 1866. Later (1886–92) he added a *Nueva colección de documentos para la historia de México* (5 vols. in 3). In 1903–07 his son, Luis García Pimentel, issued *Documentos históricos de México* (6 vols.), parts of which seemingly had been prepared from his collection for publication by don Joaquín (see Article 11 for contents). The title pages of the García Icazbalceta collections bear the name of the publishing house Andrade or Andrade y Morales, but in fact they were printed by García Icazbalceta himself on a press he had installed in his own house, about 1858. Notable also were the small editions, 300 of the first (1858–66), and 200 of the second (1886–92).

García Icazbalceta's principal historiographical monograph was *Don fray Juan de Zumárraga, primer obispo y arzobispo de México, estudio biográfico y bibliográfico*

(4 vols., 1881), which brought him fame in Mexico and abroad. It is a panoramic and detailed account of the early church in Mexico, with 64 documents as appendices. It was reissued in 1947, but modern students of ethnohistory should supplement it by use of Greenleaf's study (1961) of the Indians under Zumárraga's Inquisition.

Thus as collector, bibliographer, editor, and historian, García Icazbalceta added important elements to the deepening and widening national traditions of Mexican historical studies. Much of his work has enduring value.[9]

Alfredo Chavero, 1841–1906

There is considerably less unanimity among scholars about the place of Alfredo Chavero in the galaxy of 19th-century Mexican scholars who concerned themselves with the ancient past than about his maestro José Fernando Ramírez and his intimate colleagues and warm older friends, Manuel Orozco y Berra and Joaquín García Icazbalceta, and his contemporary, Francisco del Paso y Troncoso. Offsetting the eulogistic treatment given Chavero during his lifetime by his friend Nicolás León (1904) in biobibliographical notes to the single volume of Chavero's published *Works* are the later sharply critical remarks of him as historian by Gurría Lacroix (1952). The mixed views of his work current in his day thus continue unresolved to the present.

In scrutinizing and judging Chavero, one is struck by his diversity of activities, among which his interest in Mexican archaeology and ethnohistory was but one. Like Ramírez, Chavero was an outstanding lawyer, but unlike him and Orozco y Berra, Chavero was in high political favor following liquidation of the French Intervention.

---

[9] Other references not cited in the text are: Agüeros, 1896; C.A.B., 1870; Carreño, 1945a; Fernández Duro, 1895; Galindo y Villa, 1904, 1925, 1926; Janvier, 1938; Junco, 1940; Ricard, 1934; Vargas, 1925; Primo F. Velázquez, 1943; Wagner, 1934.

Fig. 5—ALFREDO CHAVERO. From Chavero, 1904a, frontispiece.

In addition, Chavero was a notable and well-known figure in literary and musical circles. Although he did not tower over his contemporaries in any particular manner, he was fully accepted as a peer in a wide spectrum of diverse Mexican intellectual and political circles. Here, perforce, we are primarily concerned with Chavero as ethnohistorian.

Born in Mexico City on February 1, 1841, Alfredo was the son of José M. Martínez de Chavero and María G. Cardona. After completing a training in law in the Colegio de San Juan de Letrán, he obtained his professional title in 1861, permitting him to practice in all Mexican tribunals. Already on his way to a literary and political career, Chavero married Guadalupe Rosa in 1867.

Shortly after receiving his degree, Chavero in 1862 became active in politics as a member of the Liberal Progressive Party, with which he remained affiliated for many years. Chavero was one of the few young liberals who accompanied Juárez when the latter's government was forced into exile in 1863 during the French Intervention. On restoration of the Republic in 1867, Chavero continued his political activities in Mexico City. He progressed through various posts on the city council, judgeships of lower tribunals, governorship of the Federal District, and a long service in the Chamber of Deputies, of which he was president in 1878. He was a powerful member of the "científicos" who administered the Porfirian government, and in 1892 was president of the "Junta Central Porfirista," as well as "Friends of the President" (Chavero, 1904b; González Navarro, 1957, p. 400).

A long and successful literary career paralleled his political one. Even before graduation as a lawyer he had begun (in 1850) to publishd poetry, as he did throughout his life. In 1867 when Mexico was recommencing its cultural life after grueling civil wars, Chavero was known as a young but welcome member of the literary bohemians who grouped around Ignacio Manuel Altamirano and who met weekly to raise the level of national letters (González y González, Cosío Villegas, and Monroy, 1957, pp. 754–57).

From poetry Chavero moved to drama, for which he is best known in the history of Mexican literature. His burgeoning interest in aboriginal Mexico entered into this. In 1871 Chavero provided technical advice on staging an operatic performance of "Guatimotzin," whose costumes derived from native dress as shown in Codex Mendoza (ibid., p. 567). In 1877 Chavero's own drama "Xochitl," based on native themes, was first performed. In all, Chavero wrote more than 18 operas, tragedies, and comedies, which León notes was a greater individual output than that of Corneille, Molière, or Shakespeare (León, 1904, p. vii). Related to this dramatic interest was Chavero's longstanding connection with Mexican music, especially opera. In 1895 he was a co-founder of the Philharmonic Society of Mexico, and was often reported at the opera and concerts (ibid., pp. 757, 766).

But for our narrow aims here, his purchase of the books and manuscripts of José Fernando Ramírez from the heirs on the latter's death in 1871 and his continuing intimacy with Orozco y Berra and García Icazbalceta (León, 1904, p. xx) were decisive events. Amid his other distractions and responsibilities, Chavero from 1873 began to edit texts and publish studies related to Mexican ethnohistory. Because of his literary and political activities, Chavero was elected to various learned societies in Mexico and abroad, and represented Mexico at a variety of international gatherings (León, 1904, pp. xviii–xix, xxiii). At age 65 Chavero died in Mexico City on October 24, 1906. A selected list of his works of ethnohistorical interest appears in Appendix E.

Edited Works

Perhaps Chavero's most enduring claim to remembrance rests less on his own original work than on completion and extension of Ramírez' plans to republish major native histories, and his editorship of pictorial documents, especially in connection with the Junta Colombina. It is not always clear what editorial material for texts Chavero included from Ramírez' papers and copies, and what is his own contribution.

Using the Ramírez copies, Chavero published in 1891–92 an annotated two-volume edition of the historical works of Fernando de Alva Ixtlilxochitl (see Article 32), a major source for ethnohistory. Although better than others, the Chavero edition has serious deficiencies. Much the same can be said for his edition of Diego Muñoz Camargo, *Historia de Tlaxcala* (1892b), also a major source.

Chavero seems to have been primarily

responsible for publication in that year of important Mexican pictorial documents making up *Antigüedades mexicanas* (1892a), compiled by the Junta Colombina (see below, p. 392) for the Madrid exposition commemorating the 400th anniversary of the Discovery. Chavero wrote the text volume, which describes and comments on the pictorials of the accompanying atlas which made available in full for the first time Codices Baranda, Colombino, Porfirio Díaz, and the Lienzo de Tlaxcala (see Article 23, Items 24, 72, 255, and 350).

Biobibliographies

From a rather early date until shortly before his death Chavero published a series of biobibliographical notes on colonial writers of interest to ethnohistory. Among the first of these was a pioneering study of Sahagún (1877a) which seemingly makes heavy use of an unpublished (and now lost) Sahagún bibliography prepared by Ramírez. Although reprinted several times later, the Chavero treatment, written without knowledge of the Florentine Codex and several subsequent publications of Sahagún materials (see Article 14), was generally superseded by García Icazbalceta (1886) and latter studies. Later Chavero publishd on Boturini (1886a), on Sigüenza y Góngora (1886b), on Morfi (1903e), and, a year before his death, on Veytia (1905b). His previously issued notes on Durán and Tezozomoc and essays on Motolinía, Mendieta, Vetancurt, and again Sahagún were brought together in *Apuntes viejos* (1903c), which also contains commentaries on codices (Telleriano-Remensis, Ríos, Ramírez, and Mapa Sigüenza). All these have varying but steadily decreasing value for modern scholarship.

Commentaries and Studies

Starting in 1880, in an appendix to the posthumous publication of the second volume of Ramírez' edition of Durán, Chavero from time to time published commentaries on Mexican pictorial documents. These tend to be confused and diffuse; their present value often resides in the illustrations rather than in Chavero's text. Thus his 1899 discussion of Codex Borgia parallels and repeats a less than satisfactory treatment of native religion in his 1880 commentary.

Three publications in 1901 are indeed remarkable, as in then Chavero essayed descriptions and commentaries on five pictorials in his own collection. Chavero 1–3 are falsifications (see Article 26, Items 902, 903, 904); only Chavero 4 and the Códice of Ixhuatepec (Chavero 5) are authentic native documents (see Article 23, Items 44, 167). Somewhat pathetically Chavero in the second part of the work published in full the letter from Paso y Troncoso exposing Chavero 1–3 as frauds, a fact apparently unknown to their owner until then.

Related to Chavero's comments on specific documents are various archaeological and historical studies, beginning in 1873 with his biographies of Itzcoatl (1873a) and Motecuhzoma Ilhuicama (1873b). Again these essays often are of some historical interest chiefly for the graphic materials included with them. So with various writings on the "Piedra del sol" (1877b, 1882–1903), a study of the Coatlinchan monolith (1903h), and a discussion of the "Calendario de Palemke" (1902, 1906).

Finally, worth mentioning is a summary of his views on the relations between archaeology and other sciences that Chavero gave at the St. Louis Universal Exposition in 1904. Less important are his remarks on its contribution to various arts and sciences and some of his notions. One notion was that the origin of the Nahuas should be attributed to Russia (Chavero, 1905a, p. 392). More important was his view of the Conquest, always a bone of contention between Hispanistas and indigenistas. Contrary to views imputed to him by Gurría Lacroix (1952), Chavero here attributed conquest to inexorable laws of history. He pointed out that the Indian communities were fraction-

alized, at war constantly, and could not form a national unit to assure peace and advancement of Indian welfare. Therefore they were decadent, and thus came conquest, "by inescapable laws of History" (ibid., p. 397). He added that this was merely another example of the fact that progress and justice did not necessarily go hand in hand, perhaps as a veiled apology for the Porfirian regime.

Historia antigua

Chavero's principal work was the first in a five-volume cooperative history of Mexico entitled *México á través de los siglos*, under the general editorship of General Vicente Riva Palacio. Its contributors, in successive volumes, covered Mexican history from earliest times through the Reforma. The Chavero work is entitled *Primero epoca: Historia antigua y de la conquista*. The title pages of the first editions carry no date. The Mexican edition seemingly appeared first in 1887, with a Barcelona edition from the same plates in 1888. There is a parallel "Special Edition," published under the auspices of Manuel Dublan, Secretary of State, which carries an 1889 imprint date and both Barcelona and Mexico as places of publication.

Following an extended 57-page Introduction in which Chavero discusses sources, are 912 folio, double-columned pages of text, profusely illustrated with graphic materials from codices, as well as portraits and drawings of archaeological objects. Generally speaking, the organization is chronological, divided into five books, each of which has a different number of chapters of uneven length, minutely analyzed in a table of contents at the end (pp. 913–24) which serves as an index. The basic outline of this massive volume is shown in Table 1.

The introduction is a detailed bibliographical essay on Chavero's sources. It discusses codices, linguistic sources, calendric materials, native prose documents, and colonial historians and chroniclers. There is an especially full treatment of Sahagún, taken from Chavero's own earlier 1877 essay; in it he had utilized unpublished materials by Spanish scholars like Pascual de Gayangos and Manuel de Goyochea, the American Buckingham Smith, and the notes by José Fernando Ramírez (Chavero, [1887], pp. xxxiii–xliv). He pays special tribute to Ramírez (ibid., pp. lviii–lx) and to Manuel Orozco y Berra (ibid., p. lx), whose general scheme of organization Chavero followed, omitting many things treated by the latter.[10]

Chavero stops his narrative short of that in Orozco y Berra at a dramatic point where Cuauhtemoc finally surrendered, and was brought before the victorious Cortés, ending the military phase of the Conquest. The Spanish conquest is scanted by Chavero, occupying only chapters 8–12 of his book 5 (pp. 819–911). Many topical matters, notably native writing, calendars and rituals connected with them are found in book 4 (chaps. 14–19).

His single-page Conclusion (ibid., p. 912) is in the nature of an explanation and apologia. He stated that although he had written the volume hurriedly in 20 months, it had been based on 16 years of study. He said that he had tried to be impartial and to state the truth as he saw it, but realized

his work was less than perfect. He noted new materials he had seen, but frankly told his public that he had abandoned the custom of appending footnotes, "because I did not want to appear ostentatiously erudite or fatigue the reader."

His sympathetic biographer, León, mentions that when this work appeared it "created a real revolution" among the general public. Some criticized it as a work of pure imagination; others, blaming Chavero for not following the venerable traditions of historiography, damned it as altering the documentation. León said Chavero intentionally did not cite his sources "to support his new theories, leaving it to the sagacity and diligence of his readers to uncover them" (León, 1904, p. xxii). However, in many instances, as Glass notes in Article 32 (Chavero, n.d.), the Chavero text is a running commentary on a document he mentions. In general Chavero seems faithful to the facts, but many of his interpretations have not stood the test of time.

More serious, and equally controversial, than charges of ignoring use of standard scholarly apparatus (which he also levels), are other criticisms of Chavero as an historian voiced by Gurría Lacroix (1952). These essentially boil down to a statement that Chavero's interests as a professional dramatist led him to heighten and color various scenes and episodes for literary effect, to the detriment of historical balance. Gurría Lacroix also avers that Chavero, under the influence of Orozco y Berra (whom Gurría Lacroix somewhat mistakenly labels an indigenista) and following his own liberal, indigenista political convictions in the guise of judicious balancing of accounts and sources, invariably adhered to the native version, giving his account a marked nativistic bias. Here it may be noted that Gurría Lacroix was basing his evaluation on a very small portion of the *Historia antigua*, where narratives from one or the other side, native and European, might conflict; his major citation in proof of indigenista distor-

---

[10] Here Chavero notes proudly that he introduced the legislation which authorized the government to publish the Orozco y Berra work at public expense.

tion is drawn not from the *Historia antigua* but from a separate study of Cortés' ships, written in 1876 and published by Chavero many years later (1904a).

On the more positive side, it can be said that Chavero did employ (and display through illustrations) new and important native materials not previously published, especially for the pre-Hispanic portions of his work. His preliminary discussion of sources still contains matters of interest, although much of it has been superseded. His readability is a virtue, quite appropriate for the general public to which the series was addressed.

Summary and Evaluation

Chavero was certainly not a great ethnohistorian, but he was one whose efforts over a quarter-century merit respectful mention. He was an additional important link between Ramírez' generation and that of his own, which included Paso y Troncoso, Peñafiel, and lesser luminaries. Chavero extended the horizons of Sahagún studies, edited and published previously unavailable basic texts and codices, and completed a number of specialized investigations, some up to the general standards and knowledge of the day. Unlike the vast majority of those who earlier and later dedicated themselves to ancient Mexican history, Chavero did produce a coherent synthesis, which, like that of Orozco y Berra, has been more criticized than emulated. While it is difficult, if not impossible, to assign him a fixed rank in the hierarchy of 19th-century Mexican scholarship on native history, one can see that it would have been substantially the poorer if he had decided to be merely a successful politician and playwright.

FRANCISCO DEL PASO Y TRONCOSO, 1842–1916

Modern scholarship continues to be deeply indebted to the labors of Francisco del Paso y Troncoso, less for any extended completed studies or synthesis than for a lifetime of collecting historical materials of the greatest

FIG. 6—FRANCISCO DEL PASO Y TRONCOSO. From Zavala, 1938.

importance to continuing investigations. Expanding the tradition established by Bustamante, Ramírez, García Icazbalceta, and others who had preceded him, Paso y Troncoso ransacked European repositories, ran down obscure bibliographical clues, and diligently supervised copying of a mountain of basic source material which even today has not been fully exhausted. Especially important to ethnohistorical studies were his efforts to gather and publish materials on Sahagún and, a parallel but more complex undertaking, to develop a comprehensive collection of Spanish language "Papeles de Nueva España" which would more fully document the colonial period.

Sixth son in a family of 10 born to Pedro del Paso y Troncoso and Teodora Medina, Francisco de Borja del Paso y Troncoso was born in Veracruz on October 8, 1842.[11] He

[11] To his intimate friends he was always "Borja" and very occasionally he signed articles with that name, but he is generally cited in the literature as Francisco del Paso y Troncoso (Galindo y Villa, 1922, p. 306).

was locally educated for a mercantile career, but in 1867 his family sent him to Mexico City to prepare for a future in medicine. Following work in the Colegio de San Ildefonso and the newly reorganized National Preparatory School, he matriculated in the National School of Medicine. With a noted talent for natural sciences and languages, he was an outstanding student. When a clumsy laboratory assistant ruined experiments in chemistry on which he planned to write his professional thesis during his fifth year of study, he abruptly turned to preparation of a history of medicine in Mexico. Even then displaying traits that marked his later activities, he laid out an elaborate plan that encompassed examination of Aztec science as a prelude to that in the colonial and national periods. He completed only parts of his examination of aboriginal botany, astronomy and medicine, later published in the MNA *Anales*, but he never finished the thesis or received his professional degree (González Obregón, 1939, pp. 176–78).

Paso y Troncoso determined to devote his time to history and linguistics. At the beginning of this new career, in 1883 he published a famous open letter to the Minister of Education, deploring the state of knowledge and teaching of Mexican history, with suggestions for remedies. These included reissuing in scholarly format the major chronicles, with uncorrupted texts, and seeking out basic documentation on Mexican pre-Contact and colonial history in foreign archives, especially those of Spain (González Obregón, 1939, p. 178; Carrera Stampa, 1949, pp. 3–4). He also perfected his Nahuatl, and accepted a chair in it at the National Preparatory School (1886). He began to publish erudite studies in the *Anales* of the National Museum, to which he was appointed Visitor in 1888, and successively was named acting and then permanent director (1889), a post he nominally held until his death in Florence, Italy, on April 30, 1916. As the active director between 1889 and 1892, he reorganized the

publication programs, rehabilitated the library, and undertook other salutary administrative reforms, as well as sponsoring various national scientific expeditions. When he sailed for Europe in 1892, never to return to Mexico, he had also written various studies, several of which remained unfinished and unpublished: a history of commerce, and partially edited texts (Galindo y Villa, 1922, pp. 567–68).

To celebrate the 400th anniversary of the Discovery of America in 1892, the Spanish government sponsored a large international exposition in Madrid to which foreign governments were invited to send exhibits. The Mexican government accepted the invitation, and prepared to make a major effort, one which saw mounted in Spain some 10,-000 objects filling five large exhibit rooms. As director of the National Museum in Mexico, Paso y Troncoso was chiefly responsible for gathering, describing, and supervising the preparation of this vast Mexican exhibit. The Junta Colombina (which he headed after García Icazbalceta, its nominal chairman, resigned) issued a large collection of codices, with commentary by Chavero.[12] Paso y Troncoso left for Spain on August 5, 1893, and on arrival busied himself with the compilation of a large three-volume catalog of the Mexican objects, itself a considerable scholarly contribution; the third volume was never published (Galindo y Villa [1922, pp. 321, 456–68] gives pictures and details of the Mexican exhibit). The Mexican section won many plaudits. When the exposition closed, Paso y Troncoso decided to stay on in Europe, chiefly to copy

[12] The Junta Colombina originally included as its president Joaquín García Icazbalceta (and later Paso y Troncoso), Alfredo Chavero, José María Vigil, and José María de Agreda y Sánchez, with Francisco Sosa as secretary, and Luis González Obregón and Jesús Galindo y Villa as assistants (Galindo y Villa, 1922, p. 319). Each of the latter biographized Paso y Troncoso; the 1916 Galindo y Villa summary did not appear until 1922; González Obregón published his eulogy in 1919, and reprinted it in 1939, the version here cited. The main biographical treatment is Zavala, 1939.

Sahagún manuscripts in Madrid and Italy. The closing of the Madrid exposition was the beginning of yet a new phase in Paso y Troncoso's career, his long European mission that ended only with his death in 1916.

The European Mission, 1892–1916

Zavala (1938) has abundantly documented Paso y Troncoso's activities in Europe during the 23 years he spent searching out, copying, and preparing for publication a vast store of prime documentary materials for the pre-Conquest and colonial history of Mexico. To those data later hands have added information (Carreño, 1941; Carrera Stampa, 1949, pp. 5–55).

From 1892 through 1902, Paso y Troncoso remained nominally director of the National Museum, on an extended leave of absence. In 1902 he was officially named "Director on Mission in Europe," with a research and travel budget separate from that of the museum. He based himself in Madrid and Florence, but roamed archives and libraries all over the continent: England (1896, 1910–12), Russia (1898), Germany and Austria (1898–99, 1902), Paris (1900), with various side trips from these capitals he used for his scientific gatherings. His years in Florence (1898, 1901, 1903, 1907–08, 1912, 1915–16) and in Spain (1892–93, 1903–07, 1908, 1909–10, 1912, 1913–14) placed him near the archives where the bulk of his materials were collected (Carrera Stampa, 1949, p. 6).

Paso y Troncoso saw his prime mission as twofold. First, he proposed to gather and publish as complete a corpus of Sahagún documents as possible. His interest in the great Franciscan had stemmed from the days when Paso y Troncoso as a young man had helped Joaquín García Icazbalceta prepare the latter's magisterial *Bibliografía mexicana del siglo XVI* (González Obregón, 1939, p. 185). Second, he expected to copy documentary source materials related to colonial Mexico, an elaborate group of varied papers which he generically called "Papeles de Nueva España." We treat them here in that order.

The Sahagún Corpus

Inspired by what he had learned about Sahagún from Ramírez, Chavero, and García Icazbalceta, Paso y Troncoso devoted much of the final quarter-century of his own life to gathering and publishing Sahagún materials. He accomplished only a small part of the vast publication program he evolved.

At the close of the Madrid exhibit in 1893 he went to Italy, where he first had the illustrations of the Florentino codex copied by Genaro López (1893–95); he himself copied the Spanish and Nahuatl texts of the same document. In the midst of a depression, the Mexican government furnished him no official funds for these activities. In 1895, however, he was pledged that it would assume publication costs. Paso y Troncoso then spent three more years negotiating for publication permission with the Italian government, which had also earlier given Zelia Nuttall rights to publish the Florentino. Meantime, Paso y Troncoso had begun to develop a publication program that went far beyond the relatively modest five volumes that would provide the Nahuatl text of the Florentine manuscript, the Spanish of the Tolosano, and the Florentino illustrations, all that had been authorized in 1895 because funds were limited.

In 1898 Paso y Troncoso wrote his good friend José María Vigil, outlining a group of related works that would fill 15 folio volumes (Paso y Troncoso, 1898). In addition to the first agreed five volumes, Paso y Troncoso in a sixth and seventh proposed to provide facsimiles of the Sahagún drafts in the Palace manuscript and the Academy manuscript, with an eighth volume to contain his translations of them from Nahuatl, and in it to include their illustrations. Volumes 9–11 were to form a great Sahagún Nahuatl vocabulary, in which "each word is explained, discussed and with its etymology," with comparative renderings from the Molina and other dictionaries. Finally, volumes 13–15 would consist of glosses, special topical articles, and various general indexes. He asked Vigil to impress on high officials, especially President Díaz, that getting out this monumental work was more worthy of Mexican scholarship than a re-edition of Kingsborough (evidently a competing project).

This 1898 plan underwent modification, even expansion during the following decade. In 1909, when he transmitted volume 7, the first volume fully printed during his lifetime, Paso y Troncoso briefly outlined his Sahagún program to President Díaz (Paso y Troncoso, 1909a), and at much greater length to the Secretary of State, in charge of the Office of Public Instruction and Fine Arts (Paso y Troncoso, 1909b). Advising his superiors to await further publications, Paso y Troncoso justified his issuing of these drafts before publishing the texts and illustrations of the bilingual *Historia general* (vols. 1–4) on the grounds that he could indicate by notes in the latter those passages which Sahagún had omitted, utilized, or amended (ibid., p. 75; Carreño, 1941, pp. 283–84). This obsessive urge to provide his texts with festoons of notes, comparing all possible passages, was a lifetime characteristic of Paso y Troncoso, one that reduced his completed work to only the smallest fragment of the materials he had copied and hoped to publish. Yet he felt very strongly about such notes, writing a friend in 1908, "according to my special criterion, I judge that whoever has a small store of erudition must put it at the disposition of the rest, as much for unrelated studies connected with the search for truth, which interests us all equally" (Carreño, 1941, p. 177).

The political events in Mexico from 1909 through 1916, the Mexican Revolution, meant that Paso y Troncoso received scant funds and could not continue the publication of either the Sahagún corpus or the

Papeles de Nueva España. In 1912, when there was temporary government stability, he was asked to report on the state of his mission and proposed plans. That portion of his reply relating to the Sahagún program (Paso y Troncoso, 1912) reveals a number of things. One is that despite the imprint dates on volumes 6, 7, and 8 of 1905, 1906, and 1907 (vol. 5 has no title page), none in fact had been published in those years. Volume 7 had been completed (but not generally distributed) in 1909; in 1912, volumes 5, 6, and 8 still remained in various stages of completion. He expressed hope that when they appeared, volumes 1–4, the bilingual text, would go rapidly. Further, Paso y Troncoso submitted a modified outline for the subsequent volumes, seemingly substituting for the massive Nahuatl vocabulary he had earlier envisaged a proposed series of related Latin and native texts, including Hernández' *De Antiquitatibus Novae Hispaniae*, Códice Kingsborough, and other items he had photocopied in 1912.

In 1909 Paso y Troncoso had advised his government to await distribution of the Sahagún volumes until the set was complete, the edition was primarily meant to be deposited in large research libraries. The only individuals who were to get copies of the small edition were heads of state, and certain major figures like the Duc de Loubat. Seemingly in the closing years of his life Paso y Troncoso was unable to put the final publication touches on volumes 5, 6, and 7; volumes 1–4 never even went to the printer. Hence on his death most of Paso y Troncoso's great dream of issuing the monumental Sahagún corpus and related materials was unfulfilled.

As noted below, the Mexican government, after many difficulties, repatriated part of the materials he had prepared. Among them were the printed but unbound sheets of volumes 5, 6, and 8, which seemingly the museum had bound and distributed around 1924. In 1925 it issued separately Codex Mendoza, apparently destined

TABLE 2—PASO Y TRONCOSO'S PLANS FOR PUBLICATION OF SAHAGÚN'S
HISTORIA GENERAL AND RELATED MATERIALS, 1898–1912

Volume	Plans: 1898	Plans: 1909–12	Remarks
1	Bilingual text, HG	Same	FPT copied 1893–95; ready for
2	Florentino Nahuatl		press 1912; not published. MNA
3	Tolosano Spanish		has FPT copies except bks. 10–
4			12
5	Florentino illustrations	Same	Complete 1912 except few plates and captions. MNA issued (incomplete) ca. 1924; no title page
6	PAL MS	Matritenses: Cuad. 1, Descriptions by FPT Cuad. 2, PM (PAL and ACAD) Cuad. 3, Illustrations (PAL and ACAD)	Nearly ready 1912; not published; lost Lacked captions 1912; released ca. 1924 by MNA with 1905 imprint Ibid., sometimes bound in vol. 5
7	ACAD MS	PAL MS, Mem. Español (1, 5), Mem. Escolios (1–7)	Completed and five copies transmitted July, 1909; released ca. . 1924 by MNA with 1906 imprint
8	FPT translations of vols. 6, 7; illustrations of Madrid MSS	ACAD MS, Mem. Escolios (8–11)	Lacked captions and chapter headings 1912; MNA released ca. 1924 with 1907 imprint
9	Vocabulary	Appendices: Hernández, *Memoriales* (Latin) Códice Kingsborough, Cuad. 1, Facsimile Cuad. 2, Transcription, translation, commentary by FPT on Kingsborough	Photocopied 1912; issued separately by MNA 1926 Prepared, issued 20 copies 1912 Not published; lost?
10	Vocabulary	Tezozomoc, Chimalpahin, and "others" translated by FPT	Not published; lost?
11	Vocabulary	Codex Mendoza Two codices from Escorial	Issued by MNA 1925 Unknown, photocopied 1912
12	Vocabulary		
13–14	Glosses, special article, indexes, etc.		

KEY: ACAD, Academia Real de la Historia, Madrid
HG, *Historia general*
Mem. escolios, Memoriales con escolios
Mem. Español, Memoriales en Español
PAL, Biblioteca de la Palacio Real, Madrid
PM, *Primeros memoriales*

by Paso y Troncoso for volume 11, and, in 1926, the Hernández facsimile he had expected to place in volume 9.

The bilingual text, volumes 1–4, was never published. Moreover, following Paso y Troncoso's death in 1916, part of his meticulous copy of the Florentino disappeared from his papers. Originally the Mexican government repatriated only two of his four manuscript volumes, containing books 1–6 (Nicolau d'Olwer, 1952, p. 180). They are presently found in legajos 126–27 of the Paso y Troncoso collection (INAH). In 1940 the Mexican government purchased from an antiquarian bookdealer an additional Paso y Troncoso volume, books 7–9 (Acosta Saignes, 1946, 1:iii). His copy of books 10–12 continue lost (Nicolau d'Olwer, 1952, p. 180). In addition to these small remains the Paso y Troncoso Collection in INAH now retains only various photos of the Tolosano (books 5–8) in legajos 129–31, and a fragment (fols. 1–215) of the Palace manuscript, *Primeros memoriales*, so far as Sahagún materials are concerned (Carrera Stampa, 1949, p. 29). Table 2 summarizes Paso y Troncoso's plans of 1898 and 1909–12, with notes on the results.

Plans for the "Papeles de Nueva España"

In a letter from Madrid, April 21, 1906, Paso y Troncoso outlined to the Secretary of Public Instruction his views and plans for the "Papeles de Nueva España" (Zavala, 1938, pp. 23–28). Other correspondence provides further information and detail.

Paso y Troncoso mentioned that for various reasons the material he had compiled for publication under that general title would be divided into series, each according to the class of data it contained. Each series would begin with a volume 1, and subsequent volumes would include similar documents, rather than there being only a single series with diverse materials (like DII, DIU, etc.). Series 1, which he expected to issue from Florence, would contain bibliography and be related to matters concerning sources of Mexican history. Geography, statistics, and related materials would appear in Series 2. "Histories" would comprise Series 3. Seemingly he had several others in mind. In 1906 he stated that juridical, administrative, and economic documents would each have their own series.

Carreño, who in 1936 had an opportunity to research the Paso y Troncoso personal papers (chiefly holograph notes and letters) then in private hands, casts further light on these projects. In various drafts he found that Paso y Troncoso had noted 33 documents he wanted to place in "Jurisprudence and Political Economy," with another 10 in "Commerce and Navigation," 70 in "History and Government." Part of the plan also was to publish the *probanzas*, "Information on Merits," and another group would include "Registro de Oficio," to contain various royal orders sent to Spanish authorities in New Spain. Another series was provisionally entitled "Voyages and Discoveries," in which would appear 65 items; it was here that the Baltasar de Obregón, "Historia de los descubrimientos de tierras nuevas," was originally meant to appear. Seemingly he also considered a distinct group of documents to be published on Guatemala and Central America. All of these items, of course, were to be heavily annotated (Carreño, 1941, pp. 230–35).

By 1906 Paso y Troncoso had determined that Series 4 would include works on native languages, and that an Epistolario would form Series 5. The latter was to complement the specialized topical series, and was a large compilation of varied general communications, some of which he hoped to issue in facsimile. The autobiographical statements of the conquerors and settlers seeking reward from the Spanish Crown, the probanzas, were here scheduled as Series 6. He sought approval of this general plan for the "Papeles de Nueva España," which was given in 1906 (Zavala, 1938, pp. 95–96).

Paso y Troncoso explained in another report dated April 23, 1906, his method of work. He also indicated what he planned to publish as the initial volume of Series 1, "Bibliographies." Learning that the Archive of the Indies in Seville had various unpublished finding aids, he had secured permission to have these searched, with notation made of documents relating to New Spain. In all, his employee, José J. Gómez, created about 11,000 such slips for individual pieces found in diverse parts of the archive. On review of these slips, Paso y Troncoso ordered selected documents copied for various series of the PNE. The slips themselves he proposed to publish as a catalog, more or less chronologically arranged. He mentioned that merely the listing of items in 21 legajos (file folders) of Audiencia of Mexico (60–2–16 to 36) alone would fill a 500-page printed volume (Zavala, 1938, pp. 30–33).

Geographical and statistical materials, for Series 2, lay close to Paso y Troncoso's heart (Carreño, 1941, p. 230). It was the one he had advanced furthest before his death. In a long report of June 9, 1908, he detailed the proposed contents of the 10 volumes which he expected would comprise that series. Volume 1 was to be the publication of a *Suma de visitas*, summary geographical-statistical information on numerous places at mid-16th century. Volume 2 was to include various reports, tax lists, and results of visitations, such as those by Bartolomé de Zarate and Lebrón de Quiñones, as well as assessments made on communities in Yucatan in mid-16th century. Volume 3 would publish detailed data on communities in the Archdiocese of Mexico, brought together in 1569–71 at orders of Bartolomé de Ledesma; a previous publication of the material had included only 35 of the 116 parishes covered in the whole document. Volumes 4, 5, 6, 7, and 8 were to contain *Relaciones geográficas* 1579–85, compiled in response to the 1577 order (see Article 5), successively for the dioceses of Antequera, Tlaxcala, Mexico (archdiocese), Michoacan, and Guadalajara. Volume 9 was to contain the detailed *Memoirs* of Fray Alonso de Mota y Escobar, bishop of Tlaxcala, who early in the 17th century was asked to visit and report on various parts of the realm. Finally, volume 10 would close the series with various documents on encomiendas. Specifically among them were reports on the visitation by Diego Ramírez, a report on the tributes paid to Hernán Cortés as Marqués del Valle, the Hortuño de Ibarra listing of encomiendas and encomenderos, and papers concerning perpetuity of encomiendas (Zavala, 1938, pp. xi, 62–63).

Paso y Troncoso's intentions for filling Series 3, "Histories," are not always clear.

He did expect to issue a chronicle he had located and whose author he had identified as Francisco Cervantes de Salazar, as well as the *Historia* of Baltasar de Obregón. Presumably for this series Paso y Troncoso had ordered copies of Mariano Veytia's *Historia de Puebla* and Lorenzo Boturini's *Historia general de la América Septentrional* (Zavala, 1938, pp. xi–xiii, 37, 39–42). In 1906 he thought the Veytia would fill two printed volumes and the Boturini one (Carreño, 1941, pp. 224–25).

Linguistics formed Series 4. In September, 1912, Paso y Troncoso reported that he had copied four items to fill two volumes. Two of these were anonymous 16th-century Nahuatl vocabularies. The others were Pichardo's "Diccionario de Partículas Mexicanas" and José Buenaventura Castro's 1836 "Adiciones al vocabulario misteco de Fr. Francisco de Alvarado" (Zavala, 1938, p. 96).

Various and repeated statements by Paso y Troncoso fix the preceding material as the four series clearly to form separate parts of PNE. Beyond them we are on less sure ground as to the number and contents of further series. For convenience we have assumed that the "Epistolario" about which he wrote is his Series 5, and the "Diccionario de Pobladores" a sixth, although in his erudite introduction to the correspondence of Paso y Troncoso and inventories of the papers, Zavala implies that the latter would be included among "Histories," Series 3 (Zavala, 1938, pp. xii–xiii). At this time and distance we cannot fathom where Paso y Troncoso proposed to place native chronicles, pictorial documents, partial excerpts of histories, and other items now found in the collection which bears his name. We can, however, note how much of his known plan for the PNE came to fruition.

Paso y Troncoso's Execution of the Plans

Various circumstances frustrated Paso y Troncoso's great dream of putting numerous volumes of several series each of the PNE into print and thus in hands of investigators. Later publishers, using materials he compiled, even yet have only partially realized his grand design.

At the outset, it can be said that Paso y Troncoso himself issued only portions of his Series 2, "Geography and Statistics," and one volume of one title in Series 3, "Histories." Always there seems to have been a basic subjective struggle between his laudable urge to make the documentary treasures he had uncovered available in print, and his scholarly perfectionism and innate penchant for wishing to annotate and compare every major statement in all sources of the known literature to a degree that narrowed his actual published output to a very thin trickle indeed.

In the long run, erudition won over production. The few titles of the PNE which he saw through press are heavily documented and annotated to the levels and standards of his day. The main contribution, however, remains the actual textual materials, not the notes.

Despite his statement of intentions, there seems to be no evidence that Paso y Troncoso took definite steps to edit for publication the 11,000 slips related to manuscripts about Nueva España in the Archivo General de Indias, the proposed initial volume of Series 1, "Bibliographies." In 1912 he reported he was still preparing materials for this series (Zavala, 1938, p. 95). None was published during his lifetime.

Paso y Troncoso published four relatively complete volumes, and two partial volumes, of Series 2, "Geography and Statistics." Complete were volumes 1, 4, 5, 6, and partially complete were volumes 3 and 7. Although the completed volumes bear an imprint date of 1905 or 1906, from correspondence in 1908 it would seem that actually they were not fully finished, as Paso y Troncoso expected to put preliminary matter, indexes, and (in some cases) maps in them (Zavala, 1938, pp. 59–61). However, those containing the *Suma de visitas* (vol. 1) and

three complete volumes of *Relaciones geográficas* (vols. 4, 5, 6) have been cherished and heavily used standard sources since their appearance in a small edition.

The "Descripción del Arzobispado de México" that was to form volume 3 was partially published, with an imprint date of 1905. The latter is obviously improper, as in 1908 Paso y Troncoso was still correcting proofs (Zavala, 1938, pp. 59–60). He noted in that year that the earlier publication of the same material by García Pimentel had included only 35 of the total parishes listed, but of the total 116, Paso y Troncoso's truncated version covers only about 55; nearly half the document still remains unpublished. He left unpublished a related item in the same legajo of 85 folios (170 pages), the two together amounting to 226 folios (452 pages), of which only 85 folios were included in the Paso y Troncoso volume.

Only the opening pages of volume 7, containing *Relaciones geográficas* for the archbishopric of Mexico, were ready for transmittal to Mexico by Paso y Troncoso in 1908 (Zavala, 1938, p. 63). Its imprint date is given as 1906. The publication note inside the short and incomplete volume states that from page 17 [to 39] the material was prepared in facsimile, presumably from unique page proof, and later issued by the National Museum in 1932.

The unpublished volumes remained so, for a variety of reasons. For one thing, as the Mexican Revolution broke out, funds for Paso y Troncoso's mission decreased, and his receipt of them was irregular. Once when he did get two years' allowance, he spent most of it on further photography, while works in press were withdrawn for lack of funds to pay the printer (Zavala, 1938, p. 94). Busy with his photographic enterprises, apparently Paso y Troncoso did not return proofs of the numerous corrections he had made (ibid.). At that time, 1912, he reported four complete volumes of Series 2, two partial, and four ready for press (Zavala, 1938, p. 95).

As early as June, 1908, Paso y Troncoso recalled from the press the manuscript he had prepared for volume 2. He reported that he had found serious paleographic errors in the copy made for him in Seville (Zavala, 1938, p. 60). He personally was going to collate the imperfect copy against the original, but apparently his numerous other activities delayed that important operation. In 1909, when he thought he had matters arranged to hurry various volumes of Series 2 through the press, the Spanish printers struck; by the time the strike was settled, so much important other work had accumulated in the backlog that the Paso y Troncoso volumes took a very low priority (Zavala, 1938, pp. 69–70).

Many of the same considerations which led to the truncated publication of Series 2 reduced that of Series 3, "Histories." Before his death, Paso y Troncoso saw through press only the first volume of Francisco Cervantes de Salazar's *Crónica de Nueva España.*

Bad luck had plagued Paso y Troncoso regarding that manuscript. In 1908 he had apparently found it in the National Library of Madrid and had copied it. But because of other duties and his characteristic dilatory ways, the manuscript (with his annotations) was still in press in June, 1912, when Zelia Nuttall reported finding and copying the same manuscript at the 18th International Congress of Americanists in London. In 1914 the Hispanic Society of America published the complete chronicle from the Nuttall transcript with an introduction by M. Magallón; in the same year only volume 1 of Paso y Troncoso's version had been issued. Until he died Paso y Troncoso carried on a well-bred but intense polemic concerning his own claim as the "discoverer" of the previously lost Cervantes de Salazar item.[13]

As we have seen above, at Paso y Troncoso's death various works were in the printing houses of Spain. Most of these volumes seem to have been lost or dispersed. Hence

during his lifetime Paso y Troncoso managed to publish only five complete volumes in PNE and two rather incomplete ones.

Repatriation of the Paso y Troncoso Collection

When Paso y Troncoso died in Florence on April 30, 1916, World War I was convulsing Europe, and in Mexico the military phases of the Mexican Revolution were reaching their climax. As soon as the newly stabilized Mexican government could, it began to reclaim the vast amount of material primarily deposited in Madrid and in Italy that he had collected in its name. These official negotiations with heirs and others dragged on for several years, and were only partially successful. In the process of repatriating the Paso y Troncoso Collection its original size was greatly diminished. Until detailed inventories were made in the late 1930s, losses from it continued in Mexico.

The first shipment of Paso y Troncoso's materials arrived in Mexico May 26, 1917. It proved to be merely 10 boxes of his miscellaneous printed books which bore no relation to his main mission. After prolonged correspondence the Mexican government ascertained that the banking firm of French Lemon in Italy had in its possession 21 additional boxes of manuscript copies and print, as well as another 10 boxes which Paso y Troncoso had shortly before his death asked them to collect from yet another firm; in addition were three trunks of the same materials. Negotiations slowed during the

---

[13] He had reported (August 3, 1909) that he estimated the total chronicle would fill three volumes of 400–500 pages each, that volume 1 was in press, and that he had collated the second against the original. He wrote González Obregón (Florence, August 31, 1912) that for Mexican national honor he was going to push his claim as discoverer against that of Zelia Nuttall (González Obregón, 1939, pp. 182–83). The Introduction to his volume 1 (Madrid, 1914, pp. i–x) details the dispute; Carreño (1941, pp. 236–38) discusses the dispute, and opposite page 280 reproduces FPT's draft of the first page of the "Introduction."

terminal phases of the Mexican Revolution and World War I; it was not until November, 1921, that the first 21 boxes reached Mexico. They contained primarily printed materials on Sahagún, chiefly the colored plates of the Florentine and Madrid codices.

Paso y Troncoso's heirs claimed that the other 10 boxes and three trunks of materials remaining in Italy were not the property of the Mexican government, but were personal possessions which Paso y Troncoso had willed them. However, eventually this claim was rejected. Those materials, too, finally came to Mexico in May, 1926.

Equally difficult to repatriate were masses of material which Paso y Troncoso had left in various parts of Spain. From the family of Francisco A. de Icaza were ultimately recovered three boxes, containing 1,263 legajos, which arrived in Mexico in January, 1928, followed by another five in November, with less important materials.

Licenciado Adrián F. León was the legitimate heir of Paso y Troncoso and to him rather than to the government went important materials. These came from a safe deposit vault which Paso y Troncoso had rented in the Banco Hispano-Americano de Madrid. There seemingly never was a listing or inventory of these documents, which in 1949 were in the hands of Adrián León, son of the above-mentioned Adrián. During the years the León family gave various copies and documents from this group to Federico Gómez de Orozco for his own rich private library.

The "Colección del Paso y Troncoso" manuscripts in the Archivo Histórico of the National Institute of Anthropology and History in Mexico thus does not contain the full corpus of PNE. As comparison among various lists indicates, many documents which did arrive in Mexico disappeared before a relatively definitive inventory was made by Wigberto Jiménez Moreno and Silvio Zavala; others, as we have seen, never did reach museum hands. However, the 134 *carpetas* of the "Colección del Paso y Troncoso" still contain a vast quantity of data, and great numbers of the documents which he had planned to publish as PNE.

Seemingly various official projects by the National Museum of Anthropology have been equally frustrated in completing Paso y Troncoso's publication program. At one point it was reported in 1938 that the museum expected to issue the Sahagún volumes (Jiménez Moreno, 1938). It never did so, although supplementary materials from the MNA were utilized for the 1938 and 1946 commercially issued editions of the *Historia general* (Article 14). In 1941 Carreño published an elaborate project developed earlier by Luis Castillo Ledón, director of the museum in 1936, to issue 35 volumes of the Paso y Troncoso materials, divided into seven series, apart from four more on Sahagún. The Ledón plan was never implemented. Unfortunately, irresponsible persons have been permitted access to the remnants of the Paso y Troncoso Collection, and have exploited it for often less than scholarly purposes.

Later Developments and Publications of PNE

Several later hands have dipped into the mass of material which Paso y Troncoso compiled for PNE and have utilized his transcripts or copies for publication from those copies which survive in the National Museum in Mexico. We shall briefly review these, by the series envisaged by Paso y Troncoso. Later editors have not always noted where their materials fit into his original plans.

Series 1, "Bibliographies," was respectably issued in four volumes under the general title *Indices de documentos de Nueva España existentes en el Archivo de Indias de Sevilla, 1928–1933.* With an introduction by Genaro Estrada, these were published by the Mexican Secretaría de Relaciones Exteriores as numbers 12, 14, 22, and 24 in their excellent series, *Monografías bibliográficas mexicanas.*

It is a misfortune for scholars that the unpublished portions of Series 2, "Geography and Statistics," have largely appeared under the imprint of Luis Vargas Rea. His editorial malpractices have been discussed at length in Article 11. Into these slovenly hands fell materials Paso y Troncoso had planned for volumes 2, 3, 7, 8, and 9 of Series 2 of PNE. In one general series which Vargas Rea labeled "Biblioteca Aportación Histórica," he published these, 1944–48, in a number of small, badly printed pamphlet-size volumes. Typically obtuse about actual contents, he added a misleading subtitle to volume 2 (which he subdivided into seven separate titles) that implies it contains *Relaciones geográficas* from Michoacan. In fact, there are two petitions from conquistadores and a memoria on corregimientos; the remainder of volume 2 contains Lorenzo Lebrón de Quiñones' documents which Paso y Troncoso had originally intended to have included. The Zárate reports and the Yucatecan documents Paso y Troncoso proposed for it are not included in the Vargas Rea version, nor are they in the files of the Collection for this volume.

Whether through ignorance, design, or the possibility that Paso y Troncoso copies had previously been filched from the file, Vargas Rea in his supplement to volume 3 did not complete the reports on the archdiocese of Mexico that Paso y Troncoso had planned. As issued, the supplement includes a series of views collected in 1569 concerning improvement of government and administration in New Spain; two miscellaneous documents conclude the volume. Vargas Rea broke these materials into seven separate books, paginated continuously but sold separately.

From 1944 through 1946, Vargas Rea published most of the hitherto unpublished materials Paso y Troncoso had compiled for volume 7, *Relaciones geográficas* from Michoacan. Of eight small volumes, numbers 1–4 are paged continuously, as are volumes 7 and 8, but volumes 5 and 6 each have individual pagination. Utilizing the same Paso y Troncoso files, José Corona Núñez also subsequently edited and published the same documents (Corona Núñez, 1958). Neither he nor Vargas Rea includes the map materials accompanying the original documents. Volume 8 of Series 2 was issued by Vargas Rea in 1947, in six pamphlets containing *Relaciones geográficas* of mining areas in the diocese of Guadalajara in the kingdom of Nueva Galicia. A few of these had been published as early as 1878 from unknown copies.

Finally, in 1948 volume 9 of PNE, Series 2, appeared under the Vargas Rea imprint in seven small volumes. It reproduced what Paso y Troncoso had considered to be the second part of the *Memoriales* of Bishop Alonso Mota y Escobar, a portion dealing with Nueva Galicia from a manuscript he had found in the British Museum. The first part, covering the bishopric of Tlaxcala, was to use a Spanish (AGI) manuscript that Paso y Troncoso had also copied, but when officials of the National Institute of Anthropology and History wanted it for publication, his file copy was missing. Therefore, they availed themselves of one then owned by Federico Gómez de Orozco, which possibly may have come to him through Paso y Troncoso's heirs (Mota y Escobar, 1945). In fact, the British Museum manuscript covering Nueva Galicia that Vargas Rea published had twice previously been published, also apparently from the Paso y Troncoso material, once in 1930 in very limited edition and again in 1940, recopying the 1930 edition (Ramírez Cabañas, 1930, 1940).

Thus in subprofessional dress the PNE, Series 2, have gradually become available since about 1930. In untrustworthy editions by Vargas Rea, large but not complete portions of volumes 2, 3, 7, 8, and 9 came into print, but because they appeared in limited editions they now tend to be almost unavailable. The whole Paso y Trancoso Series 2 still merits complete, scholarly republication.

Uncertain at this time is his intended placement in the PNE of a group of documents also collected by Paso y Troncoso. These are the 18th-century *Relaciones geográficas*, discussed by West in Article 10. In various complicated subseries Luis Vargas Rea also issued a number of them, in his usual unsatisfactory fashion. Possibly Paso y Troncoso intended them originally for further volumes of Series 2. Although, as West indicates, these reports are not as revealing as comparable 16th-century *relaciones*, they too warrant scholarly republication, with the added materials he noted.

There is an ironic twist to the saga of the sole title in Series 3, "Histories," that Paso y Troncoso had completed. His own edited manuscript of volume 2 of the Cervantes de Salazar *Crónica* was not among his effects which the National Museum in Mexico finally obtained. Therefore, to complete the title, the Mexican editor, Federico Gómez de Orozco, merely reprinted in 1936 the missing portion from the 1914 version published by the Hispanic Society, based on Nuttall, against whom Paso y Troncoso had so vehemently protested! Volume 2, therefore, does not carry the extensive footnotes which probably Paso y Troncoso had prepared for his own edition. Volume 3 is not heavily annotated, but does contain a few of his notes about volume 1, especially concerning the unique calendric materials.

So far as is now ascertainable, none of the titles collected by Paso y Troncoso for his fourth series, "Linguistics," has been published from his transcripts.

Series 5, "Epistolario," on the other hand, came out virtually complete in 16 sizable volumes, 1939–42, under the capable editorship of Silvio Zavala. He notes that some documents which Paso y Troncoso had earlier planned for inclusion in volumes 2 and 10 of Series 2 he had already transferred to the Epistolario, and they now appear in the published volumes of it. The 16 volumes reproduce 896 numbered items; occasionally in volumes 1–15 there is a note that the material was missing from the files. But in volume 16 a number of these missing pieces are printed from photostatic copies furnished by France V. Scholes, who had independently copied them in the Archivo General de Indias. Indexes in volume 16 aid in the use of these important Paso y Troncoso materials.

As mentioned above, a "Diccionario de Pobladores" was to be included as part of Series 3 or as a title in a sixth series. Such a "Diccionario autobiográfico de conquistadores y pobladores de Nueva España" was issued in two volumes (Madrid, 1923) with the title note "taken from original texts by Francisco A. de Icaza." Collating various notices, Zavala cast strong doubts that Icaza actually did the work, and implied as strongly as possible short of libel that Icaza, in possession of Paso y Troncoso's papers, did little more than prepare for press these 1,385 sketches copied for Paso y Troncoso, add his own name as compiler, write an introduction and prepare indexes (Zavala, 1938, p. xiii). Carreño, who knew both Paso y Troncoso and Icaza, leaves no doubt that he and others in Mexican intellectual circles (including González Obregón) were wholly convinced of the plagiarism. Carreño (1941, pp. 278–81) wrote sadly, "Icaza did not need to do this to acquire honor and fame."

In his useful summary of Paso y Troncoso's mission Carrera Stampa (1949, pp. 44–45) has localized a number of individual pieces collected by Paso y Troncoso, but published after his death by others. Little purpose would be served in repeating such information, which undoubtedly could now be greatly expanded by a search of the literature appearing after 1949. It suffices here to say that although Paso y Troncoso was unable to see the PNE published in his own lifetime, his accomplishments during that mission have proved an enormous boon to scholars seriously concerned with late native and colonial Mexico.

With this as a background, Appendix F lists selected writings and publications by Paso y Troncoso, during his life and after his death in 1916 to 1966. In this order it covers the Sahagún corpus, the PNE and other publications.

Evaluation

Time improves Paso y Troncoso's status and reputation as a major collector of materials on which to base pre-Hispanic and colonial historical investigations. As the surviving corpus that he created gradually emerges, its value steadily grows and reaffirms Paso y Troncoso's profound knowledge of the Mexican past and what would significantly document it. Certainly the most erudite Mexican specialist of his era, he allowed this deep knowledge to impede rather than advance his own direct contribution. As a collector, he attempted the nearly impossi-

ble task of faithfully reproducing basic texts, and at the same time as editor annotating them in anticipation of all the questions they raised. Perhaps the price of his perfectionism was that he was not fully successful in either role. Thus his capacities outstripped his performance, and his potentiality his achievement.

These considerations should not obscure the important and central matter. Paso y Troncoso was and remains the outstanding major Mexican investigator of his era, a fully accepted figure in the international group of his peers, which included such luminaries as Seler, Brinton, Nuttall, and other founders of the modern approaches to Middle American ethnohistory. His legacy continues to enrich these studies.[14]

[14] Other references not cited in text are: Carrera Stampa, 1963; Mendizábal, 1946; Nunemaker, 1948; Zavala, 1946, 1948.

APPENDIX A. BUSTAMANTE, SELECTED WRITINGS OF ETHNOHISTORICAL INTEREST

Studies:

1821 Galería de antiguos príncipes mexicanos. Puebla. 52 pp.
1822 Crónica mexicana, Teoamoxtlí ó libro que tiene todo lo interesante á usos, costumbres, religión, política y literatura de los antiguos indios tultecas y mexicanos, redactado de un antiguo códice del caballero Boturini. Mexico. 200 pp. [An additional "carta" remained unpublished, in possession of Joaquín García Icazbalceta in 1853.]
1826 Necesidad de la unión de todos los megicanos contra las asechanzas de la nación española y liga europea, comprobado con la historia de la antigua República de Tlaxcala. Mexico.
1829 Historia del emperador Moctheuzoma Xocoyotzin. *In* Bustamante, 1829–30, vol. 2, 46 pp. following text of Sahagún.
1835–36 Mañanas de la alameda de México; publícalas para facilitar a las señoritas el estudio de la historia de su país. 2 vols. Mexico. [Ancient history to coming of Spaniards.]

Edited Sources:

1826a Historia de las conquistas de Hernando Cortés escrita en español por Francisco López de Gómara, traducida al mexicano y aprobada por verdadera por Juan Bautista de San Anton Muñon Chimalpahin Quauhtlehuantzin, indio mexicano. 2 vols. Mexico. [Retranslation into Spanish of Chimalpahin's Nahuatl translation; Bustamante at first thought it an original native account of the Conquest.]
1826b Memoria sobre la guerra del Mixton en el estado de Jalisco. Supplement, 42 pp. *In* 1826a. [Has two lithographed native calendars in some editions.]
1826c Tezcoco en los últimos tiempos de sus antiguos reyes, ó sea relación tomada de los manuscritos inéditos de Boturini; redactada por el Lic. D. Mariano Veytia. Publícalos con notas y adiciones para el estudio de la juventud mexicana. 292 pp. Mexico.
1826d Historia del descubrimiento de la América Septentrional por Crístobal

Colón, escrita por el P. Fr. Manuel de la Vega, religioso franciscano de la provincia del Santo Evangelio de México. 250 pp. Mexico. [Partial publication, 24 of 42 chaps., of Beaumont's chronicle of Michoacan. Manuel de la Vega was the copyist.]

1829a Historia de la conquista de México por el P. Fr. Bernardino de Sahagún. 78 pp. Mexico. [Sahagún, *Historia general*, bk. 12, 1577 version.]

1829b Horribles crueldades de los conquistadores de México y de los indios que los auxiliaron, para subyugarlo a la corona de Castilla, ó sea Memoria escrita por D. Fernando de Alva Ixtlilxochitl. *In* 1829a, 142 pp. [Relación 13, "De la venida de los españoles y principio de la ley Evangélica."]

1829–30 Historia general de las cosas de la Nueva España, que en doce libros y dos volúmenes escribión el R. P. Fr. Bernardino de Sahagún, de la observancia de S. Francisco, y uno de los primeros predicadores del Santo Evangelio en aquellas regiones. 3 vols. Mexico. [Sahagún, *Historia general*, bks. 1–11. See Article 14.]

1832 Descripción histórica y cronológica de las dos piedras, que con ocasión del nuevo empedrado que se está formando en la plaza principal de México, se hallaron en ella el año de 1790, por D. Antonio de León y Gama. Mexico. [Reedition of León y Gama, 1792 (see Article 12), to which is added a long defense of the work by León y Gama, previously unpublished. García Icazbalceta (1853, p. 760) praised Bustamante for this publication, noting it "anduvo algo mas exacto que de costumbre."]

1836–38 Los tres siglos de México durante el gobierno español, hasta la entrada del ejército trigarante. Obra escrita en Ro-

ma por el P. Andrés Cavo, de la compañía de Jesús; publícala con notas y suplemento. 4 vols. Mexico. [Vols. 1, 2 are Cavo's *Historia*, covering 1521–1766; vols. 3, 4 are Bustamante's supplement, to 1821. García Icazbalceta (1853, p. 760) thought this "lo mas apreciable de sus escritos," noting a reedition in 1851; but see Burrus *in* Cavo, 1949 (Article 12).]

1840 La aparición de Nuestra Señora de Guadalupe . . . fundándose en el testimonio del P. Fr. Bernardino de Sahagún, ó sea Historia original de este escritor, que altera la publicada en 1829. . . . Mexico. [The 1585 revision of bk. 12; unique version known (see Article 14).]

1841–42 Historia de la Compañía de Jesús en Nueva España, que estaba escribiendo el P. Francisco Javier Alegre al tiempo de su expulsión. 3 vols. Mexico. [Mutilated text (see Article 13).]

1843 La aparición guadalupana de México, vindicada de los defectos que le atribuye el Dr. D. Juan Bautista Muñoz en la disertación que leyó en la Academia de la Historia de Madrid en 18 de abril de 1794, comprobada con nuevos descubrimientos. . . . pp. 53–55. Mexico. [Sahagún, *Historia general*, bk. 12, chap. 23, 1578 and 1585 versions reprinted.]

Miscellaneous:

1833 Hay tiempos de hablar y tiempos de callar. Mexico. [36-page pamphlet, autobiography.]

1834 La sombra de Moctheuzoma Xocoyotzin. Mexico. [Periodical, 12 numbers (156 pp.), 2 supps. (48 pp.).]

1840 Curiosa compilación de documentos relativos á la conquista de ambas Américas. Mexico. [Prospectus.]

NOTE: García Icazbalceta (1853, pp. 761–63) lists about 80 periodicals and pamphlets, stating the number is far from complete.

APPENDIX B. RAMÍREZ, SELECTED WRITINGS OF ETHNOHISTORICAL INTEREST

1844 Notas y esclarecimientos a la Historia de la Conquista de México del Sr. W. Prescott. *In* W[illiam Hickling] Prescott, *Historia de la Conquista de México . . . traducida al español por Joaquín Nava-*

rro. Cumplido. 3 vols.; vol. 2, xx + 124 pp. Mexico. [Paginated separately following text.]

1847a Proceso de residencia contra Pedro de Alvarado, ilustrado con estampas sacadas de los antiguos códices mexicanos, y notas y noticias biográficas, críticas, y arqueológicas . . . paleografiado del MS original el Lic. Ignacio L. Rayon. Mexico.

1847b Explicación de tres antiguas pinturas geroglíficas de los Mexicanos, con dos notas críticas sobre el Salto de Alvarado y edificación de la primera iglesia en México. Mexico. [Limited edition of 20 copies; reprint of portion of 1847a.]

1853–56 [Various articles]. *In* José María Andrade and P. Escalante, eds., *Diccionario universal de historia y de geografía.* 7 vols. Mexico. [Ramírez articles listed in González Obregón, 1898, pp. xxxiii–xxxiv.]

1854 Ixtlilxochitl (Fernando de Alva). *Ibid.,* 4:855–66.

1855 Noticia de los manuscritos mexicanos que conservan en la Biblioteca Imperial de Paris. MS. MNA/AH, copy in BNP/FM, no. 427. [Unpublished.]

1857 Descripción de algunos objetos del Museo Nacional de Antigüedades de México. *In México y sus alrededores,* app. Mexico.

1858 Cuadro histórico-geroglífico de la peregrinación de las tribus aztecas que poblaron el Valle de México, acompañado de algunas esplicaciones para su inteligencia. *In* Antonio García y Cubas, *Atlas geográfico, estadístico e histórico de la República Mexicana,* Mexico. [Unpaginated app. Reproduces Mapa Sigüenza and Codex Boturini.]

1858–66 Noticias de la vida y escritos de Fray Toribio de Benavente ó Motolinia . . . acompañadas de investigaciones sobre el origen y motivos de sus disidencias con Illmo. D. Fr. Bartolomé de las Casas. . . . *In* Joaquín García Icazbalceta, *Colección de documentos para la historia de México,* 1:1–109. Mexico.

1863 Bautismo de Moteuhzoma II, noveno rey de México. Disquisición histórico-crítica de esta tradición. SMGE, *Boletín,* 10:357–81.

1867a Historia de las Indias de Nueva España y Islas de Tierra Firme por el Padre Fray Diego Durán. . . . La publica con un atlas de estampas, notas, e ilustraciones. Mexico. Vol. 1 only. [Vols. 2, 3 later issued by MNA, 1880, with added app. by Alfredo Chavero.]

1867b Códices mexicanos de Fray Bernardino

de Sahagún. MS. [Published posthumously. See 1885b, 1903.]

n.d. [1847?–1871?] Anales antiguos de México y sus contornos. MS. 2 vols. MNA/AH. [1,022 pages, modern copies of 26 MSS in Nahuatl, largely unpublished.]

n.d. Indice biográfico por orden alfabético de los nombres que cita Antonio Remesal en la obra Historia de la Provincia de S. Vicente de Chyapa y Guatemala de la Orden de nro. glorioso padre Santo Domingo. MS. 218 pp. [LC, Rare Book Division, F 1466 R 378.]

1885a Advertencia: Anales antiguos de México y sus contornos. *In* "Anales de Cuauhtitlan," MNA, *Anales,* 1/3, Suplemento, pp. 5–6. [Preceding reproduction (Nahuatl text, translation) of AAMC, 1, 4, is Ramírez' Foreword to the collection.]

1885b Códices mexicanos de Fray Bernardino de Sahagún. RAH, *Boletín,* 6:85–124. [Posthumous publication of Ramírez, 1867b.]

1898 Biblioteca Hispano-Americana Septentrional: adiciones y correciones. . . . Luis González Obregón, ed. Mexico. [Supplementary material to Beristáin y Souza.]

1898–1904 Obras. Victoriano Agüeros, ed. 5 vols. Mexico. [Vol. 1 (1898), pp. v–xlvii, contains bibliographical sketch by editor.]

1903 Códices mexicanos de Fray Bernardino de Sahagún. MNA, *Anales* 2/1:1–34. [Incomplete.]

1944 Vida de Fray Toribio Motolinia. Col. Escritores Mexicanos, 4. Porrúa, Mexico.

1945 Peregrinación mexicana. Primera Parte. Anónimo de 1570 y Códices Telleriano y Vaticano comparados. Segunda parte de Peregrinación mexicana. Ed. Vargas Rea. Mexico.

1946–47 Moteczuma. Rafael García Granados, ed. Academia Mexicana de la Historia, *Memorias,* 5–6; *Boletín,* 1–4. [Documentary apps. include reprint of 1863, pp. 93–124.]

1948 Anales antiguos de México y sus contornos. Edited by Luis Vargas Rea. vol. 4. Aportación Vargas Rea. Mexico.

1952 Códice Boturini; interpretación. Biblioteca de Historiadores Mexicanos. Obras inéditas de José Fernando Ramírez. Edited by Vargas Rea. Mexico.

1953 [Ramírez, José Fernando. Códice Boturini, ó] Tira de la peregrinación: Interpretación. Bib. Historiadores Mexicanos.

1957 Fray Toribio de Motolinia y otros estudios. Edición, prólogo, y notas de Antonio Castroleal. Col. Escritores Mexicanos, 4. Mexico. [Reprints 1859 and 1944.]

NOTE: For comment on Vargas Rea publications, see Article 11.

APPENDIX C. OROZCO Y BERRA, SELECTED WRITINGS OF ETHNOHISTORICAL INTEREST

1853 Noticia histórica de la conjuración del Marqués del Valle, años 1565–1568. Formado en vista de nuevos documentos originales y seguida de un extracto de los mismos documentos. Mexico.

1853–54 Documentos para la historia de México. 1a serie. 7 vols. Mexico.

1853–56 [Various articles]. *In* José María Andrade and P. Escalante, eds., *Diccionario universal de historia y de geografía*. 7 vols. Mexico.

1854–55 Documentos para la historia de México. 2a serie. 5 vols. Mexico.

1855–56 Apéndice al Diccionario Universal de Historia y de Geografía. 3 vols. Mexico. [See below, 1938a.]

1856 Documentos para la historia de México. 3a serie. 1 vol. Mexico.

1856–57 Documentos para la historia de México. 4a serie. 7 vols. Mexico.

1864 Geografía de las lenguas y carta etnográfica de México, precedida de un ensayo de clasificación de las mismas lenguas y de apuntes para las inmigraciones de las tribus. Mexico.

1865 Memoria presentada a S. M. el Emperador por Ministro de Fomento . . . año de 1865. Mexico

1867 Memoria para el plano de la ciudad de México, formada de orden del Ministerio de Fomento. Mexico.

1871 Materiales para una carta geográfica mexicana. SMGE. Mexico.

1877a El cuauxicalli de Tizoc. MNA, *Anales*, ep. 1/1:3–39.

1877b Dedicación del Templo Mayor de México. MNA, *Anales*, ep. 1/1:60–74.

1877c Doctrinas en jeroglíficos. MNA, *Anales*, ep. 1/1:202–16.

1877–82 Códice Mendocino. Ensayos de descifración jeroglífica. MNA, *Anales*, ep. 1/1:120–86, 242–70, 289–339; 2:47–82, 126–30, 216–52.

1878 Ojeada sobre la cronología mexicana.

In José M. Vigil, ed., *Crónica mexicana, por Hernando Tezozomoc*, anotada por Manuel Orozco y Berra, precedida del Códice Ramírez. Pp.151–222. Mexico.

1879 Le calendrier mexicain. 3 Congrès International des Américanistes (Brussels), *Compte-Rendu*, 2:627–708.

1880a Historia de la geografía en México. Secretaría de Fomento. Mexico. [Reprint of articles which first appeared, 1876, in *La Enseñanza*, vol. 1; also reissued, 1880, by *Revista Científica Mexicana*.]

1880b–[1882] Historia antigua y de la conquista de México. 4 vols., 1 vol of plates. Mexico. [See below, 1954, 1960.]

1881 Apuntes para la historia de la geografía de México. Mexico. [Also in Secretaría de Fomento, *Anales*, 11 (1880).]

1897 El Tonalamatl. MNA, *Anales*, ep. 1/4:30–44. [Reprint of chap. 2, vol. 2, 1880b, with added illustrative material.]

1906 Historia de la dominación española en México. Bib. Nacional. Mexico. [First volume only of three; see below, 1938b.]

1938a Los conquistadores de México. Mexico. [Reprinted materials from 1855–56.]

1938b Historia de la dominación española en México. 4 vols. Bib. Histórica Mexicana de Obras Inéditas, 1–4. Mexico. [Complete MS, with introductory notes by Genaro Estrada and Silvio Zavala. Supersedes Orozco y Berra, 1906.]

1954 Historia antigua y de las culturas aborígenes de México. 2 vols. Mexico. [Partial reissue of 1880b, profusely illustrated with inferior engravings. Introductory materials by Wigberto Jiménez Moreno, Pablo Martínez del Río, E. Núñez Mata. Text arbitrarily modified, hence unreliable for scholarly use.]

1960 Historia antigua y de la conquista de México. Nueva edición preparada por A. M. Garibay K., y Miguel León-Portilla. 4 vols. Bib. Porrúa, 17–20.

Mexico. [Republication of 1880b, with discussion of Orozco's methods by Garibay and reconstructed bibliography by León-Portilla. The atlas is incomplete.]

APPENDIX D. GARCÍA ICAZBALCETA, SELECTED WRITINGS OF ETHNOHISTORICAL INTEREST

1849a Apéndice del traductor. *In* W. H. Prescott, *Historia de la Conquista del Perú . . . traducida al castellano por J.G.I.*, 2:529–666. R. Rafael, ed. 3 vols. Mexico. [Four chapters of narrative, 1549–81. This edition was reissued, 1850, with added important illustrative material.]

1849b Relación de la conquista del Perú. . . . Mexico. [Spanish translation of Pedro Sánchez, published in Italian by G. B. Ramusio, 1554.]

1853–56 [Various biographical articles (54, including José María Bustamante (1853) by JGI.] *In* José María Andrade and P. Escalante, eds. *Diccionario universal de historia y de geografía.* 7 vols. Mexico.

1858–66 Colección de documentos para la historia de México. 2 vols. Mexico. [300 copies.]

1866 Apuntes para un catálogo de escritores en lenguas indígenas de América. Mexico. [Author's private edition, 60 copies.]

1870 Gerónimo de Mendieta, *Historia eclesiástica indiana.* Con algunas advertencias de Joan de Domayguía. Sacadas de cartas y otros borradores del autor [edited by JGI]. Mexico. [See 1945.]

1875 Francisco Cervantes de Salazar, *México en 1554* [translated from Latin dialogues by JGI]. Mexico.

1877 González de Eslava, *Coloquios espirituales.* Mexico. [Edited by JGI, with introduction re colonial theater.]

1881 Don fray Juan de Zumárraga, primer obispo y arzobispo de México: estudio biográfico y bibliográfico, con un apéndice de documentos inéditos o raros. Mexico. [See 1947.]

1886 Bibliografía mexicana del siglo XVI. Primera parte. Catálogo razonado de libros impresos en México de 1539 a 1600. Con biografías de autores y otras ilustraciones. Precedido de una noticia acerca de la introducción de la imprenta en México. Mexico. [350 copies; see 1954.]

1886–92 Nueva colección de documentos para la historia de Mexico. 5 vols. in 3. Mexico. [200 copies.]

1896 Carta acerca del origen de la imagen de Nuestra Señora de Guadalupe de México. Mexico.

1896–99 Obras. Victoriano Agüeros, ed. 10 vols. Mexico. *Bib. Historiadores Mexicanos*, 1–3, 6, 9, 12, 14, 18, 20, 22. [Biobibliographical notices, 1:v–xvii. Reprinted, Burt Franklin, New York, 1968.]

1899 [i.e., 1905] Vocabulario de mexicanismos [to letter G], Luis García Pimentel, ed. Mexico. [Title page date, 1899, when terminated; cover date, 1905, when released to public.]

1941 Nueva colección de documentos para la historia de México. 3 vols.

1945 Gerónimo de Mendieta, *Historia eclesiástica indiana.* 4 vols. Mexico. [Reissue of 1870.]

1947 Don fray Juan de Zumárraga. . . . 4 vols. Mexico. *Col. Escritores Mexicanos*, 41–44. [Reissue of 1881, with added documents, introduction, index, bibliography of author.]

1954 Bibliografía mexicana del siglo XVI . . . nueva edición por Millares Carlo. Fondo de Cultura Económica. Mexico. [Revised reissue of 1886; colonial printers increased from 9 to 80; imprints increased from 118 to 180; new index.]

APPENDIX E. CHAVERO, SELECTED WRITINGS OF ETHNOHISTORICAL INTEREST[15]

1873a   Izcoatl. *In* Eduardo Gallo, ed., *Hombres ilustres mexicanos: Biografías de los personajes notables desde antes de la conquista hasta nuestros días*, 1:81–125. 4 vols. Mexico.
1873b   Motecuhzoma Ilhuicamina. *Ibid.*, 1: 127–73.
1873c   Tenoch. *Ibid.*, 1:13–33.
1875   Calendario azteca. *In* José María Pérez Hernández, ed., *Diccionario geográfico, estadístico, histórico, biográfico, de industria y comercio de la República mexicana.* . . . 4 vols. Vol. 3, appendix (2d pagination), pp. [1]–16. Mexico. [Several times revised, expanded; final version, *La piedra del sol*, 1882–1903, q.v.]
1877a   Sahagún. Estudio. Mexico. SMGE. [109 pp. First ed. of much reprinted study. Minor variation, changes in 1882, 1887, 1903c, 1904a, 1948.]
1877b   La piedra del sol: segundo estudio. MNA, *Anales*, ep. 1, 1:353–86, 2 pls. Mexico.
1878   Códice Ramírez. Duran. Tezozomoc. *In* Hernando Tezozomoc, *Crónica mexicana*, Manuel Orozco y Berra, ed., pp. 10:14, 162–67. Mexico. [Reprinted 1903, pp. 31–36; 1944.]
1880   Apéndice. Explicación del códice geroglífico de MS Aubin. *In* Fray Diego Durán, *Historia de las Indias de Nueva España y islas de Tierra Firme*, José Fernando Ramírez [and others], ed. 2 vols., atlas. Mexico. 1869–1880. Vol. 2 (second pagination), pp. [1]–172. [Chaps. 4–6 (pp. 42–93) with some omissions included in his 1887, pp. 355–84.]
1882   Sahagún. SMGE, *Boletín*, ep. 3, 6:7–42. [Reprint of 1877, with "Advertencia" giving data on acquisition, use, disposition of Ramírez' library.]
1882–1903   La piedra del sol: estudio arquelógico. MNA, *Anales*, ep. 1, 2:3–46, 107–26, 233–66, 291–310, 403–30; 3:3–26, 37–56, 110–14, 124–36; 7:133–36.
1884   [Lithographs of numerous codices in the Aubin collection.] *In* MNA, *Anales*, 2:243–45.
1886a   Boturini. MNA, *Anales*, 3:236–45. [Reprinted (1904a).]
1886b   Sigüenza y Góngora. MNA, *Anales*, 3:258–71. [Reprinted (1904a).]
[1887]   Primera epoca. Historia antigua y de la conquista. Vicente Riva Palacio, ed. 5 vols. *México a través de los siglos*, vol. 1.[16]
[1888?]   *Ibid.* [Barcelona.]
1889   *Ibid.* [Mexico and Barcelona.]
1891–92   Obras históricas de don Fernando de Alva Ixtlilxochitl, publicadas y anotadas por. . . . 2 vols. Secretaría de Fomento. Mexico. [Vol. 1, Relaciones, 1891; vol. 2, Historia chichimeca, 1892. Reprinted 1952, 1965.]
1892a   Antiguedades mexicanas publicadas por la Junta Colombina de México en el cuarto centenario del descubrimiento de América. 2 vols. Secretaría de Fomento. Mexico. [Vol. 1, text by Chavero; vol. 2, 149 pls. edited by Chavero.][17]
1892b   Historia de Tlaxcala por Diego Muñoz Camargo, publicada y anotada por. . . . Secretaría de Fomenta. Mexico. [Reprinted 1947 (added material), 1966.]
1899   Interpretación del Códice Borgiano. Obra póstuma del P. José Lino Fabrega de la Compañía de Jesús. Texto italiano pareado con la traducción castellana y seguido de notas. . . . Alfredo Chavero y Francisco del Paso y Troncoso. MNA, *Anales*, 5:1–260. [Text and translation of 1792–97 commentary.]
1901a   Pinturas jeroglíficas. Primera parte.

[15] Omitted are Chavero's numerous literary works, as well as those nearly exclusively archaeological. I am indebted to John B. Glass for use of his comprehensive, unpublished bibliography of Chavero made available in June, 1968.
[16] Various posthumous reissues, partial and complete, of [1887] not listed.
[17] Various posthumous reissues, partial and complete, of 1892a not listed.

Colección Chavero. Imprenta del Comercia de Juan E. Barbero. Mexico. 49 pp.

1901b Calendario o rueda del año de los antiguos indios: estudio cronológico. Imprenta del Museo Nacional. Mexico. 13 pp.

1901c Pinturas jeroglíficas. Segunda parte. Colección Chavero. Imprenta del Comercio de Juan E. Barbero. Mexico. 36 pp.

1902 Calendario de Palemke: los signos de los días. Memoria presentada al XIII Congreso Internacional des Americanistas. Tip. de F. P. Hoeck y cía. Mexico.

1903a Anales Mexicanos. Mexico-Azcapotzalco, 1426–1589. MNA, *Anales*, 7:49–74. [Translation by F. Galicia Chimalpopoca (1853) of a Ramírez copy of *Anales Tepanecas*, edited by Chavero.]

1903b Anónimo Mexicano. MNA, *Anales*, 7:115–32. [Nahuatl text of MS formerly in the Chavero Collection (now unknown), with incomplete translation by Aquiles Gerste, edited by Chavero.]

1903c Apuntes viejos de bibliografía mexicana. Mexico. [8 essays, 3 previously published: Códice Telleriano Remensis (pp. 5–12); Pinturas de los Soles (pp. 13–14); Peregrinación azteca (pp. 15–17); Cronistas tenochas (reprint, 1878, added material, pp. 19–36); Motolinía (pp. 37–41); Mendieta (pp. 43–45); Sahagún (reprint, 1877, best variant, pp. 47–84); Vetancurt (pp. 85–89).]

1903d Lettre préface. . . . *In* D. Charnay, ed. *Manuscrit Ramírez*. Histoire de l'origine des Indiens qui habitent la Nouvelle Espagne selon leurs traditions, pp. i–ix. Paris. [Ramírez as historian, works, and manuscripts.]

1903e Morfi. MNA, *Anales*, ep. 2, 1:52–53.

1903f Vega. MNA, *Anales*, ep. 2, 1:152–58. [Also re "Colección de Memorias de Nueva España," 32 vols.]

1903g Tovar. MNA, *Anales*, ep. 2, 1:242–46. ["Notas sobre los PP. José Acosta y Juan de Tovar," by Aquiles Gerste, edited by Chavero.]

1903h El monolito de Coatlinchan: estudio arquelógico. MNA, *Anales*, ep. 2, 1:281–305.

1904a Obras. Victoriano Agüeros, ed. Tomo I [all published], Escritos diversos. *Bib. Autores Mexicanos*, 52. Mexico. [27 works, biobibliographical introduction by Nicolás León. Fiction and geog-

raphy here omitted. 1, Sahagún [5th ed.] (1877a). 2, Sigüenza y Góngora (1886b). 3, Boturini (1886a). 4, Veytia (1905b). 5, Calendario Azteca (1875). 6, Colegio de Tlatelolco. 7, Muñoz Camargo. 7, Ixtlilxochitl (variant of 1891–92, pp. 4–6). 8, Las naves de Cortés (dated Sept. 17, 1876). 9, Tovar (1903g). 10, Fray Marcos de Niza. 11, Teotihuacan (previously published 1894, newspaper). 3 related MSS re native nobility.]

1904b Informe que rinde a los señores gobernadores de los Estados al círculo de Amigos del Sr. Gral Porfirio Díaz [por Alfredo Chavero], Presidente de dicho círculo. Mexico.

1905a Discurso pronunciado el 24 de septiembre de 1904. . . . MNA, *Anales*, ep. 2, 2:387–400. [Relation of archaeology to other sciences, and its practical value.]

1905b Veytia. MNA, *Anales*, ep. 2, 2:121–25. [See 1904a, no. 4.]

1906 Calendario de Palemke: Signos cronográficos. MNA, *Anales*, ep. 2, 3:53–96, 197–236.

n.d. [1939?] Historia antigua y de la conquista. Tomo primero. Volumen primero, [de] *México a través de los siglos*. Historia general y completa del desenvolvimiento social, político, religioso, militar, artístico, científico y literario de México desde la antiguedad más remota hasta la época actual. Obra única en su género publicada bajo la dirección del General D. Vicente Riva Palacio. 2d ed. Mexico.

1947 Historia de Tlaxcala. . . . Tomada de la edición de 1892, publicada por D. Alfredo Chavero. Primera edición ilustrada y anotada completa, corejada con el original que se conserva en al Archivo del Museo Nacional de Antropología, por Don Lauro E. Rosell y un estudio del Ing. Don Alberto Escalona Ramos, con el itinerario de los primitivos tlaxcaltecas. Mexico.

1948 Sahagún. (Vargas Rea Biblioteca Aportación Histórica, Segunda Serie). Mexico. [Reprint of 1877a edition.]

1952 Obras históricas of Fernando de Alva Ixtlilxochitl. Publicadas y anotadas por Alfredo Chavero. Nueva edición facsimilar con un prólogo del señor Lic. Ignacio Dávila Garibi. Editora Nacional. 2 vols. Mexico. [See 1891–92.]

1964 La conquista de México. Lienzo de Tlaxcala (explicación de Lienzo de Tlaxcala). Artes de Mexico. Mexico. [First published with Junta Colombina's facsimile in 1892.]

1966 Historia de Tlaxcala. Publicada y anotada por Alfredo Chavero. Homenaje a Cristóbal Colón. Ed. facsim. Oficina Tip. de la Secretaría de Fomento, 1892. Mexico. [See 1892b.]

Appendix F. PASO Y TRONCOSO, SELECTED WRITINGS AND PUBLICATIONS OF ETHNOHISTORICAL INTEREST

The Sahagún Corpus

1896 Etudes sur le Codex Mexicain du P. Sahagún conservé à la Bibliothèque Mediceo-Laurenziana de Florence [dated Moscow, 7/19 October]. Istituto Bibliografico Italiano (Firenze), *Rivista delle Biblioteche e degli Archivi*, Anno VII, 7:171–74. [Reprinted in Galindo y Villa, 1922, pp. 347–51. See also below, 1926.]

1898 Carta inédita del Sr. del Paso y Troncoso al Sr. D. José María Vigil, relativa a la publicación de la historia de Fr. Bernardino de Sahagún [Florence] 14 de junio. [Reprinted in Galindo y Villa, 1922, pp. 346–47.]

[1905a] [Historia general de las cosas de Nueva España, por Fray Bernardino de Sahagún. Tomo V. Madrid.] [Lacks title page, covers, date. Seemingly printed ca. 1903–09, but usually cited as 1905. Contains 158 numbered chromolithographs in color, made in Florence by Alejandro Ruffoni from drawings by Genaro López. These come from bks. 1–12 of the Florentino, found scattered through that manuscript, but here consolidated, without detailed captions. Most plates have more than one drawing; there are about 1,846 individual drawings. LC gift copy from Mexican government received 1924. Has blank title page with pasted printed slip: "Sahagún — Vol. V. Atlas de 158 estampas. Códice Florentino."]

[1905b] [i.e. 1912] Historia de las cosas de Nueva España por Fr. Bernardino de Sahagún. Edición parcial en facsímile de los Códices Matritenses en lengua mexicana que se custodian en las Bibliotecas del Palacio Real y de la Real Academia de la Historia. [Vol. 6.] Madrid. 1905.

[Cuaderno 1. "Descripción de los Códices," by FPT. Not published.]

[Cuaderno 2.] I. Primeros memoriales compilados en cuatro capítulos por Fr. Bernardino de Sahagún, como fundamento para escribir la obra intitulada Historia de las cosas de Nueva España. [Various folios disordered in originals placed in proper sequence by FPT.] Pp. 1–175. Real Palacio MS. Pp. 1–108 Ritos, Dioses, Cielo e infierno. Academy of History MS. Pp. 109–175 [Cielo e infierno continued, Señorío, Cosas humanas]. II. Memoriales con escolios, que comenzó a componer en dos cuadernos Fr. Bernardino de Sahagún para perfeccionar la obra general intitulada Historia de las cosas de Nueva España. Pp. 177–215. Real Palacio MS. Pp. 177–97 [cosas del cielo]. Academy of History MS. Pp. 199–215 [cosas humanas].

[Cuaderno 3. Drawings in *Primeros memoriales*]. [Issued without cover, title page, date. Often bound with Tomo V (1905a). There are 27 numbered colored chromolithographs, with captions in Nahuatl and source indications. Pls. 1–17 (Ritos, Dioses, Cielo e infierno) are in the Real Palacio MS; pls. 18–27 (Señorío, Cosas humanas) from Academy of History MS. The separate illustrations of the Madrid codices, approximately 445 separate drawings, with their equivalents in the Florentine MS, are listed in Ballesteros Gaibrois, 1964, 1:304–26, and reproduced in color photography (on very reduced scale) in his vol. 2 (1964).]

1906 [i.e. 1912] Fray Bernardino de Sahagún. Historia de las cosas de Nueva

España. Publícase con fondos de la Secretaría de Educación Pública y Bellas Artes de México, por Francisco del Paso y Troncoso. . . . Vol. 7. Códice Matritense del Real Palacio (edición complementaria en facsímile). Madrid.

Advertencia, Indice general, iv pp.

Pls. a, Bk. 4, Astrología Natural. Cuenta de los años (fol. 189). Chromolithograph in color. b, Bk. 5, Astrología Judiciaría. Cuenta de los signos (fol. 242v). Chromolithograph in color.

I. Memoriales en tres columnas con el texto solamente de una columna, escrita en mexicana por industria de Fr. Bernardino de Sahagún. Edición en facsímile de seis libros de los doce que componen la obra general intitulada Historia de las cosas de Nueva España. Pp. 1–400. [From pp. 257–79 (bk. 4), FPT notes correspondences with Florentino MS (bk. 8); notes also that Matritense del Palacio, pp. 280–386 (bk. 5) is equivalent to Florentino, bk. 4, and Mat. del Palacio, pp. 388–400 (bk. 6), corresponds to Florentino, bk. 5, but does not give detailed collations. Details on Real Palacio MS given in Ballesteros Gaibrois, 1964, 1:13–72, and correlations with the Florentine MS, ibid., pp. 181–231.] II. Memoriales en español [often cited, "en castellano"]. Edición en facsímile con la traducción del texto mexicano contenido en los Libros primero y quinto de la Historia de las cósas de Nueva España, escrita por Fr. Bernardino de Sahagún. Pp. 401–48. [Bks. 1, 5 title only of bk. 2, in Real Palacio MS, ff. 1–24v. Details in Ballesteros Gaibrois, 1964, 1:7–12.]

1907 [i.e. 1912] Fray Bernardino de Sahagún. Historia de las cosas de Nueva España. Publícase con fondos de la Secretaría de Educación Pública y Bellas Artes de México, por Francisco del Paso y Troncoso. . . . Vol. 8. Códice Matritense de la Real Academia de la Historia (Edición complementaria en facsímile). . . . Madrid. 1907.

Memoriales en tres columnas con el texto en lengua mexicana de cuatro libros (VIII á XI) de los doce que componen la obra general. Pp. 1–568. [Details in Ballesteros Gaibrois, 1964, 1:85–172, and correlations with Florentino MS, ibid., pp. 232–48.]

1909a El señor Del Paso y Troncoso a don Porfirio Díaz, 31 de julio de 1909. In Zavala, 1938, pp. 232–33 [Doc. 129].

1909b Informe al Señor Secretario de Estado y del Despacho de Instrucción Pública y Bellas Artes, 31 de agosto de 1909. In Zavala, 1938, pp. 67–79 [Doc. 35].

1912 Informe al Sr. Secretario de Estado y del Despacho de Instrucción Pública y Bellas Artes, 30 de septiembre de 1912. In Zavala, 1938, pp. 91–98 [Doc. 46].

1926 Estudios sobre el Códice Mexicano del P. Sahagún conservado en la Biblioteca Mediceo-Laurenziana de Florencia. MNA, Anales, ep. 4, 4:316–20. [Spanish translation of 1896.]

Papeles de Nueva España

First Series: Bibliographies
[not published by FPT]

1928–33 Indices de documentos de Nueva España en el Archivo de Indias de Sevilla. Introducción de Genaro Estrada. 4 vols. Secretaría de Relaciones Exteriores. *Monografías Bibliográficas Mexicanas*, 12, 14, 22, 24. Mexico. [Details on approximately 10,000 items, many of which were copied by FPT; various of these still remain in the Paso y Troncoso Collection, INAH. Complete listing of volume contents in Millares Carlo and Mantecón, 1959, pp. 79–81.]

Second Series: Geography and Statistics
Volume 1 [published by FPT]

1905 Papeles de Nueva España, publicados de orden y con fondos del Gobierno Mexicano por Francisco del Paso y Troncoso. Segunda Serie. Geografía y Estadística. Tomo I. Suma de Visitas de pueblos por orden alfabético. Manuscrito 2,800 de la Biblioteca Nacional de Madrid. Anónimo de la mitad del siglo xvi. Madrid. PNE, 1:1–332.

Contains various subsections, enumerated as follows:

i. Abecedario de las visitas de los pueblos de la Nueva Espana. PNE, 1:1–16. [Roughly alphabetical listing of 907 communities which FPT has numbered in following pages.]

ii. [Suma de Visitas]. PNE, 1:17–311. [Brief descriptions of 843 places, in roughly alphabetical order, through fol. 223r of MS, given nos. 1–843 by FPT. Important analysis, dating various entries, appears in Borah and Cook, 1960. This published version differs slightly from MS 2,800; does not include partial entries and deleted items, but paleography is generally reliable.]

iii. Relación de la visita que hizo Baltasar de Sa[n] Miguel del pueblo de Tecoantepeque y su probincia. PNE, 1:312–14. [Fols. 224r–224v of MS refer to Tehuantepec, no. 780 in previous listing, but more detailed. Dated 1550.]

iv. Relación de la visita del pueblo de Chichicapa questa en cabeza de su Magestad. Es en la comarca de Guaxaca. PNE, 1:314–15. [Fols. 225r–225v of MS. Five towns, nos. 844–48; undated.]

v. Relación de la visita de los pueblos de Coatlan y Miaguatlan y Xictla y sus sugetos, que visito Juan de Corral, vezino de Guaxaca. PNE, 1:316–17. [MS, fols. 226r–232r blank. Three towns, numbered by FPT 849–51.]

vi. Relación de los pueblos que visito Gaspar Xuarez en la provincia de Zacatula. PNE, 1:318–32. [MS, fols. 233r–240r. Undated. Nos. 852–907, apparently in geographical order.]

Volume 2 [not published by FPT; published by Vargas Rea]

1944–45 Papeles de Nueva España, coleccionados por Francisco del Paso y Troncoso. Geografía y Estadística. Tomo II. Segunda Serie. Relaciones Geográficas de Michoacán. MS de la Real Academia de Historia y del Archivo de Indias de Sevilla. Vargas Rea, ed. Biblioteca Aportación Histórica. 7 vols. in 6. Mexi-

co. Cited as VR/PNE, 2/volume: page. [Despite title, does not contain Relaciones; primarily material by Lebrón de Quiñones. Vols. 1–4 paginated consecutively; vols. 5, 6, 7 each paginated separately.]

1944a Vol. 1. Peticiones de Conquistadores; Corregimientos de la Nueva España. VR/PNE, 2/1:7–[49]. [Index, pp. 7–9, listing 6 documents, with archival indicia, all from AGI, Patronato, Papeles de Simancas.]

a. Doc. I. Extracto. Petición de Gutierre de Badajoz. n.d. VR/PNE, 2/1:11–17. [AGI, Patronato, 58–6–9.]

b. Doc. II. Extracto. Peticiones de Diego de Porras, 1527. VR/PNE, 2/1:18–22. [AGI, Patronato, 58–6–9.]

c. Doc. III. Memoria de los corregimientos de Nueva España. n.d. VR/PNE, 2/1:23–[50]. [AGI, Patronato, 2–2–4, no. 9.]

1944b Vol. 2. Comisión que dió Don Luis de Velasco. . . . VR/PNE, 2/2:51–[98]. Doc. IV. Comisión que dió Don Luis de Velasco, virrey, al Licenciado Lebrón de Quiñones, 1553. VR/PNE, 2:51–[98]. [AGI, Patronato, 5–4–3.]

1945a Vol. 3. Relación. Memoria de los pueblos de la provincia de Colima. VR/PNE, 2/3:98–[143]. Doc. V. [Lorenzo Lebrón de Quiñones]. Relación sumaria . . . de la visita. 1554. Parte 1. Memoria de los pueblos de la provincia de Colima [1551]. VR/PNE, 2/3:99–[143].

1945b Vol. 4. Memoria de los Pueblos. . . . VR/PNE, 2/4:145–[217]. Doc. V [cont'd]. . . . Parte 1. Memoria de los pueblos de la provincia de Colima. VR/PNE, 2/3:145–[217]. i, Amula, Zapotlan, pp. 145–152. ii, Abecedario de los vecinos de Colima, pp. 152–54, 161–204. iii, Cuaderno de las cedulas de los encomenderos, pp. 204–[217]

1945c Vol. 5. Relación. Segunda Parte. VR/PNE, 2/5:7–[61]. Doc. V [cont'd]. [Lorenzo Lebrón de Quiñones]. Relación sumaria. . . . Parte 2. VR/PNE, 2/5:7–[61].

1945d Vols. 6, 7. Relación, Tercera y Cuarta Parte. Carta. VR/PNE, 2/6&7:7–[130]. [2 vols. in 1.]

a. Doc. V [cont'd]. [Lorenzo Lebrón

de Quiñones]. Relación sumaria. . . . Parte 3. VR/PNE, 2/6&7:7–83.

b. Doc. V [cont'd] . . . Parte 4. VR/PNE, 2/6&7:85–120.

c. Doc. VI. [Lorenzo Lebrón de Quiñones] Carta a S. M. Antequera, 9 de abril de 1559. VR/PNE, 2/6&7:121–[130]. [Docs. V and VI from AGI, Patronato, 5–4–3.]

Volume 3 [partially published by FPT; partially published by Vargas Rea; incomplete]

1905 Papeles de Nueva España, publicados de orden y con fondos del Gobierno Mexicano, por Francisco del Paso y Troncoso. Segunda Serie. Geografía y Estadística. Tomo III. Descripción del Arzobispado de México. Manuscrito del Archivo de Indias en Sevilla. Año 1571. Madrid. Descripción del Arzobispado de México, sacada de las memoriales originales, hechas por los doctrineros ó capellanes, y compiladas por Fr. Bartolomé de Ledesma, O.S.D., Administrador del mismo Arzobispado. PNE, 3:3–167. [Responses to RC of Jan. 23, 1569, made by orders of Mexican Archbishop Fr. Alonso de Montúfar, giving data on religious establishments. Beginning with the city of Mexico, various groups of short reports touch geographically grouped doctrinas of the archbishopric, except eastern ones. Document transcribed was in AGI, Papeles de Simancas, 60–4–1. Published version covers only Mexico City and northern portion of archdiocese. The FPT volume is incomplete, partially completed by Vargas Rea, 1946–47 (listed below).]

i. [Ciudad de México]. PNE, 3:3–27. [Ten accounts by various hands giving data on ecclesiastical establishments and jurisdictions within Mexico City.]

ii. Los pueblos, minas y lugares que caen a la parte del norte de la ciudad de Mexico. Norte. PNE, 3:28–167. [Group of 45 separate descriptions by ecclesiastics of Indian doctrinas, giving many demographic data; some accounts are lengthy, with separate individual reports of component communities.

Materials cover fols. 8v–61, of apparently 141 folios, and is signed by Bartolomé de Ledesma.

1946–47 Papeles de Nueva España, coleccionados por Francisco del Paso y Troncoso. Segunda Serie. Geografía y Estadística. Tomo III. Suplemento. Informaciones secretas del arzobispado de México, 1569. Vargas Rea, editor. Biblioteca Aportación Histórica. Mexico City. 7 vols., paged continuously. Cited as VR/PNE, 3/volume:page. [These volumes continue FPT, 1905 (vol. 3). Editorial note in VR/PNE, 3/1 indicates Vargas Rea used FPT transcript from Library of INAH. The original MS is AGI, Patronato, Papeles de Simancas, 60–4–1, fols. 144–218v, covered in vols. 1–6, with further material from same legajo in vol. 7, foliation not stated. Most of the materials are "Opinions" in answer to eight queries concerning how to improve government and administration of New Spain.]

1946a Vol. 1. Informaciones secretas del Arzobispado de México. 1569. VR/PNE, 3/1:5–[44].

a. [Señor don Frai Alonso de Montúfar, Arzobispo], "Diligencias que se hizierion por orden del Arzobispado de México, para obedecer y cumplir la Real Cédula de 23 de enero de 1569 e instrucción del Licenciado Juan de Ovando. Mexico. 8 de octubre de 1569." [Archbishop's statement; VR/PNE, 3/2–6. Attachments ("Pareceres") follow.]

1946b Vol. 2. Pareceres . . . VR/PNE, 3/2:51–[91].

ii, Parecer, Luis de Castilla, Oct. 11, 1569, pp. 52–57. iii, Parecer, Bernardino del Castillo, Oct. 14, 1569, pp. 79–[91].

1946c Vol. 3. Pareceres . . . VR/PNE, 3/3:95–[140].

iv, Parecer, Juan Guerrero, Oct. 15, 1569, pp. 95–115. v, Parecer, Bach. Francisco de Carrizo, n.d. [Oct. 1569], pp. 117–[140].

1947a Vol. 4 Pareceres . . . VR/PNE, 3/4:141–[174].

vi, Parecer, Lic. Fulgenio de Vigue,

Nov. 3, 1569, pp. 142–60. vii, Parecer, Martín de Aranguren, Nov. 4, 1569, pp. 161–[174].

1947b Vol. 5. Pareceres . . . VR/PNE, 3/5:175–[231].

viii, Parecer, Don Fernando de Portugal, Tesorero, Nov. 5, 1569, pp. 175–209. ix, Parecer, Dr. Rodrigo Barbosa, Nov. 14, 1569, pp. 211–23. x, Parecer, Hernan Gutierrez Altamirano, n.d. [Nov. 1569], pp. 225–[231].

1947c Vol. 6. Pareceres . . . VR/PNE, 3/6:233–[297].

xi, Parecer, Hernan Gutierrez Altamirano, Nov. 18, 1569, pp. 234–38 [continuation of x?]. xii, Parecer, Dr. Zurnero, Nov. 19, 1569, pp. 239–41. xiii, Parecer, Dr. Zurnero, Mar. 15, 1567 [sic], pp. 241–70. xiv, Parecer, Gabriel Diez, Nov. 19, 1569, pp. 271–83. xv, Parecer, Pedro de Requena, Nov. 21, 1569.

1947d Vol. 7 Pareceres . . . VR/PNE, 3/7:301–[339].

xvi, Parecer, Bachiller Martínez, Dec. 15, 1569, pp. 301–12. xvii, Parecer, D. Francisco de Velasco, Dec. 16, 1569, pp. 313–19 [this terminates the Montúfar "Diligencias" document, followed in vol. 7 by the two next items]:

b. Mandamiento de los Alcaldes del Crimen de la Audiencia de Mexico notificando al Arzobispado y provisor de dicha ciudad para que dieran licencia para prender a las personas eclesiasticas que resultaren culpados en causa que se seguía sobre un libelo que aparecio en las puertas de la catedral. Mexico. Dec. 20, 1574. VR/PNE, 3/7:321–332. [Also from AGI, Patronato 60-4-1; editor misprints date as 1474.]

c. Auto de la Audiencia de Mexico notificando al Arzobispo y cabildo eclesiastico, para que no se representasen comedias ni otros actos en la Iglesia sin que antes se vieran en dicha Audiencia. Mexico. Dec. 10, 1574. VR/PNE, 3/7:333–[339]. [Also from AGI, Patronato, 60-4-1, foliation not provided. This terminates Tomo III, Suplemento.]

Volume 4 [published by FPT]

1905 Papeles de Nueva España, publicado de orden y con fondos de Gobierno Mexicano por Francisco del Paso y Troncoso. Segunda Serie. Geografía y Estadística. Tomo IV. Relaciones Geográficas de la Diócesis de Oaxaca. Manuscritos de la Real Academia de la Historia de Madrid y del Archivo de Indias en Sevilla, años 1579–1581. Madrid. [The RG Census (Article 8) provides full data, not repeated here.]

i. Instruction [sic] y memoria de las relaciones que se han de hazer, para la descripcion de las Yndias, que su Magestad manda hazer, para el buen govierno y ennoblescimiento dellas. PNE, 4:1–7. Cedula and instructions of May 25, 1577. [Translated in Article 5, Appendixes A, B, C.]

ii. 1. Relación de Iztepexi [Census, 57]. PNE, 4:9–23.

iii. 2. Relación de Xuchitepec [Census, 88]. PNE, 4:24–28.

iv. 3. Relación de Nexapa [Census, 73]. PNE, 4:29–44.

v. 4. Relación de Ucila [Census, 138]. PNE, 4:45–52.

vi. 5. Relación de Texupa [Census, 124]. PNE, 4:53–57.

vii. 6. Relación de Chinantla [Census, 24]. PNE, 4:58–68.

viii. 7. Relación de Tilantongo [Census, 127]. PNE, 4: 69–87.

ix. 8. Relación de Papaloticpac [Census, 78]. PNE, 4:88–99.

x. 9. Relación de Macuilsuchil [Census, 62]. PNE, 4:100–08.

xi. 10. Relación de Teticpac [Census, 119]. PNE, 4: 109–14.

xii. 11. Relación de Chichicapa [Census, 21]. PNE, 4:115–43.

xiii. 12. Relación de Tlacolula y Mitla [Census, 133]. PNE, 4:144–54.

xiv. 13. Relación de Cuahuitlan [Census, 33]. PNE, 4:155–62.

xv. 14. Relación de Atlatlauca y Malinaltepec [Census, 11]. PNE, 4:163–76.

xvi. 15. Relación de Taliztaca [Census, 94]. PNE, 4:177–82.

xvii. 16. Relación de Cuicatlan [Census, 35]. PNE, 4:183–89.

xviii. 17. Relación de Teozapotlan [Census, 109]. PNE, 4:190–95.

xix. 18. Relación de Guaxilotitlan

[Census, 46]. PNE, 4:196–205.

xx. 19. Relación de Nochiztlan [Census, 74]. PNE, 4:206–12.

xxi. 20. Relación de Teutitlan del Camino [Census, 107]. PNE, 4:213–31.

xxii. 21. Relación de Guatulco [Census, 45]. PNE, 4:232–51.

xxiii. 22. Relación de Xalapa [Census, 142]. PNE, 4:252–66.

xxiv. Suplemento. Relaciones Geográficas de los pueblos de Miahuatlan, Ocelotepec, Coatlan y Amatlan . . . Manuscrito 3,064 de la Biblioteca Nacional de Madrid. Año de 1609. Advertencia. PNE, 4:267–71.

xxv. Interrogatorio para todas las ciudades, villas y lugares de Españoles, y pueblos de naturales de las Indias Occidentales, Islas y Tierra Firme; al qual se ha de satisfazer, conforme a las preguntas siguientes, aviendolas averiguado en cada pueblo con puntualidad y cuydado [1604]. PNE, 4:46–53.
Biblioteca Nacional de Madrid, MS 3035, fols. 46–53. [Questionnaire on which following 1609 RG's were compiled:]

xxvi. 23. Descripción [1609] del Partido de Miahuatlan [Census, 306]. PNE, 4:289–300.

xxvii. Relación del pueblo de Ocelotepeque [1609] [Census, 308]. PNE, 4: 301–07.

xxviii. Relación del pueblo de Coatlan [1609] [Census, 302]. PNE, 4:308–13.

xxix. Relación del pueblo de Amatlan [1609] [Census, 301]. PNE, 4:314–19.

Volume 5 [published by FPT]

1905 Papeles de Nueva España publicados de orden y con fondos del Gobierno Mexicano por Francisco del Paso y Troncoso. Segunda Serie. Geografía y Estadística. Tomo V. Relaciones Geográficas de la Diócesis de Tlaxcala. Manuscritos de la Real Academia de la Historia de Madrid y del Archivo de Indias de Sevilla. Años 1580–1582. Madrid. PNE, 5:1–286. [Contains 8 RG's 1580–82, plus supplementary reports, 1569–71.

RG Census (Article 8) provides full data, not repeated here.]

i. 1. Relación de Tlacotalpan [Census, 134]. PNE, 5:1–11.

ii. 2. Relación de Tepeaca [Census, 110]. PNE, 5:12–45.

iii. 3. Relación de Cuzcatlan [Census, 42]. PNE, 5:46–54.

iv. 4. Relación de Acatlan [Census, 2]. PNE, 5:55–80.

v. 5. Relación de Ahuatlan [Census, 3]. PNE, 5:81–98.

vi. 6. Relación de Xalapa de la Veracruz [Census, 141]. PNE, 5:99–123.

vii. 7. Relación de Xonotla y Tetela [Census, 118]. PNE, 5:124–73.

viii. 8. Relación de Chilapa [Census, 22bis]. PNE, 5:174–82.

ix. Suplemento a las Relaciones Geográficas de la Diócesis de Tlaxcala. Manuscritos del Archivo de Indias en Sevilla. Años 1569–1571. Advertencia. PNE, 5:183–88.

x. Apuntes para la descripción de Veracruz. PNE, 5:189–201. [Arias Hernandez; Nov. 3, 1571. AGI, Papeles de Simancas, Indiferente General, 145-7-8.]

xi. Doctrinas á cargo de clérigos. Diócesis de Tlaxcala (1569). PNE, 5:202–72. [Reports supplied on orders by Bishop Fernando de Villagomez; 37 items, from AGI, Papeles de Simancas, Indiferente General, 145-7-8.]

xii. Memorias de los pueblos que doctrinaban los religiosos de la Orden de San Agustín en la Diócesis de Tlaxcala. PNE, 5:273–86. [Five reports, Mar. 1571, by monastery priors, from AGI, Papeles de Simancas, Indiferente General, 145-7-8.]

Volume 6 [published by FPT]

1905 Papeles de Nueva España, publicados de orden y con Fondos del Gobierno Mexicano por Francisco del Paso y Troncoso. Segunda Serie. Geografía y Estadística. Tomo VI. Relaciones Geográficas de la Diócesis de México. Manuscritos de la Real Academia de la Historia de Madrid y del Archivo de Indias en Sevilla. Años 1579–1582. Madrid. PNE, 6:1–322.

[Total of 19 RG's; Census data (Article 8) not repeated here.]

i. 1. Relación de las Minas de Zimapan [Census, 155]. PNE, 6:1–5.

ii. 2. Relación de Totolapa [Census, 136]. PNE, 6:6–11.

iii. 3. Relación de Ueipuchtla [Tornacustla, Census, 135]. PNE, 6:12–38.

iv. 4. Relación de Coatepec [Census, 29]. PNE, 6:39–86.

v. 5. Relación de Ichcateopan [Census, 52]. PNE, 6:87–152.

vi. 6. Relación de Citlaltomagua y Anecuilco [Census, 28]. PNE, 6:153–66.

vii. 7. Relación de Chiconauhtla [Census, 22]. PNE, 6:167–77.

viii. 8. Relación de Zayula [Census, 153]. PNE, 6:178–82.

ix. 9. Relación de Uexutla [Huexotla, Census, 51]. PNE, 6:183–92.

x. 10. Relación de Mexicatzingo [Census, 65]. PNE, 6:193–98.

xi. 11. Relación de Atitlalaquia [Census, 12]. PNE, 6:199–208.

xii. 12. Relación de Tecciztlan [Census, 116]. PNE, 6:209–36.

xiii. 13. Relación de la Villa de Tepuztlan [Census, 112]. PNE, 6:237–50.

xiv. 14. Relación de Ocopetlayuca [Census, 76]. PNE, 6:251–62.

xv. 15. Relación de las Minas de Tasco [Census, 96]. PNE, 6:263–82.

xvi. 16. Relación de Tetela del Volcan y Ueyapan [Census, 117]. PNE, 6:283–90.

xvii. 17. Relación de Tepepulco [Census, 111]. PNE, 6:291–305.

xviii. 18. Relación de Cuauhquilpan [Census, 32]. PNE, 6:306–12.

xix. 19. Relación de las Minas de Zumpango [Census, 164]. PNE, 6:313–22.

Volume 7 [partially published by FPT; partially published by MNA; completed by Vargas Rea]

1906 [i.e. 1932] Papeles de Nueva España publicados de orden y con fondos del Gobierno Mexicano por Francisco del Paso y Troncoso. Segunda Serie. Geografía y Estadística. Manuscritos de la Real Academia de la Historia de Madrid y del Archivo de Indias en Sevilla. Años 1579–1582. Tomo VII: Relaciones Geográficas de la Diócesis de México y de la de Michoacán. Años 1579–1582. Madrid. [Impresas en facsimile las portadas y pags. de la 17 hasta el final en los talleres Gráficos del Museo Nacional . . . México. 1932]. PNE, 7:1–29. [Incomplete; contains 3 RG's for archdiocese of Mexico. Remaining materials published by Luis Vargas Rea, q.v. below.]

i. 20. Relación de Teutenango [Census, 122]. PNE, 7:1–7.

ii. 21. Relación de las Minas de Sultepec [Census, 163]. PNE, 7:8–14.

iii. 22. Relación de las Minas de Temzacaltepec [Census, 103, omitting 103D]. PNE, 7:15–29. [Terminates RG's from archbishopric of Mexico.]

1944–46 Papeles de Nueva España coleccionados por Francisco del Paso y Troncoso. Segunda Serie. Geografía y Estadística. MS de la Real Academia de Historia de Madrid y del Archivo de Indias de Sevilla. Tomo VII. Suplemento. Relaciones Geográficas de Michoacán. Luis Vargas Rea, ed. Mexico City. 8 vols. Cited as VR/PNE, 7/volume:page. [Materials from FPT papers in INAH, inaccurately published in limited edition on poor paper. Pagination is continuous in vols. 1–4 (157 pages) and in vols. 7, 8 (130 pages), but vol. 5 (56 pages) and vol. 6 (50 pages) have separate pagination. Vol. 4 also bears additional subseries title: Documentos relativos a Guanaxuato. Detailed analysis of these pamphlets follows:

1944 Vol. 1. Relaciones Geográficas de Michoacán . . . VR/PNE, 7/1:5–46. [Editorial note (pp. i–iii) on Paso y Troncoso mission, and intent to publish missing materials collected for Tomo VII. Opposite p. 5 is unidentified map of Michoacan, ca. 1580? Following are four unsigned, undated documents, apparently 18th-century reports of Tepic, Sentipac, Acaponeta, Santispac.]

i. Jurisdicción de Tepic. VR/PNE, 7/1:7–12.

ii. De la jurisdicción de Sentipac. VR/PNE, 7/1:13–17.

iii. Jurisdicción de Santispac. VR/PNE, 7/1:19–23.

iv. Jurisdicción de Acaponeta. VR/PNE, 7/1:25–28.

v. [Relación de] Xiquilpa [Census, 60]. VR/PNE, 7/1:29–45.

1945a Vol. 2. Relaciones Geográficas de Michoacán . . . VR/PNE, 7/2:47–[84].

vi. Instrucsion [*sic*] y memoria de las relaciones que se han de hazer . . . VR/PNE, 7/2:47–64. [Cedula of May 25, 1577, specifying RG reports. See above Volume 4, 1905, i.]

vii. Chocandiran [Census, 60A]. VR/PNE, 7/2:62–74.

viii. Tarequato [Census, 60B]. VR/PNE, 7/2:75–[84].

1945b Vol. 3. Relaciones Geográficas de Michoacán . . . VR/PNE, 7/3:85–[112].

ix. Ynstruzion [*sic*] [Relación] del pueblo de Perivan [Census, 60C]. VR/PNE, 7/3:85–98.

x. Relación de Taymeo [Census, 93]. VR/PNE, 7/3:99–105.

xi. Relación de Necotlan [Census, 72]. VR/PNE, 7/3:107–[112].

1945c Vol. 4. Relaciones Geográficas de Michoacán. Documentos relativos a Guanaxuato. Relación de Celaya y su partido, año de 1570 [*sic*, i.e., 1580]. VR/PNE, 7/4:113–[157]. [Editorial note states that this is first of 10 volumes containing documents on Guanaxuato which he will publish to honor a forthcoming Congreso de Historia in Guanajuato. Map of Celaya-Acambaro faces p. 115 [Map List: 10], with that of Yurirapundaro [Map List: 84] opp. p. 146.]

xii. Relación de Celaya [Census, 18]. VR/PNE, 7/4:115–23.

xiii. Provincia de Ancanbaro [*sic*] [Census, 18A]. VR/PNE, 7/4:-124–146.

xiv. Pueblo de Yurirapúndaro [Census, 18B]. VR/PNE, 7/4:146–[156].

xv. Notas. VR/PNE, 7/4:[157]. [FPT notes on map of Yurirapundaro not with text in RAH, but in map section, AGI.]

1946d Vol. 5. Relaciones Geográficas de Michoacán . . . VR/PNE, 7/5:7–[56].

xv. Relación de Chitchota [Census, 23]. VR/PNE, 7/5:7–[56].

1946e Vol. 6. Relaciones Geográficas de Michoacán . . . VR/PNE, 7/6:7–[50].

xvi. Relación de Asuchitlan [Census, 7]. VR/PNE, 7/6:7–[50].

1946f Vol. 7. Relaciones Geográficas de Michoacán . . . VR/PNE, 7/7:7–[67].

xvii. Relación de Sirandaro y Guayameo [Census, 157; 157C omitted]. VR/PNE, 7/7:9–31.

xviii. Relación de Cuseo [Census, 38]. VR/PNE, 7/7:32–.

xix. Relación de Patzcuaro [Census, 79]. VR/PNE, 7/7:–60.

xx. Relación de Zinguanzingo [Census, 156]. VR/PNE, 7/7:61–[67].

1946g Vol. 8. Relaciones Geográficas de Michoacán . . . VR/PNE, 7/8:73–[130].

xxi. Relación de Chocandiran [Tingüindin] [Census, 128]. VR/PNE, 7/8:73–90.

xxii. Relación de Tamatzula, Tuspa y Zapotlan [Census, 137]. VR/PNE, 7/8:93–[130].

Volume 8 [not published by FPT; published by Vargas Rea]

1947 Papeles de Nueva España, coleccionados por Francisco del Paso y Troncoso. Segunda Serie. Geografía y Estadística. MS de la Real Academia de Historia de Madrid y del Archivo de Indias de Sevilla. Tomo VIII. Relaciones de Minas. Luis Vargas Rea, ed. Mexico City. 6 vols. Biblioteca Aportación Histórica. Cited as VR/PNE, 8/volume: page. [From FPT transcripts in INAH. Paged continuously through six poorly printed, carelessly edited small volumes.]

1947a Vol. 1. Relación de las minas, Relación de Compostela, Relación de las Minas de Xocotlan, Relación de Nuchistlan. Mexico City. VR/PNE, 8/1:7–[74].

i. Relación de las minas que ay en el Nuevo Reyno de Galizia. VR/PNE, 8/1:7–[10]. [Not an

RG, but list of mines. MS in RAH, 9–25–4.4662/II.]

ii. Relación de Compostela [Census, 31]. VR/PNE, 8/1:11–32.

iii. Relación de las Minas de Xocotlan [Census, 144]. VR/PNE, 8/1:33–57.

iv. Relación de Suchipila y Nuchistlan [Census, 75]. VR/PNE, 8/1:59–[74].

1947b Vol. 2. Relación de Minas. VR/PNE, 8/2:78–[130].

v. Relación de la Villa de la Purificación [Census, 84]. VR/PNE, 8/2:78–130.

1947c Vol. 3. Relación de Minas. VR/PNE, 8/3:135–[190].

vi. Relación de la Villa de San Martin e Llerna e Minas de Sombrete [Census, 87]. VR/PNE, 8/3:135–85.

vii. Petition. VR/PNE, 8/3:185–[190]. [Miners ask settlement of peaceful Indians.]

1947d Vol. 4. Relación de Minas. VR/PNE, 8/4:192–[260].

viii. Relación de la Villa de Xerez [Census, 143]. VR/PNE, 8/4:192–219.

ix. Relación de Poncitlan y Cuiseo [Census, 82]. VR/PNE, 8/4:221–[260].

1947e Vol. 5. Relación de Minas. Minas de Fresnillo. Nueva Galicia. VR/PNE, 8/5:263–[302].

x. Relación de las Minas de Fresnillo [Pedro de Medina] [Census, 44A]. VR/PNE, 8/5:263–79.

xi. Relación de las Minas de Fresnillo [Francisco Ruiz] [Census, 44B]. VR/PNE, 8/5:281–91.

xii. Relación de las Minas de Fresnillo [Alonso Tabuya] [Census, 44C]. VR/PNE, 8/5:293–[302].

1947f Vol. 6. Relación de Minas. Otras Relaciones de Minas de Fresnillo. VR/PNE, 8/6:305–[336].

xiii. Otra Relación de Minas de Fresnillo [Juan de Huidobro] [Census, 44D]. VR/PNE, 8/6:305–24.

xiv. Otra Relación de Minas de Fresnillo [Pedro Gaitan] [Census, 44E]. VR/PNE, 8/6:325–[336].

Volume 9 [not published by FPT; partially published by Vargas Rea; also by Ramírez Cabañas and by MNA]

1948 Papeles de Nueva España coleccionados por Francisco del Paso y Troncoso. Segunda Serie. Geografía y Relaciones Geográficas de Galicia, Vizcaya y León. Estadística. Tomo IX y Ultimo. Luis Vargas Rea, ed. Mexico City. 7 vols. Biblioteca Aportación Histórica. Cited as VR/PNE, 9/volume:page. [This group of volumes reproduces part of Fray Alonso Mota y Escobar, Obispo de Tlaxcala, *Memoriales*. Part 1, from Biblioteca Nacional de Madrid, MS 6877. Part appeared as "Memoriales del Obispo de Tlaxcala Fray Alonso de la Mota y Escobar" in INAH, *Anales*, 1:191–306 (1945); that portion deals primarily with places in the bishopric of Tlaxcala, 1608–24. Seemingly in 1930 these papers were not found in the FPT Collection; editions have been taken from a manuscript then owned by Federico Gómez de Orozco. The present portion, seemingly considered by FPT as Part 2 of the Memoriales, was copied by him from the British Museum MSS Add. 13,964, and formed legajo 105 of his materials: "Papeles de Nueva España. Segunda Serie. Complemento al Tomo IX. Alonso de la Mota y Escobar, obispo de Tlaxcala. Descripción de los reinos de Galicia, Vizcaya y León, memoriales." The latter was published, in limited edition with introduction by Joaquín Ramírez Cabañas (Mexico City, 1930), and reissued in a trade edition using the latter's edition in 1940 (ed. Pedro Robredo, Mexico City). Either or both of these versions are better for scholarly use than the Vargas Rea publication, herewith described. It has continuous pagination through seven small volumes, each given an arbitrary title to cover a portion of the material included in it.]

1948a Vol. 1. [Alonso de la Mota y Escobar]. Descripción Geográfica de los Reynos de Galizia, Vizcaya, y León. VR/PNE, 9/1:5–[36]. [Editorial note says publication of this material closes his publication of PNE materials, as well as series "Biblioteca Aportación Histórica." In a long Dedicatoria (pp. 7–13), Mota y Escobar indicates this document is in response to a 1608(?) questionnaire, but that to answer all questions for all places would entail excessive repetition, hence will generalize by geographical areas. Pp. 20–38 cover Indians, living and ancient. Banda del Norte, pp. 32–34, starts geographical coverage. On pp. 6 and 14 are unidentified woodcuts.]

1948b Vol. 2. La ciudad de Guadalajara en el siglo xvi. 1a y 2a. Salida. VR/PNE, 9/2:38–[58].

1948c Vol. 3. Pueblo de Aguacatlan, etc. VR/PNE, 9/3:59–[99].

1948d Vol. 4. Provincia de los Tagues, etc. VR/PNE, 9/4:101–[144].

1948e Vol. 5. Villa de Xerez, etc. VR/-PNE, 9/5:145–[182].

1948f Vol. 6. Villa de Saltillo, etc. VR/-PNE, 9/6:183–[220].

1948g Vol. 7. Reino de la Nueva Vizcaya, etc. VR/PNE, 9/7:221–[267].

Third Series: Histories

Cervantes de Salazar [partially published by FPT; completed by MNA].

1914–36 Papeles de Nueva España compilados y publicados por Francisco del Paso y Troncoso. Tercera Serie. Historia. Crónica de Nueva España escrita por el Doctor y Maestro Francisco Cervantes de Salazar, Cronista de la Ciudad de México. Manuscrito 2011 de la Biblioteca Nacional de Madrid, letra de la mitad del siglo xvi. 3 vols. Madrid, Mexico City.

i. Tomo I. Madrid. 1914. Introducción, pp. i–lvi; MS Map, Costas desde Nombre de Dios hasta Florida, descubiertas de 1502 a 1519, opp. p. lxvi; Libro Primero, pp. 1–69; Libro Segundo, pp. 71–166; Libro Tercero, pp. 167–331; Advertencia final: El estudio del códice continuará. Ilustración al primer tomo, pp. 337–353; Indice del primer tomo, pp. 355–363. [Introduction reviews polemic with Zelia Nuttall concerning who first found this MS. Onomastic index to Tomo I found in Apéndice, Tomo III, pp. 405–453; FPT notes on fiestas, Tomo I, chap. 19; also *ibid.*, pp. 395–401. Additional FPT notes to vol. 1 found in vol. 3, q.v.]

ii. Tomo II. Mexico City, 1936.

Talleres Gráficos del Museo Nacional de Arqueología, Historia y Etnografía. Introducción, Marcos E. Becerra, pp. i–iv; Libro Cuarto, pp. 1–270; Indice del Segundo Tomo, pp. 273–283. [Text taken by Federico Gómez de Orozco from printed version edited by Zelia Nuttall for Hispanic Society of America, hence lacks FPT notes; his annotated copies were lost following his death, April 30, 1916.]

iii. Tomo III. Mexico City. 1936. Talleres Gráficos del Museo Nacional de Arqueología, Historia y Etnografía. Introducción, Marcos E. Becerra, pp. i–ii; Libro Quinto, pp. 1–295; Libro Sexto, pp. 297–391; Apéndice, p. 393. Anotaciones de don Francisco del Paso y Troncoso al capítulo xix del Primer Libro, Tomo I de esta Crónica, pp. 395–401; Nota que contiene diversos apuntes o memorandos . . . de puño y letra de don Francisco del Paso y Troncoso . . . p. 403; Tabla onomástica de personas; instituciones, lugares y obras mencionados en el Tomo Primero, pp. 405–435; Tabla onomástica de personas mencionados en este Tomo Tercero, pp. 437–51; Algunos nuevos datos biográficos de Cervantes de Salazar, pp. 453–457; Indice del Tercer Tomo, pp. 459–481. [Text from Nuttall edition; see Tomo II. This volume contains FPT notes referring to Tomo I, q.v. above.]

Fourth Series: Language and Linguistics
No titles published.

Fifth Series: Epistolario
[not published by FPT; issued commercially]

1939–42 [Papeles de Nueva España]. Epistolaria de Nueva España, 1505–1818, recopilado por Francisco del Paso y Troncoso. 16 vols. Mexico City. Biblioteca Histórica Mexicana de Obras Inéditas, Segunda Serie, 1–16. [In 'Advertencia' to ENE, 1, p. vi, Silvio Zavala, who edited these materials, notes that index to FPT materials made by Icaza (1931) differed from plan of PNE set forth by FPT. Some documents that FPT planned to have in vols. 2 and 10 of

PNE were listed by Icaza as for ENE, hence these appear in published version of ENE. Several documents which are noted as "missing" in vols. 1–15 were later supplied, and appear in vol. 16; such substitute materials are indicated below by an asterisk.]

a. Tomo I. 1505–29. Mexico City, 1939. Advertencia, Silvio Zavala, pp. v–vii; Docs. 1–78, pp. 1–166; Indice de documentos del Tomo Primero, pp. 167–76. [Lacking: Doc. 69 (p. 71).]

b. Tomo II. 1530–32. Mexico City. 1939. Docs. 79–122, pp. 1–235; Indice de documentos del Tomo Segundo, pp. 237–44. [Lacking: Doc. 86 (pp. 25–26), Doc. 96 (p. 105),* Doc. 100 (p. 111).*]

c. Tomo III. 1533–39. Mexico City. 1939. Docs. 123–93, pp. 1–262; Indice de documentos del Tomo Tercero, pp. 263–72. [Lacking: Doc. 164 (p. 185; FPT copy in Carpeta II, Méritos y Servicios, 35 folios), Doc. 165 (p. 185; published MNA, *Anales*, ep. 4, 4:354–59), Doc. 169 (p. 191; published, DII, 14:235), Doc. 179 (p. 227; published, DII, 12:314), Doc. 180 (p. 227; published, DII, 2:179), Doc. 183 (pp. 233–34; published, DII, 42:149).*]

d. Tomo IV. 1540–46. Mexico City. 1939. Docs. 194–252, pp. 1–256; Indice de documentos del Tomo Cuarto, pp. 257–65. [Lacking: Doc. 194 (p. 1; published, DII, 14:375), Doc. 196 (p. 6), Doc. 204 (p. 32; published, *Cartas de Indias*, p. 253, no. 45).]

e. Tomo V. 1547–49. Mexico City. 1939. Docs. 253–91, pp. 1–217; Indice de documentos del Tomo Quinto, pp. 219–24. [Lacking: Doc. 257 (p. 22), Doc. 258 (p. 22).]

f. Tomo VI. 1550–52. Mexico City. 1939. Docs. 292–362, pp. 1–212; Indice de documentos del Tomo Sexto. [Lacking: Doc. 316 (p. 50; copy in Carpeta II, Méritos y Servicios), Doc. 325 (FPT copy, p. 65; in Carpeta I, Méritos y Servicios), Doc. 331 (p. 73),* Doc. 336 (p. 123), Doc. 338 (p. 124),*

Doc. 346bis, Doc. 354 (p. 172), Doc. 361 (p. 209).]

g. Tomo VII. 1553–54. Mexico City. 1940. Docs. 363–422, pp. 1–314; Indice de documentos del Tomo Septimo, pp. 315–22. [Lacking: Doc. 376 (p. 64), Doc. 402 (p. 221),* Doc. 416 (p. 290).*]

h. Tomo VIII. 1555–59. Mexico City. 1940. Doc. 423–83, pp. 1–265; Indice de documentos del Tomo Octavo, pp. 267–74. [Lacking: Doc. 439 (p. 66), Doc. 473 (p. 229).]

i. Tomo IX. 1560–63. Mexico City. 1940. Docs. 484–534, pp. 1–253; Indice de documentos del Tomo Noveno, pp. 255–61. [Lacking: Doc. 484 (p. 1),* Doc. 484bis (p. 1),* Doc. 489 (p. 53), Doc. 495 (p. 107), Doc. 497 (p. 109), Doc. 501 (p. 125),* Doc. 511 (pp. 145–46).*]

j. Tomo X. 1564–69. Mexico City. 1940. Docs. 535–623, pp. 1–313; Indice de documentos del Tomo Decimo, pp. 315–25. [Lacking: Doc. 542 (p. 21),* Doc. 563 (p. 77),* Doc. 569 (p. 129),* Doc. 570 (p. 129), Doc. 619 (p. 292).]

k. Tomo XI. 1570–75. Mexico City. 1940. Docs. 624–86, pp. 1–267; Indice de documentos del Tomo Undecimo, pp. 269–76. [Lacking: Docs. 655–58 (p. 122),* Doc. 665 (p. 135; published, JDE, 2:xxx–xxxviii [1885]), Docs. 685–86 (p. 267). See R. H. Barlow, Another Epistolario documento, *Tlalocan*, I, 1(1943):71. Doc. 665, originally omitted from PNE (t. 11, p. 135), inventory of Sta. Cruz, can be found in *Relaciones Geográficas de Indias (Peru)*, Jiménez de la Espada, ed., Madrid, 1885, t. 2, pp. xxx–xxxviii.]

l. Tomo XII. 1576–96. Mexico City. 1940. Docs. 687–743, pp. 1–203; Indice de documentos del Tomo Duodecimo, pp. 205–11.

m. Tomo XIII. 1597–1818. Mexico City. 1940. Docs. 744–98, pp. 1–390; Indice de documentos del Tomo Decimotercero, pp. 391–98. [Docs. 744–94 cover years 1597–1601, with majority concerned with details of Veracruz;

Doc. 795 is dated 1633; two lists of maps, Doc. 796 (1812) and 798 (1818), are only later items.]

n. Tomo XIV. Documentos sin fecha. I. Mexico City. 1940. Docs. 799–840, pp. 1–195; Indice de documentos del Tomo Decimo-cuarto, pp. 197–200. [Lacking: Docs. 799–800 (p. 1), Doc. 803 (p. 10), Doc. 811 (p. 28), Doc. 830 (p. 144), Doc. 831 (p. 145).°]

o. Tomo XV. Documentos sin fecha. II. Mexico City. 1940. Docs. 841–96, pp. 1–227; Indice de documentos del Tomo Decimoquinto, pp. 229–34. [Lacking: Doc. 879 (p. 168), Doc. 881 (p. 170).]

p. Tomo XVI. Apéndices e Indices. Mexico City. 1942. [From France V. Scholes, copies of missing documents: 55, 96, 100, 179, 183, 331, 338, 346bis, 402, 416, 439, 484, 484bis, 501, 511, 542, 563, 569, 655, 656, 657, 658, 831; pp. 3–93; Indice alfabético, pp. 97–204; Indice analítico, pp. 205–93; Indice auxiliar alfabético, pp. 294–310; Indice de documentos del Tomo Decimosexto, pp. 311–14.]

Sixth Series: Diccionario de Pobladores

1923 Diccionario autobiográfico de con-quistadores y pobladores de Nueva España, sacado de los textos origina-les por Francisco A. de Icaza. 2 vols. Madrid. [Zavala (1938, p. xii) clearly indicates that Icaza utilizó FPT copies, but suppressed the latter's name, adding his own; Icaza did write introduction and prepare in-dices.]

SELECTED OTHER WRITINGS AND PUBLICATIONS

Pictorial Documents (full citation and commen-tary are given in Article 32 for those marked JBG)

1882 Ensayo sobre los símbolos cronográ-ficos de los Mexicanos. MNA, *Anales*, 2:323–402. [JBG]

1886 Códice indiano del Sr. Sánchez Solís. MNA, *Anales*, 3:121–23. [JBG]

1888 Calendario de los tarascos. Museo Michoacano, *Anales*, 1:85–96. [JBG] [Reprinted, MNA, *Anales*, 4:57–63 (1897).]

1897 Los libros de Anahuac. 11th Con-

greso Internacional de Americanistas (Mexico, 1895), *Actas*, pp. 78–87. [JBG]

1898a Descripción del Códice Cospiano . . . reproducido en fotocromografía a ex-pensas de S. E. el Duque de Loubat. Rome. [JBG]

1898b Descripción, historia y exposición del códice pictórico de los antiguos Nauas que se conserva en la Biblioteca de la Cámara de Diputados de Paris. Florence. [JBG]

1912 Códice Kingsborough. . . . Madrid. [JBG]

1913 Escritura pictórica. Códice Kings-borough, lo que nos enseña. 18th International Congress of American-ists (London, 1912), *Proceedings*, pp. 455–60. [JBG] [Reprinted, MNA, *Anales*, ep. 3/4:483–99 (1913); Ga-lindo y Villa, 1922, pp. 408–12.]

1925 Colección de Mendoza, ó Códice Mendocino. . . . Mexico. MNA [JBG, "Galindo y Villa, 1925."]

Epistolario: Facsimiles (data for these are taken from Carrera Stampa, 1949, p. 36; HFC has not examined them)

n.d. Carta del conquistador Ruy Gonzá-lez al Emperador Carlos V, fechada en México el 24 de abril de 1553. Edición facsimilar. 3 fols.

n.d. Carta Latina a Felipe II, Rey de Es-paña, por el indio mexicano don Pa-blo Nazareo y su esposa doña Ma-ría, hija de don Juan Axayaca, en México a 17 de marzo de 1566, en la que explican sus genealogías, las po-sesiones de sus mayores y piden mer-cedes. Edición facsimilar. 6 fols.

n.d. Memorial de los pueblos sujetos al señorío de Tlacupan y de los que tri-butaban a México Tezcuco y Tlacu-pan. Edición facsimilar. 2 fols. [un-dated, unsigned].

Linguistic Works, Translations of Native Drama and Texts

1890 Invención de la Santa Cruz por Santa Elena. Coloquio escrita en Mexica-no por el Br. D. Manuel de los Santos y Salazar. Lo tradujo libremente al castellano. MNA. Mexico. [Biobib-liographical notes, Mexican text, FPT translation, with notes.]

1899 Sacrificio de Isaac. Auto en lengua mexicana (anónimo) escrito en el

421

año 1678, traducido al español. . . . Florence. [29 pp.]

1900 Adoración de los Reyes. Auto en lengua mexicana (anónimo), traducido al español. . . . *Biblioteca Náhuatl*, 1 (El Teatro), Cuad. 2. Florence.

1902 Comedia de los Reyes, escrita en Mexicano a principios del siglo xvii (por Agustín de la Fuente). La tradujo al castellano. . . . *Biblioteca Náhuatl*, 1 (El Teatro), Cuad. 3. Florence.

1903 Leyenda de los soles, continuada con otras leyendas y noticias. Relación anónimo escrita en lengua mexicana el año 1558. La tradujo al castellano. . . . *Biblioteca Náhuatl*, 5 (Tradiciones y migraciones), Cuad. 1 (40 pp. Florence.

1904 [with Luis González Obregón] Colección de Gramáticas de la lengua Mexicana. Tomo I. 1547–1673. MNA. Mexico. [Includes Olmos, Molina, Rincón, Galdo Guzmán, Vetancurt *Artes*.]

1907 Destrucción de Jerusalén. Auto en lengua Mexicana (anónimo), escrito con letra de fines del siglo xvii, traducido al castellano. . . . *Biblioteca Náhuatl*, 1 (El Teatro), Cuad. 4 (pp. 129–78). Florence.

1908 Fragmentos de la obra general sobre historia general de los mexicanos, escritas en lengua Náhuatl por Cristóbal del Castillo a fines del siglo xvi. . . . *Biblioteca Náhuatl*, 5 (Tradiciones y migraciones), Cuad. 2 (pp. 40–108). Florence.

Various Studies and Writings; Posthumous Publications

1885–86 Estudios sobre la historia de medicina en México. MNA, *Anales*, 3:137–235.

1886 Lingüística de la República Mexicana. MNA, *Anales*, 3:321–24.

1887a Los trabajos lingüísticos de D. Miguel

Trinidad Palma. MNA, *Anales*, 4:45–47.

1887b Lista de los pueblos principales que pertenecían antiguamente a Tezcoco. MNA, *Anales*, 4:48–56.

1890 Calendario de los Tarascos. MNA, *Anales*, 4:57–63.

1891–97 Publicaciones del Museo Nacional de Mexico. MNA, *Anales*, 4: 260–72 [Includes proposed titles in various linguistic series.]

1892–93 Exposición Histórico Americana de Madrid. Catálogo de la Sección de México. 2 vols. Madrid. [Erudite description of the Mexican exhibit. A third volume remains unpublished (FPT Collection, leg. 129).]

1897 Catálogo de la colección de Pbro. D. Francisco Plancarte. . . . MNA, *Anales*, 4:273–357.

1899 Publicaciones del Museo Nacional. MNA, *Anales*, 4:260–72.

1913 Division territorial de Nueva España en el año de 1636. 18th International Congress of Americanists (London, 1912), *Proceedings*, pp. 464–83. [Reprinted, MNA, *Anales*, ep. 3/4: 251–74.]

1926 De Antiquitatibus Novae Hispaniae. Authore Francisco Hernando. Medico et Historico Philippi III et Indiarum Omnium Medico Primario. Códice de la Real Academia de la Historia en Madrid. Edición facsimilar. MNA. Mexico. [Francisco Hernández materials.]

1927a Información de los méritos y servicios de D. Juan, señor natural de Coyoacán, y petición del mismo a Su Magestad, México, 8 de junio de 1536. MNA, *Anales*, ep. 4/5:354–59.

1927b Inventario de papeles del Cosmógrafo Alonso de Santa Cruz, año de 1575. MNA, *Anales*, ep. 4/5:360–66.

1933 Relación de las cuatro provincias en las que se divide el Reyno de Nueva España. MNA, *Anales*, ep. 4/8:386–88.

REFERENCES

ACOSTA SAIGNES, MIGUEL, ed.
1946 Fray Bernardino de Sahagún, "Historia general de las cosas de Nueva España." Noticia preliminar, bibliografía, notas, revisión y guía para estudiar a Sahagún. 3 vols. Mexico.

AGÜEROS, VICTORIANO
1896 Noticias biográficas y bibliográficas. In García Icazbalceta, 1896–99, 1:v–xvii.

ALAMÁN, LUCAS
1849 Noticias biográficas del licenciado don Carlos María Bustamante, escritas por un amigo de don Carlos y más amigo de la verdad. Mexico. [Published anonymously; see 1946.]
1946 Noticias biográficas del Lic. D. Carlos Ma. Bustamante y juicio crítico de sus obras. In Obras de D. Lucas Alamán: documentos diversos (inéditos y muy raros), 3:279–336. [Editorial Jus.] Mexico. [Reprint of Alamán, 1849.]

ALVARADO TEZOZOMOC, FERNANDO
1944 Crónica mexicana. Selección e introducción por Mario Mariscal. Secretaria de Educación Pública. Mexico.

ANDRADE, J. M., AND P. ESCALANTE, eds.
1853–56 Diccionario universal de historia y geografía. 7 vols. Apéndice al Diccionario . . . Colección de artículos relativos a la República Mexicana por los sres. José María Andrade, Manuel Berganzo, Conde de la Cortina, et al. 3 vols. Mexico.

BALLESTEROS GAIBROIS, MANUEL
1964 Sahagún, Bernardino de, Códices matritenses de la "Historia general de las cosas de la Nueva España." Trabajo realizado por el Seminario de Estudios Americanistas, bajo la dirección de Manuel Ballesteros Gaibrois. Ediciones José Porrúa Turanzas. 2 vols. Madrid.

BASSOLS BATALLA, ANGEL
1963 Importancia de la carta de división económico-administrativa de Manuel Orozco y Berra. In Temas y figuras de la Intervención, vol. 25 of Colección del Congreso Nacional de Historia para el Estudio de la Guerra de Intervención, pp. 9–16. 27 vols. Mexico.

BORAH, WOODROW, AND S. F. COOK
1960 The population of central Mexico in 1548: An analysis of the "Suma de visitas de pueblos." Ibero-Americana, 43. Berkeley and Los Angeles.

BRAVO UGARTE, JOSÉ
1946 Cuestiones históricas guadalupanas. Mexico.

BUSTAMANTE, CARLOS MARÍA
See Article 21, Appendix A.

C.A.B.
1870 Los escritos de D. Joaquín García Icazbalceta. SMGE, Boletín, 2:642–47.

CARREÑO, ALBERTO MARÍA
1941 Don Francisco del Paso y Troncoso. Divulgación Histórica, 2:175–85, 223–38, 279–89.
1945a D. Joaquín García Icazbalceta. Abside, 9:183–215 (Apr.-June). Mexico.
1945b Manuel Orozco y Berra. Academia Mexicana de la Historia, Memorias, 4:202–07.

CARRERA STAMPA, MANUEL
1949 Misiones mexicanas en archivos europeos. PAIGH, Comisión de Historia, Pub. 8, pp. 4–55. Mexico.
1963 Francisco del Paso y Troncoso. Academia Mexicana de la Historia, Memorias, 22:153–67, 209–10, 304–05.

CASTAÑEDA, CARLOS E., AND JACK AUTREY DABBS
1939 Guide to the Latin American manuscripts in the University of Texas Library. Cambridge, Mass.

CATÁLOGO
1936 Catálogo de libros y manuscritos del Sr. D. Joaquín García Icazbalceta. MS. Photostat in Library of Congress; original in University of Texas Library, Genaro García Collection.

CHAVERO, ALFREDO
See Article 21, Appendix E.

CLINE, HOWARD F.
1959 The Patiño maps of 1580 and related

documents: An analysis of sixteenth century cartographic sources for the Gulf Coast of Mexico. *El México Antiguo*, 9:633–92.

1962 The Ortelius maps of New Spain, 1579, and related contemporary materials, 1560–1610. *Imago Mundi*, 16:98–115. Amsterdam.

1964 The "Relaciones Geográficas" of the Spanish Indies, 1577–1586. *HAHR*, 45:341–74.

COMAS, JUAN
1950 Bosquejo histórico de la antropología en México. *RMEA*, 11:97–192.

CORONA NÚÑEZ, JOSÉ
1958 Relaciones geográficas de la Diócesis de Michoacán, 1579–1580. Notas por José Corona Núñez. Col. siglo XVI. Guadalajara, Mexico.

COSÍO VILLEGAS, DANIEL, ed.
1955–65 Historia moderna de México. 8 vols. to date. Mexico and Buenos Aires.

ESTRADA, GENARO
1937 *See* Teixidor, 1937.

FERNÁNDEZ, JUSTINO
1938 *See* Janvier, 1938.

FERNÁNDEZ DURO, CESÁREO
1895 El Excmo. Sr. D. Joaquín García Icazbalceta. *La Ilustración Española y Americana*, 39(6):99–103 (Feb. 15). Madrid.

GALINDO Y VILLA, JESÚS
1904 Don Joaquín García Icazbalceta, biografía y bibliografía. 3d ed. MNA. Mexico. [Separate from MNA, *Anales*, 7:520–62.]

1922 Don Francisco del Paso y Troncoso, su vida y sus obras. MNA, *Anales*, ep. 4, 1:305–568. [See Galindo y Villa, 1923.]

1923 Don Francisco del Paso y Troncoso, su vida y sus obras. Sociedad Científica "Antonio Alzate," *Memorias y Revista*, 42:135–301, 491–760. [Reissue of Galindo y Villa, 1922.]

1925 Don Joaquín García Icazbalceta. Asociación de Bibliotecarios Mexicanos, *Boletín*, 1:102–10 (Sept.).

1926 Joaquín García Icazbalceta, his life and works. *Inter-America*, 9:133–44 (Apr.). New York.

GARCÍA, RUBEN
1934 Biografía, bibliografía e iconografía de don Manuel Orozco y Berra. SMGE, *Boletín*, 44(5–8):151–335.

GARCÍA CUBAS, ANTONIO
1890 Orozco y Berra. *In* his Diccionario geográfico, histórico y biográfico de los Estados Unidos Mexicanos, 4:227–32. Mexico.

GARCÍA ICAZBALCETA, JOAQUÍN
See Article 21, Appendix D.

GARCÍA PIMENTEL, LUIS
1903–07 Documentos históricos de Mexico. 6 vols. Mexico.

GARCÍA PIMENTEL Y ELGUERO, LUIS
1944 Don Joaquín García Icazbalceta como católico, algunos testimonios publicados por su nieto. Mexico.

1950 *See* Martínez, 1950.

GARDINER, C. HARVEY
1958 William Hickling Prescott: An annotated bibliography of published works. Library of Congress, *Hispanic Foundation Bibliographical Series*, 4. Washington.

1959 Prescott's ties with Mexico. *Journal of Inter-American Studies*, 1:11–26.

1962 [ed.] Las cartas de Joaquín García Icazbalceta a William H. Prescott, Introducción y notas. . . . BNMex, *Boletín*, 13(4):3–33 (Oct.-Dec.).

GARIBAY K., ANGEL M.
1960 Estudio previo. *In* Orozco y Berra, 1960, 1:v–xxviii.

GÓMEZ DE OROZCO, FEDERICO, ed.
1927 Catálogo de la colección de manucritos de Joaquín García Icazbalceta relativos a la historia de América. Ministerio de Relaciones Exteriores, *Monografías Bibliográficas Mexicanas*, 9. Mexico.

GONZÁLEZ, LUIS
1966 Historia de la historia. *In* Manrique, 1966, pp. 46–78.

GONZÁLEZ NAVARRO, MOISÉS
1957 El Porfiriato: La vida social. *In* Cosío Villegas, 1955–65.

GONZÁLEZ OBREGÓN, LUIS
1898 D. José Fernando Ramírez (datos biobibliográficos). *In* Ramírez, 1898, 1:v–xlvii.

1919 Don Francisco del Paso y Troncoso, sabio arqueológico y lingüista mexicano. BNMex, *Boletín*, 12:167–79. [Reprinted in his 1939.]

1939 Cronistas e historiadores. Mexico. [Article on Paso y Troncoso reprinted from his 1919, pp. 175–95.]

GONZÁLEZ Y GONZÁLEZ, LUIS, EMMA COSÍO VILLEGAS, AND GUADALUPE MONROY
1957 La república restaurada: La vida social. *In* Cosío Villegas, 1955–65.

GREENLEAF, RICHARD E.
1961 Zumárraga and the Mexican Inquisition, 1536–1543. Academy of American Franciscan History. Washington.

GURRÍA LACROIX, JORGE
1952 Alfredo Chavero. BNMex, *Boletín*, 3(1):3–16.
1964 Trabajos sobre historia mexicana. INAH. Mexico.

HUERTA CASTAÑEDA, ALICIA
1942 Ideario y semblanzas históricas en la obra de Orozco y Berra. UNAM. Mexico.

IGUÍNIZ, JUAN B.
1943 Disquisiciones bibliográficas: Autores, libros, bibliotecas, artes gráficas. El Colegio de México. Mexico.

JANVIER, CATARINA A.
1938 Indice alfabético de la bibliografía mexicana del siglo XVI de don Joaquín García Icazbalceta. Traduccion y arreglo de Manuel Toussaint y Justino Fernández. Mexico.

JIMÉNEZ MORENO, WIGBERTO
1938 Fray Bernardino de Sahagún y su obra. Mexico. [Separate reprint from Ramírez Cabañas, 1938, paged in arabic numerals.]
1952 50 años de historia mexicana. *Historia Mexicana*, 1:449–55.

JUNCO, ALFONSO
1940 Joaquín García Icazbalceta. *In* his Sangre de Hispania, pp. 25–32. Buenos Aires and Mexico.

KINGSBOROUGH, LORD [EDWARD KING], ed.
1830–31 [Sahagún.] Historia universal de las cosas de Nueva España. *In* Antiquities of Mexico. 9 vols. London.

LEÓN, NICOLÁS
1904 Noticia biográfica del autor. *In* Chavero, 1904, pp. v–xxv.

LEÓN-PORTILLA, MIGUEL
1959 Orozco y Berra: investigador del pensamiento náhuatl. *In* La filosofía náhuatl, estudiada en sus fuentes, pp. 32–33. UNAM. Mexico.
1960 Bibliografía de don Manuel Orozco y Berra. *In* Orozco y Berra, 1960.

LEONARDO Y ARGENSOLA, BARTOLOMÉ JUAN
1940 Conquista de México. Ed. Robredo. Mexico.

MANRIQUE, J. A., ed.
1966 Veinticinco años de investigación histórica en México. El Colegio de México. Edición especial de *Historia Mexicana*. Mexico.

MÁRQUEZ MONTIEL, JOAQUÍN
1955 Manuel Orozco y Berra. *In* Hombres célebres de Puebla, 2:104–09.

MARTÍNEZ, MANUEL G.
1947 Don Joaquín García Icazbalceta: His place in Mexican historiography. Catholic University of America, *Studies in Hispanic-American History*, 4. Washington.
1950 Don Joaquín García Icazbalceta, su lugar en la historiografía. Traducción, notas, y apéndice de Luis García Pimentel y Elguero. Mexico. [Translation of Martínez, 1947, with added material.]
1951 Don Joaquín García Icazbalceta. *Revista Interamericana de Bibliografía*, 1:81–88.

MARTÍNEZ BAEZ, ANTONIO, ed.
1963 Tres estudios sobre don José María Morelos y Pavón, por Carlos María de Bustamante. Edición facsimilar. UNAM, Biblioteca Nacional, Instituto Bibliográfico Mexicano. Mexico.

MARTÍNEZ CEBALLOS, EVA
1931 Don Manuel Orozco y Berra. *Revista de Revistas*, no. 1084 (Feb. 8). Mexico.

MARTÍNEZ TORNER, FLORENTINO
1933 M. Orozco y Berra. *In* Creadores de la imagen histórica de México: 121 biografías sintéticas, pp. 210–13. Mexico.

MENDIZÁBAL, MIGUEL O.
1946 Francisco del Paso y Troncoso. *In* Obras completas, pp. 417–20. Mexico.

MILLARES CARLO, AGUSTÍN, AND JOSÉ IGNACIO MANTECÓN
1948 Repertorio bibliográfico de los archivos mexicanos y de las colecciones diplomáticos fundamentales para la historia de México. UNAM, Instituto de Historia, *Publicaciones*, ser. 1, 6:119–20. Mexico.

MORENO, DANIEL
1965 José Fernández Ramírez. UNAM, Facultad de Derecho de México, *Revista*, 15:487–506.

MOTA Y ESCOBAR, ALONSO DE
1930 Galicia, Viscaya y León. Bibliofilos Mexicanos. Mexico.

1945   Memoriales del obispo de Tlaxcala Fray Alonso de la Mota y Escobar. INÁH, *Anales*, 1:191–306 (1939–40). Mexico.

NAVARRO, ENRIQUE
1954   Introducción. *In* Orozco y Berra, 1954, 1:5–19.

NICOLAU D'OLWER, LUIS
1952   Fray Bernardino de Sahagún, 1499–1590. PAIGH, Pub. 142.

NUNEMAKER, J. HORACE
1948   The Biblioteca Aportación Histórica publications, 1943–1948. *HAHR*, 38:316–34.

O'GORMAN, EDMUNDO
1939a   La dominación española de Orozco y Berra. *Letras de Mexico*, 2:6–7 (no. 1, Jan. 15).
1939b   Sobre la historia de Orozco y Berra. *Investigaciones Históricas*, 1(2):127–33; 1(3):323–38. Mexico.
1966   Historia de las divisiones territoriales de México. 3d ed. Mexico.
1967   Guía bibliográfica de Carlos María de Bustamante. Centro de estudios de historia de Mexico (Condumex). Mexico.

OROZCO Y BERRA, MANUEL
See Article 21, Appendix C.

ORTEGA Y MEDINA, JUAN ANTONIO
1963   El historiador don Carlos de Bustamante ante la consciencia histórica mexicana. UNAM, *Anuario de Historia*, 3:6–58.

PALACIOS, JUAN ENRIQUE
1922   Don Francisco del Paso y Troncoso: Su magna labor de arqueología e historia de México. MNA, *Anales*, ep. 4, 1:581–88.

PASO Y TRONCOSO, FRANCISCO DEL
See Article 21, Appendix F.

PEREYRA, CARLOS
1968   *See* Salado Alvarez, 1968.

RAMÍREZ, JOSÉ FERNANDO
See Article 21, Appendix B.

RAMÍREZ CABAÑAS, JOAQUÍN
1930   Introduction. *In* Mota y Escobar, 1930, pp. 9–24.
1940   Introduction and notes. *In* Leonardo y Argensola, 1940, pp. 9–24.

RICARD, ROBERT
1934   Joaquín García Icazbalceta (1825–1894). *Bulletin Hispanique*, 36:459–71 (Oct.–Dec.). Bordeaux.

RICO GONZÁLEZ, VÍCTOR
1953   Orozco y Berra. *In* Hacia un concepto de la conquista de México.

UNAM, Instituto de Historia, ser. 1, 29:165–202.

ROJAS, ISIDRO
1900   Estudio biográfico de los vicepresidentes de la Sociedad Mexicana de Geografía Estadística. SMGE, *Boletín Especial para el Cuadragisimo Noveno Aniversario de la Fundación de la Sociedad*, pp. 3–30.

SALADO ALVAREZ, VICTORIANO
1933   La vida azarosa y romántica de don Carlos María de Bustamante. Madrid and Barcelona.
1968   La vida azarosa y romántica de don Carlos María de Bustamante. Prólogo de don Carlos Pereyra. 2d ed. Mexico.

SOSA, FRANCISCO
1884   Manuel Orozco y Berra. *In* Biografías de mexicanos distinguidos, pp. 747–65. Mexico.

—— AND OTHERS
1890   Biografía del sr. D. Manuel Orozco y Berra. SMGE, *Boletín*, ep. 4, 2:9–64. [Excerpt from Sosa, 1884, and obituaries.]

SOTO, JESÚS S.
1935   Divagaciones sobre la biografía y algo en explicación de la Orozco y Berra. SMGE, *Boletín*, 44:423–93.

TEIXIDOR, FELIPE, comp.
1937   Cartas de Joaquín García Icazbalceta a José Fernando Ramírez, José María de Agreda, Aquiles Gerste, Francisco del Paso y Troncoso. Prólogo por Genaro Estrada. Mexico.

TOUSSAINT, MANUEL
1938   *See* Janvier, 1938.

URIBE ORTIZ, SUSANA
1953   Manuel Orozco y Berra. *In* Homenaje a Silvio Zavala, Estudios históricos americanos, pp. 519–61. El Colegio de México. Mexico.
1963   Manuel Orozco y Berra en la historiografía mexicana. UNAM, Facultad de Filosofía y Letras. Mexico City.

VALTON, EMILIO
1954   Homenaje al insigne bibliógrafo mexicano Joaquín García Icazbalceta. UNAM. Mexico.

VARGAS, FULGENCIO
1925   Don Joaquín Icazbalceta y los estudios bibliográficos en México. Asociación de Bibliotecarios Mexicanos, *Boletín*, 1:98–101 (Sept. 15).